MAGISTRATES, POLICE, AND PEOPLE:
EVERYDAY CRIMINAL JUSTICE IN QUEBEC AND
LOWER CANADA, 1764–1837

MAGISTRATES, POLICE, AND PEOPLE

Everyday Criminal Justice in
Quebec and Lower Canada,
1764–1837

DONALD FYSON

Published for The Osgoode Society for Canadian Legal History by
University of Toronto Press
Toronto Buffalo London

Printed in Canada

ISBN-13: 978-0-8020-9223-6
ISBN-10: 0-8020-9223-3

Printed on acid-free paper

Library and Archives Canada Cataloguing in Publication

Fyson, Donald
Magistrates, police and people : everyday criminal justice in
Quebec and Lower Canada / Donald Fyson.

Includes bibliographical references and index.
ISBN 0-8020-9223-3

1. Criminal justice, Administration of – Québec (Province) – History –
18th century.   2. Criminal justice, Administration of – Québec (Province) –
History – 19th century.   I. Osgoode Society for Canadian Legal History
II. Title.

KEQ1170.F98 2006   364.9714090'33   C2006-903866-X   KF9223.F98 2006

University of Toronto Press acknowledges the financial assistance to its
publishing program of the Canada Council for the Arts and the
Ontario Arts Council.

University of Toronto Press acknowledges the financial support for its
publishing activities of the Government of Canada through the
Book Publishing Industry Development Program (BPIDP).

To my parents

Contents

Tables and Figures

Tables

Figures

Foreword

THE OSGOODE SOCIETY
FOR CANADIAN LEGAL HISTORY

This highly innovative study by one of the leading young historians of Quebec examines all aspects of the criminal justice system in Quebec and Lower Canada in the later eighteenth and early nineteenth centuries. The first half of the work explores the transfer and adaptation of English criminal law and courts, the appointment and character of the magistracy, and the police. The second half presents an overview of everyday criminal justice in operation. In this book Donald Fyson argues that neither the Conquest nor the Rebellions represented radical breaks with the past. Despite the Conquest, there was considerable continuity, both in structures and in personnel. Conversely, before the Rebellions, state formation was well under way, responding to the demographic, social, and economic changes that swept the colony. Criminal law and the criminal justice system were modified to suit local circumstances, and the magistracy and the police became increasingly professionalized. The relationship between the people and the system also changed dramatically throughout the period. This is perhaps best exemplified by the steady increase in the rate of criminal prosecution. From being initially relatively marginal, local criminal justice became increasingly used by both the *Canadien* and British populations of Quebec, especially in urban areas.

The purpose of the Osgoode Society for Canadian Legal History is to encourage research and writing in the history of Canadian law. The Society, which was incorporated in 1979 and is registered as a charity, was founded at the initiative of the Honourable R. Roy McMurtry, a former attorney general for Ontario, now chief justice of Ontario, and officials of the Law Society of Upper Canada. Its efforts to stimulate the study of legal history in Canada include a research-support program, a graduate student research-assistance program, and work in the fields of oral history and legal archives. The Society publishes volumes of interest to its members that contribute to legal-historical scholarship in Canada, including studies of the courts, the judiciary, and the legal profession, biographies, collections of documents, studies in criminology and penology, accounts of significant trials, and work in the social and economic history of the law.

Until earlier this year the editor-in-chief of the Osgoode Society for Canadian Legal History was Professor Peter Oliver, who had served in that role since 1979. Professor Oliver passed away in May 2006, but not before he worked extensively with the authors of our 2006 books; he is primarily responsible for seeing them through from inception to publication, as he was for all of the other sixty-three books published during his tenure of more than a quarter of a century. The Society is much indebted to him for all his contributions.

Current directors of the Osgoode Society for Canadian Legal History are Robert Armstrong, Kenneth Binks, Patrick Brode, Michael Bryant, Brian Bucknall, Archie Campbell, David Chernos, Kirby Chown, J. Douglas Ewart, Martin Friedland, Elizabeth Goldberg, John Honsberger, Horace Krever, Gavin MacKenzie, Virginia MacLean, Roy McMurtry, Brendan O'Brien, Jim Phillips, Paul Reinhardt, Joel Richler, William Ross, James Spence, and Richard Tinsley.

The annual report and information about membership may be obtained by writing: The Osgoode Society for Canadian Legal History, Osgoode Hall, 130 Queen Street West, Toronto, Ontario. M5H 2N6. Telephone: 416-947-3321. E-mail: mmacfarl@lsuc.on.ca. Website: Osgoodesociety.ca

R. Roy McMurtry
President

Jim Phillips
Interim Editor-in-Chief

Acknowledgments

I have many people to thank for their help in the lengthy transition from thesis to book. First of all, I am indebted to John Dickinson, my thesis supervisor, and the Social Sciences and Humanities Research Council of Canada (SSHRC), which funded the original research: without the thesis that SSHRC helped me complete, this book never would have been. I am also very grateful for the help of the staff at the archives, museums, and libraries that I visited for the new research I undertook for this project: the archivists at Bibliothèque et Archives nationales du Québec, and especially Evelyn Kolish and Rénald Lessard; the archivists and librarians at Library and Archives Canada, and especially Pat Kennedy; and the personnel at the Bibliothèque de l'Assemblée nationale, the Archives de la Ville de Montréal, the Musée de la civilisation, and the Musée régional de Vaudreuil-Soulanges. I also wish to acknowledge the work of the research assistants who helped out with various aspects of the project, Frédéric Chevalier, Jean-Philippe Jobin, Isabelle Malo, and Caroline Schoofs.

My thanks as well go to the Osgoode Society for undertaking the publication of this book, and especially to the late Peter Oliver, for always believing in the project, and to Marilyn MacFarlane, for her patient efficiency. My appreciation also goes out to the University of Toronto Press and its editors, Len Husband and Curtis Fahey, for their fine work and inspiring comments.

My friends at the Montreal History Group have been very supportive, as they always are. Brian Young has been a teacher and a friend since the beginning of my career; I wouldn't be in Quebec history today were it not for him, nor would this book exist without his advice and support. Mary Anne Poutanen was ever generous with her data, her home, and her food. Steve Watt shared Quebec City with me for a time, and still shares Quebec culture and information technology. And I would like to thank Bettina Bradbury, Jarrett Rudy, Alan Stewart, Colin Coates, Tamara Myers, and all the other current and former members of the Group for their help and encouragement.

Other fellow historians also deserve my gratitude. Jim Phillips has been a cheerful supporter and editor. Jean-Marie Fecteau has always given me his theoretical insights and empirical sources with the utmost generosity, even if we do not always agree. My colleagues and friends at the Université Laval listened and helped, especially Talbot Imlay, Laurent Stalder, Didier Méhu, Aline Charles, Richard Jones, Marc Vallières, Réal Bélanger, David Karel, and Sylvio Normand. Kathryn Harvey shared her take on Montreal history and on life. Jean-Philippe Garneau was always available with his erudition and his passion for the law and history of early Quebec, whether as a researcher and reader or over a meal. And Elsbeth Heaman didn't let me give up, preaching by example.

Last, and most important, my love goes out to my family. My children, Jasper and Sacha, lived through my absences. My wife, Sovita Chander, did more than endure an academic lifestyle and work schedule: she read my texts with her editor's eye and writer's mind, and she supported and inspired me while also helping me set the limits. Finally, I owe much to my parents, Bill and Raina Fyson. They took the kids and provided the beds, the meals, and the wine, but it's also from them that I learned the values of truth and justice, and thus it is to them that this book is dedicated.

Abbreviations

BAnQ-M	Bibliothèque et Archives nationales du Québec, centre d'archives de Montréal
BAnQ-Q	Bibliothèque et Archives nationales du Québec, centre d'archives de Québec
CS	Civil Secretary's incoming correspondence, LAC RG4 A1
CSL	Civil Secretary's letter books, LAC RG7 G15C and RG4 C2
DCB	*Dictionary of Canadian Biography*
JHALC	*Journals of the House of Assembly of Lower Canada*
LAC	Library and Archives Canada
RG1 E15A	Public Accounts, LAC RG1 E15A
PRDH	Programme de recherche en démographie historique
QSD	Documents of the Montreal Quarter Sessions, BAnQ-M TL32 S1 SS1
QSR	Registers of the Montreal Quarter Sessions, BAnQ-M TL32 S1 SS11
SSR	Registers of the Montreal Special Sessions, Archives de la ville de Montréal VM35

MAGISTRATES, POLICE, AND PEOPLE:
EVERYDAY CRIMINAL JUSTICE IN QUEBEC AND
LOWER CANADA, 1764–1837

Introduction

It's not a very striking tale. On Wednesday, August 11, 1830, Michel Asselin, a Montreal cabinetmaker, appeared before Thomas Andrew Turner, the sitting magistrate in the city's Police Office. In his handwritten deposition, signed with a cross, Asselin complained that the day before, while passing through the Saint-Laurent suburbs, 'il aurait été, sans cause ni provocation de sa part, attaqué, assailli et violemment frappé à coups de pied et de poing par le nommé Michel Dubois, boulanger, du même lieu' [he was, without cause or provocation on his part, attacked, assaulted and violently kicked and punched by one Michel Dubois, baker, of the same place]. Asselin demanded that Dubois be arrested. On Thursday, Dubois appeared before Turner and entered into a £10 recognizance (bond) promising to come before the city's Court of Quarter Sessions in October and to keep the peace in the meantime. The recognizance was guaranteed by Étienne Garceau, a joiner, and Amable Jeaudoin, a trader. However, there is no indication that either Dubois or Asselin ever appeared in court, or that any action was taken to enforce the recognizance.

The story told in the documents is pretty thin. The language in the deposition is formulaic; the recognizance is a pre-printed form with names, dates, and amounts filled in. Further, we know little about the protagonists, apart from Turner: a Scots immigrant and member of Montreal's anglo-Tory elites, he had been appointed to the magistracy in 1821 by that bane of *Canadien* nationalists, Governor Dalhousie, but was dropped later in 1830 as a bankrupt. The case itself provides little matter for political history, cultural analysis, or biography. Even legally, it is banal, involving no particularly interesting judicial principles. In sum, this was neither the murder trial of *La Corriveau*, nor the treason trial and evisceration of David McLane, nor the courts-martial and hanging or transportation of the *Patriotes* of 1837–8. Understandably, unlike those cases, it has attracted no attention whatsoever from Quebec historians.[1]

And yet, as much as those spectacular cases, this minor judicial event epitomizes British justice in Quebec and Lower Canada, not only in its everyday banality but also in what it suggests about crucial issues such as the contours of ethnic, class, and gender relations in a colonized and conquered society, the complex interaction between law, society, and the state, and, more broadly, the nature of the ancien-régime colonial state itself. In a time of rising ethno-political tensions in Lower Canada, leading up to the Rebellions of 1837–8, why did a *Canadien* turn to a British, Tory magistrate, and to an evidently English criminal justice system, to complain of another *Canadien*? What led an artisan to appeal to a system evidently controlled by elites? What led a man to resort to the state for a minor act of violence against him by another man, instead of dealing with it himself? To make the complaint, where did Asselin have to go, whom did he have to see, what did he have to pay? Whose language shaped the deposition, so patently not in the words of a cabinetmaker who did not sign his own name and yet neither in Turner's English nor in his hand? How was Dubois compelled to appear before Turner, in a city with no modern police force? And why did the case go no further than the initial complaint and recognizance, when, legally, it should at least have been brought before a grand jury? The two brief documents that frame this story cannot answer these questions, but, conjoined with thousands of other similarly ordinary cases preserved in the judicial archives, and contextualized with other documents, the case of Asselin and Dubois can help us reconstruct the nature, course, and experience of everyday criminal justice during a crucial period of state formation.

This is a study of everyday criminal law and criminal justice in Quebec and Lower Canada from 1764 to 1837, or from a little after the British Conquest to just before the Rebellions. Its focus is on the everyday, not in the sense of daily – as today, direct personal contact with the criminal justice system was exceptional – but in the sense of routine or ordinary. Ordinary law and justice in the colony were played out mainly at the lower levels of the justice system, around the justices of the peace and their police, where complaints like Asselin's ended up. Quebec historians, however, have paid little attention to everyday justice. We know quite a bit about the ideological significance of changes in legal regimes, the political manipulation of the justice system, the implications of martial law, the treatment of more serious crimes, and so on.[2] But we still know relatively little about the structure and operation of the lower-level civil and criminal courts, and, as for the experiences of people who came before the justice system, these come to us mainly through the work of social historians examining specific phenomena such as wife-battering or infanticide. And yet, as historians of other jurisdictions have shown, it was the everyday structures and acts of routine criminal law and justice that affected the greatest number of people, with what are often termed 'petty' cases and 'low law' making up the bulk of the work of the criminal justice system and constituting, in general, the concrete basis of the experience of justice.[3] In Quebec and Lower Canada as well, murders, highway robberies, and other high-profile crimes accounted for a small proportion of the cases that came before the courts as a whole, and highly politicized cases like those of McLane or the *Patriotes* were rare. Instead, as is the case today, most people came in direct contact with the criminal justice system through assaults, minor thefts, regulatory offences, and the like. This is not to argue that exceptional cases were unimportant to colonial society and politics, for their symbolic impact alone was profound. However, while the trial and execution of McLane undoubtedly provoked strong reactions in the *Canadien* spectators, how many also had a relative, a neighbour, or a friend who had been a plaintiff, a defendant, or a witness in an assault case or who had been fined for not maintaining the roads? Or been so themselves? Such experiences of criminal justice were very different from those of the crowd watching the butchery of McLane's corpse.[4]

My approach towards everyday criminal justice also reflects my conception of the relationship between law and society in history. Following most historical legal scholarship inspired by social history and historical sociology, I see law and justice as fundamentally being arenas for the exercise of power, both social power and state power. This power might be exercised beneficially, as is suggested by those who advance the consensual view of criminal justice and emphasize the law's positive role in dispute resolution and its acceptance by historical societies. Alternatively, it might be used to foster inequality, as argued by the proponents of the conflict model, who put the emphasis on the law as a guarantor of the social order through social control or social regulation and on popular resistance to the law. Or it might be largely ineffectual, as argued by those who underscore the marginality of ancien-régime criminal justice and the relative autonomy and self-regulation of ancien-régime societies. Nevertheless, it is power that is at the heart of all these models of the place of law in historical societies, and is a central concern in this book. Fundamentally, how did the criminal justice system function both as a source of power for those who composed it and as a source of power or oppression for those who came or were brought before it?[5]

But while the power expressed through the justice system reflected broader social and economic structures, the justice system itself, as much recent socio-legal history affirms, also had its own relative autonomy, expressed by particular rules and institutions and stemming in part from the shared practices and understandings of those who composed it. To understand the experience of criminal justice, we must also understand the normative and administrative structures that shaped and constrained that experience – that is to say, the law and the criminal justice system – as part of the broader organizational structure of the state. And we must also seek to grasp the legal culture of those who made up the system: judges, court officials, police, and so on. My intent is thus to look both at the broader social context of criminal justice and at the internal logic and functioning of the justice system, always from the perspective of understanding the relationship between law and society.[6]

My interest in the everyday criminal justice system also springs in part from an interest in the nature of the ancien-régime state, a term I use to refer to the admittedly variegated institutions of formal state authority that prevailed in Western European societies prior to the reforms of the state in the late eighteenth and early nineteenth centuries – notably the French ancien-régime state before the Revolution and the English system of 'Old Corruption' before the 1830s. Limited in scope, based on feudal power relations that precluded effective central control or even coordination, anchored in structures and practices dating back to the Middle Ages, often relatively undifferentiated from civil society, and concentrating on a limited number of functions such as revenue collection, war, and justice, these institutions of governance functioned according to a logic that was fundamentally different from the centralizing rationality of the modern, liberal, bureaucratic state as defined by

Max Weber and others. And, as Jean-Marie Fecteau and others have shown, the state structures implanted in New France, Quebec, and Lower Canada shared many of the characteristics of their European predecessors.[7] Justices of the peace and constables, for example, were institutions dating back to the late Middle Ages. Through them, the relatively weak central state in England shifted both the power and the responsibility of local social regulation onto local communities, co-opting their members, both elite and middling, into the enforcement of social norms and the exercise of power by the state on a local level and thereby ceding its sovereignty to local brokers who mediated between the central state and the local populace. In conception and in theory, these institutions were quite different from the professional magistracy and modern police forces that characterized the colony's justice system from the 1840s and far more evidently reflected a logic of attempted (though ultimately unsuccessful) social control. My use of the term ancien régime to characterize the state in Quebec and Lower Canada prior to its reformation in the late 1830s flows from the recognition of this difference between the old system and the new, though, as we will see, I question both the practical extent of the difference and the abruptness of the reforms.

The relationship between Quebec society and the ancien-régime state is a particularly interesting one, since an institution in theory characterized by rigidity and conservatism was confronted by a society undergoing rapid demographic expansion and social and economic change as well as profound political tensions. In the eight decades between the British Conquest in 1759–60 and the Rebellions of 1837–8, the small French colony along the banks of the St Lawrence, whose European population of about 65,000 was composed largely of *Canadiens*, French speakers born in the colony, was transformed into a British colony of some 600,000 inhabitants. In the 1830s, the population was still mainly *Canadien*, but waves of British immigrants, especially Loyalists fleeing the United States in the 1780s, Americans seeking land and economic opportunity in the decades following, and poor immigrants from the British Isles who arrived in increasing numbers from the 1810s, meant that a significant minority, about a quarter, were of British descent.[8] The colony's two main towns, Quebec City[9] and Montreal, grew from populations of a few thousand at the Conquest to cities of 30,000 to 35,000 people, with mixed populations of around half *Canadiens*, half British, and others. Rural society expanded as well, with new settlement areas progressively opening up on the periphery of the core seigneurial zone initially settled by the *Canadiens*, such as the Eastern Townships and the Ottawa valley, occupied in large part by British settlers. Within the older settlements, available land was increasingly occupied and a network of villages and small towns began to develop. The economy was also transformed: a commercial economy based on the export of furs and the import of European goods gave way to one based on the export of timber and grain, with the two main cities developing into commercial hubs; manufacturing began to spread in town and country, though most manufactured goods were still imported; and a largely subsistence agriculture in the countryside became increasingly connected to the market economy. All of these changes began gradually in the late eighteenth century and accelerated in the nineteenth, especially from the 1810s. Added to them were persistent political tensions, notably the classic struggles found in all white settler colonies between colonial elites and imperial interests over control of the instruments of political power, such as the legislature. In Quebec and Lower Canada, these struggles were compounded by tensions between *Canadien* elites who felt they and their compatriots were excluded from power and British immigrants who felt that their birthright should give them power over the society and politics of a colony their nation had conquered. These tensions, already present in the eighteenth century, led eventually to the violent Rebellions of 1837–8, pitting reform-minded *Patriotes* (mainly but not entirely *Canadien*) against Tories (mainly but not entirely British) in a contest that was grounded in both ethno-linguistic and social conflict.[10]

With few exceptions, Quebec historians have postulated that the state set up by the new British rulers from 1764 was unable to adapt to these rapid social and economic changes or to the accompanying political tensions. According to this view, the state prior to the Rebellions remained fundamentally unchanged, with the emergence of a modern, liberal state coming only in the 1840s. This was also a colonial state, imposed by the Conqueror on an unwilling *Canadien* population which was continually excluded from real power. The state's limited resources, combined with its lack of adaptability and legitimacy, substantially constrained its impact on society, and on rural *Canadien* society in particular, which remained largely autonomous and self-regulating. Little changed in the years between the Conquest and the Rebellions, and it was only following the Rebellions, when the liberal bourgeoisie came to power, that both British and *Canadien* elites, drawing inspiration from their European and American counterparts, radically transformed the state by modernizing and expanding it to form a powerful tool for imposing their values on society.[11]

Quebec historiography, much like that in Europe, tends to define the ancien-régime state largely in opposition to what came afterwards. Thus, one postulate is that, in the process of modernization, the state became far more extensive and intrusive. Hence, much attention has been paid to the multiplication and expansion of the various organs of the state, such as the bureaucracy or the police, and, more generally, to the way in which matters previously considered private or at least not public, such as charity, public schooling, or morality, became the purview of the state. The implication is that the ancien-régime state was much more limited both in size and in scope than its modern successor. Similarly, emphasis is placed on the growing centralization of power and control in the modern state, for example, through the creation of centralized knowledge such as censuses and scientific inquiries. And in examinations of the ancien-régime state, there is often a generalized conflation of the state and the mechanisms of government controlled by the central administration and the colonial authorities, or at least some level of government recognizable as such in modern terms, which necessarily occludes the more decentralized power and structures that prevailed before the mid-nineteenth century. Thus, analyses of the colonial bureaucracy have often been limited to paid positions under central control, leaving aside actors such as the justices of the peace, who are portrayed as largely outside the state.[12]

This stance is little different from the long-standing postulate of the fundamental weakness of the English state prior to the 1830s. And yet, in England, this view has increasingly been questioned, not only by those who emphasize the strength of the pre-reform central administration, but also by those who examine the state on a local level, where the pre-reform state was supposed to be weakest. Key to this re-evaluation is the assertion that it is simply inappropriate to apply modern conceptions of the centralized, bureaucratic state, whether Marxist, Weberian or other, to the analysis of the composition and power of the early modern state. As David Eastwood has argued regarding the venerable thesis of weak English local government resulting from lack of centralization, 'the problem with this kind of teleology is that it caricatures the eighteenth century in order to vindicate the nineteenth. It enshrines a narrow definition of administrative efficiency – essentially that of the centralized, bureaucratic state – elaborated by Benthamites and reforming Whigs in the first half of the nineteenth century, refined by

Liberal centralizers, notably John Stuart Mill, in the mid-nineteenth century, and trumpeted by the Fabians with characteristic intellectual self-assurance in the early twentieth century.' Among others, historians have shown that, at a local level, the state was in fact much more powerful than was assumed. For example, in examining the functioning of local administration by the justices of the peace, David Philips forcefully rejects the 'weak state' hypothesis and the usual opposition between central and local government and between paid bureaucracy and unpaid local gentlemen, arguing instead that any definition of the state must include the unpaid justices.[13]

In much the same fashion, my approach is focused on the local state, a term I use to distinguish what I am examining from the upper reaches of the colonial state, concentrated in the central administration. One of my principal assertions, in this book as elsewhere, is that much as in England, focusing on the state at this upper, pan-colonial level leads to conclusions about the composition, the organization, the very relevance of the state in general, and of the criminal justice system in particular which are far less tenable when we concentrate on the system at a local level.[14] This is not to imply that the local state was not intimately affected by colonial politics. As we will see, many aspects of local criminal justice were determined by colonial legislation and policies, and the justices of the peace were appointed by the central administration through a process that linked central and local interests. But a local turn allows me to offer a different perspective on questions such as the power and efficiency of the ancien-régime state and the adaptability of its structures. And it also permits a different take on the transition to the modern state, revealing preparatory developments such as the extension of social regulation, bureaucratization, and specialization in the decades before the 1830s, in contrast to a historiography that, for the most part, posits stasis before the late 1830s and then rapid change to the modern, liberal state thereafter.

Yet, in arguing that the ancien-régime state was more powerful, more efficient, and more adaptable than has previously been postulated, I am not suggesting that this benefited the population at large. Indeed, another theme that runs through this book is the extent to which the more powerful pre-reform state gave those who controlled it, essentially propertied white men, the means to exercise power over colonial society. One of the more important points raised by historians of the eighteenth-century English criminal justice system such as E.P. Thompson and Douglas Hay is that a lack of centralized control and differentiated structures did not necessarily imply a lack of power: just because the local criminal justice system was not directly an organ of the central administration in London does not mean that it could not be an oppressive burden on the popular classes.[15] My argument is thus not at all for the benevolence of the ancien-régime state or of the men who made it up, but for its potential utility as an instrument of power, though I suggest that while it could certainly serve the interests of local elites, its internal contradictions also made it a source of power for broader segments of the colonial population.

This last can be seen through two central issues that are of particular interest to Quebec historians. The first is the impact of the Conquest on law and state structures and on the place of *Canadien* elites in these.[16] The notion of a radical caesura at the Conquest has long dominated Quebec historiography: in this view, the change in regimes marked a profound discontinuity in the social, economic, and cultural life of the *Canadiens*, who were henceforth excluded from economic and political power, severed from their cultural metropolis, and condemned to subsidiary status and the search for national survival. The classic and still powerful decapitation thesis goes further, seeing in the Conquest an event that led to the wholesale replacement of the *Canadien* elite by a new, British one. British control of the institutions of governance played a key role in this process.[17] While some historians have questioned the economic and social impact of the Conquest, most have underscored how English forms of governance replaced French ones, with the exception of the civil law, and how *Canadiens*, notably elites, were largely excluded from the exercise of official power in the new institutional framework put in place from 1764. As we will see, however, the closer one looks at the actual composition and functioning of the institutions of governance, as concretely experienced rather than in their theoretical form, the less clear becomes the rupture of the Conquest and the exclusion of *Canadiens*.

This is linked to a second issue: the reaction of the *Canadiens* to the alien system of criminal justice, and their acceptance or rejection of it as a legitimate source of social power. Though an earlier Whiggish historiography suggested that *Canadiens* welcomed the overthrow of 'despotic' French criminal justice, most historians now see the impact of this shift in legal culture as being especially profound on the francophone population of the colony. A substantial part of their native legal culture, especially that which defined their relationship to the state, was replaced by an alien system which, even in its native land, had become outmoded and inadequate, ill-adapted to the fundamental transformations of society, and which remained unreformed for some eighty years. The effects on the legitimacy of the system were evident, and the incomprehension and even hostility of *Canadiens* towards this new legal culture, and towards the English colonial state more generally, was thus assured. The general view is thus of a boycott of the new English justice system by the *Canadien* population, lasting well into the first decades of the nineteenth century, which was part of the more generalized alienation of the *Canadien* population that expressed itself in the rise of *Canadien* nationalism and, ultimately, the Rebellions.[18] Again, I will show that this notion of *Canadien* rejection needs substantial revision.

To address these various issues, this study looks both at the everyday criminal justice system itself and at the interaction between the system and the people. The first half of the book concentrates more on the system: the apparatus of the criminal law and the criminal justice system at its lower levels, as seen through a focused examination of the magistrates and their police. Its chapters examine the transfer and adaptation of English criminal law and English courts, the appointment and character of the magistracy, and the police. The second half presents an overview of everyday criminal justice in operation by focusing on the treatment of 'petty' offences – complaints or prosecutions that were not destined for trial in the higher criminal courts of King's Bench or Oyer and Terminer. Its chapters examine the relevance of everyday criminal justice, the experience of people in following the routine course of justice through the system, the way criminal justice was a locus for the exercise of social power, and the extent to which it worked as an instrument of state power.

My concern for the experience of everyday justice has guided the methodological choices in this book. For one, though I am firmly convinced of the usefulness of applying current interpretive and explanatory schemas and theories to the past, I also favour attempting to see the structures and workings of everyday justice through the eyes of those who experienced them – a form of empathetic reconstruction that has some affinities with the phenomenological approach used widely in the social sciences, in its concern for understanding the world as experienced by historical actors. This shift in perspective is particularly useful in the comparative approach that is present throughout this book. For example, it is of crucial importance for historians to identify the late 1830s and early 1840s as the period when paid, professional police forces as we know them first appeared in the Canadas, one of the key acts of genesis of the modern, liberal state. But in seeking to understand how policing was experienced, we must temper our posterior recognition of the novelty of the new police by the observation that, for the tens of thousands of people arrested by constables and watchmen before the 'birth' of the police, the ancien-régime phenomenon of policing may not have been all that different.[19]

As well, my interest in everyday justice leads me away from the emphasis on representation and discourse that characterizes much current legal historiography. In part, this reflects my greater interest in the 'state system' than the 'state idea,' to follow Philip Abrams's well-known distinction.[20] But it also reflects the nature of everyday justice itself. Taken alone, cases such as that of Asselin and Dubois are not especially rich: there is not much more that can be drawn from the sparse and formulaic prose, and the spareness of the documentary record is such that most cases defy any attempt to apply the microhistorical techniques favoured by many historians of popular legal culture. It is thus tempting to concentrate only on the more detailed and fascinating cases, but while these are essential illustrative elements, they cannot be taken as representative of the general experience of everyday justice. As a result both of this and my training as a social historian, I have chosen in the second part of the book in particular to understand experience by looking at it collectively, through quantitative measures, though at the same time integrating the individual narratives of ordinary people who came before the justice system. This may seem contradictory, since one of the criticisms of quantitative history is precisely that it negates individual experience in its search for the mean, but by combining number with exemplary story, average with individual, I have tried to avoid both the impersonality of social-scientific approaches as well as what Margaret McCallum has described as the 'mere compilation of example after example ... closer to voyeurism or journalism than historical inquiry' that can come so easily from sources often filled with fascinating stories interspersed among the more ordinary ones.[21]

The sources at the base of the study are mainly the product of state institutions. First are the judicial archives of the districts of Montreal and Quebec, notably the records preserved by the clerks of the peace and of the crown. The most important of these are the registers of Montreal's Quarter Sessions of the Peace from 1764 to the 1830s; the case files of the same court, which largely survive from the mid-1780s onwards, and those of Quebec's Quarter, Weekly, and Special Sessions, which survive from about 1802 and are indexed in the *Thémis* 2 database; the scattered remaining records of the Weekly Sessions of the Peace of both districts; and the registers and case files of the colony's Courts of King's Bench, which survive partially from the 1760s onwards, though with many gaps.[22] Second are the calendars and registers of the Montreal and Quebec gaols and Houses of Correction, which have generally survived only from the nineteenth century.[23] Third are the administrative records of the city of Montreal, and in particular the registers and papers of the Special Sessions of the Peace and the accounts of the city's road treasurer, from the 1790s onwards, along with the equivalent papers of the first city council between 1833 and 1836.[24] Fourth are the various series of the colonial executive, notably incoming correspondence and documents, outgoing letter books, and papers related to public accounts and commissions.[25] And, finally, there are the various documents produced by the colonial legislature, notably the ordinances and acts of Quebec and Lower Canada through to 1836 and the *Journals* of the House of Assembly of Lower Canada from 1792 to 1836. The study is also based on several prosopographical databases concerning those involved in the administration of everyday criminal justice in the district of Montreal, notably magistrates and police.[26] Along with a wide range of complementary sources, such as newspapers, private fonds, and local histories, these form the empirical basis of my study.

This book grew out of my doctoral thesis, extensively rewritten and with an expanded focus.[27] Thus, the original study did not go beyond 1830 and was limited to the judicial district of Montreal; as much as possible, I have extended the story to the mid-1830s and to the colony as a whole. Yet most of the emphasis is still on the two largest districts of Montreal and Quebec, encompassing about 85 to 90 per cent of the colony's population; much remains to be done on criminal justice in the smaller districts of Trois-Rivières, Saint Francis, and Gaspé. The opening date, 1764, corresponds to the beginnings of British civil administration and the introduction of new state institutions based on the English model, including the criminal justice system, to a population that until four years previously had known only the 'justice criminelle du Roi'; and the study ends in the years leading up to the Rebellions.

1

English Justice in a Foreign Land

... [he said] that the conquest was in itself a misfortune; and that they must bear with a great deal, he was sensible, in consequence of it; that the criminal law must be that of the conqueror, that is, *le loi du prince*; but that they must submit to it.

– Francis Maseres on François-Joseph Cugnet, 1774

The introduction of the criminal law of England, soon after the conquest and cession, has been justly considered beneficial to Canada; and for many years, little modification of it was found necessary. But the English Code of 1763 no longer provides for every emergency in the altered situation of a colony advancing in population and commerce, and exposed to a continual influx of emigrants from Europe and from the United States of America ... Canadian legislation has not kept pace with that of England; where such great additions and alterations have been made ... and our criminal legislation in fact has remained nearly stationary ...

– Montreal King's Bench grand jury presentment, 1826[1]

It is perfectly credible that even a legal nationalist such as François-Joseph Cugnet took the imposition of English criminal law in post-Conquest Quebec as a given. After all, a common doctrine held that the public law of a conquered colony was automatically replaced by that of the conqueror. Quebec historians have generally followed this view, with the inevitability of the change usually taken more or less for granted.[2] However, constitutional arguments aside, in historical terms the wholesale imposition of English criminal law and criminal justice on the new colony of Quebec was far from preordained. In other colonies with established legal systems, British conquerors initially adopted a more flexible approach, based on legal pluralism. In New York, for example, Dutch criminal law and criminal procedure continued to have an influence for several decades after the conquest. And in eighteenth-century India, the East India Company perpetuated Islamic criminal law and justice, overlaid with British-inspired modifications, to create an amalgam of the two systems. There were thus other possible historical outcomes.[3]

In Quebec, however, formal legal pluralism was never applied to the criminal law. Under the 1763 Royal Proclamation, the law imposed right from 1764 was English, acknowledging no other legal order. As André Morel and Douglas Hay pointed out long ago, this new criminal law brought along with it a host of novelties, such as private prosecution, public trials, and the jury system, and also led to the disappearance of fundamental elements of the French criminal law, such as inquisitorial procedure, the right of appeal, judicial torture, and extreme punishments such as breaking on the wheel.[4] The new system of courts also had little in common with pre-Conquest structures: amateur justices of the peace, for example, were quite different from the professional magistrates who formed the base of the system in New France.

The undeniable formal change has led many historians to present the Conquest as a fundamental rupture in criminal justice in the colony. In this view, the reception of English criminal law created a profound discontinuity, in contrast with a much greater continuity in the private law, which, after an initial decade of uncertainty, remained essentially pre-Conquest French in inspiration. As for the administration of criminal justice, the new, English-inspired structures were a foreign system imposed wholesale on the *Canadiens* by their new colonial masters.[5] This radical shift in both criminal law and its administration is seen as all the more significant since there was then little change until the 1840s. As the Montreal grand jury suggested, criminal law and criminal justice in pre-Rebellion Lower Canada remained stuck in an ancien-régime mould.[6]

There are certainly elements of truth in these assertions of both rupture and stasis. The English criminal justice system undoubtedly did not have the same deep-rooted national and constitutional resonance for the newly conquered *Canadiens* as it did in England, and there was certainly no general legislative overhaul of either the criminal law or the administration of criminal justice until the reforms that followed the Rebellions. But this dual postulate holds up less well when we examine the system in its everyday detail, as actually implemented and thus as experienced by the colony's inhabitants. Changes in criminal law and criminal justice across the Conquest, though certain, were less dramatic than such a shift in legal cultures might lead us to expect, and the new system was far less ossified, and changed far more fundamentally, than has been suggested. To demonstrate this, the present chapter examines both the criminal law in general, focusing on the substantive criminal law, and the local administration of justice.

English Law, French Law

In his testimony during the 1774 House of Commons debates on the Quebec Act, Governor Guy Carleton was asked, 'Is there not a great difference between the criminal laws of the two countries?' His answer: 'The criminal law they [the *Canadiens*] have experienced is, in fact, not so extremely different. The mode of prosecution, the mode of deciding by the law, is very different; but the trial of great crimes, in nearly all civilized countries, is almost entirely the same.' Carleton was perhaps basing himself in part on the *Loix criminelles suivies en Canada*, a short (and incomplete) abstract of French criminal law drawn up for him by Cugnet and others that indeed, in the list of offences and their definition, suggested a close resemblance to English criminal law, though with quite different penalties.[7] But the governor was also underscoring a vital point: beyond procedural differences, there were fundamental similarities between French and English criminal law as actually experienced by the *Canadiens*. Intent on conceptualizing the Conquest as rupture, many historians have taken as their starting point the premise that the French and English criminal justice systems were fundamentally different. They might debate which system was more just, rejecting for example the Whiggish postulate of the fairness and lenity of the English system; they might disagree on the reaction of the *Canadiens* towards the conqueror's law; but the basic assumption is of two incommensurable systems.[8]

In re-evaluating this position, we can begin by examining the normativity that underlay each system, as expressed in the substantive criminal law: the range of actions required or prohibited. In the ab-

stract, the two systems expressed normativities that had some significant differences, a notable example being the much wider range of
offences penalized by England's 'Bloody Code.' And so the question
'Are there not more punishments in the law of England than in the law
of Canada?' elicited this reply from Carleton: 'I believe there are: I
cannot pronounce.' Certainly, comparing Blackstone and Hale to Muyart
de Vouglans and Jousse reveals major differences.[9] But, for the population of the colony at large, Blackstone and Hale were no more important after the Conquest than Muyart de Vouglans and Jousse before. It
meant little that the new English criminal law prohibited going about in
the forest with one's face 'blacked,' if that particular norm was never
enforced. What mattered was not the criminal law in theory but the law
they actually saw in force.

In the concrete terms of offences that the criminal justice system
actually dealt with before and after the Conquest, the pattern was
similar: a small number of serious crimes such as murder, rape, and
theft; a much greater number of minor misdemeanours, mostly assaults, with few morality offences; and a large number of regulatory
offences, such as infractions of liquor-licensing provisions, breaches of
road-maintenance regulations, and the like.[10] The bulk of these offences
were defined similarly under both the French and the English systems. For example, both systems divided ordinary homicides into the
equivalent of murder, voluntary manslaughter, and involuntary manslaughter, with widely varying penalties consequent on each.[11] Most
misdemeanours covered essentially the same actions: assaults, for example, were seen similarly under both systems. And, as we will see,
this also applied to regulatory offences. The only significant differences
in terms of offences that were frequently dealt with concerned insults,
more criminalized under the French regime than under the British, and
a new range of offences that accompanied the imposition of British civic
responsibilities, such as refusing to serve as a constable or juror.

The change in criminal law thus brought no substantial change in the
normativity that it enforced. This is unsurprising, given the broader
social constructions that underlay both systems: Judaeo-Christian traditions that penalized significant violence as well as immorality; a
fundamentally patriarchal system that in theory protected women but
in practice dealt severely with female deviance;[12] a class-based system
that ranked property crimes among more serious offences and that
used regulatory measures to attempt to impose order on what was
perceived to be an unruly population; and a shared history of gradual

expansion of the state and its desire to monopolize the use of force. But it also suggests that *Canadiens*, both elite and popular class, might have had less trouble adapting to the new normativity than we might think: quite simply, from their perspective, it was not especially new.

English Law Transformed

What, then, of the purported stasis of the criminal law following reception? Once the Quebec Act added English statutory modifications between 1763 and 1774, the only subsequent changes to the criminal law in the colony were those made by the colonial legislature, apart from a few imperial statutes that applied throughout the colonies. And scholars who have examined colonial legislation are almost unanimous in stating that changes to the criminal law were minimal.[13]

This assertion can be sustained if one adopts a narrow definition of the 'criminal law': that concerning the most serious offences (the definition of 'criminal' in some modern legal systems, such as the French). But there are problems with this definitional stance. First, it puts aside the broader sociological definition of crime as any action or inaction prohibited by state law, essential to any understanding of law and society.[14] For example, regulatory offences, which do not fall under the narrower definition of the criminal, are often as or more important in defining the relationship between individuals and the state (one of the key ends of the criminal law) than more 'serious' offences, with regulatory offences often becoming flashpoints in popular resistance to the colonial state.[15]

Secondly, the narrower definition does not acknowledge that, for contemporaries, the term 'criminal law' often had a broader significance, 'including offences we would label as sins, torts, or breaches of administrative regulations,' as Robert Shoemaker has pointed out.[16] In Quebec and Lower Canada, one can certainly find examples of the more limited definition that evidently inspired the 1826 grand jury. Thus, when in 1764 Governor James Murray's Council published an abstract of 'most of the statute laws relative to criminal offences,' it covered everything from treason and murder to extortion by threatening letter, but none of the myriad lesser statutory offences. But there are also many contrary examples, coming from jurists and judges across the period. Hence, the only significant local compilation of criminal law in the period, Joseph-François Perrault's *Questions et réponses sur le droit criminel du Bas-Canada* (1814), covered the entire range of criminal law, down to and including regulatory infractions. Or consider the language used by the Quebec City chairman of the Quarter Sessions, Jean-Thomas Taschereau, in justifying a crackdown on drunkenness in 1827: 'whenever a charge of drunkenness is laid against a person, it becomes the duty of the magistrate (in as much as drunkenness is by law a crime) to inquire ...'[17]

Adopting this broader definition of criminal law allows us to identify the period from the Conquest to the Rebellions as one of significant legal change, with colonial judicial and legislative elites adapting the law to their needs. Thus, the reception of English criminal law following the Conquest did not apply to offences defined by statutes that concerned purely 'local' situations in England rather than those intended to be generally in force throughout the realm. As the attorney general, George Suckling, declared in 1765, 'many acts of Parliament have given powers to Justices of the Peace to do, or take cognizance of matters which in their nature being local, cannot extend to the plantations.' James Marriott, the English advocate general, went even further: though a strong proponent of the automatic reception of English criminal law following the Conquest, he limited this to the *mala in se*, 'the greater crimes, such as treason and felony,' whereas the *mala prohiba*, lesser offences, were 'not governed by penal statutes antecedent to the conquest.' The limitation was generally taken in the colony to exclude such important English statutes as the Poor Laws and the game laws, crucial to defining a large part of the criminal law in England and, as numerous studies have shown, to the structuring of social relations through the criminal law. As a result, a whole range of activities that the state prohibited in England, such as moving from one parish to another, were not even technically offences in the colony.[18]

The absence of these more 'local' measures left a gap in the colony's criminal law, and, to fill this gap, local legislative bodies enacted a series of measures that created what was in essence a semi-autonomous body of colonial criminal law. Between 1764 and 1836, over 300 colonial ordinances and acts contained provisions that defined offences and attached penalties to them, covering actions ranging from counterfeiting and forgery to children begging in the countryside. This represented a substantial body of legislation: so enamoured were the colony's legislators of penal clauses that they included them in just over two-fifths of substantive ordinances and acts passed between 1764 and 1836.[19]

If we take this legislation into account, it becomes evident that, even with regard to more serious offences, colonial criminal law was not static. Before the institution of representative government, there were already a few significant changes: thus, ordinances prohibited the forging or debasing of currency other than that of Great Britain; and in 1789 petty larceny was redefined as theft of goods worth under twenty shillings, rather than one shilling.[20] Under parliamentary rule, Lower Canadian legislators followed the lead of their British counterparts in expanding the number of felonies, theoretically punishable by death. For example, each of the forty-odd acts that granted toll-bridge monopolies included a clause making destruction of the bridge or tollhouse a felony, and similar protection was accorded to equipment of the Lachine Turnpike, the Champlain and St Lawrence Railway, and the Montreal Gas Light Company. In a dozen or so acts, the legislature also specifically excluded newly created felonies from the benefit of clergy (the legal fiction that allowed first-time offenders to escape sentence of death), for example, for counterfeiting army bills, for aliens returning from banishment, for forging the seals and paper of the three banks chartered in 1820, and for embezzlement by bank officers.[21] In a sense, the Lower Canadian legislature was thus creating its own 'Bloody Code': even though none of these acts created a new class of offence, and none was a dramatic departure from English precedent, they represented the sort of 'felony creep' that had dramatically padded the English criminal code in the eighteenth century.[22]

Perjury is a good illustration both of this gradual statutory extension of offences and of its potential effects. Under the common law, perjury applied only to oaths taken with regard to civil suits or criminal prosecutions, not to oaths in general; a breach of oaths of office was not perjury.[23] But in Lower Canada, as in England, the definition of perjury was gradually expanded: between 1793 and 1836, some forty-odd statutes extended perjury to oaths ranging from that taken to claim the bounty on wolves to the qualification declarations of electors. These were not simply abstract modifications, for perjury prosecutions under the statutes could be a quite credible threat. For example, during the 1827 elections in William Henry, the attorney general, James Stuart, threatened supporters of his opponent with perjury prosecutions and pillorying if they took the electors' oath, and instituted proceedings against several of them. And the perjury provisions in an 1830 statute establishing property qualifications for justices of the peace led several to refuse the office, since, as one put it, 'a magistrate, however extensive his property may be, who shall take the oath prescribed by this law, will be liable to be prosecuted for perjury by any the most infamous scoundrel in society.'[24]

The criminal law was thus far from immobile. Still, as far as more serious offences are concerned, this was not much more than a tweaking of the system. Far more significant was the expansion of lesser offences, most of which came under the summary jurisdiction of justices of the peace. More than simply procedural enactments, these were in fact substantive criminal law, penalizing a wide range of actions from the selling of bad meat to trespassing and the refusal to answer census questions. Nor can we simply dismiss them as mere administrative measures with little bite: while most involved fines, a significant number allowed magistrates to imprison violators summarily, and the sixty-five *Canadiens* crammed into the Montreal gaol in 1778 for refusing to obey militia ordinances can testify to their potentially severe effects.[25]

Some of these 'new' offences were hardly novel, since they were analogous to similar offences in England defined by 'local' legislation that had not been received into the colony: selling liquor without a licence, for example, or using unregulated weights and measures. However, many concerned matters specific to the colony. The 1787 ordinance concerning the *corvée* (labour) duty imposed on inhabitants to provide transport for the military, which was theoretically in force to 1836 and beyond, is a good example. The preamble of the ordinance referred explicitly to 'the local position of this province' and then went on to detail offences generally unknown in England, such as failure to cart military stores, enforcing them with what were in some cases fairly substantial penalties, all tried summarily before a single justice.[26] Similarly, eighteenth-century laws that regulated contacts between the European population and aboriginal peoples, such as those banning the sale of alcohol to Natives and prohibiting settlement in Native villages, had, of course, no English counterpart.[27] Even laws with English counterparts often defined offences quite differently: hence, though England did have militia laws, the duties imposed by them were considerably less onerous than those in the colony.[28]

As well, many of these colonial modifications to the criminal law, and especially those imposing substantial penalties, concerned the relationship between state and society. *Corvée*, militia, and licensing laws all directly involved the interests of the colonial state. And, through its autonomous criminal law, the state also sought to regulate social and economic relations. For example, though various English statutes regulated parts of master/servant relationships, colonial legislation added to these and also modified them to suit colonial circumstances, as it did when it punished voyageurs for deserting on their trips inland.[29]

A substantial part of the relationship between the state and colonial society, as defined by colonial legislators, was thus not simply copied from the English experience but shaped instead by local factors. In fact, these measures, and especially those passed in the eighteenth century, harkened to the relationship between state and society under the French regime. The militia ordinances, for example, imposed many of the same obligations as before the Conquest.[30] Or consider the selection of pre-Conquest regulations presented by François-Joseph Cugnet in his two 1775 compilations, *Extraits ... des reglemens et ordonnances de police* and *Traité de la police.* Cugnet's rhetorical purpose was to contrast the good order ensured by pre-Conquest regulations with the post-Conquest anarchy that he attributed to 'la liberté Anglaise.'[31] Leaving aside Cugnet's obviously rosy view of pre-Conquest practices, his selections nevertheless include many provisions essentially repeated in ordinances passed by the governor and council in the decades following the Conquest, such as those on fire prevention in the towns, the upkeep of roads, the regulation of markets, and so on. In the three fire-prevention ordinances passed between 1768 and 1773, virtually all the obligations that were enforced by penal sanctions, whether it be having chimneys swept once a month or fixing ladders to roofs, were essentially re-enactments of pre-Conquest regulations. In the eighteenth century in particular, the substantive criminal law enacted by the legislature thus contained much that was in no way a departure from pre-Conquest law. *Canadien* inhabitants would have been quite familiar with regulations on military *corvées*, the marking of winter roads, or the sale of alcohol to Natives, and probably more so than recent immigrants from Britain or even the other American colonies.

The Justices as Legislators

But criminal legislation in the colony came from more than just the legislature. From the very beginning of civilian rule, the colony's justices of the peace made rules and regulations for the 'police' of their respective cities, the equivalent of municipal by-laws, with 'police' used in its ancien-régime sense of public order. They thereby effectively created a whole new series of offences, which they then tried themselves, in a remarkable conflation of legislative and judicial powers.

In England, justices of the peace had no formal authority to make legislation of any sort, since their function, as defined in both their commissions and the statutes, was judicial and administrative. Nevertheless, by the eighteenth century, many county Quarter Sessions had assumed this power, in effect constituting themselves as local legislative authorities and passing local ordinances on subjects ranging from road-mending to vagrancy. As one historian has pointed out, this was an unconstitutional arrogation of the legislative powers of parliament. The practice, however, was not uniformly carried over to the American colonies: at least in New England, with its strong tradition of elected local government, local legislative activity was largely the purview of non-judicial bodies such as town meetings.[32]

Though in Quebec there was at first no legislative authority allowing the justices to promulgate local legislation, they seem to have assumed that they had this power. The lack of elected town governments also created a legislative void, which the justices filled. Thus, Quebec City's justices published a first set of regulations in May 1765, dealing with the market. And in Montreal, the first record of the justices' legislative activity is in October 1765, when they issued an order that all horses be hobbled, fixing a twenty-shilling fine for each offence. Market regulations followed in December 1765, and the following April, the justices issued a series of seven orders that established what was in effect the beginnings of a municipal code for the city.[33]

This first set of Montreal regulations is worth describing at length, because in many respects it set the tone for all that would follow. The first two orders set the fees to be paid by butchers, bakers, and market vendors to the clerk of the markets, ordered the clerk of the markets to examine and stamp all weights and measures and to report all frauds, and prohibited empty carts from standing on the market-place. The third ordered all inhabitants to keep clean the streets in front of their houses. The fourth prohibited tavern-keepers from entertaining any servants or slaves, on penalty of a hefty fine of £5, a provision that extended to the entire district of Montreal. The fifth ordered all freeholders to pave or flag the footpaths in front of their houses, while the sixth prohibited the disposal of live cinders out of doors. And the seventh prohibited private lotteries. They were thus a combination of practical administrative measures, local-improvement initiatives, and attempts to impose a particular moral vision, and in that sense they were reminiscent not only of similar laws in American colonial towns but also of the police regulations in the towns of New France before the Conquest.[34]

That the justices assumed this legislative authority does not seem to have raised many objections. When the administrative structure of the colony was overhauled in 1777, following the Quebec Act and the American invasion, the Legislative Council confirmed the justices' powers over local regulation, allowing them to impose fines up to forty shillings. What objections there were came from England, where the legal officer who vetted colonial ordinances noted that 'the expression of *rules and orders touching the police* is exceedingly indefinite, and the power given by [the ordinance] very undefined and uncertain, and therefore liable to objection on this account as well as because the legislature have hereby delegated their power of legislation.'[35]

Though the measure was initially meant to be temporary, it was renewed until 1791, though still limited to the towns: an attempt in 1787 to expand the justices' powers to their entire district failed in the Legislative Council, likely owing to objections by the seigneurs.[36] In 1791, however, a permanent ordinance expanded the justices' legislative powers. It raised the ceiling on fines to £5; it declared the rules and regulations to be 'as valid and binding in the law as if the same was specifically enacted by an Ordinance of the Provincial Legislature'; it provided a partial listing of affairs that fell within the jurisdiction of the justices, referring to Quebec City's regulations as a model; it allowed the justices to make rules and regulations for any town or village with more than thirty houses when a majority of the householders filed a petition to that effect; and it may also have extended these powers to the justices of Trois-Rivières.[37] The provisions of the 1791 ordinance were essentially repeated by an act of 1802, which also required the justices to submit all regulations to the King's Bench for approval, and explicitly extended the powers to the justices of Trois-Rivières. Once again, the only objection came from London. In 1803 the Board of Trade noted (erroneously) that the legislative powers granted the justices were 'contrary to the established principles and practice of the legislature of this kingdom' and asked the governor to justify this delegation of legislative power. The answer, prepared by Jonathan Sewell, the attorney general, defended a practice that he claimed had, since 1777, 'been attended with the most beneficial consequences, promoting invariably the improvement, health, comfort and good order of those cities and their inhabitants.' As Sewell argued, the regulations were 'no more than the bye-laws of a corporate town in England,' could not run contrary to English or colonial law, and were both local and limited in operation.[38] Nine years later, in 1811, the Assembly refused to continue the justices' legislative power over smaller towns and villages, on the grounds that it had led to abuses of power (without giving any specific examples). Instead, a few years later, the legislators created their own code of municipal regulations for smaller towns that had elected trustees to oversee their application. However, the justices retained their legislative powers over the cities, which were confirmed and made permanent by an act of 1817, remained in force until the beginning of elected municipal government in 1833, and were revived when the incorporations lapsed in 1836.[39]

The 1817 act, however, led to a broader debate on the constitutionality of the justices' legislative powers. In the Assembly, the bill had been sponsored by Thomas McCord, who was also one of the chief magistrates of Montreal. Augustin Cuvillier, a future justice of the peace himself, accused McCord of having pulled a fast one on the Assembly by having them pass a bill that made the justices' powers permanent, a measure that they had always intended to avoid. Denis-Benjamin Viger, one of the leading lights in the *Canadien* party, rose in support of Cuvillier. Marshalling arguments little different from those of the English Board of Trade officials, he declared that the Assembly had acted by necessity rather than by choice:

> It was an experiment, and the powers of making Rules and Regulations of Police had as a matter of course been confided to the Magistrates of those Cities. But those Magistrates were also charged with the administration of the municipal revenues, as well as with the judicial functions relating to them. The Law therefore contained in itself principles diametrically opposed to those of the Constitution. It gave to a body of men liable to be removed from day-to-day powers repugnant in themselves, that of legislating, enforcing and judging of delinquencies committed in contravention to their acts of legislation. It was an union of the legislative, executive and judicial powers which according to the principles of the best Governments were absolutely incompatible.

Viger nevertheless added that he did not intend to accuse the magistrates in general of having misused their power.[40] Still, his position was diametrically opposed to that of Tory magistrates such as John Fletcher, Quebec City's chairman of the Quarter Sessions, who had declared in 1816 that 'the power given to the magistrates of making regulations of police relative to those circumstances on which the tranquility and good order of the lower classes of society principally depend ... should ... be limited only by the obvious principles of political œconomy and sound jurisprudence.'[41] Tory paternalism thus confronted Reform constitutionalism over the justices' power to regulate everyday life in the cities.

Regardless of the political and constitutional arguments, between 1765 and 1833, the justices in Quarter Sessions exercised broad legislative powers over local matters in the two main cities (and from 1791 or 1802 in Trois-Rivières as well), and from 1791 to 1811 they had similar powers over smaller towns and villages. As well, from 1802, Quarter Sessions could make master/servant regulations for their respective districts, a power that they retained until 1836.[42] The justices were not at all averse to exercising these regulatory powers. In Montreal, for example, they made regulations on about eighty different occasions, including eleven full sets of regulations.[43] As for the regulation of towns and villages, the Montreal justices made regulations for L'Assomption, Berthier, Boucherville, Laprairie, Saint-Denis, Terrebonne, and William Henry, though many major towns and villages in the district did not have such regulations and there was some local resistance.[44]

The full sets of urban regulations in particular are fascinating examples of legislative activity, in that they represent an early attempt at rational codification, beginning almost a century before Quebec's Civil Code. The initial regulations of the 1760s and 1770s were fairly haphazard, issued on an ad hoc basis. Already by the early 1780s, however, both the Montreal and Quebec City justices had collated and systematized their regulations, which were laid out in distinct numbered articles. The first full set for Quebec City in 1780 contained thirty-seven numbered articles divided into two sections, whereas that for Montreal in 1783 had four sections and forty-one numbered articles. By the early 1810s, the codes of both cities were published in book form, divided into thematic chapters. The 1817 regulations for Montreal, published as a bilingual compendium, contained some 180 pages with facing French and English text, just like the statute books, and was divided into nine main chapters, with 120 articles ranging in length from a few sentences to several pages.[45] In Trois-Rivières, however, with a much smaller population, no such codification was apparently attempted: even in 1830, the district's clerk of the peace was complaining that the only way to consult the regulations was by examining the original registers of the court.[46] Still, at least in Montreal and Quebec City, the rules were well publicized: as well as being printed in newspapers and in pamphlet form, they were also posted as broadsides and publicly read by the town criers.[47]

Through these municipal regulations, the justices, drawn from the towns' *Canadien* and British elites, sought to regulate such important matters as building practices, road repairs, begging, and, more generally, public conduct in the towns. Many were common-sense rules, but the regulations also reflected the changing values of these elites. Take, for example, the regulation of morality. In the eighteenth century, the few rules and regulations with a moral bent largely targeted those profiting from immoral acts. Thus, the 1766 Montreal regulations prohibiting lotteries and restricting the access of apprentices and slaves to taverns were directed only against those who ran such lotteries and taverns, and regulations from the 1780s onwards imposed Sabbatarian restrictions on carters, markets, and street-vendors.[48]

Around the turn of the nineteenth century, however, the tone of the regulations in Montreal at least began to change, with the justices' attention turning more and more to regulating actions on the part of the populace as a whole which did not fit with their conception of a well-ordered society. The first indication of this shift came in 1799, when 'idle boys' were prohibited from playing on Sundays in the Place d'Armes, with constables assigned to ensure that they did not. The new tone was clear in an 1803 regulation:

> The magistrates, seeing with concern that many young and other idle persons assemble together in numbers, on Sundays and holidays, for the purpose of play and amusement, in the streets, squares, and other places of the town and suburbs, instead of attending divine worship; and being determined to put a stop to this growing evil, do prohibit in the most positive manner all such assemblies during divine service, or from nine in the morning until five in the afternoon ... and it is also forbidden to all and every person or persons to permit or suffer, within the city or suburbs, on Sundays, any balls, assemblies, or dances, at or within their houses or outhouses.[49]

This pattern of direct intervention into public and private behaviour continued in the thirty years that followed. Thus, a regulation in 1806 made it illegal to bathe nude in the St Lawrence; regulations in 1817 also outlawed *charivaris*, skating or sliding with a sledge in the city, playing at marbles or cards in the market-place, and wheels of fortune; and regulations in 1821 added prohibitions against throwing snowballs and playing with hoops. The 1817 regulation against *charivaris* is particularly interesting, since in theory it allowed justices to deal summarily, in Weekly Sessions, with a public-order offence that they would otherwise have been brought before a jury, which René Hardy suggests shows a significant modification in elite perceptions of urban public order.[50]

These regulations are evidence of the beginnings of what would later become the Victorian bourgeois concern for morality and urban disorder, and they provide suggestive evidence that the shift towards a liberal vision of society, based on individual responsibility, began earlier than has often been postulated.[51] However, the substance of the rules and regulations also harkened back to the concern with vice that was so integral to English and colonial elite views of the popular classes in the seventeenth and eighteenth centuries. Thus, the Montreal prohibition of *charivaris* was similar to French-regime regulations, while the provisions on morality echoed those both of New France and of the American colonies.[52] The reasons for the change can also be traced to more local factors. Montreal experienced rapid growth in the first decades of the nineteenth century: a town of perhaps 6,000 people in the mid-1790s had become a small city with a population approaching 30,000 by the late 1820s. In an increasingly complex urban society, the city justices perhaps felt that extrajudicial community sanctions were no longer sufficient to regulate disorderly and immoral behaviour. As we will see, they also had an increasing capacity to intervene, with the professionalization of local justice and the growth of the police.

In Montreal, just as individual conduct judged immoral or disorderly was increasingly targeted by the justices' regulations, so too were specific groups that embodied such behaviour, at least to the elites, gradually brought under tighter legislative control. Consider, for example, the regulation of the indigent poor, beggars, and vagrants. Begging was illegal under English penal statutes, but in eighteenth-century Quebec this was difficult to enforce, since the main penalty was imprisonment in a house of correction, an institution that essentially did not exist until 1799. Though the issue seems never to have arisen, there may also have been the legal problem that the vagrancy laws were part of the English poor-law system, and thus perhaps not in force in the colony. At any rate, the justices themselves filled the legislative void with their own regulations, with a first one in Montreal in the 1760s that simply required beggars to have a pass from the local clergy, though also prohibiting outright any begging by children; the same licensing provision appears to have been continued in the 1770s, and it was included in Quebec City regulations from the 1780s. As Mary Anne Poutanen has pointed out, this was a direct continuation of pre-Conquest French practices.[53]

In the 1790s, Quebec City justices, among others, began to complain that without formal houses of correction, they could not legally enforce the English vagrancy laws: as they declared in 1795, 'many offenders go unpunished, who by law are subject to commitment to a Work-House, Bridewell or House of Correction, there being no such places of punishment to commit them to.' This was somewhat misleading, since the justices had long considered their gaols to be de facto workhouses or houses of correction. Thus, following a 1766 petition from the Quebec City justices, the executive ordered that two rooms in the gaol be set aside as a workhouse, and gaol calendars from the 1760s show the justices occasionally imprisoning vagrants in it. This apparently continued in the 1780s as well, and in Montreal the justices in the 1790s also occasionally confined men and women deemed idle and disorderly to gaol.[54]

Still, the de facto situation, which was on shaky legal grounds, became increasingly unsatisfying and as a result, in 1799, the legislature established houses of correction in Montreal and Quebec City, referring explicitly to English law through the use of the terms 'idle and disorderly persons, rogues and vagabonds or incorrigible rogues.' At first, the law simply allowed the existing gaols to be used as houses of correction (thereby confirming the de facto practice in Quebec City), and there was no further change in the regulation of begging by the justices. However, a new law in 1802 put the houses of correction on a firmer basis, providing for separate establishments, and led the justices in both Montreal and Quebec City to regulate begging more strictly. The Montreal justices opted not for the total ban under the English vagrancy laws but rather for a reformulation of the licensing system in place since the Conquest. Thus, after noting that the establishment of the local House of Correction meant that 'several provisions of the existing law in criminal cases will have effect, which by reason of the want of such houses have hitherto been dormant,' they summarized the provisions of English statute law that outlawed begging and declared their intent to put the law against vagrants and idle and disorderly persons into effect. But they then went on to declare that 'proper objects of charitable relief' could beg, as long as they appeared yearly before a committee of justices (thereby shifting the responsibility of licensing from religious to secular authorities) and wore a large cloth bearing the letters P and M on their shoulder (for 'pauper' and 'mendiant'), in the same fashion as paupers receiving parish relief in England. All who did not comply with these regulations, or who begged without permission, were to be apprehended by the city's constables and taken before a justice to be dealt with as vagrants; an American traveller in 1817 was struck by the enforcement of this measure. Similar measures were taken in Quebec City, though until 1819 permits were still granted by the clergy and then countersigned by the justices.[55]

In Montreal, the licensing system persisted until 1819, when the establishment of a house of industry led the justices to outlaw 'the pernicious practice of street-begging' as soon as the wardens of the house proved the institution capable of supporting all the indigent poor. Though the ban on begging came into force six months later, it evidently did not have the intended effect: an 1821 grand jury presentment pointed out that, while street beggars had initially disappeared, they were now back in full force. The justices' response was to return to the mixed system in effect after 1802, with a licensing system coupled with a ban on unlicensed begging; yet, once again, this did not prevent street begging, which continued through the 1830s.[56]

Overall, the development of local regulations by the justices illustrates several characteristics of colonial criminal law. First, it is evident that the criminal law did not remain essentially unchanged before the Rebellions. By themselves, neither the variable prohibition on begging, nor the outlawing of snowballs, nor even the *corvée* laws marked fundamental transformations, yet they were significant nonetheless. For it was not through major overhauls that the law was modified to suit colonial circumstances and the wishes of the colony's elites, but through piecemeal measures, enacted by the various legislative bodies under the control of colonial elites. The cumulative effect of all these changes was such that, by the 1830s, the range of actions that the state considered offences and penalized was substantially different from what it had been in the 1760s. To ignore these changes is to create the illusion that colonial elites did not regularly attempt to use the legislative process to regulate colonial society.

Second, criminal law in the colony often deviated significantly from that of England. There was no slavish repetition of British provisions; instead, legislation was responsive in large part to local circumstances. At the colonial level, laws attaching penal provisions to such matters as universal militia service, trade with Natives, and the configuration of winter roads had no real counterparts in England, which had no universal militia service, no Natives to trade with, and not enough snow to worry about winter roads. The colony's elites, on the other hand, had an evident interest in ensuring a well-regulated militia, the maintenance of trade monopolies with the Natives, and adequate winter communications. Even within the colony, legislation varied according to local circumstances. Police regulations in Montreal, for example, were not the same as those in Quebec City, each being adapted to the particular circumstances of the city and its elites. Thus, in the 1780s, Quebec City had far more elaborate regulations concerning carters, understandable given the importance of the import/export business in the city. On the other hand, the nineteenth-century moral 'turn' seems to have been less pronounced there, though regulations like one in 1827 punishing public drunkenness (in response to the colonial administration's objections to Taschereau's enforcement of English criminal law against offenders) also heralded later morality-inspired legislation.[57]

Third, much as for colonial ordinances and acts, the police regulations, especially in the eighteenth century, show the persisting influence of pre-Conquest legal norms. The most striking example is perhaps police regulations in Montreal and Quebec City that outlawed the shooting of partridges, in exactly the same terms as a 1721 police *ordonnance* of Intendant Michel Bégon; the 1811 regulations for Quebec City even reproduced the pre-Conquest *ordonnance* verbatim, including Bégon's signature at the end. Rather than wiping the slate clean and imposing an alien law, in many cases the justices, like colonial legislators, continued the pre-Conquest criminal law, de facto and even sometimes de jure.

And finally, the reformulation of the criminal law was the work not only of colonial legislators but also of the local state. Begging, for example, was criminalized and decriminalized not according to English law, or even to colonial statutes, but following regulations made by the justices themselves. And it is to the system of justices and their courts that we now turn.

The Justices and Their Courts

Much like the criminal law, the criminal justice system in Quebec and Lower Canada underwent great apparent change at the Conquest, followed by seeming stability until the reforms of the Special Council in the late 1830s. Historians have noted this and postulated both the imposition of a foreign system on an unwilling population and a blockage thereafter that was relieved only with the loosening of democratic constraints following the Rebellions.[58] And yet, at the level of the justices of the peace, the rupture-stasis model does not really hold. An

English-inspired system of local justice was transplanted at the beginning of British civilian rule, and was still in place at the Rebellions; but the system was both fundamentally shaped by local influences and underwent profound modifications.

In eighteenth-century England, as in most British colonies, the justices of the peace were the base of the criminal justice system, both in towns and in the countryside.[59] In general, justices filled four overlapping roles. First, they acted as local administrators, whose duties included the legislative functions discussed above. Second, justices were also the state's primary representatives in keeping the peace: they oversaw policing and led the civil forces of the state in the repression of popular disturbances such as labour confrontations or election riots. Third, justices had what were generally referred to as 'ministerial' functions: performing the preliminary steps in most criminal cases, such as hearing plaintiffs, issuing warrants or summonses, examining accused and witnesses, and determining whether accused should be bound over by recognizance or imprisoned until trial. And finally, justices judged offenders in a variety of venues: in formal courts of General or Quarter Sessions of the Peace, whose effective jurisdiction extended to most offences with punishments less than the loss of life and limb; in 'petty sessions,' summary hearings held with other justices with jurisdiction over a wide range of lesser statutory offences; or alone, often in their own parlours. By the mid-eighteenth century, with an ever-increasing patchwork of statutes that created new offences and put them under the jurisdiction of the justices, as well as the decline of other local courts, the various courts of the justices were the main venues for the trial of all but the most serious offences.

When the institution of the justices of the peace was transplanted into Quebec in 1764, so too were their functions, based largely on English precedent. Even more than in neighbouring colonies like New York or Massachusetts, the wording of the commissions appointing justices closely followed that used in England; accordingly, the justices in theory inherited the full panoply of peace-keeping and ministerial functions of their counterparts in England. Likewise, the court system reproduced the basic English norms: Quarter Sessions of the Peace, held every three months in Quebec City and Montreal; Weekly Sessions of the Peace, essentially regularized petty sessions, held in the two cities every Tuesday; and summary hearings outside formal courts. The justices were also to judge small civil matters, in a departure from the English model but following the practice in Nova Scotia and other colonies. Apart from the justices' civil jurisdiction, which was largely abolished in 1770, the broad outlines of the system of justices and courts thus did indeed resemble that of England and other English colonies, and hence represented a significant change from the centralized and professionalized pre-Conquest system, with its *prévôté* in Quebec City and *juridictions royales* in Montreal and Trois-Rivières, staffed by professional judges who handled most criminal cases. In broad, structural terms, the system also changed very little before the late 1830s: in 1837 there were still Quarter and Weekly Sessions, along with summary hearings. And yet, in the details of its structure, the system of justices and courts was significantly different from that in England, and also changed substantially between the 1760s and the 1830s.[60]

Legislative Stasis

Significant change did not come from the successive colonial legislatures, which did little to modify the criminal justice system at the level of the justices themselves. Until the 1780s, for example, colonial legislation made no mention of the justices' preliminary functions, apart from occasional passing reference to the procedures leading to the summary trial of specific statutory offences. Their ministerial functions in theory remained essentially the same as those of their English counterparts. Hence, instructions drawn up for the justices in 1764 by George Suckling, the attorney general, were cribbed directly from English legal authorities, and similarly, the sections in Joseph-François Perrault's 1789 French edition of Burn's *Justice of the Peace and Parish Officer* on ministerial duties were direct translations of its English source.[61] From the 1790s, there were a few modifications, most notably a number of acts in the 1790s and 1800s, during the perceived threat of French and American invasion, which prohibited justices from granting bail to enemy aliens or those accused of treasonable practices.[62] But, overall, there was little legislative modification of the justices' preliminary role, and attempts from the late 1820s to institute more substantial changes – for example, in the way justices granted bail – failed in the increasingly bitter climate reigning between the Legislative Council and the Assembly.[63]

The court structure established in 1764 also remained largely unchanged by legislation until the 1830s. Apart from the brief interregnum of 1775–6, during the American invasion, when the regular court system was in abeyance, the only significant structural changes came with the creation of the new judicial districts of Gaspé (1788), Trois-Rivières (1790), and Saint Francis (1823), each of which was given its own roster of justices and, consequently, its own system of justices' courts.[64] As for the jurisdiction of the justices' courts, the legislature also did little. The Quarter Sessions from 1764 onwards were modelled directly on English county Quarter Sessions: they were held by two and then three justices, and their criminal jurisdiction was defined not by colonial legislation but in the commissions of the justices, essentially copies of the English model. The only real jurisdictional change occurred with the creation of statutory offences in colonial legislation which were then specifically placed under the jurisdiction of the Quarter Sessions, either directly or on appeal. By this back door, in fact, the legislature progressively gave the Quarter Sessions an extensive appellate jurisdiction over many of the offences tried summarily by the justices outside the Sessions. As for the Weekly Sessions, they were not directly based on any equivalent court in the English system (though similar to the regular petty sessions held in some counties), and their general jurisdiction and functioning was also only vaguely defined. The single positive legislative directive with respect to these courts was that they be held every Tuesday, by two urban justices, with their jurisdiction defined simply as the 'regulation of the police and other matters and things' relating to the office of the justices of the peace. As well, from 1794, legislators explicitly recognized the right of justices to hold so-called Special Sessions outside the regular Tuesday courts. Apart from the extension of their jurisdiction to new statutory offences, the legislature had little else to say about Weekly Sessions.

Until the 1820s, even the summary hearings of the justices outside the formal courts remained largely unregulated. In the numerous instances where the legislature put offences under the justices' summary jurisdiction, the statutes generally stated simply that offenders were to be tried 'in a summary manner,' referring implicitly to English practices, and specified little beyond the number of justices and witnesses required, the limitation of actions, and the manner of recovering penalties. For example, colonial legislation prior to 1824 never gave the forms of the summons, warrant, or conviction that justices were to use in criminal cases, in contrast to the detailed forms given for the justices' summary civil jurisdiction.[65] It was not until 1824 that the legislature attempted to impose a more formal structure on the summary hearings of the justices. The sponsor of the bill, Jean-Thomas Taschereau, who was also one of Quebec City's chairmen of the Quarter Sessions, noted that the intent was 'to avoid unfounded suspicion against the Magistrates, which might be occasioned by the improper conduct of any individual of the body, and which might be unfavorable to the execution of the many useful laws, which were confided to the Justices of the Peace.' The resulting act, passed with little debate, did little more than reiterate standard English practices: it required justices to keep a record of all their proceedings and to submit detailed reports of all fines they collected to the clerk of the peace (which they already had to do under their commissions), and it also provided a general form for convictions.[66]

Overall, the legislative record with regard to the justices' ministerial and judicial functions was slight. Reviewing legislation alone, one might be left with the impression of an essentially English system transplanted, and then left unchanged; at best, there was a slight procedural tightening. But this impression of wholesale transplantation followed by stasis is misleading, as we can see from a closer examination of two key aspects of the system: centralization and professionalization.

Continued Centralization

Perhaps the most obvious departure from the English court system was the centralization of the courts. In England, Quarter Sessions were based on the county, and counties were small enough so that travelling to court was relatively easy, especially since in many counties the Sessions rotated between different towns. Similarly, in Upper Canada, Quarter Sessions were held in each of the growing number of districts into which the colony was divided, reaching twelve by the early 1830s.[67] In Quebec and Lower Canada, however, the courts were based on much larger judicial districts: only two initially (Montreal and Quebec), and even the creation of the additional districts of Gaspé and Trois-Rivières in the late eighteenth century left four immense districts. The district of Montreal, for example, even if restricted to its settled areas, covered an area roughly the size of southern England, with its furthest significantly settled places by 1810, Barnston and Hull, being respectively 140 and 175 kilometres from the seat of the Quarter Sessions in Montreal. As well, apart from in the Gaspé, the Quarter Sessions sat only in the district's main town. This judicial centralization was the subject of repeated complaint, and from the late 1810s proposals were made to set up additional Quarter Sessions, notably by using the electoral counties into which the colony had been divided since the 1790s.

However, the only measure taken was the 1823 creation of the district of Saint Francis, with its own Quarter Sessions in Sherbrooke. By 1824, the Assembly had reached the stage of resolving that Quarter Sessions should be established in the country parts of the province and debated a bill to that effect; similar measures were introduced in subsequent years, but all failed, often through political infighting within the *Canadien* majority. In the late 1820s, governors Dalhousie and James Kempt also decried the lack of county judicial structures. Dalhousie proposed setting up Quarter Sessions in each county, so that country justices might attend Quarter Sessions; Kempt noted the effects of centralization on colonial finances, stating that while in other colonies, as in England, 'there are county magistrates & county gaols, sheriffs of counties & clerks of the peace, and other officers attached to the Quarter Sessions,' paid for by county rates, in Lower Canada all such officials were paid for out of the general provincial revenue. But it was not until 1832 that a law finally authorized establishing Quarter Sessions in counties that built their own gaols and courthouses, and only two counties had undertaken the necessary construction before the Rebellions, with only one holding Quarter Sessions. True decentralization of the justice system would not come about in earnest until the late 1850s.[68]

Similar centralization characterized the Weekly Sessions. In England, petty sessions, the regular meetings of two or more justices, had by the eighteenth century become so formalized that some counties were divided into clearly defined geographical jurisdictions, each with its own petty sessions, clerks, and so on, which dealt with a large portion of the justices business, both administrative and judicial.[69] But petty sessions in England generally exercised jurisdiction over only their specific subdivisions of the county, giving them a decidedly local scope. The Weekly Sessions operated under no such restraint. Though clearly established at first for the purposes of urban regulation, the two justices who made up the Weekly Sessions could also try any offence that had been placed under the summary jurisdiction of one or two justices, which included most statutory offences. As a result, throughout their existence, the Weekly Sessions determined cases arising from their entire district, notably liquor-licensing infractions. In effect, the urban justices who sat on the bench arrogated to themselves a summary jurisdiction that in England was usually exercised by local rural justices.

Centralization also affected the composition of the justices' courts. In England, many county Quarter Sessions were attended by justices from throughout the county, and it was not uncommon to see twenty or thirty justices on the bench. The Sessions thus became the focus for local, county power, often as a counterweight to the centralizing tendencies of the growing central state. This Court/Country split was also reproduced the American colonies: in Virginia, for example, the system of local county courts allowed localism to dominate until well after the Revolution.[70] In Quebec and Lower Canada, though it is hard to argue that the Court had definitively won, the Country had definitely lost. As we will see, the benches of both the Quarter and Weekly Sessions were dominated by urban justices, who acted only within the confines of those formal courts. Rural plaintiffs were also far less likely to bring their cases before the urban courts. Yet, paradoxically, the capacity of the Lower Canadian state to impinge more directly upon civil society in the countryside was considerably enhanced, for urban justices, with no ties to the local community to restrain them, could enforce such unpopular legislation as liquor-licensing provisions.

Differing from the English and colonial model, the continued centralization of the formal courts nevertheless represented significant continuity across the Conquest. Criminal justice based in the main urban centres had been a feature of the pre-Conquest French regime, where few seigneurial courts heard criminal matters. For many rural *Canadiens*, as inconvenient as it might be, there was nothing new in having to travel to Quebec City or Montreal for criminal cases. And this was arguably more important for their experience of justice than the formal structure and composition of the courts.

Rural Decentralization

The continuing centralization of the justices' formal courts nevertheless masked another equally important development: the spread of summary justice in the countryside. In England, many cases in rural areas were dealt with not by Quarter or even petty sessions but by individual justices summarily disposing of cases, whether by imposing bonds to keep the peace, or summarily fining offenders, or imprisoning them in the county House of Correction.[71] And in Lower Canada as well, more and more justices dealt with matters summarily rather than sending them on to the formal courts in the cities.

As in England, the absence of almost any records of these summary proceedings makes an overall assessment difficult. There are few original records of rural justices' summary proceedings, and though they were required to account for fines they imposed summarily, few did so, with the colony's public accounts containing only scattered traces of this kind of judicial activity.[72] As for the summary imposition of peace bonds, rural justices simply kept them among their own papers, and few of these have survived. Still, rural summary hearings seem to have been rare in the eighteenth century. Thus, in 1791, of thirteen rural justices from the district of Montreal who answered a query of the Executive Council, only four declared ever having imposed fines, and only one, René Boucher de La Bruère de Montarville of Boucherville, with any regularity: between 1787 and 1789, he had imposed fines on at least twenty-three individuals, for breaking the peace, not working on the roads, or refusing to provide *corvée* labour for the king. Most justices preferred to refer cases to the urban Sessions rather than impose fines themselves.[73]

But this began to change in the nineteenth century. For example, in 1804, the *grand-voyer* (chief roads official) of the district of Montreal noted that justices in the seigneuries of Châteauguay, Sorel, and Verchères had imposed fines but not remitted the money to him. There are also indications that in some villages more regular petty sessions were being set up: by the 1810s, the justices of the peace in L'Assomption, north of Montreal, were hearing cases in the parish's church hall, in what they called Special Sessions, which even used their own specially printed summons. By the 1820s, this sort of activity was becoming quite common: at a minimum, a little over half the approximately 125 rural justices who were active in the district of Montreal between 1821 and 1830 imposed summary judgments of some sort. And inquiries in 1832 and 1833 by the Assembly into the collection of fines by justices found that many reported having collected fines though not accounting for them. Overall, there was evidently far more criminal justice in the countryside in the 1820s than there had been in the 1780s and 1790s, though it has left few traces in the documentary record.[74]

The Professionalization of the Urban Magistracy

An equally significant transformation was the professionalization of the urban magistracy. Initially, the Conquest had had the opposite effect, with the professional magistrates of the French regime replaced in part by the amateur justices who characterized the English colonial state. Yet, by this time, Britain was already witnessing the beginnings of a professional magistracy. This stemmed from two separate but interrelated concerns: on the one hand, ensuring that there were enough active magistrates to take care of criminal matters, without encouraging judicial corruption; and, on the other, ensuring that these magistrates were available when needed, both to preserve public order and to deal with plaintiffs and accused who came before them. While informal preliminary hearings held by justices in their own parlours may have sufficed for rural England, the increasing volume of the criminal work of the justices in London, coupled with rising fears about crime and public disorder, led to the establishment of public offices with magistrates in attendance at regular hours from the late 1730s, and the payment of salaries to a few particularly active London magistrates such as Thomas de Veil and the Fieldings. Regular stipendiary magistrates also appeared in Scotland, with the office of sheriff depute, and it was in Dublin that the first system of 'Police Offices' was established in 1786, with salaried magistrates and constables. Soon afterwards, in 1792, the system was implanted in London, and it also rapidly spread across the Atlantic, with, for example, a Police Office with salaried magistrates in New York from 1798.[75]

Similar developments occurred in Quebec and Lower Canada. In the first decades of British rule, preliminary proceedings in criminal matters retained the characteristic informality that they had in England outside London, or in most American colonies, with justices doing their work in their homes or offices. In Montreal, from 1768 at least, the clerk of the peace did keep a public office, the Peace Office, where among other things he was available to draw up preliminary documents such as depositions, arrest warrants, and bail bonds, if paid the appropriate fees.[76] However, there is no evidence that this was ever anything like the offices in London, with justices in regular attendance, and so seeing a justice still required a trip to his house or office. Nevertheless, the idea of professionalizing the magistracy quickly surfaced. In March 1766, less than two years after Governor Murray appointed his first justices, Adam Mabane reported to the governor and his Council on the situation in Montreal. After describing the continuing tensions between the English merchants (who composed most of the active magistracy), the military, and the French seigneurial and other elites, Mabane suggested that the only solution was the establishment of a professional, salaried magistracy. He acknowledged that this was without precedent in the colonies but argued that it was necessary, since the exclusion of Roman Catholics from public office and the commercial pursuits of most members of the Protestant elites limited both the number of potential justices and the assiduity of those appointed. The suggestion was taken up in the 1769 report submitted by Governor Carleton and Chief Justice William Hey on the reorganization of justice in Quebec: in a direct echo of pre-Conquest structures, they suggested replacing the courts of the justices with a salaried 'Officer of Justice' or 'Police Officer' in each of the three main towns. Neither plan was implemented, and the duties of the magistrates continued to be performed by unpaid or at least un-salaried justices.[77]

The first concerted attempt to establish a professional magistracy would not come until 1794, when Stephen Sewell, the solicitor general, and Thomas McCord, an active Montreal justice, established what they called a Police or Rotation Office in Sewell's house in Montreal. From the name, we may assume that they were directly inspired by the recently established English or Irish offices, the latter perhaps through McCord's strong business and family ties with Ireland. The immediate impetus, however, was not crime in general, which was little men-tioned, but rather the fear of popular unrest following riots against militia orders in May and June 1794 and the more generalized fear of American and French infiltration and secret societies, coupled with the perception that the Montreal magistracy was ineffectual.[78]

Sewell and McCord's Police Office, however, did not last, largely because of the unwillingness of the colonial administration to provide the necessary financial backing. Following the easing of tensions later in 1794, Sewell lost interest. But McCord persisted, perhaps encouraged by the small salary already granted to a 'police magistrate' in Quebec City. Echoing De Veil in 1739, he hired a house and employed three constables to summon witnesses and arrest suspects. In November, he also submitted a memorial to Lord Dorchester, the governor, asking for a salary. His request was refused, and McCord was told that Dorchester disapproved of the establishment of a Police Office. McCord neverthe-less continued the office until March at least, again submitting his expenses. This time, the reply was more tart: 'As no office of Police is allowed or considered to exist, it follows no expences incident upon such an office can be admitted' and 'His Lordship ... is at a loss to conceive how the answer to your memorial of Novr last which is in the words following "it is not in his Lordship's power to add to the salaries in the civil expenditure of this province" could give you reason to consider yourself appointed to an office with a salary.' With such strong opposition from Dorchester himself, the office was evidently doomed, and, as McCord's personal finances became increasingly pre-carious, he turned his attention elsewhere. At the end of 1796, following riots against the implementation of the new Roads Act, there was some further discussion of reviving the office, but nothing came of it. McCord almost immediately left for Ireland, probably in order to escape his creditors, and there is no further mention of the Police Office.[79] Evidently, there was as yet insufficient support for the professionalization of the magistracy. Even in London, the Police Offices were an innovation, resisted by many of the more conservative elements of society. Dorchester, by then an aging administrator intent on avoiding innovation, evidently had no intention of implementing such a novelty, even if a quarter-century earlier, as Guy Carleton, he had proposed professionalization as the ideal solution to the problems of the magistracy.

Despite this initial failure, McCord's experience in the Police Office in the mid-1790s served him in good stead fifteen years later. With Dorchester long gone and the apparently positive example of the London system, objections to the very idea of salaried magistrates and police offices held less water. Already in 1808, a Quebec grand jury had suggested naming stipendiary magistrates, and in 1809 Governor James Craig asked his Executive Council whether a paid chairman of the Quarter Sessions should be appointed in Quebec City and Montreal. Finally, in January 1810, Craig appointed Ross Cuthbert chairman of the Quarter Sessions and inspector of Police in Quebec City, at a combined salary of £500 sterling. Almost immediately afterwards, Jean-Marie Mondelet, a notary and active Montreal justice, petitioned Craig for the equivalent post for Montreal. At about the same time, James McGill, the chief executive councillor resident in Montreal and one of the leaders of the Tory faction, wrote to Craig recommending the appointment of McCord. After further consultations, in April 1810 Craig appointed McCord and Mondelet jointly police magistrates of Montreal, at a salary of £250 sterling each. The extension of the system to Trois-Rivières was already in contemplation, and a year later, Thomas Coffin was appointed chairman of the Quarter Sessions and then police magistrate there, though with a smaller salary.[80] McCord and Mondelet, who also soon added the title of chairman of the Quarter Sessions, remained in office until 1824 when they were replaced by Samuel Gale (1824–8, 1829–30), who was himself briefly replaced by David Ross (1828–9); and Coffin retained his posts until 1830. In Quebec City, there was more turnover, with the position held successively by Ross Cuthbert (1810–15), Alexis Caron (1815–21), John Fletcher (1815–23), Jean-Thomas Taschereau (1821–7), John Gawler Thompson (1823–5), and finally Robert Christie (1827–30).

Figure 1.1: Thomas McCord,
one of Montreal's first chairmen
of the Quarter Sessions,
1810–24 (1816)

Figure 1.2: Jean-Thomas
Taschereau, Quebec City's fourth
chairman of the Quarter Sessions,
1821–7 (c. 1815)

The intent with the new salaried magistrates was to professionalize both the ministerial and the judicial functions of the magistracy. Ministerially, they were to operate full-fledged Police Offices, 'similar to the Bow Street Office,' and be in constant attendance to receive depositions, issue summonses and warrants, and the like. Judicially, they were to preside in the Quarter Sessions and also attend all Weekly Sessions. In addition, they were intended to serve as the main means of communication between the central administration and the local magistracy. Their duties changed little over the period: in the late 1820s, the then-chairmen of the Quarter Sessions (the name was used interchangeably with that of police magistrate) of the three districts reported performing essentially the same tasks.[81]

While the professionalization of the justices' ministerial functions followed English precedent, the appointment of paid chairmen to preside in the justices' courts was a significant colonial innovation. Chairmen of Quarter Sessions in England and in Upper Canada were elected by their fellow magistrates, and not paid, with the position usually going to the senior magistrate present. In order to justify this expansion of the salaried colonial bureaucracy, proponents of the new system, including Craig, advanced several arguments. First, there was the fear of increasing urban disorder and of the decline of the 'police' of the cities, in the general sense of internal regulation. In suggesting a professional magistracy, the 1808 Quebec grand jury decried the 'deplorable state of the general police of this city and the disorder and depravity which prevail.' In explaining his decision to London, Craig took up the same refrain: in his words, the police of the cities 'has been the subject of universal and heavy complaint ever since I arrived,' due especially to a 'vast influx' of strangers and to an increase in 'debauchery and licentiousness.' As proponents of the scheme for Montreal stated, what was needed was a 'correct, systematic police in the city of Montreal,' which could be brought about only by 'the daily attendance in a public known office in this city, of one or more Justices of the Peace to transact the duties that must and ought (at least in the first instance) to come under the immediate cognizance of such Magistrates.'[82]

Second was the perception that the existing system of volunteer magistrates could no longer function efficiently. In 1809 several justices of the peace from both Montreal and Quebec City petitioned the governor, complaining that the volume of criminal business was such that magistrates engaged in other pursuits, notably business, were unable to give the necessary time to it, so that crimes remained unpunished, immorality was rampant, and parties suffered. They also noted that most magistrates had neither legal training nor the time to acquire the necessary knowledge of the criminal laws of England and of the provincial statutes. In justifying his appointment of stipendiaries, Craig asserted that the justices, mostly engaged in trade, often refused to act, with the Quarter Sessions often not sitting for want of sufficient justices, and that when the justices did act, being ignorant of the law, they 'very frequently commit themselves by highly improper acts.' The appointment of salaried chairmen could not but bring regularity to the courts.[83]

And, finally, there was the continuing climate of security paranoia, especially the fear of sedition and of alien infiltration. In 1810 McGill had initially suggested appointing McCord primarily so that the large numbers of aliens coming into the country might be examined by a single justice, 'by which means His Excellency would have a knowledge of those who come in than if left to the magistrates generally,' and he referred explicitly to McCord's previous experience in the mid-1790s.[84] The establishment of the new system was thus in response not only to crime and urban disorder in general but also to the immediate perceived threats to the Lower Canadian state.

Regardless of the accuracy of the affirmation of weakness in the existing system, the discourse of urban disorder, judicial inefficiency, and security threats was clear. And, remarkably, these arguments closely resembled those advanced thirty years later, in the late 1830s, to justify the re-establishment of stipendiary magistrates. As Martin Dufresne has shown, then as well the measure was justified on the basis of fear of urban disorder, of inefficiency of the existing system based on volunteer justices, and of the dangers of the prevailing political climate (in that case, the Rebellions). Though the social and political context had changed, the rationale for changes in governance remained the same.[85]

In the 1810s, the changes that ensued in the ministerial role of the justices were immediate and obvious. In Montreal, McCord and Mondelet set up the Police Office in a room of the courthouse and (according to them) kept it open every day from 9:00 in the morning until 3:00 or 4:00 in the afternoon. In other words, parties seeking a magistrate no longer had to apply to one at his home or business but could present themselves to a known public office, at set times, and expect to see a justice. The Police Office also acquired a small, salaried staff. In May 1810 McCord and Mondelet had been promised funds to pay for the operating expenses of the office and they were already employing a 'Confidential person' to inquire into aliens. By 1811, they were pressing the administration to allow them to hire clerks and messengers, and they then employed at least one constable, paying him in part from funds that were under their control as administrators of Montreal's municipal government. From 1812, as McCord explained a decade later, 'the multiplicity of business which was caused by the war in our office rendered [additional money] absolutely necessary, nor could the business be carried on without it,' and on the recommendation of a committee of the Executive Council at Montreal, the Police Office was allowed £100 Sterling per year to cover its expenses. The regular accounts submitted by McCord and Mondelet show that they hired both a clerk and a messenger, the latter of whom also acted as a constable, and that they also occasionally paid constables for making arrests and serving summonses. In 1823 the Assembly voted to increase the funding of the Police Office to £200 Sterling per year, to cover all expenses including the arrest of criminals; and from 1825, this was increased to £500 Sterling, though this also had to cover some of the fees of the clerk of the peace.[86]

Similar establishments sprang up in Quebec City and Trois-Rivières, though with some local variants. In Quebec City, the Police Office, also apparently in the courthouse, was open, in the early 1810s at least, from

8:00 until 4:00, though the magistrates may have been in attendance only for part of the day. The Police Office also had its own constables, but no separate clerks, relying instead on the clerk of the peace and his under-clerks. In Trois-Rivières, Coffin initially set himself up in rooms above the prison, though by 1822 the office appears to have been in the courthouse. He seems not to have kept particular fixed hours, though he claimed to be in attendance most days and declared that his judicial functions and ministerial duties were precisely the same as those of the other chairmen. As in Quebec City, the clerk of the peace appears to have acted as the Police Office clerk, and Coffin employed the crier of the justices' courts as the Police Office messenger. As with Montreal, both of the other Police Offices were also funded by the Assembly until the end of the 1820s.[87]

The effects on the judicial role of the justices were more subtle. Though there was no formal change in the court structures, a significant change occurred in the bench, since now there were almost always one or two professional magistrates present at both Quarter and Weekly Sessions. This did not mean an entirely professional bench: even when the position of chairman was held jointly by two justices, as in Montreal between 1810 and 1824 and in Quebec City between 1815 and 1825, the requirement that there be at least three justices to hold Quarter Sessions meant that the chairmen were always obliged to find at least one unsalaried justice to sit with them. In the mid-1820s, proposals from both Montreal and Quebec City suggested that the chairmen be allowed to pay other justices to sit with them, as was said to be the case in Halifax; one proposal even referred back to a 1388 English statute allowing justices four shillings a day for their attendance. The suggestions were rejected by Dalhousie, not because of the cost, which he acknowledged would be trivial, but 'as a system of early days, which is not creditable to the present day, if it is necessary.' And Dalhousie even questioned the need for joint chairmen, suggesting instead a single professional chairman aided by other city justices sitting in turn.[88]

Though Dalhousie envisaged unpaid justices assisting the paid chairmen in the courts, he nonetheless intended that in the cities at least, all preliminary steps were to be centralized in the Police Offices. Thus, when Chevalier Robert d'Estimauville, a Quebec City justice and former high constable, began conducting judicial business in his own home, he was strongly reprimanded; as Dalhousie noted, 'if half a dozen magistrates acted as Mr. d'Estimauville, it would be tantamount to so many police offices. It must therefore be discontinued.' Similarly, when a

Trois-Rivières justice of the peace began taking depositions and issuing warrants himself, it became grounds for his dismissal, though this may have had as much to do with the fact that he was depriving the clerk of the peace of his fees. At any rate, the intent was clear: in the towns, all preliminary steps were to pass through the public Police Offices. The shift from earlier patterns of governance was striking and meant that the administration of criminal justice in the cities had already come to resemble the sort of centralized bureaucracy that was definitively implanted from the 1840s.[89]

One major impediment to the extension of the system was that the establishments lacked formal permanence. Initially instituted by the executive, the paid chairmen and Police Offices never received legislative sanction, even though the salaries of the magistrates and the budgets of the offices were consistently paid until the end of the 1820s with the concurrence of the Assembly. In all of its legislation between 1810 and 1830, the legislature of Lower Canada seems scrupulously to have avoided explicit recognition of either the chairmen or the Police Offices. This was in contrast to the situation in other colonies: in Nova Scotia, for example, the Police Office and stipendiary magistrates in Halifax were established by statute in 1815.

The legislative void was a source of constant difficulties for the chairmen. Already in 1815, the Executive Council had refused a request from McCord and Mondelet for an increase in salary, on the grounds that there was no provincial legislation defining their duties, and when they petitioned the Prince Regent himself, the British government quickly sent the ball back to the local legislature, 'who are of course the most interested in the preservation of a good Police and the best judge of the means by which it can be attained.' McCord and Mondelet then prepared a bill to formalize their situation, allowing notably for the establishment of stipendiary magistrates (including paid assistant magistrates) and Police Offices in Montreal and Quebec City, with constables, messengers, and a fixed budget, all paid for by an additional levy on tavern-keepers. They first asked the governor to suggest the bill to the legislature by message, but when he declined, it was instead introduced in the Assembly in 1817 by Denis-Benjamin Viger, to whom Mondelet was allied both socially and politically. The bill, however, died on the table, and though McCord made a further attempt to revive the measure in 1819, nothing came of it.[90]

In part, this legislative reticence may have been due to continued resistance to the very idea of a professional magistracy, from both the

Tory and *Canadien* factions. Even in 1814, a correspondent of the Tory *Montreal Herald* noted that while the Police Office might do much good, unless the right magistrates were appointed, it could be 'converted into the greatest engine of extortion and abuse, that was ever introduced in any state.' Likewise, in discussing amendments made by an Assembly committee to the Police Office bill, McCord noted, 'You will observe the word Police erased in the amendments, 'tis considered by some a word of ill omen, and that the introduction of Police Offices must inevitably be followed by French Espionage.'[91] A professional magistracy struck at the heart of British conceptions of local governance based on the free exercise of power by lay magistrates chosen from among the elites, and hinted instead at continental authoritarianism. Coupled with the Assembly's inherent and generally well-founded suspicion of the executive, it is not surprising that few efforts were made to enshrine the Police Offices in legislation.

McCord and Mondelet's misgivings were well placed. They themselves were ousted from office in 1824 for entirely different reasons, but the problem came home to roost in the late 1820s with their successor, Samuel Gale, and the chairman in Quebec City, Robert Christie. Both Gale and Christie had attracted the ire of the *Patriote*-dominated Assembly, Gale by being one of the strongest supporters of Dalhousie's authoritarian and increasingly francophobic regime, and Christie, though generally respected for his impartiality, by his remarkably maladroit role in assisting Dalhousie in an 1828 partisan purge of the magistracy. Dalhousie had further irritated the Assembly by appointing a paid chairman in the Gaspé, thereby unilaterally increasing the colony's civil list at a time when control over finances was a key point of contention between Assembly and executive. As a result, the Assembly resolved in 1829 that the position of chairman should be abolished, and it accomplished this in 1830 by the simple expedient of refusing to vote the sums necessary for the salaries of the chairmen and the expenses of the Police Offices.

To justify the abolition, the Assembly and the *Patriote* press advanced a variety of reasons, largely based on the actions of Gale and Christie. Thus, two committees of inquiry of the Assembly in 1828–9 that touched on the state of the magistracy heard witness after witness, including a number of *Canadien* justices of the peace, declaim upon the evils of the Police Offices and the chairmen. Among other things, the chairmen in Montreal and Quebec City were accused of riding roughshod over the opinions of the other justices, of discouraging them from acting, of being agents of the central administration, and generally of acting in an authoritarian and abusive manner. The offices were also described as leading to continental despotism, municipal administrations in the style of Mangin and Delaveau, contrasted with the traditional institutions of justice inherited from the English constitution, such as the Quarter Sessions. Many of these charges were well founded, but all had applied equally in earlier years, when the Assembly had tacitly accepted the existence of the chairmen and the Police Offices. Further, as Thomas Coffin pointed out, no complaints had been raised regarding the Police Office in Trois-Rivières, yet it too was abolished along with the others. It is thus difficult to escape the conclusion that the abolition of the chairmen and of the Police Offices in 1830 was largely the result of specific political circumstances connected with the incumbents – as Christie declared, 'I feel the measure to be in a great degree personal.' The chairmen remained in office until October 1830, when both they and the Police Offices disappeared.[92]

Nevertheless, for most of the 1810s and 1820s, the three main urban centres in the colony had fixed, public offices, with stipendiary magistrates and a small staff who were in theory available every day to hear plaintiffs, issue warrants and summonses, act to impose public order, decide whether defendants should be bailed or committed to prison, and so on. Likewise, by the latter half of the 1820s, the main Quarter Sessions in Lower Canada had at least one professional magistrate on the bench, and even in the smaller districts of Saint Francis and Gaspé, it became habitual for the resident professional higher-court judge to sit as chairman. This represented a significant departure from the earlier, English-inspired practice, dependent on the willingness and availability of unpaid justices who usually dispensed justice from their homes, which still persisted outside the towns through to the 1830s.

The 1830s, in this sense, marked a partial return to older practices in the cities. The urban magistracy was once again based on voluntarism, with the duties previously undertaken by the chairmen redistributed among the city justices as a whole, as had been the case before 1810. Though chairmen still presided over the Quarter Sessions, they were now unpaid though high-status justices such as Denis-Benjamin Viger, Augustin Cuvillier or John Neilson. To law-and-order reformers such as Adam Thom and William Kennedy, authors of the report on municipal affairs for Lord Durham, the disappearance of the stipendiary magistrates was entirely negative: 'The discontinuance of these officers has been a subject of much complaint, and has proved exceedingly prejudicial to the due administration of justice.' However, while there were certainly some disruptions, they were less profound than Thom and Kennedy suggested. First, even for the justices, it was a short-lived episode. The revival of stipendiary magistrates remained on the administration's agenda – for example, it was suggested by Governor Gosford to the outgoing Montreal and Quebec City mayors in 1836 – and, after only seven years of a non-professional magistracy, by late 1837 there were professional magistrates appointed once again in both main districts. As well, despite the rhetoric, the abolition of professional magistrates seems to have had little effect on the capacity of the justice system to impose itself on colonial society, with the 1830s witnessing a significant upsurge in all aspects of the justices' work, as we will see.[93]

But, perhaps most important, from the perspective of those using or being used by the system, the formal abolition of the Police Offices themselves in fact changed things less than might have been expected. The need for a centralized, urban office, open at fixed hours, where people could go to make complaints, give bail, and the like, with a staff of professional clerks and permanent constables, had become firmly entrenched. Hence, in 1830, the functions of the Police Offices, along with their funding and a good portion of their staff, including runners and constables, were largely transferred to the Peace Offices, the offices staffed by the clerks of the peace. In Montreal, this did mean that the Police Office clerk lost his job, of which he complained bitterly, but since in both Quebec City and Trois-Rivières the Police Office duties had already been the responsibility of the clerks of the peace and their under-clerks, there was no change at all. As for the runners and constables, they continued, with the same men acting both before and after.[94]

If anything, folding the Police Offices into the Peace Offices simply increased the strength of the clerical bureaucracy, since judicial continuity was now assured by the clerk of the peace rather than a magistrate such as the chairman. This was not necessarily a positive development. In 1836, for example, the clerks of the peace in Quebec City were accused of having blank depositions and warrants signed by justices ahead of time, which the clerks could then fill out as necessary – in effect turning the magistrate's signature into a rubber stamp. But bureaucratic continuity was assured nonetheless. In fact, in both Montreal and Quebec City, the term 'Police Office' itself continued in use through the 1830s, both in common parlance and on formal documents such as depositions. This did not mean that all worked smoothly: in Montreal at least, some magistrates went back to conducting preliminary hearings at their houses or offices, and in 1834 a Montreal King's Bench grand jury complained of the lack of magistrates available to take depositions, suggesting either returning to the system of magistrates attending a public office at fixed hours or granting judicial powers to city council-lors. Still, even in Montreal, many depositions were taken before the clerks of the peace; when Montreal defendants were arrested, they appear to have been taken to the Police Office. And in Quebec City, too, most business was transacted at the Peace or Police Office. For someone coming before the criminal justice system in preliminary proceedings, whether as plaintiff or as defendant, the change would thus have seemed far less dramatic than it did from the perspective of Samuel Gale or Robert Christie. The professional system launched in 1810 lived on in another guise.[95]

Conclusion

In terms of everyday justice, neither rupture nor stasis do justice to the nature of the criminal law and criminal courts in the period between the Conquest and the Rebellions. The indisputable formal changes in laws and courts instituted by the Conquest masked a much greater conti-nuity in both. The new English criminal law actually applied was far closer to the pre-Conquest French code than formal comparisons might suggest, and in matters such as the continuing urban centralization of the courts, colonial British justice resembled very much its French pre-decessor. This is not to argue that there were no substantial changes at all during the change in regimes. The move from salaried magistrates to amateur justices, for example, represented a fundamental shift in the logic of governance, although even there we may be over-emphasizing the professionalism of the pre-Conquest magistracy: seigneurial judges, for example, were often notaries or even farmers for whom, much as with justices of the peace, judging was only a part-time activity.[96] At any rate, the adaptability of the *Canadien* population to the new struc-tures of criminal justice, which we will see in later chapters, can be attributed in part to the fact that on the ground, from the perspective of ordinary *Canadiens*, regime change was characterized as much by conti-nuity as by rupture.

Similarly, in the seven decades that followed the institution of British civil government, the law and the courts were far from immobile. The British colonial state showed itself quite capable of adapting to the changing needs of the colony, or at least of its elites, both British and *Canadien*. While there was little fundamental change in the law concerning more serious crimes, the mass of regulatory provisions adopted by the colonial legislatures and magistracy moulded the criminal law to colonial circumstances and elite desires. As for the courts, nineteenth-century developments in particular, such as the professionalization of the magistracy and the spread of justice into the countryside, suggest that far from institutional paralysis, the criminal justice system, especially at the level of the magistrates, was already undergoing many of the structural changes often associated with the growth of the modern liberal state, such as bureaucratization. Lower Canada was in fact ahead of the rest of British North America in many regards, with its system of Police Offices and professional magistrates preceding that of Halifax (1815), York (1826), and Saint John (1836).[97] This adaptability is unsurprising, given that in England similar changes were also modifying an ancien-régime justice system often regarded as static. Even so, it is clear that, instead of rupture and stasis, the earlier period is better characterized as one of both continuity and gradual change. And this also applies to the men who ran most of the criminal justice system: the justices of the peace.

2

Making Justices

The few British traders who are out of humour, because I would not make them magistrates, nor allow them to oppress the new subjects, continue to display all the malice and ire which the most bitter rancour can irritate ...

– James Murray, 1765

... there is such a want of honorable men as magistrates ... in this neglected French district, as in my humble opinion is indiscribable!!! And it is also my wish in order to Englify this French district, in spight of French influence, that the following gentlemen may be included in the commission ...

– John Antrobus of Trois-Rivières, 1811

... many Justices of the Peace, possessing every requisite qualification, and whose characters were open to no reproach, were dismissed from office ... without any form or show of investigation, or any known complaint against them ... Such was the course taken by the late administration, to revenge itself upon the Inhabitants of this Province, by attacking those citizens, who had stood forward to defend the rights of the people, and who had deserved and obtained their confidence. It was in this manner, that the Royal authority was degraded and subjected to odium ...

– Third Report of the Special Committee of the House of Assembly of Lower Canada, on the Bill for the Qualification of Justices of the Peace, 1829[1]

As the rhetoric from Murray through Antrobus to the Assembly committee suggests, the appointment of justices of the peace in Quebec and Lower Canada was often bound up in broad issues of colonial politics. And from François-Xavier Garneau forward, the justices have generally figured in Quebec historiography only at those moments when their appointment became a political issue, and in particular a facet of the ever-present national question.[2] The politicization of the commission was inevitable, since under the English system implanted in the United Kingdom and most colonies, justices were appointed by the central administration. In England, for example, the commission was controlled by Parliament, first directly through the lord chancellor's office and then indirectly through the county lords lieutenant who came to make most recommendations, and the appointment process often reflected the battles between parliamentary factions, whether royalists and republicans in the seventeenth century or Whigs and Tories in the eighteenth. In Scotland, the composition of the commission reflected the rise and fall of the political power of Jacobitism; in most British North American colonies, the appointment of justices was the governor's prerogative.[3] In Quebec and Lower Canada, despite the existence of an elected Assembly from 1792, the executive retained entire control over the appointment and removal of justices until the 1830s – a situation guaranteed to lead to confrontations with those who saw the governor's power in general as despotic, whether British merchants in the 1760s or *Canadien* nationalists and reformers in the 1820s and 1830s.

The creation of the magistracy was also linked to issues of power that went beyond general colonial politics. As in England, the institution of the justices in the colony represented a close intermeshing of interest between the central administration and local elites. In England, on the administration's side of the equation of interest, appointing members of local elites as justices co-opted them into the enforcement of laws and the application of administrative policies. For the landed gentry and other local notables, appointment served to confirm their elite status, through both the honour it bestowed and the power it gave them over the rest of the population, while at the same time ensuring that, as the principal local representatives of the state, they retained their control over local society and local affairs.[4] Similarly, in Quebec and Lower Canada, the appointment and dismissal of justices of the peace was intimately bound up in questions of local power and patronage, though these played out differently in a colony with little in the way of landed gentry, a far less rigid social structure, and the added dimension of British and American immigration and settlement in a predominantly French society.

As well, the appointment of justices was part of the larger process of colonial state formation prior to the post-Rebellion administrative reforms. In a period marked by rapid population growth, immigration, and the expansion of European settlements, unpaid appointments like those to the magistracy were one of the few ways by which the administration, constantly faced with financial constraints, could expand its administrative structures to cover the entire colony. And, though the process of appointment itself retained a decidedly ancien-régime flavour, it was far from static, moving from the personal involvement of the first governors to bureaucratic routine by the 1820s. The creation of the magistracy reflected fundamental shifts in the presence, power, and organization of a colonial state too often dismissed by historians as powerless and ossified.

Composing the Commissions of the Peace

In making up the magistracy, the usual procedure was for the governor to issue a general commission of the peace. This highly formal document wiped the magisterial slate clean by implicitly revoking all previous commissions and then appointing or reappointing a more or less lengthy list of justices. Generally issued for each judicial district, the commissions started with the ex-officio justices, usually including the members of the executive and legislative councils, the judges of the higher courts, and the crown law officers. The commissions then listed the justices appointed for the district, in order of seniority according to the date they were appointed; outlined the justices' powers and responsibilities; and designated a smaller number of them as justices of the quorum, of whom one had to be present for Quarter Sessions to be held. General commissions were a frequent occurrence: for the district of Montreal, for example, there were eighteen of them between 1764 and 1837, and they were issued for the other main districts of the colony at a similar frequency. This was more often than in late-eighteenth-century England and far more frequently than in early-nineteenth-century Ireland.[5]

General commissions were the most important event in the composition of the magistracy, often being reported in the newspapers and provoking political comment. In 1830 and 1833, for instance, the Tory

Montreal Gazette and the organ of the *Patriotes, La Minerve,* battled it out with quantitative analyses of the new commissions.[6] But in between general commissions, the administration could also name individual justices by what were known as commissions of association. The process was frequent, with governors issuing almost two hundred and fifty commissions of association between 1764 and 1837, though the practice became less frequent in the 1830s. Many such commissions of association added only a few justices, but some were almost as important as the general commissions themselves, such as that in late 1831 which added some ninety justices to a magistracy depleted by a new qualification law passed in 1830.[7]

Some general commissions followed administrative reorganizations that made the old commissions obsolete: for example, in 1776, following the Quebec Act, which had nullified all previous commissions, or in 1794, following the creation of Upper and Lower Canada. New commissions were also necessary on the death of the sovereign, as in 1820, 1830, and 1837. But the frequent renewals of the commissions were mainly due to broader concerns of state and politics. First was the fairly pragmatic need to respond to the rapid growth in the colony's European population, which rose from some 65,000 in 1764 to almost 600,000 by the mid-1830s. As Dalhousie's civil secretary declared in 1820, 'the rapidly increasing population ... requires more constant duty.'[8] Of course, the executive was not directly matching its appointments to population growth, since it had no access to detailed population figures, especially before the mid-1820s, and had not yet developed the fascination with statistics that would guide much later government activity. But as Table 2.1 shows, the end result was more or less the same. The number of justices in the commissions rose dramatically until the beginning of the 1820s and, after levelling off and even declining later in the 1820s, grew rapidly again in the 1830s. With ups and downs, this increase essentially kept pace with population growth. After an initial couple of decades with proportionately few justices, there was in general one justice to every 1,000 to 2,000 people in the two largest districts, Montreal and Quebec, and even more in the smaller districts, despite frequent complaints about the lack of justices.[9] This did not mean that the colony was particularly well supplied with justices. In the two largest districts, there were proportionately fewer justices than in the English counties, which in the 1790s generally had one justice for between about 500 and 1,200 people, or in Scotland, with one justice per 400 people in 1830. And the colony compared even less favourably with Upper Canada,

Table 2.1: Justices in selected general commissions, 1764–1837*

	Montreal[††]	Quebec[†]	Trois-Rivières[‡]	Gaspé	Saint Francis
1764	10 (2700)	20 (1600)	–	–	–
1776	12 (3500)	7 (5900)	–	–	–
1785	20 (3000)	18 (2800)	–	–	–
1788/1790	37 (1800)	25 (2100)	17 (900)	17 (–)	–
1794	72 (1200)	44 (1400)	16 (1100)	16 (–)	–
1799	85 (1200)	49 (1400)	19 (1100)	–	–
1810/1811	122 (1200)	49 (1800)	52 (600)	26 (–)	–
1815	–	64 (1500)	58 (600)	–	–
1821/1823/1824	152 (1400)	135 (800)	62 (600)	33 (200)	10 (900)
1828	173 (1500)	126 (1100)	34 (1400)	29 (300)	–
1830	138 (2000)	89 (1600)	22 (2200)	7 (1700)	25 (600)
1833	205 (1400)	104 (1500)	38 (1400)	–	28 (700)
1836/1837	294 (1100)	167 (1000)	46 (1300)	44 (300)	36 (600)

Number of justices (Population per justice)

* excludes ex-officio justices
† until 1788, excludes justices from the future districts of Trois-Rivières and Gaspé and from Upper Canada
‡ for 1828/1830/1833, excludes justices also named for the district of Saint Francis from 1823

where in the Newcastle District, for example, there was one magistrate for every 200–300 people in the 1820s and 1830s. On the other hand, there were proportionately considerably more justices than in Ireland.[10]

Related to population growth, and even more evident to administrators, was the expansion of the area of European settlement in the colony. This grew from a relatively narrow band along the St Lawrence and up some of its main tributaries, in the 1760s, to cover much of the St Lawrence basin by the 1830s.[11] While the administration had always ensured that Quebec City and Montreal had an ample number of justices, the attention it paid to distributing the magistracy elsewhere in the colony evolved considerably between the Conquest and the Rebellions. Under the early governors, there was no attempt to name justices throughout even the existing settlements, and most of those named in the 1760s and 1770s were concentrated in Quebec City and Montreal, with a few in Trois-Rivières and a few scattered elsewhere. By the 1790s, however, the administration had begun trying to expand the magistracy throughout the main settled areas of the colony. In 1794 one of the first actions of a committee struck to nominate justices was to request a list of parishes and townships, so that it could determine which had no resident justice. Similarly, the expansion of European settlement into the Eastern Townships in the first decade of the nineteenth century prompted the issuing of a new general commission in 1805 for the district of Trois-Rivières and two substantial commissions of association in 1806 for that of Montreal, mainly to add justices in the newly settled areas. This concern with expanding the magistracy to cover the colony continued into the 1820s, and by 1829, Kempt was explicitly stating his desire to name a magistrate in every parish.[12]

This did not mean that attempts to appoint justices throughout the colony were successful, for they depended on the executive's ability to identify candidates. In 1788, for example, a nomination committee noted that it could find no suitable candidates westward of Quebec City to the district of Montreal, and in 1794 the committee regretted that for most parishes without justices in the district of Trois-Rivières, 'they do not find the names of any persons therein residing recommended for that office nor have they of themselves knowledge of any.'[13] Even by the 1820s, Kempt's ideal of a justice in every parish and township was still chimerical. Thus, the 1826 commission for the district of Montreal appointed justices in only about two-thirds of places that had 1,000 or more people in the 1825 census, with no justices in such important parishes as Châteauguay or Varennes. And Kempt himself came up against a new, more restrictive qualification law in 1830, which led to the commissions of 1830 weeding out many justices and leaving many parishes and townships throughout the colony without resident magistrates. By 1833, the situation had returned to that of the 1820s: of about a hundred places in the district of Montreal with 1,000 or more inhabitants, again perhaps two-thirds had justices named to them, with a similar situation in the districts of Quebec and Trois-Rivières. By 1836–7, the administration had managed to expand the magistracy to cover most of the colony: in the district of Montreal, for example, there were only about a dozen substantial settlements, and twenty or so smaller ones, without justices named to them, leaving perhaps a tenth of the district's population without a resident appointed justice.

The bare appointment of justices does not of, course, fully reflect the magistracy's extension into the countryside. Some settlements without resident justices were close to others that did have them, such as the parishes surrounding Montreal and Quebec City. As the *curé* of Sault-au-Récollet and Saint-Joseph noted in 1820, though they had no justices, these two small parishes were so close to Montreal and the city so accessible for all his parishioners that none had ever desired a resident magistrate.[14] And conversely, as we will see, not all appointed justices acted. Still, colonial administrators were increasingly attentive to naming justices throughout the colony, and from the handful of justices in the 1760s, the potential magistracy by the 1830s had spread across Lower Canada.

Pragmatism and administrative efficiency were only some of the reasons for issuing new general commissions. Several were entirely unnecessary from a practical perspective and instead were issued largely to further the broad political agenda of the administration. Thus, in 1765, just a year after the first commission in 1764, Murray issued two different commissions for Montreal, by which he replaced seven of his original ten nominees. The intent was to address the bitter disputes that had grown up in the small British community in Montreal, between civilians and the military and within the magistracy itself. The second commission, for example, removed three justices who were seen as particularly fractious, including Thomas Walker, the main protagonist in an infamous incident where disguised military officers burst into his home and cut off his ear in revenge for his having interfered with their billeting. It followed a lengthy report on the Montreal magistracy by Adam Mabane and Benjamin Price, two councillors sent down from Quebec City to inquire into the problems at Montreal, who reported that never 'in any place had the office of Justice of the Peace sunk into so much contempt and hatred.' Similarly, in 1796, in response to popular riots around Montreal against the roads acts, the administration under Robert Prescott issued a new commission for Montreal 'in which some of the former Magistrates (who have appeared at least to connive at, if not to encourage the tumultuous meetings of the People) have been omitted; and Persons of more acknowledged Loyalty and firmness substituted in their room.' The result was an (unsuccessful) attempt to co-opt two of the administration's more vocal *Canadien* opponents by naming them justices and the addition of a number of hard-line Tories to the magistracy. And most blatantly, in 1828, Dalhousie issued new commissions to purge the magistracy of a number of *Patriote* sympathizers and, more generally, anybody who opposed his autocratic administration. This provided considerable ammunition to his political opponents, being investigated in detail by the two committees of the Assembly appointed to inquire into his administration, cited by William Lyon Mackenzie, and even reaching the Select Committee of the English House of Commons which pilloried Dalhousie's governorship.[15]

However, probably the most important reason for issuing new general commissions was turnover in the magistracy itself. The attrition rate was high: from the 1770s to the mid-1820s, about half of all magistrates disappeared from the Montreal commission every ten years, with the most common reasons being death, emigration, or appointment to an office that conferred ex-officio status. Attrition was even higher in the 1820s and 1830s, with only 48 of the 179 justices in the 1826 Montreal commission surviving through to 1837, an increase due largely to political manipulation and to the effects of the 1830 qualification act. Still, death and emigration remained key factors, and, with a few notable exceptions, the administration renewed the commissions mainly to replace justices who had moved on in one way or another.

Executive privilege was most evident in the dismissal of justices. The usual method was simply to omit a justice's name from the next general commission, although on occasion the governor might also issue a special writ of *supersedeas* explicitly revoking a justice's commission. Either way, governors wielded an essentially absolute power to dismiss at will: though their instructions enjoined them not to remove justices without 'good and sufficient Cause' and to report these cases immediately to London, there was in fact little oversight. Thus, when Murray removed Thomas Walker from the commission in 1765, he did make a report, blaming Walker's fractiousness, but though the Lords of Trade ordered Walker's reinstatement, 'as it seems unjust that a person should be turned out of the magistracy for any other cause but his misconduct therein,' Walker was never reappointed, despite considerable support from prominent public figures in England. Similarly, the instructions did not prevent Dalhousie from making his politically motivated dismissals in 1828. In the months leading up to the Rebellions, the explicit revocation of justices' commissions by *supersedeas* became an important political tool for the executive: Gosford first revoked the commissions of a number of prominent *Patriotes* such as Wolfred Nelson and Cyrille-Hector-Octave Côté, along with justices who had had the temerity to condone the anti-administration public meetings held during the summer of 1837, and then followed this up with a general commission for Montreal, in late November, which made a clean sweep of *Patriote* sympathizers. Fundamentally, this right of dismissal was entirely arbitrary: as Gosford's civil secretary asserted in 1836, in refusing to tell a justice why he had been dropped from the commission, the executive would not explain to a private individual the motives for the exercise of 'a discretion vested in it for the public benefit.'[16]

The Selection Process

The motivations for reshaping the commissions were thus varied, though all were tied to considerations of state and politics. But behind each justice on the commission lay a process of selection. Since the power to create justices of the peace was a jealously guarded royal prerogative, it was the colonial executive, the governor and his advisers in Quebec City, which was at the centre of this process. However, the selection of justices depended on the identification of 'fit and respectable characters' throughout the colony and so on the knowledge that the executive had of the colony in general and of its elites in particular. Tracing how the sources of this knowledge changed, and how the process of selecting justices was transformed, allows us to examine not only the ways in which the administrative routines of the colonial state were reshaped in this period but also centre-local power relations.

In the first decades of British rule, with a small population, a limited colonial state, and a succession of strong-minded governors, the colony's administration was highly personal, with the governor involved in the most minute of decisions. The process of choosing justices was conducted at the highest level, by the governor himself and his full Council in Quebec City. Murray, for example, was personally involved in the selection and dismissal of justices not only for Quebec City but also for Montreal.[17] The early commissions reflected this, with a preponderance of notables from the cities and few justices in the countryside, into which the knowledge of the governor and councillors penetrated far less.

Gradually, with the growth of the colony, the increasing complexity of its administrative structures, and the development of a committee system within the executive, the process of choosing justices shifted from the governor and his full Council to committees. By the later 1780s, a governor like Dorchester might decide that a new commission was needed but delegated the process of choosing justices to committees of the Executive Council. And for the districts other than Quebec, farther from the seat of the executive, the councillors might themselves delegate in turn. Thus, in considering the make-up of the Montreal commission 1788, the Executive Council committee turned to the councillors who lived in Montreal, presumably best placed to suggest 'fit characters.'[18]

Whether involving the governor or executive councillors, though, the selection of justices in eighteenth century still depended largely on the personal knowledge of high-ranking members of the executive. The 1764 commission was telling in this respect: several of the justices appointed for Montreal were identified only by their last names, reflecting the limited knowledge of the Quebec City-based governor and Council. Conversely, when the Montreal committee in 1788, under the direction of François Picotté de Bellestre, noted that 'Louis Corbin est dans la liste qu'a envoyé le greffier du conseil, mais nous ne le connoissons pas hormi que ce soit François Corbin à Sorel' [Louis Corbin is in the list sent by the clerk of council, but we do not know him, unless it is François Corbin at Sorel], they were making the correction based on direct personal knowledge.

In the eighteenth century, there was also little formal input from society at large, even from its politically active elites. Thus, while collective representations such as petitions to the governor or grand jury presentments were relatively common on a wide variety of issues right from the beginning of British rule, there were no petitions recommending specific individuals as justices. At most, there were occasional calls to increase the number of justices, which the administration generally heeded. For the 160 justices appointed for the district of Montreal in the eighteenth century, none of the wide range of sources I consulted reveals any personal recommendations whatsoever. Of course, there were no doubt informal communications of which we can know nothing, but these simply reinforced the personal nature of the process. Simply put, those who were not 'known' to the executive councillors could not become justices; as in Upper Canada, it was crucial to have an 'in' in the capital.[19]

By the end of eighteenth century, though, the colony had become too large to allow for this personal selection process to continue, and the emphasis began to shift from the personal knowledge of the executive to more local knowledge channelled through bureaucratic conduits. The executive had already recognized the limits of its knowledge by asking the judges of the superior courts for advice on adding justices to the commission, but the shift towards local knowledge was more profound. Already in 1797, when Jonathan Sewell, the attorney general, was asked to recommend justices for Berthier, northeast of Montreal, his response was based on second-hand reports: 'two have been particularly recommended ... they are both said to be men of education ...' By 1813, the executive councillors were disclaiming personal knowledge altogether, suggesting that individuals who proposed themselves as justices should be appointed only if 'recommended by more than one of the senior magistrates resident in' the county in which the applicant intends to act as a justice of the peace.' In the eighteenth century, councillors like Picotté de Bellestre would have known the individuals in question, at least by reputation, and would simply have said yes or no. By the mid-1820s, even locally based officials like Samuel Gale, Montreal's chairman, were relying on the even more local knowledge of others in making their recommendations for justices: in replying to an 1825 request for information on prospective justices in three parishes, he noted that he had delayed his response until he could receive the necessary information, and added that 'my personal knowledge does not enable me to vouch for the truth of the information received but I have no reason to doubt its correctness.'[20] The move had begun from the direct personal knowledge of colonial administrators to the administrative knowledge characteristic of the bureaucratic state.

Hand in hand with this increasing reliance on local knowledge was the growth in recommendations that specific individuals be named as justices. Here, instead of waiting for the administration to come to them for advice, members of the elites began actively seeking to fill the magistracy with their choices. In 1805, for example, Sir John Johnson, head of the Indian Department, recommended the appointment of Norman MacLeod as a justice in the new Scottish settlement in his seigneury of Monnoir. Likewise, in 1800 and again in 1809, Daniel Robertson, the former commandant of Michilimackinac and a Montreal justice in the 1760s, recommended the appointment of Daniel Sutherland, whom he referred to as a 'connection of mine.' By the 1820s, this had become commonplace. As Dalhousie's civil secretary, A.W. Cochran, declared in 1829 to an Assembly committee, 'heretofore the Justices of the Peace have been appointed indifferently at the recommendation of respectable individuals.' Though generally opposed to patronage dependent on the whim of the executive, even prominent *Patriotes* were not averse to using it when necessary. Thus, in 1824 Louis-Joseph Papineau himself asked Dalhousie that his brother, Denis-Benjamin, be appointed a magistrate for his seigneury of Petite-Nation, though he did add that he would have liked to recommend a person unknown to him. The administration obliged by naming Denis-Benjamin a justice three days later.[21]

Overall, these sort of recommendations fit the classic pattern of powerful colonial figures distributing patronage to their clients, much as in other colonies like Upper Canada.[22] Though it is often difficult to reconstruct the complex webs of alliances that led to them, we can imagine the ties that prompted Louis Poulin, the seigneur of the Île d'Orléans, to recommend Pierre Gagnon, the brother of the *curé* of the island's parish of Sainte-Famille. We can also understand the importance of family in the request by Charles-Étienne Chaussegros de Léry, one of richest seigneurs in the colony, that his son be named a justice on the father's properties in the Beauce. The importance of this sort of patronage in maintaining the local influence of patrons was underscored by James Cuthbert, the powerful seigneur of Berthier: in sending in a series of recommendations for justices, he noted that though some of those he had recommended in the past had been appointed, many more had been overlooked, and warned that should this happen again, 'the share of influence I have hitherto possessed in this section of the country and which has ever been exerted for the best interests of government, must be materially impaired.' In this case, government listened, and most of those he recommended were appointed.[23]

Had recommendations for appointments for justices come through only 'respectable individuals,' the process would have resembled the personal patronage that underlay the distribution of most colonial offices. But justices of the peace were very public officials, with considerable potential power in their communities, and, over time, these communities began to take an active interest in their appointment. A more broadly based practice developed that seems to have escaped the comment of contemporary observers: that of specific localities mounting collective petitions to have local notables appointed as justices. Petitioning for local judicial officials was nothing new, and was not particular to Lower Canada: in Upper Canada as well, local communities petitioned for the appointment of justices. In Lower Canada, however, petitioning had previously concentrated on local civil courts, and petitioning for justices became important only later. An occasional occurrence in the 1810s, by the second half of the 1820s it had become a standard means of trying to influence the executive's choice. Thus, in a list of thirty-four recommendations for justices made for the district of Montreal between June 1828 and June 1830, sixteen took the form of collective petitions.[24]

The petitions for justices reveal much about the structure of local power in the colony and the increasing involvement of local elites in state formation at a local level. Two of the earliest are an 1812 petition from Varennes, in the district of Montreal, and one in 1813 from Saint-Vallier, in the district of Quebec. The Varennes petition, signed by a dozen residents, including militia officers, two local merchants, and the local schoolmaster, recommended Paul Lussier, the seigneur, and F.-J. Trudeau, the local notary. The Saint-Vallier petition, signed by the parish's five militia captains and two other notables, recommended François Letellier, a notary who was about to establish himself in the parish. These two petitions epitomize the many that followed.[25]

First, though one might be tempted to link the practice to the arrival of anglophone settlers, especially American immigrants used to more broadly based democratic processes, it was in fact *Canadien* parishes like Varennes and Saint-Vallier that took the lead. Anglophone townships did petition for justices, but they were neither the first nor the most numerous to do so. As with many other institutions and practices imported from England, from parliamentary elections to juries, the francophone population, or at least its elites, took well to this purportedly most British form of political activity.[26] As well, collective petitions for the nomination of justices were a purely rural phenomenon. There were never any urban petitions to name specific individuals as justices, and, from the end of the eighteenth century, there were no petitions whatsoever from the two main towns complaining of a lack of magistrates or calling for the appointment of additional ones. The only petitions concerning the appointment of justices were those such as the grievance petition from Montreal in 1828, which complained of the political manipulation of the process by the Dalhousie administration.[27]

In the countryside, the interplay of local power and deference was evident. Both the Varennes and Saint-Vallier petitions were at the initiative of a small group of local elite figures, and in the case of Varennes, they were proposing their seigneur. Some petitions had the appearance of being more broadly based, such as that in 1819 from the parishes of Saint-Mathias, Sainte-Marie, Saint-Jean-Baptiste, Saint-Hilaire, and Saint-Athanase, east of Montreal, with over a hundred signatures, mainly francophone; however, with Hertel De Rouville and Sir John Johnson, the powerful local seigneurs, at the head of the list of signatories, and many of the other names in the same hand and signed with identical crosses, one wonders. The 1820 petition from forty-four mainly anglophone inhabitants of Noyan, Sabrevois, and Bleury, all signing in one way or another, was probably more genuinely broadly based, like that from sixty residents of Babyville and Sherrington 'assembled at a public meeting held in the schoolhouse.' But far more often the petitions were evidently the work of the seigneur, the *curé*, the local notary, the militia officers – or all of these.[28]

The determination of the local rural notability to keep its hold over this petitioning process is evident. Consider the case of an 1829 Saint-George petition recommending the appointment of Joshua Mandigo, from the 'habitants *canadiens*' of the parish and signed by the parish's militia officers and a large number of habitants, mostly illiterate. Whether drawn up by Mandigo himself or by one of the petitioners, the petition was obviously not the work of local elites. It was badly written, badly structured, and employed none of the usual rhetorical flourishes – for example, it described Mandigo as 'un homme qu'il est né dans la ditte place, il existe, et il a toujours existé et il espère toujours existé encor dans la ditte places' [a man born in the said place, and he has always existed and hopes always to exist in the said place]. The elites quickly responded to this challenge to their authority: in a counter-petition prepared by the notary J.-E. Faribault but signed mainly by anglophones, including three local justices, they accused Mandigo of being 'illiterate, ignorant, by business a common tavern keeper, at least retailing spiritous liquors in a public barr room [sic], and allowing it to be drunk on his counter; his mind is unstable, associates with the lowest company and in short unworthy of the public confidence and entirely unfit for the situation for which he has been recommended.' Of course, with such a disparity of recommendation and rhetoric, Mandigo was never appointed.[29]

In other cases, though, disputes over the appointment of justices reflected dissension within the local oligarchy. For example, fifteen francophone notables of Saint-Césaire, including the *curé*, three militia captains, and a notary, petitioned the governor in 1828: having heard that strangers had drawn up another petition asking for Flavien Bouthillier to be named a justice of the peace, they asked that it be rejected since it had been presented without the knowledge of the parish's *curé*, magistrate, and principal notables. Here, local ties of patronage and notability seemed to outweigh national solidarities, for the justice whom the parish francophone notability preferred over Bouthillier was William Unsworth Chaffers, a local anglophone merchant who was later a prominent anti-*Patriote*. As well, it was in fact ongoing and bitter personal conflicts within the elites that were at the root of both petitions: at almost exactly the same time, Chaffers had launched a civil suit against Bouthillier for seducing his wife, and a year later, Bouthillier would be fined for assaulting Chaffers.[30]

Taken as a group, these petitions show parish oligarchies exercising their muscle in local state nominations, much as they did in other matters such as vestries, elections, and militia operations.[31] And the petitions suggest that powerful elements within these largely *Canadien*, largely rural local communities wanted justices, and wanted them strongly enough to go to the considerable trouble of mounting collective petitions. The lack of any resident magistrates was one of the main spurs for petitioners, and most petitions expressed a general desire for magistrates before recommending any specific nominee. The language used by petitioners to convince the executive of their need for local justice, though evidently shaped by the rhetorical imperatives of petitioning, was nonetheless explicit about local need: 'personnes si utiles pour maintenir la paix et la tranquilité en et dans la dite paroisse' [persons so useful for maintaining peace and tranquility in the said parish]; 'under a deep sense of the want of a civil magistrate among them'; 'un besoin très urgent pour maintenir la bonne morale et amêner â la punition des délinquants' [an urgent need to maintain decent morality and bring delinquents to justice].[32] Even those who have generally been seen as most opposed to the intrusion of the state into local affairs, the rural *curés*, were most often favourable to the implantation of justices, and often signed at the head of the petitions. As was the case with local civil courts, far from seeing magistrates as an unwanted intrusion by a foreign-dominated colonial state, local francophone elites complained when they were absent and actively sought out their appointment, much like their counterparts in Upper Canada.[33]

However, while local petitioning might be important, it was no guarantee of success. Thus, the 1812 Varennes petition was approved by the Executive Council, but for some reason Lussier and Trudeau were not commissioned, and as for the 1813 Saint-Vallier petition, though it too was approved, Letellier moved to Rivière-Ouelle instead, farther down the St Lawrence, and was only appointed a justice much later.[34] Still, about half of those recommended by petition were eventually appointed as justices; local input was evidently becoming an accepted part of the appointment process. But this 'democratization' could go only so far, since the Tories who dominated the administration, just like their counterparts in England, were inherently suspicious of any popular initiatives. Thus, in 1820, David Ross, king's counsel at Montreal and future chairman, accused the people of Chatham of acting 'rather in the Radical stile' in recommending justices, and in 1822 W.B. Felton, Tory patron of the Eastern Townships and soon to be named to the Legislative Council, was even more scathing in his dismissal of popular participation in the nomination process:

On the subject of these recommendations of the people I think it necessary to state that the most infamous characters alone are brought forward in this manner. The respectable people of the country abstain from such measures, knowing that a few bottles of rum will at any time obtained [sic] signatures to any representation. Besides the principle, as introduced from Vermont savours too much of democratic practices and if countenanced by you will assuredly place the country at the disposal of factious and unprincipled demagogues.

The discourse of Ross and Felton might have been lifted directly from contemporary English anti-reformers.[35]

By the 1820s, the appointment process was thus very different from what it had been in the eighteenth century. Councillors and other highly placed colonial politicians might still intervene in the process to make personal recommendations, but this was exceptional. Instead, local initiative and local support were becoming increasingly important in the decisions made by the executive on whom to name as justices. Letellier, for example, the prospective Saint-Vallier justice, had initially proposed himself, but he had been refused by the Executive Council and so had returned to the parish to get up a petition in his favour. And this local power was not channelled through existing formal political structures, for, unlike in Upper Canada, there was no particularly prominent input from members of the Assembly into the appointment process. Though, like Papineau, they might on occasion propose justices, they did so most often in their role as members of local elites. As Denis-Benjamin Viger, a leading *Patriote*, declared before the House of Commons committee in 1828, 'we have sometimes imagined that the choice [of magistrates] was not always good, but the governor exercised his prerogative; it is left by the law to his judgment, and we have not interfered.'[36]

As the number of recommendations to the magistracy continued to increase, the executive was forced to develop the means of vetting those recommended. The establishment of salaried local judicial officials, the chairmen, gave the administration an ideal conduit for local knowledge, especially in the districts farther from the capital, and in the 1810s the executive began referring recommendations for the magistracy to the chairmen in Montreal and Trois-Rivières. By the late 1820s, almost all recommendations were systematically referred to them, often in batches at a time. For the district of Quebec, closer to the seat of power, individual recommendations seem only infrequently to have been referred to the chairmen, at least formally; the executive evidently had other sources of local knowledge, or perhaps simply consulted the local law officers informally.[37]

The making up of the general commissions illustrates this growing importance of the local judicial bureaucracy. Those of 1810 and 1811 for Montreal and Trois-Rivières were still referred to committees of the Executive Council, but by 1815, that for Trois-Rivières was referred directly to Coffin, the chairman there. For the 1821 commission for Montreal, the executive initially relied on Charles Marshall, the solicitor general, then resident in the city. Apparently with little knowledge of the countryside, he wrote a circular letter to the curés of the district's Catholic parishes, asking them for their suggestions. This was a decidedly unusual step, and a particularly incongruous one for a Tory who would later be one of the key architects of the unabashedly assimilationist Union Bill of 1822. Despite many helpful letters from the curés, no doubt pleased at being consulted, and assistance from the resident Montreal judges, Marshall botched the job, producing lists filled with errors. The resulting commission angered many justices by not respecting the habitual order of seniority, by excluding many senior justices from the quorum, and by dropping justices who had not previously acted. The executive then turned to McCord and Mondelet, the chairmen, who showed their superior knowledge of the district by sending in a detailed, annotated list of the justices on the current commission plus their suggestions for additions, all of which allowed the executive to produce a second, corrected commission. The chairmen henceforth became central figures in making up the general commissions and remained so until the end of the 1820s. Even in Quebec City, at the seat of the executive, it was the chairmen by the mid-1820s who drew up the lists of nominees.[38]

In turning to the chairmen and other local officials, the executive was asking them not only for knowledge of the individuals recommended but also for knowledge of their districts. By the nineteenth century, the administration had established the policy of not naming justices unless there was truly a local need. It was the chairmen who were most often asked to make the call, based on their local knowledge. In 1822, for example, when referring a Varennes petition to the Montreal chairmen, the executive asked them to report not only on the fitness of the proposed justice but also on the necessity of the appointment. Mondelet, himself originally from Saint-Marc, only a few kilometres away, replied that not only was the proposed justice unacceptable but there were five justices in Boucherville just a league and a half away and another at Verchères two and a half leagues away.[39]

Yet the power of the chairmen over the composition of the commission, initially a question of administrative efficiency and local knowledge, soon became enmeshed in colonial politics. In making up the 1828 commission, Dalhousie asked Robert Christie, the Quebec City chairman, to comment on the existing commission and to note in particular 'such as from misconduct or other causes it may be necessary or expedient to leave out of the new commission,' a reference that Christie understood to include political opposition to the administration. This became one of the many grievances of the Assembly against the Dalhousie administration. The power of the chairmen over the nomination process had already begun to arouse the ire of the *Canadien* majority from the mid-1820s, when in both Quebec City and Montreal the chairmen in office were prominent supporters of Dalhousie's administration, and from 1825, successive bills for the qualification of justices sought to ensure that they were nominated on the advice of the Executive Council and/or judges, rather than the chairmen. It was in 1829, however, following Dalhousie's purge of magistrates in 1828, that discontent over the nomination process boiled over, becoming a central issue in both of the Assembly committees that examined the state of the magistracy. As well as hearing testimony identifying justices dismissed for political reasons, the committees focused on the role of the chairmen in selecting justices. Witness after witness declared that, in excluding Dalhousie's political opponents from the commission, the chairmen had subverted the independence of the judiciary and had served as the governor's 'organs' in his quest to force both the magistrates and the people to 'crouch and bend to the pleasure of the executive.' Christie, who was also a prominent moderate Tory member of the Assembly, was specially targeted, with accusations that he had boasted about his power over the commission and had used his seat to spy for the administration; this led eventually to the unfortunate saga whereby Christie was repeatedly expelled from the Assembly, only to be re-elected by his constituents. Vallières de Saint-Réal, the sponsor of the 1830 qualification bill, charged that there had been a conspiracy led by Dalhousie to destroy the liberties and energies of the country, with Christie as the instrument. The *Patriote* majority was not at all wrong: private communications of both Christie and Coffin show that they did indeed recommend explicitly political dismissals. But, rather than trying to fix the process, the reformers' response, as we saw, was to abolish the office of chairman.[40]

Beginning with the new commissions in 1830, the executive resumed closer control over the nomination process, although still relying heavily on local knowledge. When Kempt began in the summer of 1829 to put together the commissions, he tried to distance himself from the practices of his detested predecessor. Thus, though the chairmen were still in office, he avoided any reference to them. Instead, he reverted to a more personal mode of proceeding, relying on information gathered on his tour through the colony and soliciting prominent local individuals for suggestions. In a colony with over a half-million inhabitants, the return to older methods was difficult. The selection process became a lengthy one, 'of so much delicacy and difficulty that it has been necessary to proceed with great caution,' as Kempt admitted to his superiors. The commissions did not issue until October 1830, and he was still unable to find enough suitable candidates. And this more direct involvement of the colonial executive continued later in the decade. Local communities and local elites continued to send petitions and recommendations for justices to the governor. He in turn might accept or reject them directly, or send them for comment to a variety of presumably trustworthy individuals with local knowledge, such as judges, individual members of the Legislative Council (though the council itself was largely left out of the loop), or, in the more conciliatory mood of the earlier 1830s, *Patriote* Assembly members. Even in the heightened political climate of the later 1830s, governors threw their nets wide in gathering information on potential justices. In 1836, for example, Gosford asked Pierre-Dominique Debartzch, one of the more nationalist *Canadien* legislative councillors, for his advice in making up the commission; Debartzch in turn asked Jacques Viger, the nationalist ex-mayor of Montreal, for his input, which he willingly provided; and this may help explain why a number of avowed *Patriotes* ended up being appointed to the resulting commissions. The more personal nature of these consultations is clear from the assertion by Stephen Walcott, Gosford's civil secretary, that the general commissions of 1836 and 1837 were prepared 'from the best sources of information within my reach,' though apparently assisted by the *Patriote* Jean-Joseph Girouard.[41]

The return to a nomination process less dependent on local officials in 1830s, however, did not necessarily mark a retreat in the bureaucratization of the process that was already well under way. For example, from the 1810s onwards, the executive had gradually put in place measures to ensure that justices who were appointed were actually willing to act. In England, appointment to the magistracy was distributed as much for the honour it bestowed as for the concrete actions that justices might undertake on the part of the state, and little attention was paid to whether appointed justices actually acted; this was also the case in American colonies such as Massachusetts. The executive in Quebec and Lower Canada, however, had long adopted the more utilitarian stance that only justices willing to act should be appointed. Already in 1765, Murray had justified the dismissal of one justice in part because he had refused to act, and in renewing the commission in 1788, Dorchester suggested that inactive justices should not be reappointed. In the eighteenth century, however, this largely remained a pious wish, since potential justices seem not to have been asked whether they were willing to act, and those who did not act were not systematically removed. Even in 1810 and 1811, when new commissions for the districts of Montreal and Trois-Rivières were drawn up, the executive councillors apparently thought inactivity no bar to renewal, and in the Montreal commission at least, a dozen justices who had not even taken the oaths of office were reappointed.[42]

By 1815, however, this had changed, with the executive seeking to exclude justices who did not qualify themselves (by taking the oath of office) and act – those who, as Thomas Coffin put it, 'take the advantage of the mark and exemption derived from the commission, without rendering any service whatever.' But the executive was still faced with the problem of determining who had, and who would, act. In 1815, for the smaller district of Trois-Rivières, Coffin was more than happy to identify those who had not qualified. But for the district of Quebec, the executive took a different, more systematic course, sending out circular letters to all justices who had not qualified and to all prospective new justices, asking them if they intended to qualify and act, and dropping those who declined. Initially, the principle was unevenly applied: thus, in 1821, though the executive had directed Marshall, the solicitor general, not to suggest any justices who would not act, he still proposed renewing the commissions of several superannuated Montreal justices, so as not to deprive them of 'a compliment which their long services would seem to entitle them to, and the withholding of which, I have had occasion to observe, would be rather sensibly felt.' By the mid-1820s, however, the administrative check on justices' willingness to act was being used before almost all general commissions, and in 1830 every one of the hundreds of proposed justices was sent a printed circular letter asking him if he intended to qualify and act and, if he accepted, a second letter reminding him to qualify. This practice continued in the 1830s, with circular letters sent out and the clerks of the peace asked to identify justices who had not qualified or acted.[43]

Willingness to act thus became not only a deciding factor in selecting justices but also a bureaucratic necessity. At least nine Montreal justices were dropped from the 1826 commission simply because they did not respond to the circular letter, and many more suffered the same fate in 1830, including four who answered too late; one of these, Ignace Gaucher *dit* Gamelin of Soulanges, practically begged to be reinstated but was left off nonetheless. Still, the executive reserved the right to bend this rule on occasion, as when William Hallowell, a Montreal Tory, was reappointed in 1826 and 1828 despite never having qualified himself since his first appointment in 1822. And the verifications were not perfect: at least two justices reappointed to the 1828 commission were already dead. Still, by the 1820s, bureaucratic supervision of the nomination process had become entrenched, giving the executive far greater control over those it named to the commission; and by 1830, the process had been enshrined as a set of 'rules' in an internal memorandum.[44]

The process of selecting justices and making up the commissions justices thus changed profoundly from the 1760s to the 1830s, though there were some fundamental constants. From an entirely centralized procedure based on the personal knowledge of the governor and his councillors, the executive had moved by the 1820s to one heavily dependent on local knowledge, funnelled to Quebec City directly via petitions or through local officials such as the chairmen and the clerks of the peace; and though local officials became less systematically involved in the 1830s, the dependence on local knowledge remained. Local elites thereby became involved in a key part of the royal prerogative, with the nomination of justices often reflecting local power dynamics – quite different from the top-down view of patronage and state power often portrayed in Quebec historiography.[45] Nevertheless, as the Assembly repeatedly pointed out, the executive retained its arbitrary power over appointments to important positions such as those of justice of the peace, a power that in the hands of men like Craig, Dalhousie, or Aylmer could readily serve to further partisan political ends. This interplay between local power and central authority was characteristic of ancien-régime states on the English model; what was new was its increasing systematization.

Choosing 'Fit and Respectable Characters'

Once the executive had decided that the appointment of a justice was necessary, there was still another essential question: Was the person proposed fit to be included in the commission? The answer to this was influenced by questions of politics and power, but also by notions of propriety. Thus, though the first commission issued by Murray in 1764 was dictated by the practical necessity of implementing his instructions to appoint justices, his specific choices, a mix of merchants, soldiers, and civil officials, were an obvious attempt to balance the two main British factions, the merchants and the army. As Murray noted regarding his Montreal appointments:

> ... the civil establishment was by no means relished by the troops, as the new magistracy must be composed, agreeable to my instructions, of the very merchants they held so much in contempt ... Unluckily the merchants at Montreal the most proper from their circumstances and understanding to be made Justices of the Peace were those who had had the most disputes with the troops. I was aware of these disagreeable circumstances at Montreal and remedied them as much as possible by joining with them half pay officers in the commission of the peace and even by borrowing some from the Regt. on duty there, and it was strongly recommended to live in peace and harmony there.[46]

As Murray's difficulties imply, he was not free to select whom he wished as a magistrate, for his choice was limited by his instructions, which in this case banned Catholics. And he was also guided by a concern for naming those 'most proper from their circumstances and understanding' as well as by political considerations. Throughout the period, the choice of justices was shaped both by formal criteria and by more informal notions of what constituted 'fitness' for the position.

Formal Criteria

Though the system of appointing justices in Quebec and Lower Canada was in theory the same as in England, there were substantial differences in the formal criteria that determined who legally could be named a justice. Some criteria were evidently the same: for example, justices had to be men.[47] But others differed significantly. Thus, Catholics were excluded from the magistracy in England by virtue of the Test Act, which in essence required them to abjure their faith as a condition of accepting office. This was initially applied in Quebec, thus barring from the commission all but the handful of Protestants in the colony, almost all British. However, the Quebec Act soon removed this disability by providing a special oath for Catholic officeholders. This was in marked contrast to England's other predominantly Catholic colony, Ireland, where the Test Act barred Catholics from the magistracy, and also two other British North American colonies with substantial Catholic populations, Maryland and Pennsylvania, though it was not without precedent: in Acadia, for example, British governors had appointed a Catholic justice in the 1720s.[48] The dispensation extended only to Christians, however: in 1830, the Executive Council objected to only one justice in the list submitted them, Samuel B. Hart, 'who, being a Jew, they are of opinion cannot take the oaths of qualification.' This rebuff precipitated a series of petitions and representations by Hart and other members of the Jewish community, which led eventually to the watershed colonial statute of 1831 that extended full civil rights to Jews in Lower Canada and the appointment of three Jews to the commission of 1833. However, since the oath of office retained Christian references, two of the three refused to swear, and the status of Jewish justices of the peace remained unclear until just before the Rebellions.[49] Still, with this exception, from 1775 onwards governors were bound by no formal rules relating to the religion of appointees. As we will see, this had a profound impact on the character of the magistracy and thus on how colonial society at large experienced the criminal justice system.

Another important difference between England and Quebec was the disregard of property qualifications. In England, property qualifications ensured that justices were drawn only from the propertied elites. Most English justices had to possess property yielding an annual income of £100 and were in theory subject to heavy penalties if they acted without being qualified. However, this in fact had little impact since the local gentry who usually composed the magistracy easily met the qualifications. In Quebec immediately after the Conquest, however, the application of English property qualifications would have excluded almost all Protestants in the colony. Murray thus disregarded it and appointed property-less merchants and army officers. After 1775, with the rehabilitation of Catholic landowners and the rapid growth of anglophone landholding, this should have been less of a consideration. However, successive administrations continued to ignore property qualifications, preserving their freedom to name whomsoever they chose. This was in marked contrast to Upper Canada, where justices were required to have the requisite property, although it was similar to the situation in both Ireland and Scotland.[50]

This departure from English norms provided reformers with considerable political ammunition and, from the middle of the 1820s, became one of the avenues the Assembly exploited to attack what it saw as the administration's despotism. Bills to establish qualifications for justices were thus passed by the Assembly in each session from 1825 onwards, with provisions based directly on English precedent: notably, justices were to swear that they owned a certain minimum value of real property, and sheriffs, coroners, and practising lawyers were excluded. However, for the administration, the bills became symbolic of the Assembly's attempt to usurp executive power and were repeatedly rejected by the Legislative Council. The issue of qualification was also raised by the Assembly's representatives before the House of Commons committee in 1828 and became central to the Assembly's 1829 inquiries into the magistracy, which heard evidence that in the three main districts, some justices owned no property whatsoever and others were bankrupt. With the conciliatory Kempt at the head of the executive, the Assembly's bill was finally passed in 1830, setting the qualification for justices at £300 total worth of real property, or £150 in the Eastern Townships and the Gaspé.[51]

The debates that surrounded the successive qualification bills reflect in a microcosm the broader political debates in the colony. The bills' supporters, mainly members of the *Canadien/Patriote* party and more moderate reformers, argued that the measure was simply meant to ensure that justices who were sued for misbehaviour could be held accountable, rejecting any charge that they were trying to apply the 'aristocratic' principles that in fact underlay the English property qualification. The insistence on real property, however, perpetuated a long-standing debate in the colony over the relative rights and responsibilities of landed wealth and merchant capital, with the reformers leaning towards the former and the Tories the latter. As Papineau argued in 1830, in a colonial setting moveable property was too easy to transfer and disguise, especially since many of those who lived in apparent opulence had no intention of staying in the country. Only real estate gave true security, and at any rate, if those without real property wanted to become magistrates, all they had to do was buy land. The bills also reflected the reformers' more general attempt to curb the power of the administration – what Papineau described as 'the caprice of the Governor' and 'the enormities committed by the Executive' – by establishing legislative parameters for its actions.[52]

As with other measures such as the qualification and summoning of juries, the bills' proponents referred back to fundamental ideological principles, and despite the rise in *Canadien* nationalism, their point of reference in the late 1820s was still England. Hence, in a report to the Assembly in 1829, Vallières de Saint-Réal, the main sponsor of the qualification bill, gave what was in essence a lecture on the history of the justices in England, reaching back to the Middle Ages. His underlying argument was for a return to the purity of the English constitution, which had been sullied by successive colonial administrations and in particular that of Dalhousie. Much of the *Patriote* rhetoric on the importance of landed property was similar to that used to defend the primacy of landed property in the appointment of English magistrates until the 1830s, thereby excluding the rising commercial class. And when one *Patriote* member, Thomas Lee, suggested that justices be elected, as they were in the United States, his proposal was shot down by leading reformers such as Vallières de Saint-Réal, Denis-Benjamin Viger, and John Neilson. As Vallières de Saint-Réal argued, the office was not elective in England, and 'we must not pretend to more freedom than John Bull. John Bull is subject to a limited monarchy; we must not claim to ourselves a Republican government.' Even Papineau himself, later a proponent of elected magistrates, did not support Lee. Similarly, the 92 Resolutions of 1834, though they decried the composition of the magistracy, did not call for their election. Popular election of magistrates, which was being raised as an issue in Upper Canada at the same time, would gain widespread support only much later, with the radicalization of the *Patriotes* in the immediate lead-up to the Rebellions. As with many other issues relating to institutional change before the early 1830s, the reform discourse on the justices remained fundamentally conservative and centred on the British model, rather than overtly Republican and nationalist, as has sometimes been argued.[53]

Nevertheless, the bills were bitterly opposed by hard-line Tories, who had a quite different view of the English constitution and many of whom were deeply suspicious of anything that might increase *Canadien* power. They saw the bills as an assault on the royal prerogative and viewed the insistence on real rather than personal property as a veiled attack on the merchant class to the benefit of the landholders in general and the Assembly in particular. As Samuel Gale declared in 1828, the measures

> would have excluded intelligent men of monied property or independent incomes and particularly mercantile gentlemen, in the towns, and would have substituted for them, a half-educated class of thriving [sic] notaries and small householders and farmers who might be ready to swear them-

selves worth £100 per year. And it would have thus promoted an object which certain individuals in the Assembly appear from their conduct to keep steadily in view, the placing [of] civil power and the authority of the state, in the hands of persons sufficiently raised above the lower orders to be useful instruments in misleading them, but not sufficiently distinguished from them either by professions character or education to be qualified to become leaders themselves.

In 1830 Henry Mackenzie was, if possible, even more vitriolic, openly playing the card of national conflict: 'in this country, real property is almost exclusively possessed by persons little moved from ignorance, of French origin indisposed to persons of British birth, in habits of systematic opposition to the measures of Administration, and the mere tools of a faction whose ostensible purpose is the enjoyment of the Constitution in its fullest purity, but of whose ultimate aim none who know them can have a doubt.' Tory justices also resented the Assembly's imputations: as Edward Cartwright, a Trois-Rivières justice and former army captain, put it in 1829: 'when I read in the newspapers, the debates in the House of Assembly, and my feelings hurt by the unhandsome tone they spoke in of the magistrates, I declined any further attendance ... after what has been said ... I have no wish to be a Magistrate.' They also intensely disliked the requirement that they swear an oath as to their property holdings and the detailed clauses of the bills that set out how justices could be sued for non-compliance. After the bill passed in 1830, several, including Mackenzie, refused to qualify even if they had the necessary property. Still, even among Tories, the act gained a measure of acceptance, and when the Assembly renewed it in 1836, the Tory-dominated Legislative Council assented, in marked contrast to its refusal the previous year to renew a qualification bill for jurymen.[54]

Tory rhetoric aside, the property qualification finally imposed by the 1830 act was in fact relatively minimal: £300 at an annual yield of 5 per cent was equivalent to an annual value of only £15, far less than that in England or even Upper Canada. To put this in context, already in the early 1810s, the average annual rental value of a stone house in Montreal was well over £50. As for rural areas, Papineau was probably exaggerating when he declared that half of all household heads had property worth £1,000 or more, and Durham even more so when he noted that the qualification 'is so low, that in the country parts almost everyone possesses it.' Still, as in England, the qualification was low enough that few members of landed elites were excluded.[55]

The process of putting together the 1830 commissions that followed the new property qualifications nevertheless showed that a significant number of existing justices could not meet even these limited requirements. In the district of Montreal, of 173 justices named in the 1828 commission, 93 were not reappointed; by contrast, Dalhousie's purge of 1828 resulted in at most nineteen justices being dropped. Though, as we saw, many removals were the result of death or emigration, twenty-two justices stated that they were disqualified by the act, six refused to qualify under it, and another twenty simply ignored the circular letter asking them if they were qualified. The disqualification removed some particularly active magistrates, especially in the countryside: as John Yule of Chambly noted rather pathetically, 'by misfortune in business, I have become so reduced in my circumstances as to render it intirely out of my power, to express myself qualified, to continue to serve in the Commission of the Peace; as required by the Statute of last session. On retiring from an arduous duty, which I have had the honor so long to exercise, tho' with but slight ability; I hope I may have merited, a small share of esteem, from an indulgent community.'[56] Whatever Yule's merits as a justice, however, the act was certainly having the desired effect.

Politics of all stripes, from the national to the personal, played out in the debates over the qualification of justices. For example, the exclusion of practising attorneys, though firmly established in English precedent, was probably directed at Gale, the hated Tory chairman at Montreal, who had always continued to practise as a lawyer; this allowed the Assembly to take away not only his salary as chairman but also his status as a magistrate. But political considerations, notably Tory resistance, also meant that from 1775 until 1830 there were few formal criteria restraining the administration's choice of candidates. Did this imply, as Papineau charged in 1829, that 'dismissions and appointments have been made without respect to character, influence, property or ability for the office,' that in fact 'the Provincial Administration has established no rule, and has imposed upon itself no restraint,' as the Assembly claimed?[57] Not at all. Instead, petitions, letters, and reports both for and against the nomination and dismissal of justices show that the executive was guided by a shifting, fluid, but nevertheless definite set of desirable magisterial qualities, neatly summed up in the governors' instructions. From Dorchester in 1791 through Gosford in 1835, governors were enjoined to ensure that councillors, judges, and justices of the peace were 'men of good Life, well affected to Our Government, and of abilities suitable to their Employments.' And, along with local need and willingness to act, these qualities of respectability, loyalty, and competence were the main measures of potential and actual justices. The rub came in the definition of these qualities by the administration.

Respectability

The first quality sought in a justice was respectability: to be 'of good life,' as the instructions put it. As Dorchester declared in 1794, 'the appointment of fit and respectable characters to fill the magistracy is a matter of the first importance'; and this had not changed by 1830, when Kempt declared that he had chosen justices among 'those persons of the greatest respectability in the community.'[58] But what exactly was meant by 'respectable,' an epithet used so often in petitions and recommendations as to seem almost trite?

First, of course, respectability meant morality – as another clause in the instructions stated, 'in order to discountenance Vice and promote the practice of Virtue to the utmost of your Power, we do hereby strictly command and enjoin you, to appoint no Person to be a Justice of the Peace, or to any Publick Trust or Employment, whose notorious ill Life or Conversation may occasion Scandal.' Already in 1765, when justifying the dismissal of two bankrupt Montreal justices, Murray commented that since the justices were the only magistrates at Montreal, 'it is necessary at least that they should be esteem'd honest men,' though in this case he may have been concealing political motivations; and as Mondelet put it in describing the principles he and McCord sought in recommending justices, 'nous exigeons des moeurs' [we insist on morals]. In similar fashion, though evidently acting for political reasons, Samuel Gale also appealed to morality in justifying the dismissals of 1828: 'no names of former Justices of the Peace were omitted without strong reasons such as convictions, criminal offences, degraded moral character, intemperance or misconduct.' 'Involved in debt contracted in a most dishonorable way,' 'is accused of a degrading crime,' 'unfit from inebriety and other causes'– all these were epithets attached to justices dismissed from the commissions.[59] Overall, though, few justices were removed from the commissions for outright criminal behaviour, and usually this happened only in particularly egregious cases. John Scriver and Joseph Odell, for example, were both removed for being manifestly involved in smuggling. Other justices suspected of criminality or immorality were nonetheless left in the commission, like William Bullock, charged in 1819 with forgery, or Martin Strong Parker, sued in 1822 for practising medicine without a licence. As Charles Marshall, the solicitor general, admitted in 1820, 'many persons have, at different times, been put into the commission, by no means unobjectionable,' but, because of the shortage of qualified individuals, especially in the countryside, he had omitted justices only in the few instances where he had heard of actual misconduct.[60]

Respectability also included class, ethnicity, race, age, and temperament. Justices were to be gentlemen, 'in character and habits of association better than that of the mass of the people.' Carleton's dismissal of the colony's justices in the 1760s is well known: 'there was not a Protestant butcher or publican, that became as bankrupt, who did not apply to be made a Justice.' Class and ethnic considerations also barred men such as Thomas Dunn of Hemmingford, 'a low bred vulgar Irish emigrant,' according to the report on the popular petition in his favour. As for race, while it was never explicitly raised, there was never any discussion of appointing Natives as justices: in 1820, for example, when recommending the appointment of justices for Sault-Saint-Louis (Caughnawaga), a Native village near Montreal, the *curé* recommended two Europeans. Justices were also to be mature: in not recommending Joseph-Édouard Faribault *fils*, son of a local potentate, Gale noted that he was 'a very young man and although his character be perfectly fair it may be matter for reflection whether it would not be proper to defer his solicited appointment until his age shall be somewhat more mature and his character more firmly established.' Finally, respectability also meant even-temperedness. In recommending new Montreal justices in 1765, for example, Mabane and Price noted that 'the point we had chiefly in view was to find out persons well inclined to one another unbyased by party spirit and who should enter into the office without having former resentments to gratify and at the same time who had firmness to execute the office with impartiality & justice.' Similarly, in the nineteenth century, one potential justice was dismissed as 'certainly not a respectable character, for the last years he is known to have been extremely litigious, taking up and conducting petty suits for others as well as himself,' while another was dismissed as turbulent and quarrelsome and thus little suited to keeping the peace. Instead, what was sought was the man who 'pour son affabilité, son esprit de conciliation et son intégrité, réunit tous les suffrages' [by his affability, his spirit of conciliation and his integrity, is supported by all], as the *curé* of Sainte-Scholastique put it.[61]

Surprisingly, three aspects of respectability were relatively unimportant. The first was family connections: so important for the appointment of justices both in more established societies such as England and Wales and in colonies such as Massachusetts or Upper Canada, they were rarely mentioned in discussions of potential justices in Quebec and Lower Canada. In most cases, recommendations concerned the merits of the justice himself, with references to family at best expressed in general terms such as 'des meilleures familles' [of the best families] or 'de famille ancienne' [of an ancient family]. In relations between local, especially rural, society and the colonial administration, family was evidently secondary in establishing respectability. This was perhaps the reflection of an increasing distance between Court (the central administration) and Country, as we saw in the nomination process, but also of the fluid social structure of the colony. In the early nineteenth century, traditional seigneurial elites were in flux and many local notables were either *Canadiens* recently acceded to elite status or recently arrived British and American immigrants; for them, appeal to family brought little status.[62]

The second aspect little considered was wealth. In England, landed fortune was the backbone of respectability, and some lords lieutenant even went so far as to consider anyone engaged in commerce or the professions as unsuitable for the bench, whatever their property holdings. In Quebec and Lower Canada, despite the Assembly's assertion that property was entirely disregarded in the appointment of justices, landholding was in fact often considered, with Mondelet, for example, stating that he and McCord recommended only landholders, 'des personnes qui tiennent au sol.' However, recommendations rarely went beyond the bare assertion of property ownership, and wealth was never a quality mentioned by the executive. Rather than being a sign of egalitarian principles, this was simply a reflection of the tenuous state of fortunes, especially in the countryside, which had nothing like the landed gentry of England.[63]

The last aspect virtually absent from the evaluation of justices' fitness was piety. Recommendations for justices, even those from *curés*, made little mention of religious beliefs. These could actually be a bar to the magistracy, since, unlike in England, the executive consistently refused to appoint active clergymen. In England, clerical justices had become increasingly popular in the late eighteenth and early nineteenth centuries, for they were more likely to act than the rural gentry who had previously dominated the commissions; by 1830, clergymen composed perhaps a quarter of qualified justices overall, and over 40 per cent in several counties.[64] In Quebec and Lower Canada, however, Catholic *curés* were obviously not suitable as representatives of the anti-papist English monarchy; nor it seems were members of the 'established' Church of England, or indeed almost any clergymen. In the district of Montreal between 1764 and 1837, for example, there were only a handful of clergymen appointed. Only one, John Doty, the Anglican minister of Sorel in the 1780s, ever acted with any regularity, and his appointment proved an unmitigated disaster. He became heavily embroiled in disputes between the different Loyalist factions at Sorel, using his powers as a justice to further his own faction As a board of inquiry noted in 1787, 'we are induced to believe that the ministry of the gospel is disturbed, and that in the present circumstances the publick receives little benefit from the magistracy being vested in the hands of the clergy, when other subjects can be found.'[65] Doty was dropped from the commission in 1788, and though the principle was never explicitly stated, all successive administrations consistently avoided naming active clergymen to the commission. After all, Protestant ministers could hardly have been expected to be impartial in cases opposing Catholic *Canadiens* and Protestant immigrants. In this respect, the colony was closer to more religiously heterogeneous British possessions like Ireland, Scotland, or Upper Canada, where equally few clerical justices were appointed.[66]

In general, notions of respectability took much the same form as in other contemporary societies, but with significant local differences. Morality, class, age, and an even-tempered disposition were all relatively universal and self-evident qualities sought in magistrates. However, the particularities of a colonial society composed of two very different ethno-religious groups meant that factors such as family, wealth, and religion were of far less importance than in England or even in neighbouring Upper Canada.[67]

Loyalty

The second quality noted in the governors' instructions was that justices should be 'well affected to Our Government' – in a word, loyal. In a recently conquered colony, close to a hostile neighbour, in an empire that saw itself in constant danger, it is not surprising that epithets like 'a good subject' and 'a loyal subject' came up frequently in discussions around the fitness of justices. But, as studies on colonies such as Upper

Canada have shown, loyalty was a fluid concept, readily manipulated. In Quebec and Lower Canada, in a political community increasingly split over the question of parliamentary power and executive privilege, and with strong-willed and confrontational governors like Murray, Craig, Dalhousie, and Aylmer, the test of loyalty to the British crown often became conflated with that of support for the governors, leading to the sorts of political dismissals already discussed. And more generally, loyalty could also be seen to mean being British-born, and thus, not being French or American. John Antrobus's declaration in 1811 as to the need to 'Englify this French district' therefore went hand in hand with that of Henry Cull (an active Eastern Townships magistrate and militia officer), who asserted that it was 'as necessary to Englify the Yankees as it is to unfrenchify the Canadians.' Even when they were not explicitly anti-French or anti-American, statements referring to 'the zealous attachment he bears to His Majesty's person and government, he being a British Born subject' appealed to a hierarchy of loyalty in which both *Canadiens* and Americans were subordinate if not excluded.[68]

The conflation of loyalty and Britishness played out in the inclusion or exclusion of *Canadiens* in the commission. From the beginning, the executive was faced with the difficulty of governing a society with a substantial *Canadien* majority, both among the population at large and among the local elites who were essential in implementing local governance. Already in 1766, Adam Mabane raised the possibility of the appointment of Catholic *Canadiens* as justices, though he rejected it as 'perhaps improper,' and the report of the English attorney and solicitor generals in the same year suggested something similar, though the ideal would be to name Protestant *Canadiens*.[69] Murray had in fact already taken this latter step, appointing pre-Conquest Protestant merchants Jean Dumas Saint-Martin and François Lévesque to the 1764 commissions for Montreal and Quebec respectively, along with other francophone Protestants who had arrived with the British army. But it was the removal of bars on Catholic officeholders following the Quebec Act that allowed the executive to follow the British practice in many conquered colonies, from New York to India, of co-opting local elites into the lower levels of judicial administration.[70] At the same time, though, from Carleton in the 1770s through Milnes and Craig in the 1790s and 1800s and Dalhousie and Aylmer in the 1820s and 1830s, many governors became deeply suspicious of *Canadien* loyalty. This difficult balance between the practical need to co-opt local elites and the desire to create a loyal, British magistracy was directly reflected in

Table 2.2: Proportion and number of francophone justices in selected general commissions, 1764–1837*

	Montreal	Quebec	Trois-Rivières	Gaspé	Saint-Francis
1764	10% (1)	15% (3)	–	–	–
1776	58% (7)	57% (4)	–	–	–
1785	50% (10)	44% (8)	–	–	–
1788/1790	65% (24)	56% (14)	76% (13)	41% (7)	–
1794	60% (43)	64% (28)	88% (14)	19% (3)	–
1799	42% (36)	55% (27)	79% (15)	–	–
1810/1811	41% (50)	45% (22)	50% (26)	12% (3)	–
1815	–	64% (41)	48% (28)	–	–
1821/1823/1824	42% (64)	61% (82)	48% (30)	18% (6)	0% (0)
1828	32% (56)	49% (62)	35% (12)	14% (4)	–
1830	43% (59)	44% (39)	64% (14)	0% (0)	0% (0)
1833	32% (66)	45% (47)	63% (24)	–	0% (0)
1836/1837	43% (127)	63% (105)	70% (32)	36% (16)	0% (0)

* excludes ex-officio justices

the fluctuating proportion of francophone justices appointed to the commission.

As Table 2.2 shows, the commissions from 1776 to the mid-1790s almost always included a majority of francophones in each of the major districts, reaching notable highs of two-thirds, three-quarters, or even more francophones in the 1780s and early 1790s – this despite Dorchester's bitter disappointment at *Canadien* neutrality during the American Revolution. But, with the development of what Murray Green-wood has termed a 'garrison mentality' among British elites in the mid-1790s, preoccupied with potential *Canadien* disloyalty, along with the further political crisis under Craig, the growth of *Canadien* nationalism, and the concomitant desire to anglicize the colony as much as possible, the tide shifted.[71] By the early 1810s, francophones were in the minority in all but the district of Quebec. The decline continued through the 1820s, especially in the districts of Montreal and Trois-Rivières, culminating with Dalhousie's commissions of 1828.

Little wonder, then, that by the 1820s the ethnic composition of the magistracy had become the focus of complaints by *Canadien* nationalists regarding the appointment of justices, with, for example, one of the 1829 Assembly committees declaring that the low number of locally born justices had 'given birth to, feelings of a most painful nature to the inhabitants of the Country.' Under later governors, the proportion of francophones continued to fluctuate according to the executive's political stance. Kempt's commission of 1830 was explicitly conciliatory, like his overall policies, and his declared intent to appoint justices 'without distinction of party,' manifested through his appointment of a number of prominent *Patriotes*, seems to have been appreciated, but the satisfaction was short-lived. Aylmer returned to Dalhousie's policies – he appointed fewer francophones and excluded from the commission two Montreal magistrates who had been involved in the murder charges against troops who had killed several people during the 1832 Montreal West Ward election riots – which led to the issue of the ethnicity of appointed justices rebounding. This issue entered the anti-administration 92 Resolutions voted by the Assembly in 1834, though the charge that in the commission of 1833 only one-third of justices appeared to be of French origin, essentially true overall, applied less to the districts of Quebec and Trois-Rivières. Finally, Gosford initially returned to Kempt's approach: as he put it in his letter to Debartzch, 'I am anxious to avoid making this a political transaction, my sole object is, to obtain men of integrity, & independence, & in whose character, judgment, and discretion, the public may place confidence,' and his initial commissions included large numbers of francophones. But this stance did not survive the increasing defiance of colonial authority by nationalist and reform-minded elites, and by mid-1837 he was dismissing many of the magistrates he had appointed just a few months before.[72]

However, loyalty was not an overriding criterion. Many *Canadien* magistrates accused of 'disloyalty' were never dismissed: thus, though a number of justices helped organize highly publicized meetings in the spring of 1834 in support of the 92 Resolutions, none was removed, or even admonished. And many of those dismissed by one administration were reappointed by another. Eustache-Ignace Trottier Desrivières Beaubien, for example, was appointed in 1790 under Dorchester, dismissed in 1796 under Prevost, reappointed in 1799 just before Prevost left, dismissed in 1810 by Craig, and reappointed in 1815 by Drummond, only to die a year later. Further, while several justices were retired army or navy officers, serving military officers were almost never appointed justices after the early 1760s. Even a military governor like Dalhousie rejected their appointment as 'not ... adviseable,' and it was only in the wake of the second Rebellion, in November 1838, that Governor John Colborne appointed thirty-five British officers to the commission in the district of Montreal, so as to expedite proceedings against rebels.[73]

Perhaps most indicative of the often pragmatic approach to the loyalty question was the appointment of non-Loyalist Americans to the commission. It was most often Tories at the fringes of power who played the anti-American card: men such as John Hill Roe, who accepted nomination in 1830 with the statement that 'there being but American Justices of the peace heretofore appointed in this quarter [I] do think that my services as a British born subject may be of some use.'[74] In contrast, successive administrations frequently named Americans to the commission, especially in the newer settlements near the American border. Thus, excluding Loyalists and their descendants, at least eighty justices named in the district of Montreal between 1800 and 1833 (and probably far more) were American-born immigrants who had arrived long after the Revolution. These included men who had evidently participated in the republican forms of governance so abhorred by conservatives, such as a former county court judge and Vermont's former secretary of state. This was in contrast to Upper Canada, where the appointment of American-born magistrates to the commission declined substantially after 1815.[75] In a colony where substantial areas had limited immigration from Britain even after 1815, the executive had little choice but to rely on local elites, whether they were American or *Canadien*.

The ambiguous status of loyalty as a criterion for appointment is also suggested by the justices' political leanings. Overall, as Table 2.3 shows, I have been able to identify the approximate political orientation of about half of the justices named in the district of Montreal between 1764 and 1833. Unsurprisingly, loyalty to the British crown was a key factor: few of the justices appointed in the 1760s, for example, joined the American rebels, even though many were American merchants. But the magistracy was not necessarily a slavish reflection of the administration. Thus, in eighteenth-century Quebec, members of the English party outweighed those of the French party, even though it was the latter who were most favoured by the governors. Conversely, under the parliamentary system in Lower Canada, while Tories were by far the largest group of appointed magistrates, there was still a significant minority of reformers and *Canadien* nationalists, including vocal members of the *Canadien/Patriote* party. As Gosford declared to one *Patriote* justice in 1837, in admonishing him for presiding at an anti-administration meeting, he 'conceived that your principles were liberal but loyal, and friendly to good order, and under that impression nominated you with your own consent to the Magistracy.'[76] As elsewhere, governors in Lower Canada had to balance loyalty with political expediency; though

Table 2.3: Political orientation of justices in the district of Montreal, 1764–1833*

First named 1764–1791		First named 1793–1833	
Orientation	Number	Orientation	Number
Unknown	55	Unknown	· 268
Total known	47	Total known	288
English party	27	Tory	173
French party	15	Moderate reformer or nationalist	43
American rebel	3	*Canadien / Patriote* party	58
Other	2	Mixed	2
		Other	12

* excludes ex-officio justices and justices whose commissions were immediately abrogated

this did not prevent them from dismissing justices who went beyond the bounds of what the administration considered acceptable political activity.

Competence

The final quality sought in colonial appointees to the magistracy was that they be competent: 'of abilities suitable to their Employments,' as the royal instructions put it. In the case of justices, competence meant both innate intelligence and education, with each coming up again and again in recommendations, though generally in a negative sense. In 1820, for example, Marshall, the solicitor general, decried that 'the greatest and most obvious defect in the general state of the magistracy, consists in the want of a sufficient number of persons, especially in the country parishes, competent by the education, ideas, and habits, to fill so important of office.'[77]

The administration sought to ensure the competence of the magistracy in part through the use of the quorum clause in the commission. In England, the quorum clause was initially designed to ensure that justices could not undertake significant judicial actions, notably holding Quarter Sessions, without the presence of experienced or knowledgeable magistrates. The clause had become meaningless by the mid-eighteenth century, since it was usual to include all but one justice.[78] In Quebec, the quorum was also at first a mere formality, with all justices included from 1765 through to 1785. In 1788, however, the new administration under Dorchester limited the number of quorum justices to the first three or four regular justices in the commission (ex-officio justices were always on the quorum), probably as part of the general attempt to reform the colony's administration. This meant that in the district of Montreal, for example, only a tenth of justices were on the quorum. Though this severe restriction of the quorum was subsequently relaxed on the grounds that it made the holding of Quarter Sessions difficult, the policy of limiting the quorum continued through to the 1830s, at least in the main districts of Quebec and Montreal, where in general only between a quarter and a third of justices were included. In the smaller districts, however, because of the small number of justices and the difficulty of getting them together to hold sessions, far more justices were included.[79]

The utilitarian bent of the quorum is suggested by the fact that, in the two main districts, it was heavily weighted towards urban justices, who regularly comprised half or even two-thirds of the quorum despite making up a far smaller proportion of appointed justices. This reflected the centralization of the Quarter Sessions in the city but also confirmed the hold that urban magistrates had on the system. On the other hand, there was no general attempt to use the quorum clause to relegate *Canadien* justices to secondary status.[80] While francophone justices were under-represented in the quorum in the district of Quebec, compared to their presence in the commission as a whole, this was largely a reflection of their smaller numbers in Quebec City itself, and in fact, in the districts of Montreal and Trois-Rivières, they were if anything over-represented on the quorum. Indeed, in 1830, while the proportion of francophone justices dropped to about 40 per cent on the commissions of Montreal and Quebec, in both they made up more than half of the quorum justices.

Another utilitarian skill was language, with bilingualism an obvious advantage for justices. As G.W. Allsopp suggested regarding magistrates in 1830, 'altho' the English language is a desirable acquirement the French is the most necessary in the country parishes.' Appeal to language skills could nevertheless also link back to the question of ethnicity and loyalty. Thus, while recommending two bilingual candidates for Berthier in 1797, Sewell, the Tory attorney general, also declared that though there were many eligible shopkeepers and substantial farmers, 'for want of knowledge in the English language they are not likely to acquire the forms of office which are frequently essential, nor competent information on the criminal law which they are to administer which is entirely in English.' Lack of English had not previously barred the appointment of francophone seigneurs and merchants to the commission, and Sewell's apparently utilitarian contention was questionable: after all, this was less than a decade after Perrault's translation of substantial portions of Burn's *Justice of the Peace*, including forms for arrest warrants and other documents. Instead, Sewell's pronouncement must be seen in the context of the more general francophobia he shared with the other members of the British ruling elite at the time.[81]

While education, experience, and language were thus important skills in potential or actual justices, specific legal training or knowledge was rarely an issue. When prospective justices had legal training, it might be cited as a plus: thus, when Micah Townshend recommended Solomon Bingham for Saint-George, he took care to specify that Bingham 'has had a collegiate education, studied law with a view to practising it, was for some years a judge of one of the county courts of Vermont, has a naturally strong mind, and is in general far the best acquainted with the principles of law, of any person within the parish.' However, an equally common sentiment was that too much legal training could be a dangerous in a magistracy based on the principle of lay participation: one of the complaints against Samuel Gale was that 'being a Lawyer, [he] certainly exercises a great influence over the minds of his colleagues on a question of Law.'[82] Of the three basic qualities sought in justices, competence, as expressed through intelligence and knowledge, was probably the least important. Rural justices in particular were appointed not so much for their competence as for their local notability, in an attempt to cement the otherwise loose ties between local communities and the central state.

Why Become a Justice?

The colonial administration could, of course, nominate men as justices of the peace, but it still remained up to the nominee to accept. The motivations of these men are often hard to fathom, since few left any personal reflections on their role, but extant letters of both acceptance and refusal, especially in the nineteenth century, give some hints.

The two reasons most often evoked for accepting the magistracy were loyalty to the crown and desire to serve the public. Loyalty, as we saw, was an important though not overriding criterion in the selection of justices, so it is not surprising that nominees, both British and *Canadien*, expressed their attachment to Britain. As Pierre-Amable Boucher de Boucherville put it in 1830, 'if the duties of Magistrates are laborious, their worships are well repaid; first, by doing that which every subject ought to be proud of: eg serving in a conspicuous manner their sovereign and their country.' Another justice, Owen Quinn, conflated loyalty, constitutionalism, and religion: 'I beg leave to offer my services to His Excellency in the faithful discharge of the duties thereof, with unremitting loyalty, and zeal, to the Happy Constitution under which I was born, and through Almighty God am destined to live.' But equally important was the notion of public service, evoked time and again: as Jean-Baptiste-René Hertel de Rouville stated, 'vue la grande nécessité d'un juge de paix dans cette partie ici de notre District et les demandes réitérées des habitans de mon comté, je ne puis point me refuser à accepter cette distinction malgré toute la répugnance que je ressens pour tous emplois publics' [given the great necessity of a justice of the peace in this part of the District and the repeated demands of the inhabitants of his county, he could not refuse this distinction despite his aversion to any public employment]. Though such declarations were largely rhetorical (among his other public positions, Hertel de Rouville was both a member of the Assembly and lieutenant-colonel of the county militia battalion), it is difficult to dismiss entirely the impetus of public service in the constant activity of many unpaid justices. That left the question, of course, as to which 'public' was being served, which we will examine in the second part of the book.[83]

Loyalty and public service were reasons that could be openly evoked, but other motivations evidently also came into play. Some justices served for financial reasons: professional magistrates like the chairmen, most notably, but also rural justices who charged fees for depositions and warrants, though the income derived from this was probably too limited for there to be any of the 'trading' justices found in parts of England.[84] On a more sordid note, some justices entered the magistracy essentially for ulterior motives: Scriver, the justice accused of smuggling, used his position to obstruct the actions of customs officers. But above all, as was the case wherever the English system of justices of the peace was implanted, the magistracy was a means of exercising local power. For seigneurs such as Hertel de Rouville, being active justices who mediated disputes between their *censitaires* and ensured the building of roads on their lands was a natural extension of the paternalistic vision they had of themselves as seigneurs. The same also held for the growing class of rural merchants and professionals, seeking to distinguish themselves from *habitant* society in general. And in the cities, many justices served as much in order to participate in municipal government, primarily through the Special Sessions, as out of a desire to act in criminal matters.[85]

A further spur to acceptance of the commission was the honour the magistracy bestowed. This was perhaps the principal motivation of most justices in England, and colonial justices did regularly refer to the honour of the appointment: as Boucher de Boucherville declared in 1830, a second reward for justices was 'being gratified with the approbation of the Executive Government who places none in the commission, but to those in whom His Excellency trusts.' Once appointed, justices were very sensitive to the 'stigma' of being removed, with several magistrates who had been dropped declining to be renamed in later commissions. Justices also sometimes specifically asked to be named to the quorum or objected when they were not included in it, and a justice left off the quorum could become the subject of unflattering comment. Even the order in which justices were listed in the commissions, reflecting seniority based on date, became a point of honour when it was not respected, as in the first Montreal commission in 1821; and when the justices dismissed in 1828 were reintegrated in the commission of 1830, care was taken to insert their names according to their previous seniority, as some explicitly requested in their letters of acceptance.[86]

But the importance of the honour of the magistracy should not be over-emphasized. Seniority, as determined by the order in the commission, was as much a practical question of power as a matter of honour. The senior justice in a parish or township had important administrative powers: signing the certificate necessary for obtaining a tavern licence, organizing the public meeting to elect roads officials, acting as school visitor, keeping the minutes of petty sessions (and thus controlling the patronage position of clerk), and so on.[87] As well, while justices could benefit from adding the honorifics 'esquire' or 'JP' to their names, the importance of this is far from clear. Thus, justices had no special rights to the term 'esquire': among suitors using the honorific in civil court documents from the 1790s to the 1820s, only a third were current justices, another third had other formal reasons for using it (judges, councillors, attorneys, and the like), and another third had no apparent reason at all, apart from social status.[88] As for adding 'JP' to their signatures, this was uncommon, apart from in public documents such as depositions or petitions where it was legally important that justices identify themselves.

If many members of colonial elites were more than willing to accept nomination as justices, some were not. Refusals were far less common than acceptances, with few before the mid-1820s; even under the 1830 qualification law, which alienated many otherwise qualified justices, about two-thirds of qualified nominees accepted the position. But the reasons for refusal are instructive nonetheless. Apart from resistance to the qualification law and the usual excuses of old age and other incapacities, by far the most frequent reason cited was the time that the essentially unpaid position required. 'Point d'argent, point de Suisse' [no money, no mercenary], as a Quebec district nominee declared in refusing the position – especially appropriate since he was in fact Swiss. And a Montreal candidate was said to have refused because of 'the incroachments to which his leisure might be exposed, and the inconvenience inseperable from a kind of business towards which his previous habits had produced no predeliction.' More occasional were refusals related to competence: lack of sufficient knowledge of either French or English, for example, or of the criminal law. Some candidates were even more candid about the drawbacks of the position: as C.-P. Huot of Baie-Saint-Paul put it:

Je suis Notaire et absolument sans fortune, j'ai trop besoin de la faveur du public pour pouvoir accepter une place dans la nouvelle commission pour la paix. J'ai servi comme juge de paix depuis plusieurs années, et j'ai eu occasion d'observer que pour remplir dignement cet emploi il faut être indépendant, car on ne peut que se faire des ennemis dans l'exécution de cette charge, surtout parmi des gens sans connoissance.

[I am a notary and entirely without fortune, I have too much need of public favour to accept a place in the new commission of the peace. I have served as a justice of the peace for several years, and I have observed that in order to fill the position with dignity one must be independent, for one cannot but make enemies in carrying out this duty, especially amongst those of little understanding.]

But for most nominees, the burdens associated with being named to the commission seem not to have outweighed their desire to be justices, whether this was out of loyalty, public service, or personal interest.

Conclusion

It is easy to see the creation of the magistracy purely from a central perspective, with the executive attempting to impose its will throughout the colony by its control of this essential position. This was certainly the view presented by the *Canadien/Patriote* party in the 1820s and 1830s. However, in a rapidly expanding colony, the executive in Quebec City could have only limited knowledge of the men it had to find to fill the commission, and especially so in districts like Montreal whose inhabitants had less intercourse with the colonial capital. The executive thus relied increasingly on local information channelled through local officials such as the chairmen, whom it trusted to identify those who were fit and those who were not. The first decades of the nineteenth century also saw the increasing involvement of local communities in the selection of magistrates and thus in local state formation. Central-local relations were reversed, with local knowledge and local concerns playing a key role in the composition of apparently centrally controlled institutions such as the commission of the peace.

Still, a close examination of the appointment process suggests that the administration also kept an increasingly close watch over magistrates, not so much in what they did as whether they did it. This oversight argues against the notion of a magistracy essentially free of central bureaucratic control, and suggests instead significant autonomous administrative development in the colony long before the Rebellions.[89] And the final make-up of the commission remained largely under executive control, with the first legislative measures coming only in 1830. Further, with the disregard of property qualifications and the inclusion of Catholics from 1775, the executive could appoint just about whomsoever it chose – as long as they were Christian and male. The executive could and did also dismiss at will, and successive administrations showed a ready willingness to manipulate the commission for political ends. Taken together, these factors could easily have produced exactly the sort of magistracy that many writers have assumed and then condemned: of low status and little competence, grossly unrepresentative of the predominant culture, dominated by administration yes-men, and of little consequence. But it did not, and the face of criminal justice that presented itself to the colony's people was far from that portrayed by critics like Antrobus or the *Patriotes*.

3

The Character of the Magistracy

La plainte pour viol n'étant pas suffisament prouvée, suivant mon examen et mes interrogations, j'ai donné mon warrant pour fournir reconnoissance de sa comparution à Montréal et ai cru que la douceur de nos loix exigeoit cette indulgence de la part du magistrat, qui suivant moi, doit être le protecteur et non le tiran des sujets de sa majesté.
[The accusation of rape being insufficiently proven, according to my examination and investigations, I issued my warrant for him to give surety for his appearance at Montreal and believed that the lenity of our laws required this indulgence on the part of the magistrate, who according to me, must be the protector and not the tyrant of His Majesty's subjects.]
– Michel-Eustache-Gaspard-Alain Chartier de Lotbinière to John Reid (1806)

Corriger le bas peuple de ses défauts est chose très difficile; il ne voit que d'un oeil méchant les institutions établis pour réprimer l'immoralité.
[Correcting the common people's faults is very difficult; they see the institutions established for repressing immorality only in the worst light.]
– Jean-Marie Mondelet to Lewis Foy (1811)

I cannot but express my regret, that among the few institutions for the administration of justice throughout the country which have been adopted in Lower Canada from those of England, should be that of unpaid justices of the peace ... When we transplant the institutions of England into our colonies, we ought at least to take care beforehand that the social state of the colony should possess those peculiar materials on which alone the excellence of those institutions depends in the mother country ... most disreputable persons of both races have found their way into [the commission], and still continue to abuse the power thus vested in them. Instances of indiscretion, of ignorance, and of party feeling, and accusations of venality, have been often adduced by each party. Whether these representations be exaggerated or not, or whether they apply to a small or to a large portion of the magistracy, it is undeniable that the greatest want of confidence in the practical working of the institution exists.

– Lord Durham, *Report on the Affairs of British North America* (1839)[1]

Taken in and of themselves, the comments of Chartier de Lotbinière and Mondelet reflect two very different visions of the role of justices of the peace. The first was firmly grounded in the paternalism that informed members of the traditional *Canadien* elites – such as Chartier de Lotbinière, the seigneur of Vaudreuil – and epitomized what Norma Landau has termed the 'patriarchal' model of the English justice as voice and protector of his community.[2] The second, uttered by a self-made man, a rural notary who had moved to Montreal less than a decade before and had recently been appointed joint head of the city's magistracy, exemplified the views of the new urban bourgeoisie of the nineteenth century, condemning the immorality of the urban popular classes. But the circumstances of these comments also reveal something else, suggested in Durham's description of the magistracy: dubious judicial behaviour, if not outright misconduct, on the part of both of these experienced justices.

Chartier de Lotbinière was discussing the complaint of seventeen-year-old Marie Clausien *dit* Lapensée against Louis de Coigne *fils* for bastardy and rape. Technically, he was not wrong in granting bail, since even in rape cases this was at the discretion of the justice. But the plot thickens when we realize that the forty-year-old de Coigne was married, had fathered at least two previous illegitimate children (a fact that was no doubt well known locally, since the children had been baptized in a local parish church), and was the son of Louis-Mars Decoigne, Chartier de Lotbinière's fellow justice in Vaudreuil. Apart from the evident conflict of interest, de Coigne's previous history could well have disqualified him for bail, as a person charged with a serious felony and, in Blackstone's words, 'not being of good fame.' However, Chartier de Lotbinière protected his fellow member of the local elites and fellow man. As in so many other rape cases, the word of the victim was not enough. Further, Chartier de Lotbinière's own sexual morality was perhaps questionable – in 1789 he was apparently described as a scandalous lecher whose residence was a miniature bordello. As such, it is perhaps unsurprising that de Coigne was never convicted of the rape. Instead, he became a justice himself in 1815. Convicted of extortion in 1824 for demanding payment for felony warrants and dropped from the next general commission, he certainly qualified as one of Durham's 'most disreputable persons.'[3]

Mondelet, for his part, was trying to justify having knocked down Jean-Baptiste Gauthier *dit* Saint-Germain, who had then launched a prosecution against him for assault and battery in the Quarter Sessions, Mondelet's own court. The letter to Foy accompanied a petition to the colony's administrator, Thomas Dunn, asking him to discontinue Gauthier *dit* Saint-Germain's prosecution by *nolle prosequi*. This was a most inappropriate request in the absence of the explicit consent of the private prosecutor (which Mondelet nonetheless tried to imply he had), and the argument was grounded more on social solidarity than on legal principle: if his request were not granted, 'nous serons forcés de voir commettre le crime et de garder le silence de crainte de nous voir insultés par ceux qui mériteroient nos censures, car dans le cas actuel, je n'avois d'autre dessein que de faire rentrer en lui même un homme très fréquemment ennivré, et en lui portant le main sur l'estomac, de l'éloigner de moi pour éviter ses crachats ... mais la plus petite secousse renverse celui que les liqueurs accablent' [we would be forced to see crime committed and keep quiet for fear of being insulted by those who deserve our censure, for in the present case, I had no other design but to constrain a man frequently drunk, an[d] in putting my hand on his stomach, to distance him from me so as to avoid his spitting ... but the smallest shake knocks over those afflicted by liquor]. Dunn quite rightly refused, but Mondelet's self-interested actions continued: at his own trial before the Quarter Sessions, he appears to have sat on the bench during the proceedings, and even delivered the charge to the jury, though at least when found guilty he did not participate when the other justices imposed a nominal one-shilling fine on him.[4]

It is easy to find other instances of misconduct or outright malversation on the part of magistrates. Take the magistrates in the district of Montreal as an example. In the 1760s the conduct of the justices throughout the district was such as to lead the executive to revoke their civil powers almost entirely in 1770. Among other things, they were accused of issuing blank warrants to bailiffs and plaintiffs, fomenting disputes, and charging excessive fees. In the early 1800s, Oliver Barker, a Compton magistrate, was accused by Henry Cull, a fellow magistrate, of taking money from American banks and even from the legislature of Vermont in order to catch the forgers who had set up shop on the Lower Canadian side of the border. Turning the tables, in 1814 Barker himself accused his fellow magistrates of improperly issuing certificates to Americans coming into the province. Magistrates near the American lines seem to have been particularly prone to abusing their powers. As we saw, both Joseph Odell (of Odelltown) and John Scriver (of Hemmingford) were dismissed as magistrates for being involved in smuggling. Scriver had also been convicted and fined for selling liquor without a licence, and he was not alone: in 1810 McCord and Mondelet, Montreal's newly appointed chairmen, suggested that several justices had applied for and received tavern licences and retailed liquor, 'a thing we humbly conceive to be highly improper, as those very men may be the judges, on complaint made before them, of the conduct of people in the same profession.' And other justices were also accused of improperly collecting fees.[5]

The situation was no different elsewhere in the colony. In the district of Trois-Rivières, the magistrate of Saint-Pierre-Les-Becquets, Joseph Dionne, was accused in 1811 of being 'at the bottom of all the quarrels and difficulties which abound in this place' and of privately disposing of fines imposed by him. In the words of the commentator, 'considering that an ignorant, meddling and vindictive magistrate is a very great plague I think the Parish of St. Pierre would be better without one than with such one as Mr. Dionne.' Likewise, in the district of Quebec, Dougald Fraser of Matane was accused of using his position as magistrate to harass one Denis *dit* Lapierre, who had married a local heiress and thereby spoiled Fraser's hopes of getting her property.[6]

All of these instances of misconduct lend weight to the criticisms levelled by contemporaries, not only outsiders like Durham but also colonial reformers like the *Patriote* press, which in the late 1820s and 1830s frequently pointed to the incompetence and self-interestedness of the magistracy.[7] And it is these perspectives that have informed most historiographical interpretations since. In judging the character of the magistracy between the Conquest and the Rebellions, Quebec historians have generally followed the lead both of contemporary critics like Durham, who is often cited, and of older English historiography. From the Webbs forward, English historians drew largely on contemporary discourse in order to characterize the pre-reform English justices as either corrupt tyrants, such as the 'trading' justices of London, or lackadaisical do-nothings, such as the gentleman-justices in the counties more interested in hunting and imbibing than in justicing.[8] Similarly, with regards to Quebec and Lower Canada, the picture of the magistracy could have been written by the Webbs themselves: inefficient, negligent or even entirely inactive, self-interested, fractious, tyrannical, capricious, corrupt, lacking legal education and training, with little knowledge of French or of local customs, a bench discredited and in disarray.[9]

There is much in these critiques that is valid. Most justices were certainly not legal professionals and lacked formal legal education; their actions often did not live up to current or even contemporary standards of administrative efficiency; and as we saw, they could certainly act self-interestedly. But, as more recent work on the pre-reform English system suggests, we must also be careful before accepting the views of contemporary reformers and other critics at face value. Thus, Carleton's oft-cited characterization of the justices in the 1760s as bankrupt butchers and publicans should be contrasted with Murray's statement that many of the justices were 'worthy men who very disinterestedly give much of their time and attention to the public': neither was particularly accurate.[10] And, while the views of Durham and other critics on the ineffectualness and corruption of the justices in the 1820s and 1830s are crucial in reconstructing contemporary reformist discourse, neither is a reliable indication of what the character of the magistracy actually was. For that, we must turn to a closer examination of the men who made up the magistracy.

This is not the same, however, as an examination of the make-up of the commission of the peace, such as that presented in the previous chapter. While studying the commission is important in understanding state formation and centre-local relations, the experience of people who actually came in contact with the justice system was shaped not by the potential magistracy that the commission represented but by the men who actually acted as justices. To a plaintiff or a defendant, what mattered most was who was sitting in their parlour, or in the Police Office, or on the bench, receiving complaints, ordering arrests, imposing punishments. Likewise, as much as the executive might want to extend representatives of the state into all the corners of the colony, justices who never acted were invisible; and conversely, those who acted more than others imprinted their character more firmly on the relations between criminal justice and colonial society. Any examination of the magistracy itself, from the point of view of the people, must therefore concentrate on those who actually acted.

Magisterial Activity

Historians have generally assumed, following what has often been suggested for England and its colonies, that most justices in Quebec and Lower Canada never acted. This was also the view of some contemporary administrators, such as Dalhousie, who complained that 'very few individuals therefore can be induced to take the oaths to act, except those residing in the principal towns.'[11] There are two common ways of measuring whether justices regarded their appointment as more than simply honorary. The first is whether they qualified themselves to act by taking the oaths of office. In the district of Montreal between 1803 to 1820, about 70 per cent of justices appointed for the first time took the oath of office; almost half did so within three months of being appointed, three-quarters within a year, and all but twelve within two years. Most thus, at the very least, went to the trouble of qualifying themselves to act.[12] The other measure is of actual activity, as revealed in sources such as depositions and recognizances, gaol registers, or fines returns. As Table 3.1 shows, in the district of Montreal, justices were far more likely to act than has often been suggested. Between 1764 and 1836, a little under 650 justices individuals were appointed justices in the district of Montreal. Of these, about two-thirds were active at least once in criminal matters, and another 10 per cent had apparently qualified themselves but were not demonstrably active in criminal matters. In other words, at least three-quarters of justices were at least willing to act, and perhaps two-thirds actually did so; these figures are much higher than the usual estimates for England or Ireland at the same time, which generally range between a fifth and a third, and approach the highest figures for Upper Canada, where estimates range from a small fraction to 80 per cent in one rural district. The district of Montreal was not an exception: in the district of Quebec, based on very partial sources, at least 60 per cent of the justices on the commission in the 1820s acted at least once in criminal matters, and more than 80 per cent of those on the commissions of 1830 and 1833 did so. In part, this reflected the colonial administration's enforcement of the principle that appointed justices must qualify by taking the oath, but it also suggests that, on the whole, those who were appointed were willing to act if necessary.[13]

Table 3.1: Active and qualified justices in the district of Montreal, 1764–1836

	1764–1836	1764–1788	1788–1810	1810–1830	1830–1836
On the commission*	639	53	219	361	243
Active at least once in criminal matters in the period	431 (67%)	38 (72%)	133 (61%)	234 (65%)	151 (62%)
Apparently qualified but not proven active in criminal matters**	50 (8%)	2 (4%)	33 (15%)	40 · (11%)	42 (17%)
Not proven active or qualified	161 (25%)	13 (25%)	53 (24%)	87 (24%)	50 (21%)
Active only while ex-officio	15	8	9	4	5

* Justices are included in each period during which they were on the commission, apart from those appointed in the general commission at the end of each period. Excludes ex-officio justices and those whose commissions were annulled almost immediately

** Justices who took the oath or performed an administrative action suggesting they were qualified

The magistracy encountered by the people was embodied in these individuals who acted as justices. For the district of Montreal between 1764 and 1836, if we add the fifteen justices who were only ever active while appointed ex-officio, this gives us a group of a little under 450 men who formed the active magistracy, and on whom the remainder of this chapter is largely based. Understanding their character allows us to understand whom plaintiffs and defendants faced when they came before the criminal justice system of the state.

Thumbnail Sketches of Active Justices

To begin, consider the following six justices, all among the more active magistrates of the district of Montreal. Three were from Montreal itself: Daniel Robertson, Jean-Marie Mondelet, and Samuel Gale. And three were from the countryside: Michel-Eustache-Gaspard-Alain Chartier de Lotbinière of Vaudreuil, Calvin May of Saint-Armand, and Joseph Douaire de Bondy of Berthier.

Daniel Robertson (1733–1810) was appointed a justice in 1765, part of Murray's response to the problems with his first set of Montreal justices. Robertson was at the juncture of three of the city's main elite

Figure 3.1: Daniel Robertson (c. 1804–8)

factions. He was an ex-army officer, having been present at the capture of Montreal; he had strong links with the colony's British merchant community; and, through his marriage to Marie-Louise Réaume in 1760, he was connected to an important *Canadien* merchant family. Robertson was a highly active magistrate through the 1760s and thus one of the more important faces of justice at Montreal. Like his fellow justices, however, he became embroiled in local politics. Despite his army background, he sided firmly with other merchant-justices in disputes with the military over matters such as billeting and impress warrants, and was also condemned by the Huguenot justice Pierre Du Calvet as the opinionated and oppressive leader of a league against him. As well, Robertson was part of the Montreal justices' common front against the Council's investigation into the abuse of their civil jurisdiction, and when this was stripped from them in 1770, he ceased to act, like most of the city's other British justices, and eventually left the colony. Almost thirty years later, after a long career in the military, he returned to Lower Canada, acquiring substantial landholdings in the township of Chatham and living there and in Montreal until his death. He was reappointed a justice in 1799, but his interest was apparently only in the honour the position bestowed, for while he insisted on being named to the quorum, there is no evidence that he ever acted.[14]

Figure 3.2: Jean-Marie Mondelet (c. 1807)

Jean-Marie Mondelet (1771–1843) was born in Saint-Charles or Saint-Marc, the son of a local doctor. Educated in Montreal and Quebec City, he returned to Saint-Marc to practise as a notary. His local prominence and education, along with important connections in Montreal, probably led to his appointment as a justice in 1798, at the young age of twenty-seven. He initially acted only occasionally, but after moving to Montreal in mid-1802, he became one of the city's most active magistrates, part of a small group of francophone justices who dominated the Montreal magistracy in the first decade of the nineteenth century. Like most of these, Mondelet was connected to the *Canadien* party, sitting for it in the Assembly. But he shied away from its more forthright actions, refusing to endorse the confrontation with Craig and even reporting on anti-administration colleagues. It was probably this loyalty, combined with judicial experience and a passable command of English, that led Craig to name him joint chairman in 1810, a position that allowed Mondelet to dominate Montreal's magistracy until 1824.

The most conscientious justice in the district, Mondelet attended most sessions of the justices' courts and, from 1810, sat most days at the Police Office. But, as we saw, this dedication to 'public service' did not stop him from acting in his own interests when necessary. Mondelet was the target of fairly frequent accusations of malversation and incom-

Figure 3.3: Samuel Gale (1850s)

petence. In 1803, for example, Christopher Carter, a long-time William Henry justice, complained that Mondelet had damaged his reputation by issuing search warrants against him for stolen goods, which Carter had in fact seized as a magistrate. In 1810 Mondelet almost caused a diplomatic incident by summoning a visiting Spanish dignitary, Don Joseph Gonzales, to appear at the Police Office and produce his papers. And in 1815 he became embroiled in a bitter affair for refusing to sign a warrant at the request of Samuel Park, a fractious Montreal furniture manufacturer, who had turned up at his house rather than going to the Police Office.

Despite holding many government posts, including coroner, Mondelet maintained his ties to the moderate wing of the *Canadien* party. As a result, one of the key representatives of the administration in Montreal was constantly the target of veiled criticism in the Tory press, while receiving only lukewarm praise from moderate reformers. Along with the other Montreal justices, Mondelet frequently asserted the magistracy's independence from the administration in Quebec City, much like Robertson. Though this was tolerated in the 1800s and 1810s, it led to a series of conflicts with the Dalhousie administration in the 1820s, and eventually to Mondelet's dismissal as chairman in 1824 and as a justice in 1828. Unlike most of the other targets of Dalhousie's purge, however, Mondelet was not reinstated in 1830, since the qualification act specifically excluded coroners.[15]

Samuel Gale (1783–1865) was in many ways Mondelet's opposite. His parents, ardent Loyalists, moved soon after his birth to Quebec, where his father occupied a variety of high positions in the colonial bureaucracy. Gale himself studied law and began practising in 1807 in Montreal; his clients ranged from Lord Selkirk to parties in assault and battery cases in the Quarter Sessions, where he argued (and lost) many cases before Mondelet. Gale was a committed Tory, with unabashedly francophobic views: in 1825 he declared that, should the 'frenchification' of the province continue, he would rather return to the United States than remain in an only nominally English colony. This ideology, along with a strong commitment to the colonial administration, made Gale popular with Dalhousie, who chose him to replace McCord and Mondelet as chairman in 1824.

Gale and other similarly minded Tory justices dominated the commission in Montreal through the late 1820s and became a focal point of *Patriote* attacks on Dalhousie's administration, attacks that eventually led to the abolition of his position. Gale himself had not been contented with the chairmanship, which he claimed cost him dearly in lost professional income, and was constantly seeking a better place; for example, he threatened to resign in 1827 when he was not appointed sheriff. As a practising lawyer, he was dropped from the 1830 commission, but his loyalty was eventually rewarded by Aylmer, who appointed him a judge in 1834 over the strong objections of the *Patriote*-dominated Assembly.[16]

The three justices from outside the city were of a different sort. Michel-Eustache-Gaspard-Alain Chartier de Lotbinière (1748–1822), the seigneur of Vaudreuil and Rigaud, came from a long-established pre-Conquest seigneurial family which included two judges of the *prévôté* in Quebec City. In many ways he fit the stereotype of the post-Conquest *Canadien* seigneur: a military background, including service as a boy during the Seven Years' War; a brief and disappointing sojourn in France; assumption of the family's estates in the early 1770s; and a ready willingness to accommodate himself to the new English system. This was in stark contrast to his father, Michel Chartier de Lotbinière, who in the 1770s spoke out against English law, including English criminal law, and in 1776 renounced his British citizenship and became involved with the American rebels. The father's disloyalty was, however, no taint on the

Figures 3.4 and 3.5: Michel-Eustache-Gaspard-Alain Chartier de Lotbinière
(1763 and 1809)

son: in 1785 he was appointed a justice, joining several other conservative seigneurs on the commission, and in 1796 he was named to the
Legislative Council. His successful transition across regimes and centuries is suggested by the portraits he chose to represent himself (Figures
3.4 and 3.5), the first a classic French aristocrat (a portrait he had
recopied in the mid-1780s), the second a solid member of the nineteenth-century gentry. Chartier de Lotbinière acted as a justice regularly but infrequently from the mid-1780s to the mid-1810s, leaving
most of the judicial business to another Vaudreuil justice of lower social
status, Louis-Mars Decoigne, a retired military officer. From 1814, he
stopped acting altogether, probably for the same reasons of age and ill
health which led him to resign his colonelcy in the militia. His attitude
towards the magistracy was perhaps best summed up in the opening
line of an 1809 letter: 'Je me suis trouvé obligé d'agir comme magistrat
dans une affaire très désagréable ...' [I have been forced to act as a
magistrate in a most disagreeable affair ...].[17]

Calvin May was far less prominent. Perhaps born in Connecticut in
1765, he was most probably a Loyalist immigrant, apparently established in the Eastern Townships by 1792 like several others of the same

name. He eventually settled at Philipsburg in Saint-Armand, where he practised as a doctor and, like many other substantial township settlers, engaged in land speculation. His appointment as a justice in 1797 came along with that of five others who fit the same profile of land speculator/professionals and marked the beginning of the administration's attempts to implant the magistracy in the area along the American border, with more than twenty-five justices there by 1810. Many acted only rarely, but some, like May, formed the core of the region's active magistracy. This did not mean that they knew what they were doing: in 1802 May, along with four colleagues, wrote to the governor that 'it will afford us much satisfaction was our duty and authority as Magistrates more clearly defined, as we have in sundry instances experienced much embarrassment for the want of competent knowledge thereof.' And, as with Chartier de Lotbinière, May's interpretation of the criminal law could be flexible. In 1809 he and two other Saint-Armand justices were sued for assault and false imprisonment, having sent a local farmer, William Babcock, to the House of Correction; however, at the urging of May's counsel, Samuel Gale (then a twenty-six-year-old lawyer), the jury found against Babcock. More egregiously, in 1823, May quite illegally signed an arrest warrant against John Johnson for a theft committed in the United States, outside his jurisdiction, which led to Johnson being forcibly and illegally extradited by Montreal constables, one of the events that led to Dalhousie's removal of Mondelet. Yet May, though accused of being either ignorant or corrupt and receiving a strong rebuke from the executive, was not dismissed and continued acting as a magistrate until 1830, when he declined being reappointed owing to 'my age and state of health.'[18]

Finally, Joseph Douaire de Bondy (1770–1832) was born in Verchères, the son of a local merchant. He too became a merchant, and moved to Quebec City, where he married. Sometime between 1798 and 1806 he moved again, this time to Berthier, where he apparently established himself in the village, remaining until the late 1820s at least. Despite his moves, Bondy fit the classic pattern of a local notable: as well as being a justice from 1806 until 1828, he was also commissioner for the trial of small causes between 1808 and 1810 and again from 1821, and a member of the Assembly from 1816 to 1820. Politically, he was sympathetic to the *Canadien/Patriote* party; in 1827 he signed arrest warrants against unqualified electors who had voted for the Tory attorney general James Stuart; and in 1828 he was identified by the Assembly as one of those dropped from the 1828 commission for political reasons. His political leanings, however, did not deter him from being one of the most active justices outside Montreal, and one of the few who regularly accounted to the central administration for fines he imposed. As for his dismissal by Dalhousie, this may also have been the result of an over-eager interpretation by a committee intent on finding additional examples for a case which, as we saw, was already well proved, since in November 1824 Bondy had informed the administration that he was resigning as a magistrate because of bad health, though he did continue to act on occasion.[19]

The six justices shared some important characteristics. All were drawn from the colony's educated elites and were men of some local prominence at least. But they ranged in social place from Bondy, the local merchant, to Chartier de Lotbinière, the seigneur and member of the Legislative Council. They represented both of the colonists' dominant ethno-cultural groups, with political views ranging from extreme British Toryism to *Canadien* nationalism and firm reformism. And their legal training and competence spanned the spectrum from Gale, the professional lawyer, to Chartier de Lotbinière, who applied his own rules of common sense and equity whatever the formal law. These elements of commonality and diversity were characteristic of the active magistracy as a whole, and thus of the face which the criminal justice system presented to the people.

Relative Activity

While all six of these justices were highly active, not all 'active' magistrates were equally so, and even among justices who were consistently active, there were significant variations. Both Calvin May and Jean-Marie Mondelet were consistently active from about the late eighteenth century to the end of the 1820s, but while in that period Mondelet produced thousands of documents, committed perhaps a thousand prisoners to gaol, and sat in judgment on several thousand cases in both Quarter Sessions and Weekly Sessions, May committed perhaps twenty-five prisoners to gaol, produced perhaps a hundred documents, and never sat on the bench of the Montreal courts. As Figure 3.6 shows, throughout the period, two-thirds or more of the work of the justices in the district of Montreal was performed by the ten most active justices, with the possible exception of the bench of the Quarter Sessions in the 1830s; and from 1810 to 1830, half or more of the work was done by the three most active justices – a concentration of magisterial work similar to that found in England.[20]

Figure 3.6: Proportion of justices' work by most active justices in the district of Montreal

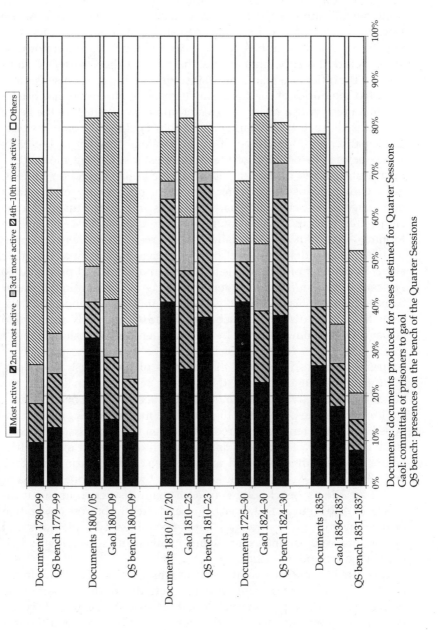

Documents: documents produced for cases destined for Quarter Sessions
Gaol: committals of prisoners to gaol
QS bench: presences on the bench of the Quarter Sessions

One reason for the concentration of magisterial work was the professionalization of the magistracy in the 1810s and 1820s. As we saw, one of the many complaints against the chairmen was their monopolization of judicial business: as Jean-Philippe Leprohon noted in 1829, 'before the appointment of a chairman of the Quarter Sessions holding the office as a place, the Magistrates organized themselves and executed the duties of their office by turns; but since there has been a chairman receiving a salary the greater number of Justices of the Peace have ceased to act.'[21] This harkening back to a golden age of magisterial participation was something of an overstatement: even in the early 1800s, before the creation of the chairmanships, the ten most active magistrates in the district of Montreal, including Leprohon himself, dealt with perhaps 80 per cent or more of preliminary matters and dominated the bench of the Quarter Sessions, in a district that had some eighty-five justices on the commission in 1799 and twenty-five in Montreal itself. But professionalization did result in further concentration. While Mondelet and McCord were chairmen, they alone made about 85 per cent of committals to the common gaol and produced 80 per cent of preliminary documents, a concentration continued under Samuel Gale and David Ross. If gaol committals are any indication, the same held in the district of Quebec: in the 1810s and early 1820s, 70 to 90 per cent of committals were by the chairmen, and only slightly fewer in the late 1820s. In both districts, the abolition of the position of chairman in 1830 did spread the business of the magistracy among more justices, but even then, through the 1830s, it remained in the hands of a few active justices, much as had been the case before 1810.

Throughout the period, the highly active magistracy was thus composed not of the tens or hundreds of men on the commission but of a small core group of at most a dozen magistrates in each main district before 1810 and after 1830, and as few as two or three during the 1810s and 1820s. This was not much larger than the professional judiciary, with four King's Bench judges in each main district from the 1790s onwards. And it meant that, even before and after the professionalization of the magistracy, the men most often encountered by plaintiffs and defendants were not untried amateurs but men with substantial experience in the routines of justice.

This core of highly active magistrates was also heavily urban. In the district of Montreal, for example, in any period and for any part of the justices' work, the three most active justices, and at least half of the ten most active, were always from the city. In part this reflected the fact that the majority of cases originated in Montreal itself, but it was also another manifestation of the urban centralization of justice. There was a striking contrast between the highly active justices of the city, for whom justicing was at least a weekly and often a daily pursuit, and the mass of active justices in other parts of the district, for whom justicing was most often a very occasional activity.

Geographical Distribution

While the relative activity of justices was important, what mattered even more to plaintiffs and defendants, especially outside the cities, was the presence of a justice willing to act, regardless of whether he acted one, ten, or a hundred times a year. And this presence of the active magistracy outside the cities changed dramatically across the period, as Figure 3.7 shows.

Initially, the active magistracy was concentrated almost exclusively in the cities, and this had changed little by the end of the 1780s. In the district of Montreal, there were only a handful of active justices in the rural areas, where 90 per cent of the population lived, and two-thirds of the active magistracy was in the city itself. This represented a significant continuity with the centralization of criminal justice during the French regime and contrasted with eighteenth-century England and its American colonies; and it suggests the relative weakness of local justice in the countryside. From the end of the eighteenth century, however, the situation began to change, with the administration's concerted effort to appoint justices in most localities. By the end of the first decade of the nineteenth century, there were far more active rural justices, though there were still large areas without. Local justice had begun to spread in the countryside, but it was only a beginning. As the number of justices on the commission increased, along with the administration's efforts to ensure that those appointed were willing to act, the active magistracy extended further through the countryside. By the early 1820s, there were active justices spread through most of the district, and by the 1830s, despite Tory complaints that the property qualifications had seriously depleted the magistracy and deterred many men from acting, most areas had at least one active magistrate.

Concretely, these changes meant that rural plaintiffs had far greater potential access to justice: whereas in 1785 Noël Ainse, a Chambly habitant, had to travel to Montreal to make his complaint before James McGill against one Thevenot for smuggling near Saint-Jean, by 1830 he

Figure 3.7: Places in the district of Montreal with active justices

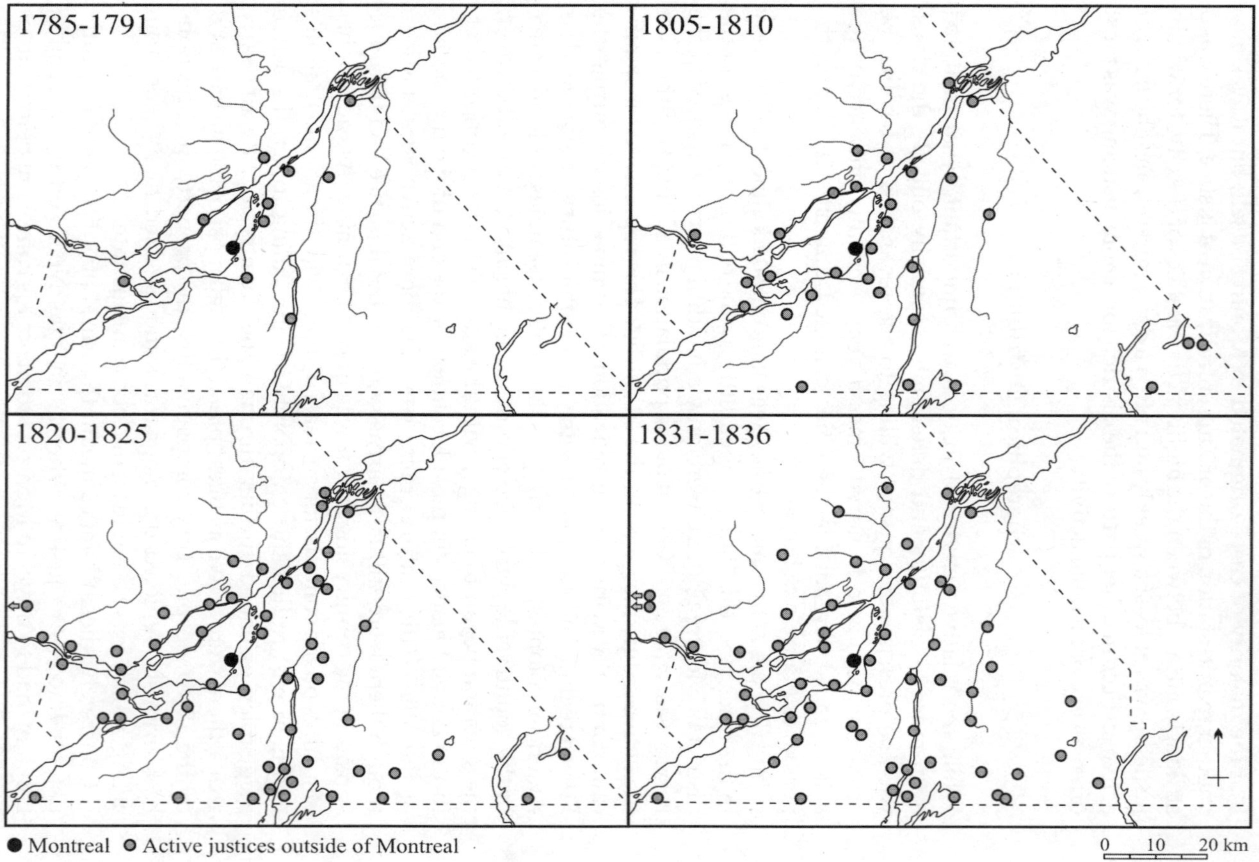

1785-1791

1805-1810

1820-1825

1831-1836

● Montreal   ○ Active justices outside of Montreal

0   10   20 km

might have had his pick of a half-dozen active justices along the upper Richelieu, including William Macrae, the local customs officer. In addition, there were far more justices available to enforce state regulations such as the roads and militia laws. However, there were still gaps in the system: not only were there a few significant settlements with no justices appointed at all, some also had appointed justices who never acted. In Berthier, for example, the only active magistrate in the late 1820s, Charles Morrison, had died by 1832, and his replacements from 1830, Pierre-Louis Panet and Norbert Eno, do not seem have been active in criminal matters. Still, this did not mean that Berthier plaintiffs had to travel all the way to Montreal; instead, in the 1830s, they went about twenty kilometres westwards to Saint-Paul-de-Lavaltrie, where both Jean-Olivier Leblanc and Barthelemy Joliette were active justices.

The spread of justices throughout the district also meant that non-Montreal justices began to play an increasingly important role in the preliminary steps in criminal cases originating outside the city. In the eighteenth century, with few justices outside Montreal, rural plaintiffs most often came to Montreal, with about two-thirds of their depositions before 1800 taken before urban justices. By the 1820s and 1830s, however, this changed dramatically: even considering only the depositions of rural plaintiffs that ended up in the Montreal court records, about two-thirds were taken before rural justices. Evidently, the spread of active rural magistrates meant that access to local justices was far easier in the 1820s and 1830s than it had been even in the 1790s.

The Ethnic Face of the Magistracy

Active as they might be, and spread through town and country, there is still the issue of the character of the men who were magistrates, which, as we saw, has been consistently criticized, from the *Patriotes* and Durham down to modern historians. One especially important issue, given the imposition of a British system of criminal law on a French population and the rise of *Canadien* nationalism, was the ethnic face of the magistracy. In general, the contention has been that the colonial magistracy was significantly and even grossly under-representative of the *Canadien* majority, which explains *Canadien* alienation from the system; further, it is said, even when *Canadien* magistrates were appointed, they were either reluctant to act or were discouraged from acting.[22] Yet, as we observed in examining the make-up of the commissions, the situation was not nearly so clear-cut, with francophone jus-

Figure 3.8: Francophones among appointed and active justices in the
district of Montreal, 1765–1836

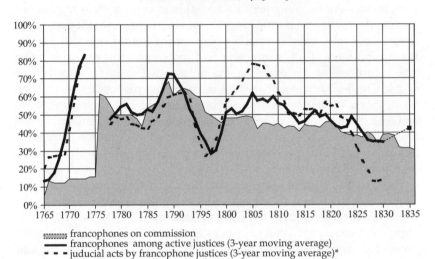

::::::::: francophones on commission
———— francophones among active justices (3-year moving average)
- - - juducial acts by francophone justices (3-year moving average)*

* insufficient data beyond 1830

tices in the majority in some districts during long periods. This also
extended to the active magistracy. In the district of Montreal, as Figure
3.8 shows, apart from the late 1790s and the late 1820s, as many or more
active justices were francophones than their place on the commission
might suggest. Between 1800 and 1825, for example, while the proportion of francophones on the commission was between 40 and 50 per
cent, they accounted for between 50 and 60 per cent of active justices
and an even higher proportion of judicial actions. Evidently, *Canadien*
magistrates, far from shunning judicial activity, were more prone to act
than their British counterparts: even among the joint chairmen, Mondelet
was more than twice as active as McCord.

Consider also the involvement of francophone justices in three important roles of the justices, where many plaintiffs and defendants were
likely to meet them: hearing preliminary complaints in cases destined
for the justices' courts (based on justices taking depositions and recognizances and issuing warrants), committing prisoners to gaol (mainly
reflecting their actions in more serious criminal cases), and sitting on
the bench of Quarter Sessions. As Figures 3.9 through 3.11 show, apart
from three brief periods, francophone justices played an important and
sometimes dominant role in all three of these aspects of the justices'
work in the district of Montreal. And as Figure 3.12 shows, a similar

Figure 3.9: Francophone justices hearing complaints in the district of Montreal, 1785–1835

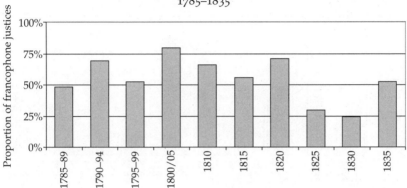

Figure 3.10: Francophone justices committing to the Montreal gaol, 1810–37

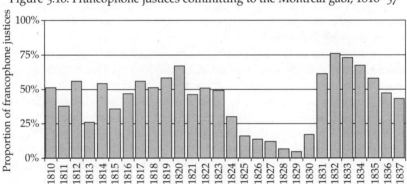

Figure 3.11: Francophone justices on the Montreal Quarter Sessions bench, 1764–1837

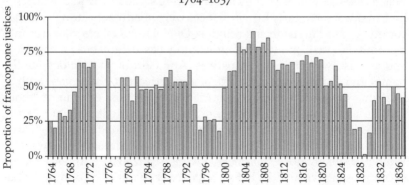

Figure 3.12: Francophone justices committing to the Quebec gaol, 1813–37

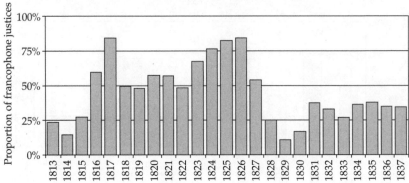

situation prevailed in the district of Quebec from the mid-1810s to the mid-1820s, with half or more gaol committals being by francophone magistrates between 1816 and 1827, though this was followed by a sharp drop-off thereafter.

The variations in the ethnic character of the active magistracy were linked to the specific circumstances of different periods, notably the interplay of power and ethnicity. Take the first decade of British civil administration in Montreal. As most writers have noted, the exclusion of Catholics from the commission meant that British justices dominated in the 1760s. The only active francophone before 1768 was Jean Dumas Saint-Martin, the pre-Conquest Huguenot merchant. Despite Dumas's assiduity, this meant that British justices made up over three-quarters of those on the bench of the Quarter Sessions, giving the court a decidedly British cast. British predominance is also suggested by the handful of remaining depositions and other preliminary documents in King's Bench cases, of which over 80 per cent were signed by British justices.[23] Still, many of these early British justices were not divorced from *Canadien* society, nor its language and religion. Daniel Robertson's marriage into a prominent pre-Conquest *Canadien* family has already been mentioned, and at least two other active justices, Ann Gordon (a man despite the name) and Francis Mackay, were also married to *Canadiennes*, with at least one of Gordon's children buried in a Catholic ceremony; James Cuthbert had enough knowledge of French to write it; and one justice, Thomas Lynch, appears to have been a closet Catholic, or at least cared little about Protestantism, since two of his children by Rosamonde Winter (probably not a *Canadienne*) were baptized as Catholics. Of the seven most active justices before 1770, only two, Isaac Todd and Thomas Brayshay, had no demonstrable personal connection to *Canadien* society. This may help explain why, as we will see, *Canadiens* did not shun the courts of the justices even at this early period.

But the composition of the Montreal magistracy changed dramatically from 1770. In 1769 Dumas was joined in the active magistracy by Pierre Du Calvet, another pre-Conquest Huguenot merchant, and in 1770 by John (Jean) Marteilhe, another merchant of Huguenot descent and French birth.[24] At the same time, after the loss of their civil jurisdiction, most British justices ceased to act entirely. Their place was taken by the three Huguenots, who performed virtually all the business of the justices until 1775. As a result, the bench of the Quarter Sessions became resolutely francophone; and though none of the three was *Canadien*, *Canadiens* coming before the court would have at least been encountering men who understood their language and, in the case of Dumas Saint-Martin and Du Calvet at least, their culture as well. If anything, it would have been British plaintiffs and defendants who were alienated from this court, since only Marteilhe understood English.

This decade was a harbinger of future patterns. When British elites pulled back from acting as justices, *Canadiens* occupied the space vacated; but *Canadien* elites also pulled back from the magistracy at other moments. Thus, with Catholic emancipation under the Quebec Act and the inclusion of a number of prominent *Canadiens* in the commission of 1776, *Canadien* elites seem to have been more than willing to take on the responsibilities of the magistracy in the 1770s, 1780s, and early 1790s, composing up to 70 per cent of active justices in the district of Montreal and hearing between half and two-thirds of preliminary complaints for lesser cases. Still, some urban British justices were also highly active: the bench of the Montreal Quarter Sessions was about evenly divided between the two main ethnic groups, and British justices carried out about two-thirds of preliminary proceedings for more serious criminal complaints. Further, the situation may have been different in the district of Quebec: between 1776 and 1788, there were only four *Canadiens* among the twenty-two justices who took the oath of office, though this increased to fourteen of twenty-seven between 1788 and 1789.[25]

Tensions between the *Canadien* and British communities in the mid-1790s, however, led to a dramatic decrease in the number of active francophone justices, who made up fewer than a third of justices on the Montreal Quarter Sessions bench between 1795 and 1799 and were often absent altogether. But this changed again in the first decade of the nineteenth century, with *Canadien* justices once again dominating. The francophone presence waned somewhat in the 1810s and early

1820s, with the appointment of McCord as joint chairman along with Mondelet, although Mondelet was more assiduous than McCord and most of the other highly active justices were *Canadiens*; still, outside Montreal, the appointment of increasing numbers of British justices in the countryside was also reflected in their increasing presence in the active magistracy. From the mid-1820s, the change in the ethnic character of the magistracy became more pronounced. In Montreal, Mondelet and McCord were replaced by Gale, ending the practice of joint British and *Canadien* chairmen, whereas in Quebec City the chairmanship passed to Christie; as well, Dalhousie continued to reduce the number of *Canadiens* on the commissions. This led to British justices dominating criminal proceedings in the later 1820s, at least in the two main districts. The situation reversed once again in 1830, with the abolition of the chairmen, the removal of a significant number of Dalhousie's largely anglophone appointees, and the appointment of a few more francophone justices. In the district of Montreal at least, despite their limited place on the commission, francophones accounted for a much larger part of the justices' business in the early 1830s, committing over three-quarters of prisoners to gaol in 1832–3 and making up about half of the justices on the Quarter Sessions bench or hearing preliminary complaints, though this began to decline in the mid-1830s. In the district of Quebec, British magistrates continued to dominate judicial business from the late 1820s until the Rebellions.

The magistracy that plaintiffs and defendants encountered, far from being uniformly dominated by men foreign in language and custom to the *Canadien* majority, was thus, for most of the period, composed in significant part of members of *Canadien* elites. This varied across time and place, however, even in the two largest districts, and matters were often quite different in the smaller districts, with, for example, no francophone justices whatsoever in the district of Saint Francis. The ethnicity of the magistracy was still important, especially when active magistrates were francophobes, as was the case in Montreal in the late 1820s. But what set justices such as Jean-Marie Mondelet, Jean-Thomas Taschereau, or even Joseph Douaire de Bondy apart from their neighbours was not their language but their social status.

Magisterial Prominence

If the ethnic character of the active magistracy fluctuated considerably, the same was not true of the justices' social status. It has sometimes been suggested that part of the problem with the colonial magistracy was that the justices were generally of lower status than the justices in England.[26] Undeniably, colonial justices could not match the grandeur of the English county commissions, which usually included most of the local nobility and the more substantial gentry. However, the prominence of the English justices in the eighteenth century, and especially those who acted, should not be overstated.[27] Further, the lower relative status of colonial justices was no more than a reflection of the fact that colonial elites were less wealthy than those in England. What mattered more was their relative place within the society of which they were a part. And as Table 3.2 shows, if occupation can be taken as an indication of status,[28] the vast majority of the men who made up the active magistracy, at least in the district of Montreal, were drawn from the colony's elites, both colonial and local.

The active justices were almost all businessmen, landowners, or professionals, both private and government, but in proportions that made the Montreal magistracy quite different from that of England or other colonies. Significant landed wealth, for example, was far less important than in England, reflecting both the smaller number of large landed estates in the colony and the importance of trade and the professions among colonial elites. Thus, whereas active English county justices were most often landholders and clergymen, the Montreal justices were more often businessmen and professionals, especially in the nineteenth century. And unlike the colony's Assembly, or the magistracy and Assembly in Upper Canada, no rural *habitants* were justices, whatever their local prominence, and only a few British farmers became magistrates.[29] Further, while there were some differences between *Canadien* and British justices, notably in the weight of the liberal professions, both were about equally active in business and landowning; this reflects the important but often-forgotten presence of *Canadien* elites in trade, especially as local rural merchants. There were also some variations between town and country, and between the eighteenth and nineteenth centuries, reflecting more general trends such as the rise of the liberal professions.

Though the justices were thus almost all drawn from local and colonial elites, with the emphasis on trade and the professions, their relative position within the elites was more variable. Some active justices were clearly at or close to the top of colonial society: seigneurs such as Chartier de Lotbinière, for example, or leading merchants such as James McGill or Augustin Cuvillier. As one rough indicator, about 30 per cent of the active justices in the district of Montreal have merited full biographies in the *Dictionary of Canadian Biography* (*DCB*), with a similar

Table 3.2: Occupations of active justices in the district of Montreal, 1764–1836

	All	Franco-phone	Anglo-phone	Mont-real	Rural	18th c.	19th c.
Active justices	446	183	263	128	340	113	377
Profession unknown	30 (7%)	7 (4%)	23 (9%)	3 (2%)	28 (8%)	1 (1%)	30 (8%)
Profession known	416	176	240	125	312	112	347

1. By profession (justices with multiple professions counted more than once)

	All	Franco-phone	Anglo-phone	Mont-real	Rural	18th c.	19th c.
Business	207	83	124	73	144	53	175
	(50%)	(47%)	(52%)	(58%)	(46%)	(47%)	(50%)
Merchants/traders	207	83	124	73	144	53	175
Land	139	61	78	29	119	39	118
	(33%)	(35%)	(33%)	(23%)	(38%)	(35%)	(34%)
Seigneurs	53	37	16	16	42	20	41
Rural landowners	31	11	20	7	26	9	26
Farmers	40	3	37	–	40	2	38
Urban rentiers	9	6	3	6	4	7	8
Land agents	15	7	8	1	15	3	12
Liberal professions	85	49	36	20	70	13	80
	(20%)	(28%)	(15%)	(16%)	(22%)	(12%)	(23%)
Notaries	38	37	1	10	31	6	36
Lawyers	5	3	2	5	–	1	4
Doctors	25	4	21	5	21	4	25
Surveyors	16	7	9	1	16	2	14
Educators	2	–	2	–	2	–	2
Clergy	1	–	1	–	1	1	–
Government	79	26	53	37	53	38	54
	(19%)	(15%)	(22%)	(30%)	(17%)	(34%)	(16%)
Civil	47	17	31	26	28	22	33
Military	31	9	22	10	25	16	20
Other	1	1	–	–	1	–	1
	(<1%)	(<1%)	–	–	(<1%)	–	(<1%)
Artisans	1	1	–	–	1	–	1

2. By exclusive category (justices counted in one category only)

	All	Franco-phone	Anglo-phone	Mont-real	Rural	18th c.	19th c.
Business only	36%	32%	39%	45%	32%	34%	36%
Business and land	10%	11%	9%	8%	11%	10%	10%
Land only	16%	15%	18%	6%	20%	13%	17%
Liberal professions	15%	23%	9%	10%	17%	6%	17%
Government	11%	6%	15%	14%	9%	21%	8%
Mixed/other	12%	13%	10%	18%	12%	15%	12%

proportion among active justices in the district of Quebec between 1810 and 1835; by comparison, the equivalent figure for justices in the Niagara district in Upper Canada is less than 10 per cent.[30] There was nevertheless a large difference between urban and rural justices: while almost 55 per cent of active Montreal justices have full biographies in the *DCB*, this is true of only about 20 per cent of active rural justices. About a tenth of active justices in the district of Montreal also became members of the executive or legislative councils, the most powerful political bodies in the colony, and about a sixth were elected to the Lower Canadian Assembly at some point. Many active justices were not of this prominence, with Joseph Douaire de Bondy and Calvin May being good examples: one a local merchant, the other a local doctor, and neither meriting more than a passing mention in the local histories of their respective areas. But most justices were men of at least local importance, with a substantial minority prominent in the colony as a whole.

Most justices were also well established before being appointed, with an average age of forty-two at first appointment, both for *Canadien* and for British justices. The average age of justices active in any particular year ranged from the mid-forties to the mid-fifties, depending on the period. The only notable exception was the period before the Quebec Act, with some especially young justices, such as twenty-three-year-old Isaac Todd. Overall, however, the men before whom plaintiffs and accused appeared were mainly middle-aged: neither upstart youngsters like Todd nor ancient and decrepit Dickensian justices.

There were, of course, justices whose social prominence was more than doubtful: Francis Noble Knipe, for example, a merchant-justice who went bankrupt in 1766 and left for England in 1767, or Jean-Jacques Jorand, an active Montreal justice at the turn of the century who was later reduced to being a court copyist. And there are others whose utter invisibility in any of the prosopographical sources or local histories consulted suggests very strongly a lack of local prominence. But considered as a whole, the prominence of the active Montreal justices certainly does not give the impression of a magistracy composed of marginal men. In sum, class distinguished the magistracy far more than ethnicity: when Louis Saint-Amant, a Vaudreuil habitant, was arrested by the bailiff Jean Simard Aymond in 1798 and brought before Michel-Eustache-Gaspard-Alain Chartier de Lotbinière, what he saw was not so much a fellow *Canadien* as his seigneur.

Magisterial Knowledge

Plaintiffs and defendants thus faced men who were generally prominent and mature. But were they competent or, as has been asserted, 'generally untrained and often ignorant of the law and procedure'?[31] If the latter, this might indeed have discouraged people from bringing complaints before the justices, and would have justified the condemnation of contemporaries such as Durham and the *Patriote* press.

That few justices had formal legal training in the criminal law is undeniable. That was the whole point of a system that sought to co-opt elites into the administration of the criminal justice system. A few were lawyers, in particular professional magistrates such as Gale or John Fletcher, the Quebec City chairman in the late 1810s and early 1820s, described by Aubert de Gaspé as having an encyclopaedic knowledge of the criminal law, always ready to justify his decisions with antiquated English statutes (of which he did indeed own an almost complete set).[32] Likewise, justices who were notaries were trained to deal with legal forms and documents, which made up a major part of the justices' work. And in the eighteenth century, several of the judges of the Common Pleas acted regularly as justices, such as René-Ovide Hertel de Rouville, who had studied law during the French regime and been *lieutenant général civil et criminel* in Trois-Rivières. However, lawyers, judges, and notaries constituted a small proportion of active justices (10 per cent at most in the district of Montreal), with the others having no formal legal training whatsoever.

Legal training or a judgeship did not necessarily mean respect for the law: Hertel de Rouville, for example, was frequently condemned for acting arbitrarily.[33] Nor did a lack of formal legal training necessarily mean a lack of legal knowledge. To take perhaps the most striking example, McCord, the joint Montreal chairman between 1810 and 1824, though having no formal legal training, had an extensive knowledge of criminal law. On coming into office in 1810, he collected copies of most provincial acts and ordinances, and in 1815 he helped prepare an index to the ordinances and acts of Lower Canada that was so well received that James Reid, the chief justice of Montreal's King's Bench, suggested he prepare a general digest of the criminal law of England (though this never materialized). Similarly, Mondelet vaunted his 'unremitting application ... to the study of the criminal law prevailing in this country' and claimed to have 'methodically studied and knows the principles of the civil and criminal laws,' claims supported by the King's Bench judges; and Thomas Coffin, the Trois-

Rivières chairman, could cite Hawkins, Blackstone, Burn, and Bacon.[34]

Still, magisterial ignorance was certainly an issue, especially in the countryside, and was raised regularly in correspondence with the central authorities. As Alexander Wilson, a Côteau-du-Lac justice, put it in 1817, 'the Country Justices are often at a loss how to act, for want of the necessary books to educate them.' The administration was of little help: even in 1837 Gosford rejected the suggestion of issuing printed instructions for the guidance of country justices, 'it being quite beyond his province to furnish general rules for this purpose.' At the same time, some rural justices were quite evidently knowledgeable of the laws they applied: in defending himself against a complaint in 1824, for example, John Yule, the active Chambly justice, listed off the relevant statutes and explained in detail why his actions were justified. And, on the whole, the depositions, warrants, recognizances, and other papers sent in even by rural justices followed the proper forms. 'Warrant irregular, also the recognizance' may have been how Montreal's clerk of the peace characterized documents sent in by Louis-Mars Decoigne of Soulanges; but on another document sent in by Paul Roch de Saint-Ours of L'Assomption, he marked, 'This recog. is well drawn up in good form and stile.'[35] The question then becomes, how did these untrained justices know what to do?

Manuals and Laws

One way that lay justices had access to legal knowledge was through published laws and lawbooks. For English law, few justices followed Fletcher's lead in collecting the masses of English statutes; instead, like English justices, they had recourse to justices' manuals, mainly imported from England. The most widely used manual in England at the time was Burn's *Justice of the Peace and Parish Officer*, in numerous editions from the mid-eighteenth until well into the nineteenth century, which included both a detailed discussion of offences (arranged in alphabetical order) and forms for warrants, depositions, recognizances, and the like. Along with Blackstone's more scholarly *Commentaries*, Burn was the main reference for justices in the colony. A dozen copies of Burn were distributed to Murray's new justices, and when law officers communicated with justices, it was Burn they referred to. Burn and Blackstone were the most common books on the criminal law found in private libraries in Montreal and Quebec City in the late eighteenth and early nineteenth centuries, and the estate inventories of several active urban justices mention them: Jean-Philippe Leprohon of Montreal, for example, had a copy of Burn, as did Thomas Wilson of Quebec City, and James Finlay of Montreal had both.[36]

Burn and Blackstone, however, were not enough. First, Burn was in English only, a major hindrance to *Canadien* magistrates. In launching a project in 1789 to translate Burn into French, Joseph-François Perrault claimed that while *Canadiens* occupied many judicial positions, including the magistracy, they were unable to consult English lawbooks. Consequently, they were beholden to their English-speaking colleagues for assistance, colleagues who had acquired superiority over them not only by the knowledge they brought from Europe but also by the ease with which they could consult English authors. Despite a significant list of subscribers, including many justices, Perrault managed to produce only a translation of the sections of Burn describing the general powers and duties of justices and other judicial officers and general procedures such as arrest warrants and recognizances, leaving out the bulk of the work which described and discussed specific offences. However, since forms were an important part of justices' work, even this limited translation was significant, and it appears to have had an effect: of 130 subscribers in the district of Montreal, about 50 were current or future justices, and half of the district's francophone justices active between 1789 and 1800 were had been subscribers, including Paul Roch de Saint-Ours but not Louis-Mars Decoigne – which perhaps explains their differing competence. And Perrault could replace Burn, as it did for Pierre Foretier, another very active Montreal justice, though he also had Blackstone (although perhaps in translation).[37]

Besides being in English, Burn, like Blackstone, covered only English law. Unlike in the American colonies, there were no lawbooks describing local legislation until a half-century after the Conquest, with the 1814 publication of Perrault's *Questions et réponses sur le droit criminel*. Like his previous compilation of civil law, this was destined primarily for law students, but it was also useful for magistrates: at the back it incorporated a range of examples of documents produced by country magistrates in the district of Quebec (perhaps prepared from actual models that Perrault had come across in his work as clerk of the peace). Yet Perrault's work was evidently useful only for those magistrates who read French; manuals in English destined for Lower Canadian justices did not appear until well after our period, long after the first Upper Canadian manual in 1835.[38]

One reason may be that, for local legislation, justices had another more readily accessible source: the colonial acts and ordinances themselves. Until 1794, justices were essentially left to their own devices, though all laws were published in the *Quebec Gazette* in both English and French and there were also several published collections. From 1794, however, all justices were entitled to copies of all new colonial legislation, and in the late 1820s justices of the quorum also received a copy of all pre-1792 ordinances still in force. This gave Lower-Canadian justices better access to statutory law than their counterparts in England, for example, where systematic distribution of the statutes to justices and other officials, though beginning in 1797, was much more limited. As in England, Lower-Canadian justices were attentive to their right to have copies of the statutes, complaining when they did not receive them, and the estate inventories of justices like Foretier, Finlay, and Wilson show that they kept them. It is no doubt this that allowed a justice like Yule to list off the relevant provincial statutes.[39]

Clerks, Law Officers, and Colleagues

Beyond manuals and laws, justices could get help from other legal officials and each other. Justices of the peace in England and the colonies often relied heavily on their clerks for legal advice. Their main assistant was usually the clerk of the peace, generally a paid professional whose main responsibilities were to create and manage the records of the justices' courts and organize the courts themselves. Clerks of the peace were among the first officials appointed by the new colonial administration in 1764, with the office a career appointment that attracted long-serving public officials. Between 1764 and 1837, there were only six clerks of the peace for the district of Montreal, with the office dominated by three clerks, John Burke (1764–87), John Reid (1787–1811), and John (Jean-Baptiste) Delisle (1814–38). Similarly, in the district of Quebec, while there were more clerks (ten in all between 1764 and 1837), this was only because of the practice, from 1777, of having joint English and French clerks; the clerkship was dominated by long-serving men such as David Lynd (1777–1802) and Joseph-François-Xavier Perrault (1815–53).[40]

Over the period, the professionalism and specialization of these clerks increased significantly. In Montreal, the first clerk, Burke, was not only clerk of the peace but also English-language clerk of the Common Pleas, a position that no doubt took up far more of his time. Described by one historian as 'eminently honest, but very indifferently educated, and of no particular ability,' he had been appointed when he was just twenty, apparently with no formal legal training. Surviving registers suggest that he kept the records of the justices' courts very poorly, and in 1791, when asked by the Executive Council to justify a substantial discrepancy between the amount of fines imposed by the justices' courts and the amount he had remitted to the receiver general, he replied disingenuously that 'he had either thrown aside or destroyed as useless, the lists and memorandums [of fines paid] ... some letters [of pardon] from the Governor's secretary ... were filed in the office and neglected to be marked on the books ...'[41]

Burke's successor, John Reid, was more competent and kept far better records. A former schoolteacher, he had served as Burke's assistant and was well-enough respected to have James Stuart, the colony's future attorney general and chief justice, placed with him for legal education; he was also related to Thomas McCord by marriage. Like Burke, Reid also became clerk of Montreal's civil courts, meaning that the clerkship of the peace was only one of his concerns. Reid attempted to create a family dynasty by having his son, Alexander, appointed clerk in his stead in 1812. But, though Alexander was the first clerk trained as a lawyer, ill health and perhaps negligence made him unable to perform his job properly, and at any rate he died in 1814.[42]

John Delisle, who replaced Reid and remained in office until his retirement in 1838, was far more meticulous and competent. Delisle (baptized Jean-Baptiste) came from one of Montreal's most prominent legal families: his father and grandfather were important Montreal notaries, and his brother Benjamin was Montreal's high constable in the 1830s. John ensured his dynastic succession by having his son, Alexandre-Maurice, who trained as a lawyer, named joint clerk of the peace and of the crown from 1833 (positions that he held until the early 1860s); other sons included Adelphe, Montreal's high constable in the later 1820s, and Jacques-Guillaume, water bailiff of the Trinity House (the body that oversaw inland shipping) in the early 1830s. The Delisle family's hold on the judicial bureaucracy in Montreal was such as to provoke snarky comments in the *Patriote* press. John Delisle's appointments were certainly lucrative: the net income from the clerkship of the peace alone was between £350 and £500 per year at the beginning of the 1820s, and after the disappearance of the Police Office in 1830, it rose to about £1,000. Despite his evident distribution of bureaucratic patronage to his family, however, Delisle was an accomplished bureaucrat. His training, like John Reid's, was through apprenticeship: he had entered the office of the clerk of the peace in 1798 as an assistant clerk, at the age of eighteen, and thus had sixteen years' experience before becoming clerk himself. He kept excellent judicial records and maintained a small staff of subclerks, who from 1828 included Alexandre-Maurice. Further-

more, he was clerk only of the peace and the crown, and thus specialized in criminal business.[43]

In Montreal, the succession of Police Office clerks from 1810 to 1830
were also generally legal professionals, though, given the much lower
income (a salary of £60–£100 per year plus fees), the position was less
attractive. Of seven clerks in all, four were lawyers at the beginning of
their careers, including Charles-Elzéar Mondelet, Jean-Marie's son and
a future Superior Court judge. However, the choices were not always
felicitous: the first clerk, John Tarver, apparently perfectly honest while
in office in Montreal, had previously been convicted of forgery in New
York, and the clerk for most of the 1820s, James Prest, formerly a banker
and merchant in Malta, seems to have 'absconded' to Philadelphia in
March 1829, though the exact circumstances are unclear.[44]

The Quebec clerks of the peace were also increasingly professional.
The first clerk, Williams Conyngham, was described by James Murray
as 'the most thorough paced Villain who ever existed,' and his implication in political machinations rapidly led to his dismissal in 1765. His
effective successor, James Shepherd (1765–75), was far more honest
but, like Burke in Montreal, apparently had no legal training. This was
also the case of David Lynd, the next English-language clerk, though,
before becoming clerk of the peace, he had already been clerk of the
Common Pleas and of the crown. The later English clerks, however,
George Pyke (1802–12), William Green (1812–32), and Alexander Stewart
Scott (1832–42), were all trained as lawyers and associated with the
colony's upper legal circles. Pyke eventually became advocate general
and then a King's Bench judge; Green articled with Attorney General
Jonathan Sewell; and Scott was junior partner to the moderate *Patriote*
lawyer and future judge Joseph-Rémi Vallières de Saint-Réal. The French-
language clerks all had legal training. The first, Nicholas-Gaspard
Boisseau (1777–95), had even been clerk of New France's Conseil
supérieur until the Conquest and French-language clerk of the Common Pleas afterwards; the legal competence of his successor, Joseph-
François Perrault (1795–1815), is evident in his publications; and he was
in turn succeeded by his son, Joseph-François-Xavier Perrault, also
trained as a lawyer.[45]

By the 1810s, much as in England, some justices outside the main
cities were also being assisted by clerks, with depositions and other
documents sent in to Montreal frequently not in their own hand. Initially, the practice was doubtful, since a clerk could charge fees for
documents that a magistrate could not, and a Trois-Rivières justice was
accused of extortion in 1817 for having allowed fees to be paid to his

clerk. However, the legislature was indirectly acknowledging the practice by the 1820s, and in 1833 an act explicitly regulated the fees of clerks employed by country justices. Some clerks were local notaries, as in the case of Charles H. Gauvreau of Baie-Saint-Paul, whose (unsuccessful) 1815 petition to become a justice not only underscores the use of clerks but also the importance of their legal knowledge: 'as I am establish [sic] here in my capacity of a notary public, all and every depositions in that line are generally written by me, our magistrates having so much of their own business and besides as they are not accustomed to take affidavids in the regular form of law.' Since many justices in the 1820s were also commissioners for the trial of small causes, they may also have employed the clerks of these courts in their business as justices: this was the case of Antoine Delisle, the clerk of Joseph Vignau, a Boucherville justice and commissioner.[46] The importance of clerks in both town and country as sources of legal knowledge and general assistance for the justices cannot be overstated, though it is largely occluded in official records that put the emphasis on magisterial legitimacy. As an 1843 poetical description of the Upper and Lower Canadian courts put it, 'benches of Justices appear / In Petit, or Four times a year / While thousand Squires send forth their thunders / Clerks taking care, they make no blunders.'[47]

One concrete way the clerks of the peace assisted justices was by providing forms for judicial documents. In 1767, for example, Burke asserted that he had taken 'pains to serve oblige and assist His Majesty's Justices of the Peace in said district in the fforms and proceedings of their office [and] furnished each with the fforms of all sorts of process, recognizances, and warrants.' As well, printing accounts from the 1760s onwards show the Montreal and Quebec clerks purchasing pre-printed forms, and the earliest consistently surviving Sessions documents, in Montreal from the mid-1780s, show these forms in frequent use for many common preliminary documents. This no doubt reflected the clerks' desire to simplify their daily business, but it also helped to ensure that justices did not make errors of form that might lead to legal challenges – an especially important consideration for rural justices, who did not always have access to trained clerks. In 1817, for example, Thomas Coffin, the Trois-Rivières chairman, suggested that townships magistrates be provided with 'printed forms of depositions, examinations, convictions, warrants etc. with such instructions, in regard to their proceedings, as they may appear to be in need of.'[48] While there is no evidence that the administration ever took this step, from the 1810s some rural justices in the district of Montreal at least began to use pre-printed forms, especially for recognizances and warrants. Sometimes their forms were identical to those used in Montreal, including typesetting errors, though with place names left blank, suggesting that the printer who prepared the Montreal forms simply ran off extra copies. Others appear to have been specially ordered, such as the warrants used by Lawrence Kidd of Laprairie in the mid-1820s, which were printed up with his name already filled in. Though most documents prepared by rural justices in the 1820s and 1830s were still in longhand, the spread of pre-printed forms into the Lower Canadian countryside suggests not only the routinization of their activity but also the importance of their work: forms were useful only if there were significant numbers of people likely to come before the justices.

Justices could also consult the law officers of the crown for legal assistance. In 1809, for example, the acting attorney general, Edward Bowen, advised a Gaspé justice on a murder and a Quebec City justice in the case of a suspected French spy. Since such consultations were costly, the executive generally tried to restrict them to special cases: as the civil secretary declared to Peter Roe, a Leeds justice who repeatedly pestered the administration for advice in the mid-1830s, while the government was willing assist justices, 'yet it cannot take upon itself to give directions and advice in the ordinary details of Magisterial Duties.'[49] But even less serious cases could raise complex legal issues that justices could submit to the crown law officers. Thus, in 1814, Thomas McCord wrote Stephen Sewell, the solicitor general, regarding a problematic Weekly Sessions case:

> The Case. A brings an action against B as his apprentice requiring him to finish his time. In support of his claim to B's service A produces a paper which he calls an indenture or engagement said to be passed before a notary by which B is said to be bound. To this B's attorney excepts and pleads Inscription en faux. The court having taken the plea in consideration adjudged that the exception be maintained. A by his attorney insists that the court is not competent to take cognizance of the plea of Inscription en faux to that the Court of Kings Bench alone can decide on the validity or falsehood of a notarial act. My own opinion is that the law having given the Court of Weekly Sittings or two magistrates the right to judge the matter in dispute they have necessarily a right to enquire into the validity of any paper exhibited as a proof of an engagement ...[50]

Not only does this show the involvement of the crown law officers, it also suggests the potential complexity of cases brought before the Weekly

Sessions and the role played by lawyers in establishing the justices' courts as an area of legal debate (to which we will return); and it underscores McCord's own legal competence, since what he presented was not a description of the specific case but rather a classic legal syllogism.

Finally, justices could also gain legal knowledge through collegial interaction with their colleagues, and especially, for urban justices, by sitting on the bench of the Quarter Sessions with other more experienced justices. In 1819, for example, John Fletcher, the Quebec City chairman, described how the court decided on judgments:

> A time is appointed, usually on the last day or the last day but one of the Session, for the consultation on this part of our duty. Not only every magistrate who sat on the trial, but every other gentleman in the commission who chooses to attend is considered as having a voice; as is the case in the Court of King's Bench in England on verdicts given at the Assizes or at Nisi Prius in London or Westminster on Crown issues emanating from thence. Our number is usually from 3 to 5. The Chairman reads his notes carefully, with the addition of such comments on the evidence, the deportment of the witnesses, etc. which he feels right, and concludes with offering his own opinion as to the nature and extent of the judgement. Every magistrate present does the like; and the sentence ultimately agreed upon becomes accordingly the result of the aggregate judgement of the whole Court.

This did not necessarily lead to domination by the professional chairman. In the case presented by Fletcher, for example, concerning a particularly violent assault, all agreed that the plaintiff's evidence was exaggerated, but they differed on the punishment that should be imposed, with Fletcher proposing the mildest sentence; the final sentence was a compromise between the opinions of the five justices who heard the case.[51]

Though they rarely sat in Quarter Sessions, country magistrates acquired legal experience from their frequent service as King's Bench grand jurors, much as in England. While jury service was limited to the towns in the eighteenth century, it was extended into the countryside from the 1810s. In the district of Montreal, about three-quarters of active urban justices from the 1780s to the 1820s, and a little under half of rural justices active in the 1810s and 1820s, had served on King's Bench grand juries, often multiple times. Jury service exposed justices to the sorts of felony cases they might deal with at the preliminary stages, in a court staffed by professional judges and law officers, and the charges of chief justices were often explicitly directed at magistrates. As one grand jury put it in 1812, in arguing for the extension of jury service to rural justices, 'the Magistrate, from the additional knowledge and insight he might there acquire, would learn to bring to Justice, in a regular and legal manner, the offenders brought before him.'[52]

Magisterial Competence

The justices were thus not bereft of sources of legal knowledge, especially in the cities but also in the countryside. And while, as we saw, there are many examples of magisterial incompetence, many justices demonstrated a concrete ability, when they wanted to, to conform to the law. Take the question of justices acting without proper authority, such as after their commissions had been revoked: among all the justices active in the district of Montreal between 1764 and 1836, only two definitely acted after they were dropped from the commission.[53] Or again, consider the extent to which the justices in Quarter Sessions respected the obligations imposed on them as to time of sitting (dictated by the legislation), number of justices required (two or three depending on the period, as dictated by the commission), or the necessary presence of a justice of the quorum. It has been suggested that in Quebec City the justices were extremely lax in this regard, but this may have been largely *Patriote* rhetoric: in 1835, for example, the executive responded to a complaint from the City Council, that justices held Weekly Sessions irregularly, by pointing out that records demonstrated the Sessions had been held on all but two statutory occasions since 1833. Likewise, a detailed examination of the Montreal Quarter Sessions records shows that, apart from a few brief periods, the justices conformed almost exactly to their legal obligations. In this they were helped by the clerks of the peace, as when John Reid pointed out in 1791 that the court could not hear a case since the only quorum justice on the bench was also a material witness and would have to leave the bench to testify. Periodically, there were more serious problems with justices' attendance: in the district of Trois-Rivières, for example, two entire Quarter Sessions were not held in the mid-1810s because not enough justices showed up, and the failure of justices to attend Weekly Sessions in particular was regularly decried from the 1780s to the 1820s. But these problems were related not to knowledge but to assiduity, and despite the entirely volunteer nature of the position, such incidents were in fact quite uncommon. Even in the 1830s, after the return to a voluntary magistracy, there were only two instances where Montreal Quarter Sessions sittings had to be put off until the next day for want of magistrates, and the justices regularly drew up lists distributing Quarter Sessions and Weekly Sessions duties among themselves.[54]

This mix of competence and incompetence, assiduity and laxity is also evident in the justices' actions in felony cases. In theory, under the Marian bail and committal statutes in force in the colony as in England, justices were the front line in the investigation of felonies, with the responsibility of holding preliminary inquests and assembling witnesses for trials before the higher criminal courts. Though a detailed study of felony proceedings remains to be undertaken, a cursory examination of the remaining records of Montreal's Court of King's Bench, from the 1810s, suggests that many country magistrates did follow the basic provisions of the Marian statutes, recording the statements of plaintiffs and witnesses, binding them to appear at the next session of the King's Bench, taking the examination of prisoners and either committing or bailing them, and sending in the necessary papers to judicial authorities in Montreal. In this respect, they were no different from their counterparts in Upper Canada.[55] As in Upper Canada, however, the practice was far from uniform. In 1816, for example, the attorney general complained that magistrates in the district of Trois-Rivières had become 'so negligent in investigating criminal offences that it is almost impossible in the short time allowed by law for holding criminal pleas within this district to bring the offenders to justice,' since prisoners were committed to gaol without written depositions or examinations and without witnesses being bound over, as the Marian statutes required. Likewise, in 1825, John Fletcher, by then provincial judge of Saint Francis, noted that the depositions accompanying five prisoners accused of forgery were sufficient to ascertain the general truth but 'far too imperfect' to allow for charges to proceed, since 'the magistrates are far too little accustomed to business of so intricate a nature.' In the early 1810s, even McCord and Mondelet came under criticism from Chief Justice James Monk for failing to prepare proper depositions against people accused of treasonable practices.[56]

Further, even when they respected the forms, country magistrates in particular tended to minimize their preliminary investigations in felony cases, most often limiting themselves to the evidence necessary to justify sending the accused to gaol (generally the plaintiff and a small number of other witnesses) and binding over the plaintiff to prosecute, rather than assembling the full range of witnesses necessary for trial and binding them all. Rural justices did sometimes undertake more extensive investigations. In 1818, for example, Léon Lalanne, a Philipsburg justice, chided McCord and Mondelet for having prematurely issued an arrest warrant in a forgery case, since he had been trying to set a trap for the ringleaders. Cases such as this, however, were exceptions.

Since justices often bound only a few witnesses for trial, if any at all, this was not enough for a full prosecution. As a result, the crown law officers were forced to take over witness management themselves by issuing subpoenas to all witnesses before the sessions of the higher criminal courts; these were served either by the high constable or by special bailiffs, at considerable expense, especially outside the cities. In the early 1820s, the administration, faced with a major cash crunch, decided to direct magistrates to apply the Marian committal statute strictly by binding over all necessary witnesses, but this manifestly did not work, since the executive was soon forced to return to the old system. In more serious criminal cases, the justices thus limited their role to preliminary arrest and commitment, rather than being public prosecutors who prepared cases beforehand.[57]

Still, if justices were unwilling to go to the trouble and expense of conducting full-scale criminal investigations, this does not mean that they were incompetent or lackadaisical. There are few examples of rural justices willingly refusing to deal with serious criminal cases, though this did occur: in 1827, for example, William Woods, a Sainte-Marie justice, was accused of interfering in proceedings in a murder case before Philip Byrne, another justice, in order to keep witnesses back from trial, out of kindness towards the accused. But Byrne's own actions in the same case, and the thousands of people in the Montreal and Quebec gaols on felony charges ranging from larceny to murder, are testimony to the assiduity of many justices. There are also ample examples of rural justices following up on cases they had sent in to the law officers: a rural justice carefully sending a covering letter separate from his package of depositions and examinations, with an example of the wax seal he had used, since he suspected that the bailiff carrying the package might tamper with it; or another responding to the clerk of the crown's criticism of his proceedings by citing passages from Blackstone. And, while Woods was also accused, in 1828, of refusing to attend a criminal court as a witness in a case of attempted murder begun before him, stating that 'he would not attend, altho' he might get subpoenas or anything else sent to him, (for he had attended at some of the courts and had not been paid for it) unless he was brought by main strength' and that 'he would see the Attorney General damned before he would go to Montreal to attend the Court,' rural magistrates regularly appeared as witnesses at the King's Bench trials of prisoners they had sent to gaol.[58]

Conclusion

From the perspective of those caught up in the system, there was certainly no void in the administration of local criminal justice from 1764 to the Rebellions. This was especially true in the cities themselves, which always had at least a small core of active magistrates, along with formal courts, but from the early nineteenth century onwards, there were also active justices spread throughout more and more of the countryside. Though these justices were certainly in no way representative of the colony's population, this was a function of class more than of ethnicity. The British policy of co-opting local elites into colonial administration worked relatively well: not only were many *Canadien* members of the elites named to the commission, they were also quite willing to act as representatives of the British colonial state. And the power and prestige of these magistrates came from their positions in their respective communities and in the colony as a whole.

In this respect, the magistracy in Quebec and Lower Canada conformed to the ancien-régime English ideal of local justice based on the power and status of local elites, rather than on obscure men endowed with bureaucratic power. Even salaried justices such as McCord, Mondelet, and Gale in Montreal, Taschereau and Christie in Quebec City, or Coffin in Trois-Rivières derived their social prominence not from their judicial activities but from other spheres of their lives: McCord from his urban landholdings, Mondelet from his notarial activity, Gale from his law practice, Taschereau from his seigneuries, Christie from his literary activities, Coffin from his business and seigneurial interests, and all from their political connections. While the bureaucratization of the magistracy was certainly beginning, this was still a transitional phase between the old regime and the new, which would be definitively implanted from the late 1830s.

Despite their mostly amateur status, the justices before whom plaintiffs and defendants appeared were also far from uniformly unskilled, inept, and incompetent. This is not to suggest that the justices were fair-minded, selfless public servants who impartially judged their fellow citizens. Many were partial and arbitrary; they were driven by interests of class and even of party; some displayed a striking lack of judicial knowledge and judicial judgment. But, in general, they were not bumbling amateurs with little education and even less knowledge of the law. Instead, many justices had a relatively solid grasp of the laws that governed their conduct, and when they ignored them, as Chartier de Lotbinière did in the case of Louis de Coigne, they did so not out of ignorance but deliberately. Further, incompetence or malversation did not necessarily lighten the impact of the system on the colony's people: when Oliver Barker, the magistrate in the pay of the American banks, committed felons to prison, as he did on several occasions in the 1800s and 1810s, it did not change their experience to know that he may have done so for personal financial gain. Downplaying the impact of the justices on colonial society ignores the experiences of the thousands of other people on whom their impact was great indeed; and it does not explain why, if the system was in the disrepute suggested by Durham, thousands of people went to the trouble of appearing before a justice to make a complaint. But for the criminal justice system to have any significant impact on the colony's people, there was another essential element: the police.

4

The Police before the Police

There is not, nor for years past has been a Bailiff or Constable in the whole Province.
- Preamble to a bill 'for Protecting the Province, by Increasing the Security of the Public Peace,' presented in the Legislative Council, 1787

We were rather unfortunate in making immediate search, as there is no constable or militia officer within the limits of the borough [of William Henry]. The jury of inquest have made every inquiry possible and all to no purpose, and the citizens have in general submitted to a search.
- Moses Holt to Jonathan Sewell, regarding the murder of J. Palley and his maidservant, 1796

Under a temporary Act, Quebec and Montreal were watched and lighted, after a sort, down to May 1836. The funds were altogether unequal to the proper support of these essential branches of civic government. Lamps fed with oil were distributed at intervals 'few and far between'; and the guardianship of the night was intrusted to a meagre selection of the class of veteran servitors, of whose impotency for all useful purposes the people of London were cognizant before the establishment of 'the New Police.'
- William Kennedy and Adam Thom, 'General Report of the Assistant Commissioners of Municipal Inquiry,' Durham Report, appendix C (1839)[1]

As much as magistrates might embody the criminal justice system, without officers at hand to carry out their orders, as Moses Holt's complaint suggests, the justices were largely powerless, since they generally did not themselves engage in the labour of law enforcement. Both Holt's observation on policing in William Henry, one of the colony's larger towns, and the preamble to the 1787 bill, presented by William Smith, the colony's new chief justice, imply what many historians have asserted: that the colonial state was singularly ill-equipped when it came to policing. And Kennedy and Thom's report suggests that things had not improved much over the next decades. This is in accord with the standard historiographical account, wherein New France's relatively effective law-enforcement system was swept away by the Conquest, replaced by a version of the English policing system that had all of the inconsistencies and inefficiencies of its parent. After a brief and unsatisfactory experiment with bailiffs named in each parish, policing in the countryside was transferred to the militia captains, who remained virtually the only agents of the criminal law until after the Rebellions. In the cities there were essentially no police at all until the establishment of an unpaid citizen constabulary in 1787, supplemented from 1818 by small paid night watches. Policing in both rural and urban areas of the colony relied on untrained, unpaid, and thus unprofessional individuals, who acted reluctantly if at all. The result, according to this view, was a police that was disorganized, untrained, and disregarded by the population, and a criminal justice system without the means to exert its will. Only the city watchmen even remotely resembled a modern police, and these 'veteran servitors,' as Thom and Kennedy put it, were as notoriously inefficient as their London counterparts. It was not until the reforms of the Special Council after the 1837–8 Rebellions that the colony saw its first modern, professional police; before then, the only reliable instrument of state power was the army.[2]

Like interpretations of the criminal justice system as a whole, this account of the colonial police fits into the broader interpretation of the ancien-régime colonial state: weak and ineffective, grafted onto an alien and unwilling society, and largely unchanging until the profound transformations leading to the implantation of the modern liberal state in the years following the Rebellions, exemplified by the new professional police. And yet there was quite evidently some policing going on, at least from the perspective of the 10,000-odd people confined in the Montreal gaol on criminal charges between 1811 and 1836, the 8,500 in the Quebec gaol in about the same period, the thousands more in the two cities' houses of correction, the thousands more imprisoned overnight by the 'veteran servitors' in the city watch-houses, and the thousands again who were arrested and brought before justices but released or bailed. And just a year before Holt's complaint, Andrew Kollmyer, identified by James Sawers, another William Henry justice, as the 'constable in William Henry,' participated in arresting a French spy, though he soon left to become a professional constable and bailiff in Montreal.[3] In other words, policing in Quebec and Lower Canada was far more complex than the classic tale based on laws and elite complaints, illustrating once more how the ancien-régime state in theory and in discourse did not correspond to how it was experienced in practice.

The existing historiography of the police in Quebec and Lower Canada is largely inspired by classic approaches to pre-reform policing in the Western world, and especially in England and its colonies. For many years, whether writing from a law-and-order, liberal, or Marxist position, English police historians posited a 'revolution' in policing in the middle third of the nineteenth century and a correspondingly sharp dichotomy between the ancien-régime and the modern police. The pre-reform era was one of unpaid, unwilling constables and corrupt, inefficient watchmen, mired in structures and practices dating to the Middle Ages, isolated from state control, and completely inadequate to the realities of industrialization and urbanization. This changed only with the Peel reforms of 1829, which led to the birth of efficient, state-controlled police forces stressing prevention over response. For Whiggish historians, this was a classic example of nineteenth-century rational progress; for later, more critical historians, the 'Peelers' were rather one of the new mechanisms of social control that emerged with the formation of the nineteenth-century bourgeois state; but for both, the ineffectiveness of the old system was both manifest and essential in explaining what followed.[4] The historiography of policing in England's North American colonies and the early United States long followed a similar trend, with emphasis on disorganized and inadequate colonial law enforcement and a sharp break towards the middle of the nineteenth century.[5]

More recently, writers on the police in both England and the colonies have begun reassessing the pre-reform police. Many scholars now suggest that the development of the 'new' police in England can be traced back much farther than 1829, pointing out that the 'old' police underwent considerable reform throughout the eighteenth century. Others note that the old system itself cannot be dismissed so easily: on the one hand, it could work quite well for everyday crimes such as petty thefts and assaults, and on the other, its corruption, inconsistency, and inability to deal with large-scale popular disturbances did not preclude its being an everyday burden on the disadvantaged. The London Watch dismissed by Kennedy and Thom, for example, was in fact far more efficient than contemporary critics made out.[6] There has been less of this sort of re-evaluation of the 'old' police in North America, though there are some suggestive studies.[7] Questions are thus being raised both about the irrelevance of the old police and about the radical break between the old police and the new.

Part of the problem is one of definition. Definitions of 'police' adopted by historians range from the general eighteenth-century sense of public order or social regulation, especially (but not exclusively) in urban centres, to the modern sense of bureaucratic and hierarchical state institutions responsible for maintaining public order and preventing and detecting crime. The first definition is essential for understanding how elites conceived of public order, as Martin Dufresne has shown for Quebec City, but is not especially useful for exploring the specifics of how the criminal justice system actually exerted its will on people, since it conflates much of the local criminal justice system, including laws, magistrates, and constables, along with local administration in general, under the heading of 'police.'[8] The second definition, which is that adopted by many police historians, corresponds to the specific structures that grew up in Europe in the eighteenth century and came into their own in the nineteenth, but, since it is ultimately derived from the discourse of early-nineteenth-century reformers as to what the police *should* be, it cannot but emphasize the differences between the old police and the new. For example, it has led to the common practice in English and colonial police history of talking about 'policing' or 'law enforcement' before the nineteenth-century reforms and 'police' after, thereby defining away the police before the police. Further, the emphasis on bureaucratic structure and control attaches greater importance to the form of the police than to the everyday reality of policing and the experience of being policed; hence the common notion that since the 'new' police were permanently appointed and salaried, this made them fundamentally different from the annually appointed and fee-remunerated constables who preceded them. Searching backwards from the modern definition of police has also led historians to what has been called 'a classic instance of the historical fallacy of presentism,' focusing only on the most evident ancien-régime policing institutions and thereby underestimating both the extent and the impact of the ancien-régime police.[9] Hence the assumption that, because there were no constables in Montreal and Quebec City before 1787, the cities had no police. And yet, if this was so, why did Edward William Gray, the sheriff of Montreal, pay a carpenter in 1781 for '8 rods for the bailiffs,' rods or staves being the traditional symbol of authority of English parish constables?[10]

To account for both the rods and the bailiffs mentioned along with them, this chapter draws on a definition of police adapted to the more fluid nature of ancien-régime state authority, while still focused on the concrete impact of the criminal justice system itself, notably its deployment of coercive force. Thus, the police addressed in this chapter are those who, under explicitly delegated state authority, habitually acted as intermediaries in the initial stages of conflictual relations between the criminal justice system of the state and members of society at large, notably but not exclusively by detecting crime and by making arrests; who could (but did not necessarily) employ coercive force in doing so; who did not themselves have the formal discretion to judge offenders; and who were recognizable as judicial intermediaries by the people they were policing. They were thus distinguished by both their function and their powers, by their position between state and society, by the moment of their intervention, and by their legitimated (though frequently challenged) authority but not by the specifics of their organizational structure. They can be conceived as agents of the state, with special powers, rather than as private individuals exercising powers generally endorsed by the state (such as people who separated brawlers or private guards). The policing tasks they regularly undertook involved more than routine non-conflictual administrative tasks such as summoning witnesses or keeping juries, or punishments meted out after judgment, though the police were often involved in those as well. But the police discussed here were not necessarily part of any formal bureaucratic hierarchy, nor under any sort of direct administrative control, with authority often delegated at several removes from the central administration; and they were both full-time and part-time, paid by salary and by fee. This broader definition still does not cover all law enforcement in Quebec and Lower Canada, for state officials without the right to use coercive force, such as roads or police inspectors, were involved in the detection and prosecution of offences. But, even concentrating only on the more coercive aspects of policing, the police between the Conquest and the Rebellions were quite different from what has been postulated by reformers like Kennedy and Thom and by historians since.[11]

Bailiffs and Militia Officers, 1764–87

The first two decades of policing under British civil rule illustrate the limits of applying a modern definition of police to an ancien-régime state, and also caution against a too-ready acceptance of the picture laid out in legislative theory and contemporary discourse. In theory, the only police in Quebec between 1764 and 1787 were the parish bailiffs and then the militia captains. In practice, however, it was men like Gray's 'bailiffs,' invisible in colonial law and discourse, who carried out much of the policing in the colony, both in town and in country.

Along with establishing criminal courts and naming justices and clerks, one of the first actions of the new British colonial administration in 1764 was to organize policing. Under the military regime, policing functions previously exercised in New France by militia captains, bailiffs, and the small *maréchaussée* had mostly been taken on by militia officers, especially sergeants, though some French-regime bailiffs also continued to act. But with the decision to abolish the militia in 1764, the administration had to look elsewhere for its police. The obvious choice was a system of parish constables supplemented by urban watches, as in both England and many colonies. But there were difficulties. Constables, while probably part of the common law system received into Quebec,[12] were usually nominated by courts of medieval origin such as the Sheriff's Leet or by Anglican parish vestries, neither of which existed in the new colony, and anything but a volunteer watch would have required direct taxation, which the new administration could not impose. The 1764 ordinance that set up the courts thus took a different route, providing for the nomination of a bailiff and two sub-bailiffs for each parish, including the urban parishes of Montreal and Quebec City. Echoing English traditions of local autonomy, and in a departure from the more centralized pre-Conquest style of governance, six men were to be elected annually by an assembly of the parish's householders; then, to maintain central control, the list was sent in to the central administration, which selected three of the men named. As with parish constables, this was meant to be avocational community policing: no one was to be elected more than once until everyone in the parish had served, although, in the interests of continuity, one of the two sub-bailiffs was to continue as bailiff in the next year.

Though the ordinance made no distinction between town and country, in practice two different systems developed. In most rural parishes, bailiff elections were held regularly, and, since the administration almost always chose the first three names on the list sent in, local autonomy was essentially complete. The rule against repeat service was often disregarded, with some bailiffs serving two, three, or even more years running, but there was nevertheless frequent rotation: about a thousand different men served as parish bailiffs in the district of Montreal alone, almost all *habitants* and solid members of their local communities, out of an adult male population of perhaps 5,000–6,000. With a few minor modifications, this system remained in place until 1775: existing bailiffs were temporarily continued in office following the coming into effect of the Quebec Act, but, with the chaos engendered by the American invasion and the restoration of the militia later in the year, the institution withered away, and a 1777 ordinance formally transferred most of the bailiffs' duties to the militia captains.[13]

Rural parish bailiffs were meant to assume many of the functions performed by militia captains and bailiffs under the French regime and by parish officials in the English system, especially constables. Thus, they had judicial duties, including the resolution of certain minor civil disputes and the service of process in civil cases; administrative duties, especially overseeing public works; and policing duties, notably arresting criminals and conveying them to the next parish to be sent on to the urban gaols, and detecting and prosecuting offences against the roads laws.[14] Though a full evaluation of the work of rural parish bailiffs remains to be done, bailiffs seem to have been little involved in coercive policing. For example, in the sparse remaining criminal justice documents, there are virtually no references to parish bailiffs making arrests. Their main activities seem to have been administrative, notably overseeing roads repairs, and while they may have prosecuted people for not repairing the roads, that was probably the extent of their policing activities.[15] In part, this was because the justices of the peace, who were those who gave orders for arrests and the like, were concentrated almost exclusively in the cities, but it also reflected the serious limits of a truly community-based system of avocational police.

When the militia captains definitively took over the bailiffs' functions in 1777, the administration evidently intended them to act as police, since they were explicitly given the powers of peace officers, namely to arrest anyone for crime or breach of the peace and bring them before the nearest justice. As well, militia captains were to arrest all deserters and all strangers suspected of sedition or assisting the enemy and also to enforce roads regulations. Almost every parish had one or more militia captains, so that in theory there were police spread throughout the rural parts of the colony. In terms of both their formal police functions and their geographical distribution, there was thus continuity from the system of parish bailiffs, and even in personnel: more than a third of rural militia captains in the district of Montreal in 1779 had previously been parish bailiffs.[16]

In practice, however, like the bailiffs they replaced, the rural militia captains were largely divorced from the criminal justice system. There are occasional references to them making arrests or conveying prisoners, and, when prisoners escaped from the urban gaols, the sheriffs dispatched circular letters asking rural militia captains to watch out for them. It was probably also militia captains who launched at least some of the fairly frequent prosecutions of *habitants* for roads offences. But apart from that, they seem to have played a relatively minor policing role.[17]

Instead, if any individuals in the countryside can be described as police, it was semi-professional bailiffs who began to appear in the countryside from the late 1770s. The replacement of parish bailiffs by militia captains had left a hole in the system of civil process-serving in the countryside. As a result, some rural inhabitants began acting regularly for the civil courts, often referring to themselves in official documents as *huissiers* or bailiffs. While their main business was serving civil process, they also acted in criminal matters on occasion, making arrests for justices and the like. These were men like Jean-Baptiste Kerle *dit* Bellegarde of Chambly, a former French soldier who had been a parish bailiff in the 1770s. In 1783 he arrested Joseph Morin for selling liquor without a licence and brought him to Montreal by order of the justices, and his profession at his death in 1809 was listed simply as 'huissier.'[18]

The closest thing to police in the colony before 1787, however, were neither parish bailiffs, nor militia captains, nor even rural civil bailiffs. Throughout the period, both Quebec City and Montreal had a small group of generally long-serving justice professionals who acted both for the civil and the criminal courts. Étienne Plantade *dit* Chateauverd, for example, was a bailiff in Montreal over two decades, from the mid-1760s to the mid-1780s, serving civil process, making arrests in criminal cases, summoning witnesses, and attending punishments; his only formal appointment was as one of Montreal's parish bailiffs between 1768 and 1773. And Simon Mazurier, another Montreal bailiff in the 1760s, was never formally appointed to any position whatsoever; but this did not prevent him being stabbed to death in 1769 while trying to arrest Louis Bourgoin *dit* Versailles for assaulting Joseph-François Villiers, another long-serving Montreal bailiff.

These professional urban bailiffs were largely the creation of judicial officers who were faced with the practical necessity of enforcing their orders. Thus, each district had a deputy provost-marshall, or sheriff, generally a long-serving justice professional: Gray, the Montreal sheriff, was in office from 1765 to 1810, and his counterpart in Quebec City, James Shepherd, formerly clerk of the peace, was in office from 1776 to 1816. As elsewhere, sheriffs were responsible for carrying out the orders of both the civil and criminal courts and for judicial administration more generally, including process serving, arrests, summoning witnesses and juries, collecting fines, organizing corporal punishment, and overseeing the gaols.[19] And, as elsewhere too, the sheriffs generally did not perform these tasks by themselves. Instead, they named subordinate officers to help them, and the sheriffs of both Montreal and Quebec each kept a small roster of professional bailiffs, about a half-dozen in each city, to whom they directed their orders. Plantade, for example, was one of the bailiffs of Gray, the Montreal sheriff, from 1767 to 1784 and perhaps earlier. The sheriffs' bailiffs spent most of their time serving civil process in both town and country, but Gray's accounts show him making regular payments to bailiffs like Plantade for criminal matters such as pursuing and arresting offenders, for which he then claimed compensation from the central administration.[20] This represented a crucial break with the philosophy that in theory underlay the English policing system, where the financial burden of policing was supposed to lie not with government but with victims.

Plantade did not act only for the sheriff. In 1784, for example, he claimed payment from Burke, the clerk of the peace, for 'la charpentier prize et amenné en ville a la cour après avoir trouvé du butain vollé ches il et entres ces mains et par ordre de la cour cherche son fils en plus de vingt maisons dans la boue et a la plui' [the carpenter taken and brought to town to the court after having found the stolen property at his house and in his hands and by order of the court having searched for his son in more than twenty houses in the mud and the rain]. 'La cour' in this case were the justices of the peace who endorsed his account. Urban justices seem to have decided from the very beginning that what they needed at their disposal was not avocational bailiffs elected each year from among the citizenry, but justice professionals.

Thus, during the time of the parish bailiffs, justices in both Montreal and Quebec City subverted the relatively democratic system of parish bailiff elections, with the tacit concurrence of the executive. In Montreal, apart perhaps from the very first year, the bailiffs were not elected by parish assemblies but instead named by the city's justices, who kept many of the same individuals in office year after year: for example, both Jean-Christophe Decoste and Joseph-François Villiers between 1765 to 1769, and Plantade, Jean-Baptiste Decoste, and John Divine from 1768 until 1773. In Quebec City, there was more rotation, but there were also many bailiffs named repeatedly, such as John Buchanan and Mathieu Hianvieu *dit* Lafrance, both appointed 1767–73. In both cities as well, there were far more bailiffs appointed than the three specified in the 1764 ordinance: in Montreal, a high bailiff and six to seven sub-bailiffs; and in Quebec City, up to thirteen sub-bailiffs in the city and its suburbs. Finally, in both cities, there were almost no nominations at all after 1771, with the same bailiffs kept in office until 1775.

But this was not all. In England, justices could swear in constables other than those regularly nominated by the parish vestry, and could name whomever they chose to execute their warrants.[21] The Montreal justices at least evidently took this to mean that they could appoint their own bailiffs in addition to the parish bailiffs, bypassing the central administration completely. In 1766, for example, the justices called twelve bailiffs to appear at Quarter Sessions, of whom only five were on the list of parish bailiffs; and between 1766 and 1770, they named more than two dozen 'justices' bailiffs,' for both Montreal and the rural parishes. The rural parish bailiffs seem to have been connected only to the justices' civil jurisdiction. However, the urban justices' bailiffs were in fact often the same individuals whom the justices appointed as parish bailiffs and who also served as sheriffs' bailiffs. François Husson *dit* Lajeunesse, for example, was sworn in as a justices' bailiff in Montreal in 1767, was a parish bailiff between 1770 and 1773, and also acted as a bailiff for Gray. Likewise, in Quebec City, Hianvieu was not only parish bailiff between 1767 and 1773 but also one of the sheriff's bailiffs from 1766 to the 1780s. The position mattered less than the individual, so that, when the system of parish bailiffs disappeared in the mid-1770s, it did little to change the situation of these bailiffs: the sheriffs and justices simply continued to employ them and pay them to do exactly what they had done before.

Though, like their rural counterparts, most of the city bailiffs probably spent most of their time on civil matters, the justices who administered the cities clearly intended them to act as parish constables as well, and considered them to be a corps under their control. Consider an order the justices made in Montreal Quarter Sessions in 1766:

> The bailiffs to distribute the city into wards ... and each one is to take his ward and to have the same in good order. Bailiffs to pay a fine of forty sols for misbehaviour ... are to see the streets properly clean'd and looked after and that no disorderly houses are kept in their wards ... 1st. De Cost père has for his ward, from Mr. Gray's Provost Martial to Quebec Gate ... 8th Ward Farrel called the Swiss the suburbs of Quebec and the commons.[22]

This harkened back to the system of ward constables found in many colonial cities and shows a concern for policing urban disorder long before the nineteenth century. Whether this was actually followed is less clear. Certainly, in 1769 Pierre Du Calvet intimated that the justices' and sheriffs' bailiffs were still concerned with the 'police' (public order) of Montreal; likewise, in 1767 the Montreal justices ordered 'city bailiffs' to attend the market in rotation, being paid a half-dollar per day by the clerk of the market and forfeiting a half-dollar for each non-attendance, a system continued until 1773 at least. The administrative reorganization of 1775–7 had little effect on the involvement of bailiffs in this sort of urban policing: thus, in 1783, Joseph Minot petitioned the Montreal Quarter Sessions for special privileges since he had been useful in keeping good order in the market, and twice in 1786 the justices ordered bailiffs to patrol the city's streets in the aftermath of fires. Bailiffs also participated in the symbolism and ritual of criminal justice: they attended executions and punishments ordered by the criminal courts, and were provided with the traditional symbol of the constable's authority, the painted staff, featuring the king's arms.[23] And the justices also exercised disciplinary control over their bailiffs, fining them when they neglected to appear in court, or forgot their staves, or disobeyed orders. When in 1781 Plantade refused to attend the punishment of a prisoner, Gray, the sheriff, asked the justices in Quarter Sessions to discipline him, referring to him as 'one of the huissiers or bailiffs of this Court,' and the court threatened to have him arrested unless he appeared and explained himself; however, when in 1784 Plantade again refused to help put a prisoner in the stocks, saying 'that he can never serve on such like punishment,' he was simply dismissed from his post and prohibited from acting as a bailiff.[24]

In each city, there was thus a core of long-serving, active bailiffs who at least on occasion acted as police, even if that was not their only or even primary occupation. And these bailiffs were also the recognizable and known faces of justice. When Mazurier was killed in 1769, for example, one of the assailants spotted another bailiff, Pierre Cazelet, in the street and cried, 'Aha, here is also another villain of a Bailiff, I'll do for him also.'[25] A closer analysis of these bailiffs is instructive. In Montreal, some twenty-five bailiffs acted as police between 1764 and 1787. Two-thirds were francophones, mostly Catholics, reminding us that bailiffs, like most other lower-level state officials, were not covered by the Test Act.[26] At least a third were ex-soldiers, which meant that they had some experience with arms, and indeed they seem often to have carried both swords and pistols. Despite being soldiers, the urban bailiffs were not necessarily uneducated. Since an essential part of their work for both civil and criminal justice was making returns of process, most were able to write, though, like Plantade, often imperfectly; one, Joseph Gabrion, eventually became a schoolteacher and then a notary. The bailiffs were also generally mature men, neither youths nor super- annuated: most were in their thirties or forties when they first acted, and their average age at mid-career was forty-three. Many also had long-term careers as officers of justice, of which policing was only a part: more than fifteen of the Montreal bailiffs (of whom most were francophones) were active for five years or more, and three (Plantade, Joseph Minot, and Jean-Baptiste Flamand) acted for almost the entire first two decades of British rule. Not all fit this pattern: Titus Simons, for example, a Loyalist immigrant, acted as a bailiff only in 1785, when he was just twenty years old, and by 1789 was a merchant in Kingston. But most were justice professionals.

This professional status is especially evident in the remarkable conti- nuity among the men who worked as bailiffs across the Conquest. In Quebec City, five of the eight French-regime bailiffs, including Hianvieu, were still active in the later 1760s, forming the core of the deputy provost marshall's bailiffs there. For these men, their profession was acting for the justice system, whatever it might be; thus, when Charles- Philippe Jailliard appealed to the Quebec Common Pleas in 1783 to 'le rettablire dans: Sça premier; fonction Dhuissier ... pour luy faire gagner Sa vie' [to reinstate him in his first position, of bailiff, to allow him to gain his living],[27] he was appealing to the court not to end a career that had spanned more than thirty years, starting in 1750 under the French regime. But even in Montreal, where there was more turnover because the position of bailiff disappeared during the military regime, two of the city's six pre-Conquest bailiffs, Jean-Baptiste Decoste and his son, Jean-Christophe, continued under British civil government, with Jean-Baptiste being one of the city's leading bailiffs. The regime might have changed, but there was even more continuity in the face of the police than in that of the justices.

It was these professional urban bailiffs who were at the heart of coercive policing before 1787. Thus, in Montreal, almost all references to policing within the city concerned these urban bailiffs. John Divine and Jean-Baptiste Flamand, both long-serving city bailiffs, acted as peace officers in breaking up a fight in the streets in 1769, while in 1785 Plantade asked to be paid for taking up sheep-stealers, and Joseph Minot for arresting Charlotte Lepine and two others, by order of 'Monsieur Maguil ecuier et juge de paix.'[28] And these urban bailiffs also acted as police in the countryside, though increasingly supplemented from the 1780s by professional rural bailiffs such as Bellegarde. Rural forays could take urban bailiffs far from their base and sometimes put them in great danger: in 1768, for example, one of the Quebec sheriff's bailiffs, Clément Choret, was shot and killed in Kamouraska, 150 kilometres downriver from Quebec City, while trying to arrest Pierre Mathieu *dit* Belarbre.[29]

Professional bailiffs, therefore, were the mainstays of everyday policing before 1787 and policing was only occasionally undertaken by others. While both Quebec City and Montreal were garrison towns, with guards posted in different parts of the city, the role of the military was limited, with only occasional references to soldiers involved in everyday policing. In 1769, for example, after Mazurier's murder, the other bailiffs proved unable to overcome the resistance of the killer and his family, so Gray, the sheriff, called on the military. But British administrators were highly reluctant to use the military against civilians except when absolutely necessary. In 1764 Quebec City's justices asked that soldiers act as watchmen, given 'the present inability of the inhabitants of said city, to maintain a sufficient body of watchmen for the safeguard of their effects at night,' but this seems not to have been followed up. And, even during the period of martial law that followed the American invasion, there were only two arrests of civilians by the army, though in the late 1770s and early 1780s the military occasionally arrested those accused of treasonable practices, such as Pierre Du Calvet or Valentin Jautard.[30] Likewise, there was little formal policing by ordinary citizens. Justices did occasionally use private individuals to make arrests: in 1771 Donald Mackay of Berthier was appointed by special warrant by James Cuthbert to investigate the murder of Donald Morrison, a peddler, and eventually arrested Baptiste Dufour at the Baie du Febvre, spending three days searching for Morrison's body 'as the prisoner would not tell where it was' and eventually prosecuting the case in the Montreal King's Bench. But this was a rarity. Similarly, while there was a temporary voluntary watch set up in Montreal in November 1783, 'for the safety of the town on account of many robberies committed,' it lasted only a month, and another thirty-five years elapsed before the town had a permanent watch.[31]

The system of policing through 1787, then, was far different from that outlined in colonial legislation. The ordinances attempted to emulate the English system and make policing the responsibility of unwilling amateurs, the parish bailiffs until the mid-1770s and the militia captains thereafter. But, in practice, everyday policing was largely the work of justice professionals, especially the small group of urban-based bailiffs employed by the justices and the sheriffs. None of this was in any way illegal, but it created a policing system quite different from the decentralized system of parish constables found not only in England but also in most English colonies. At the same time, this policing system corresponded little to what later reformers, and historians, would look for in police. For example, though bailiffs were on occasion paid out of public funds, most of their income was probably derived from payments by private parties: in justifying his request to be reimbursed for arresting the sheep-stealers, Plantade noted that Burke had promised to pay him even if the parties refused. Most government payments to bailiffs directly involved government interest in one way or another, such as the arrest of soldiers involved in criminal acts or disobedient militiamen.

At least in terms of its structure, the policing system in Quebec resembled far more the system in place before the Conquest. In his criminal justice functions, the sheriff filled a position similar to that of the *prévôt de la maréchaussée* in New France, whose duties were to search for criminals and oversee some executions. The city bailiffs played a policing role similar to that of both the *prévôt*'s *archers* (soldiers) and urban civil bailiffs, going from the cities where they were based into the countryside to arrest offenders, and, like the *archers*, attending punishments and executions. And, as in New France, civil bailiffs in the countryside also acted on occasion in criminal matters. Even the urban centralization of the police was the same. There were, of course, differences between the two systems: while the *archers* were salaried, uniformed, and apparently dealt only with criminal matters, the city bailiffs were paid in fees, most often coming from the parties themselves, and also operated extensively in civil matters. But, in practice, both were quasi-professional urban police capable of reaching on occasion into the rural areas of the district.[32]

Policing in Quebec in the two decades following the Conquest, however, suffered from the same shortcomings as other ancien-régime police systems. Even with the professional bailiffs there were discipline problems, and not just missed court sittings or forgotten staves: in 1765, for example, the high bailiff of Montreal, James Crofton, was convicted in Quarter Sessions for refusing to serve an arrest warrant, and the sheriff complained in 1784 that the bailiffs in general refused to put prisoners in the stocks or the pillory. In two cases in 1769, bailiffs were also prosecuted for extortion, having charged higher fees than allowed by the justices. And the bailiffs themselves had problems getting assistance from the public: during Mazurier's murder in 1769, other bailiffs repeatedly called for assistance in the name of the king, but received none.[33] It was in part because of these sorts of problems that the existing system of policing came under criticism in the mid-1780s, leading to a further reorientation in 1787.

Reforming the Police in the 1780s

Police reform in the 1780s was part of the general re-examination of the state of the colony following the turmoil of the American Revolution and the Loyalist influx. Policing was addressed briefly by Executive Council committees in 1786–7 that examined the justice system and the state of commerce and police (in its older sense). After hearing evidence from a number of sources, the committees concluded that the structures of policing were woefully inadequate: that there were no bailiffs or constables; that the militia captains were not required to arrest offenders but simply had the power to do so; and that, in the cities, the justices lacked the ability to enforce their orders regarding local administration. The committees blamed these structural inadequacies for what they saw as the gross defects in the practice of policing, and of the criminal justice system as a whole: as the committee on commerce and police said of Quebec City, 'The regulations that are made ... are but little attended to, and ill executed, the Magistracy is unconnected without a head, and without inferior officers to put the laws in force, their mandates want efficacy and do not enforce subordination in the people.'[34]

The committees' conclusions regarding policing at least were largely hyperbole, for, as we saw, there were certainly bailiffs in the years before 1787. Nevertheless, their views were accepted with little question and an ordinance was prepared to address them. There was some disagreement between the members of the English and French parties on exactly how policing should be reorganized: the former suggested that the Quarter Sessions of each district appoint high and petty constables throughout their district, while the latter, probably fearing the power that this would give urban justices, used their majority to limit the justices' powers to the cities. The ordinance therefore reinforced the militia officers' responsibility for policing in rural parishes but also directed the justices of the peace in Quarter Sessions to appoint each year as many people as they felt necessary within the cities of Quebec and Montreal 'for carrying into execution the orders and decrees of the several courts, and to preserve the public peace therein.' Every appointee was to serve for a year under a hefty penalty for non-compliance, but with exemptions for all civil and military officers and a variety of others including doctors and schoolmasters.[35]

By this system, which in theory formed the basis of policing in the colony until the Special Council's reforms in the late 1830s, the Legislative Council once again attempted to give the colony the sort of decentralized, avocational, involuntary police that historians have posited for England and other English colonies. And the colony's administrators also attempted to curtail government's financial involvement in police: in 1788, for example, the committee on public accounts refused to reimburse the Montreal sheriff for policing performed by his bailiffs, on the grounds that this was now the responsibility of the peace officers named in the ordinance.[36] But, as was the case in 1764 and 1777, the policing system that actually followed was not that envisioned by the lawmakers, either in the cities themselves or in the countryside.

Urban Policing from 1787: Constables and Substitutes

In the cities, justices were quick to take advantage of their new powers. The ordinance did not specify how they were to choose constables, or even use the word 'constable' at all, but the justices in both Montreal and Quebec City evidently decided to follow the English model of citizen-constables, where the office rotated among heads of households owning or renting property above a certain value. In July 1787 the Montreal justices had their crier make up lists of householders liable to serve as constables, much as he was accustomed to doing for jurymen, and in November they appointed twelve householders, six in the city itself and two each in the Quebec, Saint-Laurent, and Recollet suburbs. Constables were also named in Quebec City in August, though the exact nomination process is less clear. And though the system was not formally extended to Trois-Rivières until 1821, constables were already being named there in the early 1790s.[37]

The justices in Montreal were soon confronted with the difficulty of enforcing this involuntary service, even for such occasional duties as attending the Quarter Sessions, let alone for actual police actions such as arrests. More than half of the citizen-constables did not show up at the opening of the April and July Quarter Sessions in 1788, and as late as October, the justices were still using a professional bailiff to watch over the juries during their deliberations, a job supposedly part of the constables' unpaid duties. Probably because of this, when four of the twelve householders nominated as constables in 1788 asked to provide substitutes to serve in their place, the justices readily agreed and swore the substitutes into office, along with another. The ordinance made no provision for this sort of substitution and its legality was doubtful, although it was a widespread practice in both England and the American colonies.[38]

In Montreal, the practice of using substitute constables quickly became entrenched and remained in place until 1820. In 1789 eight of the twelve constables nominated by the justices appointed substitutes, including four of the substitutes named in 1788, and by 1790 only one of the constables nominated by the justices was serving in person. Overall, of a little over 550 constables nominated by the Montreal justices between 1787 and 1820, only about a quarter served in person, with the remainder appointing substitutes. In Quebec City, substitutes were also allowed until the early 1820s at least. Though the extent of the practice is unknown, it was enough to provoke public criticism, to which the city's high constable replied (erroneously) that it was difficult to stop citizens from making use of a privilege allowed by law.[39]

The popularity of substitution is understandable, given the very real burdens of serving as a constable. All constables were expected to show up at the opening and closing of each Quarter Sessions and King's Bench; to act in turn as bailiffs in those courts during their sessions by keeping juries and prisoners; to attend, in rotation, the Weekly Sessions, at least until 1820; and to attend all corporal punishments and executions. And the Montreal justices were fairly vigilant in enforcing this attendance: between 1790 and 1820 they imposed over a hundred fines,

Table 4.1: Professions of Montreal constables, 1787–1820

| Profession | Nominated | Did not serve* | Nominated and serving | Serving | | | |
| | | | | In person | | By substitute | |
				#	%	#	%
Merchants	154 (20%)	38	116 (21%)	0	0	116	100
Other elites	8 (1%)	6	2 (0%)	0	0	2	100
Retailers/traders	71 (9%)	13	58 (10%)	7	12	51	88
Tavern-keepers	94 (12%)	17	77 (14%)	23	30	54	70
Farmers	13 (2%)	5	8 (1%)	4	50	4	50
Artisans	232 (31%)	43	189 (34%)	63	33	126	67
Other popular class	2 (<1%)	–	2 (<1%)	2	100	0	0
Unknown	185 (24%)	76	109 (19%)	33	30	76	70
Total	759	198	561	132	24	429	76

* exempted, did not appear, or reason unknown

ranging from a couple of shillings to a pound, on constables who did not show up in Quarter Sessions. Further, constables were expected to assist the justices, again without pay, in such socially unpopular tasks as suppressing riots and charivaris. And citizen-constables serving in person could not offset these unpaid duties by fees for paid services, such as making arrests or serving summonses, since, as we will see, these were monopolized by professional police. Hence, the office was to be avoided if at all possible.

As Table 4.1 shows, the Montreal justices nominated constables from a range of social classes, from merchants down to artisans, but with few labourers.[40] The largest group of nominees, perhaps a third, were artisans, but another fifth were merchants, including a few prominent members of the city's business community such as John Molson (nominated in 1802) and Alexander Auldjo (nominated in 1795, just a year before he became a justice of the peace). Still, the broad exemptions under the ordinance meant that many members of the elites were automatically exempted: in 1796, for example, the attorney general advised the justices that the ordinance's reference to 'civil officers' being exempted included professionals holding commissions from the crown, such as notaries and land surveyors, and the exemption of militia officers and of justices themselves also meant that many of the most prominent members of the city's elites never served. As well, while the ordinance made no mention of gender, and in England women were not automatically excluded (since they could provide substitutes), the Montreal justices limited their nominations to men only.[41]

Table 4.2: Professions of Quebec City constables, 1798–1822

Profession	#	%
Merchants	30	7
Other elites	1	1
Retailers/traders	4	1
Tavern-keepers	91	22
Farmers	3	1
Artisans	253	62
Other popular class	16	4
Other	10	2
Total	408	100

The status of the nominees becomes understandable when we consider that substitution functioned as a form of indirect taxation. There are no records of the arrangements between nominees and substitutes, but the situation was probably similar to that in England, where most substitutes were paid by the nominees. This allowed justices to place some of the burden of policing on members of their own social class without incurring the resistance that would inevitably have ensued had merchants like John Molson been forced to serve summonses or watch over prisoners in court. As well, as in London in the late seventeenth century, many of the artisans appointed were more substantial trades-men, such as bakers, butchers, or master shoemakers, who had the means to pay for substitutes. This was regressive taxation, however, and substitution was not equally accessible to all nominees: while all merchants appointed substitutes, buying their way out of this 'civic' duty, a significant minority of artisans did not, serving in person instead.[42]

In Quebec City, as Table 4.2 shows, the justices proceeded differently, with a far more evident class bias. Merchants were rarely named; instead, almost two-thirds of nominees were artisans, and the few 'merchants' named were probably smaller shopkeepers. As in Montreal, however, the Quebec City justices appointed few labourers – as the high constable explained in 1821, he had personally visited all those appointed, both to ensure their respectability and to avoid any injustice such as calling out poor folk whose families would suffer in consequence. The Quebec City justices did appoint more tavern-keepers, but the burden of the office certainly did not fall largely on them. Instead, it was squarely directed at the more prosperous ranks of the labouring population.[43]

Even in Montreal, the class interests underlying the system become clear when we consider what happened after 1821, when the justices abruptly disallowed substitution and returned to a system of citizen-constables serving in person. McCord and Mondelet explained this rather disingenuously to the Executive Council in 1822:

> Heretofore, by some strange inadvertence, the magistrates have followed what was considered the practice in England, and appointed a certain number of inhabitants, being householders, to act as constables for one year, and as in England a constable is a parish officer, they were taken from the whole community, not exempt, and where the person nominated did not chose to serve in person, he was allowed to provide a substitute. This was attended for some time back with much inconvenience, as the substitutes produced were mostly very indifferent characters, or very ignorant, and the office fell into disrepute. To obviate this unpleasant circumstance, we have endeavoured to provide a set of men to do the duty, who know each other, respectable tradesmen, who agreed to volunteer it, provided no substitutes were received.[44]

It is scarcely credible that these experienced magistrates inadvertently allowed the appointment of substitute constables for over a decade. Rather, the change roughly coincided with the professionalization of the Police Office constables and the establishment of the watch, both discussed below, which rendered the system of substitutes largely unnecessary. Almost immediately, the justices ceased appointing members of elites as constables; the vast majority of constables from 1821 onwards were artisans, tavern-keepers, and other retailers, as in Quebec City. The burden of policing had shifted definitively away from the city's elites.

The system of substitutes gave the cities exactly what the Legislative Council apparently had not intended, a police that was composed largely not of citizen-constables but of justice professionals or semi-professionals, with a small core of active, professional police. In Montreal, of the original five substitutes appointed in 1788, at least three had previous policing experience, including Jacob Marston, who had been a bailiff since 1783 and, with his wife, keeper of the courthouse since 1786.[45] And, of substitute appointments made between 1788 and 1820, over 80 per cent were of individuals who acted as substitutes two times or more, and 60 per cent were of twenty-eight individuals who acted as substitutes five times or more. In other words, of the approximately 550

constable appointments made by the justices, about half were monopolized by a small group of long-term, habitual substitute constables.

To put this into concrete terms, consider the constables appointed by
the justices in Montreal in 1800 and 1815. In 1800 the justices appointed
seventeen constables, of whom only three served in person. Of the
fourteen substitutes, only two had never been constables before, while
seven had been substitutes continuously since 1795 or earlier, and two,
Marston and Philippe Garnot, had been bailiffs even before the establishment of the constables in 1787. Further, twelve of the fourteen
substitutes were named as substitutes again in the following year.
There was less continuity in 1815: more citizen-constables served in
person (six of twenty-two appointed), though this still left sixteen substitutes, and of the substitutes, half had never been constables before.
However, there were still six constables who had been substitutes since
before 1810, including Frederick Charles, first appointed in 1795, and
Gaspard Degan and Claude Thibault, both substitutes since 1806. And
twelve of the substitutes were appointed again in 1816, re-establishing
the strong pattern of continuity.

The ethnic and class profile of the Montreal substitutes closely resembled that of the city bailiffs who preceded them. Of the approximately 150 individuals named as substitutes between 1788 and 1820,
about two-thirds were francophones, mainly *Canadiens*, including five
of the seven substitutes who served ten years or more. The remainder
were a mix of British and a smaller number with Germanic names, in all
likelihood former soldiers. As well, as one might expect, they were
generally drawn from the popular classes, mainly labourers and artisans. Many of the substitutes were neither professional nor even semi-
professional police but simply place-fillers for the nominees; as the
attorney general described the substitutes in Quebec City, 'they are
generally worthless and useless, and will take any thing that is given to
them.' Many were probably artisans or labourers for whom acting as a
constable was a part-time pursuit undertaken in addition to a primary
occupation: Jacques David, for example, a substitute between 1815 and
1818, was a shoemaker. These likely had the same relationship to policing as nominees who served in person, simply filling the basic requirements of showing up at the various courts and on occasions such as
executions where all constables were expected to attend. Thus, there is
no record of David ever acting as police, although he was once fined for
not attending the Quarter Sessions.[46]

Among the 150 substitutes, however, there were thirty-one who acted as police with more regularity. Of these, seventeen were *Canadiens*, but only four were British, the rest having Germanic names, though some were integrated into the *Canadien* community through marriage. In this respect, they were similar to rural civil bailiffs in the 1780s and 1790s, most of whom were *Canadiens*, along with a few assimilated Germans, and they also marked a continuity with the police of Montreal before 1787. Even more than in the magistracy, the coercive face of British justice in Montreal was not very British at all.

Many of these active substitutes were justice professionals. For some, the office of substitute constable was only one of several concurrent state positions, usually connected with the justice system. Until 1810, several of the active substitutes were professional bailiffs who acted for both the civil and criminal courts, just as the bailiffs had done before 1787. Some even moved from being substitute constables to holding more permanent, salaried state positions: after coming to Montreal from William Henry, Andrew Kollmyer was an active substitute constable from 1795 to 1802, a civil bailiff at the same time, the main sheriff's bailiff in 1803–6, and finally, from 1807, town crier, a post he held until 1817.[47]

But professional bailiffs aside, the justices also encouraged the existence of a small corps of semi-professional, full-time police by creating a number of semi-permanent, paid police positions and awarding them to long-serving, active substitutes. Funds available to the justices for policing purposes in Montreal were non-existent before 1796, and limited thereafter. A 1796 act imposing local rates only allowed the justices to use £30 for 'general purposes of police' other than public works, an amount that had to cover everything from burying dead animals through arresting beggars and vagrants to the services of the town crier, and though this was raised to £100 in 1802, it was still clearly insufficient to support any kind of professional police establishment.[48] However, this did not deter the justices, especially under Thomas McCord and Jean-Marie Mondelet in the 1810s, who paid little heed to the legislated limits: when a committee of justices examined the city's finances for 1817–18, they found that the police fund had expended over £250.[49] There were also other funds on which the justices could draw, including the £100 per year that was granted by the central administration to cover the expenses of the Police Office and salaries paid directly by the central administration. In all, the justices had enough resources at their disposal to ensure that a small core of active substitute constables received what was in effect a base salary, to which they added whatever fees they could collect either from private individuals or from the central administration.

The most important of these paid positions created by the justices was that of high constable. In eighteenth-century England, high constables were appointed annually from among the middling members of the community, their chief responsibility being to oversee the petty constables. In Quebec and Lower Canada, however, the position was both salaried and more permanent. In 1795 the Montreal justices chose one of the most active substitute constables, Jacob Marston, an American Loyalist immigrant and former land agent of the governor of New Hampshire, and kept him in office until 1820. From 1796, Marston, though appointed by and responsible to the justices, was paid an annual salary of £20 by the central administration, and from 1799 the justices themselves added an annual stipend of about £5 for attending them in Special Sessions. Marston also received substantial fees from both government and private parties for making arrests, serving summonses and subpoenas, summoning the other constables, and performing a wide variety of administrative services for the justices. Finally, from 1802 until 1815, he and his wife received another £80 per year from government as keepers of Montreal's new courthouse (they had lived in the old one for free since the mid-1780s). Altogether, this made a not insubstantial income for the justices' high constable, derived largely from the public purse, and allowed Marston to be very much a full-time criminal justice professional.[50]

Apart from the high constable, the Montreal justices also established other minor paid positions for constables. From 1799 at least, they revived the practice of having constables attend the market, but rather than rotating these duties among all constables, in 1800 they appointed Louis Sabourin, one of the long-serving active substitutes, as market constable, paying him £4 per year. They kept paid constables, generally long-serving active substitutes, in the markets until 1817, with the two market constables in that year making about £20. As well, from at least 1814, the chairmen, Mondelet and McCord, also employed a 'runner' for the Police Office, at a salary of £18–£20 per year, who acted as both a messenger and a constable; and once again they filled the post with active substitute constables, the last, Louis Marteau, being in office from 1816 to 1830 and continuing to act for the Peace Office in the 1830s. Finally, the justices also made occasional lump-sum payments to professional substitutes that were clearly intended as income supplements: £5 to Claude Thibault in 1811, for example, ostensibly for delivering notices to tavern-keepers regarding strangers but, in reality, as McCord noted, 'being fully due for many services to the police office not provided for.'[51]

The effect of all of these payments was that, between 1800 and 1818, the justices kept between two and four professional substitute constables on the public payroll in one way or another: in the early 1800s, Jacob Marston and Louis Sabourin; around 1810, Marston, Claude Thibault, Jean-Baptiste Morin, and perhaps Mikel Souther; and in the later 1810s, Marston, Thibault, Louis Marteau, and perhaps André Boileau. Along with one or two other long-serving substitutes to whom the justices regularly directed warrants and other orders but who were never given salaried posts, such as Andrew Kollmyer and Frederick Schmidt in the late 1790s and early 1800s, Jean Bauert in the late 1810s, and Frederick Charles throughout, these formed the core of professional police in Montreal.

This core of professional constables developed a professional identity, much as bailiffs had during the French regime. Thus, a petition presented to the justices in July 1809 Quarter Sessions from 'all of the constables belonging to the said court,' signed only by Marston, Thibault, Charles, and Morin, complained that 'it is, and hath been customary in this city for the Bailiffs of His Majesty's Courts of King's Bench to execute nigh all the warrants & summons that herto [sic] hath been issued from the Clerks [of the peace] office, to the great damage of us, constables' and asked that in future all warrants and summonses be directed to them alone.[52] The constables' assertions were not true: almost all extant arrest warrants and summons from the period were directed to serving substitute constables, mostly the small group of professional substitutes identified above. They essentially monopolized the business: as Jacob Marston, Montreal's high constable, declared in 1817 regarding the ordinary constables, 'it hath hitherto been customary to summon to constables only to attend on the Court of Quarter Sessions of the Peace.'[53]

Though the picture is sketchier for Quebec City, it seems that a similar system existed there as well. The Quebec City justices had appointed a high constable from 1788, and, as in Montreal, the position was a permanent one, with only three different high constables until the early 1820s. From 1814, the central administration paid a small annual stipend, and the position was held by individuals with other salaried state offices. The first high constable, Hugh Mackay, was the keeper of Quebec City's special gaol in the 1790s, and his successors, John Bentley

(1798–1813) and Robert Chevalier D'Estimauville (1814–23), were also the capital's chief public works officials, under the authority of the justices. But Bentley and D'Estimauville were less exclusively concerned with criminal justice than Marston in Montreal, and also of higher social status: Bentley was a distinguished musician and organist of both the Catholic and Anglican cathedrals, while D'Estimauville, an immigrant French nobleman, was also the Quebec district's deputy *grand-voyer* and would become a highly active justice of the peace from 1823. In Quebec City, therefore, the high constableship was still very much a part-time affair, an adjunct to other positions, as D'Estimauville himself put it, and part of the ancien-régime system of multiple 'places,' while in Montreal it was well on the way to becoming a principal, professional justice profession.[54]

There are also indications of a small core of professional constables in Quebec City, as in Montreal. Gabriel Landry, for example, was named a constable almost every year from at least 1798 until his death in 1806; he was active as a constable in prosecuting unlicensed tavern-keepers and people who infringed the police regulations; he seems also to have been a crier in the justices' courts; and, though the constable lists gave his profession as shoemaker, his death certificate identified him simply as *huissier*. His son, Michel, petitioned to replace him as constable, and occasionally served as such; more important, he would become crier of most of the courts in Quebec City, with his sons in turn following suit. Like the Delisles in Montreal, but at a much humbler level, the Landrys were a judicial dynasty, launched by Gabriel. And there are others as well: John Johnston, for example, named as a constable in various years between 1804 and 1814, identified as a tavern-keeper in the lists but as a bailiff elsewhere, and in 1812 briefly serving as gaoler.[55]

From the 1790s to the 1810s, policing in the cities was thus the business of a voluntary, vocational police force, with considerable continuity in personnel and dominated by a small number of paid justice professionals, which in many ways resembled the system in place before 1787. Even the accoutrements were the same, with the constables in both cities receiving staves of office just like the bailiffs'. But the urban police also resembled their pre-1787 counterparts in another way: the system did not necessarily function as it should, largely because of the police themselves. Frequent fines on constables for not attending the Montreal Quarter Sessions suggest discipline problems, though the core of active substitutes was far less likely to be fined. Some of the most active professional police in Montreal were themselves accused of engaging in criminal activity. Mikel Souther, for example, was indicted in the Quarter Sessions in July 1815 for keeping a brothel, and not reappointed as a substitute after that. And finally, while the system of paid substitutes may have sufficed for everyday policing, it was not up to the task of controlling mass challenges to authority. Consider the following account submitted by Marston, the Montreal high constable, for his efforts in suppressing a charivari in November 1816: 'summoning all the constables to be and appear at the Court House this evening at 6 o'clock with their staves in order to stop the sheverree people from a riot in the streets and disturbing Milote house and preventing the mobb doing damage by order of Mr. Mondelet ... attending and patrolling same night with 3 constables others runaway ... [next night] patrolling all night with 2 constables only all the others runaway first of the evening myself knocked down by the mobb and nigh murdered.' And even if they did not run away, constables expected to be paid for their services, even when suppressing public disturbances; in 1817, for example, the high constable charged a fee to the returning officer in a Quebec City by-election for his efforts in controlling election violence.[56]

Partly because of these sorts of problems, in the late 1810s, policing in Montreal at least began to come under increasing criticism from the city's elites, corresponding to the changes in elite attitudes towards crime noted by Jean-Marie Fecteau. Thus, in 1816 the *Montreal Herald*, in describing a robbery, noted that 'we cannot help pointing out to the Magistrates the necessity of establishing a more rigid system of police for the better protection of the lives and property of the citizens.'[57] Again, as in the late 1780s, the result was significant structural changes, with the establishment of a professional watch and of professional constables attached to the Police Office, along with the disappearance of the system of substitute constables; but at the same time the system in the 1820s maintained many of the same basic characteristics as that which preceded it, both in its organization and in its personnel.

Urban Police Reform in the Late 1810s

In 1816, John Fletcher, Quebec City's chairman, was invited by the acting governor, Major-General John Wilson, to put in writing his thoughts regarding the 'general Improvement of the Police of Quebec.' The lengthy document he prepared demonstrates the fundamental shift already occurring in the meaning of the term 'police' itself: while Fletcher did address the subject of police in the older sense of public order, he put the emphasis on the police in the new sense then gaining ground in England, a force of men for maintaining law and order. The first three points of his document proposed a complete reorganization of the police:

> 1stly Of the Establishment and maintenance of a body of Police Officers attached to the Public Offices as is the case in London
> 2ndly Of the division of the City into Wards or divisions, and the Establishment of a local subordinate police for each of them
> 3dly Of the Nightly Watch or patrole

On police officers, he noted that, while the annual appointment of constables might suffice for country parishes and villages, it was not suited for large towns, since it was necessary to employ 'those only who have served a considerable apprenticeship to the business of repressing rapine and plunder,' 'a body of men of activity and intelligence whose sole duty it is to render themselves acquainted with all the different artifices by which depradations are carried on, the most frequented streets of the depredators and even with the persons and characters of the most notorious amongst them.' He proposed hiring four of them, at £25 per year each, attached to the Police Office. On ward police, he suggested that the town be divided into six or eight wards, with a tradesman or artisan appointed ward constable in each, with a small £10 salary, and inferior constables at their disposition, echoing policing systems elsewhere in North American colonial cities such as Boston or Saint John. Finally, as to establishing a stipendiary watch, 'as is done in every other city of equal population, throughout the civilized world,' he was pessimistic, given 'the excessive degree of public outcry which even the slightest pecuniary impost occasions in this province,' which he attributed mainly to the *Canadiens*, more than willing to serve government in person but extremely averse to any form of payment. Since a night watch throughout the city and suburbs at £4,000 per year was unrealistic, the ward constables and subordinates should do occasional rounds instead, with assistance from soldiers of the nearest guardhouse.[58]

The ideas expressed in Fletcher's proposals were already circulating. A bill to set up watches in Montreal and Quebec City had been introduced earlier in the year but failed to pass; and in 1818 the grand jury of the Montreal Quarter Sessions echoed Fletcher's first and third points, as well as his use of the word police:

... they cannot but express their sincere regret that depradations to an alarming extent have untill very recently been committed within the precincts of this city, that in order to assist the magistracy in the prevention of crimes as well as in the detection of offenders they are of opinion that a certain number of active, intelligent, and vigilant persons should be appointed by them as Police Officers whose duty should be exclusively to search after and execute the orders of the Magistrates in the detection of culprits in a similar manner as those employed by the Police Officers [sic] in London and that they should receive an annual salary in compensation of their service. The jurors are also of opinion that the lighting of the streets and the establishment of a general nightly watch would tend most materially to secure the repose and preserve the property of the citizens during those hours where these hordes of depredations let themselves loose to prey on the public.[59]

Nor were these ideas entirely novel, even in the colony. During Thomas McCord's abortive attempt to set up a Police Office in 1794–5, he regularly employed constables for serving summonses and arresting suspects, and as we saw, the Montreal Police Office had a salaried runner who was also an active substitute constable. As for a watch, the idea had been bandied about since the eighteenth century. In 1764, when Quebec City's justices asked that soldiers act as watchmen, it was to be 'under the same orders and regulations as the nightly Watch of the City of London,' while in 1779 Montreal residents presented a petition to the justices stating that 'a town watch for the better security of the place against accidents by fire or otherwise would be essentially necessary this season,' and both cities saw other temporary watches from time to time. But none of these measures was permanent, and some encountered resistance from the highest quarters: as we saw, McCord's attempt to set up a staffed Police Office was squashed by Dorchester, and when Montreal residents went ahead in 1779 and set up a citizen's watch without the approval of the executive or the magistracy, Haldimand asked the sheriff to inquire into it 'as such a proceeding seems altogether new and extraordinary.'[60] The reforms of the late 1810s were both more permanent and more fundamental.

High Constables and Police Constables from the 1820s

The reforms in the police attached to the Police Offices, like the earlier creation of semi-permanent salaried posts, were local initiatives of the justices, without executive or legislative sanction. In Quebec City, by the 1820s, permanent constables were attached to the Police Office, under the direction of the chairmen, and received a salary of £10 to £20 per year, though most of their income still came from fees or, more dubiously, the selective prosecution of unlicensed tavern-keepers. Apart from their remuneration, these police constables, between two and four at any particular time, were increasingly similar to the 'modern' police that would follow them after the Rebellions. They were permanently in office across long periods and generally named separately from the usual constable-nomination process; they derived their livelihood from their 'humble situation,' as one called it, and referred to themselves as 'police constables'; they were issued belts, swords, and guns as part of their office and asked to return them when they left; and they were subject to discipline by the supervising magistrates. At the end of the 1820s, for example, two of the four Police Office constables were fired by Robert Christie for having complained to the executive about his not paying them. Along with the city's high constable, and a further small group of long-serving but unsalaried constables, these police constables formed the professional police force of Quebec City. The system continued into the 1830s despite the disappearance of the Police Office, with three of the four police constables who had served in the late 1820s still in office until 1832 at least, and incorporation changed little, since the City Council had responsibility only for the watch and for its own police regulations. Like the police that were to follow them after the Rebellions, however, the Quebec City constables represented a significant shift from the older system of bailiffs and substitutes in one important respect: few were *Canadiens*, with both high constables and eight of the ten most active constables in the 1830s being British. Like the magistracy itself, the face of the police in Quebec City was increasingly alien to the *Canadien* majority.[61]

Similar developments reshaped the Montreal police in the 1820s. By the end of the 1810s, the system of maintaining a small core of full-time, professional substitutes had begun to crumble. Jacob Marston, the incumbent high constable, was in his sixties and by 1822 was described as 'notoriously superannuated.' Further, in 1818–19 financial constraints compelled the justices to suspend payments to the market constables and then to abolish the posts permanently.[62] At the same time that the old system was being dismantled, though, the justices were putting in place a new system of professional police entirely separate from the constables named under the 1787 ordinance. In 1817, using their powers to appoint special constables, McCord and Mondelet had begun employing Richard Hart, in addition to Jacob Marston and two other regular substitutes attached to the Police Office, and in 1818 they asked Hart to act as their main Police Office constable. At first he worked in concert with Marston but eventually displaced him and the other substitutes, and by 1821 Marston had resigned as high constable in favour of Hart, in return for a £60 pension. McCord and Mondelet also housed their constable in rooms in the courthouse, to keep him near to their office. Hart hired deputies to assist him, whom the justices generally named as special constables attached to the Police Office. Thus was launched a new system of professional policing.[63]

The modern conception of state-supported policing embodied in this new system, completely at odds with the philosophy behind the 1787 ordinance but in line with the thinking of Fletcher in 1816, becomes evident if we consider the accounts the police constables submitted to government in felony cases. In 1817 Hart, Marston, and the other police constables charged fees for executing at least 79 arrest or search warrants; in 1818 this number rose to 89; in 1819 it jumped to 204; and in the first nine months of 1820, it rose again to 275. For all of this police activity, Marston and Hart expected to be handsomely rewarded: between November 1818 and September 1820, for example, their accounts totalled over £800 in expenses and fees for themselves and their 'recors' or assistants (usually the other police constables), a huge increase from the average of perhaps £50 per year charged by Marston in earlier years. The charges for arresting a single offender were sometimes outrageous: for instance, substantial mileage fees meant that, for a single search and arrest at Sainte-Anne amounting to one day's work, Hart charged over £7. This was thus a potentially profitable business, and seen as such by the principles: in 1819, when Hart concluded a private agreement with Marston to share the duties of the offices of high and police constable with him, they also agreed to split the profits and losses as if it were a business partnership. The constableship, though foreshadowing professional, state-remunerated police, was still in transition between private place and bureaucratic position.[64]

The clash between old and new conceptions of the organization of policing became the focus of disagreement between the judicial establishment at Montreal – especially McCord and Mondelet – and the central administration, with the chairmen pressuring the administration to appoint a police office constable at a fixed salary as in London, and the administration resisting any increase in the civil list at a time when expenses were becoming a point of contention with the Assembly. Thus, the executive refused to pay more than a fraction of Hart and Marston's accounts and in 1822 even suspended the five-shilling payments it had been making since 1796 for the arrest of felons, on the grounds that the constables appointed under the 1787 ordinance should perform the service for free. Citizen-constables, of course, did nothing of the sort, and for about a year, as one Montreal newspaper pointed out almost every time it reported on a robbery, the city's professional police officers had to rely on whatever they could get from private individuals, a return to the older, victim-supported conception of policing. But the financial situation eventually stabilized: by the end of 1823, the Police Office's budget had been increased to £200 per year, including payments for apprehending felons; from 1821, the justices also granted Hart a salary of £50 to enforce the city's police regulations; and in 1822 the justices readily acceded to his petition that only he and the 'under constables' be allowed to serve warrants issuing from the Police and Peace Offices, giving him effective control over the lucrative business of everyday policing in the city. At the same time, McCord and Mondelet suppressed constable substitution in 1821, and thereafter, apart from occasional riots or fires, the citizen-constables named under the 1787 ordinance had little to do with everyday policing. The position came to be seen largely as a burden, with reformers even charging that constable nominations were intended to punish the administration's opponents.[65]

Though a permanent, professional police was now established under the direct control of the professional magistrates, there were still difficulties. Hart continued to have trouble getting paid for his earlier work, and he was also terminally ill. He died in 1823, and his successor, Archibald Henry Ogilvie, was in office less than six months before being sacked for participating in the John Johnson affair that led to Calvin May being censured. The justices' next appointment, of Adelphe Delisle, was sounder but led them into direct conflict with Dalhousie, who had his own candidate. In response to the justices' refusal to cede their local autonomy, he revoked Delisle's salary and then removed McCord and Mondelet as chairmen. Yet, after this dubious start, policing in Montreal once again became the business of a small group of long-serving, largely francophone, professional constables centred on the high constable. Delisle remained in office until his death in 1831, regularly receiving his £50 salary for enforcing police regulations, submitting accounts averaging about £50 per year through the Police Office for arrests and searches, and, from 1826, once again receiving a salary from the central administration, to all of which was added the fees he claimed from private parties. After he died in 1831, Delisle was replaced by his uncle, Benjamin, a former soldier in the Canadian Fencibles and John Delisle's brother, who remained in office beyond the Rebellions.[66]

The Montreal justices also continued to appoint police constables, with two to four in office at any one time; these included Louis Marteau, who was still receiving his salary as runner of the Police Office, and Antoine Lafrenière, who was in office from 1827 until the early 1830s. Likewise, paid constables reappeared in the markets, though they were now hired by the market clerks; by the mid-1830s, there were three or four of them. Nor did the disappearance of the Police Office in 1830 mean the end of professional constables like Marteau or Lafrenière, who simply continued under the Peace Office, named as special constables by the justices and sometimes still referred to as police constables.[67] And, as in Quebec City, administration by the Montreal City Council between 1833 and 1836 changed little, apart from transferring the high constable's responsibility for enforcing police regulations to a new municipal official, the police inspector, who complained bitterly of being under-funded and without constables to help him (though by the mid-1830s the duties were split between two different officers). In 1836, in its petition for renewal of incorporation, one of the City Council's complaints was that it lacked any control over the constables. In the mid-1830s, the Montreal professional constabulary thus closely resembled that of the late 1820s. It was composed of the high constable, Delisle, Louis Malo, and at least three other constables, Henry Hébert, André Dubé, and Joseph Potvin, referred to as 'connétables employés au bureau de la Police' [constables employed in the Police Office]. These were full-time police: together, they made about 200 arrests each quarter. Citizen-constables appointed under the 1787 ordinance did sometimes participate in policing, but most of the work was carried out by the professional constables or by the watch. And, unlike in Quebec City, this professional constabulary was apparently entirely composed of *Canadiens*. The face of the Montreal police had changed little since the 1760s.[68]

Despite undeniably being professional police, however, the high and police constables in both Montreal and Quebec City, like the professional substitutes who preceded them, certainly did not live up to the ideal of impartial defenders of the law, and were frequently accused of the arbitrary use of power and the circumvention of legal procedures.

One of the more egregious was the John Johnson affair, which led to Ogilvie's removal from office. On the strength of Calvin May's warrant, Ogilvie, police constable Antoine Lafrenière, and Benjamin Schiller (the deputy quartermaster of the Montreal watch) seized Johnson in Montreal and forcibly removed him to the United States, where he was wanted for theft, into the waiting hands of an American sheriff's officer. This led to the trial and conviction of Ogilvie, Schiller, and Lafrenière and their dismissal as police officers, and, as we saw, the censure of May and (eventually) the dismissal of Mondelet. As David Ross, king's counsel in Montreal, put it, 'this transaction is most disgraceful to the administration of justice in this country, as it but too clearly evinces that its under officers can lend themselves to do most illegal acts.' Police constables, including Adelphe and Benjamin Delisle, the high constables, were regularly accused of complicity in 'compounding,' the dropping of a complaint in return for payment. This seems to have been elevated into a system in Quebec City in the late 1820s, tacitly approved by the magistrates, while in Montreal, Benjamin Delisle was accused of selectively prosecuting tavern-keepers at the same time as he turned a blind eye to unlicensed houses kept by his cronies. The Montreal police constables were also heavily involved in the disastrous Montreal election riot of 1832: while the high constable, Delisle, was praised for his habitual calm neutrality, Louis Malo seems to have acted partisanly for the Tory forces, leading the hundreds of special constables, mostly Tories, who had been sworn in by Tory magistrates and who were a significant factor contributing to the riot that resulted in military intervention and the death of civilians. But none of these examples of malfeasance or political partisanship changed the fact that men like Ogilvie or Malo were undeniably professional police, nor lessened the burden of their activities on those they arrested, legally or illegally; and the police constables in this respect were behaving no differently from the urban police in Quebec through the rest of the nineteenth and much of the twentieth century.[69]

The Watch

In contrast to the police constables, the city watches were on firmer footing, since they were set up under acts of the legislature. Under the 1818 watch act, the justices of the peace of Quebec City and Montreal could organize a night watch made up of a foreman and up to twenty-four watchmen (increased to forty-eight in 1823), paid for by duties on tavern-keepers and auctioneers. In 1833 jurisdiction over the watches were transferred to the new city councils, but when the incorporations were not renewed in 1836, the watch expired along with the city councils.[70]

The Montreal watch provides a good example of how rapidly the justices proceeded. Within a matter of days of the passing of the 1818 act, they decided that the watch was to consist of a quartermaster at £75 per year, a deputy quartermaster as £50 per year, and eighteen watch-men at three shillings per day; struck a committee of five justices (all *Canadiens*) to oversee the watch; and appointed Emmanuel D'Aubreville as quartermaster, with instructions to find eighteen watchmen. A week later, they approved a set of eighteen regulations for the watch drawn up by Mondelet; appointed Antoine Lafrenière (the future police consta-ble) as deputy quartermaster; ordered that the watchmen whom D'Aubreville had by now recruited enter into notarized engagement contracts for six months; and resolved that the watch begin its activities the following week. The Quebec City justices followed a similar course, including the regulations and notarized contracts.[71]

The justices clearly intended their watches to be effective forces, modelled after the parish watches in England which, by the early nineteenth century, were far more organized, disciplined, and effective than has often been assumed.[72] The watches also represented a concrete concern not just for the protection of property but also for regulating urban society more generally. In the preamble to his regulations for the Montreal watch, Mondelet declared, 'L'on appelle Guêt un certain nombre d'hommes forts, robustes, et actifs réunis en corps, dont le devoir est de faire la veille dans les rues toute la nuit pour empêcher les déprédations, les vols et la commission de tous crimes ou délits qui affectent la société, ne fut ce qu'en troublant son repos' [The Watch consists of a certain number of strong, robust and active men, united in a body, whose duty is to watch the streets all night to prevent depreda-tions, thefts and the commission of all crimes or misdemeanours which affect society, even if only in troubling its repose]. And the Quebec City regulations provided a detailed list of those the watch was expected to arrest, including people breaking the peace; 'night-walkers, malefac-tors, rogues and vagabonds, and other loose, idle and disorderly per-sons' (terms lifted directly from English vagrancy statutes); people loitering in any 'Square, Street, Court, Lane, Yard, Alley, Passage or Place'; those against whom a hue and cry had been raised, or delivered to the watch by respectable householders; and, underlining the municipal purpose of the watch, people emptying dirt into the streets and refusing to identify themselves. Watchmen were to take their prisoners to the watch-house or gaol and bring them before a justice in the morning, ushering in an era of summary imprisonment that reshaped urban policing through the nineteenth century.

The regulations also saw the watches as regular and disciplined police forces. The officers were to keep detailed records of all that transpired and to make frequent reports to the justices, and they were held responsible for all aspects of the watch's operation and the actions of the watchmen. The watchmen themselves were subject to fines for disobedience or for leaving their posts, and immediate dismissal for corruption or drunkenness. In both cities, they were also issued standard equipment, with the emphasis on identifying them as public officers: in Quebec City, a coat, a constable's staff (with the king's arms), a rattle, and a numbered lantern; in Montreal, a staff, a whistle, and a badge marked G.R., to which were later added cloaks, caps, and grapnels.[73] As for distribution, the Quebec City regulations set up two watch-houses and specific stands for the watchmen in both the city and the suburbs, complete with watch-boxes. The Montreal regulations were less specific, leaving the arrangement up to the quartermaster and the committee of justices to whom he reported every week, and there were initially complaints that the watchmen did not keep to specific posts; however, by the mid-1820s, they were distributed as in Quebec City, and separated into two shifts.[74]

Though the watches were modelled after ancien-régime institutions, their target population, their emphasis on controlling urban public space, their uniforms, and their discipline also evoked later fundamental changes in policing. The watches were in essence transitional institutions towards the new police of the late 1830s. But this did not mean that the watch system actually set up was entirely satisfactory. One problem was the chronic shortfall in watch revenues. Already in 1819, the Montreal justices complained that the duties set aside to pay for the watches, amounting to about £1,600 per year, were insufficient to maintain a watch in both city and suburbs, and proposed more than tripling the annual budget. Their request was ignored, and instead revenues declined steadily, to about £1,300 in 1822. In 1823 duties were increased but revenues increased only slightly, to around £1,700–£1,800; they increased again in the 1830s, reaching a high of over £2,400 in 1833, but this did not even match the increase in the city's population, which had almost doubled since 1818. Nor did anything change substantially under the city councils, with continuing complaints that watch funding was wholly insufficient.[75]

Funding restrictions inevitably affected the size and distribution of the watches. In Quebec City, the watch seems to have stayed at the full strength envisaged by the legislature, though even this was sometimes insufficient: magistrates in the late 1820s claimed that they were often forced to call on the military for assistance in quelling disturbances, given the small number of watchmen. In Montreal, revenue shortfalls in 1820 led the justices to cut the number of watchmen by a third and discontinue lighting the city, though by 1824 the watch had once again grown to four officers and twenty men; by 1832 it had at least twenty-nine men and two officers, and there was a similar number of regular watchmen under incorporation, rising to perhaps thirty-one men by 1835. Still, even with those, the watch concentrated its efforts on the city centre, where merchants and other elites had their businesses and homes, with far less presence in the working-class suburbs. At the same time, these numbers should be put into perspective: Paris in 1789, an extremely well-policed city, had a guard composed of about a thousand individuals for a population of about 650,000, or one per 650 population; the equivalent for Quebec City in the mid-1830s was about one watchman per 625 population, and for Montreal, one per 1,000. This is not to suggest that Montreal and Quebec City were as well policed as Paris; most notably, the watches were, of course, only night-time institutions. But it does allow us to nuance the view that the watches were so small as to be ineffectual.[76]

In terms of ethnicity and class, the Montreal watchmen were much like the substitute constables, with the two groups even overlapping at the beginning, as many watchmen also served as constables at the same time. Like the substitutes, watchmen were primarily francophones: about two-thirds overall, including almost all the officers. The ethnic character of the Montreal watch fluctuated considerably, however, with more diversity at the beginning and end of its existence (in the mid-1830s, there were apparently both a 'Canadian' and an 'Irish' list of replacement watchmen) but an almost exclusively francophone watch in the late 1820s and early 1830s. In Quebec City, the watch was initially only about 40 per cent francophone, and though by the later 1820s and into the 1830s the proportion of francophones had climbed to about half, the watch never had the strongly francophone character it had in Montreal. Nevertheless, Louis-Bazile Pinguet, the Quebec City foreman throughout most of the period, under both the justices and the corporation (and likewise head of the police after the Rebellions), was a *Canadien*, along with several of his deputies. As with the magistracy and constabulary, the face of the watch was not necessarily that of the Conqueror.[77]

The watchmen's social status and background also resembled that of the constables, mainly labourers and artisans, but with a strong military element as well. Pinguet, for example, had been assistant adjutant-general of the Lower Canadian militia during the War of 1812, while D'Aubreville, the foreman of the Montreal watch until 1827, was a former officer who had fought in Swiss regiments. Both cities' watches also included a number of continental Europeans, mainly with Germanic names, who were in all likelihood former soldiers, along with men like William Macdonald, a Montreal watchman in the mid-1830s who had previously served twenty-two years in the 79th regiment. In this respect, the watches resembled professional police in other colonial cities, also often former soldiers.[78]

However, despite the military background of some watchmen, the watches did not necessarily work as the justices' regulations intended. The Montreal watch, for example, was frequently the subject of complaints. In 1823 a Quarter Sessions grand jury accused the watchmen of frequenting brothels while on duty, and their officers of being drunk and absent from their posts, of joining the men in gambling, of receiving prostitutes into the watch-house, and of appropriating the watch's firewood for their personal use – conduct that led the grand jury to conclude that 'a watch so conducted is no protection to the peaceable citizens of Montreal.' In 1827 three of the watch's officers, including the foreman, D'Aubreville, were fired for drunkenness and neglect of duty, after complaints from the watchmen themselves. And there were frequent accusations levelled against the watch and watchmen in the city's Tory press, usually centring around their inability to stop thefts. Nor did this change under incorporation, with further complaints against misconduct by officers and watchmen continuing through the 1830s, some coming from watchmen themselves.[79]

Antipathy towards the watch's officers came from *Patriotes* as well as Tories: the 1827 purge, for example, was at the initiative of a committee composed entirely of *Canadiens* and supported by justices from both political factions, while at another level, in 1820, André-Auguste Mallard was accused of assaulting D'Aubreville and calling him 'un mouchard de la ville et des magistrats, un espion des Anglais et un traitre à sa patrie' [an informer for the city and the magistrates, a spy for the English and a traitor to his homeland]. But the broader complaints against the watch as a whole were generally the product of hostility on the part of the town's British and Tory elites, rather than any reflection of the reality of policing. The most striking instance of this occurred in the mid-1830s, when the watch came under control of the *Patriote*-led City Council. Soon after entering office, the council set up an inquiry into the watch, which concluded that the foreman appointed by the justices, Pierre Rottot, a former lieutenant in the Canadian Chasseurs and Tory supporter, was undisciplined, intemperate, and a bad book-keeper to boot; the council replaced him with their own nominee, Augustin Fréchette, a bankrupt merchant and *Patriote* sympathizer. Then, during an election in 1834, the council decided to use the watch to maintain order, so as to avoid the partisan violence and bloodshed of the 1832 elections. This was seen by Montreal Tories as a blatant attempt by *Patriotes* to control the polls, especially since the council had quite illegally increased the number of watchmen by several hundred. Tories organized their own forces, essentially bullies, and watchmen and Tory bullies clashed repeatedly, with the watch-house being sacked, pitched battles being fought in the streets, and, eventually, the watch being forced for several months to abandon its posts and make its rounds as a group, if at all. The conflict over the watch became an important factor in the non-renewal in 1836 both of Montreal's charter and of the watch act, leading to the disappearance of the watch in May. With Quebec City's charter also not renewed, the watch disappeared there as well, though in both cities temporary patrols were organized for a few months in 1837–8.[80]

But British and Tory antipathy towards the watch had deeper roots than the 1834 elections. Many members of the British elites had long resented the watchmen's attempts to control their often rowdy amusements. In 1819, for example, a correspondent of the *Montreal Herald* complained that while the watch did little to stop charivaris, they were all too ready to come down on gentlemen:

A short time ago a Gentleman was passing to his lodgings, and in the moment of hilarity happened to utter something in imitation of an Indian yell. Immediately one or two of these Night Guardians came up and desired that he would go peaceably, stating, it was their orders to permit no noise to be made in the streets. The gentleman expostulated, a whistle was given, and he was immediately surrounded and conveyed to the Guard House. Shortly afterwards he was summonsed to give bail for his

appearance before the magistrates. Here was prompt duty executed. But
to interrupt a Charivarie! there's danger in it!

And there are many other examples of such conflicts. In 1821 a large
crowd of probably British rioters was carrying out a charivari in front of
the widow Hutchison's house, when the watch intervened and made
several arrests; and in 1834 a crowd assaulted the watch-house, broke
the windows, burst in the door with battering rams, and rescued the
prisoners. On a more individual level, in 1825, two British lawyers and
a nephew of the sheriff assaulted a *Canadien* watchman when he ac-
costed them on their leaving Rasco's Hotel, a favourite elite drinking
establishment, wrenching away his staff, and later gathered a crowd of
their friends to assault him and other watchmen (including Rottot, the
future foreman), with the sheriff's nephew declaring, 'By God I will
beat the watch-men every night after this,' and the crowd eventually
moving off singing, 'We will fight and conquer again and again.' In
1830 one of the same lawyers, Campbell Sweeney, was involved in
another affray with the watch and vowed, 'I will in future carry pistols
in my pockets and shoot every watchman who will attack me in the
same manner as I was tonight.' Even Thomas McCord's own son,
William King (later a police magistrate), was accused of insulting and
assaulting watchmen, including the foreman D'Aubreville, in the company of a number of other young British elite men. Conflicts over the
watch spilled over into the magistracy itself: in 1828–9 David Ross, then
chairman, hired a former Dublin police officer, William Moon, to spy
on the largely *Canadien* watch, without informing the other members of
the watch committee, which so incensed *Canadien* magistrates that they
used it in their testimony before the Assembly as yet another example
of the tyranny of the chairmen. Tory criticism of the watch was thus
shaped by both class and political considerations. In contrast, *La Minerve*,
while it criticized the under-funding of the watch, steadfastly defended
the watchmen and 'notre Guet' [our Watch] and praised the diligence
with which it carried out the difficult mission imposed on it – a striking
departure from the paper's regular denunciations of the justices themselves and their constables.[81]

Beset with problems the watches certainly were, resulting from inadequate funding, poor leadership, and, in Montreal at least, the antipathy of part of the city's elites. Nor were the watches complete police
forces: they functioned only at night, and certainly in Montreal, their
coverage of the suburbs was limited at best. And yet, like the police

constables, they cannot be dismissed as easily as many historians have done, especially from the point of view of those arrested by them. Consider that in the one year for which we have a fairly good record of the Quebec City watch's activity, 1827–8, watchmen and constables together arrested at least 900 people (excluding deserting seamen), and probably more, many of them for public-order offences, giving us a minimum arrest rate of about 38 per 1,000 population. In 1845 the equivalent figure under the new police was more than double, at about 85 per 1,000, but by 1854 it was back to 60 per 1,000, or perhaps one and a half times as much as under the old, and supposedly ineffectual, system of police constables and watchmen. The new police was certainly more active than the old, but the difference was more one of degree than of orders of magnitude.[82]

One testimony to the relative efficacy of the urban police is the relative infrequency of recourse to the army or urban militia. When Aubert de Gaspé in his 1866 *Mémoires* asserted that the only policemen in his childhood were the soldiers of the guard,[83] he was reflecting the prevailing mid-Victorian view on the birth of the modern police, not the reality of his childhood. Soldiers sometimes assisted in making arrests, especially in cases involving other soldiers, but military arrests of civilians in peacetime were exceptional, apart from in a handful of high-profile political cases. Soldiers also enforced state power during riots, charivaris, and other mass disturbances, but, even then, authorities were reluctant to call on the troops, with few instances before the Rebellions. As for the urban militia, it was only rarely involved in policing of any sort. In 1823, for example, a nightly charivari lasting three weeks challenged the Montreal magistrates' control of their city. The justices eventually called on the militia, but only after first deploying the watch and their own constables, then calling on the military, and then swearing in special constables. And even when they eventually turned to the militia, one of the city's commanders refused to help them, since he was not authorized to do so under the militia law. In short, instead of being the iron core of law enforcement under the ancien régime, military policing was an uncommon and sometimes weak reed.[84]

Rural Policing from the Late 1780s

As in the cities, policing in the countryside from the late 1780s to the 1830s did not correspond to what was envisaged by those who framed the 1787 ordinance. The ordinance placed the burden of rural policing on militia officers and sergeants, an intent consistently repeated in legislation through to the 1830s.[85] But, as before 1787, militia officers were in practice not the main agents of the criminal justice system in the countryside. As Richard Hart put it in 1823:

> The executive has been led to believe that the militia officers in the several parishes in the district are capable and competent for the purposes of executing the various warrants against persons in their vicinity, and that they are to do so by law is the case, but as sanguine as the expectations may be that the public duty can be done in this way ... the government can scarcely expect an officer of militia or any other to leave his business and go to execute a warrant and when he may have to spend money in doing it for love of country alone and without remuneration for his time or expenses ... I have endeavoured to put into execution the wish of the executive by calling upon officers of militia in the country parish [sic] to execute several warrants and which has failed twice out of three times. In calling upon an officer of militia to execute a warrant he knows better than to refuse but what is his reply: he tells you that the man who warrant is against lives three or four miles from him and that he the officer cannot walk there he has no horse, he do not feel well, he has a ferry to cross for which he must pay and has no money, but concludes by saying pay my expenses and I will go. Will the law fine this man? No, his excuse appears reasonable.[86]

Though Hart was evidently seeking to justify his own services and fees, his comments underscore a fundamental point: unpaid policing simply did not work, especially when there were professional police paid for their services.

Hart's assertions are borne out when we look at rural policing itself. Justices in the district of Montreal almost never directed arrest warrants against rural inhabitants to militia officers, nor did the sheriff employ them. And among the hundreds of prosecutions in both Quarter Sessions and King's Bench for assaults on officers, which show policing at its most active and conflictual, only a handful involved assaults on militia officers arresting prisoners. Even in matters directly concerning the militia or the army, such as desertion or disobedience, justices sometimes looked elsewhere: thus, when in 1814 Étienne Hénault, a militia captain from Beauharnois, complained to the local justice of the peace, François Tremblay, that Albert Mercier had been threatening him and making every effort to stop militiamen obeying his orders, Tremblay directed his arrest warrant not to any of the other local militia officers but to Charles Gabrion, a local bailiff, who arrested Mercier and took him to Montreal. Despite the legislative provisions, justices evidently preferred to avoid using militia officers as police. And so, when in the mid-1830s the colony's attorney general, Charles Richard Ogden, made the surprising and probably erroneous assertion that militia officers could not be compelled to follow justices' orders, the practical effect on the ground was probably less important than it might seem.[87]

Militia officers and even ordinary militiamen were nevertheless sometimes involved in policing, especially in the remoter areas of the colony. In 1823, for example, Benjamin Spearman, a militiaman from Odelltown, south of Montreal, and a former farrier in the Irish mounted police, was seriously wounded while trying to arrest a dozen men suspected of attempted murder, on orders from Robert Hoyle, a local justice. Like the army in the cities, rural justices sometimes called on the militia for assistance when suspects made concerted efforts to resist. Thus, when Jean-Baptiste Barbier *dit* Pretaboir *fils* resisted being arrested by Charles Lamothe, a Saint-Denis bailiff, on an assault warrant from Pierre Guerout, Guerout issued a further warrant ordering all militia and peace officers to assist, which had the desired effect: Pretaboir was arrested three days later and eventually fined forty shillings. But even then, militia officers were not necessarily reliable. In 1794, for instance, Jacob Marston was sent to the countryside to arrest Alexis Vaillant, one of the leaders of a crowd of voyageurs who had pulled down the pillory in Montreal and thrown it into the river. Marston reported that he was unable to make the arrest, since Vaillant 'shut himself up in his house, armed, and that the officers of the militia would not furnish him with the necessary assistance to effect his apprehension.' Coming only a month before more generalized resistance to a militia mobilization ordered by Dorchester, this incident underscored the extent to which the militia was an unreliable instrument of state power, though this did not save Vaillant from having to leave the colony to avoid being taken. Or again, in 1836, the colonial administration admonished Captain Alexander Cattanach for entrusting a warrant he had received from a Leeds magistrate, against one Catherine Lennox, to a boy, who lost it, and further declaring that he would sooner give up his commission than execute the warrant (a course which the administration denied him).[88]

Militia officers were also more often involved in conveying prisoners to the urban gaols after pre-trial examination. Thus, in 1824, Charles Charland, a Berthier-based King's Bench bailiff, claimed expenses for arresting Louis Latoure *père*, Charles Latoure, and Jean-Marie Latoure at Berthier for stealing from a carding mill, taking them before Joseph Douaire de Bondy, keeping them overnight, and conducting them and the stolen goods to the nearest militia captain, to be transferred from captain to captain to Montreal; the calendars of the Montreal prison show that the Latoures were committed one day later. For some strategically placed militia officers, this could become a heavy burden: in 1834 the militia officers of Lévis, across from Quebec City, complained that since all prisoners from the south shore of the St Lawrence necessarily passed through their parish, their duty was very heavy, and asked that bailiffs or constables be appointed to help them. But even in this respect, militia officers were not reliable agents of the state, since they sometimes exercised their own form of discretionary justice by allowing prisoners to escape. This seems to have been especially true of militia officers in the townships south of Montreal, along the American border. As Oliver Barker of Stanstead put it in 1814, in justifying having paid bailiffs to convey a prisoner to Montreal, 'it would have been of no use to have attempted to have sent him by way of the militia as there never was a man ordered to be sent to gaol from this country in that way who reached Montreal.' But militia officers elsewhere in the colony were also unreliable, and often failed to convey prisoners securely.[89]

Since militia officers were unreliable even for conveying prisoners, let alone for arrests, it is not surprising that both urban and rural justices mainly relied on others for coercive policing in the countryside. For this work, Montreal district justices generally used urban constables, who, like the city bailiffs before 1787, occasionally made forays at the justices' behest into the rural parishes around Montreal. With the increasingly active rural magistracy in the 1810s, the urban police's penetration in the countryside likely decreased, except briefly in the latter part of the decade: the accounts of Hart and Marston between 1817 and 1820 show that they made almost a hundred trips into the countryside to arrest prisoners in crown cases, often accompanied by other police constables as assistants.[90] The financial difficulties of the Police Office establishment in the 1820s diminished this sort of urban reach into the countryside, though it continued in especially lucrative matters such as prosecutions for selling liquor without a licence.

But, while urban police were sometimes active in rural areas, it was mainly rural inhabitants who acted as police for the justices, especially by the 1820s and 1830s, when criminal justice in the countryside was increasingly the business of rural justices. In 1822, for example, Charles Kilborn and Selah Pomeroy hired Andrew Patton, a Stanstead-based bailiff of the Court of King's Bench, to convey John S. Moores and Isaac Worthers to gaol. Worthers had been committed by the justices twice before but, though sent off with militia officers, he did not make it to Montreal and simply returned. Patton, on the other hand, 'was faithful in the discharge of his duty, altho' at great expence to him, being at a time the roads were bad and great danger in crossing the stream,' and both Moores and Worthers ended up in the Montreal gaol.

In the district of Montreal, a wide range of rural inhabitants acted as police, almost none of whom was a peace officer under the 1787 ordinance. They form a disparate group, from Henry Boright, a Saint-Armand blacksmith employed in 1827 by Jonas Abbott, the local justice of the peace, to arrest several people for kidnapping and take them to Montreal, to King's Bench bailiffs such as Charland or Patton. As before 1787, many appear to have been semi-professional bailiffs whose main business was probably serving civil process for the King's Bench or, from the 1820s, acting as commissioners for the trial of small causes. Some were employed on a semi-regular basis by local justices in criminal matters: for example, Gilles Guerbois, a Vaudreuil bailiff active between 1799 and 1825, or Francis Hogel, a Saint-Armand bailiff active between 1820 and 1830. The existence of this network of rural justice officers acting for the justices was tacitly acknowledged by an act of the legislature in 1833, which sought to regulate their (sometimes exorbitant) fees.[91]

Country bailiffs and urban constables were the main police active in the Lower Canadian countryside, but they were not the only ones. Consider an anecdote related in Félix Gatien's 1831 *Histoire du Cap Santé*. In 1808, Gatien related, a bill was passed to maintain good order in churches. Jean-Baptiste Dubord, the parish's *curé* and one of the bill's supporters, told the outgoing churchwardens that it was up to them to act as church constables. A pew was set up at the church door for the last three outgoing churchwardens; a cloak like a beadle's, a sash for slinging across the shoulder, and a constable's stave were made up; and each of the three churchwardens in turn, for a year, donned the uniform and acted as constable. This lasted until 1820, when a churchwarden, repulsed by the unpleasantness and the insults his predecessors had endured, refused to act. Thus ended Dubord's police establishment. From 1808 to 1821, successive acts had made churchwardens responsible for keeping good order in and around churches on Sundays, in effect, acting as police. Perhaps because of the difficulties in Cap-Santé, a new act was passed in 1821, allowing justices to appoint one or two constables to assist the churchwardens in their duties. This had apparently already been resorted to in at least one parish: in 1819 François Séguin, the church constable of Sainte-Marie, prosecuted Louis Choinière *dit* Sabourin, a Beloeil habitant, for being drunk in the church during divine service, to the great scandal of those present, and, at the end of the service, having at the church door flung blasphemies and insults at the churchgoers. Though in most parishes it was probably the church-wardens who continued to maintain order, church constables were nevertheless appointed in several rural parishes in both the districts of Quebec and Montreal: thus, Pierre-Louis Deligalle was named the church constable of Sorel in September 1821, and in April and May of the following year he prosecuted François-Paul Plante, Jacques Saint-Martin, and Louis Lelendre for being drunk on Sunday and Jean-Baptiste Lemery for indecent behaviour in church.[92]

For a short time, there were also constables named to enforce the police regulations that were sporadically extended to rural towns and villages. An 1802 act had made this the responsibility of local roads officials, but when it did not produce the desired results, a further act in 1807 allowed the Quarter Sessions to appoint police inspectors and constables for towns and villages on petition of the majority of house-holders. Until 1810, inspectors and constables were appointed in this way in several villages. However, the 1807 act was not renewed in 1811, and under an 1818 act, which once again set out general police regula-tions for towns and villages, only police inspectors were appointed, whose role was more as public prosecutors than police: in William Henry, for example, the police inspector from 1818 was Henry Crebassa, a local notary and justice of the peace.[93]

Since most of the offences that church and village constables and police inspectors were supposed to regulate were dealt with summarily before rural justices, for whom almost no records have survived, it is difficult to form any idea of how this system worked. There is, how-ever, one suggestive scrap of information: some of these men were in fact the sort of semi-professional rural justice officials described above. Thus, Charles Charland, the King's Bench bailiff, was appointed village constable of Berthier in 1809; and Deligalle, the church constable of William Henry, was also a King's Bench bailiff. Once again, the rural policing system was more professional than the legislative provisions might suggest. None of this changed the very evident fact that there were far fewer police, and thus far less policing, in the Lower Canadian countryside than in the cities. But it does caution us against assuming too rapidly that because militia officers were ineffective police, the criminal justice system, and the state as a whole, was essentially powerless in the countryside.

Conclusion

The history of the police in Quebec and Lower Canada illustrates many of the points that I have made about the everyday criminal justice system in the colony. First, there were significant differences between the system in theory and as it concretely presented itself. Despite the implantation of citizen policing on the English model, most active police were in fact justice professionals or semi-professionals, a pattern established in the first decade of British rule and continued until the 1830s. The face of the police was also far more *Canadien* than we might assume in a conquered colony. The continued reliance on French-regime bailiffs for policing in the first years following the Conquest set the tone for what was a classic instance of British indirect colonial rule, with the colonial state co-opting members of the colonized community into enforcing its orders. This reliance on *Canadiens* as police was such that some policing institutions, such as the Montreal watch, became political tools in the hands of those opposing colonial domination, in their struggle for electoral control with the Tories. Most police, however, whether *Canadien*, British, or other, continued to serve their colonial masters. Louis Malo, for example, was not only deeply involved for the Tories in the 1832 Montreal election but was also one of the constables whose forays into the countryside to arrest *Patriote* leaders helped spark the 1837 Rebellions, and while some rural bailiffs did become involved in the *Patriote* uprising, others remained committed to the existing system.[94]

Like the criminal law and the magistracy, policing also changed fundamentally across a period often seen as one of stasis. These changes occurred largely at a local level, and often through decisions made by local officials such as the justices rather than by the colonial executive and legislature. It was above all these local decisions that brought the system increasingly closer to a modern idea of professional police, frequently despite resistance from central authorities more concerned with economy. The shift was nevertheless not a smooth progression,

with many false starts and backward steps, just as in the professionalization of the magistracy. The disappearance of the city
watches from 1836, for example, made the criminal justice system
appear that much weaker in the cities and therefore fuelled calls for
policing reform that led to the new police institutions, which were
already being contemplated before the outbreak of armed conflict in
1837.[95] But these gaps in institutional coverage must not lead us to
dismiss policing as a whole, nor to underestimate the capacity of the
system to respond even to these difficulties. In Quebec City, for instance, though the disappearance of the watch provoked a near-panic
in the newspapers, it had little effect on the capacity of the state to arrest
and imprison everyday offenders.

The watches, of course, concerned only the towns, and, as with the
justice system as a whole, there were fundamental differences between
town and country. In the nineteenth century, the cities had increasing
numbers of what cannot be described as anything but full-time, professional police, beginning with the high constables and culminating with
the watch and police constables of the 1820s and 1830s. Rural areas
were less policed, especially since parish bailiffs and militia officers had
little to do with the criminal justice system except in specific circumstances. Still, the countryside was far from devoid of local police, such
as civil bailiffs or church constables. And when Delisle, Malo, and other
Montreal constables made their forays into the countryside prior to the
1837–8 Rebellions, it was not an unusual occurrence but rather a journey that urban police had made many times before, though generally
not for such political reasons.[96]

This is not to argue that the Quebec and Lower Canadian state was
well endowed with police, compared either to the police structures of
other contemporary states such as France or to the system put in place
in the late 1830s. There were far more police after the Rebellions, at least
temporarily, though, by the 1850s and 1860s, there were about the same
number of professional policemen per population in Montreal as there
had been in the mid-1830s, and in fact fewer in Quebec City.[97] Nor is it
to minimize the differences between the 'old' and the 'new' police:
permanent salaried positions, more bureaucratic organization, and even
uniforms changed the nature of the occupation. And the old system
was neither rationally constructed, nor suited to centralized control and
bureaucratic organization, nor anything but venal, nor at all free from
corruption and malversation. But concentrating too heavily on the form
of the police can lead to ignoring the material impact of their actions on

those who experienced them. To take constables as an example, that they were appointed every year and paid by fees does not mean that they were less permanent or well remunerated than professional police officers; that they were not part of a formal bureaucratic hierarchy does not mean that they were disorganized; that they wore no uniforms does not mean that they were not recognizable as police in the local community; and, in general, that they were not 'police' in the usual modern sense does not mean that they had little impact on society. From the perspective of 'Elaine Fortier, Dabby Lorimier, Angélique Clément, Lizette Brazeau, Scolastique Sans Chagrin, one Bouchard, two of the name of Brunelle, and two of the name of Charpentier,' brothel-keepers and prostitutes arrested in Montreal in December 1817, it did not matter that Jean Bauert and his three assistants were acting not within the confines of a hierarchical police structure but for a justice of the peace to whom they were informally attached, and not disinterestedly, but for the substantial fees, over £5; nor that Bauert himself, six years later, was arrested and imprisoned for breaking into and robbing the Police Office itself.[98] They were arrested and sent to prison nonetheless. And it is to the relationship between the people and this system of law, justices, and police that we now turn.

5

The Relevance of Criminal Justice

... from the litigious spirit of the Canadians in this district, my time is so taken up with my duty to the Crown and Publick, that I have scarce a moment to myself.

– Edward Abbott to Frederick Haldimand, 1782

En 1781, le nombre de ces réfractaires [aux] corvées s'étoit prodigieusement amplifié dans le district de Montréal ... une désobéissance, de nécessité, à la Police, est punie en crime volontaire & public; les réfractaires condamnés à l'amende de cinq liv. st.; & les impuissans d'indigence, claquemurés dans une indigne prison. Juste Ciel! des bêtes de charge qui regimbent contre un joug trop pesant, à qui on les attèle, pourroient-elles être plus sévèrement fustigées? Pauvres Canadiens, bridés, emmuselés, entravés & fouettés ainsi, sans pitié, sous le garrot! Bataille, première bataille de Québec, nous frapperez-vous toujours?

[In 1781, the number of those who refused the corvées increased dramatically in the district of Montreal ... a necessary disobedience to the Police is punished as a wilful and public crime; those who refuse condemned to a £5 Sterling fine; and the indigent who cannot pay clapped in a disgraceful prison. Great Heavens! beasts of burden who chafe against too heavy a yoke, to which they have been attached, could they be more severely punished? Poor *Canadiens*, to be bridled, muzzled, hobbled and whipped so, without pity, strangled! Battle, first battle of Quebec, will you always afflict us?]

– Pierre Du Calvet, 1784

Il n'y a pas d'autorité dans les villages, cependant l'ordre public s'y maintient mieux que dans aucun autre pays du monde. Un homme commet-il une faute, on s'éloigne de lui, il faut qu'il quitte le village. Un vol est-il commis, on ne dénonce pas le coupable, mais il est déshonoré et obligé de fuir.

[There is no authority in the villages, nevertheless public order is better maintained than in any other country in the world. If a man commits an offence, he is shunned, he must leave the village. If a theft is committed, the guilty party is not denounced, but he is dishonoured and forced to flee.]

– John Neilson in conversation with Alexis de Tocqueville, 1831[1]

Abbott, Du Calvet, and Neilson have left us three entirely different visions of the relevance of criminal justice to rural *Canadiens*. Abbott, a Saint-Jean justice, was asking for another justice to assist him. He gives the impression of hordes of habitants beating down his door to complain against each other, though for what is unclear, since there are few extant traces of Abbott's work. In contrast, Du Calvet was writing in vitriolic condemnation of Haldimand, who had arbitrarily imprisoned him and who was vigorously enforcing the laws that forced habitants to transport military stores. For Du Calvet, British criminal justice was a source of brutal oppression of the conquered by the Conqueror, a continuation of the battle of the Plains of Abraham, though he also lauded the humanity and justice of Montreal magistrates who refused to punish refractory *habitants*. And for Neilson, Lower Canadian parishes were self-regulating oases, where official justice was marginal at best. As he put it, 'à vrai dire, chaque paroisse est une famille' [in truth, every parish is a family] – but *good* families, which did not need regulation. In the countryside, there was nothing rarer than a theft or other offence, since country people were singularly honest and moral, in contrast to the relaxed morality of urban middle-class *Canadiens*.[2]

Each of these three visions exemplifies one of the broad approaches adopted by historians in examining the relationship between society and ancien-régime criminal justice systems. The first, with affinities to Abbott's discourse, suggests that ancien-régime criminal justice was a consensual instrument for community dispute resolution. This was the traditional view of English criminal justice, and in modified form it still informs the interpretation of many contemporary scholars. Its proponents argue that, while there were obvious limits to consensus in institutions operated by the state and controlled by privileged white men, criminal justice was nevertheless fairly well accepted by, integrated into, and used by the community at large, who were thus generally convinced of the system's legitimacy, or at least of its utility.[3] Another approach emphasizes conflict, social control, and oppression, much like Du Calvet. This conflictual view of ancien-régime criminal justice is exemplified by the Marxist analyses that historians such as E.P. Thompson have applied to eighteenth-century England, where the law is one of the main tools that elites used to control the popular classes.[4] Other historians, however, have questioned the very relevance of ancien-régime criminal justice, postulating instead its marginality in dispute resolution – not for the idyllic reasons suggested by Neilson, but because justice was shunned by local and especially rural communities. This is the view of many criminal justice historians in France, for example, from Nicole and Yves Castan forward. Criminal justice under the ancien régime, particularly in rural society, was neither a privileged arena for community dispute settlement nor a mechanism of social control, but rather an institution of last resort when community-based arbitration had failed. As such, its impact on society at large was minimal: it operated on the margins of the community, aimed at members who committed especially horrific and unusual crimes or those individuals who were not integrated into community structures, such as slaves and vagabonds.[5]

Each of these views has found its echo in Quebec historiography. Thus, liberal anglophone historians of the first half of the twentieth century emphasized consensus and legitimacy, asserting that the largely *Canadien* populace found the criminal justice system implanted by the British administration both fair and useful. The conflictual view dominated the historiography in the 1970s and 1980s, recast to include ethnic conflict and colonial domination as principal factors along with class. Most recently, the vision of a socially marginal criminal justice system has found its expression in the work of scholars who stress how little official justice was integrated into community life in the period before the Rebellions.[6] And yet, as I will argue in the next four chapters, none of these views adequately grasps the complex nature of the relationship between the people and criminal justice from the Conquest to the Rebellions. In a sense, the perspectives underlying the statements of Abbott, Du Calvet, and Neilson were all accurate, even though each held only part of the larger picture.

This chapter begins by exploring the social relevance of everyday criminal justice to the people of Quebec and Lower Canada – not just rural *Canadiens*, though they were by far the largest group, but all those who made up the colony's increasingly complex society. It concentrates above all on recourse to the system, and it does so by asking several basic questions. How frequently did people come before the everyday criminal justice system? How was this affected by the geographical deployment of the system, notably the difference between town and country? Did *Canadiens* use the justice system established by the Conqueror? What offences led plaintiffs and defendants to find themselves before the justices and the courts? And to what extent did people avoid the criminal justice system altogether? Through these questions, we can begin to assess the three models of consensus, conflict, and marginality, and, more broadly, to think about the legitimacy of the system in the eyes of the people.

Seeking out the Justices

Perhaps the most basic issue in considering the social relevance of criminal justice is how often people had direct contact with it, notably by making a complaint or by being targeted by a prosecution. Of course, this is only part of the story, since, as Douglas Hay points out, a single manifestly unjust treason trial might make more of an impression than an entire year's worth of equitable everyday contacts.[7] Further, beyond plaintiffs and defendants was the whole slew of bail guarantors, witnesses, jurymen, and so on who also came in contact with the system. Nevertheless, the number of plaintiffs and defendants is a good starting point. There was a vast difference between the few people who went before the criminal courts in eighteenth-century Languedoc and the huge numbers who sought out local magistrates in nineteenth-century Philadelphia, prompting the historian of the first to argue for the marginality of criminal justice in dispute resolution while that of the second emphasizes its centrality.[8]

One of the greatest challenges in evaluating how many people came in contact with ancien-régime criminal justice is the plurality of places of contact. For example, many early studies of criminal justice in early-modern England were based only on the higher courts, leading to partial views of the overall rate and nature of recourse to criminal justice.[9] In Quebec and Lower Canada as well, while King's Bench cases were of undeniable importance both numerically and ideologically, they still represented a relatively small proportion of contacts between colonial society and the criminal justice system of the state, as we will see. This chapter thus attempts to cover the whole range of contacts between the people and the system.

Since overall criminal statistics began to be collected in Quebec only from about the mid-1840s, any evaluation of the activity of the criminal justice system depends on surviving judicial records. Though Quebec is comparatively well endowed with these, there are still many lacunae. For example, there is no way of knowing the number of cases heard in the Montreal Weekly Sessions before 1779 or, with a few exceptions, in any of the justices' courts in Quebec City in the eighteenth century. Still, piecing together information from various sources, we can arrive at some estimates of the number of complaints that came before the various elements of the criminal justice system in the two main districts of Quebec and Montreal. These estimates are set out in Table 5.1; there, the only significant overlap is between Quarter Sessions complaints (complaints initially destined to become cases in the Quarter Sessions) and formal Quarter Sessions court cases – cases were a subset of complaints, since, as we will see, many complaints never ended up in court. The numbers are based only on defendants, since information on plaintiffs is often missing from the records, but, given that there were almost as many plaintiffs as defendants (depending on the court, the ratio was between 0.8:1 and 1:1), the numbers provide a good general idea of both. Table 5.2 then puts these numbers together so as to come up with the total number of defendants complained of to the criminal justice system, adds the ratio to population, and, for comparison, also includes numbers for New France.

These numbers are only approximations and are subject to the vagaries of sampling. As well, the tables do not cover several important venues. They exclude felony complaints that were sent on by justices but never indicted in King's Bench – though, given the eagerness of the colony's various attorneys general for the lucrative fees an indictment brought, there were probably few of these. They also exclude a few courts that occasionally imposed penal sanctions, such as the Trinity House and the Court of Vice-Admiralty. More significantly, they omit summary complaints handled with fines or peace bonds imposed by rural justices, as well as misdemeanour and felony complaints dismissed by justices at the initial hearing, since the records for these simply have not survived. Still, taken as best-guess, minimum estimates for the various venues represented, the two tables do allow for several observations.

Table 5.1: Defendants complained of annually before the criminal justice system[10]

Period	Complaints and summary proceedings				Formal court cases		
	Summary complaints for peace bonds and fines*	Quarter Sessions complaints	Masters' complaints against seamen**	Summary imprison-ments***	Weekly and Special Sessions†	Quarter Sessions	King's Bench
District of Montreal							
1767–1773	?	?	–	?	?	13	10
1779–1788	?	75	–	c.10	c.90	39	11
1805	?	c.110	–	c.40	c.190	59	c.30
1815	c.80	c.360	–	c.30	c.150	158	87
1820	c.170	c.390	–	c.70	c.150	221	c.140
1829/1830††	c.130	c.310	–	c.120 †††	273	92	182
1835	c.130	c.880	–	c.150	293	426	209
District of Quebec	Summary Quarter Sessions complaints						
1766–1769	?		–	?	?	14	21
1787–1788	?		–	?	30	25	c.20
1805	c.70		–	?	c.120	?	c.35
1815	c.350		c.50	c.80	c.100	?	c.120
1830	c.550		c.100	c.250	c.165	c.250‡	c.110
1835	c.1100		c.525	c.400	c.200	c.290‡	c.115

'c.' indicates minimum estimates. Some figures are averages of years in the period.

* urban justices only; rural figure unknown

** Quebec only; Montreal cases included elsewhere

*** excludes pre-trial commitments and commitments on judgment of the formal courts; for Quebec City, also excludes seamen

† excludes tax-recovery cases

†† 1829 for formal court cases, 1830 for complaints and summary proceedings

††† does not include House of Correction commitments

‡ inferred from number of indictments

Table 5.2: Defendants per population, 1710s–1830s[11]

Period	Place	Population	Defendants per year	Rate per 1000
1710s	New France	22,000	c.33	1.3
1750s	New France	60,000	c.95	1.3
1748–1759	New France (royal courts excluding police)	60,000	c.21	0.35
1766–1769	District of Quebec (indictments only)	34,000	c.35	1.02
1767–1773	District of Montreal (indictments only)	34,000	c.23	0.68
1779–1788	District of Montreal	56,000	c.170	3.1
1805	District of Montreal	198,000	c.375	3.1
	District of Quebec	78,000	c.210	2.7
1815	District of Montreal	266,000	c.640	3.8
	District of Quebec	98,000	c.700	7.2 (6.7)*
1820	District of Montreal	200,000	c.920	4.6
1830	District of Montreal	419,000	c.970	3.5
	District of Quebec	147,000	c.1600	11.0 (8.3)*
1835	District of Montreal	305,000	c.1700	5.7
	District of Quebec	167,000	c.2400	14.2 (11.0)*

* parentheses indicate rates excluding masters' complaints against seamen

First and most obviously, the vast majority of people involved in criminal complaints came before the justices only, with relatively few ending up in front of the Court of King's Bench. This predominance of the justices was similar to the situation in England but took on a different character in the colonial setting. For *Canadien* plaintiffs and defendants, it meant that the face of the criminal justice system they actually came in contact with, even in formal court cases, was usually not the august and mainly British judges of the King's Bench but rather the justices, many of whom were also *Canadien*.[12]

Second, people seem to have come before the criminal justice system no less frequently after the Conquest than before. Unfortunately, we have little information on the summary jurisdiction of the justices in the first decade of British rule. Nevertheless, under the British system, indictments brought in the Quarter Sessions and King's Bench, for which we do have records, occupied roughly the same position as criminal cases formally brought before the royal courts in New France, and dealt with roughly the same range of offences. In these venues, there were proportionately about twice as many cases in the decade after the Conquest as in the decade before. Of course, as Douglas Hay has pointed out, many of those before the courts in the early years of British rule, and in the Court of King's Bench in particular, were not *Canadiens*. However, in the Montreal Quarter Sessions and King's Bench together, there were still about twelve francophone defendants per year between 1767 and 1773, which works out to a rate of 0.36 per 1,000 per year – almost exactly the same as in the royal courts in New France as a whole in the 1750s (0.35 per 1,000). In the district of Quebec in 1766–9, the equivalent rate for francophones was if anything a little higher, about 0.43 per 1,000. When we also consider that up to 90 per cent of the accused in the 1750s were soldiers, which was also the case for many of those accused in the King's Bench after the Conquest, it seems likely that *Canadien* civilians found themselves before the criminal justice system at least as often after the Conquest as before.

Third, in a period often described as one of stasis, the relative number of people who came in contact with the criminal justice system increased quite dramatically. Based on the records of the Quebec King's Bench and prison, Jean-Marie Fecteau placed the beginning of this rise at the very end of the 1820s and linked it mainly to the increase in summary imprisonments for vagrancy, with recourse to the regular courts remaining steady; from this he postulated both a saturation of the regular court system and the beginnings of a fundamental transformation of the penal economy.[13] In the district of Montreal, while the rise in the 1830s is evident, already in the 1810s, with summary imprisonment still relatively unimportant, there were proportionately almost twice as many defendants as in the eighteenth century, and probably more given the lack of sources on the summary activity of rural justices. The district of Quebec saw an even more dramatic increase in prosecution rates from the early nineteenth century until the 1830s, even if we exclude masters' complaints against seamen, which inflate the numbers since seamen were non-residents. Though partly attributable to the rise in summary imprisonments, this was also the result of a fourfold increase in the number of people who made complaints to the justices for matters intended to be heard in Quarter Sessions, notably for assault. This fairly dramatic rise between the eighteenth and nineteenth centuries, coming before the remodelling of the criminal justice system from the late 1830s onward, matches a similar pre-reform rise in England, where it is attributed not to an increase in crime but to a growing propensity to prosecute.[14] And it also suggests an ancien-régime criminal justice system that was capable of expanding to meet the new demands placed on it.

There were nevertheless some important differences between the districts of Quebec and Montreal. Some related to broader structural factors: for instance, as we will see, the higher prosecution rate in the district of Quebec was partly due to the fact that Quebec City itself accounted for a larger share of its district population than Montreal, since urbanites were far more likely to come before justice than people from rural areas. But the higher number of summary commitments in Quebec City, and the large numbers of complaints by masters against seamen for desertion and the like, also reflect a justice system that presented itself differently, and had different concerns, than the system in Montreal.

When people came before the justices, they also increasingly saw them outside the formal courts. In the district of Montreal in the eighteenth century, about 40 per cent of complaints never came before the formal courts; this had risen to about 50 per cent by the mid-1810s and over 60 per cent in the late 1820s and the 1830s. The trend was more marked still in Quebec City. Even excluding masters' complaints against seamen, complaints dealt with outside the formal courts already made up about 60 per cent of all prosecutions in 1815, and about 75 per cent in 1835. This was due to two fundamental shifts in the way people interacted with the criminal justice system. First, as we will see, there was an increasing proportion of complaints initially intended for trial in Quarter Sessions but dropped before making it to court, the reflection of a system with a strong dose of prosecutorial discretion. Many of the complaints that never made it to Quarter Sessions were in fact being dealt with summarily – for example, by the imposition of a bond that required the defendant to appear at the next Quarter Sessions and to keep the peace in the meantime. This was the other major change: the rise in importance of the summary jurisdictions of the justices in the first decades of the nineteenth century, including not only the summary imprisonment of vagrants and prostitutes but also the imposition of peace bonds in cases of threats or minor assaults and summary fines for statutory offences. The trend is especially evident in the cities, but there are also strong indications that rural justices increasingly exercised their summary powers to impose peace bonds and fines. Though it is impossible to estimate the numbers of these, consider the rough notebook kept by Henry Crebassa and Robert Jones of William Henry, which appears to cover their summary judgments between April 1822 and December 1823. In what they referred to as a 'Cour special de la paix,' they dealt with twenty-nine criminal cases and thirty-two defendants altogether, or about twenty per year, compared to perhaps a half-dozen defendants each year in cases sent in to the Quarter Sessions and King's Bench from William Henry and the surrounding parish of Sorel. And they were not alone: in five months in 1819, for example, Joseph Porlier of Saint-Hyacinthe heard five criminal cases, the equivalent of about a dozen a year, with one involving ten defendants accused of not repairing the roads. Even if these justices were exceptional, just fifteen more like them would add another 350-odd defendants to the total number of complaints heard in the district of Montreal in the early 1820s, or more than a third again to the 900-odd defendants estimated in Table 5.1; and, with evidence of many highly active rural magistrates in the early 1820s, this does not seem at all far-fetched. As the public accounts committee of the Assembly noted in 1826, 'from the whole body of magistrates throughout the province, no fines appear to have been received, although it is very probable many were imposed, levied, and recovered in virtue of the existing laws.' Indeed, by the early 1830s, the fines imposed by rural justices in the district of Montreal probably added up to as much as those imposed in the city's Weekly Sessions, which by the late 1820s heard about three hundred cases per year.[15] If we add the recognizances summarily imposed by justices, which in the case of Crebassa and Jones amounted to a little under a third of all cases, we can suggest that rural justices probably tried hundreds of people summarily each year whose fate is entirely unknown to us.

We can also look more closely at how the frequency of people's contacts with the justices changed over time. For the district of Montreal, this is possible for Quarter Sessions cases and for Quarter Sessions complaints, to which we can add (from about 1810, and for urban justices only) complaints resolved summarily (Figure 5.1). Since these cases and complaints largely involved matters in which plaintiffs at least moved of their own volition to settle their personal differences, notably assaults, they provide a fairly good measure of the willingness of people to have recourse to the courts. For the district of Quebec, the Thémis 2 database allows a rougher measure of the evolution of the total number of complaints of all nature preserved in the records of the clerk of the peace (Figure 5.2).

In both districts, recourse to the justices progressed in what can best be described as a series of steps, both up and down. While there are several possible explanations, likely factors included changes in the organization and composition of the magistracy itself as well as the shifting political climate. Thus, the sharp rise from 1810 in both Montreal

Figure 5.1: Montreal Quarter Sessions cases and complaints, 1765–1837*

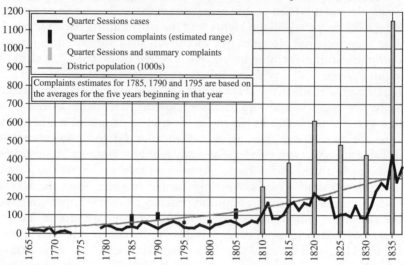

*by number of defendants

and Quebec corresponds evidently to the opening of Police Offices and the appointment of professional chairmen, which made making a complaint that much easier. Conversely, in the district of Montreal, drops in the 1790s and 1820s corresponded to times when relations between the *Canadien* and British communities deteriorated and when the bench became dominated by francophobic Tories. This does not mean that there was a generalized boycott of the justice system, especially in the late 1820s, when complaints declined less sharply than cases, but it does suggest that people were less willing to pursue a personal complaint, such as for assault, as far as the formal court with its British magistrates, and thus, perhaps, that they were less convinced of its legitimacy or at least of its responsiveness to their needs. Their attitude was perhaps captured in an 1830 critique of the chairmen that appeared in *La Minerve*. Noting the decline of the 'antique and constitutional' institution of the Quarter Sessions, the paper claimed that the court had been reduced to judging prosecutions for debauchery or orgies in the suburbs, for fights and fisticuffs between lower-class citizens, and for infractions of police regulations. In the eyes of *La Minerve*, the Quarter Sessions had become nothing more than a police court, inspiring disgust in all decent people and discouraging them from serving as witnesses or jurors; indeed, country jurors could not under-

Figure 5.2: Complaints in the records of the Quebec clerk of the peace, 1802–36*

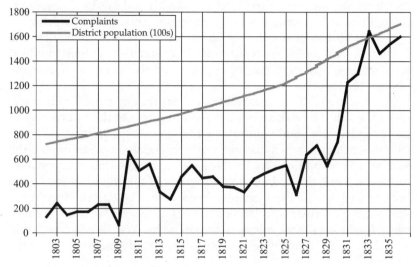

* by number of defendants

stand why they had to come from so far to witness demoralizing scenes to which they were so little accustomed.[16] While this was no doubt an exaggeration, the dismissal of Gale and the transferral of the Police Office's functions to the Peace Office do appear to have reversed the tendency: by 1835, the number of complaints had shot up once again beyond the levels of the early 1820s.[17]

In the district of Quebec, there was no apparent boycott of the justices, with instead a plateau in complaints in the 1810s and 1820s. Even when the Police Office and the chairman were under bitter attack in the Assembly, people kept coming before the justices. Again, this may have been linked to the character of the men on the bench. As we saw in chapter 2, until 1830, the magistracy in the district of Quebec as a whole was far more francophone than in Montreal. And in the late 1820s, the chairmen in Quebec City were Jean-Thomas Taschereau and then Robert Christie, both Tories but neither as objectionable as the francophobic Gale – Taschereau had previously supporrted the *Canadien* party and was even briefly imprisoned in 1810 for 'treasonable practices,' while Christie, though vilified by the Assembly for his role in shaping the 1828 commission, was generally considered a moderate. Equally striking is the rise of complaints in the 1830s, immediately following the abolition of the position of chairmen. As in Montreal, and despite the predictions of disaster on the part of Christie and the other incumbent chairmen, the judicial restructuring evidently did not lead to judicial chaos. Even setting aside summary imprisonments, most of which were sworn by official prosecutors such as constables and watchmen, the number of complaints for assault and battery and the like almost doubled between 1830 and 1835, far outstripping the rise in population of the city and its district.

Unfortunately, these figures do not allow for any meaningful observations about the relationship between recourse to the justice system and broader economic patterns. In England, both Douglas Hay and John Beattie have shown that in times of higher food prices or war, the number of prosecutions for thefts went up, but, as Robert Shoemaker has pointed out, this did not hold for many of the offences tried by the justices, such as assaults. Certainly, in the case of Quebec, neither figure shows any particular correlation to economic events such as the sharp rise in food prices in the colony in the late 1820s. Was there a correlation with theft prosecutions? Only a more focused study, based on all courts, will tell.[18]

We can also ask how people's recourse to the criminal courts in Quebec and Lower Canada compared to that of other societies with similar justice systems. Take the most evident comparison, eighteenth-century England. In Essex at the end of the eighteenth century, a county with a population of about 200,000, there were perhaps 35 indictments for violence and 120 for property crime each year in the Assizes and Quarter Sessions together. The district of Montreal had proportionately similar though slightly lower numbers: in the 1780s, with a population one- quarter that of Essex, there were a little under 30 indictments altogether in the King's Bench and Quarter Sessions for violence and property crimes (for about 40 defendants), and in the early 1810s, with a population of about 150,000, perhaps 110 indictments (for about 150 defendants). And this was considerably higher than other English counties. In eighteenth-century Staffordshire, for example, with a population reaching 250,000 by 1801, there were perhaps 80 indictments per year; and in eighteenth-century Lindsey (a division of Lincolnshire), with a population of perhaps 250,000, there were fewer than 20 indictments for assault each year, and perhaps 75 complaints of all types in the sessions rolls, including petty administrative matters. In Montreal, even in the 1780s, with a population one-fifth that of Lindsey, perhaps 25 people were indicted for assault each year, and there were perhaps 75 Quarter Sessions complaints and twice that many again in all the courts. The formal criminal courts in Quebec were thus proportionately almost as active as those in a central county like Essex, more active than those of Staffordshire, and far more active than those in a peripheral, largely rural region like Lindsey. On the other hand, the Quebec courts saw nothing like the activity of the courts of London, which, as John Beattie has pointed out, were exceptional. Of course, in many parts of rural England, most criminal matters were dealt with not in the formal courts but before the justices in petty sessions and summary hearings, though it is difficult to get an idea of how many people came before the justices in this fashion. In Essex, it was probably hundreds every year; in Staffordshire, it was perhaps as many again as there were indictments; in Lindsey, however, summary judgment by justices was much rarer. As we saw, the Quebec and Lower Canadian justices' exercise of their summary jurisdiction is also difficult to measure, but in the rural areas of the colony, at least by the early nineteenth century, it was probably somewhere between Essex and Lindsey.[19]

The American experience also provide points of comparison, at least for the eighteenth century. In North Carolina in the 1760s, by far the peak decade for pre-Revolutionary criminal prosecutions, there were 150 prosecutions per year for serious offences such as assaults, thefts, and so on, for a white population of about 120,000. In the district of Montreal in the 1780s, there were about 95 complaints per year for similar sorts of cases, for a population of about 60,000, which is within the same order of magnitude. In the 1720s, there were about 5.3 indictments per 1,000 male adults in New York City, and 5.4 in Richmond County, Virginia; the equivalent figure for the district of Montreal as a whole was about 2.3 in the late 1760s and early 1770s and 3.1 in the 1780s, and, as we will see, the urban rates were much higher. In pre-Revolutionary Massachusetts, the rate for all prosecutions in the Superior and General Sessions between 1760 and 1774 was about 0.9 per 1,000, roughly comparable to the overall rate of indictment in the district of Montreal.[20]

Elsewhere in British North America, there have been relatively few studies of prosecution rates. Still, in both the small, largely rural Newcastle and Niagara districts of Upper Canada in the late 1820s and early 1830s, there were perhaps three cases taken to Quarter Sessions cases each year per 1,000 population, whereas the equivalent rates in both the districts of Quebec and Montreal were about one per 1,000 per year. Evidently, Upper Canadians came in contact with their Quarter Sessions far more frequently than Lower Canadians, but this is perhaps a misleading comparison, since the Quarter Sessions was the main court in these districts, with no equivalent of the Weekly Sessions and apparently little summary activity before 1834.[21]

What all of these admittedly rough comparisons suggest is that, in Quebec and Lower Canada, recourse to the criminal justice system by plaintiffs – and the consequent weight of the system on defendants – was not out of line with that in other societies with similar justice systems. Of course, the total numbers were still small: even in 1835, perhaps 4,000 defendants for a population of over 450,000 in the two main districts. This was nothing in comparison to the 40,000–60,000 cases per year in mid-nineteenth-century Philadelphia, with its half-million people, or the over 250,000 annual prosecutions for wood theft alone in Baden in the 1830s and 1840s, for a population of about 1.3 million.[22] Likewise, far more people came in contact with civil justice than with criminal. In 1787–8 the clerks of the Montreal and Quebec Common Pleas reported that there were about 3,500 cases before the courts, while there were probably no more than 800 defendants in criminal cases. In 1815 there were about 4,500 new civil cases in the inferior and superior terms of the Montreal and Quebec King's Bench, compared to at most 1,500 criminal defendants. And in 1834, there were about 9,500 civil cases launched in the Montreal King's Bench, including circuits, dwarfing some 1,700 criminal defendants in the district; and this does not even include the numerous cases tried by the rural civil courts of the commissioners for the trial of small causes.[23] Still, consider that in the fifteen-year period between 1779 and 1793, at least 1,600 people were charged in the Montreal Quarter and Weekly Sessions alone, of whom only about 12 per cent were there more than once, along with another 150 or so in the King's Bench. Similarly, in the seven years between 1815 and 1821, the equivalent number was perhaps 4,500, with a repeat rate of perhaps 17 per cent, plus another 800-odd in the King's Bench.[24] Or again, the total number of people formally charged in the lower courts in the district of Quebec between 1802 and 1837 was at least 30,000, to which should be added another 3,000-odd in the King's Bench.[25] Adding plaintiffs and witnesses would at least double if not triple these numbers, even accounting for multiple prosecutions by official prosecutors and their witnesses. We then begin to approach a not insignificant proportion of the population at large that had direct personal contact with the criminal justice system of the state – a system that quantitatively at least, can hardly be described as marginal.

Town Justice, Country Justice

Overall prosecution rates are nevertheless misleading, since they lump together town and country. A commonly noted feature of ancien-régime criminal justice systems is their urban bias: they were largely institutions designed for, targeted at, and used by an urban population, and in particular the population of metropolises or larger regional towns. This is one of the main points of those who emphasize that, in ancien-régime societies, official criminal justice occupied a marginal place in the resolution of rural community tensions, or in the imposition of state authority outside the cities. Thus, it has often been suggested that village communities in large portions of France, the continent's seemingly most centralized and powerful nation-state, came in contact with the criminal justice system only rarely. The rural propertied elites in eighteenth-century England were more successful in using the criminal law as a means of controlling their tenants and servants, but, even there, studies have shown that people from rural areas were far less likely to come before the courts than Londoners. As for New France, about 60 per cent of criminal cases that came before the royal courts originated in the three main towns, which constituted at most 20 per cent of the colony's total population.[26]

In Quebec and Lower Canada, urban dwellers were also heavily over-represented in the criminal justice system. Figures 5.3 and 5.4 show the proportion of urban parties in the two main districts in various venues. In the district of Montreal, in both the eighteenth and nineteenth centuries, about 60 per cent of plaintiffs and accused in Quarter Sessions complaints were from Montreal, rising to 70 per cent in 1835, while the city accounted for at most 10 per cent of the district's population throughout the period. The Montreal Weekly Sessions was an equally urban court, with in general about 70–80 per cent of parties from the cities. The only exception was the brief period of the Revolutionary War, when, as Du Calvet noted, large numbers of rural inhabitants were fined for refusing to transport military stores. The urban bias was if anything heavier in the district of Quebec, where in the nineteenth century 70–85 per cent of those involved in Quarter Sessions complaints, and up to 90 per cent of those involved in Weekly Sessions complaints, came from Quebec City, while the city's population accounted for perhaps 15 per cent of that of the district as a whole.

What this meant was that prosecution rates in the towns were far higher than those in the countryside. The rates for Montreal and Que-

Figure 5.3: Proportion of urban parties, district of Montreal

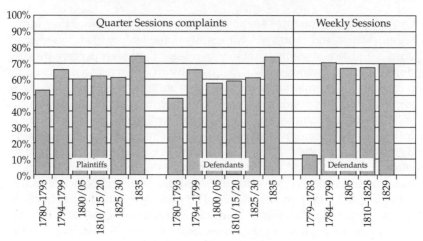

Figure 5.4: Proportion of urban parties, district of Quebec

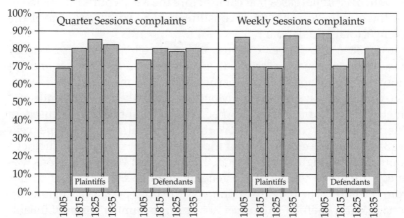

bec City were fairly similar: in Montreal, the rate rose from about 25 per 1,000 in the 1810s to a little over 40 per 1,000 in 1835, and in Quebec City, excluding masters' complaints against seamen, from about 20 per 1,000 in 1815 to over 50 per 1,000 in 1835. Recourse to the criminal courts was much less common outside the cities: for example, based only on surviving records, rural prosecution rates in the district of Montreal varied between 1 and 1.5 per 1,000 between 1810 and 1835. Of course, as we saw, in the nineteenth century at least there were more rural residents coming before the criminal justice system than the records of the urban courts suggest, since many cases were handled by rural justices alone, but this could not have made up for the striking urban bias. For instance, during the eighteen months covered by the William Henry justices' notebook in the early 1820s, there were a total of twenty-nine defendants in criminal cases dealt with summarily, along with another two to three defendants sent on for trial each year to Quarter Sessions or King's Bench. With William Henry and its surrounding parish of Sorel having a population of a little over 4,500 in 1825, this yields a prosecution rate of a little over 4 per 1,000 population per year, or perhaps a tenth of the Montreal rate for 1820 (a little under 40 per 1,000). To put it another way, for rural prosecution rates even to reach half of those in the city, there would have had to have been about 1,500 summary complaints per year before rural justices in the early 1810s, and about 5,000 in the mid-1830s, figures that are very unlikely.

Various reasons have been suggested to explain the lower propensity of rural people to come before the criminal justice system. As Allan Greer has suggested, following a well-established historiographical path, there may simply have been less crime in rural areas. This was certainly the view expressed by Augustin Cuvillier, a moderate reformer and one of Montreal's leading justices, when he addressed the Quarter Sessions grand jury in 1836. Stating that the rapid progress of crime was limited mainly if not entirely to the city, he suggested that the country parishes offered barely a single case of serious crime – new proof, if any was needed, that the agricultural population maintained the moral rectitude that had so strongly contributed to its well-being. But Cuvillier's assertions are impossible to gauge. As many historians have asserted, the number of assault cases that turned up in the criminal courts had little to do with the number of assaults actually committed, and this was even more true of the whole range of lesser regulatory offences. There is, however, one firmer indicator that the countryside may in fact have been more peaceful: the murder rate seems to have been quite a bit higher in the cities than in the countryside. Likewise, the sorts of transgressions increasingly targeted and punished by the justice system, such as prostitution and vagrancy, were far more common in a port city such as Quebec or a commercial crossroads like Montreal than in the countryside.[27]

Another frequent explanation for the urban bias of criminal prosecution is the weakness of the ancien-régime state in the countryside and the consequent difficulty of access for rural inhabitants. As we saw in previous chapters, there were two different justice systems in the colony: a well-established, increasingly professional system in the two main towns at least, and a much less well-established one elsewhere, with amateur justices and part-time bailiffs scattered unevenly across the countryside. With such a significantly different presence of the tangible manifestations of criminal justice, it seems hardly surprising that recourse to criminal justice was different in town and in country. Still, as we also saw, by the 1820s at least, if a plaintiff wanted to make a complaint, there was probably an active justice within a few kilometres, and a bailiff or constable willing to serve the warrant or summons if paid the appropriate fee. The geographical distribution of the justice system was thus less and less a factor. At any rate, the absence of resident magistrates was not necessarily a brake on recourse to or contact with the justice system. Take the example of Île Jésus, north of Montreal. By the late 1810s, the 5–6,000 inhabitants of the island's four parishes had limited options if they wanted to deal with a resident magistrate: the only one was Joseph Lacroix, a justice since 1791 who was becoming old and rather infirm. Yet, all the same, there were seven or eight Quarter Sessions complaints per year involving residents of the island, some begun before magistrates in the two neighbouring villages of Terrebonne and Saint-Eustache, just across the Rivière-des-Prairies, but most before magistrates in Montreal, a relatively short distance away.

There is also the view that rural communities were essentially self-regulating and less willing to accept state justice as a legitimate form of dispute resolution. As Neilson suggested, rural communities were more independent and closed, with stronger community mechanisms for conflict resolution, and thus less likely to resort to an external justice system to resolve disputes that only involved community members. They were also more liable to resist criminal justice when it was imposed on them, and even in cases where the interests of the state were most directly involved, such as assaults on tax-collectors, rural communities were often able to repulse royal justice. Thus, when they did come in contact with the criminal justice system of the state, it was as a last resort, in extraordinary cases which they could not resolve themselves or in which the state's interest was particularly strong.[28]

While there is no doubt some truth to this view, the rejection of official criminal justice by rural communities was far from uniform. Local communities, as we saw in chapter 2, regularly petitioned for the establishment of justices of the peace among them. Of course, the petitions were most often inspired by local elites, but these elites were not only local seigneurs or merchants, who might be expected to benefit directly from the power wielded by justices of the peace, but also other groups, such as local clergy, for whom the criminal justice system could well have been seen as a competitor to their own forms of dispute resolution. Thus, there is little evidence that local clergy actively resisted the official criminal justice system or sought to discourage people from having recourse to it. Instead, many *curés* were more than happy to have justices around to bolster their authority. In 1829, for example, the *curé* of Sainte-Marguerite-de-Blairfindie signed at the head of a petition that declared the urgency of appointing justices in the parish, since its youth were growing up in the habit of not being corrected for their sloth and vice, to the great detriment of agriculture and industry. The petition noted the difficulty and cost of having prompt access to justice, and listed off the specific provincial acts that it felt were not being enforced as a result. The *curé* was asking not for protection against outsiders but for a tool of social regulation within his parish, on matters such as idleness, vice, and immorality which we might have expected he would have considered to be the responsibility of the church itself. And this was not a unique case: the *curé* of Pointe-Lévy, across from Quebec City, wrote to his local assemblyman bemoaning the lack of justices to deal with the minor altercations that occurred from time to time, while the *curé* of Sainte-Scholastique asked the administration for a local justice because his parishioners were frequently obliged to bring their affairs before a justice in the neighbouring parish, up to five leagues away. Even the *curé* of Cap-Santé in the 1820s and 1830s, Félix Gatien, a critic of the British colonial administration and a faithful follower of the doctrine of resistance by the church to state interference in matters such as education, nevertheless related the story of a chorister who in 1808, after disturbing the congregation four Sundays in a row by quitting the choir and singing loudly in his pew, was finally tamed by having him brought before a justice and fined. *Curés* also wanted active justices: as the *curé* of Saint-Antoine, near Cap-Santé, declared, it was worse to have a justice in whose presence the law was broken with impunity than to have no justice at all. While a complete examination of clerical attitudes towards the justice system as a whole remains to be undertaken, it is certainly difficult to argue that the rural Catholic clergy uniformly discouraged their parishioners from appearing before the justices.[29]

Table 5.3: Time between incident and complaint, Montreal Quarter Sessions complaints, 1780–1835

	Same day	Next day	2 days	3–5 days	6–10 days	11–30 days	31+ days
Montreal plaintiffs	31%	40%	10%	10%	4%	4%	2%
Non-Montreal plaintiffs	16%	26%	14%	17%	10%	11%	6%

A more concrete indication that rural communities integrated local criminal justice into their own dispute regulation is the place of residence of those involved in complaints, for lesser offences such as assaults, that were either resolved summarily by justices or that were destined to be heard in Quarter Sessions. Among complaints that involved parties from outside of the city, about 70 per cent involved plaintiffs and defendants who came from the same parish, seigneury, or township, with another 10 per cent only involving people from neighbouring places. A significant part of the criminal justice system at the level of the justices thus did not at all fit the pattern of an ancien-régime criminal justice system outside the towns that was used only to deal with outsiders. There are certainly examples of rural inhabitants using the justice system to deal with aggressions by strangers, such as the 1830 complaint of Joseph Beaudreau and Amable Dufresne, Longue-Pointe farmers, against Joseph Beauchamp, who declared himself to be from Saint-Roch, for stealing their chickens and a harness; and Gatien, the *curé* of Cap-Santé, complained that the justices in his parish were cowards for not having dealt forcefully with thefts and other offences committed by transient soldiers. But these were a minor part of how rural residents used and were used by the criminal justice system.[30]

Consider as well the amount of time it took for a plaintiff to make a complaint, which, for the district of Montreal, is summarized in Table 5.3. If the criminal justice system was used only as a last resort, we would expect to see a significant delay between the date of the crime and the date that the plaintiff appeared before the justice, as other forms of dispute resolution were tried first. Certainly, rural plaintiffs took longer to go before a justice than their urban counterparts: only about 40 per cent made their complaint the same or the next day, compared to over 70 per cent for urban plaintiffs. However, over half made their complaints within two days; and if we consider only complaints that rural plaintiffs made before rural justices (thus excluding those who made their way to Montreal to complain), about half made their complaints within a day, 60 per cent within two days, and 70 per cent within three days. At most, therefore, rural plaintiffs may have taken an extra day or two to make their complaints, which is not surprising given more difficult access to justice in the countryside. This suggests that, when rural people went before a justice, it was not as a reluctantly used last resort but as a viable response to situations in which they felt aggrieved. No doubt it was not the only response, or even perhaps the most important, but it was not a last-ditch measure either.

The under-representation of rural parties in the records consulted for this study also probably reflects in part an unwillingness of people from outside the city to go before the formal urban courts rather than an outright avoidance of the criminal justice system. Most of the judicial records that have survived concern cases that in one way or another made it to town. But there are indications that, in the areas farthest from the cities, justices were more likely to impose, and plaintiffs to accept, a resolution that did not involve a costly trip to town, at least in the sorts of less serious cases that were decided by the justices themselves. Thus, all eight of the assault cases recorded in the notebook of Crebassa and Jones, the William Henry justices, were resolved by imposing a recognizance to keep the peace on the defendant rather than sending the matter on to trial in Montreal, and consequently none of these cases shows up in the central judicial records.[31] And even in cases initially destined to be heard in Quarter Sessions, it is quite likely that, just as in England, rural justices may not have sent the documents to town if the dispute was subsequently settled.[32]

At any rate, we cannot assume that the preponderance of urban dwellers was the result of a classically marginal ancien-régime criminal justice system and, more generally, a weak ancien-régime state. As I have shown elsewhere, this same pattern of a much stronger presence of urban dwellers in the criminal justice system also held true through the nineteenth and well into the twentieth century. Thus, between 1880 and 1960, conviction rates for the judicial district of Montreal, consisting mainly of the city and its surrounding suburbs, were between fifteen and forty times higher than those in largely rural districts elsewhere in the province. At the beginning of the twentieth century, the conviction rate for what had been, a hundred years earlier, the rural parts of the district of Montreal was only 0.3 per thousand for indictable offences and 1.2 for summary offences – not much different from what it had been in the early nineteenth century.[33]

Canadiens and British Criminal Justice

This same ambiguity is evident in the relationship between the majority *Canadien* population and criminal justice. Most historians have argued that, in the decades between the Conquest and the Rebellions, *Canadiens* were alienated from the criminal justice system of the state and avoided it as much as possible as an illegitimate imposition by the Conqueror. Louis Knafla puts it bluntly: 'English criminal law was superimposed on a French-speaking society, the law was despised from the outset, and hostility increased from the 1790s down to the mid nineteenth century ... the alienation of the *Canadiens* to the English [has] become a permanent scar on the face of the country.'[34] In a more nuanced form, this notion of a *Canadien* 'boycott' of the criminal justice system, a 'passive, yet steadfast, resistance,' is present in the work of most who have written on the subject.[35]

Most of this argument is based on the higher criminal courts, where, indeed, *Canadiens* were heavily under-represented. Though more than 95 per cent of the population in the first decade of British rule was *Canadien*, non-francophones made up two-thirds or more of defendants in the King's Bench between 1764 and 1775. Likewise, in the late eighteenth and early nineteenth centuries, as Jean-Marie Fecteau has shown, defendants in the Quebec King's Bench were largely non-*Canadien*. Similarly, less than half of prisoners committed to the Montreal gaol for felonies in the 1810s and 1820s were francophones, when they made up perhaps 80 per cent of the district's population. Of course, it was not defendants who could choose to boycott the criminal justice, but even among plaintiffs or victims in King's Bench cases, only about a third were francophones in the eighteenth century, and a little over 40 per cent in the nineteenth.[36]

At the everyday level of the justices, however, things were more ambiguous. As Figures 5.5 and 5.6 show, francophones were indeed consistently under-represented in all of the justices' courts and in both the districts of Quebec and Montreal. Non-francophones made up less than 5 per cent of the population of the district of Montreal until the mid-1780s and perhaps 20–25 per cent by the 1820s, with an even smaller proportion in the district of Quebec. And yet they consistently represented at least 30 per cent of parties in the eighteenth century and

Figure 5.5: Francophones before the justices, district of Montreal, 1765–1835

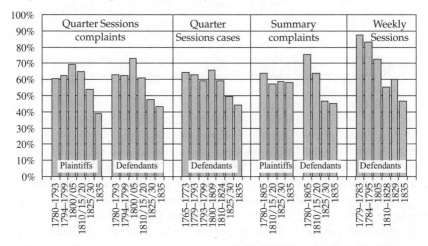

Figure 5.6: Francophones before the justices, district of Quebec, 1805–35

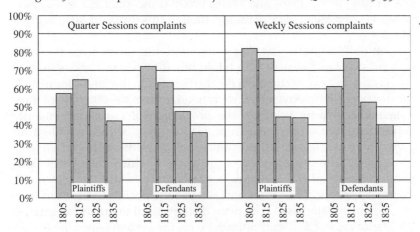

over half by the later 1820s and 1830s. Still, in both districts, until the early 1820s, francophones were in the majority among parties, generally making up 60–70 per cent of both plaintiffs and defendants. And, in the last two decades of the eighteenth century, about 80 to 85 per cent of defendants in Montreal's Weekly Sessions were francophones, approaching their proportion in the population at large.

Table 5.4: Francophones among urban and rural plaintiffs, Montreal Quarter Sessions and summary complaints, 1780–1835

	1780–93	1794–9	1800/05	1810/15/20	1825/30	1835
Rural plaintiffs	77%	74%	89%	76%	57%	65%
Urban plaintiffs	45%	56%	61%	58%	56%	37%

The apparent under-representation of francophones was also partly a reflection of the urban bias of the courts discussed above. As Table 5.4 shows, francophones made up between 70 and 90 per cent of rural plaintiffs in Quarter Sessions and summary complaints in the eighteenth and early nineteenth centuries, and though this dropped dramatically in the late 1820s, it was back to 65 per cent in the mid-1830s. In contrast, they generally made up a little over half of Montreal plaintiffs, apart from the mid-1830s. If we consider that the population of Montreal by 1832 was only half-francophone, while that outside of the city was perhaps 85 per cent francophone, we can see that, in both cases, francophones were far less under-represented than the overall figures show. If anything, in the 1810s and 1820s, urban francophones seem to have been over-represented as plaintiffs, though this dropped off sharply in the 1830s.

Even the decline in *Canadien* recourse to the courts from the 1820s onward was less clear-cut than might initially appear. For one thing, it seems only to have occurred in the districts of Quebec and Montreal. In the district of Trois-Rivières, if we can judge from the ethnicity of those indicted in Quarter Sessions, the proportion of *Canadiens* remained between 70 and 90 per cent from 1827 to 1835, with no evident decline.[37] Further, consider the ethnicity of plaintiffs in minor violence cases brought to the attention of the justices, which are a particularly good indicator of the willingness of plaintiffs to use the system. As Figure 5.7 shows, while there was an absolute decline in the number of francophone plaintiffs in both main districts until the 1820s, suggesting the beginnings of a disenchantment with the system (since the francophone population itself was increasing, even in the cities), by 1835 the number of francophone plaintiffs in these cases had rebounded to earlier levels. What masked this was the remarkable surge in complaints by anglophones in both cities, two or three times as many in the 1830s as they had been in the 1820s. The reasons for this upsurge in anglophone recourse to the courts remain to be explored; given that it was essentially an urban phenomenon, perhaps, as Jean-Marie Fecteau

Figure 5.7: Ethnicity of plaintiffs in violence cases, 1805–35

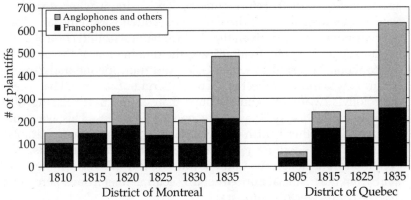

has suggested, it was linked to the difficulties faced by recent immigrants in integrating themselves into the host society, though Fecteau is referring mainly to the summary imprisonment of the urban poor. Certainly, looking back from the late 1840s, Robert Christie blamed immigration for what he saw as a dramatic upswing in crime between 1800 and 1820.[38]

Finally, just like rural inhabitants, when *Canadiens* made complaints, they were generally complaining against each other. Table 5.5 presents the ethnic mix of parties in Montreal Quarter Sessions complaints. Cases where parties came from more than one ethnic group were very much in the minority, and cases where there was at least one francophone plaintiff and one anglophone defendant were no less common than the opposite. There is thus little evidence of *Canadien* reluctance to use the courts against each other, and it is also difficult to see the justice system as mainly a locus of ethnic conflict, or of British domination over *Canadiens*.

Table 5.5: Ethnicity of parties in Montreal Quarter Sessions complaints, 1780–1835

Francophone parties only	43%
Anglophone or other parties only	29%
Mixed	29%
Francophone plaintiff and anglophone defendant	12%
Anglophone plaintiff and francophone defendant	12%

The *Canadien* majority, far from boycotting the everyday criminal justice system, was therefore quite at home using it when necessary, even among themselves. If there was a boycott, it was in the late 1820s, which is not surprising given the political battles around control of the magistracy and, in Montreal at least, the domination of the bench by francophobic Tories like Samuel Gale. And francophone under-representation was more a reflection of the differing urban/rural balance of the colony's two main ethnic groups than of any particular hostility towards the justice system on the part of *Canadiens*. This was quite different from other British colonies, such as Ireland, where Catholics were clearly less willing to make complaints than Protestants, and, even in those societies, the Catholic attitude towards the law stemmed more from the financial burdens of prosecution than from a perception that the courts were illegitimate.[39]

There are, of course, examples of explicit ethnic conflict played out in the criminal justice system. Corvée prosecutions of the sort condemned by Du Calvet, or the political prosecutions of leading members of the *Canadien* and *Patriote* parties, inevitably took on an ethnic character. And even setting aside these high-profile but infrequent cases, there were examples among the everyday cases heard by the justices. For example, Jacques Gagné, a Quebec City shoemaker, was accused in 1810 by John McDonald of declaring that 'si Je pouvoit faire un fusil capable de tuer 25 anglois a la fois, Je le ferois et si tous les *Canadiens* etoit comme moi je serai le premier de faire cela' [if I could make a gun that could kill 25 English at a time, I'd do it and if all *Canadiens* were like me I'd be the first to do it], and also, that 'si tous les *canadiens* voulaient dire comme moi, on ravagerait tous les anglais J'irais a la tete et je tirerais moi meme sur le gouverneur' [if all *Canadiens* thought like me, we'd ravage all the English I'd be at the head and I'd shoot the governor myself]. This was at the height of the political crisis under Craig, following his dissolution of the *Canadien*-dominated Assembly and his suppression of the *Le Canadien*, the principal French-language newspaper. But even in this case, the ethnic dimension of the prosecution was modulated by the fact that Gagné's other accuser was Michel Cameron, whose name, use of French in his deposition, and marriage to a Catholic suggest someone who straddled the cultural divide. And, at the level of everyday justice, cases such as Gagné's were very much the exception; Gagné himself seems to have been a tumultuous person, frequently accused of various assaults and disturbances by both *Canadien* and British men and women.[40]

The Reasons for Justice

Another way of understanding the relevance and legitimacy of everyday criminal justice is by considering the offences that led people to appear before the justices. This sort of analysis has been fundamental to many of the longest-running debates in criminal justice history. For example, those who advocate the conflict theory of criminal justice argue that, since most people brought before the courts in the eighteenth and nineteenth centuries were accused of theft and other property crimes, the criminal justice system was evidently at the service of men of property who used it to defend their wealth. More recently, criminal justice historians inspired by Norbert Elias have turned this argument on its head, arguing that the decline in violent crime before the courts and the corresponding rise in property crime are firm proof of Elias's view of the 'civilizing process' that has transformed Western society since the Middle Ages.[41] Of course, historiographical debates aside, from the perspective of a brothel-keeper in Quebec City or Montreal, it was evidently of great importance whether her neighbours dealt with prostitution informally or simply ignored it, as was the case in the eighteenth century, or regularly had prostitutes arrested and imprisoned, as they increasingly did in the nineteenth.

There are evident methodological problems with any attempt to categorize the vast range of individual circumstances that led people to complain. Still, if only for heuristic and comparative purposes, this section adopts some fairly standard criminological categories. Violent offences and property offences are relatively self-explanatory, with the provisos that most riots (which were directed against specific people) are classed among the former, and the relatively small number of burglary and robbery cases among the latter. Offences against the state are those that were direct attacks on state power, such as assaults on officers, refusal of militia service, or counterfeiting, along with misconduct by state officials. Offences related to the licensing of alcohol sales pose a special problem, since they were on the frontier between revenue matters and morality, and have thus been classed apart. Offences against morals denote victimless vice-related offences such as prostitution, gambling, non-violent infringement of sexual mores, Sabbatarian infringement, and alcohol-related offences beyond simply licensing. Public-order offences cover a range of individual behaviour – such as disturbing the peace, drunkenness, and vagrancy – that challenged increasingly bourgeois notions of proper public conduct. Regulatory offences cover all other victimless offences such as infractions of the roads acts and ordinances or of the police regulations. Labour designates the many quasi-civil cases of master/servant and master/seaman relations dealt with in the criminal courts. Finally, a residual category includes such offences as libel and bastardy that do not easily fit into the others. If these categories are taken as heuristic devices rather than definitive characterizations, they are useful in comparing different courts, places, and periods and are roughly comparable to the categories used by others who have studied historical crime.

While several studies on Quebec and Lower Canada have concentrated on specific sorts of cases, such as prostitution, infanticide, or master/servant relations, little attention has yet been paid to the overall reasons for which people came in contact with the colony's criminal justice system. The only systematic analysis has been that of Jean-Marie Fecteau, based on Quebec King's Bench indictments and gaol committals. For the period to 1815, Fecteau found that while the greatest number of defendants in King's Bench were charged with property offences, these did not dominate, unlike in Europe. This changed dramatically in the 1820s and 1830s, with property offences rapidly coming to outweigh all else, though Fecteau refrains from linking this to the broader economic interests of the colony's elites. Imprisonment underwent a different evolution: between the 1810s and the 1830s, the proportions of prisoners committed for violence and for property offences remained roughly equal, though with a tendency towards more property offences, but there was a dramatic upsurge of imprisonments for public-order crimes such as vagrancy and prostitution. Fecteau links this shift mainly to changing attitudes towards the prison as a form of social discipline.[42]

As Figure 5.8 shows, Fecteau's findings for the Quebec King's Bench also applied in general to the district of Montreal, though property offences dominated even more, apart from late 1790s, which saw high-profile prosecutions against those suspected of plotting to overthrow the government. From the early 1810s, there were even more defendants charged with property offences, accounting for three-quarters of all defendants by the mid-1830s. Conversely, the proportion of those indicted for violent offences declined substantially, becoming a minor part of the court's business.

As we saw, however, the King's Bench was only one of the many judicial venues where plaintiffs and defendants came in contact with criminal justice, and, numerically, it was far from the most important.

Figure 5.8: Offences in the Montreal King's Bench, 1767–1835

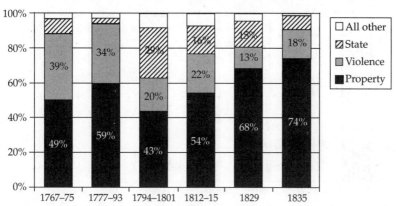

Most people came only before the justices, in venues ranging from summary hearings to formal courts. The extant sources allow us to form an idea of the types of offences heard in several such venues, though not all. For the district of Montreal, the analysis is based on Quarter Sessions complaints and Weekly Sessions convictions and cases (Figures 5.9 and 5.10). For the district of Quebec, the Thémis 2 database gives information on Quarter Sessions complaints and Weekly Sessions complaints and cases, though the latter are probably incomplete for some years (Figures 5.11 and 5.12).

As these figures show, when people came before the justices, it was for offences quite different from those prosecuted in King's Bench.

Figure 5.9: Offences, Montreal Quarter Sessions complaints, 1765–1835

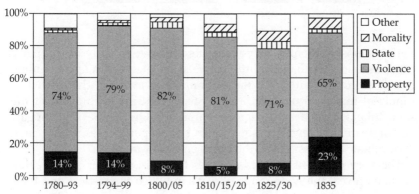

Figure 5.10: Offences, Montreal Weekly Sessions, 1779–1835

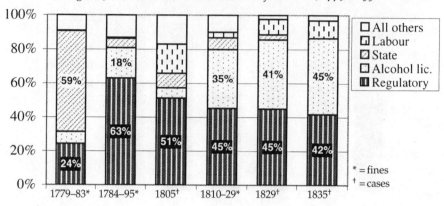

Figure 5.11: Offences, Quebec Quarter Sessions complaints, 1805–35

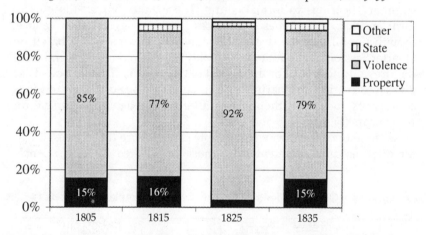

Perhaps most evidently, they were there relatively rarely for property offences, and this changed little between the eighteenth and the nineteenth centuries, with only the beginnings of a rise in the district of Montreal in the 1830s. This was in sharp contrast to England at the same time, where, despite regional variations, Quarter Sessions in particular heard an ever-increasing number of property cases, which came to dominate the Sessions by the nineteenth century.[43]

The very different profiles of cases heard in Quarter and Weekly Sessions reveal the wide range of ways in which the justices and their

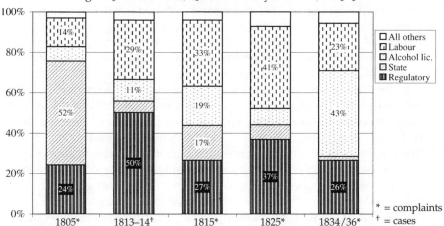

Figure 5.12: Offences, Quebec Weekly Sessions, 1805–36

courts fit into the social order. Nor was this the only difference from England. In Quebec and Lower Canada's Quarter Sessions, throughout the period, plaintiffs and defendants were largely involved in interpersonal violence cases, mostly various types of assault, which accounted for two-thirds or more of the complaints and cases before the court. By contrast, in much of England at the same time, even in the eighteenth century, assault cases generally made up between a quarter and a third of the Quarter Sessions' business, with highs of a half reached only in remoter areas like Lindsey or Northumberland. The importance of violence in Quebec and Lower Canada's Quarter Sessions was more reminiscent of the justices' courts in Middlesex in the late seventeenth and early eighteenth centuries, before the eighteenth-century upsurge in property crimes, and it was similar to the situation in other British North American colonies, such as Nova Scotia or Upper Canada, where assault cases also dominated in Quarter Sessions.[44]

The 'colonial' pattern of the Quarter Sessions gave these courts a flavour that their counterparts in England, increasingly concerned with enforcing property relations, were beginning to lose. As we will see, all but the most serious violence cases were treated differently from felonies, with the emphasis put on prosecutorial initiative rather than state vengeance, and, just as in civil cases, there was a great deal of latitude for private settlements that would take the cases out of the court system. As well, assaults were offences that, by definition, were not victimless. Every one of the thousands of assault complaints in the Montreal and Quebec sessions files from the 1780s to the 1820s involved at least one person who claimed to have been threatened or hurt, and most of these victims were private individuals, appealing to the courts for the redress of private wrongs, whether real, perceived, or constructed. And, as we will also see, plaintiffs and accused in assault cases were largely from the same social class.

In the Weekly Sessions, on the other hand, most defendants were accused of victimless offences: disobedience of the *corvée* and militia laws, unlicensed liquor-selling, not performing statutory labour on the roads, breaking fire, market, or health regulations, and so on. The Weekly Sessions was thus a prime venue for the exercise of power by the state at a local level. Prosecutions against those who refused to work on the roads or broke fire regulations may have had a flavour of community sanction, but they were still prosecuted under official regulations and, as we shall discover, largely by official prosecutors. While, as already noted, Weekly Sessions cases mainly targeted city dwellers, the courts also reached out to exercise state power over the whole district. Thus, in liquor-licensing cases, which made up an increasingly large proportion of cases in Montreal Weekly Sessions (rising from about 20 per cent in the eighteenth century to over 40 per cent in the 1820s and 1830s), some 60 per cent of those convicted in the 1810s and 1820s were from outside the city, ranging across the entire district. And it is hard to argue that enforcement of the *corvée* service reflected anything but the desires of the central administration to control rural inhabitants. Further, almost all charges in the Weekly Sessions stemmed from local criminal provisions, whether colonial acts and ordinances or regulations made by the justices themselves. This gave the Weekly Sessions a particularly local flavour, and it was here, for example, that the justices enforced their own legislative enactments.

Below the two formal courts of the justices lay their summary jurisdictions, which, as indicated earlier, are largely invisible in the documentary record. For the city of Montreal itself, scattered complaints preserved in the case files for matters not destined for trial at Quarter or Weekly Sessions give some hints of this activity. Though the eighteenth-century records are scanty, a little under half of defendants altogether were accused of various combinations of threats and assaults, one-third for offences against public morality (though these came from only two large prostitution cases), one-sixth for deserting service or other labour offences, and the remainder for various other offences. In the nineteenth century, of about 730 defendants in summary complaints in the sample years between 1800 and 1835 where the offence is known, about 400 were accused of threats and violence, 140 with labour offences, 80 with public-order offences such as vagrancy, and another 80 with morality offences such as prostitution (though as Mary Anne Poutanen has shown, the last two categories were largely interchangeable insofar as disorderly women were concerned). This nevertheless grossly underestimates the number of people summarily convicted of vagrancy and prostitution, since up to 1830 at least, it seems that many were committed without any formal record of the complaint being kept by the court clerks: thus, between 1810 and 1819 there are only fourteen complaints in the Montreal case files for prostitution and female vagrancy, but between April 1811 and December 1815, there were at least seventy-four women committed for these offences to Montreal's House of Correction.[45] Overall, justices in Montreal in their summary hearings outside formal court dealt with two different sorts of people: on the one hand, those who complained of assaults and threats where the justice summarily imposed recognizances; and on the other, specific groups on the margins of society who offended against the social order as conceived of by the justices, mainly prostitutes, vagrants, and disobedient servants.

In Quebec City, the sorts of complaints that plaintiffs sought to have handled by the justices summarily, outside their formal courts, were similar to those in Montreal. Thus, of the approximately 1,250 prisoners committed summarily to the Quebec gaol between 1815 and 1830, about three-quarters were there for morality and public-order offences such as vagrancy and prostitution, with, as Jean-Marie Fecteau noted, a marked rise in these offences from the late 1820s. And the case files of Quebec's clerk of the peace contain numerous complaints about threats and abusive language which could have been dealt with only by peace bonds, since they were not indictable offences. The one significant variation in Quebec City was the increasingly large number of desertion prosecutions under the merchant seamen's acts, which, as Table 5.1 shows, reached about 100 complaints per year by 1830 and over 500 per year by 1835. Quebec City, as a major North Atlantic port, was part of a trans-Atlantic justice system in which shipmasters used the criminal justice system to discipline their crews, while seamen pursued their masters for wages. This discipline extended also to summary imprisonment: between 1817 and 1821, an average of forty seamen per year were committed to the gaol, and though after 1821 the gaoler no longer recorded these imprisonments in his official register, other sources show that the practice continued.

With regard to summary hearings outside the cities, the evidence is even scantier. For the district of Montreal, there are a few surviving records where rural justices sent in fines and also specified the offences. The forty-odd cases from the late 1780s and 1790 suggest a pattern similar to that of the Weekly Sessions, with offences against the roads and militia laws dominating. Thus, in March 1790 François Malhiot, of Verchères, fined François Parizeau and two others for not repairing the king's highway, while in March 1789 Joseph Boucher de La Bruère de Montarville, a Boucherville justice, fined Baptiste Cicotte twelve *livres* for having refused to cart wood for the king.[46] The picture from the late 1820s and early 1830s is slightly different: of fifty-four defendants, thirty were fined for regulatory offences and minor offences against the state, with roads and militia offences predominating, but another thirteen were fined for offences against public morality, most for causing disorder in church on Sunday, and eleven for trespass under an agricultural-improvement act. The notebook kept by Crebassa and Jones, the William Henry justices, is probably representative of the business done in the summary hearings of rural justices. Overall, they required all nine defendants in assault cases to enter into recognizances to keep the peace, fined or found against thirteen *habitants* in roads and fences cases (along with another two in which the case was settled before judgment), fined another four defendants for drunkenness or disorderly conduct in church and another for selling liquor on Sunday, disciplined one *sous-voyer* (minor roads official) for not doing his duty, heard one deposition in a bastardy case, and imposed a fine in a case in which the clerk forgot to mention the charge.[47]

Given the fragmentary nature of the sources, it is risky to try to put together all the numbers so as to come up with a composite picture of the sorts of matters that were brought before the criminal justice system as a whole. Figure 5.13 nonetheless attempts this for all but complaints dealt with summarily by rural justices. Though the proportions should be treated as rough estimates, the figure suggests several things. First, while the criminal justice system could and certainly did serve to protect property, most people who came before it were not there because of property crime. Violence, on the other hand, was fundamental to the system. In the eighteenth and early nineteenth century, between a quarter and a third of all complaints concerned violence of one sort or another, from threats to murder, and from the 1810s on, the proportion surged to between 40 and 60 per cent. This corresponded to the opening of the Police Offices and the spread of the active magistracy into the countryside, both of which made it easier to make a complaint; but it

Figure 5.13: Offences, all complaints

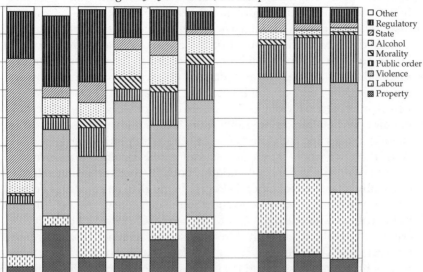

also suggests a criminal justice system to which people were increasingly willing to turn. Violence and theft, however, never dominated, with a varying mix of other circumstances bringing people before the justice system. In the eighteenth century as a whole, the sorts of offences dealt with by the Weekly Sessions, notably those that involved public obligations, made up half or more of all matters brought before the criminal justice system. And, in the nineteenth, we can perhaps see the beginnings of the rise in the prosecution of public-order and morality offences, heralding the changes that would transform the focus of criminal justice in the 1840s and beyond. In fact, the overall figures presented here, as we will see, probably underestimate this trend, since the increase in these prosecutions was also accompanied by an increase in prosecutions for other offences, notably those involving violence.

Avoiding Criminal Justice

There is thus evidence that criminal justice was integrated into everyday dispute resolution, even among rural *Canadiens*. And this impression is strengthened if we examine the relationship of criminal justice to other forms of dispute resolution, both state and non-state. Consider first the place of the civil courts in the resolution of potentially criminal disputes. Complaints for interpersonal violence, for example, could be launched either in the criminal or the civil courts, as a breach of the king's peace or as personal injury to the plaintiff. In eighteenth-century England, civil actions for assault and unlawful imprisonment were quite common, and in some courts in England, such as the King's Bench, interpersonal violence cases were often prosecuted as both criminal and civil matters at the same time, which allowed the plaintiff to claim damages and the state to fine or otherwise punish the defendant. And in New France, actions for assault could become either criminal or civil, with the same court judging both.[48] After the Conquest, and especially after the separation between the English criminal and French civil law systems, there was no court with such concurrent jurisdiction in the colony, and plaintiffs had to choose whether to launch a civil or criminal complaint, or both. Most chose the criminal side, with few interpersonal violence cases brought before the civil courts. Thus, there were a little over 30 such actions in the superior terms of the Montreal Common Pleas between 1770 and 1795, and a little over 150 in the Montreal King's Bench between 1795 and 1827; even the latter amounted to perhaps five suits per year, compared to over 400 violence complaints per year on average brought before the justices in the same period. Nor were assault suits common in the inferior terms of the civil courts. While a complete analysis remains to be done, a brief survey of the registers of the Montreal circuit courts reveals almost no suits for assault, although there were occasional suits for insult and defamation. Sometimes, aggrieved parties launched concurrent actions in the civil and criminal courts. In 1796 defence counsel in one such civil case (David Ross, the future chairman) argued that 'it is contrary to the law of the land for a plaintiff to have both a criminal and a civil prosecution for one and the same offence.' The response of the plaintiff's counsel (James Reid, the future King's Bench chief justice) illustrates the limits of a criminal action and the rationale for blending civil and criminal concerns. 'Inasmuch as by the present constitution of the courts of justice in this province,' he argued, 'all suits of a criminal nature are prosecuted in the name of the public, and for the ends of public justice only, in which the party complaining receives no damage or satisfaction for the injuries he hath sustained,' the stopping of the civil case would mean that 'the ends of justice would not be served.' The court sided with Reid, and concurrent civil and criminal complaints in assault cases continued in the nineteenth century, with the principle reaffirmed in another King's Bench decision in 1818.[49]

Civil assault cases nevertheless remained a rarity and, in superior terms at least, involved cases that were especially serious in some way, such as an apprentice tied up and beaten until he could not sit down, or a fight between members of Montreal's small Jewish synagogue during divine service. The reasons for this are evident. In superior terms, even launching a civil suit was a complicated and costly affair, necessarily involving lawyers, and with no certainty that there would be any particular effect on the defendant. Even if the plaintiff won the case, it might take months before the defendant had to pay anything other than his own legal fees. In a criminal assault complaint, on the other hand, the costs of the initial deposition and warrant were within reach of even labouring people, and since an arrest was generally made quickly, the victim of an assault could have the satisfaction of seeing the aggressor punished immediately, and if the result was pre-trial imprisonment, even if only for a few days, the effect was even stronger.[50]

Outside state justice entirely lay its informal counterpart, community mediation. As a complement to the argument of the marginality of criminal justice in ancien-régime societies, many historians have suggested that what usually took its place in dispute resolution was extrajudicial mediation, or infrajustice. Similarly, Quebec historians have suggested that rural *Canadiens* in particular frequently bypassed the courts by turning to local notables such as the militia captains or the *curés* to resolve their disputes.[51]

It is certainly possible to find examples of infrajudicial proceedings. In the 1760s and 1770s, there were a handful of cases of notarized reparations for insults, which could potentially have been brought before the justices of the peace through the imposition of peace bonds, though these tended to go before the civil courts instead. And, though perhaps referring more to civil than criminal justice, a meeting of the inhabitants of the parishes of Repentigny and Saint-Sulpice, northeast of Montreal, under the guidance of their *curé*, declared against the establishment of a local court by using the familiar terms of community mediation: the erection of a new court in the area 'animera l'esprit processif, déja trop répandu, et lui fairoit perdre de vue la méthode gratuite qu'elle veut introduire de se faire juger par ses amis' [would foster litigiousness, already too widespread, and lose sight of the free method envisaged of being judged by ones friends]. Likewise, in accepting appointment as a new magistrate in 1830, Jean-Antoine

Bouthillier, a Beauport notable, stated that 'I am the more disposed to undertake it, that during fifteen years residence in this parish I have been very often applied to in affairs requiring the interference of a magistrate, a great number of which I have succeeded to settle "à l'amiable."'[52] But how important really were infrajudicial proceedings in the dispute-settlement process, and did they lead to avoidance of more formal criminal proceedings?

First, it is essential to have some clarity as to what infrajustice means. As Benoît Garnot has pointed out, the term has been used so loosely that in some cases it has been extended to virtually all forms of formal and informal dispute resolution outside the courts, thus becoming co-valent with the everyday negotiations of normal social life and losing any analytical value. For example, Martin Dufresne's work on criminal justice in Quebec City defines infrajustice simply as modes of resolution that operate in parallel with the courts, which, among other things, leads him to argue that because relatively few assault cases from rural areas ended up in the Sessions papers, infrajudicial resolution of assaults must have been common. Evidently, most minor disputes, violent or otherwise, were addressed without going to court, but such is the case even today: most cases of minor interpersonal violence, for example, are not reported to the police.[53] Still, this observation does not help us understand the place of more formal alternate forms of dispute resolution.

A more useful definition of infrajustice in criminal matters, similar to that adopted by Garnot, restricts it to proceedings that sought to replace the criminal justice system with something analogous: for example, where two people, in a dispute that could have been brought before the criminal courts, sought out a third to mediate, with the third person often of higher social standing (in a rural parish, the local priest or seigneur, for instance), or when opponents entered into formalized agreements to resolve potentially criminal matters, again often with the involvement of third parties as guarantors (such as witnesses or notaries). However, infrajustice must be distinguished from the settlement of complaints already brought before the courts, for, while infrajustice sought to remove the courts from the dispute-resolution process, informal settlement of lesser criminal complaints such as assaults was, as we will see, an integral and accepted part of the ancien-régime criminal process. And the entire civil justice system was founded on the freedom of plaintiffs to discontinue their action at any time and settle privately.

Of course, measuring infrajudicial proceedings, even in this more restrained sense, is difficult, especially if mediation was entirely oral. In Europe, most evidence of infrajustice comes from the notarial archives: instances where victims of potentially criminal acts, such as violence or theft, entered into mutual agreements with their aggressors. Quebec and Lower Canada had the same notarial system as civil law countries such as France, so that, if notarial settlements were an important feature of dispute resolution, we would expect them to turn up with some regularity. But, in fact, while arbitration was a common (and legally accepted) form of proceeding in civil matters, such as claims for damages, it seems not to have been used with any regularity for cases that could have gone before the criminal courts. For example, in the two decades following the Conquest, the *Parchemin* database describing extant notarial records until the mid-1780s contains no reference whatsoever to the terms assault, theft, or murder, and infrajudicial settlements are no more common in the decades afterwards.[54]

The paucity of mentions of failed attempts at infrajudicial mediation in court documents is another indicator of their relative unimportance. In Europe, failed settlements often led victims to turn to the courts, in whose records historians can pick up the trail, and there are also instances of this for New France.[55] The Quebec and Lower Canadian judicial archives also provide examples. In 1820 an altercation broke out between Daniel Tuttle, a Barnston farmer, and Ebenezer Bacon, a bailiff from Hatley. Tuttle called Bacon 'a damn'd lyer a damn'd rascal and many other hard things, and accused him of whipping his father and turning him out of doors'; Bacon spat in Tuttle's face, and Tuttle reciprocated; and both exchanged threatening words, with Tuttle taking off his coat and rolling up his sleeves. Before the matter went any further, others who were present convinced them to stop and submit their differences to Levi M. Emerson and William Weeks, who 'did dictate to the said Tuttle and Bacon how they should settle and that they did agree to settle their dispute on the conditions by us proposed and both acknowledged themselves satisfy'd.' Tuttle and Bacon 'parted on apparently friendly terms.' Despite the infrajudicial settlement, however, things apparently soured, for about a week later Tuttle went before Phineas Hubbard, a local justice, and swore out a complaint against Bacon. Tuttle pursued the case right to indictment in Montreal Quarter Sessions, and after the grand jury found a bill against Bacon for assault, the latter pleaded guilty and was fined twenty shillings.[56] But this case is exceptional: in the extensive court records examined for this study, it is the only clear example of such an instance of failed arbitration by people entirely outside the justice system.

All of these observations are tentative, not only because arguments from an absence of indications in the sources are, of course, relatively weak, but also because there is as yet no in-depth study of infrajustice in post-Conquest Quebec. Nevertheless, the evidence so far for infrajudicial activity is scanty at best, consisting of a few isolated examples such as the Tuttle and Bacon affair or Bouthillier's affirmation and occasional mentions by outside observers. No doubt, many potentially criminal disputes were settled outside the courts: as Allan Greer points out, offenders may have been punished by community mechanisms such as shunning, and the relatively low number of cases of violence brought before the courts indicates that either this was an especially peaceful society (which its homicide rate, higher than that in England at the same time, suggests was not the case) or that most instances of ordinary violence were resolved extrajudicially.[57] It is also clear that violent mechanisms of popular justice such as riots, charivaris, and even revenge killings were not uncommon features of colonial society. But this was true right through the nineteenth century, and their mere presence tells us little about the place of the criminal justice system in dispute resolution, or the willingness of people to resort to it. The point is not that disputes were always brought before the criminal courts. It is rather that, when victims did decide to go beyond the informal individual or community-based sanctions common to all societies, they more often turned to the criminal justice system than some other alternative. And, when they did so, they must at least have believed that the criminal courts allowed them to exercise some form of social power, however limited.

Conclusion

Quantitative analyses can evidently go only so far in judging the different historiographical models of the relationship between the people and ancien-régime criminal justice, but they do give us some initial insights. In the first place, it is clear that marginality alone is an inadequate framework for understanding this relationship. Certainly, Abbott's complaints about the burden of dispensing justice on account of the litigiousness of rural habitants seem far-fetched: there were few rural plaintiffs in the eighteenth century, and even in the 1820s, there were fewer than twenty complaints of all types each year in a large settlement like William Henry. Had Abbott been an urban justice in the 1830s, however, his complaint would have been more grounded, since by then the everyday work of urban justice was a time-consuming affair. Still, even in the countryside, criminal justice was not marginal: Neilson's picture of bucolic peace in the early 1830s is belied by the regularity with which rural people made complaints to the justices, even if they came nowhere near to matching the litigiousness of city dwellers. And the relative unimportance of both civil justice and infrajustice in resolving criminal disputes also underscores the place of criminal justice.

Secondly, the pattern of offences suggests that neither the consensual nor conflictual models can satisfactorily encompass how people in Quebec and Lower Canada related to criminal justice. Ordinary assault cases, which dominated in the Quarter Sessions and made up a large proportion of offences overall, represented ancien-régime criminal justice at its most public-service-oriented, for no one was forced to launch an assault complaint and justices were generally open to plaintiffs dropping their complaints. In property cases, the justice system evidently had far more potential to act as an instrument of class domination, but theft and the like made up a small proportion of offences, even when all criminal courts are taken into account. Ethnic conflict comes through in the prosecution of specific regulatory offences such as breaches of the *corvée* laws, which, as Du Calvet correctly though perhaps hyperbolically asserted, represented the dominating power of the Conqueror at its most bare. But even these did not dominate, except perhaps briefly in the early 1780s, and most regulatory prosecutions were more an expression of the growing weight of the state, whether on tavern-keepers or property owners. More important in the long term was the beginning of attention paid to public-order and labour offences. Through these, class and gender conflict became an increasingly important feature of the justice system, and one that would come to dominate in the remainder of the nineteenth century. The everyday criminal justice system was thus a venue both for community dispute resolution and for the imposition of the will of those with power, both social and political.

As for the relevance of criminal justice to the *Canadien* population, it seems evident that, while they were less likely to come before the justices than the colony's British subjects, it is hardly fair to characterize the justice system as essentially concentrated on and used by the British population. Consider the attempted arrest of Joseph Dupras *dit* Pratte in Terrebonne in 1797, as narrated by Charles-Baptiste Bouc, the local member of the Assembly. A riot was taking place in the parish, and Bouc saw one Mr Destimonville seized by the neck. When he tried to free him, Dupras stepped forward and shouted, 'Etrangles ces sainé Englois en me parlant vous mavez atrapé lanné derniere vous mavez voulu epouventé en menpêchant daller a Montreal pour moposé auz bille des chemains mais je nest pas voulu vous ecouter et parse que nous avont manquer notre coup tueons pandant que nous pouvont nous somme dans un temps de liberté' [Strangle these damn English and then talking to me you tricked me last year, you wanted to frighten me into not going to Montreal to oppose the Roads Bill but I didn't listen to you and because we failed let us kill while we can we are in an age of liberty]. Bouc asked a bailiff to arrest Dupras, but the bailiff was hit several times and his constable's staff seized. A militia sergeant then arrived with six men but was also mistreated, and Dupras fled, swearing at and insulting the officers and all those in authority.[58] The case appears to underscore the extent of rural *Canadien* hostility towards all things British, including the justice system. But, though Dupras's defiance of authority is undoubted, everybody named in the case was *Canadien*: not only the parties and witnesses but also Félix Jolie, the Lachenaie justice of the peace before whom Bouc made his statement, Pierre Panet, the justice who joined Jolie in having Dupras arrested and bound to appear in Quarter Sessions, and most likely the bailiff and the militiamen. Dupras's experience of justice was therefore an entirely *Canadien* one, which is perhaps why, despite his defiance of the 'sainé Englois,' Dupras, or at least his attorney, turned up in the Montreal Quarter Sessions as he had promised, though whether this indicated his acceptance of the system's legitimacy seems doubtful. Overall, *Canadien* recourse to and participation in the criminal justice system provides little evidence of widespread rejection of the system's legitimacy, as Neilson would have had Tocqueville believe, but the extent of *Canadien* acceptance of it remains an open question. Of more immediate concern to Dupras and others was what they experienced once they came in contact with everyday criminal justice.

6

Experiencing the Everyday Course of Criminal Justice

The King agt. Geo, a Negroe. John Grant Prosecutor. George the Defendant arraigned for Stealing Two Pieces of Silk Ribbon Value Eleven pence Sterling. Pleads Guilty. Ct. That he the said George between the hours of Nine and Ten O'clock in the forenoon on Friday the 2d Day of August be Stript Naked to the Waist and tyed at a Cart Tail at the Goal and there to receive 10 Stripes & at Mr. Deschambaux Corner 10 Stripes and at the first Street this side the Generals 10 Stripes and at Mr. Landrieves Corner 10 Stripes and proceed to the Court Corner and there receive 10 Stripes & on the Parade 10 Stripes.

– Montreal Quarter Sessions register, July 1765

Un querelleur m'acoste et m'insulte. Je le menace de lui donner des coups de baton. Il n'est pas le plus fort, et prudemment il s'esquive. Mais toute réflexion faite il s'en va chez un magistrat devant lequel il prête serment que d'après les menaces que je lui ai faites il craint pour sa vie, et demande pour cette raison qu'on m'amène devant lui pour m'obliger à donner caution que je garderai la paix à son égard et envers tous les sujets de sa Majesté et à faute de ce faire de m'envoyer en prison. Le Juge à Paix comme de droit lance son mandat d'arrèt. Un connétable ou officier de paix en est chargé, il vient me prendre chez moi et me conduit devant le magistrat. J'ai su qu'il falloit donner des cautions, j'en suis muni. Me voilà devant le magistrat qui me fait part de la déposition, faite coutre moi. On dresse le cautionnement, il est donné. Je suppose que l'affaire est finie, je fais ma révérence à son honneur et veux partir. On m'arrête, on me dit que j'ai quelque chose à payer. Je demande comment cela se peut? ...

On me répond que l'on va m'envoyer en prison si je ne paye pas d'abord cinq shellings pour le greffier ou commis qui a dressé la déposition de mon adversaire, cinq shellings pour avoir écrit ce mandat d'arrêt, cinq shellings à l'officier de paix qui m'a rendu le service d'exécuter l'ordre et de m'amener devant le magistrat, enfin cinq shellings pour le cautionnement qu'on ne pouvoit refuser d'admettre.

[A quarreller accosts and insults me. I threaten to hit him with a stick. He is not as strong as I, and prudently runs away. After reflection, however, he goes before a magistrate, before whom he swears that because of my threats, he fears for his life, and thus asks that I be brought before the magistrate to be made to enter into a recognizance to keep the peace towards him and all His Majesty's subjects, failing which that I be sent to prison. The justice of the peace, as is his right, issues his warrant. A constable or peace officer is charged with it, he arrests me at my house and brings me before the magistrate. I knew that one had to bring guarantors, I have them with me. There I am before the magistrate, who acquaints me with the deposition against me. The recognizance is made up and entered into. I suppose the affair is over, I salute his honour and want to leave. I am stopped, I am told that I have something to pay. I ask, how is that possible? ... I am told that I will be sent to prison if I do not pay, first, five shillings for the clerk or scrivener who drew up my adversary's deposition, then five shillings for having drawn up the arrest warrant, five shillings to the peace officer who rendered me the service of executing the warrant and bringing me before the magistrate, finally five shillings for the recognizance which could not be refused me.]

– Anonymous correspondent, *La Minerve*, 1827[1]

Once plaintiffs had decided to complain, they engaged themselves and defendants in a judicial process which fundamentally shaped their experience of everyday criminal justice. As many historians have noted, the routes that people followed to, through, and out of criminal justice systems based on the English model were as varied as the range of matters brought before the system and the patchwork of officials and jurisdictions that made it up. Even within any given jurisdiction, the possible courses of justice varied widely. Peter King, for example, has described the procedural routes taken by those accused of property offences as a corridor of interconnected rooms or stage sets, each with doors leading eventually to conviction but also with exits, both legal and illegal.[2] The individual experiences of plaintiffs and defendants were also affected by a range of other factors, such as the type of

offence, the choices of decision makers including plaintiffs, police, magistrates, and jurors, and the resources, financial and otherwise, of participants. The course they took might consist in nothing more than a
displeasurable and perhaps costly visit to a justice, as in the case of *La
Minerve*'s correspondent, or might extend to the whole panoply of
preliminary imprisonment, jury trial, and subsequent corporal punishment, as was George's experience. In the case of a defendant who was
never arrested, it might amount to no experience whatsoever.

What George and *La Minerve*'s correspondent each experienced did
have some commonalities. Both encountered the everyday criminal
justice system through Montreal's justices of the peace, and both came
out of the encounter punished. Further, both were punished at the
initiative of a private plaintiff, rather than an official prosecutor. And in
both cases, there was nothing especially extraordinary about the course
that justice took. However, there were few other similarities. George,
possibly a slave, was prosecuted by a fur-trading merchant for petty
theft and brought to trial in the Quarter Sessions, most likely after first
undergoing preliminary imprisonment in the gaol. The grand jury seems
to have found the bill of indictment, and since George pleaded guilty,
his fate was then decided by the justices on the bench, two merchants
and a former army officer. George's punishment, a painful, terrifying,
and humiliating public experience, was the very image of what we
think of as ancien-régime punishments, mirroring similar punishments
in both New France and England.[3] It also reflected the importance that
merchant-justices placed both on property crime and on crime by those
on the margins of society. The experience of *La Minerve*'s correspondent
was quite different. After being threatened with imprisonment if he did
not pay up, this evidently literate individual ended up shelling out £1 in
fees, a considerable sum which he nevertheless apparently had at his
disposal. No pre-trial imprisonment or whipping through the town for
him, but instead a case settled the same day, with a hefty hit on his
pocketbook. His experience was not terrifying, but alienating nonetheless – as he declared bitterly, 'Il se trouve ici des personnes d'une
scrupuleuse conscience qui appellent cela de la justice' [There are people
here of a most scrupulous conscience who call that justice]. Here was a
man confronted by a judicial bureaucracy which, in his eyes, had ex-
torted money from him. This was perhaps particularly galling since,
given his affinity for *La Minerve*, he most likely did not share the
political beliefs of the men he encountered in the Police Office.

While we know a great deal about extraordinary proceedings in treason trials or under military justice,[4] we have little direct testimony of how ordinary people experienced the everyday course of criminal justice in the colony, criminal or civil, beyond occasional complaints about the legal proceedings themselves. At best, we have a few newspaper and travellers' accounts written by educated and generally reform-minded members of the elites, but their views are inherently biased. Thus, can we really take at face value Tocqueville's oft-cited description of a civil court case in Quebec City in 1831 as 'quelque chose de bizarre, d'incohérent, de burlesque même' [something bizarre, incoherent, even burlesque], due to the mixing of French and English, of Catholicism and Protestantism, of the customary and statute law of England and France, coming as it did from a young noble visitor who nostalgically saw the *habitants* as unspoiled relics of an ancien régime long lost in France and the clergy as the enlightened leaders of *Canadien* society?[5] Or the almost caricatural depictions of justices in the reform press of the late 1820s and 1830s, when the goal of this commentary was to discredit the Tory-dominated administration, in the face of equally blatant truth-manipulation from the Tory press? Instead, using both quantitative evidence and individual examples, this chapter attempts to reconstruct what plaintiffs and defendants might have experienced as they took their course through the everyday justice system, from the moment of the initial complaint to final resolution of their case.

Pre-trial Proceedings

As *La Minerve*'s correspondent's experience suggests, one of the most important (though least studied) aspects of British criminal justice was pre-trial procedure, most of which took place before justices. The orality of many of the proceedings means that official documents are often silent on all but the formal steps, but we can still make a few observations on the nature of these initial encounters between the people and the system.

First, what characterized these proceedings was the heterogeneity of experiences and courses they engendered. Consider the following examples, both from 1800 and involving *Canadiens* charged before the justices in Montreal. The complaint of Pierre Goguet, a Saint-Hilaire habitant, against Baptiste Bazinet, his tenant farmer, and Charlotte Brouillet, Bazinet's wife, for assaulting him when he asked for two days' labour, followed what can be termed the 'normal' route for assault cases. The assault occurred at seven o'clock in the morning on 6

September; by some time later in the same day, Goguet was in Montreal complaining to Jean-Jacques Jorand, who issued an arrest warrant directed to one 'Guyon huissier,' presumably the local bailiff, who had perhaps accompanied Goguet to Montreal; three days later, Bazinet and Brouillet were before Jorand to enter recognizances to appear at the Quarter Sessions in October; but the case proceeded no further, or at least did not appear in the registers of the court. Another procedure altogether applied in the complaint of William Martin, Montreal's inspector of chimneys, against Louis-Charles Foucher, the colony's solicitor general and future justice of the King's Bench, for erecting an enclosed wooden staircase beside his house on the Place d'Armes. On Thursday, 1 May, Martin visited the house with Gilbert Miller, a carpenter, as a witness; on Saturday, 3 May, Martin swore out a *qui tam* complaint (whereby a prosecutor sued on his own and the King's behalf) against Foucher before Charles Blake. Blake issued a summons to Foucher to appear in the Weekly Sessions at 10:00 the following Tuesday morning; sometime in the intervening three days, the summons was served on Foucher, most likely by one of the city constables; and on Tuesday, Foucher himself appeared before Blake, John Richardson, Robert Cruickshank, William Maitland, and James Hughes to plead not guilty, only to see himself found guilty two weeks later.[6]

The ways to and through the justice system, before trial, were as varied as those in England, even if we consider only legal routes. Figure 6.1 summarizes these routes, moving from the initial offence in the top left corner to trial at the bottom right. The possible courses are indicated by broken lines for the plaintiff and solid ones for the defendant, with steps involving police indicated by dotted lines. As complex as it already is, the diagram leaves out a number of special procedures, such as habeas corpus applications, that applied in only a limited number of cases.

At the first stage, the complaint itself, having ready access to a justice was crucial. Most plaintiffs started off by appearing before a justice to swear out a deposition and procure a warrant, as was the case with the 'querelleur' of *La Minerve*'s correspondent. In some cases, they might go first to a bailiff or constable. In 1825, for example, Lazare Beauvais, of Caughnawaga, was at Pierre Reider's in Châteauguay when he was hit by Jacques Duquet, a local labourer. He then went to the house of Charles Dewitt, the bailiff of Châteauguay, but on leaving the house Duquet ran up to him, declaring, 'Puisque tu veux m'en faire coûter, je veux te battre à ma fantaisie' [Since you want to make me pay, I want to

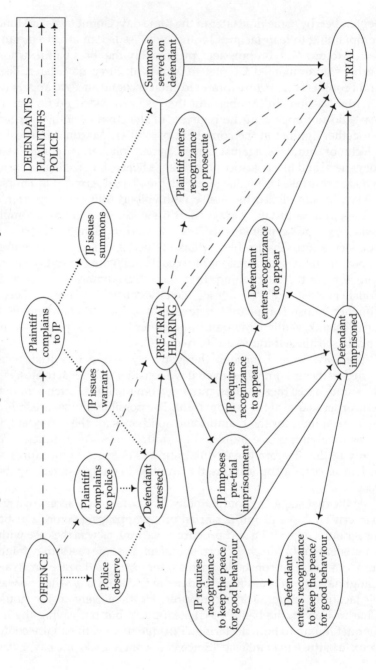

Figure 6.1: Common pre-trial routes of criminal complaints

DEFENDANTS ——→
PLAINTIFFS – – →
POLICE ·······→

OFFENCE

Plaintiff complains to police

Police observe

Plaintiff complains to JP

JP issues summons

JP issues warrant

Defendant arrested

Summons served on defendant

Plaintiff enters recognizance to prosecute

PRE-TRIAL HEARING

Defendant enters recognizance to appear

JP requires recognizance to appear

JP imposes pre-trial imprisonment

Defendant imprisoned

JP requires recognizance to keep the peace/ for good behaviour

Defendant enters recognizance to keep the peace/ for good behaviour

TRIAL

beat you as much as I want], and proceeded to hit him repeatedly until bystanders pulled him away. In other cases, plaintiffs might first draw up the deposition themselves, or have it drawn up by a notary or lawyer, as seems to have become increasingly common in the 1830s, after the closing of the Police Office. But passing through a magistrate's parlour or the Police or Peace Office was an essential step, since it was the justice who had to accept or reject the complaint and then decide what to do next.[7]

From the defendant's point of view, what came next was crucial in determining the experience of justice: an arrest or a summons. Which of these courses was taken depended less on the discretion of the justice than on the nature of the offence. Defendants were generally arrested if accused of felonies, common law misdemeanours such as threats, assault, or keeping disorderly houses, and most statutory offences punishable by summary imprisonment, such as desertion or vagrancy; in the latter, as we will see, it was increasingly the police themselves who acted directly as plaintiffs. For most other statutory offences, especially those involving breaches of the regulatory provisions of acts, ordinances, and police regulations, defendants were summoned rather than being arrested. The difference was crucial, for, if arrested, a defendant had to go almost immediately before the justice, just like *La Minerve*'s correspondent, and undergo the public humiliation of marching through the streets or countryside accompanied by a bailiff or constable who was generally a long-serving professional and thus well known to the inhabitants. If a defendant were summoned, on the other hand, the process instead resembled that used in minor civil cases. The summons was served on the defendant (often not even in person), thereby considerably diminishing the accompanying social stigma. And it was generally returnable several days later, either before the justice or one of the formal courts, a pause that gave defendants time to organize their defence.

The role of police was also central at this stage of the proceedings, whether the encounter with them was direct or indirect. In most cases, police were acting reactively, as process-servers, serving warrants or summonses at the behest of plaintiffs after a complaint to a justice. But in the nineteenth century, as we will see, in the increasing number of cases of people accused of vagrancy and disorderly conduct, the police acted as plaintiffs as well as police, both arresting the defendant and swearing out the complaint. In addition, the relationship between police and the people they arrested went beyond simple conflict and domination. Until 1810, for example, at least in the district of Montreal, it was a common practice for a constable or bailiff to arrest a defendant, take him or her before a justice, and then immediately turn around and become one of the defendant's guarantors on their bonds. In Montreal, the practice was stopped in 1810 as 'very improper and in-compasible [sic] with the said office,' but it continued sporadically in rural areas.[8]

After being arrested or summoned, defendants who did not head straight for court generally underwent a preliminary hearing before a justice. This was more or less elaborate depending on the nature of the offence, and especially on whether the defendant was accused of a felony, and thus subject to the Marian bail statutes, or of another offence such as assault, for which there were fewer legal guidelines. As we saw, some justices undertook fairly substantial preliminary hearings in felony cases, including interrogations of defendants. These could be harrowing for defendants: Christian Shavers, an accused thief, said in 1795 that 'being somewhat intoxicated in liquor and never in all of my life brought before a magistrate before that I was so much terrified that I scarcely knew where I was or what I said,' though he may have been evoking terror to discredit what had evidently been a confession.[9] Preliminary investigations and hearings in misdemeanour cases were much more rudimentary. Few if any witnesses were heard beyond the plaintiff, and there does not appear to have been much in the way of questioning of the defendants. More often, as in the case of La Minerve's correspondent, the defendant was simply read the deposition and he or she either gave the necessary bail or was committed to gaol. Both plaintiffs and defendants were generally present at these hearings, and in some cases even at the original complaint. We can only imagine what this meant: not only the tensions caused by deposing in front of one's aggressor, often soon after the aggression, but also the satisfaction of seeing that aggressor in custody.

Important as well for the experience of plaintiffs and defendants was that justices could legally resolve many cases at this preliminary stage of the proceedings, thereby making appearance in a formal court unnecessary. In the case of both felonies and misdemeanours, justices could decide after the preliminary hearing that there simply was not enough evidence to support the complaint and refuse to proceed further by requiring bail or committing the defendant to gaol. Thus, in his notebook in July 1819, the Saint-Hyacinthe magistrate Joseph Porlier recorded a case where James Moses, a farmer, prosecuted Michel

Chauvin for stealing his hay. Porlier had Chauvin arrested, but, after hearing the parties and the witnesses, he dismissed the case and ordered Moses to pay all costs.[10] In England, perhaps a quarter of property crime accusations were dismissed in this way, but though the lack of any consistent records for individual justices makes it impossible to judge the scope of pre-trial dismissals in the colony, justices seem generally to have erred on the side of caution, committing accused to gaol on the strength of the plaintiff's evidence alone without a full pre-trial investigation. As in the case of *La Minerve*'s correspondent, in a wide variety of misdemeanour cases, from assault through disturbing the peace to prostitution, justices could also bind over the defendant to keep the peace towards the plaintiff and/or be of good behaviour, most often for six or twelve months, by imposing a recognizance (bail bond) generally ranging from £10 to £100, often for £20, along with two guarantors for half of the amount each. This was a common practice: judging from the case files in the sessions papers, Montreal justices in the 1810s and 1820s imposed peace bonds in about a quarter of assault cases that came before them, with the remainder sent on for trial in the Quarter Sessions.

It was only in cases where the justice felt that the offence was too serious to warrant the imposition of a peace recognizance, or where he did not have the jurisdiction to impose a formal settlement, that plaintiffs and defendants in felony and misdemeanour cases found themselves sent on to a formal court. A key magisterial decision here substantially affected the defendant's experience: whether he or she was imprisoned while awaiting trial or allowed to enter into a recognizance to appear at the court. In most serious felonies, such as murders or robberies, justices were not supposed to bail defendants but instead send them to gaol, and they seem generally to have done so: among a small sample of defendants indicted in Quebec King's Bench in the 1810s, 1820s, and 1830s for serious violence-related crimes, such as murder and robbery, at least 85 per cent can be positively identified as having undergone some form of pre-trial imprisonment. These defendants might stay in gaol only briefly, until released under habeas corpus, or for a long time, until the next session of the bi-yearly criminal courts. In misdemeanours, pre-trial imprisonment was less usual, since defendants were legally allowed to find bail, and most were able to. Still, if a defendant could not immediately find sureties to appear or keep the peace, a justice could instead send him or her to gaol, so that even for minor offences, defendants could find themselves imprisoned without actually being convicted of anything, though often they were bailed soon afterwards. And this was not a rare occurrence: the rate of pre-trial imprisonment for cases of lesser violence from the 1810s to the 1830s, in both Montreal and Quebec City, varied between about 10 and 25 per cent with the high point coming in the 1820s and a sharp decline in the 1830s, perhaps related to the replacement of professional chairmen by unpaid justices. Justices had broad powers to imprison suspects even before trial, which was crucial not only to the experience of defendants but also to the decisions that plaintiffs took.

These preliminary proceedings before the justices closely resemble what has been described for English justice in other settings. However, despite this fundamentally English cast, the process was also not that different from pre-Conquest French procedures. Thus, both before and after the Conquest, regulatory offences were dealt with summarily before judges or magistrates, under procedures that seem to have been similar, involving summons rather than arrests. For other offences, the process started in both systems with a complaint, generally by a private individual, which followed the same basic form (a general description of what had happened and its results). One important difference with French procedure was the moment of arrest of the suspect, which came earlier under the English system and was at the discretion of the justice rather than a crown prosecutor. In more serious cases, though, as we saw, justices might sometimes undertake preliminary investigations, just as under the French system, and their preliminary hearings were analogous to the *informations* of the French system, with statements from the principal witnesses, including a medical or coroner's report if necessary, and all relevant papers then forwarded to the state prosecutor for examination and action. Even the voluntary examination of defendants was analogous to the *interrogatoire* under the French system, although it came earlier, generally at the same time as the preliminary hearing, and, as the name implies, was less rigorous, since defendants could not be compelled to give evidence against themselves under oath and many simply denied involvement. Finally, pre-trial imprisonment was broadly similar to the French system, where suspects in more serious cases (those subject to the *procédure extraordinaire*) might spend months in prison.[11]

Alongside formal pre-trial procedures, justices might engage in other proceedings that sought to direct plaintiffs and defendants away from the formal courts. In eighteenth-century England, especially in cases of minor violence and theft, magistrates were allowed and even encouraged to mediate disputes rather than send them on to formal trial, in what Gregory Smith has called a 'culture of arbitration,' which fit perfectly with the paternal notions of local elites.[12] And, though the evidence is necessarily scanty, justices in Quebec and Lower Canada also acted as mediators. The Chevalier de Niverville, a Trois-Rivières justice, explained in 1791 that he had never submitted any fines to government because, having never received any instructions on his role, he always acted as arbitrator in disputes brought before him. This had generally worked quite well, and when the parties remained unreconciled, he condemned them to pay the bailiff's fees. Likewise, a failed arbitration lay behind the complaint that James Sawers, a William Henry justice, sent on to Quarter Sessions for trial, involving the assault of Pierre Prévost on Antoine Frapper *père*:

> having heard what both parties had to say, I determine that the defendant pay to the plaintiff all the charges of the constable, the witnesses, the time the plaintiff's husband has been sick, and the surgeon's bill, all which amount to a little more than thirty shillings *at this time*. The defendant will not pay more than six dollars; and the plaintiff will not put up with that small sum, not knowing how much the surgeon's bill will amount to; so not agreeing to my determination, they chuse rather to carry the cause in before the next Court of Quarter Sessions of the Peace ...

Sawers, indeed, seemed to favour imposing these sort of settlements, sometimes even abusively. In 1800, for example, he was sued by Pierre Grignon, a Berthier habitant, for having had Grignon arrested for insulting one Josephte Rivard, summarily trying him, and forcing him, on pain of sending him to prison, to sign an apology which would be posted at the door of the Berthier parish church and of several other churches in the region – a punishment entirely unprovided for in English or colonial law, though not technically illegal. And Sawers was not alone: Philemon Wright, a justice of the peace and the leading figure in Hull, declared that his 'zeal for to keep the peace of the country; was generally crowned with success, and we accordingly saved expences in the law by the adjustment of grievances nearly by the rule of equity.' But mediation could turn to outright misconduct. Patrick Conroy, a long-serving magistrate, was dismissed from the commission in 1810 because he had offered to free a prisoner accused of theft 'if the parties choose to settle it here, pay the charges and me something for my trouble.' The charge was likely a felony, and what Conroy was suggesting was compounding, a serious offence, which subsumed the criminal law to private concerns.[13]

Prosecutorial Initiative and Discretion

Conroy's suggestion nevertheless raises a key aspect that shaped the course of justice and was one of the most striking features of ancien-régime criminal justice based on the British model: the importance of prosecutorial initiative and discretion. In England, until the nineteenth century, most cases brought before magistrates and judges, from simple assaults to murders, were prosecuted by private individuals, at their own initiative and expense, with little intervention by the state. The flip side of this prosecutorial initiative was prosecutorial discretion: if the plaintiff decided not to pursue the case, the state did not generally step in, allowing the case to drop. This is often presented as one of the fundamental differences between continental criminal justice systems and those of Britain and its colonies, though it is becoming increasingly clear that discretion was important in ancien-régime France as well. The persistence of private initiative as the basis of criminal prosecution is also presented as one of the fundamental weaknesses of the system, one that eventually led to its being replaced by state-based prosecution, which, in England at least, became the job of the new police. There are, of course, many nuances to this broad picture: for example, in more serious cases, plaintiffs were often bound over by recognizance to prosecute in court, meaning that it was harder for them to abandon the prosecution. But in England at least, it was private initiative that characterized criminal justice in what Peter King has called 'the golden age of discretionary justice.'[14]

In Quebec and Lower Canada, as in the American and British North American colonies, the situation was more complicated. In more serious cases the state was more directly involved in prosecution: thus, King's Bench cases were prosecuted not by victims but by the colony's law officers, to whom justices sent in the results of pre-trial hearings. And, as we will see in chapter 8, the rise of public prosecution in other cases was one of ways in which the everyday criminal justice system was transformed in the nineteenth century. However, as Martin Dufresne has shown for assault cases in Quebec City in the 1830s, much as Allen Steinberg found for Philadelphia in the first half of the nineteenth century, for less serious complaints, and notably assaults, the system still retained a strong flavour of private initiative and prosecutorial discretion.[15]

It is indeed in complaints for interpersonal violence that we see the strongest evidence for this. In England, as has often been pointed out, judicial officials often treated assault cases more as if they were a civil case between two parties than a matter involving the public, though this attitude was beginning to change in the later eighteenth century. The situation in New France prior to the Conquest was little different; there, too, assault cases were often left to the initiative of the private plaintiffs, despite the theoretical involvement of the *procureur du roi*. And the same applied in our period, with magistrates quite open to stopping court proceedings if the plaintiff requested it. Thus, the registers of the Montreal Quarter Sessions regularly record assault cases discontinued on the plaintiffs declaring themselves satisfied. Until 1810 at least, this often occurred even after indictments had been found by the grand jury, underscoring even more forcefully the fiction of prosecution by the king. While parties sometimes formally appeared before the court and asked its permission to stop the proceedings, the informality of these sorts of discontinuance can be seen in the clerk's laconic note in the 1785 case of Joseph Dufau against Joseph LaRocque for assault, in which the jury had found a true bill: 'Mr. Justice Foretier represents that [Dufau] had declared to him that he was satisfied,' on which the case went no further. And this sort of magisterial acquiescence also extended to cases that had not yet come to court. In 1820, for example, William Kell, an Argenteuil justice, wrote to the clerk of the peace in Montreal regarding an assault complaint he had sent in; the parties, he declared, 'both came to me this morning saying that they had agreed and settled their affair and did not wish to have it go any further and they pray that you will have the goodness to stop the proceedings that their names may not be called in Court, and their bails saved, if this will not be granted have the goodness to acquaint me with it, that they may appear and save their bail. Murphy has writ to his attorney to the same effect to stop the proceeding.'[16]

Further, while they regularly required plaintiffs in felony cases to enter into recognizances to prosecute before the King's Bench, Montreal's magistrates at least infrequently imposed such recognizances on plaintiffs in assault cases, much as in England. Thus, in violence complaints destined for the Montreal Quarter Sessions between 1780 and 1835, there were more than ten times as many recognizances to appear imposed on defendants than recognizances to prosecute. And, even when recognizances were imposed on plaintiffs, they were almost never forfeited if the plaintiff chose not to prosecute. Thus, in 1809, the new attorney general, Edward Bowen, suggested that recognizances were 'considered a mere idle force and consequently little attention is paid to it by which means many culprits go unpunished, the prosecutor frequently neglecting to appear though bound to do so by the tenor of the recognizance.' Little, however, changed and in the mid-1830s plaintiffs could still be fairly sure that their recognizances to prosecute would not be enforced. On an entirely different level, the reliance on private prosecutorial initiative might extend even to the transmission of information between rural justices and urban court officials. Though many justices sent in the necessary papers themselves, the civil secretary in 1835 suggested to one justice that he have such documents delivered by the prosecutor, 'whose interest & duty alike tend to ensure the safe delivery of the papers to the Clerks of the Peace.'[17]

There were some limits to the openness of the justices to prosecutorial discretion, even in assault cases. When it suited them, justices could revert to the fiction that all criminal prosecutions were at the suit of the king. In 1787, for example, John Graize was found guilty in Montreal Quarter Sessions of an assault and battery on Josette Girard. Graize's counsel moved that judgment be arrested, since Girard was not present when the jury delivered its verdict, as required by law; but the justices dismissed the motion, since 'the prosecution being at the suit of the crown, there was no necessity for the prosecutrix being present.' More important, from the 1810s, there were attempts on the part of the justices to exercise more control over assault prosecutions. In 1819, for example, John Fletcher explained why the justices had convicted Jacques Blais of assaulting Michel Patris and sentenced him to two months in gaol, despite an apparent agreement between the two:

> I rather think that the prosecutor and defendant had subsequent to the bill being found but previous to the trial either made up the difference between them without leave of the court or entered into some negociation for that purpose, but the case appearing to the court to be of such a nature as to render it incompatible with their duty to permit a private arrangement between the parties (and which indeed is scarcely ever done by us after the return of a true bill by the grand jury) the case was ordered to proceed.

In Montreal Quarter Sessions as well, after 1810 there are few examples of cases being discontinued at the explicit request of the parties once a bill of indictment had been found, although, of course, the plaintiff could simply not turn up to prosecute – which, as we will see, happened frequently.[18]

Coming to Trial

Once they came to trial, the experience of plaintiffs and defendants also depended fundamentally on the nature of the procedures undertaken and the court involved, whether a summary hearing before a single justice, a Weekly or Special Sessions hearing, or a Quarter Sessions jury trial. As elsewhere, summary hearings, whether before urban or rural justices, were often brief affairs.[19] In the case of summary convictions for prostitution, vagrancy, or ship desertion, for example, while there are no direct accounts of trials, there is no indication that any witnesses were heard beyond the plaintiff. And the few records we have of rural hearings before justices mostly show them taking place a few days after the initial complaint and summons, again with few if any witnesses heard. Even before rural justices, though, hearings could be more complex. The 1814 prosecution launched by Médard Bruguière, one of the militia captains of the village of L'Assomption, against Augustin Lacroix, a baker, for refusing to provide *corvée* labour for the king, was heard before three of the village's justices. Lasting over two different sessions, it involved a challenge to jurisdiction, four prosecution witnesses, the production of documentary proof, and a dissenting opinion by one of the three magistrates. In its complexity, it thus rivalled many King's Bench criminal trials. Still, this example notwithstanding, judicial proceedings were probably often quite informal, as evoked by this account of an habitant tried before a rural justice for a roads offence:

> Interrogé par le Magistrat, l'habitant voulut donner ses raisons pour se défendre. Le Magistrat l'interrompit et lui dit qu'il avoit menti; le Défendeur ayant voulu s'expliquer, le Magistrat revint à cette expression favorite, et finit par le menacer de le mettre à la porte. On pense bien que tout cela ne se disoit pas de la manière dont on dit *Je vous aime.*
>
> [Questioned by the magistrate, the inhabitant sought to give his reasons for his defence. The magistrate interrupted him and told him that he lied; the defendant wanting to explain himself, the magistrate came back to his favourite expression, and ended up putting him out. One can imagine that all of that was not said in the same manner as one says I love you.]

And indeed, rural justices were accused on several occasions of not allowing defendants a full defence.[20]

Trials in both the Weekly and Quarter Sessions were more formal experiences. In both courts, plaintiffs and defendants faced a bench composed of two, three, or more urban justices, far more accustomed to trials than their rural counterparts, and in fact professional jurists in the 1810s and 1820s, along with a full panoply of court officials, including clerks, criers, and constables. Cases before the urban courts were part of a much larger bureaucratic routine: while a rural justice might hear at most a few cases per year, both Weekly and Quarter Sessions, at least in Montreal and Quebec City, were dealing with hundreds of prosecutions each year by the early nineteenth century.

There were nevertheless significant differences between the two courts, including the number of cases dealt with each sessions. Even in the early nineteenth century, the Montreal Weekly Sessions in general dealt with only three to four different cases each session, along with administrative business, a number that had risen only to about five per session in the late 1820s. Even if spectators were present, this meant that the hearings were most likely relatively intimate affairs. In Quarter Sessions, however, the caseload was much higher, with each session of the courts in Montreal and Quebec City dealing with dozens and, by the 1830s, hundreds of different cases. Individual plaintiffs and defendants were thus lost among the throng.

As well, judging by the few remaining records, summary proceedings in Weekly Sessions were often similar to those before rural justices, with only a few witnesses called, and sometimes just the plaintiff, and judgments imposed on the spot. Some trials were more complex, with multiple witnesses and lengthy testimony, but these seem to have been the exception.[21] Trial in Quarter Sessions, at least for indictable offences, was a far more involved and no doubt alienating judicial experience. These trials involved the same multiple steps as in England and its other colonies: the crier calling over each case and the parties involved at the beginning of the Sessions; plaintiffs and their witnesses giving secret testimony before the grand jury, which found or rejected the bills; the court clerk reading the indictment to the defendant, followed by his or her plea; the plaintiff and witnesses swearing their oaths and testifying before the trial jury, which found the defendant guilty or innocent; and the bench pronouncing judgment. As a result, the length of summary proceedings before the justices and before the Weekly and Special Sessions was very different from that of jury trials in Quarter Sessions. In summary proceedings, little time generally passed between the initial complaint and final resolution by the justices. When people were arrested as vagrants or prostitutes, they were almost invariably brought before a magistrate the same day or the next (if arrested during the night) and judged on the spot. Summary hearings before rural justices also generally happened rapidly, with only a few days between the initial complaint, the summons, and the judgment. Even in the more formal Weekly Sessions, three-quarters or more cases in the Montreal court were determined in a single session. Some Weekly Sessions cases could drag on through multiple continuations, but these were rare. In cases destined for Quarter Sessions, on the other hand, months might pass between the initial complaint and the trial itself. Then, the full process was often spread out over the entire ten-day period of the session, with each step coming on a different day, meaning that plaintiffs and defendants had to devote more than a week to getting their dispute formally resolved before the court. And, since defendants generally had the right to traverse their case, which involved putting it off until the next session after they had pleaded not guilty, many cases stretched out over two or even more sessions.

Another thing that distinguished the experience of Quarter Sessions from that of all other proceedings before the justices was the presence of juries. As I have argued elsewhere, the jury was a crucial institution in the colony, a means whereby the middling ranges of colonial society were co-opted into the operations of both criminal justice and local administration. For plaintiffs and defendants, juries in Quarter Sessions also represented yet another level of formality, as well as exposing them to the judgment of other members of society. As was true of England and other societies, despite the rhetoric of trial by peers, juries in Quebec and Lower Canada were far from representative of the population as a whole. Just like the justices, juries were entirely male. As well, in Quarter Sessions before the late 1820s, virtually all jurors were drawn from the towns, meaning that rural parties were submitting themselves to the judgment of city dwellers. The class composition of the jury was also unrepresentative, especially at the level of grand juries. Until the early 1830s, Quarter Sessions grand jurors were generally drawn from the middling or upper reaches of colonial society: in the eighteenth century, they were often made up of leading merchants, apart from those who were also justices, and though in the nineteenth their status declined, most Montreal grand jurors until 1832 were still middling traders and shopkeepers. While a study of trial juries in the colony has yet to be undertaken, property qualifications meant that they were also generally drawn from the 'respectable' ranks of property holders. On the other hand, juries were ethnically mixed. From the very beginning of British rule, the sheriffs who composed grand juries applied the principle of *de mediate*, with jurors being half-*Canadien*, half-British. In trial juries, the principle was followed less strictly, but, in general, a *Canadien* defendant could expect to be judged by a jury composed of at least half *Canadiens*. For a brief period under an 1832 jury-qualification law, grand and trial juries were much more broadly based, drawn from the district at large and mostly *Canadien* habitants, but, owing to wrangling between the *Patriote*-dominated Assembly and the Tory-dominated Legislative Council, the law was not renewed in 1835. In practice, though, juries remained more broadly based, at least in terms of ethnicity: in Montreal, after a brief return to the *de mediate* principle in 1835, the 1836 and 1837 Quarter Sessions grand juries were once again composed largely of *Canadiens*.[22]

As elsewhere, jury deliberations in Quebec and Lower Canada were often rapid. Though most juries do seem to have retired to consider their verdicts, few remained out for long, and juries deliberating for more than a day were rare. As well, the solemnity of jury proceedings was often dubious. In 1791, for example, William Harkness was found guilty in Montreal Quarter Sessions of assaulting Jean-Baptiste Hervieux. Harkness protested that the jury had 'separated themselves from each other after being charged by the court and before bringing in their verdict; that they withdrew from the place where they were put under the charge of the constable, and some of them were seen talking to people in the streets, all of which he is ready to prove.' In a direct contradiction to that trumpeted fundamental principle of the English criminal justice system, the impartial jury, the court replied that 'the same even if proved is not sufficient to annul the verdict,' and fined Harkness fifteen shillings. What is equally instructive, the justices on the bench included James McGill and Pierre Guy, then the two most experienced justices, as well as Thomas McCord, the justice who, twenty year later, would be praised for his intimate knowledge of English law; all three were also frequent members of King's Bench grand juries. Their decision was thus unlikely to have been the result of ignorance; it may have had more to do with the fact that McGill and Guy, like the plaintiff Hervieux, were all Montreal merchants.[23]

Nevertheless, we must not overestimate the importance of juries in shaping the courses that plaintiffs and defendants took through the everyday criminal justice system. There were no juries outside the King's Bench and Quarter Sessions, which meant that they played no part in determining what happened to those tried before the justices for vagrancy, disobedience as apprentices and servants, or street prostitution, nor for breaches of colonial statutes or police regulations. Even in

Quarter Sessions, it was only common law offences such as assault and battery and larceny that were subject to the full panoply of jury trial, whereas statutory offences such as bastardy or weights-and-measures offences and administrative offences such as defaulting constables or jurymen, all of which made up perhaps a third of cases heard by the Montreal court, were tried summarily by the justices themselves. And many complaints for assault and the like never actually made it to trial before the courts. Overall, it was thus a small minority of criminal complaints that were determined even by a grand jury: in the district of Montreal in the nineteenth century, something around a quarter, and in the district of Quebec, decreasing from perhaps a quarter in the mid-1810s to less than 15 per cent in the mid-1830s.

A final and crucial aspect of trials before the justices, whether summary or in formal courts, was that they were public affairs, open to whatever spectators happened to be interested. Even the few accounts we have of hearings before rural justices often mention the presence of onlookers, sometimes as many as ten or twenty.[24] This initially shocked some elite observers more used to the French system. In 1765, for example, Christophe Pélissier, a Quebec City merchant, protested to Murray and his Council about an assault case against him in Quebec Quarter Sessions. Among other things, he complained of the humiliation of undergoing a public trial on the simple word of a plaintiff. It was mortifying, he declared, for a man of honour and sentiment to endure, in open court, humiliations that he did not deserve, especially since ill-intentioned men, informants, would almost always find the means to oppress the innocent from the moment of their deposition, regardless of the defendant's witnesses. However, Pélissier, an educated and fairly recent immigrant from France, was hardly representative of the *Canadien* community, fleeing to the United States during the Revolution.[25] There is otherwise little indication that the *Canadiens* in general objected to the public nature of criminal court proceedings, but, even so, that feature of the justice system did mark a significant change from pre-Conquest procedures based on private trials in closed courtrooms.

Professional Assistance

Plaintiffs and defendants, however, did not necessarily face the justices or the courts alone. Representation by counsel had strong roots in the colony's legal culture, both before and after the Conquest, and, though most of lawyers' business was made up of civil cases, they were nevertheless frequent players in the justices' courts, from the Quarter Sessions down to summary hearings before individual rural justices. The limits on defence counsel under English law applied only to capital crimes, which the justices' courts could not try, so that defendants were not necessarily thrust without assistance into the legal arena, as was probably the case in the higher criminal courts in the eighteenth century. And, while criminal prosecutions in the King's Bench were generally undertaken by crown law officers, these took little part in cases before the justices, where private prosecutors dominated.[26]

That lawyers were regular participants in Quarter Sessions trials is evident from the benches reserved for them in the courtrooms, at least in the nineteenth century, and from occasional comments such as that of McCord and Mondelet in 1823 that 'all the advocates are in the habit of attending the Court of Quarter Sessions,' or the brief description by John Lambert in the early 1800s that in Quarter Sessions 'counsellors attend and argue for their clients, who are put to great expense for summonses, fees, &c.'[27] It is harder to tell how many plaintiffs and defendants were actually represented by counsel. The Montreal Quarter Sessions registers suggest that attorneys were involved in at least a quarter of indictable cases overall, with counsel for plaintiffs specifically mentioned somewhat more often than for defendants (about 15 per cent for the former and 10 per cent for the latter), but these numbers were undoubtedly low, since the registers generally noted the presence of attorneys only when they made procedural motions, which generally happened only once an indictment had been found.

Further, it was not only in Quarter Sessions that parties had counsel. Newspaper accounts of Weekly Sessions cases suggest that lawyers were a frequent presence there as well, cross-examining witnesses, making motions, and so on, and the Montreal Weekly Sessions register for 1835 shows attorneys present in over half of cases. In the registers these were mentioned far more often for defendants than for plaintiffs, but, tellingly, the printed forms used for complaints and convictions in liquor-licensing cases in the 1820s, among the most common heard before the court, explicitly included a line for the plaintiff's attorney's. Lawyers were also sometimes present in summary trials before rural justices, though, given the concentration of the bar in the cities, this must have been a less common occurrence. Most likely they were involved mainly in cases where the stakes were higher, as in a case in Berthier in 1833 in which several inhabitants were tried before a justice for cutting down a maypole and saved from conviction only by the presence of a Montreal lawyer. And some plaintiffs might be accompanied by lawyers all the way through the process, right from the initial complaint, though the extent to which plaintiffs first went to lawyers, rather than directly before the justices or their clerks, is almost impossible to determine.[28]

Though the attorneys of plaintiffs and defendants were sometimes relatives or friends, most were professional lawyers, both British and *Canadien*, members of the growing colonial bar. A full study of legal practice in the colony awaits, but it seems that in the nineteenth century at least, *Canadien* lawyers were just as likely to be present in Quarter Sessions as their British counterparts, and in the 1835 Weekly Sessions register, about 40 per cent of the lawyers were *Canadiens*. This puts the lie to the long-standing assertion that *Canadien* lawyers basically avoided criminal practice because of the preponderance of English, and instead confirms the impression one gets from reading contemporary accounts such as Aubert de Gaspé's *Mémoires*, which, without comment, relates two cases in which he appeared as an attorney before Quebec City's Quarter Sessions in the 1810s.[29] More important, it meant that for plaintiffs and defendants who could get access to counsel, language was no barrier, since both francophone and anglophone lawyers were ready to practise before the justices.

As has been noted for other courts elsewhere, the presence of lawyers fundamentally affected the character of the proceedings.[30] For one thing, the justices' courts were regularly the site of detailed legal arguments which were no doubt over the heads of most of the participants. Thus, in 1780, François Duaine was prosecuted in Montreal Quarter Sessions for engrossing wheat, contrary to a proclamation of the governor. James Walker, appearing for Duaine, argued that the proclamation 'whereon the prosecution is grounded is not a law, but as notice and warning to the public; that the act of parliament of the 5th and 6th of Edward the 6th whereon [the proclamation] is founded is repealed by an act of parliament of the 12th George the Third and produces said last mentioned act of parliament therefore prays the defendant may be dismissed and discharged.' The court agreed with this essential though technical distinction and dismissed the case. Likewise, in the 1833 Berthier maypole case discussed above, the Montreal lawyer successfully argued that the justice had exceeded his jurisdiction; as *La Minerve*'s correspondent remarked, if the lawyer had not been present to make his motion, the magistrate, who evidently believed that he had jurisdiction since he was sitting for this case alone, would no doubt have condemned the accused, against both law and justice. Defence lawyers intervened on a variety of different technicalities: pleas of misnomer or of want of form, to have indictments thrown out; challenges to the court's jurisdiction over various offences; assertions of improperly followed pre-trial procedures; and so on. Sometimes these motions were successful, other times not. But they suggest that lawyers gave the court an atmosphere of legal formality that might otherwise have been lacking. In recommending that Samuel Gale be associated with them as one of the paid magistrates of Montreal, McCord and Mondelet argued that the presence of the bar made it essential that the Quarter Sessions 'should be held by experienced justices versed in the criminal and civil law.'[31]

As this last suggests, the presence of the bar before the justices affected power relations in the court, bringing two models of justice into conflict: the paternal power of untrained justices and elite grand juries against the professional power of lawyers. This sometimes led to open conflict between justices, jurors, and lawyers. In 1815, for example, McCord and Mondelet attributed moves to discredit their Police Office clerk to the bar, since 'like all other magistrates who are determined to do their duty with steady impartiality we no doubt have made ourselves enemies ...' They described an incident where a young lawyer before them in the Police Office contested the fees paid to their clerk, calling them 'a damned extortion, for which he was ordered out of the office.'[32] Similarly, in 1823 the Montreal Quarter Sessions grand jury castigated a lawyer who had dared criticize one of their decisions: 'The Grand Jurors ... express their dissatisfaction at some observations which fell from John Boston, Esquire, one of the Barristers, touching a rejected Bill, and conceive it highly indecorous on the part of any individual, to offer the slightest animadversion on their award, which in every case is decisive, without being subject to further consideration. The Great Palladium of British Liberty, is the right which is intrusted to Jurors and the smallest innovation on this prerogative, is calculated only to inspire the warmest indignation and calls for a severe reprimand from the Court.'[33] For plaintiffs and defendants, the presence of lawyers thus meant that the court was not a monolithic structure of judicial power, but rather a theatre of frequent tensions between different factions of the law.

Nevertheless, even considering the limits of the sources, it is clear that not everyone had access to professional assistance. Lawyers were costly, and their fees not always regulated by an official tariff. An attempt by the Montreal justices to regulate attorneys' fees in 1810 was abandoned by 1811, and by the early 1830s, when the justices in Quebec City and Trois-Rivières had established tariffs that allowed them to tax costs, there was still no tariff in Montreal.[34] Still, some lawyers seem to have worked on speculation, counting on a judgment in favour of their client and an order for the payment of their fees. This was probably what was understood in the letter of recommendation written by Alexander Mabbut, a L'Assomption justice, 'to any Gentleman of the Bar at Montreal' in favour of Jean Smith, a Berthier watchmaker, and Josephte Chenette, his wife, in their complaint against Jean-Baptiste Christin *dit* Saint-Amour, whom Mabbut described as 'a man of wealthy connections and property.' The case was eventually taken on by Peter Rossiter, a lawyer just starting out on his career.[35]

This was not necessarily a sure proposition: in 1831, for example, Aaron Philip Hart and Sabrevois de Bleury, two Montreal lawyers, complained to the justices in Quarter Sessions that in the absence of a regular tariff by which losing parties could be taxed for their opponents' legal fees, they frequently found themselves unpaid even after winning, since their clients had no money left after paying the court costs themselves.[36] But it did mean that less-well-off plaintiffs and defendants could get access to professional assistance. While elite and middle-class defendants in Montreal Quarter Sessions were more than twice as likely to be represented by counsel as artisans and labourers, it was still almost a tenth of the latter who had representation, and, overall, most of those represented by counsel before the justices, whether plaintiffs or defendants, were farmers, artisans, or labourers. Evidently, the cost of representation was not so prohibitive as to limit it only to those with ample financial resources. At the same time, this access to counsel did not extend to marginalized people such as beggars, vagrants, or street prostitutes. They were generally prosecuted by public officials, such as constables, who were not liable to have attorneys' fees charged against them; there is no evidence that any were ever defended by attorneys pro bono, and, as a result, they were almost never represented by counsel.

The Language of the Law

Another fundamental aspect of the experience of justice was the language of the proceedings. The language of the law has often been seen as alienating populations from the justice system, whether it be the use of dead languages, such as Latin in England until the seventeenth century, or the deployment of specialized terminologies that only the initiated could understand. This was especially so in conquered colonies, where the imposition of the Conqueror's law implied the use of the Conqueror's language. Quebec is often seen as a case in point, especially since the prevailing view is that, at the Conquest, French lost its status as a public language, becoming at best a language of translation (and poor translation at that). And one of the more persistent stereotypes regarding criminal justice in the years between the Conquest and the Rebellions, from Garneau forward, was that it operated in English only, a language that few *Canadiens* understood, with English judges, English documents, and English law officers. This has been used to help explain the hypothesized alienation from, even boycott of, the criminal justice system by the *Canadien* majority, as well as the purported shunning of criminal practice by *Canadien* attorneys. The contrast is made with the civil courts, which operated in a mix of English and French and were thus more accessible to the *Canadien* population and lawmen alike.[37]

As always, there is some truth to this view. Thus, in the King's Bench, most documents and proceedings were in English only, although *Canadien* witnesses testified in and were cross-examined in French.[38] And, following English statutory requirements, indictments in all courts, including Quarter Sessions, were always written in English. But the anglicization of criminal justice did not extend throughout the criminal justice system, and especially not to everyday justice at the level of the justices. Instead, linguistic practices were substantially reshaped by the practical imperative of large numbers of francophones among the parties, the officials, and, as we saw, even the magistrates.

Take, for example, the language of preliminary documents such as depositions, warrants, and recognizances. These were the documents that framed much of the everyday interaction between people and the justice system: depositions, for example, were meant to reflect the stories of those who were complaining or testifying, and were read back to the deponent by the magistrate or clerk before being signed, while warrants were often read out on arrest. Far from being in English only, throughout the period they might be in either English or French, depending on the language of the party whom it concerned and the justice who was making it out. For example, when Marguerite Babineau of Vaudreuil complained in 1820 to André-Dominique Pambrun, the local justice, that Antoine Chenier had kicked her and hit her with a rake, when she was four months' pregnant, both the deposition before Pambrun and the arrest warrant that he issued to Gilles Guerbois, the local bailiff, were entirely in French, although, when Guerbois brought Chenier before John Mark Crank Delesderniers, another Vaudreuil justice, Delesderniers wrote out Chenier's recognizance to appear in English. In the case of depositions at least, bilingualism was even mandatory, since magistrates and clerks were generally required to take down depositions in the language of the party deposing, and could be censured by the higher courts if they did not. Furthermore, bilingualism went beyond the linguistic capacities of individual justices, with printers' accounts from the eighteenth century forward showing justices and clerks ordering forms for warrants and recognizances in both English and French, and many instances of anglophone justices using French forms.[39]

Nor was this all. Evidently, proceedings before single rural justices would have been in French when all participants, including the justice, were francophone. But bilingualism also extended to the more formal courts of the justices. Thus, the Quarter Sessions did not operate solely in English but rather in a mixture of French and English, depending on the parties of the case. Testimony was in the language of the witness; lawyers presented arguments in both English and French; justices charged juries in either language, and sometimes in both; and even the official judgments recorded in the registers were sometimes written in French, the product of a clerk simply transcribing the language used by the bench. It was only for indictments that English unilingualism was the rule. Since indictments were read out twice, on arraignment of the defendant and at the beginning of trial, their language was not trivial, and would certainly have given an English cast to the proceedings. The unilingualism of the written indictments became a particular problem in the early 1830s, when changes in jury-selection procedures led to grand juries generally composed almost entirely of unilingual francophones, who had to rely on the presence of bilingual jurymen to translate the substance of the indictments for them – an imperfect solution at best.[40]

This is not to say that the extensive use of French in the criminal justice system was accepted without criticism. Already in the 1770s, Francis Maseres asserted that all criminal procedure should be in English only, with interpreters used as necessary, and even suggested that this be written into the Quebec Act.[41] His suggestion was not heeded, and for the next half-century the bilingualism entrenched in the civil courts was also the rule in much of the criminal justice system, especially at the level of the justices. By the 1820s, however, in the context of rising interethnic tensions, bilingualism in the courts was once again becoming a matter of controversy. The issue was particularly debated in the civil courts, with the Montreal judges, for example, briefly adopting a policy that summons should be in English only, except for *Canadiens* born before the Conquest,[42] but it also spilled over into the criminal courts. Thus, the clerk of the peace in Trois-Rivières from 1826, David Chisholme, a radical and somewhat francophobic Tory and sometime editor of the *Montreal Gazette*, adopted the practice of composing depositions in English only, regardless of the language of the deponent. When censured for this by a committee of the Assembly in 1836, as part of a general condemnation of his practices, Chisholme replied with a lengthy defence in which he sought to demonstrate 'the absurdity as well as impolicy of taking down depositions in the French language' since 'the whole of the criminal laws of England must be enforced in the language of that country' and, at any rate, no such provision was made for native languages in Scotland, Ireland, or Wales. Even Chisholme admitted, however, that the oral parts of criminal proceedings were necessarily bilingual.[43] Anglicization also began to creep more subtly into the everyday practices of the magistrates: thus, in Montreal, printed-form recognizances in the 1820s and 1830s were generally in English only, though country justices continued to use French forms. While depositions remained in the language of the deponent, by the late 1820s, under the watch of the francophobic Samuel Gale, French had almost entirely disappeared from the registers of the courts.

As well, at the level of individual justices, language could be a problem, especially in the countryside. John Yule, for example, the especially active Chambly justice, was described in 1824 as alienating *Canadiens* because of 'being unable to speak, write, or understand their language and having no one in his employ capable of doing so for him ... The Canadians ... must feel, and do feel, that it is a great hardship to submit all their differences to a man incapable of understanding them, and dependant on chance for an interpreter being present.' Indeed, on his appointment in 1815, Yule had warned that 'want of proficiency in the French Language must be a great obstacle in my way of making myself useful in such capacity.' On the other hand, there are also contrary examples: in the 1825 complaint of Aaron Osborn against William Carden, before William Woods of Sainte-Marie, while the parties and the justice were English-speakers, all the documents, from deposition to recognizance, were in French, and in a hand suggesting the presence of a clerk.[44]

In general, though, Tocqueville's observation of habitual bilingualism in the civil courts applied equally well to the courts of the justices. This was undoubtedly aided by the bilingualism of many of the justices, and especially the chairmen, as well as of their clerks. The more formal criminal courts, the Quarter and Weekly Sessions, also generally had paid interpreters on hand. And accommodation was made for people who spoke neither English nor French: for example, the number of discharged German soldiers in and around Montreal following the American Revolution was such that the courts employed a special German interpreter.[45] Accordingly, in going before a justice to make a complaint, or even going to court as a witness or spectator, *Canadiens* were hardly entering a necessarily unilingual English arena. Instead, both *Canadien* and British participants in criminal justice would have experienced a criminal justice system that was fundamentally bilingual, in some instances coming in contact with anglophone justices and English-language documents, in others, francophone magistrates and forms.

The Outcome of Complaints

Being named in a criminal complaint did not really matter to a defendant if it had no real impact. Thus, William Lampher and Jacob Tyler could complain to James McGill that Louis Dupré, Michel Belhumeur, Baptiste Lousignan, Baptiste Rose, and Augustin Saint-Sauveur *dit* Lecuyer had invaded their house in Varennes, but since there is no indication that anything ever came of this complaint, its practical impact on Dupré and the others was nil.[46] Of the 3,000-odd defendants named in Montreal Quarter Sessions complaints sampled between 1780 and 1835, only about a quarter reached some formal resolution in the court itself, and only half of those were found guilty. From this we might conclude that the criminal justice system was not 'working' for plaintiffs, in that they could get it to convict their opponent only about one time in eight. But, if we look more closely at where this sort of filtering was happening, and what happened to those who were not filtered out, we find a somewhat different picture.

Take a hundred defendants named in Montreal Quarter Sessions complaints between 1780 and 1835. Of these, seventy-nine came in contact with the criminal justice system at least once, usually appearing before a justice to enter into a recognizance to appear, indicating that the initial actions of the police were successful. This represents a 'clear rate' of 79 per cent; by comparison, in Quebec today, the clear rate for those charged with non-sexual assault (which has the highest clear rate among common Criminal Code offences) is 85 per cent, and 75 per cent in Canada as a whole.[47] As for summary complaints, those heard before Montreal justices in cases of interpersonal violence, the only ones for which it is generally possible to know whether the defendant ever came in contact with the system, the clear rate was 74 per cent. Given that both of these rates are based on actually finding and matching the appropriate documents in the archives, they are probably low; so, at a cautious estimate, a plaintiff who went before a justice could expect that, three-quarters of the time or more, there would be some real impact on those against whom he or she complained.

In Quarter Sessions complaints, the filtering continued on the route to a formal court case. In strict legal theory, once a defendant had appeared before a justice and entered into a recognizance to appear at the next Quarter Sessions, the case should ultimately have ended up before the grand jury. Neither the justice nor the plaintiff had the right to discontinue the action, since the king's peace had been broken and any fine imposed belonged to the king; the only important legal ways in which a case could be stopped before reaching the grand jury were if the king's attorney discontinued the case by *nolle prosequi* or if the court itself issued an order in a case where there was not enough evidence to lay an indictment, both rare occurrences. But this formal requirement was often disregarded. Thus, among our seventy-nine defendants who actually came in contact with the system, only forty-one would turn up listed as defendants in the registers of the Quarter Sessions, with the bulk of the remainder having been bound over to appear but evidently not doing so. Of these forty-one, somewhere between thirty and thirty-eight actually appeared in court, with the sketchiness of the court records making it harder to be more precise. In other words, the minimum attrition rate between appearance before a justice (79 of the original 100 defendants) and appearance in the formal court of Quarter Sessions (38 defendants), was perhaps half, and, overall, from being named in a complaint (100 defendants) to appearing in court (38 defendants), almost two-thirds. Most of this filtering came at the second stage of a criminal process, between a defendant's appearance before a justice and in Quarter Sessions itself, and was the result of the sort of prosecutorial initiative discussed above.

Filtering continued once the case reached court itself. Of defendants actually named in the Quarter Sessions registers, only between a half and two-thirds ever received a formal verdict from the court, somewhat lower than what Norma Landau found for eighteenth-century London. For the rest, the plaintiff might appear in court to declare himself or herself satisfied or might simply default (allowing the defendant to go free); in up to a third or more cases, depending on the period, the case simply disappeared from the registers with no explanation whatsoever. This became increasingly problematic in the nineteenth century. As Augustin Cuvillier, presiding at the Montreal Quarter Session in 1836, noted in his charge to the grand jury:

> ... il ne se juge pas la dixième partie des cas d'assaut et batterie qui sont couchés sur les registres de cette cour, les parties entrant en accord avant la réunion de la cour, ou étant détournés de poursuivre par les frais et les délais. Il ne peut résulter de ce simple fait beaucoup d'inconvénient pour le public, mais il est arrivé souvent que des individus ayant des familles à faire subsister, sont demeurés en prison jusqu'à la réunion de la cour, pour n'avoir pas pu trouver des cautions, et qu'alors les accusateurs n'ont pas paru, ou n'ont pas voulu poursuivre. Vous avez là un exemple d'un droit légal exercé d'une manière rigoureuse et impitoyable aux dépens de tout sentiment d'humanité.
>
> [... not one tenth of assault and battery cases entered in this court's registers are ever judged, since the parties come to agreement before the meeting of the court, or are dissuaded from prosecution by costs and delays. This simple fact cannot lead to any great inconvenience for the public, but it has often happened that individuals with families to support have remained in prison until the meeting of the court, for want of guarantors, and that then the accusers have not appeared, or have not wanted to prosecute. There is an example of a legal right exercised in a rigorous and unpitying manner to the exclusion of all sentiment or humanity.]

And Cuvillier was not far off the mark: in 1835, of almost seven hundred defendants charged with violence in depositions, only a little over a tenth ended up with their case resolved by a trial jury, although, if we add bills not found by the grand jury, that proportion rises to about 20 per cent.[48]

A formal verdict could come in a variety of guises. In summary trials, the justices could dismiss a case or summarily impose a fine, whereas, in trials on indictment, the grand jury could reject the bill of indictment, the defendant could plead guilty, and the trial jury could render a verdict of guilty or not guilty, with a range of other less important possibilities as well. In Quarter Sessions, jury verdicts appear to have followed much the same pattern as in the King's Bench, studied by Jean-Marie Fecteau. Thus, the grand jury rejected bills presented to them about 15 per cent of the time in the eighteenth century and about 20 per cent in the nineteenth; and trial juries found defendants guilty about 65 per cent of the time in the eighteenth century and between 55 and 60 per cent in the nineteenth. Putting these together, in perhaps half of cases where the final decision rested with a jury (which, as we saw, were a minority of all cases), the decision was in favour of the plaintiff about half the time and the defendant the other half. Going before a jury was thus very much a toss-up.[49]

An action that had reached Quarter Sessions could have one of four main outcomes. It could end with a decision against the defendant, where the defendant either pleaded guilty or was found guilty by the court or the trial jury. It could end with a decision in favour of the defendant, by being dismissed by the justices, the grand jury, or the trial jury. It could be resolved before any formal decision by the judicial system, either by the plaintiff declaring his or her satisfaction or by simply not turning up to prosecute. Finally, it could come to no result at all, at least as far as the registers of the court show (though, given the changing practices of the clerks, these last two categories were often difficult to distinguish). As Table 6.1 shows, the mix of these possible outcomes shifted frequently over time. In the period immediately following the beginning of British rule, as Douglas Hay observed, the pattern was very much the same as that in England, with a little under half of outcomes going against the defendant.[50] However, in the rest of the period, a different pattern emerges. Between 1779 and 1793, cases in the court were especially likely to be resolved, and less than a third of defendants who appeared in the registers had outcomes that went against them. Between 1794 and 1799, under Tory justices, the situation was closer to that before 1773, though with a higher proportion of cases that were not formally decided. But from 1800, regardless of the composition of the magistracy, the proportion of outcomes against defendants declined steadily, so that by the end of the 1820s and beginning of the 1830s, less than a quarter of defendants in the registers had outcomes that went against them. This was largely due to the greater proportion of cases that were not formally decided by the court (reach-

Table 6.1: Results of Montreal Quarter Sessions cases, 1764–1835*

Result	1764–73	1779–93	1794–99	1800–9	1810–23	1824–30	1835
Against defendant	46%	28%	41%	39%	28%	22%	22%
For defendant	37%	20%	24%	25%	27%	28%	32%
Resolved	8%	31%	17%	13%	13%	18%	5%
No result	7%	19%	15%	23%	31%	32%	41%
Other	2%	2%	3%	1%	<1%	<1%	<1%

* Results by defendant

ing almost half of all cases during the last two periods) but also reflected an increasing proportion of defendants who had formal outcomes in their favour. In the eighteenth and early nineteenth centuries, formal decisions went more often against defendants than for, but the situation had reversed by the 1820s and 1830s. From the plaintiffs' point of view, it was thus increasingly difficult to get the courts to decide against their opponents, which is one factor that helps explain why so many dropped their cases before they came to a formal conclusion.

If we turn away from the Quarter Sessions to the other venues in which the justices judged offenders brought before them, a different picture presents itself. Though the sources for understanding the fate of defendants in Weekly Sessions are limited, since most of the records concern convictions only, defendants nonetheless pleaded or were found guilty far more often than in Quarter Sessions: about 60 per cent of the time between 1779 and 1784, in 1805, and again in 1835, though the figure was only about 40 per cent in 1829. The conviction rate was even higher in the trials of those accused of militia and *corvée* offences in the late 1770s and early 1780s, between 60 and 75 per cent.[51] As for the proceedings of justices outside the formal courts, where they imposed summary fines or imprisonment, it is difficult to judge what happened to defendants, since almost all surviving records list only convictions. In regulatory offences, justices seem to have tended towards the side of plaintiffs: thus, fourteen of the sixteen defendants in regulatory offences before Crebassa and Jones, the William Henry justices, were found guilty, while the other two settled with the prosecutors, and all but a few of the extant appeals and certioraris from justices' decisions in rural petty sessions were for convictions. Likewise, there is little indication that urban justices were anything but harsh in dealing with the vagrants, prostitutes, and beggars brought before them; discretion came instead at the level of the police, who chose whether or not to make an arrest. At least in desertion cases, however, as Ian Pilarczyk has found, while justices sided with masters about two-thirds of the time, and thus in a sense found their servants guilty of desertion, many servants were simply ordered to return to their masters, rather than punished by the court – yet another form of filtering.[52]

The scope and variation of all of this filtering has significant implications for understanding the meaning and impact of the criminal justice system. The extent to which plaintiffs dropped their cases before trial has been taken both as evidence of their desire to avoid the formal criminal courts as much as possible and as a sign of the weakness of a criminal justice system that was unable to enforce its own decrees. But, as we saw, private settlement of disputes was in no way incompatible with formal criminal justice, since, at least in assault cases, justices were not only allowed but even strongly advised to encourage parties to settle before they reached a formal case. Instead, the high clear rate combined with the large attrition before a case reached the Quarter Sessions suggests a criminal justice system that was not at all impotent but that still left the initiative to p laintiffs, for whom the simple fact of having an aggressor arrested may have been redress enough. 'I felt quite pleased this morning when I saw my antagonist in the hands of your constable,' declared Robert Bartly, a British Army lieutenant stationed in Odelltown, to Philip Byrne, regarding Hendrick Oastrum, who had threatened Bartly; 'the inhabitants here are all delighted to see him on his way to St. Johns. He came to my house and begged my hand on a thousand times. I think a trip to St. Johns will be a great use to him.'[53] At the same time, the fate of defendants in Weekly Sessions and summary cases shows a system that was far more perilous for them than the Quarter Sessions might suggest, and that could, as we will see, serve in the exercise of state power.

Punishment and Costs

Another thing that helps explain the extent to which prosecutors exercised their discretion in dropping Quarter Sessions cases is that, when a case actually came to a formal conclusion, with a punishment imposed, this was entirely out of their hands and brought them nothing. Punishment under ancien-régime criminal justice is often associated with the terror and spectacle of corporal punishments and executions. As George's experience shows, punishment by the justices could be a terrifying experience, even if they could impose nothing that led to the loss of life

Table 6.2: Select punishments imposed in Montreal Quarter Sessions[*]

	Corporal punishment	Imprisonment	Fine	Recognizance
1765–1799	7%	8%	61%	23%
1800–1830	3%	35%	60%	15%
1835	–	52%	40%	10%

* Percentages represent the proportion of defendants on whom that punishment was imposed, and thus may add up to more than 100 per cent.

or limb. Whipping could be severe: Aubert de Gaspé, for example, decried the practice of the Quebec City chairman, John Fletcher, of ordering convicts whipped not for a particular number of strokes but rather until their back was bloody, the standard practice in England. Corporal punishment was also imposed through the pillory, an instrument common enough that it featured on at least one eighteenth-century map of Quebec City and was also occasionally the target of resistance on the part of crowds seeking to prevent prisoners being pilloried or even destroying the pillory itself.[54] Corporal punishment, however, made up a small proportion of the punishments imposed on those found guilty by the justices. As Table 6.2 shows, even in Quarter Sessions, though it was a normal part of the proceedings, it was never imposed on more than a small fraction of defendants. It was also a practice in decline, being proportionately twice as frequent in the eighteenth century as in the nineteenth, and not used at all by the Montreal justices in 1835, though the Quebec City justices still imposed both whipping and the pillory until the 1830s.[55]

In contrast, imprisonment was increasingly imposed as a punishment by the justices. As both Jean-Marie Fecteau and Martin Dufresne have pointed out, this was partly a reflection of the rise of summary prosecutions for vagrancy and morality offences from the late 1820s, which were generally punished with imprisonment either in the gaol or in the House of Correction. But even in Quarter Sessions, imprisonment became more and more part of the experience of the condemned: relatively rare in the eighteenth century (though no less common than corporal punishment), in the first three decades of the nineteenth century about a third of those sentenced by the justices in Quarter Sessions had some form of imprisonment as part of their punishment, a proportion that rose to over half in 1835 (though this concerned a comparatively small number of cases). This shift towards the new mode of punishment was already well under way in the first decade of the century, providing yet another example of changes in ancien-régime penal practices that significantly predate the reforms of the late 1830s.

By far the most frequent punishment imposed by the justices, however, was not pain or loss of freedom but a fine. For statutory offences, which made up the bulk of those tried summarily by the justices alone or in petty or Weekly Sessions, the penalty was almost always a specific fine laid out in the act or ordinance, ranging from a few shillings to the £10 Sterling fine for selling liquor without a licence and beyond. Here, as we will see, the interest of the prosecutor was far more at stake, since in most cases they received half of the fine imposed – which helps explain why so many more of these cases were carried through to judgment. And since justices were bound by the statutory provisions to impose the set penalty, a plaintiff setting out on a prosecution knew exactly what the reward would be at the end of it, if a conviction could be secured.

In common law offences such as assaults or petty larceny, on the other hand, justices in theory had a much greater latitude, with the discretion to impose whatever sentence they chose short of those that involved loss of life or limb. The sentences in consequence varied greatly: for assault, from the sixpence fine on Catherine Jolicoeur in 1809 to the six months in gaol on John Whealon in 1780; and for petty larceny, from the half an hour in the pillory on Mary Campbell in 1793 to the half a year in the House of Correction at hard labour plus thirty-nine lashes in the market-place on Jean-Baptiste Mathieu in 1811.[56] However, the Montreal justices in general followed some standard sentencing practices, based on the offence. In about 90 per cent of cases involving interpersonal violence (mainly assaults and batteries), they imposed a fine and/or a recognizance to keep the peace. Unlike in eighteenth-century London, where nominal one-shilling fines were by far the most common, the Montreal justices imposed a wide range of fines, varying from sixpence to £100. The median fine was 7.5 shillings in the eighteenth century and ten in the nineteenth, and most fines were relatively moderate: about 80 per cent were £1 or less and a third five were shillings or less.[57] The other 10 per cent of sentences involved imprisonment of one sort or another, often in combination with a fine and a recognizance to keep the peace. In contrast, 90 per cent or more of convictions in cases involving property and public morality (largely petty larceny and prostitution-related offences) resulted in imprisonment or corporal punishment, mostly from a month to six months in the common gaol or, in the nineteenth century, the House of Correction.

Hence, in cases in which interests of class and state were not paramount, which was most cases involving interpersonal violence, defendants could expect to face little more than a monetary penalty, in many cases amounting to a relatively small sum. But, when considerations of class and elite morality were stronger, defendants were punished much more harshly. In all of this, however, the plaintiff had little interest, beyond the satisfaction of seeing his or her opponent punished, since even in the case of fines, all went to the king.

Beyond the punishments formally decreed by justices, there were other costs involved with making a complaint or being accused of a offence. Most evident were police and court costs, which in many cases tried before the justices were paid not by the state but by the parties. Costs were paid by the crown in all cases heard in King's Bench, but this was far less common in the justices' courts, where prosecutorial initiative was the rule. In assault cases in particular, plaintiffs were generally responsible for most initial costs, such as the payment of constables and witnesses and the fees for drawing up the bill of indictment; which may explain the indignation of La Minerve's correspondent at being asked to pay.

Unfortunately, there is not enough surviving information on costs for an in-depth analysis. Tables of fees and the few remaining bills of costs show that, in general, the bulk of the expense of a complaint came not during the preliminary proceedings but once a case reached a formal court. In the prosecution that Rose Beaulieu launched in 1820 against Joseph-Norbert Faribault, a Montreal law student, for assault and battery, the pre-trial costs were twelve shillings sixpence for the deposition, warrant, and arrest, whereas drawing up the indictment alone cost one pound two shillings sixpence, along with more than £2 in other court costs, all of which Beaulieu would probably have had to pay in advance. Even the twelve shillings sixpence represented a considerable outlay, the equivalent of perhaps a week's unskilled labour. Though this was still within reach of many people, the costs of a full Quarter Sessions case must have been prohibitive to most. In Weekly Sessions the costs were lower but, according to the Trois-Rivières clerk of the peace in the mid-1830s, David Chisholme, still amounted to perhaps thirty shillings per case. And the cost of arrests in rural areas could be prohibitive, with some bailiffs' bills as high as two or three pounds.[58]

Costs are another crucial factor in explaining the reluctance of plaintiffs to move beyond the level of preliminary proceedings. A formal court case, especially in Quarter Sessions, was potentially very expensive. As a Montreal King's Bench grand jury, half made up of justices, put it in 1828:

> The present mode of prosecution in the Court of Quarter Sessions is attended with very bad effects, almost ruinous to both the private prosecutor and the person accused. The prosecutor being bound to prosecute at the next session of that court is compelled to pay, without the prospect of being reimbursed, heavy fees to the officers of the court; he must pay the witnesses attending the grand jury when they are deliberating on the bill of indictment, and he must again pay them when they attend at trial; in many instances the trial is postponed in consequence of the illness of a material witness, when he and his witnesses are again obliged to attend. A prisoner who pleads to an indictment and endeavours to put off his trial, is seldom tried before the second or third session from that in which the bill of indictment is laid before the grand jury; consequently the prosecutor and his witnesses are obliged to attend the Court of Quarter Sessions during three and sometimes four terms. This is particularly burthensome when the parties are from a remote part of the district, and it cannot be a matter of surprise that many petty offenders are knowingly permitted to escape, or that they should be tried in the Courts, where the prosecution is carried out at the expense of the Crown.

While this last was probably a veiled response to the Assembly's charges against the attorney general, James Stuart, for prosecuting cases in King's Bench that could have been tried in Quarter Sessions, it also expressed the growing frustration with the burdens of private prosecution. Until the 1820s, justices regularly awarded costs to the victorious party, but then there was the problem of actually collecting the amount. Thus, in Beaulieu's case, Faribault did not pay, so the justices had to issue process against him for the amount owing. Yet there was still no certainty that, even with a guilty verdict, the plaintiff could recoup costs, since it was unclear whether justices could imprison defendants until costs were paid, as they could for fines. Further, though the non-payment of fines and costs in many statutory offences, such as those involving liquor licensing, allowed justices to order constables and bailiffs to seize and sell the defendants' goods, by warrant of distress, their right to do so in common law offences, such as assaults, was less clear. Finally, from about 1830, King's Bench decisions challenged the right of justices to impose costs at all, though even in 1835 the Montreal justices reaffirmed the principle in a tariff of allowed fees.[59]

With costs so difficult to recoup, especially in assault cases, it is no wonder that they formed part of the settlements by which plaintiffs and defendants sometimes stopped such prosecutions, and which, from the defendant's point of view, took the place of the punishments imposed by the justices. Unfortunately, unlike in eighteenth-century London, only scattered pre-trial settlements have survived, generally consisting in costs and some form of monetary compensation. In February 1804, for example, Joseph Potevin of Baie-Saint-Paul, east of Quebec City, launched a complaint against Clément Corneau for assault and battery. The case was brought before the July Quarter Sessions in Quebec City, but Corneau neglected to appear. Instead, the parties came before Louis Bélair, the local justice of the peace who had heard the initial complaint, and stated that 'voûlan terminer leurs Diffiqultté pandant dans la présente Cession de Cartier de la paix qui ce tiens presentemens a quebec' [wishing to end their difficulty during the present Quarter Sessions presently being held at Quebec], Potevin would declare himself satisfied before the court, in return for thirty-five Spanish dollars 'pour c'est frais, le voyage de quebec et mauvais traittement qu'il a reçue ... sans préjudice au droit de Sa Majesté s'il y en à' [for his fees, the trip to Quebec and the ill-treatment he received ... without prejudice to the rights of His Majesty if there are any]. Unfortunately for Corneau, however, in this case the proceedings had already gone too far, and he was eventually convicted.[60]

The reliance on monetary penalties and fees underscores the class bias of the justice system. Simply put, a ten-shilling fine for assault imposed on a merchant or professional was no more than a pinprick, just like the pound or two in court costs. *La Minerve*'s correspondent, for example, had no trouble with this outlay. For a better-off artisan or an average farmer, this was a hefty sum, but still within reach. For an unskilled labourer, on the other hand, two or three pounds represented several weeks' labour, and if he or she was in prison, there was no means of working to make the sum. Consider the case of Pierre Julien, an illiterate labourer convicted of assault in April 1817 in Quebec Quarter Sessions and sentenced to one month in gaol, a fine of £5, and to find security to keep the peace. Having served his sentence, he (or rather, someone writing for him) petitioned the governor for remission of the fine, stating that he could not pay and that he and his family had much suffered by the previous hard winter. The pardon request was rejected, and Julien stayed in prison another month, finally finding the means to pay the fine at the beginning of July. Or again, take the situation of John

McClure, a Quebec City labourer convicted of assault in April 1829 in Quarter Sessions and sentenced to pay a forty-shilling fine. In his pardon petition, written in his own hand, he asserted that 'he has no friends, but an aged Mother whom by his industry he has assisted to support, he has not the means to raise one shilling.' Despite his evident education, McLure was also evidently a marginal member of local society: he had been accused of larceny by several people only a few months before, and, unable to pay the assault fine, he remained in gaol until August. Still, even hefty fines of £5, £10, or more were not necessarily out of reach of most defendants, whatever they might say in pardon petitions. For example, Joseph Tanguay, a farmer from Saint-Charles Rivière Boyer, southeast of Quebec City, was convicted in 1816 of assault, fined £20, and committed to gaol until the fine was paid. Two days later, his counsel, Jacques Leblond, presented a pardon petition stating that since Tanguay could not and would never be able to pay, he must remain the rest of his life in prison. He lived with his family on a pension of £25 per year, the petition asserted, and had only a small lot of thirteen *perches* in front which he had not been able to cultivate for the last two years, lacking both means and good health. This was the very picture of rural poverty (though already his use of a lawyer spoiled the picture a bit), but when the pardon petition was refused, he paid up in full and was discharged four days later. The Quebec gaol registers, in fact, show few people imprisoned for non-payment of a fine for more than a few days, though this in no way diminished the financial burdens that these fines placed on people with limited resources.[61]

At the same time, the reliance on fines could sometimes work in favour of poorer people. In some cases, notably for infractions of their own regulations, justices could not imprison for non-payment of the fine, so there was no punishment at all if the offender had no means to pay. For example, an 1831 petition to the Montreal justices complained that the regulations against nude bathing were not being enforced because children and men of no standing in society, who were most likely to infringe, escaped punishment on account of their youth or poverty; it suggested that instead constables be empowered to take offenders before a justice to pay the fine immediately or be imprisoned.[62]

Beyond monetary costs, there were also more general social costs associated with being the target of a criminal complaint, even before the justices and even if the case did not make it to court. Consider the civil complaint that Joseph Loizel, a Saint-Marc farmer, launched in 1800 against Christophe Marchesseau, parish notable and militia captain, for damaging his reputation. Marchesseau arrested Loizel in his barn, told him he was to be taken before Jean-Marie Mondelet (then still a rural notary and justice), put him in a cart driven by one Roc, and set off, following in his own cart and with two others filled with people whom he had ordered or asked or hired to convey Loizel. Loizel was thus ignominiously conveyed to Mondelet's, a league away, and en route was exposed to the ridicule and mockery of the population. At Mondelet's, where Loizel stayed several hours, Marchesseau accused him of various (unspecified) crimes and obliged him to seek sureties among the neighbours, under a two-man guard. Marchesseau also represented him as so guilty that Loizel's guarantors refused in the end to bail him, and to regain his liberty he was obliged to accept certain (unspecified) conditions imposed by Marchesseau, pay him for his time and travelling, and also pay the people whom Marchesseau had brought to depose against him. Marchesseau's complaint had never left the parish and may never actually have been a formal complaint at all, but the militia captain had Loizel punished nonetheless, both financially and socially. This procession was perhaps an exceptional event, but even a simple arrest could incur social stigma. When a correspondent of *La Minerve* remarked three people dressed in charivari costumes being conducted through the streets of Montreal by the high constable, he was struck by the injustice of it: 'Je demanderai seulement s'il était décent, s'il était de droit d'exposer ainsi à la risée générale, aux huées de la populace assemblée, 3 individus qui ne devaient pas être regardés comme coupables' [I would ask only if it was decent, if it was legal to expose to general ridicule, to the hoots of the assembled populace, three individuals who should not have been regarded as guilty].[63]

As Martin Dufresne has suggested, these broader social costs cannot be ignored in seeking to understand the experience of defendants who came before the justices. Still, few cases refer to these other costs, making them difficult to analyse. Was being accused of assault, arrested by a bailiff, and brought before a justice really a profound social stigma for *Canadien* habitants in general, or did they simply shrug it off as part of the normal litigious relations in which they often found themselves? Since all we really have are the complaints of those who felt slighted, or the scattered accounts of resistance towards the law, making any such judgments about them is extremely hazardous.[64]

Appeals and Pardons

As the petitions of Julien and Tanguay suggest, judgment by the justices was not necessarily the end of the formal legal process. Similarly, when Foucher, the solicitor general with the hazardous staircase, was condemned in Weekly Sessions to pay a £20 fine and demolish the staircase, he did not pay up. Instead, he appealed his case to Quarter Sessions, and when his appeal was dismissed by the justices, appealed again, this time to King's Bench.[65] In all cases, it was theoretically possible to override the justices' judgment, either through appeal to a higher court, as in the case of Foucher, or by petitioning the governor for pardon, as in the cases of Julien and Tanguay. In the case of many statutory offences tried summarily by the justices, either alone or in petty or Weekly Sessions, legislation provided for an appeal to Quarter Sessions, which thus in theory had broad powers of oversight. This applied only to statutory offences judged summarily by the justices, however, and there was no appeal in indictable offences such as assault or larceny. But, much as in England and the American colonies, all cases before the justices could be removed by certiorari into King's Bench at any point in the proceedings, effectively giving the King's Bench both oversight and appellate jurisdiction over the justices' courts. Further, the governor, as the king's representative, could pardon anyone convicted of virtually any offence other than treason or wilful murder, as well as remit corporal punishment, imprisonment, or the king's share of fines. Finally, during the brief period of elected municipal government in the 1830s, when the crown's portion of fines for infractions of municipal by-laws went instead to the corporations, city councils could also remit this share.[66]

With the notable exception of one type of conviction, however, people convicted before the justices rarely continued their cases beyond judgment. Appeals and removals by certiorari were uncommon: in the district of Montreal from the 1790s to the 1820s, for example, there were only about twenty appeals to Quarter Sessions and about thirty removals by certiorari from the justices' courts into King's Bench. Further, the latter were almost all effectively appeals of judgments by justices alone or in petty or Weekly Sessions, with only a couple of instances of cases in progress in Quarter Sessions removed by certiorari. Neither the King's Bench nor the Quarter Sessions thus exercised much in the way of oversight, with justices essentially left to their own devices. As for pardons, few people convicted of assault, theft, or other indictable offences before the justices asked for pardons or for their punishments to be remitted: in the district of Montreal from the 1780s to the 1820s, there is evidence of fewer than ten such clemency petitions, and though the practice was somewhat more common in the district of Quebec, perhaps because the governor was on the spot, there were at most two or three a year there in the 1810s and 1820s. This was in contrast to the more serious offences heard in King's Bench, where those convicted systematically sought pardons, and of which some seven hundred were granted from the 1790s to the mid-1830s.

People judged by the justices avoided appeal and clemency procedures for fairly evident reasons. An appeal from a summary conviction was a lengthy and costly process, almost inevitably involving lawyers, and the punishments imposed by the justices in cases that could be appealed, generally moderate fines, were not worth the effort. Further, there was no guarantee of success: in appeals to the Montreal Quarter Sessions, for example, appellants were successful only a little over a third of the time. Much as Douglas Hay has shown for England, the higher criminal courts were decidedly biased towards the justices: as Montreal's acting chief justice, James Reid, declared in 1821, 'we find it to be the policy of the law, to protect the justice of the peace the most, and even in his errors, where there is no corruption, to treat him with lenity, from the principle on which his office is held.' As for clemency requests, though a single clemency petition was no doubt cheaper than an appeal, the fines imposed by the justices in most of the indictable cases they heard in Quarter Sessions again made such a petition not worth the trouble and expense. Only when the justices imposed harsher punishments did this become worthwhile, and, as we saw, the Montreal justices rarely imposed such punishments. Indeed, the somewhat more frequent use of corporal punishment by Quebec City justices is perhaps another explanation of the more frequent clemency petitions there. Thus, when in 1819 Bertin Becquet, a private in the 60th Foot, was convicted of assault with intent to murder in the Quebec Quarter Sessions, he petitioned the governor to reduce the justices' sentence, which included being kept in solitary confinement on bread and water in a dark cell of the gaol, whipped until his back was bloody on two separate occasions in the Quebec City market-place, and wearing a blackboard with his name and crime on it during the ordeal, all of which, he said, would drive him to suicide from the shame. Nothing so harsh or as shaming had been imposed by the Montreal justices since the beginning of British rule, with the whipping processions of prisoners like

George. And, in Bertin's case, his petition worked, to a degree: the second whipping was remitted. Likewise, most of the fines imposed under colonial or local legislation were hardly high enough to warrant the trouble of mounting a pardon petition. Thus, in Montreal, there were no petitions whatsoever for the remission of fines imposed under the justices' police regulations before 1833, and perhaps a dozen to the City Council for fines (almost all substantial) imposed under the by-laws.[67]

The one significant exception to defendants' perhaps unwilling acquiescence to the justices' judgments were petitions for remission of the king's share of the substantial £10 fine imposed in cases of selling liquor without a licence. Relatively rare in the eighteenth and early nineteenth centuries, petitions for remission of liquor-licensing fines became increasingly common from the 1810s and, especially, the 1820s. Between 1810 and 1830, for example, in the district of Montreal, at least 200 such petitions were presented, accounting for over 90 per cent of all requests for clemency from people judged in the justices' courts, and in 1836 alone there were over sixty such petitions from the district of Quebec. So common did they become that the central administration fell back on a system much like that used in considering petitions for justices, with the petitions sent to the chairmen for their report and, after the chairmen were abolished, to the clerks of the peace, for submission to the sitting magistrates.[68] Even in these cases, it was only a minority of people who appealed for clemency: in 1829, for instance, while about sixty people were convicted of selling liquor without a licence in the Montreal Weekly Sessions, only about a quarter seem to have filed petitions for the remission of the king's share of the fine. But this was still by far the most common form of appeal from the justices' judgments. On occasion, the central administration sought to discourage such appeals, declaring in 1822 to the Montreal chairmen that 'the frequency of similar applications (almost daily) from this offence [is] very fast increasing & it therefore becomes necessary in order to check the evil, to be more circumspect,' but this changed little, with pardon petitions and recommendations continuing through the 1820s and 1830s; even in 1837, the administration was seeking to stem the flood by refusing to remit more than half the king's share.[69]

The reasons for the popularity of these petitions were simple. They could save defendants more than £5 for what was no doubt a much smaller outlay in hiring a lawyer or notary to draw up the petition. And they succeeded at least two-thirds of the time, and probably more. In them, we find the discourse of deference and paternalistic mercy that so characterized ancien-régime criminal justice systems. Petitioners pleaded their good character, their poverty and large families, their ignorance, the illness that had prevented them from taking out a licence. At the same time, they recognized their fault, and by the late 1820s defendants were beginning to plead guilty so that they could benefit from a favourable recommendation from the justices. This was an essential part of the game of having a fine remitted, and the chairmen in particular seem increasingly to have been willing participants: thus, while in 1810 McCord and Mondelet refused to recommend a petition on the grounds that to pardon one would encourage others to offend in the hopes of also gaining pardon, by the early 1820s they were regularly recommending petitioners for remission.[70]

As in pardons more generally, the criteria for a favourable recommendation centred not on the specifics of the case, which the chairmen rarely reported on, but on the deserving nature of the culprit. As Gale noted in a report on two separate petitions, 'I am told and I believe truly, that he is an honest man in his dealings with others, that he is poor and has a large young and helpless family, and a troublesome wife; these are serious claims to commiseration,' and 'her sex and the good recommendations she has produced, seem to entitle her to favorable consideration.'[71] Indeed, the petitions of women convicted of selling liquor without a licence were almost never rejected. Again, the central administration tried half-heartedly to counter this, with Dalhousie stating that he did not consider 'the pleading of poverty alone on the part of the offenders sufficient of itself to warrant his interference with the decision of the law,' but again, little changed. At the same time, this concentration on the character and circumstance of the deserving culprit, rather than on the specifics of the case, helps explain why vagrants, prostitutes, and the like summarily sentenced to long terms of imprisonment at hard labour in the houses of correction, who in theory could also have presented clemency petitions, never did so. Aside from not having the financial resources to consult a lawyer to draw up the petition, they would no doubt have had little chance of success in proving that they merited clemency. And so they remained imprisoned, while at least some unlicensed tavern-keepers avoided paying their fines.

Conclusion

Examining the course of everyday criminal justice underscores the point brought out by the stories of George and *La Minerve*'s correspondent: the difficulty of making broad generalizations about how plaintiffs and defendants experienced the justice system. Depending on whether they came before the justices in the eighteenth or in the nineteenth century, whether they were urban or rural, what offence they were accused of, what court they came before, and, perhaps most important, the individual circumstances of their character and their case, the course of proceedings could vary enormously.

This variation in part reflected the discretion that, as many historians have noted, was built into the ancien-régime criminal justice system. The experiences of both plaintiffs and defendants were shaped by the discretion of others: the discretion of plaintiffs in pursuing their cases; the discretion of justices in accepting complaints, issuing warrants, imposing punishments, and, sometimes, arbitrating differences; the discretion of governors in pardoning; even the discretion of defendants in accepting the terms of settlements. All of this was expressed in a constant filtering of complaints and cases, which certainly made the experience of everyday justice far from certain.

But discretion and uncertainty are unsatisfactory characterizations. The system did have a logic of its own, which was far from arbitrary and which profoundly shaped the experiences of those who came before it. *La Minerve*'s correspondent, for example, knew exactly what was going to happen when he was arrested, to the point of bringing his guarantors with him. Whether a defendant was arrested or only summoned depended not so much on the choice of the plaintiff or the justice as on the nature of the offence, as laid down in laws and bureaucratic routines that were fairly strictly followed. Similarly, the vastly differing experiences between those who came before the formal courts, notably the Quarter Sessions with its panoply of lengthy procedures, and those who were judged summarily in the Police Office or the justice's parlour, depended on well-established practices that funnelled cases to one or the other according to relatively coherent rules. And, at the other end of the experience of justice, the punishments that defendants faced were constrained by laws and legal customs that made it relatively easy for plaintiffs and defendants to predict what it was that would happen once a verdict was delivered – not certainty of punishment, but good probability nonetheless. With many lesser punishments strictly laid out in colonial statutes and municipal regulations, and everyday offences such as assaults punished in set ways, punishment under the ancien-régime system of everyday justice was far from arbitrary, and little more so than under the reforms of the 1840s. Even the ultimate example of ancien-régime discretion, the executive pardon, came to be dominated by a bureaucratic regimen that the executive itself seemed unable to control. This did not mean that the system was rigid, and it evolved over time. But it nonetheless constrained the experience of justice far more than notions of discretion and uncertainty suggest.

Beyond the system of laws, procedures, and institutions, other broader constraints also shaped the experience of justice. Geography was key: in minor regulatory cases, for example, rural parties generally found themselves before rural justices, quite different from the experience of their urban counterparts before the Weekly Sessions. Social class, too, was a powerful factor in shaping experience, much more so than ethnicity. Linguistic alienation was simply not very much of a factor in an everyday justice system which was functionally bilingual. On the other hand, the financial character of most punishments, the burden of court costs, the charges for hiring lawyers to conduct cases or make appeals and petitions – all meant that those with fewer resources were more deeply affected by the system. And, when we consider as well the much harsher punishments meted out on those who threatened property relations and middle-class morality, we cannot but be persuaded of the class bias of the system. Yet, despite this evident bias against them, popular-class people continued to come before the justice system, not only as defendants but also as plaintiffs. John McClure, for example, the labourer imprisoned for several months in 1829 because of his inability to pay his fine, was back before the justices again in early 1830. This time, however, it was not as a defendant but rather to complain against William Moffet and Augustin Dallaire for assault with intent to murder.[72] It is hard to accept that McClure believed in the inherent justice of the system, since it had treated him so unjustly. Instead, what he was most likely seeking was social power.

7

Criminal Justice and Social Power

The road system has always been a most fruitful source of petty penal litigation in this province. The moment neighbours quarrel, the first thing they do in order to gratify their animosity is to prosecute one another for some breach of the road law, an offence easily substantiated against almost every landholder in the country. Such prosecutions are of course legally resisted, not only with the view of escaping the prescribed penalties, but also in the hope of gaining a judicial victory over private vindictiveness. Lawyers are employed, and the French Canadian will spend his last penny to get the better of his antagonist; the consequence is, that many of the habitans have been driven to want and even to beggary by this propensity to litigation, a passion so congenial to the natures of an ignorant and semi-civilized people ... if there were no other blemish in the road laws of Lower Canada than the facility which they afford to the litigious propensities of the French Canadians, no time ought to be lost in applying a remedy to the evil.
　　　　　　　 – Testimony of David Chisholme, Durham Report, Appendix C

... last evening he was violently assaulted, beat, bruised and otherwise ill-used without any just provocation, by one Lowell, who lives with Mr Hall of Montreal, Hatter. Wherefore Depont. prays Justice in the premises.
　　　　　　　 – Deposition of John Bill against Jacob Lowell, 29 April 1793

... on Sunday the twenty Eighth instant between the Hours of Eight & Nine

O'Clock in the Evening he was assaulted by John Bill ... Chair maker without any provocation or reason, and therefore prays process against him.
– Deposition of Jacob Lowell against John Bill, 30 April 1793

Yesterday about nine o'clock I saw a woman whose name I do not know, beat severely her child in the passage of a house situate in Notre Dame Street, facing nearly the house of S. Sewell esquire, and the child now in the Police is the same who was beaten, and I believe this child's life would be endangered by its being returned to the care of its mother who is a prostitute a drunkard and a woman of great violence of character.
– Deposition of William Bingham against Mary Burk, 1830[1]

Chisholme's disdainful comments on *Canadien* petty litigiousness, Bill and Lowell's mutual accusations, and Bingham's complaint against Burk highlight the everyday criminal justice system as an arena for the exercise of social power. Chisholme, the francophobic Tory who had previously decried the absurdity of bilingual criminal justice, saw roads prosecutions as tools that had little to do with any actual offence, serving simply to gratify the vindictive litigiousness of the *Canadiens*, egged on by lawyers. This was fairly hypocritical, because Chisholme himself had been dismissed as clerk of the peace for the district of Trois-Rivières in 1836 in part for having transformed assault complaints into indictments for attempted murder, which allowed him to charge fees against government. As an Assembly committee noted wryly, it seemed as if 'the mild and peaceable habits which happily form the character of the inhabitants ... [have] almost instantaneously been changed for the worse, to the alarming degree that, with few exceptions, every quarrel, generally of such petty consequence in other sections of the province, has been there, for several years past, attended with violence and a thirst for blood.' But Chisholme's observations nevertheless underscore an important feature of everyday criminal justice: its instrumentalization by the population as a source of power, even by rural *habitants*.[2]

Bill and Lowell's mutual complaints also suggest instrumentalization, since they were classic instances of what is termed the cross-bill. Despite the respective affirmations of peaceable conduct and unprovoked assault, some sort of minor quarrel got the two fighting. The next day, Bill was angry or hurt enough to go before John McKindlay, a Montreal justice, and swear out a complaint so as to have Lowell arrested. Once arrested, Lowell was brought before Thomas McCord, where he turned the tables and swore out his own complaint. Bill was then arrested, and brought before McKindlay, now as a defendant rather than a plaintiff. Despite the back and forth between different justices, both complaints went no further; there is no sign that either man ever appeared in court. Here, a criminal complaint became part of a game of tit for tat, with no apparent desire to take the matter as far as a court case.

Bingham's deposition provides an entirely different view of how power played out in the criminal justice system. At one level, it can be read as a classic case of a concerned citizen denouncing the brutal violence of a drunken woman on her child, epitomizing a system protecting the powerless. But the complaint also represented a structural imbalance of social power between accuser and accused. Burk had little power: a woman and a prostitute, she was arrested several more times in the 1830s and early 1840s, and, though she was married, her husband was also on the margins of urban society. Her accuser, William Bingham, was both a man and of an entirely different social class. The son of a leading American merchant and Federalist senator, he was also the husband of the seigneuress of Rigaud, Marie-Charlotte Chartier de Lotbinière, the daughter of the patriarchal and morally flexible Vaudreuil justice. The power imbalance, both of class and of gender, was evident, and influenced the course of the complaint. Despite the contradictions of a plaintiff who claimed not to know even the name of the accused but could nonetheless swear to her character, profession, and consumption habits – and despite the fact, that a few years earlier, Bingham had been successfully sued in the King's Bench for a false accusation of forgery – Burk's child was seized and taken to the Police Office, an event rare in itself. Burk subsequently spent seven weeks in prison before being discharged at the end of the next Quarter Sessions, unable to find bail. Whether her child was then returned to her is unknown.[3] The criminal justice system could thus be a source of social power, but it also reflected the structural inequalities that underlay Quebec and Lower Canadian society. And it is both the instrumentalization and the structural biases of everyday criminal justice that this chapter addresses.

Instrumentalizing Criminal Justice

Many historians who have considered the relationship between social power and criminal justice in Quebec and Lower Canada have studied the extent to which it functioned as an instrument of social domination, a tool in the hands of those with social power against those without. This might be the domination of the propertied over the poor, of employers over labourers, or the gender domination that – as Mary Anne Poutanen has so clearly shown – characterized the regulation of prostitution in Montreal. All of this fits more generally with the conflictual view of a criminal justice system used by the ruling classes to advance their interests.[4]

As we have already seen, there is certainly much truth to this view of a criminal justice system that explicitly involved class and gender domination, even at the everyday level of the justices. Complaints for petty larceny and prostitution were by the very nature of the offence directed against popular classes and women, and, though in Quarter Sessions at least they were numerically far outweighed by cases of interpersonal violence, their effects on the defendants in particular were far more devastating. But, while class and gender domination clearly explains some aspects of the everyday criminal justice system, and helps us to understand the variable experiences of people who came before the justices, it is insufficient to account for all or even most of the thousands of everyday criminal complaints where the plaintiffs were ordinary men and women – complaints that, as we will see, dominated large parts of the criminal business heard by the justices.

As we saw in the last chapter, prosecutorial initiative and discretion were key to determining the everyday course and experience of justice. But prosecutorial discretion also meant prosecutorial power, a power that began right from the initial stages of a complaint. Regardless of whether an accusation was for felony or misdemeanour, credence was generally given to the plaintiff, with the accused most often ending up before the justices prior to any preliminary examination of witnesses. This was especially so in less serious cases such as assaults, as the grand jury of the Montreal Quarter Sessions remarked in 1830: '... they consider the practice of issuing warrants for the apprehension of persons complained against without instituting further enquiry than that contained in the examinations on oath of the plaintiff as injudicious and tending to involve vexatious and expensive litigations which in many instances might be avoided.'[5]

Though, as we saw, justices encouraged private settlement, excessive instrumentalization could be frustrating for some. In 1825 Jonas Abbott, a Saint-Armand justice, wrote to the clerk of the peace in Montreal to explain why he had not written out in full the recognizances of the parties and witnesses in the complaint of John Gibson Jr, a Sutton farmer, against Thomas Waters, 'a transient person,' for assaulting him:

> I have heretofore been in the habit of making out recognizances at full length, which has occasioned me a great deal of writing, and in some instances have transmitted bonds, which have been taken on the most flagrant kind of assault and battery, neither the plaintiff nor respondent has appeared, the bonds never called for, and here the matter ended – the whole country in this part of the relm is well apprised of this – and many of our inhabitants dont hesitate to break the King's peace every day of their lives – give bail for their appearance at the General Quarter Sessions of the peace – and laugh at the magistrate the moment recognizance is entered into ... I feel very confident that neither the plaintiff, respondent, or witnesses will appear at court, my reasons for so believing is that the parties have been to me requesting that I would not send the papers to Montreal, saying they could settle the matter amongst themselves.[6]

The local criminal justice system was being used as leverage in local disputes but bypassed when it became too cumbersome: just as Abbott predicted, there is no mention of the case in the Quarter Sessions registers. In this case and, from Abbott's comments, many others, the criminal justice system of the state was clearly a tool, to be used as necessary and discarded when no longer needed. What suited many people outside the cities was having their opponent brought before a justice, without having to make the lengthy and costly trip to town.

Vengeance and Cupidity

There were, however, less edifying aspects to the instrumentalization of justice. As Chisholme's comments suggest, complaints before the justices could sometimes stem from fairly base motives of vengeance and cupidity. For example, as in the roads prosecutions cited by Chisholme, the system could essentially become a tool for vengeance. Thomas McCord summed this up in his charge to the grand jury of the Quarter Sessions in 1811: 'The Officer of the Crown will have nothing to lay before you of a higher nature than Assaults and Batteries ... The trifling and inconsiderate manner in which many accusations are preferred, is indeed much to be deplored, and particularly when the principal motives seem to be most contrary to the principles of religion, those of hatred and revenge.'[7]

Unlike McCord, we generally do not have access to the oral testimony of witnesses before the justices, and it is often difficult to discern motives from the few documents that have been left. Still, much as Douglas Hay suggests for eighteenth-century England, and Martin Dufresne has found for assault cases in Quebec City in the 1830s, many complaints were probably launched from motives that went beyond redress for the actions described in the complaints. Cross-bills for assault, such as those of Bill and Lowell, are the most evident vengeful use of the criminal justice system, and were a regular feature in Quarter Sessions. They accounted for perhaps 10 per cent of all such complaints brought before the justices, with the proportion staying relatively steady across the period. Other prosecutions were also sometimes more clearly actuated by a desire for revenge. In 1829, for example, William Square, a Montreal grocer, was prosecuted for having sold liquor without a licence to John Lane, who had occupied a part of his premises 'and lived on terms of intimacy and friendship with him.' After his conviction, at the prosecution of Adelphe Delisle the high constable, Square claimed that all he had done was share two glasses of spirits with Lane without payment, but that

> since the 17th day of May last, several misunderstandings and altercations have taken place between the said Lane and your Petitioner, and your Petitioner was under the necessity of causing him to be arrested for an aggravated assault committed by the said Lane with a hammer upon your petitioner, and also for a forcible detainer of part of your petitioner's house; in consequence of which the said Lane hath manifested strong malice against your petitioner and expressed determination of being revenged of him. Actuated by that malicious and vindictive feeling the said Lane made the said complaint and upon his evidence in support of the prosecution, your petitioner was condemned.

David Ross, who reported on the pardon petition, said that he believed Square, even though on the evidence he and the other justice on the bench had been obliged to convict him. Similarly, in 1829 Adam Handyside, a Montreal distiller, was convicted of the same offence. As Gale remarked in his report on Handyside's pardon petition, one of the witnesses 'frankly avowed that his motive for giving the information was to punish Mr. Handyside for personal violence and for refusing to pay his wages.' Some witnesses were also more directly actuated by greed, being paid by the prosecutor for the testimony. Such was the case of Christie Berg, a witness for Alexandre Charmon in his liquor-licensing prosecution against George Jenkins in Quebec City in 1813, who declared under oath that Charmon had offered him a pair of shoes in consideration of his testimony.[8]

As Douglas Hay has noted, the victims of malicious prosecutions had little recourse, since the legal remedy, a civil suit, was an expensive affair. And this applied in particular to the sorts of cases heard by the justices, where the stakes were lower. Thus, there are only seven suits for malicious prosecutions in the case files of the Montreal King's Bench between 1794 and 1827, and all concern prosecutions for felonies. At any rate, the maliciousness of a prosecution did not preclude its being founded in fact. As Gale noted in Handyside's case, 'the motives of informants can rarely be expected to be of the purest description; but altho in the present instance vindictive feelings may have caused the information to be given, proof has not been confined to the evidence of the informer, and the investigation has disclosed a long continuance of practices which the law inhibits, and which have been declared under oath to have been carried on with the concurrence of the petitioner.' And though Berg's testimony was rejected by the presiding justices, Charmon's prosecution of Jenkins was successful on the basis of other testimony, despite a defence plea of malicious prosecution.

Concurrent with its use as an instrument of vengeance, the everyday criminal justice system could also serve the interests of cupidity. In regulatory offences, prosecutorial cupidity was built right into the system, since almost all colonial acts and ordinances that defined new offences followed the English practice of providing that a proportion of the fine be paid to the prosecutor, usually half, in order to encourage private prosecution and thus save the state the expense of having to set up its own system of public prosecution. This applied even in offences that directly affected matters of state revenue, such as infractions of the licensing laws. When one petition for remission of a liquor-licensing fine, for example, described the main witness as having acted 'par des motifs bas et honteux, séduit d'ailleurs par l'appat d'un gain sordide' [from low and shameful motives, and furthermore seduced by the lure of sordid gain], there was no doubt a great deal of truth in the assertion, for the witness's share, even when split with the constable who was the main prosecutor, could amount to over £2. This goes a long way towards explaining why plaintiffs carried so many more Weekly Sessions cases through to judgment, in contrast to the high rate of cases dropped in Quarter Sessions complaints.[9]

But beyond the legally encouraged cupidity of the informer, greed could also motivate a malicious prosecution and subsequent offer to settle. This comes through most clearly in the practice of compounding, or offering to withdraw a prosecution in return for money, which in felony cases was considered an especially serious offence; as we saw, the mere suggestion of it led to the dismissal of at least one justice. Technically, even agreements between parties in assault cases constituted compounding, since the suit was the king's, but, as already noted, justices and law officers had little problem with this sort of settlement. More problematic in their eyes was compounding in regulatory offences, since the crown thereby lost its share of the fine: it was on this basis that in 1815 Joseph Robert launched a complaint against François Marois, who had begun prosecuting him for selling liquor without a licence but then agreed to drop the case for 150 *livres*, or a little over £6.[10]

Protection and Power

We take a far too bleak view of people's recourse to everyday criminal justice, however, if we see it only as a question of vengeance and cupidity. In other cases, people appealed to the law as a source of the power they lacked, and, despite its frequent use by the powerful to impose their will on the powerless, everyday criminal justice could also serve as a tool for those with little power to protect themselves. Perhaps the clearest example of the social power that the everyday criminal justice system could provide, and the very real limits of this power, was the experience of women who made complaints for domestic violence.

Unlike in France and New France and perhaps more clearly than in England, courts and justices in Quebec and Lower Canada, much like those in the United States, generally considered that husbands did not have the unrestrained right to assault their wives, and battered wives could lodge a formal complaint against their abusers.[11] For some women, the police and the courts were an important tool in responding to violent physical abuse from their husbands. In 1830 Catherine Robertson made a deposition against her husband, David, a Montreal comb-maker:

My husband has frequently abused ill treated and used personal violence towards me and threatened to deprive me of life; that he has in the violence of his passion on some occasions thrown down the stove at the risk of setting the house and neighbourhood on fire, broken the furniture and inflicted severe blows on me. That last night he beat me again, knocked me down and jumped with his feet upon my body in such wise as to endanger my life. That on a previous occasion three days before he jumped with his feet upon my body and injured me so much that in consequence I vomited shortly after about two quarts of blood. And I verily believe that I shall be deprived of life by his violence unless he shall be imprisoned or compelled to give security.[12]

After the latest assault, she went to her next-door neighbour, Andrew Watt, a cooper, who called the watch and had her husband taken into custody. The criminal justice system had not protected her from her husband's violence, but it had provided a means for her to shield herself from her husband after the fact, at least temporarily.

Ian Pilarczyk has suggested in his study of domestic violence in Montreal at the end of our period that police and courts often took domestic violence very seriously,[13] and this view that wife beating was a particularly grave form of assault also held earlier. Consider, for example, the deposition that George Sery, Jean-Baptiste Castonguay, Louis Sabourin, and Jean-Baptiste Morin, all long-serving Montreal constables, made on 2 January 1800 against Joseph Joutras. Joutras being at home in the faubourg Saint-Laurent, drunk, Madame Dorleans, with whom he lodged, sent for Sery to restore the peace at her house. After arriving, the constables removed Joutras's wife, Marie Dorée, from his grasp, since he was threatening to kill her and had seized a chair to strike her. They also deposed that Joutras was dangerous, repeating, 'Il faut que je te tue' [I must kill you] over and over again to his wife, and that to avoid misfortune Joutras had to be secured.[14] This was an unusually proactive intervention by city constables, who generally acted only after a warrant had issued. Likewise, even though the colonial administration normally assumed the cost of prosecutions only in felony cases, Richard Hart, Montreal's police constable and then high constable in the late 1810s, went so far as to charge his fees in several cases of wife battering to the government, alongside charges for arresting thieves and murderers, although these were later disallowed along with most of his other charges.[15] Further, husbands who battered their wives were much more likely to end up in gaol on preliminary imprisonment than those in assault cases in general: while wife batterers made up only a small proportion of defendants brought before the Montreal justices in the 1810s and early 1820s, they accounted for up to a fifth of prisoners committed to the gaol on assault charges in the same period, although it is difficult to know whether this was as a result of the justices refusing to bail on the basis of a reasonable fear of possible murder, under the Marian bail statutes, or the community in general refusing to enter into bail for wife batterers. Whatever the reasons, the willingness of justices to send wife batterers to prison must have been one of the reasons that women were willing throughout the period to bring these complaints before the formal criminal justice system. Finally, in the few cases of domestic violence that went to trial in the Quarter Sessions, the justices were unwilling to impose any limitation on the rights of wives to testify against their husbands. Thus, in 1815, at the trial of Michel Bourgoin *dit* Bourguignon for assaulting Marguerite Laurin, his wife, Bourgoin's lawyer objected to the admissibility of Laurin's evidence, 'the said being against her husband,' but the justices on the bench overruled the objection and admitted Laurin's evidence.[16]

The case of Laurin and Bourgoin was exceptional in that it went to full trial at the Quarter Sessions. More typical was that of Marie Sançon and her husband, the butcher Jean Lessart (or John Lesser). In January 1798 Sançon appeared in the Montreal Quarter Sessions to ask that Lessart be compelled to enter into a recognizance to keep the peace, and the court accordingly ordered a six-month recognizance, which Lessart entered in to. Three months later, however, Sançon was back in court along with her husband, and 'acknowledged that her fears derived from the ill-treatment and menaces of the said John were removed, and prayed a discontinuance of her complaint against him, and that he might be discharged from his recognizance.'[17] While women made consistent complaints against their husbands for battering them, they almost never pursued these complaints as far as a formal court case. Instead, in almost every case, wife batterers were arrested and then either bound to keep the peace or, in default, imprisoned. Of the few complaints of spouse abuse that became cases in the Montreal Quarter Sessions, most were resolved by the court summarily imposing a recognizance to keep the peace.

This summary resolution of spouse abuse, though, was an ambivalent tool for women. Peace bonds and summary imprisonment had the advantage of giving battered women an immediate respite from their husbands, allowing the justice system to intervene immediately in cases of domestic violence, but this was only because of an unwieldy court system where assault victims could wait as long as three months until the next sitting of the formal court, the Quarter Sessions. Further, as both Pilarczyk and Kathryn Harvey have shown, since most battered wives who made complaints were from the popular classes, they faced significant costs when they took their husband to court, both in terms of the expense of going to trial – which, as we saw, could be substantial –

and in terms of the loss of the income of their economic partner.[18] Victors in regular assault cases could expect to have the court order the defendant to pay costs, at least until the early 1830s, but in the case of battered women, the money came straight from their own family economy.

Moreover, not all battered women had equal access to the justice system. For one thing, most of the surviving complaints by battered women come from the cities themselves. In part, this is a reflection of the absence of records of the summary resolution of cases by rural justices, and there are indications that battered women from outside the city sometimes appealed to local justices. Thus, the notebook of Crebassa and Jones, the William Henry justices, records the cases of Nathalie Braux (asking for security of the peace against Pierre Baillac *dit* Lamontagne, her husband) and Mary Valois versus Antoine Valois (for assault, though the relationship in this case was not specified), in both of which the justices imposed a recognizance to keep the peace. And there are also several cases in which women travelled from rural parishes to complain against their husbands before urban justices. Thus, Magdeleine Allard, the wife of Charles Maillou, a Saint-Denis farmer, came before Jean-Marie Mondelet on 16 September 1820 to complain that her husband had been beating her for several years, and a week earlier had wounded her in the leg and thrown her from the bed onto her child's cradle. Mondelet issued an arrest warrant, and four days later Maillou was in Montreal entering into a recognizance to keep the peace for six months.[19] Nevertheless, complaints for domestic violence remained a largely urban phenomenon, with rural women more rarely using the justice system for that purpose.

Ethnicity and class also seem to have played a role in deciding whether battered women would resort to the justice system. *Canadien* women were perhaps comparatively less willing to bring domestic-violence complaints before magistrates than their anglophone counterparts: while domestic-violence cases accounted for about a third of the complaints made by British women, the proportion was only half that among *Canadiennes*, though in absolute terms there were still more of the latter who complained. And domestic-violence complaints were made almost entirely by women from the popular classes, with very few cases involving elite women.[20]

In addition, as most studies of domestic violence have shown, recourse to the justice system was not a first-line defence, and battered women usually went to the justice system only after prolonged abuse: about three-quarters of the complaints that battered women made explicitly mentioned prolonged physical and/or verbal abuse. This was not because justices required proof of long-term abuse to act: even Samuel Gale was willing to impose a recognizance to keep the peace on the basis of a deposition wherein when Mary Flynn accused James Dogherty of threatening to kill her with a table fork while he was drunk, without any mention of any physical or prior verbal abuse.[21] But, generally, it was only when abuse reached an intolerable level that women were willing to go before a justice.

Further, despite the occasional intervention of constables in particularly egregious cases, we must not think that the justice system was particularly proactive in dealing with domestic violence. In the first place, not all justices were equally willing to facilitate domestic-violence prosecutions. Thus, in Montreal, under the Tory chairmen of the late 1820s, Gale and David Ross, though the number of women bringing complaints involving domestic violence before the justices in Montreal remained steady, the number of wife batterers committed to gaol dropped sharply. And consider the comments made by Chartier de Lotbinière, the aristocratic Vaudreuil justice, in a covering letter enclosing the documents relating to the complaint of Magdelaine Treslerd, the twenty-year-old daughter of one Treslerd, against her father for beating her on several occasions. In explaining why he had not required Magdelaine to enter into a recognizance to prosecute, he stated that 'dans les divisions et difficultés de famille, il faut autant que possible, laisser une porte ouverte aux accomodements' [in family discords and difficulties, one must as much as possible leave open the door to accommodations]. Likewise, Austin Cuvillier, Montreal's leading magistrate in the mid-1830s, was reported to have declared that husbands had the right to correct their wives, much like masters their servants.[22] None of this suggests that justices were particularly sensitive to the problems of battered women. At most, the criminal justice system took a neutral stance, as is evident from the fact that it was not only wives who could turn to the justice system against their husbands, but also husbands against their wives: in the district of Montreal until 1835, in about 10 per cent of domestic-violence cases in all, it was husbands who were complaining against their wives for physical abuse.[23]

Finally, even if police and justices had all the will in the world to stop spouse abuse, there were severe limits to the extent to which the justice system could really protect women from abusive husbands. Abusive husbands were well aware that they could be arrested: John Skelton, for example, a Montreal butcher, declared to Marie Gosse, his wife, that if she didn't have him arrested, 'elle se souviendrait de lui' [she would remember him]. But this did not stop them beating their wives. Marie-Josephte Brais, the wife of Toussaint Renaud *dit* Desloriers, a Longueuil farmer, declared in December 1830 that her husband had beaten her so much that fifteen days ago she had been obliged to have him arrested, but he had continued and so she had to leave the house with her children. And Marie-Louise Saint-Aubin of Saint-Laurent stated that Antoine Legault *dit* Delorier, her husband, who was a habitual batterer, threatened to burn their buildings. In these two latter cases, the threat was all the more credible in that they took place in rural areas, where, as we saw, there was far less presence of both police and justices – one reason why Saint-Aubin came before the Montreal justices to complain was that her parish had no resident justice. And one case in particular illustrates the very real limits of soliciting judicial intervention, that of Marie Reeves, the wife of François Vinet *dit* Souligny, of Longue-Pointe. As a result of her husband's abuse, Reeves had on several occasions resorted to the justice system, and on 28 September 1821 she had him arrested and committed to gaol. A month later, Vinet managed to mortgage his property to procure bail, and on 1 January 1822 he murdered Reeves by hitting her repeatedly with a piece of firewood. As Ian Pilarczyk has shown, wife murder was an uncommon but nevertheless regular feature of life in Montreal. But its potency as a threat against wives comes through clearly in the 1835 deposition of Rachel-Charlotte Desautels against her husband, the notary Joseph-Hilarion Jobin, for threatening to do to her 'ce que Dewey avait fait a sa femme' [what Dewey did to his wife], Dewey having been found guilty of murdering his wife and executed after a sensational and highly publicized trial in Montreal a couple years earlier.[24]

Nevertheless, women continued to come before the justices with complaints against their husbands, and the very fact that these often poor, often illiterate, often francophone wives were willing to use the power of the state to counter the physical power of their husbands testifies to their belief that it could serve their needs, however poorly. And in many cases, these women were successful in their attempts to exercise this limited power. Take the case of Josette Levasseur. In 1784 she charged her husband, Jean-Baptiste Racine, with 'treating [her] ill.' By the time the case came to trial, Racine had been in prison eight days, and Levasseur simply did not appear to prosecute any further.[25] That this encounter with the justice system stopped Racine from beating her, however, is doubtful.

Negotiation and Reparation

While most battered women who appealed to the justice system were probably seeking direct protection, criminal complaints could also fit into a larger process of negotiation and reparation, adding weight in the balance of a plaintiff who was otherwise disadvantaged. Consider the assault complaint that Margaret Farrell, an unwed mother, made against John Crooks, a Montreal miller, in 1835. Farrell related that Crooks had fathered her child, which was born the previous year, and ever since had given her a dollar a week as maintenance. However, when Farrell had recently asked for her dollar, Crooks refused and assaulted and kicked her. While initially this might seem simply a case of a woman prosecuting a man who had beaten her, the complaint was also perhaps designed to force Crooks to keep paying: the complaint came five days after the assault, which strongly suggests a period of negotiation.[26]

As in the case of Farrell and Crooks, the process of negotiation and reparation that lay behind many criminal complaints is lost to us, and we are reduced to conjecture. But there is no doubt, as Martin Dufresne has argued, that complaints before the justices, especially those concerning interpersonal violence, were sometimes, perhaps even often, used as leverage in larger disputes. One of the best examples of this is bastardy cases. Prosecutions for bastardy had a long history in England, allowing for the father of an illegitimate child to be sued for the costs of childbirth, the expenses of raising the child, and punitive damages. The English bastardy laws were not, however, progressive instruments for the protection of single mothers. They formed an integral part of the Poor Laws, and their main intent was to avoid bastard children becoming a burden on the parish and thus on its propertied ratepayers. And the complement to suing the father of a bastard child was punishing the mother for fornication, usually by a term in the local House of Correction. Similar proceedings were used in the American colonies, although bastardy prosecutions themselves were perhaps rarer.[27]

The practice was transferred to Quebec following the Conquest: as early as 1767, Catharine Bauparlant prosecuted Joseph Dondaneau (unsuccessfully) for bastardy in the Montreal Quarter Sessions. But in the colony, bastardy prosecutions took on a different tone. There was never any question of punishing the mothers of bastard children, unlike in the American colonies, where such prosecutions were frequent, in part because mothers could be punished only if the child became chargeable to the parish, which was impossible since the English Poor Laws were never applied in Quebec. In Quebec, bastardy prosecutions became instead a means for single mothers, or their parents, to seek financial redress from those who had impregnated them. They thus followed the practice of New France, where Marie-Aimée Cliche found almost a hundred cases where women launched legal proceedings against men who got them pregnant. Unlike those in New France, however, bastardy cases after the Conquest were definitely criminal matters: this is the only way that they could have been received into the colony after 1775, when French civil law came back into effect, and they had been specifically determined to be criminal matters by English court decisions which were later used as authorities in Lower Canada. Further, bastardy complaints followed the same course as assault complaints: defendants were subject to arrest immediately after the complaint, in contrast to the summons used in civil cases; they were bound over for trial, just as in misdemeanour cases; and those found guilty were subject to immediate imprisonment if they did not immediately pay. As in master and servant cases, however, suits were never in the name of the king, but rather the plaintiff, and cases were determined summarily by the justices, in Quarter Sessions, rather than by jury trial.[28]

Bastardy cases primarily involved *Canadiens*, who accounted for about 90 per cent of both plaintiffs and defendants, and they were largely a rural phenomenon. None of the women was from the elites, since the key to a bastardy case was proving that the mother was unable to support the child herself, but, as Cliche found in New France, some of the men being sued were clearly members of the elites, such as in the cases of Catherine Lebeau's prosecution of Dr George Plunket of L'Assomption in 1785 or Rebecca Samuel's prosecution of Samuel Judah, an important Montreal merchant, in 1781. The prosecution thus became a way of offsetting the unequal power relations otherwise present between ordinary women and elite men. However, in other cases, the defendant was also clearly not well-off: when François Dirigé *dit* Laplante was condemned to pay £3 to Marguerite Varin in 1790, he was given fifteen days to find the money 'on account of his poverty.'[29]

The question that arises immediately is the extent to which these suits were at the behest of the woman herself, rather than of her parents. Constance Backhouse has shown that nineteenth-century seduction suits in Canada had little to do with the woman who was seduced and were instead instances of the father suing for damages to his possessions. The bastardy cases that came before the justices of the peace in the district of Montreal in the eighteenth century, however, were more ambiguous. As was true in New France, some cases were clearly launched mainly at the impetus of a man, generally the woman's father or employer. Thus, there is little doubt that when Henry Stodt, of Varennes, was charged with bastardy in 1788 for having impregnated Lisette, a Native slave of Joseph Ainse, it was Ainse who was suing Stodt for damage to his property. In other cases, the record is more obliquely suggestive of paternal involvement: for example, Marguerite Bertrand's prosecution of François Lantier in 1792 was conducted for her by her stepfather, ostensibly because the eighteen-year-old was too ill to appear in court. On the other hand, there were at least five widows who prosecuted men for bastardy; several of the single women who brought suits were fatherless; and, even among the single women, many were willing to go to considerable trouble to ensure that their cases were successful, as when Marie-Louise Reine, a nineteen-year-old, travelled all the way from Yamaska to Montreal to swear her complaint against Pierre Petit *fils*. In these cases, it is more difficult to deny agency to the women involved.[30]

Part of the reason that women were willing to launch bastardy suits was their effectiveness, for, in the Montreal Quarter Sessions after 1779, they were consistently successful: until 1794, in every case where the woman persisted to a full trial before the justices, the man was found guilty. The proceedings in these trials were not at all what one might expect from an otherwise evidently patriarchal system. First, unlike in rape trials, the justices were usually more willing to believe the word of the woman than of the man she was accusing or of witnesses brought up against her. Thus, at the bastardy trial of Lantier, in October 1792, Lantier's attorney presented a witness who claimed to have heard Bertrand accuse Lantier of liking her sister more than her, and threatening that 'je me ferai attraper par quelque autre et je dirai que c'est toi, et j'en ferai serment, et que ce serment seroit sans aucune consequence' [I will get myself caught by someone else and I will say it was you, and I will swear to it, and the oath will be of no consequence]. But the justices nevertheless found Lantier guilty. Further, the justices were clearly more concerned with compensating the woman than with the fiction of ensuring that the child did not become a burden on the parish: thus, they made several awards in cases where the child would manifestly not become a burden on anybody, since it was dead. Even in the matter of custody, the justices did not entirely follow the patriarchal model that would later come to dominate: for instance, in Catherine

Parranteau's prosecution of Simon Frichet *fils* in April 1782, they awarded Parranteau £4 for 'lying in costs' plus two shillings sixpence per week for the child's first five years, whereupon the father could take the child 'unless the mother chooses to keep it at her own costs and expences.' And the justices also did not hesitate to enforce their sentences: Étienne Grinier of Repentigny spent three months in prison because he was unable to satisfy the court-imposed payment to Thérèse Latouche. This is not to say that the justices' decisions were uniformly favourable to women. In the case of Lantier, for example, they refused to order him imprisoned until he made his payment to Betrand. And, in the two bastardy cases involving elite defendants, the justices gave custody of the children to the fathers, though they were to remain with their mothers while still young. But, in general, a man facing a bastardy suit ran a high risk of having the decision go against him.[31]

The threat of a bastardy suit was thus a powerful weapon to induce an illegitimate father to make some sort of arrangement with the woman he had impregnated. One such arrangement was marriage. Thus, in January 1786, Marguerite Lavigne, the young *engagée* of Jean Monjean, a Varennes habitant, travelled to Montreal to complain that after Monjean repeatedly asked her to sleep with him and promised marriage, preying on her weakness, she finally gave in, but on her becoming pregnant, though she had asked him to marry her, he replied that it did not regard him. On Lavigne's complaint, Monjean was arrested by the local bailiff at seven in the morning, but the complaint went no further, probably because in April 1786, a month after the birth (and death) of the child, Monjean married Lavigne, with the couple having six more children by 1798. Similarly, in January 1794, Marguerite Lacoste, a thirty-nine-year-old Boucherville widow who had had thirteen children with her previous husband, launched a bastardy complaint against Paschal Daudelin, fourteen years her junior; her child, Félicité, was born in March. The complaint was obviously an insufficient incentive, for the case went on to full trial, and in July, Daudelin was condemned to pay forty shillings for lying-in expenses, the same sum retroactively to Félicité's birth for maintenance, ten shillings per month for future maintenance, plus twenty shillings in court costs, and to be committed until the whole was paid. This provided the necessary leverage for Lacoste: a month later, in August, she and Daudelin married and legitimated Félicité, though the child died three months later. Of eighteen bastardy cases where the parties were identifiable from parish records and the man was not already married, ten resulted in marriages, and in fully half of all bastardy suits the woman either declared herself satisfied or simply dropped the prosecution. And beyond the bastardy cases that were actually brought before justices, how many suits were threatened but never carried out?[32]

Yet bastardy cases also illustrate how, while the criminal law could be a source of leverage, the legalistic decisions of the justices who made up the Quarter Sessions could severely curtail this tool, for after 1795 bastardy prosecutions ceased entirely. In that year, David Ross, the young lawyer who three decades later would become Montreal's chairman, argued that the complaint of Anne Grandmaitre, a twenty-three-year-old Châteauguay woman whose parents were both dead, against Joachim Foubert should be dismissed since 'there is no law in force in this country that authorises the Justices in sessions to take cognizance of complaints of this nature.' Ross was correct, since the bastardy laws were part of the Poor Laws and had thus not been received into the colony. After deliberating, the justices agreed and dismissed the complaint, despite the arguments by Grandmaitre's lawyer, Louis-Charles Foucher, that 'there is a law which authorises the Justices in sessions to take cognizance of complaints of this nature and that since the establishment for [sic] the Quarter Sessions in this province they have uniformly taken cognizance of such complaints.' Subsequently, justices refused to hear bastardy complaints, as 'not being within the jurisdiction of this court,' and it became a fixed part of colonial judicial opinion that 'that part of the Criminal Law of England which relates to this subject is not applicable to the state of society here, nor in accordance with our Institutions.' One of the principal ways in which women, and rural women in particular, had used the criminal justice system in the eighteenth century had thus disappeared. While civil suits remained an option, all that remained on the criminal side was an even more directly instrumental use of the system, as in the assault prosecution that Farrell launched against Crooks.[33]

Bastardy cases, just like malicious or greedy prosecutions, or appeals to justice by battered women, change our perception of the relationship between people and criminal justice. Not only do they underscore the instrumentalization of the law, they also suggest an explanation as to why so many ordinary people had recourse to it: not because they necessarily believed in its legitimacy, but because they considered that it could, after all, serve their purposes, if only imperfectly.

The Structural Biases of Justice

As bastardy cases suggest, the distribution of social power in colonial society was shaped not only by the will of plaintiffs but also by the structural biases built into the fabric of society. Ethnicity is the most evident of these in a colonized society: colonizers and the colonized, British and *Canadiens*, evidently did not have the same access to power. But, as we saw, ethnicity was not a strong determinant of recourse to the criminal justice system, nor of the experience of justice. Further, as many historians have shown, seeing the distribution of social power only through the lens of ethnicity distorts the nature of the colony's society, which, like its Western equivalents, was also fundamentally structured by class, gender, and race. This was a highly inegalitarian society, with a well-entrenched class system and social inequalities even among *habitants*; a patriarchal society, in which women were denied many rights, including, for most, the right to vote; and a fundamentally racist society, which accepted the slavery of Blacks and Natives until the end of the eighteenth century, while, in the case of Natives in particular, marginalizing them and infantilizing their culture. And these three basic structural determinants of class, gender, and race shaped how the everyday criminal justice expressed social power.[34]

Class

As with geography and ethnicity, the class of plaintiffs and defendants played an ambiguous role in shaping their contacts with the criminal justice system. Take the basic question of who was prosecuting whom. One of the strongest arguments of the consensual view of the English system is that the parties involved were generally not from the elites who, according to the conflict theorists, used the criminal law to defend their interests. Instead, most were from the middling and popular classes, and most cases involved little in the way of class conflict.

To form some idea of the social class of parties, Figures 7.1 and 7.2 present the approximate occupational structure of plaintiffs and defendants before the justices. Parties are broken down into seven socio-professional groups: elites, especially merchants and members of the liberal professions; 'middling,' comprising those who were definitely not part of the elites but also not really part of the popular classes, such as clerks, mid-level government bureaucrats, and small shopkeepers; skilled labourers, especially artisans; farmers; 'yeomen,' who were most

Figure 7.1: Occupations of parties, district of Montreal, 1785–1835

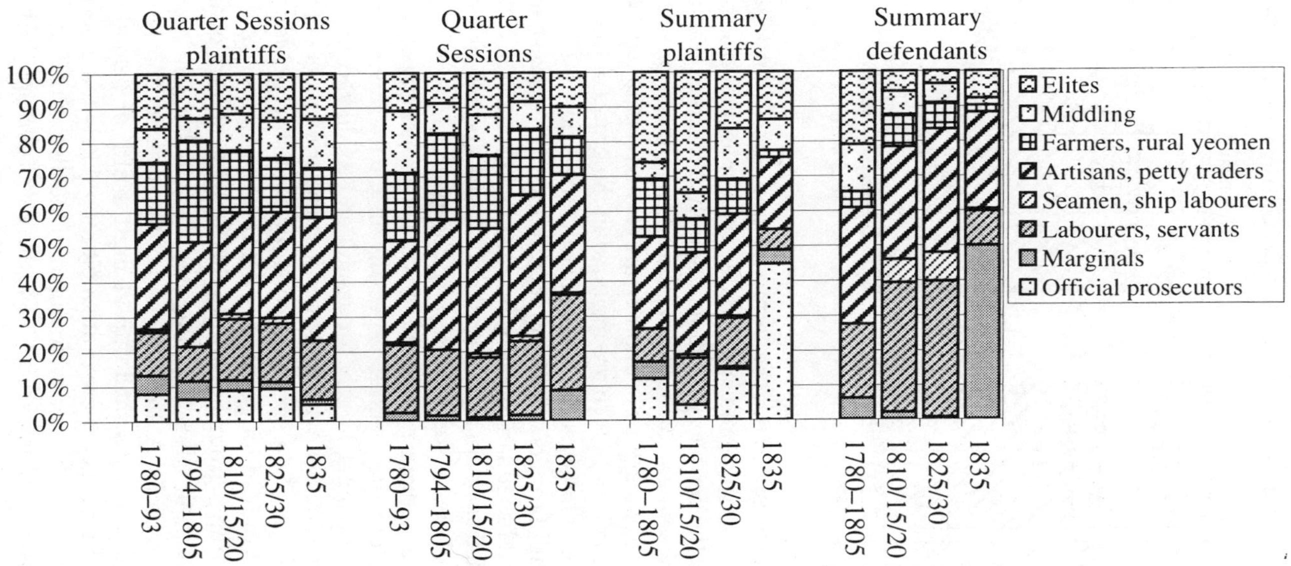

Quarter Sessions plaintiffs
Quarter Sessions
Summary plaintiffs
Summary defendants
100%
90%
80%
70%
60%
50%
40%
30%
20%
10%
0%
1780–93
1794–1805
1810/15/20
1825/30
1835
1780–93
1794–1805
1810/15/20
1825/30
1835
1780–1805
1810/15/20
1825/30
1835
1780–1805
1810/15/20
1825/30
1835
Elites
Middling
Farmers, rural yeomen
Artisans, petty traders
Seamen, ship labourers
Labourers, servants
Marginals
Official prosecutors

Figure 7.2: Occupations of parties, Quebec Quarter Sessions complaints, 1805–35

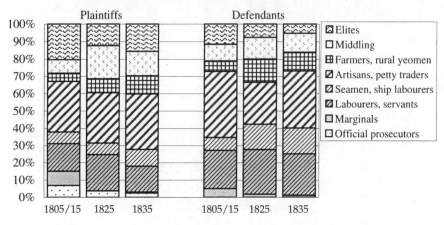

likely farmers, though the term was imprecise;[35] unskilled labourers, including servants and apprentices; and a marginal group including all those on the periphery of colonial society, such as vagrants, prostitutes, ordinary soldiers, or indentured seamen. Official prosecutors, generally police of one type or another, are classed separately. Women whose occupation is not given are included in the group of their husbands or fathers. Obviously, occupational structure is only a rough measure of class, with farmers, for example, ranging from poor sharecroppers to well-established landowners; but just as for offences, if the categories are treated as heuristic tools rather than strict representations of reality, they do allow for some interesting observations.

What is perhaps most striking is the heterogeneity of the people who came before the justices, especially in Quarter Sessions complaints. These complaints, largely for assault and the like, conform best to the consensual model, with most parties neither members of the elites nor at the bottom of the social structure. In the district of Montreal, the elite group accounted for perhaps 15 per cent of plaintiffs, and even adding the 'middling' group only raises this figure to about a quarter. Further, members of the elites were only slightly more likely to be plaintiffs than to be defendants. At the other end of the scale, the marginal group and unskilled labourers made up at most a fifth of defendants until the 1820s, though they were quite a bit more likely to be defendants than plaintiffs. The situation was similar in the district of Quebec. However, in the district of Montreal at least, there was perhaps the beginning of a

Table 7.1: Pair-wise comparison of class of parties in Montreal Quarter Sessions complaints, 1780–1835*

Defendants Plaintiffs	Elites	Middling	Farmers, rural yeomen	Artisans, petty traders	Labourers, apprentices, servants	Marginals
Elites	46	20	24	60	34	11
Middling	12	24	17	64	59	14
Farmers, rural yeomen	16	9	157	33	36	6
Artisans, petty traders	39	56	28	252	99	26
Labourers, apprentices, servants	21	17	27	85	99	2
Marginals	1	3	5	31	6	4

* Numbers are absolute numbers.

more class-oriented system in the 1803s, with marginals and unskilled labourers making up almost 40 per cent of defendants overall in 1835, as against perhaps 15 per cent of plaintiffs.

If we look at who was complaining against whom, in Quarter Sessions, we can also see how little of the business of the justices in Quarter Sessions complaints had to do directly with class conflict, and even less with elites using the system against the popular classes. Table 7.1 presents the numbers of plaintiffs and defendants from each group who complained against each other, based on plaintiff-defendant pairs, with unskilled labourers and marginals grouped together. About 40 per cent of these pairs involved people from the same group, and about another 25 per cent involved only plaintiffs and defendants who were definitely from the popular classes; in other words, perhaps two-thirds of these pairs involved no evident class conflict.

Another way of analysing the social class of plaintiffs, at least in Quarter Sessions cases, is through their literacy, or, rather, their capacity to sign depositions and other documents. As Table 7.2 shows, about half of the plaintiffs were unable to sign, reflecting a justice system used in large part by people who came from the popular classes. At the same time, the capacity of plaintiffs to sign was consistently above the averages that have been found for Quebec and Lower Canadian society as a whole. For example, only about 10 per cent of rural francophones in

Table 7.2: Plaintiffs' capacity to sign in Montreal Quarter Sessions cases, 1780–1835

	1780–1800	1825	1835
All	49%	51%	57%
Urban	57%	52%	61%
Rural	32%	46%	39%

	Urban	Rural
Anglophone men	85%	79%
Francophone men	49%	26%
Anglophone women	44%	43%
Francophone women	20%	16%

Quebec, both men and women, could sign their names; the percentage of plaintiffs in Quarter Sessions cases who could do so was one and a half times higher for women and more than double for men. Similarly, as late as 1840, only about 60 per cent of rural anglophone men could sign their names; among Quarter Sessions plaintiffs, this reached almost 80 per cent. As for urban-dwellers, only about 30 per cent of men in Quebec City could sign their names, a rate lower than even francophone men who made Quarter Sessions complaints in Montreal.[36] All of this bolsters the impression that those who made complaints before the justices, while mainly not members of the elites, were nevertheless not entirely representative of colonial society as a whole.

The class bias of the justice system was also clearly evident in other aspects of the criminal justice system. As Jean-Marie Fecteau has shown, defendants in the King's Bench, which increasingly concentrated on property crime, were overwhelmingly from the margins of society, although whether the plaintiffs in these cases were necessarily members of the elites awaits further study.[37] Summary complaints were also more clearly shaped by class considerations. In Montreal, as Figure 7.1 indicates, an increasingly large proportion of defendants in summary complaints were unskilled labourers or marginals, about half in the 1810s and 1820 and reaching 60 per cent by the mid-1830s, reflecting both the importance of breach-of-service complaints, whether of voyageurs, apprentices, servants, or mariners, and, as Mary Anne Poutanen has shown, increasing summary arrests and imprisonments of vagrants and prostitutes.[38] And in Quebec City, at least in the nine-teenth century, the large numbers of complaints against sailors for desertion, and against vagrants and prostitutes, ensured that the everyday justice system was increasingly concerned with class. On the other hand, those most often targeted by complaints in the regulatory-offence cases that dominated in the Weekly Sessions were middling and even elite members of society: those who had land abutting a road they did not keep up, for example, or retailers selling liquor without a licence.

Class also had some effect on the course a complaint took, though not as uniformly as one might expect. Thus, the clear rate for complaints by elite complainants, at 77 per cent, was only slightly higher than that for unskilled and marginal complainants, at 71 per cent, but the rate at which elite complainants took their complaints to Quarter Sessions was much higher, at 48 per cent, compared to 33 per cent for unskilled and marginal complainants. And this is complemented by another trend: for elite defendants, the clear rate was 82 per cent, but for unskilled and marginal defendants, it was only 69 per cent; and, while the rate of pursuance to the Quarter Sessions was 46 per cent for elite defendants, it was only 23 per cent for unskilled and marginal defendants. Complainants from the top of the social hierarchy, though only slightly more likely to be successful in having a tangible effect on their opponents than those at the bottom, were quite a bit more likely to pursue their complaint to a formal court, but, at the same time, elite defendants, probably because they were easier to find, were more likely to be forced to go before a justice, and also to have their case move on to a formal trial. In court, the story was similar. Again considering only cases involving interpersonal violence, while elite complainants had a decision in their favour about 45 per cent of the time, the proportion for unskilled and marginal complainants was much lower, about 25 per cent. On the other hand, elite defendants had decisions against them about half of the time, while unskilled and marginal defendants experienced this result only about a quarter of the time. While complainants from the bottom of the social hierarchy were less likely to have a case decided in their favour, they were also less likely to have it decided against them. Just like the evidence concerning offences tried in the various courts, all of this suggests that while the criminal justice system was certainly not primarily a locus for class conflict, it was not at all class-neutral.

Gender

Another structural bias of the justice system was gender. Studies of eighteenth- and nineteenth-century criminal justice systems in Europe

Figure 7.3: Women before the justices, 1765–1835

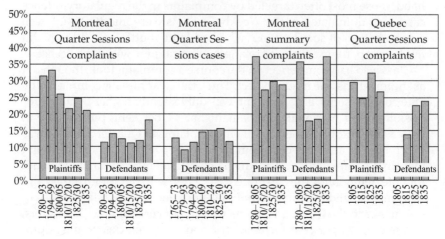

and North America have demonstrated that the presence of women was variable, depending on the place, time, and court, but almost always far lower than that of men.[39] The same held true for Quebec and Lower Canada. As Jean-Marie Fecteau has shown, women played a small role in the higher criminal courts, accounting for under 5 per cent of defendants in the Quebec King's Bench between 1775 and 1840.[40] This was gendered justice, but to the disadvantage of men. Yet the situation was more complex at the level of the justices. As Figure 7.3 shows, among people who brought complaints before the justices for matters such as assaults and petty thefts, dealt with by Quarter Sessions, women were certainly in the minority, but a significant minority: between 25 and 30 per cent of plaintiffs, though only about 10 to 20 per cent of defendants. The presence of women was quite different in other parts of the everyday justice system, however. In the Weekly Sessions, for example, women barely appeared at all: never as plaintiffs and only rarely as defendants, accounting for less than 4 per cent of those convicted in the court in Montreal. The Weekly Sessions was a venue primarily concerned with enforcing formal obligations to the state, and such obligations were directed primarily at men, both as property holders and as citizens. Women were exempted from some of these obligations simply because they were women, as was the case for

Figure 7.4: Women as defendants in the criminal justice system, 1712–1835

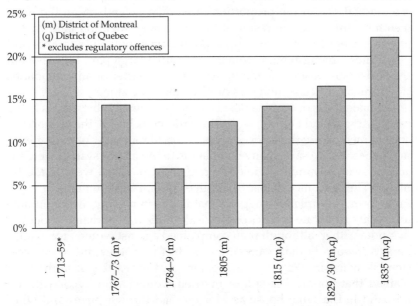

militia service, but in other instances their exemption was based not directly on their sex but on their lack of property. Hence, in the few cases where women did appear, they were mostly widows charged with offences contingent upon the ownership of property, such as selling liquor without a licence, not levelling the snow in front of their lands, or refusing to have their chimneys swept. On the other hand, there were proportionately far more women among the offenders that the justices committed summarily: in the Montreal House of Correction, for example, women often made up half or more of prisoners. This was because summary justice and especially summary imprisonment often concerned marginal groups such as servants, vagrants, and prostitutes where women were heavily if not exclusively represented. Even here, however, there were variations: in Quebec City, the summary conviction of mariners for desertion concerned only men.[41]

Figure 7.4 gives an overall picture of the presence of women before the criminal justice system, at least as defendants, from the era of New France to 1835. There was relatively little change across the Conquest, though with a small drop, and the small proportion of woman defendants in the 1780s reflects the temporary importance of regulatory cases in Weekly Sessions, notably for militia violations. On the other hand, the gradual rise in the proportion of woman defendants in the nineteenth century was the result of the increasing attention paid by the justice system to urban marginal populations, notably vagrants and prostitutes, among whom women made up a large part. Still, even in the mid-1830s, women made up less than a quarter of all defendants: the criminal justice system was directed far more at men.

The male focus of criminal justice is in itself remarkable, for, as in the case of Asselin and Dubois, with which this book began, the preponderance of men before the justices gives us a different view of masculinity in Quebec. As we saw, many complaints to the justice system were for acts of relatively minor violence, and most of these were made by men.[42] The very fact that artisans like Asselin were willing to make these formal complaints suggests that it was in no way dishonourable to appeal to the state in cases of physical conflict rather than responding in kind. Further, although men complained against women for assault far less frequently than women did against men, they did so on occasion, as when in 1825, Pierre Monjon, a Montreal blacksmith, complained that Sophie Perrault, a married women who lived with her husband in the same house as Monjon, had thrown plates and other articles capable of harming him at his face. Evidently, Monjon's conception of masculinity did not in any way preclude him from having a neighbour's wife arrested and bound to keep the peace, rather than dealing with it himself. Nor did Samuel Davis, a Montreal furrier, see any shame in making a complaint in 1835 against Sarah Oxbey, a blacksmith's wife, who tried to stab him with a carving knife, which was only 'with great difficulty wrested from her hand by 6 men who were present.' Neither Monjon nor Davis pursued the complaints to formal trial, but there were occasionally men who appeared in open court to prosecute women for physically assaulting them.[43]

The complexity of gender relations and roles is also highlighted by the marital status of women who made complaints. Historians have often assumed that, under English law, since married women ceased to be persons and became instead *femes covertes*, they simply did not appear in the legal system, apart from in special cases such as spousal abuse. Work on the status of *femes covertes* in the American colonies, however, suggests that married women were more active in practice than their formal status under the law might suggest; for example, they were not spared from prosecution because of their status.[44] The legal

Table 7.3: Marital status of female plaintiffs in Montreal Quarter Sessions complaints, 1780–1835

	Unmarried	Married	Widowed	Unknown
All 1780–99	18%	66%	7%	9%
Francophones	18%	66%	7%	8%
Anglophones	19%	68%	6%	6%
All 1800–35	13%	59%	10%	18%
Francophones	10%	63%	8%	18%
Anglophones	19%	50%	13%	18%

status of women was more complicated in Quebec and Lower Canada because of the co-existence of French civil and English criminal justice systems, though in theory the English rules should have applied in criminal cases. Yet, as Table 7.3 shows, there was apparently little impediment to married women making complaints in their own names: even if we assume that all women whose marital status was not explicitly mentioned in the court documents were single, almost two-thirds of the women who brought complaints before the justices were married, with little difference between francophones and non-francophones in the eighteenth century, though perhaps there were proportionately fewer married anglophone women in the nineteenth. Further, few depositions by women bothered to include the formula required by the Coutume de Paris, whereby women declared themselves duly authorized by their husbands. Finally, these women were almost all not simply adjuncts to a male plaintiff: over 90 per cent made their complaint alone, and only 5 per cent were making a complaint in conjunction with a man.

Equally interesting is the large proportion of *Canadien* women who made complaints before the justices. *Canadiennes* made up about three-quarters of female plaintiffs before the Montreal justices in the eighteenth century, and two-thirds in the nineteenth, outstripping the proportion of *Canadien* plaintiffs overall: even in 1835, when francophones made up only perhaps 40 per cent of all plaintiffs, about half of women who made complaints were francophones. This certainly modifies a more traditional view of the passivity of *Canadien* women.

More revelatory of the gendered bias of the criminal justice system were the significant differences in the reasons for which women and men came before the justices. As Figure 7.5 shows, women encountered everyday criminal justice in five main ways, in ascending order of

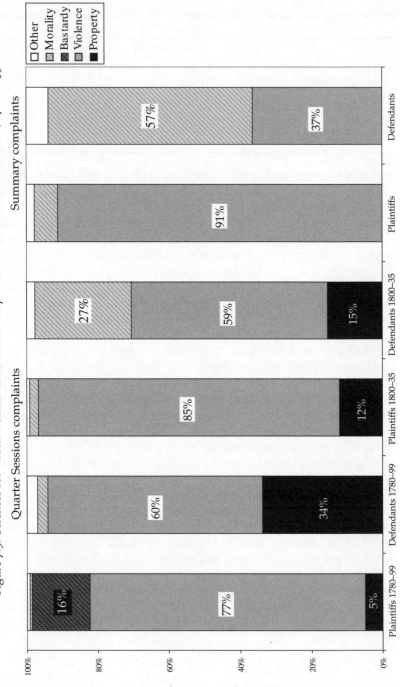

Figure 7.5: Offences for which women came before the justices in the district of Montreal, 1780–1835

Table 7.4: Gender and the course of complaints, Montreal Quarter Sessions, 1780–1830*

	Dropped before Quarter Sessions	Results in Quarter Sessions			
		No resolution	Settled	For plaintiff	For defendant
Female parties only**	66%	11%	17%	44%	28%
Female plaintiff, male defendant	68%	24%	17%	30%	29%
Male plaintiff, female defendant**	77%	7%	20%	40%	33%
Male parties only	70%	22%	17%	34%	26%

* calculated on the basis of results by defendant
** small number of cases makes the breakdown of Quarter Sessions results unreliable

numerical importance: as plaintiffs in bastardy cases, at least (as we saw) in the eighteenth century; as defendants in property cases, largely petty larceny; as defendants in the whole nexus of morality and public-order offences centred on prostitution and vagrancy; and as both plaintiffs and defendants in violence cases, essentially assault, including domestic violence (though these were a small minority of women's violence cases as a whole). There were some overall similarities with the pattern for men, such as the predominance of cases involving violence, but also some striking differences. Thus, of course, men were never plaintiffs in bastardy cases; women, on the other hand, were almost never accused of offences against the state, such as assaulting police. Likewise, few women appeared before the justices on service-related charges: employers clearly disciplined their female servants in other ways. The small number of women lodging complaints for property offences, such as theft or vandalism, is not at all surprising, since married women and minors, who comprised the vast majority of women, were largely excluded from the formal ownership and control of the sort of property liable to be stolen or damaged. And, as for public-order offences, such as prostitution or infractions of municipal regulations, such offences were almost invariably prosecuted by men, with women coming before the justices as defendants. Overall, the ways in which women encountered the justice system of the state thus reflected their formally subordinate position in property relations and state structures. When they came before the justices as plaintiffs in particular, it was in ways intimately connected to their own bodies, and what they were seeking to protect was themselves.[45]

On the other hand, gender did not play much of a role in determining the course of a case once a complaint had been made. As Table 7.4

shows, women were only slightly more likely than men to pursue a complaint as far as a formal case in Quarter Sessions, and once there, there was no dramatic variation in the results of cases, especially if we compare the two most frequent scenarios, where women complained against men and where men complained against men. This mirrors the situation in England, where there were significant gender differences in trial results and sentencing in higher courts, with female defendants treated far more leniently, but not at the level of Quarter Sessions.[46]

In general, there is no doubt that the justice system was an inherently gendered institution: the justices, the clerks and other officials, the constables and bailiffs, the members of the jury, and the attorneys were all men; the laws and the lawbooks were all written by men. And thus, when a woman ventured into court, or even into the office of a justice to lodge a complaint, she was entering an essentially masculine space. But, as in other Western societies, this did not stop many women from making complaints, and, as far as Quarter Sessions complaints are concerned, mainly assaults and thefts, they were far more likely to come before the justices as plaintiffs than as defendants, far more likely to be seeking out the justice system as a source of power than being sought out by it. This suggests that women were far from excluded from the public sphere in the colony. André Lachance, examining the criminality of women in New France, argued that their low rate of delinquency resulted from their adherence to a traditional domestic role in the private sphere of the home. And yet these same *Canadien* women, or their daughters or granddaughters, seemed quite willing to enter the very public sphere of the post-Conquest legal system in order to challenge those who had wronged them, suggesting something other than a simple public/private dichotomy – much as historians have been finding in other British North American contexts.[47]

Race

In colonial societies, another powerful structural bias was race, which shaped the experience and meaning of criminal justice. Indeed, when the conflict model of ancien-régime criminal justice is transposed into the colonial context, it is above all racial domination that is seen as the main feature of criminal justice in early colonial societies from India to South Africa.[48]

The situation was different in Quebec and Lower Canada: instead of being a locus of racial domination, the criminal justice system was above all a marginal part of the lives of non-Europeans. As one might expect, Blacks and Natives did appear as defendants before the justices, ranging from George, who, as we saw, was whipped through Montreal in the mid-1760s, to Paul and Jean-Baptiste Sacoyatinta, Caughnawaga Natives, arrested in 1830 for being drunk and disorderly in the city's Old Market and assaulting a market constable who admonished them.[49] True, in Quarter Sessions complaints, non-Europeans were quite a bit more likely to appear before the justices as defendants rather than as plaintiffs – Natives about twice as likely and Blacks about four times as likely – which suggests that, for those on the margins of European society, the courts of the justices functioned more as instruments of oppression than as sources of power. However, unlike in other white settler societies such as the Spanish colonies or South Africa, the business of the justice system (at least at the level of the justices) was little concerned with the enforcement of European domination. Non-Europeans represented only a small number of defendants, about 1 per cent in Quarter Sessions complaints in the district of Montreal between 1780 and 1835 (split evenly between Natives and Blacks); and of prisoners committed to the Quebec gaol between 1813 and 1837, also about 1 per cent (of whom three- quarters were Black).[50] For Blacks at least, this was in part because they made up a tiny proportion of the colony's population, though there are no exact figures.[51] Natives also formed a small part of the St Lawrence valley population, having been decimated by disease and warfare. But as well, in contrast to rural *Canadiens*, some Native communities actively resisted the European criminal justice system as a challenge to traditional authority structures. As the *curé* of Sault-Saint-Louis (Caughnawaga) explained in 1820, after his recommendation of two Europeans as justices, he had been obliged to appease the village chiefs, who did not want a justice of the peace. They believed (no doubt with some foundation) that once a justice was established in their village, their authority would be undermined and they would be regarded as nothing, while the justice would reign supreme.[52]

Not all Blacks and Natives rejected the legitimacy of European criminal justice, and some appeared before the justices as plaintiffs. Thus, in 1799, Agathe Sagosennageté, the wife of Thomas Arakouanté, a Caughnawaga trader, travelled to Montreal to complain to Patrick Murray that Otiogwannon Ontsientani, one of the Caughnawaga chiefs, had, a few days previously, entered her house and told her that he would forcibly prevent her from attending church, and the next day he repeated his threats, so that she had not gone to church for fear of his violence. About a week later, Ontsientani was arrested by Jacob Marston, the high constable, and taken to Montreal, where he entered into a recognizance to appear at the next Quarter Sessions. John Lees was thus only technically correct when he stated in 1801, in sending in the complaint of Pierre Tehasitaere against Thomas Awessassiion for hitting him on the shoulder with a rock and then hitting him several times on the head with a drinking glass, that 'I suppose it is the first instance of an Indian prosecuting another in a judicial manner for a beating; however I think it full time that the gentry should be brought under the civil law and encourage it as much as I can.'[53] Thomas Arakouanté was a frequent user of the criminal justice system, and this may help explain the later hostility of the Caughnawaga chiefs to the appointment of a justice. Likewise, consider the case of Catherine D'Amour, a Black woman and the wife of William D'Amour, who in 1795 accused Marie Lapierre, the wife of Pierre Henri, of stealing several items of clothing from her. Lapierre was indicted in the Quarter Sessions and faced a full jury trial, though she was eventually found not guilty. And Blacks occasionally brought prosecutions against each other: in 1835, for example, Jean François, a Black Montreal labourer, accused William Montgomerie, possibly a Montreal innkeeper, and William Johnson, a Black man who had come to Montgomerie's with François, of robbing him of a silver watch and a large sum of cash.[54]

As Helen Stone, Denis Delâge, and Étienne Gilbert have shown, in the case of Natives, this sort of recourse to European justice was rare, and especially so in the eighteenth century: between 1760 and 1820, Delâge and Gilbert found only 180 criminal cases involving Natives, of which few concerned disputes between Natives. With some notable exceptions, such as Arakouanté, Natives preferred to resolve their disputes through traditional structures such as band councils. Here we see clearly the rejection of the legitimacy of official criminal justice and its marginalization through active resistance by local communities, which throws into sharp relief the extent to which *Canadiens* did not share in this perspective.[55]

The relationship between the colony's Black community and the criminal justice system was less clear-cut. As Frank Mackey has shown, Blacks were often ill-used by the criminal justice system; and yet, they still appealed to it. An example of this ambivalence is the Betsy Freeman affair. Freeman, also known as Betsy Marvin, was a fourteen-year-old Black girl in the service of Ann Marvin (née Gelston), from North

Carolina, who accompanied her mistress on a trip to Montreal in June 1836, staying at the house of James Adams Dwight, an American-born watchmaker who was married to Ann Marvin's sister. Members of the city's Black community suspected that Freeman was a slave, and Alexander Grant, a leading member of the community, encouraged her to desert and gave her refuge in his house. Ann Marvin, however, was under the care of Dr Daniel Arnoldi, one of the city's more active justices, who no doubt encouraged her to swear out a complaint of desertion against Freeman, on the strength of which Arnoldi issued a warrant for her arrest. The next day, Freeman was arrested by Benjamin Delisle, the high constable, and taken before Arnoldi, in his own office rather than at the Police Office, accompanied by Grant.[56]

The preliminary hearing was a contentious affair, which gives some flavour of what might go on before a magistrate. According to the later testimony of Freeman and Delisle, Freeman first declared that she had been whipped by Ann Marvin, but then changed her story. Grant refused to accept Freeman's declaration that she was an indentured servant, not a slave, saying that 'he would protect a hundred coloured folks if they would come in here, that he knew the law as well as any man and that it did not allow any slaves here and that I should not go back to my mistress and said to the doctor that he would keep me in spite of him,' and insisted on reading aloud from a book on slavery, despite both Arnoldi and Delisle trying to silence him. All agreed that Arnoldi ended up grabbing Grant by the collar and forcibly ejecting him; Grant also said that Arnoldi kicked him. Freeman returned to her mistress, entirely voluntarily according to her later testimony, but only after being threatened and browbeaten by Arnoldi, according to Grant.

Grant then filed an assault complaint against Arnoldi and also, on the advice of Cyrus Brewster, an American-born hardware merchant, sought a writ of habeas corpus to have Freeman released as an illegally detained slave. Accompanied by Brewster, he went first to see a lawyer, Charles-Ovide Perrault, and then in the evening they all went before Samuel Gale, by then a King's Bench judge, accompanied by Delisle (presumably so that the writ could be served immediately). Gale took Grant's deposition and then, after first agreeing to issue the writ, put the case off until the next morning before the full court. Fearing that Ann Marvin would spirit Freeman away, Grant and five or six other Blacks gathered at Dwight's house to prevent this. After first demanding that Dwight hand over Freeman, which he refused, saying that she was not a slave, they continued around the house for several hours and, according to Dwight and his family, broke his windows, stuck a gun and a sword in, fired a shot, and left only when it was starting to get light. The habeas corpus writ was granted the next day, but at the hearing on the writ a couple of days later, Freeman asserted again that she was an indentured servant rather than a slave, and had no desire to leave Ann Marvin; the court told her that she was free to do as she pleased. A few weeks later, Arnoldi's trial came on in Quarter Sessions, with Delisle, Freeman, and Grant called by the prosecution. Grant's testimony inculpated Arnoldi, but, as we saw, Freeman and Delisle blamed Grant instead. However, despite being directed to acquit Arnoldi by the presiding magistrate, James Millar, the jury found Arnoldi guilty, and the justices fined him ten shillings. The administration in Quebec City subsequently took the unusual step of sending Arnoldi a letter telling him to consider himself struck from the commission of the peace, but after Arnoldi mounted a vigorous defence of his actions, including depositions from Freeman, Delisle, and several others and declarations from the magistrates on the bench, the order was rescinded, and Arnoldi never formally dismissed. Finally, Grant and two others were indicted in September King's Bench for riot for their role in the disturbance at Dwight's house, but the trial testimony was ambiguous: Dwight, his family, and several other witnesses declared that Grant and the others had acted violently, while defence witnesses, including Brewster's brother and business partner, William, argued that it was an unknown sailor who caused all of the ruckus and that Grant and his compatriots had simply kept a peaceful vigil on the house; Grant and the two others were found not guilty.

The truth in all of this is difficult to tease out. Though there is little doubt that Grant was convinced that Freeman was a slave or at least in danger of being enslaved, Freeman repeatedly asserted that she was free and blamed Grant for convincing her to desert by telling her 'he had known many folks who had come on here as servants with their masters and who had been foolish enough to go back again and were sold for slaves.' She also declared that it was Grant who had prompted her to tell Arnoldi that she had been whipped and that she was a slave. This, of course, could have been testimony induced in a frightened fourteen-year-old by her mistress, but Freeman repeated her story on at least three occasions, in June, July, and September. Grant's charges against Arnoldi have a ring of truth, and in fact no one denied the physical violence, but the testimony of both Freeman and Delisle as to Grant's passionate desire to ensure that Freeman was not returned to her mistress also rings true. While the *Patriote* press simply reported that Arnoldi had been convicted, Arnoldi in his defence suggested that the jury had been influenced by other considerations: Louis Malo, the Quarter Sessions crier, asserted that a jury member had told him, 'On le tient le bonhomme on va le faire suer' [We hold the fellow we'll make him sweat] (though Malo's Tory partisanship makes this testimony suspect), while other jurymen who were present but had not served on Arnoldi's trial jury claimed that the verdict had surprised everybody and that members of the jury had told them afterwards that they had not understood the charge of the presiding magistrate, James Millar, because he spoke French poorly. Further, Arnoldi's petition was somewhat grudgingly supported by Jacob De Witt, a leading moderate *Patriote* supporter.[57] As for the action at Dwight's house, the defence of an unknown sailor who caused all of the noise and damage seems fairly unlikely, though so too does the testimony of Dwight and his family as to the ferocity of Grant and his companions.

Apart from the insights that it provides into the functioning of the criminal justice system, the whole affair suggests that the Black community both acknowledged the legitimacy of the law and the criminal justice system and also distrusted it. On the one hand, Grant appealed to the courts both for the habeas corpus and in the assault case, and defence testimony at the King's Bench riot trial claimed that he had told his companions to let the law take its course. Race seems to have played little part in both of his legal victories, namely, Arnoldi's conviction and Grant's acquittal. And Delisle acted more as an intermediary than an enforcer: at the hearing before Arnoldi, for example, when Grant refused to be silenced, Delisle ignored an initial order by Arnoldi to arrest Grant, and at the King's Bench trial, though called by the crown, Delisle gave testimony favourable to Grant and the others. At the same time, Grant and the other members of the Black community evidently had little confidence that the system would safeguard Freeman, taking her protection into their own hands prior to the issuing of the habeas corpus writ. As well, Grant seems increasingly to have become a pawn in a larger affair, woven into the conflict between Tories and *Patriotes* over the Montreal magistracy. Cyrus Brewster, who counselled Grant to use the law, was Jacob De Witt's nephew, and thus linked to the *Patriotes*. The lawyer who took on Grant's case, Charles-Ovide Perrault, came from a leading *Patriote* family (and was subsequently killed in the battle of Saint-Denis). And the *Patriote* press, notably *La Minerve* and the *Vindicator* (published by Perrault's brother),

308 Magistrates, Police, and People

used the incident to lambaste Arnoldi and the administration as well: when it was learned that Arnoldi's dismissal had been revoked, *La Minerve* commented that this augured ill for the new commission of the peace that it was thought was about to issue. As for Freeman, she claimed that she herself was a pawn, but of Grant, though once again it is almost impossible to discern what she actually thought of the Montreal law. At any rate, she eventually returned to North Carolina and may still have been living there in 1850, apparently a free woman.[58]

Conclusion

Considering the exercise of social power in the everyday criminal justice system leaves us with something of a paradox: a system that was at once definitely used by the elites for their own purposes, and to a certain extent biased in their favour, but also used by colonial society more broadly. The structural inequalities built into the colony's society, around class, gender, and race, certainly played out in the everyday criminal justice system, which was thus far from being a neutral service-oriented state institution. However, the system was not primarily oriented towards class, gender, or racial domination. Women and popular-class people came before the court both as plaintiffs and defendants: as Mary Anne Poutanen has shown, even prostitutes, certainly at or near the bottom of the social hierarchy, though they themselves were heavily targeted by the criminal justice system, used the system to charge other prostitutes and clients with assaults and other crimes.[59] And while, for Blacks and Natives, the system was essentially marginal to them, they were also marginal to it, unlike in many other colonial societies. Overlying all of this was the instrumentalization of justice, which was a regular though often hidden feature of complaints that people made to the justices, whether for protection, negotiation, or malice. Instrumentalization, indeed, explains recourse to the criminal justice system far more than inherent belief in its justice or legitimacy.

The complexity of ordinary people's relationship to the system can be summed up in the complaint that Marie-Louise Goder, the wife of Pierre Labadie *fils*, of Vaudreuil, made in September 1810 before Louis-Mars Decoigne, the local justice of the peace (and father of Louis de Decoigne, bailed a few years earlier by Chartier de Lotbinière). Goder stated that, while she was at Pierre Vadeboncoeur's house with several other people, Vadeboncoeur 'a etté le cuë à la main pisser dans [son] visage' [with his cock in his hand pissed in her face] and then threw her to the ground, helped by one Joseph Pilon. While Vadeboncoeur held Goder down, Pilon lifted her skirts and began to fondle her, and, though one Françoise LaBeaux managed to get Pilon off of Goder, Vadeboncoeur immediately took his place. Decoigne issued an arrest warrant to Gilles Guerbois, the local bailiff, which resulted in Vadeboncoeur and Pilon appearing before the justice a few days later and entering a bond to appear at the Quarter Sessions in October. The case was entered in the registers of the court as a charge of assault and battery against Vadeboncoeur and Pilon, but was dropped since Goder did not appear to press her charges; there is no indication that any of the parties ever made the journey to Montreal.[60]

The case illustrates many of the points I have made concerning social power and the everyday criminal justice system, in this and previous chapters. Though urban cases dominated the justices' business, rural inhabitants did use the courts, and did so even for the resolution of local tensions: everyone involved in the affair, from the victim, Goder, to the bailiff, Guerbois, belonged to the same local, rural community. There is no direct evidence of ethnic or class conflict, since all the parties seem to have been *habitants*. And here was a case of a woman who used the justice system to respond to a serious aggression against her, but for whom this tool did not perhaps answer all of her desires. Thus, for example, what could probably have been charged as attempted rape was first constrained by Decoigne to 'insulte, viollence et assot' [insult, violence and assault] (the words he used in the warrant), which required only an arrest and a bond to appear, rather than committal to the Montreal gaol, and then, in the registers of the court in Montreal, to simple assault and battery, a charge devoid of any connotation of sexual violence. And though called as defendants in the October sessions, Vadeboncoeur and Pilon defaulted, and the case went no further; as far as they were concerned, the power of the state ended with their arrest by Guerbois and their appearance before Decoigne. Did this therefore mean that the everyday criminal justice, and the Quebec and Lower Canadian state more generally, was powerless?

8

Criminal Justice and State Power

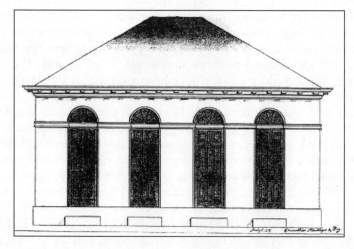

Les Privés ou il y a tant de communication se trouvent non seulement comblés mais entourées de tant d'ordures qu'ils sont inaccessibles et que même dans les chaleurs ils vont devenir une nuisance publique.

[The Privies where there is so much traffic are not only filled but even surrounded by so much filth that they are inaccessible, and in the heat they will become a public nuisance.]

– Jacques Terroux, keeper of the Montreal courthouse, April 1815

Building Privys as per accompanying plan, with a vault 10 feet deep. Masonry of Pierre Epaisseur, door jambs, sills and caps of Cut stone, moulded belts and pilastors, Ashler plinths, Imitation venetian windows, with venetian blinds, the Roof hipp'd and covered with tin the inside to be finished correspondent, and lath'd and lastered – £379–16–2
– Chevallier, Phillips and Try, plan and estimate for new privies
of the Montreal courthouse, July 1815

... [vers minuit] il aurait trouvé sous la halle du nouveau marché de cette ville, une femme de *couleur*, dont il ne connait pas le nom, qui s'est nommé Ann Taylor (au bureau de Police), couchée sur un banc après *forniquer* avec un soldat, que le déposant l'aurait arretée, fait prisonniere, et conduite au Guet comme étant une prostituée et une femme de mauvaise vie.
[... around midnight he found under the new market hall of this city, a woman of colour, whose name he does not know, who called herself Ann Taylor (at the Police Office), lying on a bench fornicating with a soldier, whom this deponent arrested, took prisoner, and brought to the Watch house as a prostitute and women of ill fame.]
– Antoine Charbonneau, Montreal watchman, 1819[1]

The state of the privies in the Montreal courthouse epitomized the majesty of criminal justice in Quebec and Lower Canada. The grandiose plan for neo-Palladian public privies, an evident attempt to reinforce the legitimacy of justice through architecture, was never carried out – the cost was prohibitive. Instead, the King's Bench judges recommended that the existing privies be emptied and repaired and chimneys built to take care of the smell, at a cost of about £50. The privies were also a fundamental part of the experience of criminal justice. Though the colonial legislature had spent thousands of pounds on a majestic new courthouse described by Joseph Bouchette as 'extremely airy and agreeable,' what struck passers-by more forcibly were the disgusting odours; as a grand jury stated, the privies were 'highly injurious to His Majesty's Subjects, passing and repassing in the King's Highway.' Anyone coming to the Montreal courthouse in the early 1810s to make a complaint, undergo a trial, or testify as a witness would evidently be well advised to make prior arrangements or face the terror of the privies. This was in contrast to the judges, magistrates, and other officials, whose rooms were fitted up with locked water closets which allowed them to avoid the undignified recourse to the public facilities and thus, even at this most banal of levels, preserve the majesty of justice.[2]

Majesty and terror are, of course, two motifs intimately associated with the power of ancien-régime criminal justice. As Douglas Hay noted long ago, the evident weaknesses and shortcomings of ancien-régime criminal justice was compensated for not only by the public terror of executions and other corporal punishments but also by public majesty, which helped legitimize judges and courts in the eyes of the population. The arrest of Ann Taylor shows the majesty and terror of the law in a quite different light. There was nothing majestic about the watchman who made the routine arrest, which followed a set pattern leading inexorably from overnight detention in the no doubt dank holding-cell of the watch-house to appearance in the Police Office the next morning. The magistrate on duty, Alexander Henry, ordered Taylor committed until the last day of the Quarter Sessions, which was then sitting; the justices on the bench then committed her and several other women to the city's House of Correction for three months' hard labour for being 'incorrigible vagabonds'; and on the expiry of the three months, Taylor was once again brought up before the justices and summarily recommitted for another three months. As Mary Anne Poutanen has shown, this was a harsh process which the watch, constables, and justices had followed many times before, and would do many times again – a process whose repetition was fast becoming one of the routines of the exercise of power by the state in the city.[3]

This final chapter turns back to the system itself, and its capacity to impose itself on the people both symbolically and practically – a capacity that, we will see, changed considerably over the period, notably in the cities but also in the countryside. The chapter first considers the majesty of justice as a source of power for the state, as expressed through architecture, symbol, and ritual. It then evaluates how everyday justice served the coercive power of the state by examining the rise in public prosecution and summary trials, the enforcement of punishments, and the state's capacity to deal with active resistance to the justice system.

The Majesty of Justice

Previous chapters explored the human face of everyday criminal justice, represented by the magistrates, police, and other officials who largely embodied it. As we saw, these made the system less alienating and perhaps more legitimate through drawing on local elites and the local population, both *Canadien* and British, as justices, officials, and police. But the system was not composed only of individuals. When an accused was judged by a magistrate or judge, his or her experience of the event was bound by the space in which it took place (the magistrate's parlour, the Police Office, the public courtroom) and shaped by the symbols and rituals that structured the proceedings (the dress and demeanour of the officials, the act of reading the complaint and writing out the warrant of committal, and so on). For example, it has been suggested that the symbolism of English criminal law translated poorly to the colony after the Conquest, and especially to its *Canadien* majority, who were repelled by its Britishness and thus avoided it.[4] But, as already explained, such avoidance applied far more to the superior criminal courts than to the justices. In this respect, the possible role of architecture and ritual is tantalizing: it would have been far more alienating, awe-inspiring, even terrifying, for a *Canadien* to be tried before the colony's British chief justice, in full judicial regalia, in a courtroom with the king's arms, than before a *Canadien* or at least francophone justice, most likely in everyday dress, in his own home.

The Architecture of the Law

The most permanent and concrete public manifestations of the majesty of criminal justice in the colony, as elsewhere, were buildings, notably prisons and courthouses. While much attention has been paid to the ideology of changing prison architecture, historians have also begun exploring the architectural impact of courthouses and courtrooms.[5] This is key to understanding everyday criminal justice because, while the prison might strike the imagination as one of the more terrifying aspects of ancien-régime justice, most people who came in contact with the system did so in the magistrate's office or the courtroom. In the countryside, this might be nothing more than the justice's own parlour, but in the towns where more formal courts met, justice generally had a more formal setting, epitomized by the courthouse, which expressed the majesty of justice as much as the prison expressed its terror. The development of courthouses in the colony's two main cities illustrates both the possibilities and the limits of the majesty of justice, as well as providing insights into continuity and change in the experience of justice across the Conquest and into the early nineteenth century.

In pre-Conquest New France, royal justice was meted out in purpose-built courtrooms closely associated with the secular arm of the state. In Quebec City, the courts were held in the Intendant's Palace, which, with its accompanying buildings, including the prison, constituted a nexus of political and administrative structures that made up one of the main poles of official power in the town. In the lesser jurisdictions of Montreal and Trois-Rivières, the *salles d'audience* that served as courtrooms shared buildings with the prisons. These formal and above all non-public settings (in theory, the inquisitorial system excluded the public from all court sittings) were in marked contrast with those in England and the American colonies, where not only was criminal justice a public affair but, in smaller towns, even more formal courts were often held in informal public settings such as inns.[6]

The setting of criminal justice in post-Conquest Quebec was a blend of these two different traditions. On the one hand, the pre-Conquest courtrooms were deemed unsuitable, partly because of the deteriorated state of the buildings but also perhaps because the public sessions so essential to the legitimacy of British criminal justice would have been impossible in the small rooms set aside for hearings under the French regime. But, on the other hand, there was no need to resort to more informal settings, at least for the courts themselves. With the criminal justice system concentrated almost exclusively in the two main towns, with Catholic institutions dependent on the good will of the executive for their survival, and with the extensive property of important religious orders forfeited to the crown, the colonial administration had at its disposal a range of official and institutional buildings dating from the French regime, ready to be reused as courthouses.

In Montreal, the French-regime prison and *salle d'audience* had been abandoned by the beginning of British civil government, as was another building chosen for the courts: the *maison du greffe*, owned by the Seminary of Montreal. As the name suggests, this building was intimately associated with pre-Conquest justice. Under the French regime, as local seigneur, the Seminary maintained possession of the *greffe*, or judicial archives, and rented them and their *maison* to the court clerks. This feudal practice expanded under British civil administration, with the government renting the building from the Seminary until the end of the eighteenth century and using it not only for the clerks but also for all court sittings apart from King's Bench criminal sessions. While there was a distinct incongruity in the king's courts being held in a building rented from a Catholic religious institution, this also represented, for participants, a concrete sort of continuity. In the pre-Conquest system, much of the preliminary business of the courts, the kind dealt with by justices, had taken place before the *greffier royal*, in the *maison du greffe*, which was thus probably as much associated with royal justice as the *salle d'audience*. And this association simply continued under British rule. Even the location of the building marked continuity with existing power structures: it was in the western half of the city, diagonally across from the Seminary's main building, just down the street from the Catholic parish church, and far from the symbols of British official power in the city's eastern section. Much like the criminal law itself, the British courts fitted themselves into pre-existing structures.

But the courts also appropriated these structures. Thus, the *maison du greffe* rapidly became known simply as 'the (public) Courthouse' in English and the *'chambre d'audience'* in French, though the pre-Conquest term *'Greffe'* also remained in common use for the building. Either way, it was a readily identifiable public building, used as a spatial referent (as in 'at the end of François Street near the court house') and explicitly associated not only with justice but also more generally with the exercise of public power by the colonial state: for example, it was used for officially sanctioned public meetings in the 1760s, and, on the visit of Prince William Henry in 1787, the justices and judges ordered the bailiffs to illuminate its windows. Further, judicial functions were increasingly consolidated in the courthouse. The clerks were all there by the late 1760s, including the clerk of the peace, and, while the criminal sessions of the King's Bench were initially held in the former chapel of the Recollet monastery, periodically fitted up as a courtroom, by the 1780s they too had been transferred to the *maison du greffe*. For plaintiffs and defendants, this had become Montreal's principal judicial building.[7]

In Quebec City, the Intendant's Palace in the Lower Town was abandoned after the Conquest, partly through a desire to dissociate British administration from this symbol of French rule. The new rulers set up their courts instead in a variety of former religious buildings scattered through the Upper Town. Thus, in the 1760s, the chapel of the Bishop's Palace, rented from the bishop, was turned into a sessions house for the justices and also used to hold sessions of the King's Bench, while, from the 1770s, courts were also held in the former Jesuits' College and its adjoining chapel, in the market-place across from the French cathedral. In seeking justice, participants therefore moved from the Lower Town to the Upper, and from the former centre of secular power to buildings previously associated with the church. Further, instead of a single identifiable locale, they now had to seek justice in several different sites, with the court clerks, for example, initially doing business from their own private offices in other buildings yet again. The repurposing of religious buildings as courthouses, however, did represent a form of continuity. Whether it was simply a practical decision to make use of existing spaces (as with the use of a hall in the Ursuline convent for the trial of *La Corriveau* during the military regime, because the Military Council's room in the Château was too small), or a deliberate attempt to draw on the existing symbolism of these buildings, people coming before the courts in Quebec City were doing so in architectural settings that had been conceived, both inside and out, to express institutional power. However, the institution whose power they now expressed was no longer the church, but the British state. This was a concrete reminder of the victory of British and Protestant power over French and Catholic hierarchy, much like that expressed in representations of Quebec City's ruined public buildings in post-Conquest British prints. And the Britishness of the setting of justice in Quebec City was further reinforced later in the eighteenth century. By the 1790s, the courts were mostly being held in the Jesuits' College, which also housed the offices of the clerks, including the clerk of the peace. Unlike the courthouse in Montreal, however, this was a multi-purpose building, also used as one of the city's main barracks and housing the Presbyterian chapel. Far more than in Montreal, parties in court cases, both criminal and civil, thus had to enter directly into a space largely dominated by entirely British institutions, the army and one of the major churches.[8]

In both Montreal and Quebec City, then, people encountered the courts in formal buildings intimately associated with the colony's power structures, not in the informal locales often found elsewhere. And, through decorative renovation, attention was also paid to solidifying the presence and majesty of British justice in these French relics. In Montreal, for example, when the Recollet chapel was used periodically in the 1760s and 1770s for sessions of the King's Bench, it was fitted up by a British carpenter who used green cloth for the judge's seat and added a canopy over his head, fastening the whole with gilt-headed tacks and taking it down again after the session was over. Likewise, in Quebec City, when the chapel of the Bishop's Palace was used for criminal sessions, a carpenter installed a 'Great Table' (presumably for the clerks, other officials, and possibly lawyers, as was the custom in England and its colonies) and a prisoners' bar, which were taken down

Figure 8.1: Richard Short, 'A View of the Inside of the Jesuits Church' (c. 1759)

and stored in the garret between sessions. And the courthouses in both Montreal and Quebec City were furnished with the royal arms, from the 1780s if not earlier, a symbolic affirmation considered so important by imperial authorities that Carleton's 1775 instructions as governor explicitly ordered that 'Our Arms and Insignia be put up not only in all such Churches and Places of holy Worship, but also in all Courts of Justice; and that the Arms of France be taken down in every such Church or Court, where they may at present remain.'9

However, in Montreal and Quebec City alike, both the majesty and the Britishness imparted by these eighteenth-century courthouses were compromised. For one thing, plaintiffs swearing out criminal complaints in the eighteenth century seem often to have done so not in the courthouses but rather in the houses of the cities' justices of the peace. It was only in the later stages of proceedings that the different courthouses were in play. Further, even once parties went to court, the recasting of the old French religious buildings they saw was only superficial, since there was no money available for major architectural modifications, leading inevitably to a mixing of the symbols of power, both French and British, religious and secular. Without major renovation work (of which there is no evidence in the public accounts), it would

Figure 8.2: Richard Short, 'A View of the Jesuits College and Church' (c. 1759)

evidently have been difficult to erase completely the ornamental rich-
ness of the interior of the chapel of the Jesuits' College, so closely
associated with 'papism,' that is visible in the well-known engraving by
Richard Short,[10] and, of course, impossible to change its outside form,
so far from the neo-Palladian and neo-Classical styles then in favour for
official buildings in England (Figures 8.1 and 8.2).

The buildings themselves also became increasingly unfit. By the 1790s,
juries, justices, and judges were repeatedly complaining of Montreal's
courthouse, which they described as a 'tottering building,' too small,
with a bad roof, its walls held up by temporary props, and the ceiling
barely attached to the walls. This was an issue of both image and
practicality: as a 1796 petition stated, the courthouse, 'independent of
the precarious and uncertain title under which it is held, is as unbecom-
ing that decency and dignity, due to the administration of justice, as it is
injurious to the health of those, whose duty, or business, may necessarily require their attendance therein.' In Quebec City, the judges, after
noting that the courthouse in the Jesuits' College was 'literally in a
barrack,' complained that their sittings were 'disturbed over head,
below, and on each side, by annoyances of various descriptions so
disgraceful to the administration of justice, that it would be unbecom-

ing even to specify them,' leaving us to speculate as to just what they might have been.[11] It is thus hard to imagine anyone coming to court in the eighteenth century being struck by the majesty of British justice, or alienated by its Britishness. Instead, they would have experienced justice in settings that were an amalgam of both French and British influences, much like the law itself, the magistracy, and the police.

Late-eighteenth-century complaints about the courthouses, coupled with more readily available funds from the newly constituted legislature, led to a significant change in the architectural setting of justice at the turn of the nineteenth century: the erection of new purpose-built courthouses in both Montreal and Quebec City. Though generally treated from the internal perspective of the colony, such as the development of the 'garrison mentality' among the British elite in the 1790s and the concomitant desire to ensure a more definitively British architectural presence in the cities, this was also part of a larger movement in North America towards legitimizing the law through architecture. In the United States, for example, Martha McNamara has shown how judicial architecture was reshaped in the late eighteenth and early nineteenth centuries as part of the drive towards the professionalization of the law by attorneys. Specialized courthouses replaced multi-purpose buildings or informal locales, so as to emphasize the independence of the legal profession; courthouses were located away from the markets so as to exclude the taint of commercialization; and courthouse design itself emphasized rational professionalism over the public spectacle of the law. A similar process was at work in Lower Canada, though the role of lawyers themselves is less evident. The result, architecturally, was much grander, and more British.[12]

In Quebec City, the new courthouse built between 1799 and 1804 was an integral part of the formation of a new nexus of official power around the Place d'Armes. This period saw the construction on the Place d'Armes of both the Anglican cathedral and the courthouse, in the neo-Palladian style that epitomized eighteenth-century British conceptions of official architecture,[13] joining other official buildings such as the governor's residence and the Assembly. The courthouse itself was the joint creation of the French-trained but anglophile architect François Baillairgé, the military engineer William Hall, and the anglifying attorney general Jonathan Sewell. In its style and its scope, it was clearly meant to contribute powerfully to both the majesty and the Britishness of justice in the colony's capital, and, at a cost of some £13,000, it was one of the most expensive building projects in the colony to date. Joseph

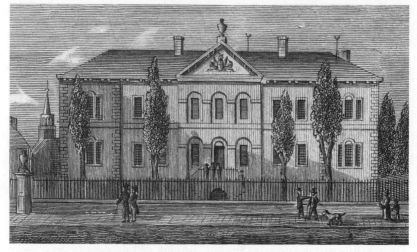

Figure 8.3: Montreal courthouse, 1801–44 (c. 1839)

Bouchette described it in 1815 as 'a large modern stone structure ... presenting a regular handsome front ... the embellishments of this edifice, both interior and external, are in a style of simplicity and neatness; the arrangements for public business methodical and judicious; the whole may be considered a great ornament to the city, and does honour to the liberality of the province, thus to provide for the easy and expeditious administration of justice.'[14] Bouchette's emphasis on modernism was misplaced: neo-Palladianism as a dominant style, even in official buildings, had been in decline in England since the 1780s, and essentially disappeared from the 1810s, so that the choice of this style in the late 1790s was already a conservative statement, harkening back to English courthouses built earlier in the eighteenth century. Still, it was certainly a far cry from the hubbub of the recycled Jesuits' College.[15]

In Montreal as well, the new courthouse (Figure 8.3), built at the same time (1799–1801) and following the same plan and neo-Palladian style as that of Quebec City, was the first step in the creation of an official space around the governor's official residence, eastward along Notre-Dame Street. The first major post-Conquest public building in the city, the courthouse marked the beginning of the anglicization of public architecture in Montreal, and was soon to be joined in close proximity by a new gaol (1808–12), Nelson's monument (1809), and the

Champ de Mars itself, a parade ground laid out on the site of the former fortifications (1813). The courthouse quickly became one of central architectural features of city, mentioned favourably in travellers' accounts. Even a highly critical American traveller like Joseph Sansom declared that 'before I quit Montreal, I shall not do justice to its Public Edifices, without mentioning, as a handsome Structure, the Government House, for the administration of Justice, &c. with the king's arms, in the pediment, elaborately executed in Coades artificial stone.' Having the king's arms imported from England (at a cost of over £250) rather than painted or created by a local artisan was symbolic of the determination to emphasize imperial ties through architectural statement, much like the adoption of neo-Palladian style.[16]

As well as solidifying the Britishness of the architectural space into which plaintiffs and defendants would have had to penetrate, the courthouses also symbolized increasing judicial efficiency and bureaucratization. Quebec City joined Montreal in having virtually all judicial functions henceforth consolidated in one courthouse, from the clerks' offices to the courts themselves. Gone were the days of dispersal across the city, with only preliminary hearings still sometimes heard in justices' houses, and, as we have seen, from the 1810s these too became concentrated in the Police Offices, also located in the new courthouses. Even when the Police Offices were abolished in 1830, many preliminary hearings continued to be held in the courthouses, under the auspices of the clerks of the peace.

The internal layout of both buildings reflected the hierarchy and importance of the courts and dictated the experience of those coming before justice. Each courthouse had two main courtrooms, one for the Quarter Sessions and other justices' courts, and the other for the King's Bench, both civil and criminal. The Sessions courtroom and clerk of the peace's office, those most heavily used in criminal justice, were on the ground floor, immediately on entering, while the larger and more prestigious King's Bench courtroom was upstairs. In Quebec City, the Police Office was also downstairs, while in Montreal it was up a flight of stairs from the Peace Office. As in similar structures in the United States and England, the new courthouses innovated by reserving separate rooms not only for the courts and their clerks but also for lawyers, juries, and auxiliary judicial officials such as sheriffs. The courtrooms themselves were also spatially segmented, with reserved areas not only for judges, trial jury, and accused, as had always been the case, but also for members of the bar, grand juries, and various judicial officials. In

1820, for example, Montreal's justices ordered that none but lawyers enter the benches reserved for them. Even in the Police Offices, attention was paid to this separation of justice and public: Montreal's chairmen, McCord and Mondelet, sought to exclude what Mondelet referred to as 'les importuns' [the intruders] by having their 'sanctuary' (that is, their desk) raised on an eight-inch platform and separated from the public by an ornamental balustrade. Just as in the United States at the same time, the definition of courtroom spaces reflected not only the increasing professionalism of the legal professions but also their increasing separation from the population as a whole.[17]

The atmosphere of sober dignity and of majesty was also reinforced by the interior decorations and fittings. In Montreal the courthouse was painted in white, yellow, and green, and the judges' desks covered with fine green cloth. Green was a colour long associated with justice, used regularly in the eighteenth-century courtrooms, and its continued use pointed to continuity even within this new structure. The flooring in the courtrooms was of oak, though cheaper pine was used elsewhere in the building. Venetian blinds and extensive hardware fittings, including door locks imported from England, added to the building's prestige. Finally, to reinforce royal authority, the king's arms were repeated inside each of the two courtrooms, on canvas paintings imported from London, though set within gilt frames made locally.[18]

The transformation of the architectural setting of justice was striking. Those participating in criminal justice in Quebec City and Montreal moved from makeshift and hardly majestic courtrooms in the eighteenth century, housed in French-regime buildings, to much more impressive and British courthouses in the nineteenth. And plaintiffs and defendants now had to penetrate an increasingly professionalized and segregated space which embodied the power of the colonial state. The change in the experience of justice is undeniable.

Still, the new architectural majesty of justice was only relative. For one thing, even an interested observer like Bouchette emphasized not the majesty of the courthouses but their efficiency, using adjectives such as plain, handsome, modern, simple, neat, methodical, and judicious. More important, problems developed quickly. By 1815, the keeper of Montreal's courthouse was complaining that, apart from the smelly privies, soldiers lodged in the basement as a guard were urinating in the corridors, had ripped up floorboards to deposit waste, and were even cutting down the building's supporting beams, while the tables, benches, desks, and seats of the judges (presumably including their fine green cloth) had been ruined. Extensive repairs were needed for a building barely a decade old, and even these did not stem the tide: in 1827 a grand jury declared that 'the Court House of this District is going rapidly to decay from the want of the necessary repairs; the roof also appears so defective in several places as to admit water in a way which must destroy the walls in a few years.' By the early 1840s, the Montreal courthouse was described as entirely inadequate, much like the eighteenth-century one, though its destruction by fire in 1844 definitively solved the problem. Things were no better in Quebec City. In 1814 the King's Bench judges complained that the new courthouse was in such bad repair that rain poured through the roof and ceiling onto the seats of the grand jury, to their great discomfort. And in 1830 a grand jury warned that the courthouse might fall down soon if it was not repaired, since its eastern end was cleft from top to bottom.[19] The majesty of the city courthouses – as well as the legitimacy of the justice system that could be derived from architectural statement – thus rapidly became somewhat threadbare. Even the undeniable Britishness of the courthouses should not be overstated, despite the royal symbology. Though the architectural style of the courthouses was undoubtedly British in inspiration, and probably struck *Canadiens* as such, this did not necessarily distinguish them from courthouses south of the border: late-eighteenth and early-nineteenth-century courthouses in Massachusetts, for example, drew inspiration from many of the same British pattern-books, and eighteenth-century American architecture in general was heavily influenced by neo-Palladianism, so that for an American visitor or immigrant to Lower Canada, the architectural face of justice in the nineteenth century was not much different from what presented itself to the south.[20]

This same overall trend held for the public gaols in the two main cities. Following developments elsewhere in the West, these went from makeshift and reused buildings in the eighteenth century to more solid, purpose-built structures in the nineteenth, designed with efficiency and reform in mind. But the new prisons also fell far short of expectations. The French-regime prisons were abandoned soon after the Conquest, and prisoners lodged instead in repurposed buildings: in Montreal, a wing of the Jesuits' College from 1765 until it burnt down in 1803 (though elsewhere as well on occasion), and in Quebec City, initially in the Royal Redoubt, a French-regime fortification that had also served as a barracks, and then, from 1789, in part of the New or Artillery Barracks, also a pre-Conquest military building. In both cases, these makeshift gaols provoked a string of complaints, in particular regarding

Figure 8.4: Montreal gaol, 1811–36 (c. 1839)

their insecurity (guards often had to be posted in the cells to ensure that prisoners did not escape) and their unfitness as places of confinement (such as the lack of separation of even male and female prisoners or the generally unsanitary conditions). Various projects were launched for building new gaols, including both a rejected ordinance and a failed lottery scheme, but nothing came of them until the early nineteenth century, when new gaols were finally built in Montreal (1808–11) and Quebec City (1810–14).[21]

Aside from the political disputes that arose regarding the funding of the construction of the gaols,[22] the architecture and setting of these buildings, like the courthouses, were designed to solidify the presence of British justice. They, too, were large-scale construction projects, incorporating neo-Palladian elements, and were soon identified as among the main public structures of the cities (Figure 8.4). In 1811 the *Montreal Herald* described the new gaol as 'elegant, ornamental, and commodious,' while Bouchette in 1815 called it a 'substantial, spacious building ... disposed with every attention to ... health, cleanliness, and comfort.'[23] But this tune changed rapidly, and the new gaols rapidly lost their sheen of elegance and salubrity: as a reader noted in a letter to the *Herald* in 1817, the first thing that struck visitors was 'the unwholesome and offensive smell issuing from the debtor's room ... As to the state of the felon's apartments it is such as cannot be described without creating the most disgustful idea.'[24] Backward, insufficient, crowded, and unhealthy, the gaols were seen as a breeding ground for the criminal class and a disgrace to an increasingly liberal society. By the 1830s, yet another gaol was being built in Montreal, at the Pied-du-Courant, though in Quebec City the gaol was not replaced until the 1860s. Even more than the courthouses, the gaols were hardly likely to impress with their majesty. At best, like common gaols later in the nineteenth century, they might inspire terror, through the squalidness of their living conditions more than any deliberate architectural device.[25]

Outside the two main cities, justice was architecturally even less majestic. In smaller districts, purpose-built courthouses and gaols came considerably later. In Trois-Rivières, for example, the administration continued the practice of reappropriating French-regime religious buildings, and, since these were poorly heated in the winter, the courts on occasion were forced to sit elsewhere. It took three decades for new buildings to be erected, once again in the neo-Palladian style (which by then was seriously outdated), with the gaol completed in 1819 and the courthouse in 1822.[26] In the Gaspé, new combined courthouses and gaols were planned from 1808 for New Carlisle and Percé but took longer to complete: in 1814 for New Carlisle, and not until 1828 in Percé. Even then, courts held in other parts of the district had to make do without: the first Quarter Sessions in Douglas Town, in 1824, for example, was held in the open air.[27] In the district of Saint Francis, the courthouse at Sherbrooke was described in 1836 as an 'old wooden building ... little better than a common shed,' which was so unstable that the keeper and his family abandoned it during a winter storm for fear of it falling down. The brick gaol, built in the mid-1820s, was more solid but still seen as 'manifestly insufficient.'[28] Finally, outside the main district towns, there were no purpose-built courthouses or gaols at all before the mid-1830s, and then only in Saint-Hyacinthe (1835) and Napierville (1836).[29] Coming before criminal justice in the 'country parts' of the colony generally meant penetrating the private space of a justice of the peace, in his parlour or *étude*, thereby reinforcing, as in England, the paternalistic character of the system. Still, even in rural Lower Canada, the nineteenth century witnessed the beginnings of change: by the 1810s, some rural sessions were being held instead in more public settings, such as priories.[30]

On the whole, throughout the period, it was not through its architectural presence that British colonial justice inspired awe in the populace, whether *Canadien* or British, and thereby contributed to the legitimacy of the colonial state. Even in the two main cities, it was not until the early nineteenth century that the courts and gaols were housed in more imposing buildings, and these were vaunted more for their efficiency than for their majesty. Elsewhere, architectural changes came later still, if at all. But there nonetheless was a distinct change in the architectural setting of justice, starting around the beginning of the nineteenth century: the increasing formalization and specialization of judicial space. Judicial architecture in eighteenth-century Quebec was a classic ancien-régime mixing of old and new, decaying and patched-up, British and French, and in this respect far different from judicial architecture in the American colonies, where courts in larger towns often sat in townhouses explicitly devoid of the religious symbolism shunned by Puritans. In the nineteenth century, however, Lower Canadian judicial architecture, both inside and out, reflected a judicial system that was increasingly professionalized and bureaucratized, much as in the neighbouring states. In the cities at least, the architectural experience of justice in the 1830s was thus quite different from that of the 1760s and, if anything, for ordinary suitors and especially *Canadiens*, more alienating.

Symbols and Rituals of Authority

Symbolism and ritual were crucial to the power of all ancien-régime institutions which otherwise lacked the coercive might to enforce their will, and lay at the heart of the legitimization of the authority of British criminal justice, both in England and in its colonies.[31] In Quebec and Lower Canada, there is certainly ample evidence of the attention paid to ritual, ceremony, and symbolism in the colony's criminal courts. This was especially true in the higher criminal courts. The King's Bench judges in Quebec City and Montreal wore the traditional wigs and robes of English judges, and, from the mid-1780s at least, they required both court officials and attorneys to be dressed like their counterparts in Westminster Hall, to reinforce the Britishness of the setting. And right from the 1760s, magistrates, bailiffs, gaolers, coroners, and other judicial officials were commanded to attend the criminal sessions of the King's Bench, with opening ceremonies that included the usual processional entries and formal addresses to the grand juries, the latter often panegyrics on English criminal justice.[32] The same approach extended to the courts run by the justices of the peace, who also sought to legitimize their exercise of authority through ritual and symbolism. The opening ceremonies of Quarter Sessions at least were similar to those used in the King's Bench, though on a smaller scale. In both the eighteenth and nineteenth centuries, all bailiffs or constables were summoned to attend; the justices' commissions were ceremoniously read; the grand jury was 'called over' and sworn; and the senior magistrate (from the 1810s, the chairman) charged the grand jury, in terms similar to those used by the colony's chief justices. The justices also sought to instil proper decorum in their courtrooms, with constables summoned every court day to maintain order, a task undertaken by the court criers as well. The concern for order is evoked in Thomas McCord's charge to the Montreal's Quarter Sessions grand jury in 1810, which he closed by observing: '[T]hat as [the court] is determined to hold its sessions with that regard to the solemnity and decorum of its proceedings which becomes the administration of justice, it will exercise its severity against all persons who shall neglect the duties which propriety and respect impose upon them. It is upon the observance of a proper discipline that the welfare of a community depends; it is from a rigid adherence to the rules of a court and from causing its proceedings to be respected, that must flow the respect which is paid to the court itself.' In Quebec City, Christie, the chairman in the late 1820s, even tried to exclude one of his fellow magistrates from the bench because, in Christie's opinion, he was not properly dressed, an assertion that the magistrate vigorously denied: 'I was decently dressed, in the way I generally am; and I think I have gone to see the Governor on business, in the same sort of dress I then wore.'[33]

Much as was the case for judicial architecture, there also appears to have been an increasing attention paid to ensuring that these rituals and symbols were specifically British. Take, for example, the ceremony of swearing on the Bible before testifying. In the eighteenth century, at least in Montreal, it was a Catholic Bible that was used. However, from 1795, in the context of the developing 'garrison mentality,' Montreal's judges and justices substituted an English Bible. This caused considerable and continuing anxiety among the Catholic hierarchy, but it also meant that the symbolism of the ritual of oath-swearing was significantly altered: Aubert de Gaspé even suggests that the fact of swearing on the *'book* anglais' led *Canadiens* to believe they were not perjuring themselves if they lied under oath, though he also noted that, by the mid-1810s, a compromise had been reached by adding a crucifix on the cover of the English Bible. At any rate, Catholic bibles continued to be used: when witnesses were sworn on 'les Stes Evangiles' during a summary hearing in the priory of the village of L'Assomption in

1814, odds are that the Bible in question was not the King James version.[34]

The concern for majesty and image also affected the police. As Montreal's high constable put it in 1822, officers had to have 'the means of appearing genteel and respectable before the public, which always gains an officer respect and without which neither him nor the law is respected.' Though most surviving documents are silent on the rituals of arrest, there are occasional glimpses of how these, too, sought to reinforce the legitimacy of the proceedings: arrests in the name of the king, laying a hand on the shoulder, symbolically showing the warrant with the king's arms, and so on. Officers who neglected to follow these rituals, especially the showing of the warrant, could find their actions declared illegitimate by the courts. More concretely, as we saw, from the 1760s forward, bailiffs, constables, and watchmen carried a formal symbol of authority: the long staff, painted dark blue and featuring the royal arms or a crown. Altering the staff removed its legitimacy as a symbol of authority. Thus, during the violent Montreal by-election of 1832, when there were not enough staves for all of the special constables named by the magistrates, the available staves were sawn into halves or thirds. This became an issue in the public inquiry that followed, because of the alteration of the length and the absence of the requisite crown on the sawn staves. The king's authority, whether printed or painted, was taken seriously: a warrant ripped by a defendant was seen as especially heinous, while a half-satirical description of a charivari in Montreal in the early 1820s noted that 'wooden sabre encountered watchman's baton, in irreverent disregard of the G.R. marked on it.'[35]

Ensuring that rituals projected the majesty and authority of justice, and thereby reinforced its legitimacy, was thus a concern at all levels of the system. However, in practice, majesty at least was regularly compromised. Even at the level of the superior criminal courts, the judges had to contend with the fact that colonial courtrooms were not, in fact, Westminster Hall, though they did share some of the same inconveniencies. In the eighteenth century, the chapel of the Bishop's Palace in Quebec City, initially used for the criminal sessions of the King's Bench, was so cold that the chief justice ordered a special foot stove, creating the distinctly undignified image of a judge shivering and/or warming his bunions. Similarly, in the 1790s, the lack of a separate jury room in the Jesuits' College forced juries to deliberate life-or-death verdicts in a 'common alehouse,' thus undermining the solemnity of the ritual of jury deliberation (though echoing both British and American practices).

The Jesuits' College was also a pungent place, much like the later Montreal courthouse: in 1785 a grand jury complained of 'the great quantity of dirt & filth heaped in the yard of the Jesuits College the stench from which is ... very offensive to the neighbourhood & to every person passing the street leading thereby.' And even in the 1810s and 1820s, when Quebec City had acquired its fine neo-Palladian courthouse, the judges complained that in their courtroom (used for both civil and criminal pleas), the light reflected off the tin roofs of the buildings opposite directly into their faces; this was quite different from the Old Bailey in London, with its artfully placed mirror to reflect light into the face of the prisoner in the dock, and suggests squinting judges instead.[36] At the level of the justices and their courts, majesty was even more problematic. In Trois-Rivières, illumination was also an issue. On the one hand, the justices there complained that light from the courtroom windows glared directly into their eyes, making it painful for them to conduct their business (and again suggesting squinting justices). On the other, they frequently had to hold sessions by candlelight and complained that the courthouse keeper would not furnish them with candles. The justices also noted, rather plaintively, that 'the Chairs provided for the Bench, being very small and entirely made of Wood, are neither appropriate nor comfortable for Persons who are obliged to sit a long time,' which calls to mind a picture of magistrates shifting uncomfortably about on their seats during trials.[37]

More generally, the few direct accounts we have of the atmosphere in the courthouses, even in the nineteenth century, hardly give the impression of hushed dignity or solemn majesty. Much as in England, Quarter Sessions brought together a 'great concourse of people' who milled about in the passageways when they were not in the courtroom.[38] The atmosphere in the courtroom seems to have resembled the sort of 'participatory theatre' evoked by Peter King, as is suggested, for example, by Aubert de Gaspé's description of jurors and spectators laughing during one of his pleas before Quebec City's Quarter Sessions, or by the case of Mathew Floy, accused in 1835, during April Quarter Sessions in Montreal, of causing disorder and scandal in the courthouse by drunkenly insulting members of the bar. Outside the courtroom, everyday life also spilled over into the courthouses. Minor judicial officials such as the courthouse keepers and criers lived in the courthouses with their families, raising the spectacle of domestic tumult. In Montreal, they occupied most of the basement, while in Quebec City they temporarily took over the trial jury room. Since most officers lived by fees rather than by salary, constables and bailiffs gathered at the courthouse doors seeking customers, with Montreal's high constable lamenting that he was 'compelled to stand daily at the entrance of the courthouse and there to cavil and solicit employment with all other inferior officers.' And, of course, the smells did not go away: in 1830 a Montreal grand jury complained of the heaps of dung that lay around the courthouse and gaol, echoing the 1815 complaint regarding the privies.[39] Imagine as well a plaintiff going before the chairmen to make a complaint in the 1810s and 1820s. Balustrades and platforms regardless, the Police Offices were small, cramped places: in Montreal, twenty feet on each side, with large cupboards on the walls; in Trois-Rivières, 'a closet of about 9 feet by 13'[40] – all of which implied that magistrates, plaintiffs, and defendants were often in close physical proximity. If this was the atmosphere in the city courthouses, hearings at the other end of the scale, before rural justices, in their homes or in local public buildings, can hardly have had much of an atmosphere of ritualistic majesty at all. Susan Lewthwaite has suggested that local justice in Upper Canada presented little in the way of majesty,[41] and, though we have little evidence for the atmosphere in these settings in Quebec and Lower Canada, there is nothing to lead us to suppose it was any different.

And so the rituals of justice were far from majestic, whatever the intent of judges and magistrates. Instead, at the everyday level of the justices, what replaced rituals was routines, and increasingly bureaucratic ones at that. This is what *La Minerve*'s correspondent experienced in going to the Police Office: not terror, but red tape, just like that which still ties up the bundles of documents in the records of the clerks of the peace. A good illustration of the increasing prevalence of bureaucratic routine is the use of pre-printed forms, which reduced individual parties and their stories to filled-in blanks on documents. As we saw, already in the eighteenth century, clerks were providing the justices with pre-printed forms for routine documents such as arrests and summons. Individuality nevertheless still came through in the lengthy depositions that clerks or justices laboriously wrote out, often pages long, and the parchment indictments, beautifully inscribed in copperplate. From the 1810s, however, indictments for assaults and batteries, the most common type of case heard in the Quarter Sessions, became pre-printed forms, on regular paper, rapidly filled out by the clerks. By the late 1820s, even the official records of summary convictions, in Weekly Sessions or of vagabonds, were entered on pre-printed forms, reducing parties and their punishments to the names, amounts, and dates filled in. The only documents that were still regularly written out in full were depositions. In Montreal at least, some of these were on pre-printed paper, headed by the king's arms and with filing information on the back, and the depositions themselves became increasingly perfunctory, often no more than a few lines stating the bare fact of the offence committed. Individual stories and circumstances became subsumed to the press of impersonal bureaucratic routine.

Allen Steinberg has described the courts of mid-nineteenth-century Philadelphia, with their crowds of parties and spectators, their dirt and noise, as hardly awe-inspiring, but rather, to the largely working-class litigants, as familiar places, not that different from their homes and neighbourhoods.[42] I would not go so far for the criminal courts in Quebec and Lower Canada, whose atmosphere – architectural, symbolic, and ritualistic – had little in common with that found in the house of a *habitant* or artisan. But certainly, architecture, symbolism, and ritual, as they actually manifested themselves, were weak reeds on which to base the legitimization of British justice in the eyes of the colony's population. They may have played more of a role in alienating the *Canadien* population through their essential Britishness, but even this seems doubtful, especially in the eighteenth century but in the nineteenth as well. What replaced majesty and domination was utilitarianism and bureaucracy. As Norma Landau has argued for the Quarter Sessions in London, at the level of everyday criminal justice, it was less awe and terror that characterized the interaction between the population and the state than bureaucratic process. In Quebec and Lower Canada too, if alienation there was, it stemmed more from the alienation common throughout the Western world that accompanied the rise of the bureaucratic state.

The Bureaucratic Power of Ancien-Régime Justice

It may seem anachronistic to evoke the bureaucratic power of an ancien-régime institution like the everyday criminal justice system. After all, the growth of bureaucracy is usually associated with the rise of the modern, liberal state, which did not appear in Quebec until after the Rebellions. But, as many scholars of ancien-régime justice and police suggest, the routines of governance and of everyday discipline that underlay later developments of the modern state had their roots in the older system. We can see this by examining several aspects of how the power of the state was expressed through the everyday criminal justice system in Quebec and Lower Canada: the growth of public prosecution; the rise of summary justice; the enforcement of judicial orders; and the fate of those who resisted the everyday state.

The Growth of Public Prosecution

As we saw in chapter 6, at the level of the justices, private initiative played a significant part in the prosecution of offenders in such matters as assault. However, this reliance on private prosecutors, so central to the English model, was never fully realized in the colony, with public prosecutors playing a key role in a number of areas. King's Bench cases were the most notable example, but even in the sorts of cases decided by the justices, public prosecutors became increasingly important.

Take the prosecution of regulatory offences. Despite the provision in most offences for the informer to get a share of the fine, in practice it was difficult to induce private individuals to prosecute cases in which they were not personally interested, especially where the fine (and thus the prosecutor's share) was low. Partly this was a question of costs: a private prosecutor had to assume the initial costs, might have to pay the full costs if the prosecution was unsuccessful, and had no certainty of recouping costs even if the defendant was found guilty. But it also stemmed from the revulsion that such proceedings could induce. As the Quebec City chairmen declared in 1822, even in the case of lucrative prosecutions for selling liquor without a licence, the prosecutor's share of the fine was 'by no means a sufficiently powerful incentive to induce the generality of mankind to incur the odium which is always cast on the character of an informer.' As a result, it tended to be public officials who undertook the prosecution of such offences.[43]

The prosecution of offences against the militia and *corvée* laws is a case in point. In these cases, finding a private individual willing to take on such an unpopular role was almost impossible, and generally not even considered. When hundreds of *habitants* were prosecuted for these offences in the district of Montreal in the late 1770s and early 1780s, under orders from the administration, it was the clerk of the peace, John Burke, who undertook the prosecutions. And the same thing happened in 1815 and 1816, when John Delisle, the clerk of the peace, and David Ross, at that point king's counsel, were ordered to prosecute *corvée* infractions, with the result that 'many person in different parts of the said district were prosecuted, which had the desired effect of making the inhabitants more obedient to the corvey law.'[44] In both cases, direct state interests dictated recourse to public prosecution.

These were limited instances, but we can see a more general rise in recourse to public prosecution in the enforcement of the justices' police regulations. In the eighteenth century, in the face of the evident reluctance of private parties to prosecute, the Montreal justices half-heartedly tried to assign the responsibility for police regulations to officials under their authority, first to the bailiffs in the 1760s and then to the clerk of the peace in the 1780s, but this functioned only sporadically. Likewise, in the 1780s, the administration appointed salaried inspectors of police in both Quebec City and Montreal to enforce the regulations, but those appointed only occasionally carried out their duties and the positions eventually became sinecures. There were some areas where public prosecution of police regulations and similar statutory offences was more solidly established, such as those concerning the markets and fire regulations, since they were under the specific oversight of officials such as the clerks of the markets or the chimney inspectors, but these were few. By the nineteenth century, with growing concern for well-ordered urban space, this could no longer be tolerated. The justices increasingly incited their clerks of the peace to prosecute infractions of the police regulations, but, as this became impossible with the rise in judicial business, they turned elsewhere. By the 1820s, as we saw, the Montreal justices were paying a substantial salary to their high constable to prosecute infractions of the police regulations, and, under incorporation, this became the responsibility of specifically designated public officials, the police inspectors.[45]

Nor was public prosecution of regulatory offences limited to the cities. In the countryside, there were also increasingly active public prosecutors among the various officials concerned with the public roads, notably the roads inspectors and *sous-voyers* named throughout the countryside under the various roads acts from 1796 on, as well as the fence and ditch inspectors named from 1824 under the agricultural improvement acts. While the dearth of records of summary proceedings of rural justices, along with the lack of any substantial studies of the operation of the roads and agricultural improvement acts in the nineteenth century, make it difficult to evaluate the activity of these officials, the fact that prosecutions by them form a substantial part of the few summary records that remain suggests that they were increasingly active. In 1830, for example, *La Minerve* described a case where fence and ditch inspectors had pursued a dozen *habitants* before a local justice for not doing their share of work on a watercourse common to three adjoining parishes. The *habitants* turned around and sued the inspectors before another justice for having illegally issued the work orders; the inspectors riposted and had the *habitants'* goods seized to satisfy the fines and costs; and the *habitants* in turn riposted by suing the inspectors in King's Bench. This flurry of litigation belies once again the notion of a rural society that regulated its own affairs outside the formal law, and highlights the role of local officials acting under the authority of their office for the ostensible benefit of the wider community. Of course, these local officials were also members of their rural communities – the *sous-voyers* and fence and ditch inspectors were in fact *habitants* elected by parish assemblies, which is what may have inspired Chisholme's comments on malicious roads prosecutions between *habitants*. And *sous-voyers* and other roads officials were also regularly prosecuted for not doing their duty. But they were nevertheless local officials, part of the state at a very local level and participants in the growth of public prosecution.[46]

The significance of public prosecution can be illustrated by a series of cases in Montreal Weekly Sessions in 1805. Christopher Georgen, then acting clerk of the market, launched suits against five members of Montreal's elites for buying provisions outside the market. These included David Alexander Grant, the wealthy seigneur of Longueuil; the Honourable Isaac Ogden, one of the judges of the King's Bench; two prominent *Canadien* merchants; and, to cap it all, John Reid, the clerk of the peace himself. Despite Reid's somewhat specious plea that he only bargained for his chickens outside the market and paid for them in it, the justices on the bench, John Richardson and François Desrivières, condemned all five to fines of twenty shillings plus costs. Though a hefty fine for a labourer earning two shillings a day, this was peanuts for men like Grant and Ogden. But it was likely particularly galling to Ogden in particular, since both Richardson and he were leaders of Montreal's francophobic Tory elites. Still, Georgen's attention to his duty in this instance does not seem to have harmed his career, since two years later the Montreal justices made him keeper of the House of Correction. Georgen, a former German mercenary who had successively been a tailor in Kingston and then a trader and auctioneer in Montreal, was part of Montreal's embryonic local state bureaucracy. By making an example of elite figures who were flouting the very regulations they were supposed to be supporting – and, in Reid's case, helping to enforce – he was apparently simply doing his job as an official prosecutor. But he was also protecting the fees he made from market-sellers. In this instance, the criminal justice system thus served the state and private interests at the same time.[47]

The best example of the rise of public prosecution through the conjunction of private and public interests is the involvement of constables in the prosecution of licensing offences, especially selling liquor without a licence. As we saw, these cases formed an increasingly significant part of the business before the justices in Weekly Sessions. When the British parliament enacted the Quebec Revenue Act in 1775, on which these prosecutions were based, it no doubt had in mind the system used earlier in the century to control gin-houses, in which prosecution rested on a network of informers associated with the excise officers, who were encouraged to prosecute for their hefty £5 share of the fine, another £5 going to the poor of the parish in which the prosecution was launched. Indeed, the fine imposed in Lower Canada was exactly the same, £10 Sterling split between the prosecutor and the crown, and the motivations similar. This was an offence that lay on the boundary between state interest and moral regulation, but where the state's interest was very much in play, since licensing fees were an important source of revenue for the colonial executive. The preponderance of revenue over morality becomes clear when we consider that few tavern-keepers were prosecuted for an issue more obviously linked to morality, selling liquor on Sundays, and official correspondence regarding licensing prosecutions generally concerned revenue rather than morality.[48]

In the eighteenth century, liquor-licensing prosecutions were mainly initiated by private individuals, such as the licensed Montreal tavern-keepers in the 1760s who launched prosecutions against their unlicensed competitors. But, from the late 1810s, the main prosecutors had become professional constables. Of 68 cases in the Montreal Weekly Sessions in 1829, 41 were prosecuted by Adelphe Delisle, the high constable, or the police constables Louis Malo and Antoine Lafrenière, whereas in 1835 Benjamin Delisle, Adelphe's successor, prosecuted all but 18 of the 127 cases.[49] As we saw, these prosecutions were one of the ways in which urban justice reached out into the countryside to exercise its control, and again, it was urban constables who were the plaintiffs in many of these cases, even at a period when policing in rural areas was increasingly carried out by rural police.

It is difficult to know whether these rural prosecutions by urban constables represented cases in which the constables actually went into the countryside, or whether they simply acted as prosecutors for cases brought to them by informers. Much like excise officers in England enforcing the Gin Acts, constables and other public prosecutors relied on informers to assist them. This was necessary both because most legislation required a prosecutor as well as a witness and because the constables and other officers themselves, as long-serving officers, were often known to offenders, who would refuse to sell to them. Sometimes the officers seem to have been little more than figureheads, with the informers being the main motors of the prosecution. But officers were also actively involved in the recruitment and management of networks of informers. Consider a case in the Montreal Weekly Sessions in April 1829 where William Moon, the former watch spy who had by then become a Montreal police constable, prosecuted Michael Gibson for peddling without a licence at Longueuil. The main witness was one James Tooner of Montreal, Moon's assistant on a speculative foray into the countryside to catch offenders. Tooner testified that Moon paid him a dollar a day to travel with him; that he had been with Moon for three days, and had received ten shillings; that Moon had asked Gibson the price of a handkerchief and, on being told nine pence, had declared himself a constable and seized Gibson's goods. After a lengthy cross-examination and countering testimony, where Tooner was effectively accused of offering to compound with another peddler, the justices found Gibson guilty and imposed a fine of £5 plus costs. Similarly, the inspector of weights and measures established under an act in 1799 was to detect and prosecute all retailers using false or unregulated measures. In Montreal, the inspector in the 1810s and early 1820s, William Mechtler, regularly employed informers to buy small quantities of goods from grocers or shopkeepers suspected of using unregulated measures and then to testify against them: Régis Laplante was a witness in twelve such cases in Quarter Sessions in July 1816, and William B. Thompson in nine in July 1818. An article in *La Minerve* in 1833 even accused constables of using children as young as twelve as informers in liquor-licensing cases.[50]

As Martin Dufresne has suggested, these cases represented a conjunction between public and private interests, not only in the type of proceeding adopted (the *qui tam* action, where a private individual prosecuted both for himself and for the king) but also by virtue of the fact that constables gained considerable reward from their prosecutions. *La Minerve* was scathing in its condemnation of the practice of sharing fines between the king and the prosecutor. After denouncing police inactivity in the case of the wife murderer Dewey, the editorialist added that this was especially striking given that, for the least infractions of the police regulations, the town's citizens were continually exposed to vexatious and arbitrary fines, sought by men whose lack of courage kept them from exercising the most important part of their office but whose avarice and desire to profit from half the fine made them so ingenious and active that they went far into the countryside to seek out those who sold liquor without a licence. As the paper declared, 's'il fallait ici dérouler tout le tableau d'iniquités et d'intrigues qui sont la suite de ces poursuites de spéculations ou de passions, qu'il serait hideux et qu'il représenterait sous de noires couleurs les mouchards du jour!' [If we had revealed the full portrait of iniquities and intrigues that result from these prosecutions arising from speculations or passions, how hideous it would be and darkly it would represent the informers of the day!] And, while the paper admitted that this was done in the name of order and the public good, the means employed to reach the ends were too often accompanied by immorality and 'font d'un objet de bien public une mine exploitée aux profits d'hommes déhontés, nourris dans la fainéantise et guidés par les passions et l'intérêt' [make of the public good a mine exploited for the profit of shameless men, nourished in sloth and guided by passion and interest].[51] While this was no doubt exaggerated, private interest could outweigh public interest even for constables, as when they compounded with offenders so as to drop the prosecution on payment of their costs. In Quebec City, the practice had become elevated into a system by the late 1820s: as Joseph-François-Xavier Perrault, the Quebec City clerk of the peace, noted in testimony before the Assembly in 1830, 'Do you not consider that the practice of permitting parties to compound with the Informers operates as a direct encouragement to sell without License, and causes a great diminution of the Public Revenue? No doubt of it; it causes a very material diminution of the Revenue.'[52]

Nor were prosecutions for selling liquor without a licence an efficient way to discourage the practice. The recurrent prosecutions and convictions suggest quite otherwise, and grand juries and newspapers repeatedly complained of the evils of unlicensed tavern-keepers. The reason for this, however, was less the incapacity of the justice system than the incoherence of the licensing system, where the costs of a licence, especially from the late 1810s onwards, could outweigh the costs of a conviction. As David Ross, acting as agent for the provincial secretary in Montreal, explained several times, many tavern-keepers were probably tempted to take their chances without a licence, though many also took out their licences.[53]

But, whether or not they were effective in stemming the problem, these prosecutions nevertheless represented the growth of routine public prosecution. The regularity with which liquor-licensing prosecutions were brought by constables, or even weights-and-measures prosecutions brought by Mechtler (who prosecuted almost a hundred people between 1816 and 1820), suggests a bureaucratic process which the constables and other official prosecutors repeated again and again, regardless of the individual they were prosecuting and against whom they more than likely held no personal grudge. Those convicted of licensing offences who petitioned for pardon, for example, while they might raise the issue of greed on the part of the informer, never did so against the constables, who appear to have been seen as simply part of the system.

As well as the growth of public prosecution in regulatory offences, there was also the growth of the principle of at least partial public responsibility in many of the sorts of cases heard by the justices in Quarter Sessions. Consider the question of who was responsible for paying court fees. In felonies, no fees were charged the plaintiff for the initial depositions, warrants, recognizances, and so on; arrests of felons were generally made at the expense of the crown and prosecutions were conducted at crown expense by the attorney general, with witnesses summoned and paid for their attendance. As we saw, in minor misdemeanours such as assaults, it was generally the plaintiffs themselves who had to pay, at least initially, though the defendant might sometimes be asked to pay for the warrant and recognizance. However, there was also an intermediate category between felonies and minor misdemeanours. As the Quebec clerks of the peace put it in 1817, 'in such cases of misdemeanours as it is considered equally interesting to the person injured as to the public to prosecute, payment of the fees has always been made by the prosecutor, whereas in felony and such gross misdemeanours as involve the public welfare, fees are never charged to the private individual.' This latter category, which initially included such evidently state matters as assaults on officers, was increasingly broadened in the nineteenth century to include matters more generally related to the 'public welfare,' such as brothel-keeping, larceny, and riots. There was some resistance to this on the part of economically minded administrators, especially in the context of constant financial crises and battles with the Assembly over revenues. Thus, the committee on public accounts in 1827 rejected the claims of the Quebec City clerks of the peace for the prosecution of nuisances on the grounds that 'in England these and other expenses are borne exclusively by the parties and not by the public.' Still, by the early 1830s, it had apparently been settled that government paid for all cases in Quarter Sessions apart from simple assault. By 1836, the Quebec clerks of the peace were even separating assaults into two classes: those where 'the public safety, peace and tranquility, or an assault with an intent to commit felony, renders it absolutely necessary to proceed against the offending party, which is then denominated a "public case," and in which the party complained of is proceeded against by us at the public expense,' and those involving 'simple differences between individuals where the party preferring the charge has himself to disburse the costs of the proceedings, and which is termed merely a "private case."' By the mid-1830s, only assaults were excluded from the definition of public cases, and not all of these. This still meant that the majority of cases heard before the justices were paid for by private parties, but the change in the conception of what constituted a public case was already well under way long before the changes of the late 1830s.[54]

Once these public cases reached the Quarter Sessions, they were often prosecuted not by the original plaintiff but by whichever law officer of the crown happened to be available – in Montreal, for example, initially the clerk of the peace but then, by the later 1810s, generally the solicitor general or the king's counsel. Even in larceny cases, where there was definitely a private victim, the sort of public prosecution that characterized the King's Bench became increasingly common before the justices as well. In the eighteenth century, larceny cases in Quarter Sessions were generally prosecuted by the victims, as in England. However, from the 1810s at least, and perhaps earlier, the prosecution of larceny cases before the justices became an increasingly public affair. By the 1820s, larceny victims evidently still had to take the initiative to make a complaint to a justice, but once the case reached this stage it became a crown case, with court fees charged to the central administration and the case prosecuted by the crown law officers. When the Montreal King's Bench grand jury complained in 1825 of the burdens of prosecuting in Quarter Sessions, they were thus referring mainly to assault cases.[55]

A final and highly significant change in the nineteenth century was the rise in the prosecution of victimless public-order offences, prosecuted by official prosecutors rather than by private citizens. Thus, as

Mary Anne Poutanen found, women in Montreal accused of vagrancy or prostitution were most likely to be first arrested and then prosecuted by city constables or watchmen. Further, as we have seen, in both Montreal and Quebec City, these sorts of summary arrests formed an increasingly large part of the business of everyday criminal justice, and, by the mid-1830s in Montreal, about half of all summary complaints were by official plaintiffs, such as constables and watchmen. In Quebec City, the change was even more complete: virtually all of complaints against prostitutes, vagabonds, and so on were launched by these sorts of official prosecutors. This foreshadowed what was perhaps the major transformation of criminal justice in the mid-nineteenth-century, the increasing concentration of the everyday criminal justice system on marginal urban populations, and was linked to another development that began the transformation of colonial criminal justice: the rise of summary justice.[56]

The Rise of Summary Justice

In Quebec and Canadian historiography, the rise of summary justice and the decline of the jury trial has often been seen as the result of the mid-nineteenth-century revolution in government and the rise of what has elsewhere been termed the 'policeman state,' with its increasing attention to the regulation of everyday behaviour and consequent need for expeditious justice. However, studies of England have increasingly pointed out that summary justice was of great importance there long before the mid-nineteenth century, despite being entirely contrary to the fundamental ideological premise of a system based on the jury trial.[57]

In the eighteenth century, though the evidence is scanty, it seems likely that apart from summary trials in the more formal courts, notably in the Weekly and Special Sessions, summary justice was a minor part of the criminal justice system. The surviving Montreal records of the 1780s and 1790s, for example, contain few peace bonds, with almost all defendants being bound over for trial at Quarter Sessions. As for summary fines, the centralization of the court system meant that justices in the cities never imposed them outside their formal courts of Weekly or Quarter Sessions. And, as we saw in chapter 1, summary imprisonment of beggars and vagrants was also rare because of the limits of the carceral system. Overall, summary justice, while it did occur in the eighteenth century, was fairly uncommon.

It was in the first decades of the nineteenth century that summary proceedings rose rapidly in importance. As noted in chapter 1, rural justices were increasingly active in summarily determining complaints, though quantifying their activity is virtually impossible, and the same shift happened in the cities as well. By the late 1820s, Robert Christie, the Quebec City chairman, was noting that in one year his business had consisted of 400 arrest warrants in criminal cases, including misdemeanours; 128 warrants against deserting sailors, of whom 86 were summarily convicted; 144 cases heard in Weekly Sessions; and 65 summary convictions under the vagrancy laws. If we estimate that at least 50, and probably more, of the misdemeanour arrests led to summary resolution by peace bond, this means that of all the complaints brought before him, Christie resolved about a third summarily. This proportion continued to climb, notably because of the increase in summary imprisonment of vagrants and prostitutes and summary prosecutions under the merchant seamen's acts (which rose tenfold between 1815 and 1835). By 1835, about half of the complaints brought before the city's justices were dealt with summarily, outside the formal courts, and such was the importance of summary convictions of vagrants and prostitutes that, by the late 1820s, the clerks of the peace were using special pre-printed forms for them. Similarly, in Montreal between 1820 and 1835, the city's justices resolved summarily, by the imposition of peace bonds, about a third of all violence complaints brought before them, and they increasingly committed people summarily, even when sitting in Quarter Sessions. The lower number of summary commitments in Montreal compared to Quebec City (Table 5.1), and the absence of any significant number of seamen's desertion cases, meant that in 1835 only about 20 per cent of complaints brought before the Montreal justices were dealt with summarily, but, if we consider convictions only, about half of those punished by the justices were punished by summary judgment imposed outside the formal courts of Quarter and Weekly Sessions. And, like their Quebec City counterparts, by late 1836 Montreal justices began using pre-printed forms for depositions against vagrants and prostitutes, suggesting the increasing importance of this type of business.[58]

There were limits, however, to the summary business of urban magistrates. As explained earlier, urban justices almost always imposed fines only when sitting in the formal courts, not only in the eighteenth century but also in the nineteenth. Thus, in 1833, of fifty-two justices from the district of Montreal who reported imposing fines in summary hearings, only two were from the city, while in the district of Quebec, all of the fourteen justices reporting were rural. This was in contrast to American cities such as Philadelphia and Boston, where local magistrates often held their own summary hearings in their homes or businesses, in effect leading to the setting up of so many local neighbourhood courts.[59]

Perhaps the most striking feature of the growth of summary justice in both cities was the rise of summary imprisonment. As we have seen, following the establishment of houses of correction from 1799, and definitively from 1802, summary imprisonment of marginalized members of society became a regular feature of urban life in the colony, especially in the 1820s, though perhaps more so in Quebec City than in Montreal. The houses of correction were not always on stable legislative ground, shutting down, for example, for a year at a time in 1810–11 and 1816–17, for two years in 1827–9, and again from 1835, when their enabling acts were not renewed. But this did not spare those who were targeted by summary imprisonments, since, in the interim, justices simply committed vagrants, prostitutes, and disobedient servants to the gaol instead, and even the term House of Correction continued to be used.[60]

Gaol and House of Correction records also underestimate the actual number of people summarily imprisoned, since they do not cover people imprisoned overnight by watchmen and constables who were not subsequently charged. Thus, in Quebec City, from the early 1820s at least, it was standard practice for the watch and the constables to take people they had arrested to the gaol and commit them overnight, before taking them to the Police Office the next morning, when they might or might not be recommitted on formal charges. The gaoler did not enter these people into his official register, since he had no warrant or deposition to justify their imprisonment. But in his daybook, after the regular committals which he wrote out in full, he made a brief note of the type 'seven men by the watch' or 'three men and a woman by the constables.' The only daybook to have survived, the 'Daily report of committals etc.' covering one year in 1827–8, a period when there was no house of correction, shows some 688 committals of this sort, when only 525 prisoners were regularly committed and entered in the official register, including about 150 committed summarily by the justices for vagrancy and the like. The absence of any names makes it difficult to say how many of the 688 summarily committed by the watch and constables were subsequently recommitted on formal charges; almost 400 (and probably more) were most likely not, because there are no corresponding committals in the day or two following their imprisonment. In other words, this sort of very summary imprisonment by the watch and constables was probably about as important as regular committals of all types, and certainly more important than summary committals by the justices themselves, which, even when the House of Correction was in operation, did not exceed 250 per year in the 1820s. An 1828 Quebec City grand jury (including nine urban justices) complained of the practice, noting especially that the gaoler charged fees for the release of prisoners committed by the watch. Whether there were any changes as a result is unknown, though the large number of vagrancy complaints sworn by gaol turnkeys between 1833 and 1836 suggests the persistence of this practice of imprisoning arrestees the night before and taking them before the justices the next morning. In Montreal, summary imprisonment by the watch was even less formal: those arrested were taken to the watch-house, kept overnight in what became evocatively known as the 'Black Hole,' and, if no formal charges were to be laid, as was usual in simple cases of drunkenness or rowdiness, released the next morning. This was the experience, for example, of François Forrioso and 'Duffy, Irishman,' brought in by the watch on the night of 11–12 June 1832 and released the next day. However, the lack of any substantial surviving watch records makes it difficult to know whether this happened as frequently as in Quebec City. Similarly, many of those arrested for vagrancy and disorderly behaviour by the police after the watch disappeared in 1836 were apparently not formally imprisoned: for the second quarter of 1836, the high constable reported thirty-six arrests for vagrancy, plus another thirty for disturbing the peace, when the gaol records show perhaps thirty-two people being committed for these offences. The existence of this sort of informal punishment, though difficult to measure, may help explain why the summary punishment of vagrants in Montreal, though rising substantially from the early 1830s, appears from the court and gaol records to have been less frequent than in Quebec City.[61]

Summary imprisonment thus became an increasingly common feature of urban life. On the other hand, while rural justices were increasingly active in imposing fines and peace bonds summarily, summary imprisonment was rare outside the cities. In the nineteenth century, rural justices did occasionally commit vagabonds and disobedient servants to the gaols and houses of correction, as in the case of Baptiste Rochefort *dit* Gervais, a voyageur committed to the Montreal House of Correction in 1806 by Pierre Bouthillier and Francis Winter, Châteauguay justices, for deserting the service of Alexander Simpson; or that of Reine Ouellet, committed to the Quebec gaol for fifteen days in 1822 by Amable Dionne, a Kamouraska magistrate, for 'indecent and irreverent behaviour' in the parish church.[62] But these cases were infrequent. Thus, between May 1827 and April 1829, when the absence of a house of correction in Montreal meant that all summary commitments were to the gaol, rural justices committed only eight prisoners summarily. And rural justices in the district of Quebec almost never committed summarily: between 1813 and 1837, they sent at most twenty people to the Quebec gaol for summary imprisonment. The reasons for this are evident: it was far too much trouble to send a prisoner accused of a minor offence to Montreal or Quebec City, especially when the poverty of those generally involved in cases of vagrancy or desertion meant that there was no hope of holding them to pay the considerable costs involved. How Dionne got Ouellet all the way from Kamouraska to Quebec City remains to be explained.

Overall, by the 1830s, far more cases were dealt with summarily by the justices than ever made it to the formal courts, both in the cities and in the rural areas of the colony. And this shift in the nature of justice began long before the 1840s, though it certainly continued to accelerate thereafter. However, the move towards summary justice was neither coherent nor rapid enough for many who grew increasingly impatient with the existing system. In 1829, for example, a Montreal Oyer and Terminer grand jury decried what it called the triviality of many of the offences brought before it, and called for justices to be given powers 'similar to those they possess in England for the summary punishment of small offenses,' most likely referring to petty thefts. And in 1837 a Montreal Quarter Sessions grand jury called for the establishment of a police court under a police magistrate, to deal with many of the offences they were forced to determine. The issue for them was one of their own time, of efficiency, and of the public good:

> Not only are the individuals composing Grand Juries taken away from their respective businesses for several successive days, but a number of others summoned as petit jurors, while the ends of Justice could be much more effectively and expiditiously attained, by the most of the cases being tried by a Police Magistrate. For the length of time that frequently elapses between the commission of an offence and a Bill of Indictment being laid before a Jury for consideration, witnesses are not forth coming when called for, and in consequence the Criminal, much to the public injury,

escapes whereas if brought before a Police Court, when the circumstances are fresh in the recollection of those concerned, and the witnesses on the spot, no such thing would occur.

And just the following year, across the gulf of the Rebellions, the Montreal Police Court would indeed begin its operations, marking the definitive triumph of summary justice.[63]

The Enforcement of Judicial Orders

Another way of gauging the transformation of the coercive power of the everyday criminal justice system is to examine the system's capacity to enforce the orders it made. On the one hand, little seems to have changed in the enforcement of recognizances imposed by the justices. As we saw, the justices rarely imposed recognizances to prosecute, or enforced those they did impose. The situation was a little different when it came to recognizances entered into by defendants, to appear in court or to keep the peace. Unlike in England, the justices rarely declared recognizances forfeited by estreating them, whereby they became a civil debt to the crown. Thus, in the late 1810s, the Quebec City chairmen claimed that a forfeited £20 recognizance that they had themselves collected 'is the only sum which has ever been actually paid into the revenue out of the many thousands which have become due on forfeited recognizances since the Conquest.' While this may have been an exaggeration, even when recognizances were more systematically estreated, as the Montreal chairmen briefly did in Quarter Sessions cases in the early 1810s, there was no guarantee that the crown law officers would actually collect. Even in the mid-1820s, the attorney general was arguing that it was impossible to collect on forfeited recognizances since there was no court of exchequer in the colony, and, though a few recognizances forfeited in criminal cases do appear to have been collected in the later 1820s, these almost exclusively concerned King's Bench cases. Despite sporadic attempts by the administration to tighten up the enforcement of recognizances, little changed, in part because of resistance on the part of judicial officials. Thus, in 1823, the Quebec clerks of the peace, while stating that forfeited recognizances in their office amounted to some £5,000 per year, also questioned 'whether the putting forfeited recognizances in suit might not, while opening a source of revenue, tend to impoverish that source by putting parties more on their guard than they have been, and rendering them less willing to contract an obligation under the certainty of its being enforced,' though they also acknowledged that stricter enforcement of recognizances might bring an extra two thousand pounds in revenue. By the mid-1830s, forfeited recognizances were still not being collected in the Quebec Quarter Sessions. However, entering into a recognizance to prosecute or to appear was more than just a symbolic gesture, the respect for which depended less on the will of the state than on that of the parties. When defendants did not respect recognizances to appear, for example, the Montreal justices at least regularly issued bench warrants for the arrest of the defaulter, which often had the desired effect.[64]

The situation evolved more significantly with regard to the capacity of the justices to enforce punishments imposed by them. In cases before the Quarter Sessions, the Montreal justices generally did not impose a sentence unless the defendant was before them in court, and they generally specified that the defendant was to be committed until the sentence was satisfied. As a result, almost all defendants fined in the Quarter Sessions paid their fines: about 95 per cent between 1788 and 1795 and about 90 per cent between 1811 and 1823. This high rate of payment shows the power that the court could exert if necessary to enforce its orders, which was no doubt a strong inducement to pay.

The enforcement of fines imposed by the justices in Weekly Sessions and summarily was initially less sure. Justices generally could not summarily imprison those who simply refused to pay fines imposed upon them for regulatory offences and the like, although, as in civil cases, they could seize the defendant's goods to make good the fine, through a warrant of distress.[65] The only notable exception was fines imposed on those who directly affronted the interests or sensibilities of the elites or the state, as in deserting servants or those who misbehaved in church, in both of which cases a defendant not paying the fine could be summarily committed. This was how Cézaire Archambault came to be in the common gaol of Montreal in September 1825, committed by Barthelemy Rocher for not paying the £1 fine he had imposed for indecent behaviour in the church of Saint-Roch. And the same held true for offences where the state was more directly involved, notably those against the militia ordinances and defendants who would not or could not pay the hefty £10 Sterling fine for selling liquor without a licence; in both cases, those convicted could be committed to gaol summarily.

In the eighteenth century, the justices apparently had great difficulty enforcing the punishments they imposed in Weekly Sessions. Thus,

John Burke, the clerk of the peace, was asked to explain the difference between the amount of fines actually imposed in the Weekly Sessions between 1779 and 1787, totalling about £1,700, and the amount that he could account for, totalling £1,150. He replied that 'a great number of persons fined, from time to time, had not paid their fines, some from poverty and distress, having neither goods or any sort of moveables or other sort of effects or property whatsoever, others from having gone away, from their places of abode to some different distant parish or place so as not to be found, so that their fines could not be recovered, and tho warrants were issued against several of them, for the purpose of levying their fines, it was to no effect.'[66] But this still meant that two-thirds of fines were either paid or accounted for in some other way, such as being remitted.[67]

By the nineteenth century, the collection of fines imposed in the Montreal Weekly Sessions became more sure. Thus, between April and November 1810, after the opening of the Police Office, the justices imposed fines totalling about £250. Of these, they had collected £143, but £65 of the remainder was owing by a single person who had bought regimental effects from soldiers and been committed to gaol in default of payment, so that only £41, or less than a fifth of all fines imposed, remained either uncollected or unpunished.[68] Further, though it is impossible to know the total number of convictions for selling liquor without a licence, and despite the frequency of pardon petitions, over three hundred people paid their £10 Sterling fines in these cases between 1811 and 1826, probably encouraged in the latter part of this period by several imprisonments of defaulters by the justices in 1819 and 1820. There was, however, at least one area in which the enforcement of fines was not so certain: those imposed with regard to the rules and regulations of police made by the justices themselves. Thus, a return of such fines imposed in Montreal between 1821 and 1824 listed seventy-eight defendants who had not paid, beside some of whom was the notation 'nulla bona,' indicating that a warrant of distress had been issued but the constable or bailiff who attempted to serve it had been unable to do so. As the Montreal justices lamented in 1827, their inability to imprison those who did not pay the fines meant that 'poor rogues and vagabonds, of all the most likely to become delinquents, commit with perfect impunity offences and indecencies for which all the better classes would be punished' – punished through the seizure of their property.[69]

Yet, despite its flaws and imperfections, none of this suggests a justice system that was unable to impose itself. Almost all defendants fined in the Quarter Sessions paid up; when a prostitute or a vagrant was committed summarily to the gaol or the House of Correction, she or he was definitely committed; though a significant proportion of people fined summarily or in the Weekly Sessions did not pay, most did; and non-payment was not without its risks, at least in cases such as selling liquor without a licence, where a defendant's goods could be seized and sold and he or she imprisoned.

Resisting the State

A final way of approaching the everyday criminal justice system as an instrument of power for the state is to examine resistance to the system and the system's ability to respond. This has often been pointed out as a fatal flaw in ancien-régime criminal justice: even if the system might work fairly well in ordinary cases, it was simply unable to respond to any sort of mass resistance to its authority, except through the brute force of military intervention. A full study of resistance to the state would have to go far beyond the bounds of the everyday criminal justice system discussed here, notably because many of these incidents ended up before the superior criminal courts. But, even staying at the level of the justices and their police, we can make a few observations.

Certainly, as we have already seen, there are regular examples of resistance to the everyday criminal justice system. Thus, there was often generalized distrust and even hatred of the police, whatever their form. Throughout the period between the Conquest and the late 1820s, bailiffs, constables, and watchmen filed a steady stream of criminal complaints against people who had insulted, threatened, or assaulted them, from John Divine and Jean-Baptiste Flamand, city bailiffs who in 1769 charged Augustin Loiseau and Alexis Rencontre with attacking them on Saturday night when they came to investigate a noise in the street and a woman crying, to Adelphe Delisle, who in 1830 charged a Dr Leslie, whom he did not know but could point out, with assault and battery. Overall, police filed perhaps four hundred such complaints in the district of Montreal between 1800 and 1835. Assaults on justices were far less common, in part because they were not often themselves involved in the physical work of enforcing the law, but they did occur on occasion. Thus, of some eighty prisoners committed to the Quebec gaol between 1813 and 1837 for resisting police or magistrates, only six were accused of threatening or assaulting justices, the rest being imprisoned for their actions towards constables and watchmen.[70]

While a thorough study of assaults on judicial authorities, attempted rescues, and the like is beyond the scope of this book, they followed patterns similar to those in eighteenth-century England.[71] A few cases illustrate the degree to which popular resistance to the police and the law could go. In 1806 John Marstene, a Montreal bailiff, was ordered by the Quarter Sessions to arrest Thomas Garoniontée, a Caughnawaga Native, for assaulting Thomas Arakouanté (once again before the courts), and he took along with him Frederick Charles, one of the long-serving Montreal constables, as an assistant. But, when Marstene attempted to arrest Garoniontée, he was 'surrounded by a large crowd of savages, not less than fifty in number, who was armed with clubs and sticks, saying to me, they had not any business with the Montreal law,' and was forced to retire. Likewise, in 1820 Catherine Meloche, the wife of a Sainte-Geneviève tavern-keeper, complained to William Smith, a Saint-Eustache justice, that she had been assaulted in her house by Thomas Cousineau, a Sainte-Geneviève joiner. Smith accordingly issued an arrest warrant to Narcisse Béllair, the local bailiff, who, with his *recors*, Baptiste Cousineau, went to Thomas Cousineau's house. According to the declaration that Béllair made later,

> à l'instant que j'ai été entré dans la maison dudit Cousineau pour lui fair un devoir par corpt de la part du roi le dit rébelle sest mit en défence dun gros batont et les manches de chemise retrousé jusquau [gros] du corpt en me tretant avec toutes les injures les plus atroces et même en jurent et blassefaiment contre les ordres du roi et en jurent contre sa majesté et acompagnié de sont frer qui lacompagne et qui le conseile à désobeyre au dit warrant
> [as soon as I entered the house of the said Cousineau to arrest him in the name of the king the said rebel defended himself with a big stick with his sleeves rolled up to his body and treated me with all manner of the worst insults and even swearing and blaspheming against the orders of the king and swearing against His Majesty, accompanied by his brother who accompanied him and counselled him to disobey the said warrant]

And there is no record that the case proceeded any further than that. In this case, resistance had been successful.[72]

Nor was resistance limited to men. In 1823 William Woods, the Sainte-Marie justice of the peace, ordered François Leclaire, a local bailiff, to arrest Marie Dubois on the complaint of five Sainte-Marie farmers for having left her husband, Augustin Labonté, of nearby Saint-

Mathias, and lived for the last two years with one François Daunais to the great scandal of all, for having had a child with Daunais, for having had sex in front of one of the plaintiffs, and for assaulting and threatening two others. When Leclaire went to arrest Dubois, she refused to open her door and said that, while she would go before a justice at Chambly, a little farther away, she would not go before Woods, 'parce qu'il était trop crasseux, trop veaurien quil netoit pas Juge à Paix qui avoit été cassé' [because he was too foul, too worthless that he was not a justice of the peace that he had been dismissed] – no doubt a reference to Woods having been forgotten in the second commission of 1821 (though this had already been rectified by a commission of association in 1822). Woods himself added that, when Leclaire finally did bring Dubois before him, assisted by Ambroise Bédard, a militia captain, she not only confirmed what Leclaire alleged but declared that Woods was 'aussi saleau quelle et quelle ne samusoit quavec des saleau' [as much a scoundrel as she and that she only amused herself with scoundrels]. On her refusing to give security for her good behaviour, Woods issued a warrant to commit her to gaol, in which he accused her of keeping a 'mauvaise maison' [bad house] – in essence, accusing Dubois of prostitution. What happened to her then is unknown, though the fact that the documents ended up in Montreal suggests that she was probably committed to gaol. A Marie Dubois was indeed indicted in October sessions, but for larceny rather than for assault or for keeping a disorderly house. Still, as in England, resistance to police was overall very much a male affair, with over nine-tenths of defendants being men.[73]

Resistance to state law could also take more passive forms. One popular form was convincing witnesses in liquor-licensing cases not to testify. In 1827, for example, Alexander Fraser of Sainte-Scholastique, north of Montreal, launched licensing suits against a half-dozen people in the area. Fraser had had his witnesses subpoenaed to testify at the Weekly Sessions, and had offered to pay their expenses, but when he tried to gather them to go into town, they demurred. On asking them why, one told him that he did not know what to do 'as he was told many things,' and John Earl, a local merchant who was also present, told Fraser that the witnesses would not go, declaring, '[I]t is a shame for you to be so mean to prosecute these people when you are able to live without it, these are dirty tricks, and I hope these people will not do as you. You know these people cannot gain their livelihood after this, as the principal men of the place are engaged in this & they will no longer assist you.' It turned out that Earl and two others, Joseph Boutron *dit* Major and Louis Dumouchel, had offered the witnesses substantial sums of money not to testify, and also, when Fraser came looking for them, hid them in Boutron *dit* Major's barn and under his bed. The net result was that the witnesses stayed behind, and Fraser's suits failed.[74]

Popular dislike of the police and the law was perhaps best exemplified in 1799 by John Sparrow, a Montreal carter: when Jean-Baptiste Castonguay, the market constable, asked him to move his cart and showed him his constable's stave, Sparrow refused, showed his backside to the constable, and then hit him in the face. But Sparrow did not get away with his resistance: Castonguay collared him and took him before Pierre Foretier to enter into a recognizance to appear at the next Quarter Sessions, where he was found guilty, fined forty shillings (which he paid), and forced to enter into a recognizance to keep the peace for six months.[75] And indeed, as we saw, the police were considerably more capable than reform discourse and later historians would have us believe. Thus, for every charivari that spun out of control, how many revellers were arrested and locked up by the watch? Or take the 1835 incident involving Montreal's high constable, Benjamin Delisle, and a carter named Jean-Baptiste Charbonneau. Delisle recounted that he had arrested Charbonneau on a warrant for assault and battery on one Josephte Fabien and hitting her with a knife. In the Peace Office, Charbonneau began to resist and also was unable to find acceptable guarantors. As a result, Delisle, with great difficulty, conducted him to the gaol; once there, Charbonneau threw himself on Delisle and tried to hit him, but was prevented by someone else. Charbonneau's resistance to the police and the law did not get very far at all.[76]

Still, the everyday criminal justice system was certainly best at responding to everyday resistance, not the sort of mass resistance that characterized moments such as the American invasion in 1775–6, the Roads Act riots of 1796, the militia enrolment riots of 1812, the Montreal election riot of 1832, or, of course, the Rebellions of 1837–8. Faced with those, the ordinary system was incapable of responding, and the colonial state fell back on military repression. But then, this was also the case for the 'new' system in the mid-nineteenth century, when, if anything, police and magistrates were even more challenged by the riots and labour actions that characterized social relations in a rapidly urbanizing and industrializing society.

Conclusion

Quebec historians have often shown how the criminal justice system of the state could serve as a brutal instrument of naked repression, whether it be the militiamen locked up in the 1770s and 1780s or the *Patriotes* hanged or transported in the late 1830s. Though the ultimate form of state power remained the army, criminal justice was an essential tool as well. But this is not the type of justice we have explored in this book. Military tribunals, imprisonment without *habeas corpus*, packed juries, and Baconian judges were all extraordinary measures, applied selectively in an evident effort to shape justice to the ends of political expediency, imperial interest, and ideological imperative, all expressed through the exercise of state power. The everyday criminal justice system, on the other hand, is often seen as having been more an impediment than an aid to state power. After all, why was it necessary to suspend *habeas corpus* or proceed with military tribunals, unless the ordinary system of judges and juries, even in the higher courts, could not be bent to these political ends?

Part of the problem, it has been argued, is that most of the ordinary criminal justice system – and especially the level of the justices – still functioned essentially according to the logic of private prosecution. Thus, despite the evident role played by police in the detection and prosecution of crimes, despite the increasing involvement of the crown in prosecutions, the criminal justice system in Lower Canada, even in the 1830s, remained stuck in an ancien-régime mould. This sort of argument, however, neglects the fundamental changes we have seen in this chapter, between the Conquest and the Rebellions, which made the criminal justice system more and more an instrument of state power and state domination – the domination not of the central administration but of the local judicial bureaucracy of magistrates, police, and clerks who made up most of the system. The architecture of justice changed substantially, from repurposed French-regime buildings to purpose-built English ones, giving the judicial bureaucracy its structural base, and legal routines became increasingly bureaucratic as well. And the rise of public prosecution and of summary justice, and the ability of the system to enforce its orders and deal with ordinary resistance, also underscore its everyday power.

A pathetic instance of this triumph of the everyday state and of bureaucratic routine over the individual is the case of Jane Laughlin. A Quebec City prostitute, she had been in and out of the gaol and House of Correction since the late 1810s. On the morning of 3 May 1827, she was found dead of exposure on the Plains of Abraham. Tucked into her bosom was a printed form, the record of her conviction for being an idle and disorderly person, filled out with her name, the date she was convicted (30 April), and her sentence, one month in the House of Correction. Laughlin had pleaded guilty, which probably meant that she had wanted to be committed, perhaps to avoid the inclement weather. But, fatally for her, the legislation establishing the House of Correction expired the next day, on 1 May, and the keeper, strictly adhering to the law, turned out all of the prisoners. Laughlin had been doubly slighted by the system. Seeking shelter by using the criminal law, she had been denied it because of a bureaucratic decision. And the last contact between her and the criminal justice system was not the keeper or even a constable but this impersonal printed form, the most cursory of documents, clasped to her breast like a prized possession. It was not even signed by Robert Christie, the justice who had sentenced her knowing full well that it was purely for the form, since she would be kicked out the next day. After all, she was just one of the thousands of women and men who filed through the Police Office in Quebec City in the 1820s and 1830s and were used by this increasingly impersonal system – though, in this case, she may well have been trying to use the system herself.[77]

Conclusion

But now the growings of the State
Arrangements new, do soon create.
Old things must pass away, and other
Take up their place, and make fresh pother.
– Plinius Secundus, *Curiae Canadenses,
or, the Canadian Law Courts* (1843)[1]

With these couplets, Plinius Secundus, whoever he might have been, launched a lengthy doggerel description of changes wrought in the Lower Canadian court system at a time when criminal justice, the criminal law, and the state in general were being profoundly reshaped. His perspective fit perfectly with that of contemporary reformers: his 'old things,' the court system that had endured since 1794, were to be swept away by the 'arrangements new' established on a more rational basis, under legislation passed by the appointed and authoritarian Special Council which replaced Lower Canada's democratic institutions following the failed Rebellions. In a similar fashion, as historians have shown, the police and the magistracy were also transformed, with the establishment of large police forces and stipendiary magistrates in both city and countryside – 'fresh pother' for those who argue for the importance of the late 1830s and early 1840s as a key moment in state formation in Canada.

My intent in this book has certainly not been to minimize these changes, nor to ignore, as Robert Storch has put it, 'what was genuinely new in nineteenth-century criminal justice history … [in] the temptation to collapse it entirely into that of the eighteenth century or earlier by overemphasizing earlier precedents and trends.'[2] From the perspective of the history not only of ideas and ideologies but also of practices and lived experiences, criminal justice and policing after the Rebellions, at least in the cities, was different from what it had been even in the 1820s and early 1830s – though, as I have suggested elsewhere, it is dangerous to generalize from the cities (and from Montreal in particular) to the countryside, since in rural areas and smaller urban centres, the transformation of criminal justice came about far later.[3] But, in seeking to avoid the teleological pitfall of searching for evidence of modern structures in ancien-régime practices, we must not fall into the equally dangerous trap of ignoring the very real changes that took place under the old system, nor of downplaying the impact of the system on the colony's inhabitants, in the search for a rupture marking the transition from the ancien régime to the new order. Similarly, in identifying pivotal moments in state formation, we must not overemphasize the changes brought about in the early 1760s by the transition from one ancien-régime colonial system to another, in the search for a rupture between the French regime and the British and for further evidence of the colonial domination and interethnic tension that inarguably followed the Conquest. The rejection of the stasis/rupture model of state formation lies at the heart of this book's discussion of the criminal justice system in Quebec and Lower Canada.

One of my principal arguments has thus been that the ancien-régime criminal justice system in the colony, and the colonial state as a whole, was not at all the rigid, toothless, unchanging, miniature 'Old Corruption' that has long been postulated. Colonial state formation, especially at a local level, was a continuing process that characterized not only the years after the Rebellions but the period before as well, responding to the demographic, social, and economic changes that swept the colony. Many of those who have concentrated on the changes of the late 1830s and early 1840s have presented the preceding system as almost timeless, with the 1830s taken as a good enough sample of the ancien régime, a starting point from which later changes were launched.[4] But, just as in France prior to the Revolution and England prior to the revolution in government, the ancien-régime system in the colony changed dramatically in the eighty years between the Conquest and the Rebellions.

In the mid-1760s, in a small, recently conquered colony, criminal justice was both occasional and exemplary. State justice was meted out largely in the two main towns, by largely British magistrates, the product of a system of courts and laws newly imposed by the Conqueror. The Conquest itself brought both change and continuity, in the nature of the criminal law, in the structure of the courts, and in the personnel who embodied both. British criminal law replaced French, though in practice the two normative systems were similar, at least in terms of the law as actually applied at the level of the justices. In practice, this law was not that different from that of New France before the Conquest. The definition of common offences was similar, and a substantial part of the criminal law was more local than English, based as it was on colonial ordinances and local regulations. Courts and procedures also shifted dramatically in theory, with a British system that brought innovations such as justices of the peace, private prosecution, and jury trial, though in many respects, such as the centralized justice system, the architectural setting of the law, and even the nature of preliminary proceedings, the new system closely resembled the old. At this everyday level, there was strong continuity between the two criminal justice systems, whatever the formal laws might be. And, while British judges and magistrates replaced *Canadien* ones, there was far more continuity across the Conquest among judicial auxiliaries such as court officials and police. Even the exclusion of *Canadiens* from the magistracy was only temporary. Nevertheless, despite this continuity, the new system had many of the vices often imputed to ancien-régime criminal justice: untrained and sporadically active magistrates, at best moderately competent officials, makeshift settings, and a hodgepodge of laws. Though not shunned by the population, whether British or *Canadien*, it was hardly central to formal dispute resolution or the exercise of social power, in the way the civil courts were. And as a tool for the exercise of power by the state, though it might work fitfully, as *Canadien* militiamen found out a decade later, it was hardly terror-inspiring or even that frightening.

By the late 1820s and early 1830s, everyday criminal justice had been transformed, with profound changes occurring in the nineteenth century, and especially from the 1810s, many of which prepared the ground for what was to come in the criminal justice system of the modern, liberal state. It was no more terrifying than the eighteenth-century system but had become commonplace, routinized, bureaucratized. In other words, it was well on the way towards the system progressively put in place through the nineteenth and early twentieth centuries. In a rapidly expanding colony that brought together people of varying and often clashing ethnic backgrounds and social classes, it was well integrated into the mechanisms of dispute resolution as one of several options available to those who felt wronged, though the structural biases inherent in a capitalist and patriarchal society meant that this option was far from being equally available to all. Its flexibility opened a space for the use of power by those often thought to have been largely excluded from it, just as it allowed them to abuse this power for motivations of revenge or greed. It also offered the state itself (or, rather, the British and *Canadien* elites who controlled the state) a relatively powerful, though often faulty, tool to regulate Lower Canadian society. And, by way of magistrates and police of various types, it was spread throughout the colony, though still heavily concentrated in urban centres. In this, the early decades of the nineteenth century were the key period. This was a period when it was not only the ideas of criminal justice reform that were circulating in Lower Canada. Substantial reforms were being concretely implemented, though mostly on a local level, under the radar of those who have looked at the state from the top down. These included the ongoing adaptation of the criminal law to local circumstances and the changing values of the colony's elites, both through colonial legislation and local enactment; the changing practices in the nomination of justices and the increasing control exercised over them by central authorities; the extension and professionalization of the magistracy and the police; the solidification of the architectural presence of the law through the building of new courthouses and prisons; the decrease of public and corporal punishments; and the rise of public prosecution and the increasing recourse to summary justice and summary imprisonment.

These processes of change and adaptation by no means conformed to some Whiggish view of the ongoing progress of the state, for colonial state formation was marked by both advances and retreats. Thus, the implantation of British criminal law and British criminal justice in the 1760s was in no way the glorious advance later enshrined in liberal historiography, though neither was it the profound rupture bemoaned by mid-twentieth-century neo-nationalist historians. And the 1830s, if anything, saw something of a regression in the organization of the everyday institutions of criminal justice, on account of the political crises leading up to the Rebellions: the deprofessionalization of the urban magistracy and, eventually, the disappearance of the city watches harkened back to an eighteenth-century model which had been on the road to disappearance in the first decades of the nineteenth. Still, this seems to have had relatively little impact on the capacity of the system to deal with the increasing business before it.

Nor did these transformations of everyday criminal justice apply equally in all parts of the colony. There were in fact at least two quite different criminal justice systems, one in town and one in the countryside. While both changed substantially over the period, it was in different ways. In the cities, where criminal justice had always been strongly anchored, the story was that of professionalization and specialization, accompanied by the rise of public prosecution and of summary justice. In the countryside, it was more the simple expansion of the presence of criminal justice. Rural justices of the peace are a case in point. Appointed from among local elites, generally firmly embedded in their local communities, often supported by petitioning campaigns launched by the local oligarchy to ensure the selection of one of their own, they served the classic dual purpose of reinforcing local power structures and providing the colonial administration with relatively competent and essentially costless representatives. Some rural justices were undoubtedly corrupt or petty tyrants, but most were probably not; most seem to have done a fairly good job within the limits of their appointment; most were probably actuated by a sense of paternalistic responsibility and a desire to ensure that they, and not others, had the power to regulate their local communities. This system did not disappear with the reforms of the state following the Rebellions, and unsalaried justices of the peace remained the backbone of the rural criminal justice system in Quebec right through the nineteenth century, despite the gradual extension of professional magistrates and more formal courts into the countryside. In the 1890s, for example, rural justices determined about four times as many cases as salaried district magistrates.[5] And the groundwork for this later system was laid with the extension of the rural magistracy in the 1810s, 1820s, and 1830s.

Throughout the colony, in both town and country, the nature and thus the experience of criminal justice altered profoundly between the Conquest and the Rebellions. Yet, while both events launched periods of accelerated change, neither was a moment of complete rupture that bracketed an otherwise undifferentiated period of colonial rule and ancien-régime stasis. And, as I have argued for other aspects of state formation, such as local government, this suggests that the accepted periodization of state formation in Quebec and Lower Canada needs to be rethought, to incorporate incremental change from the early decades of the nineteenth century in particular rather than stasis followed by a sudden and dramatic shift following the Rebellions. Even the post-Rebellions shift itself needs to be relativized, since comparing institutions and practices in the immediate pre-Rebellion period to those immediately afterwards can lead to identifying differences that may be less striking, though no less present, in a longer-term perspective. Thus, the 'arrangements new' that Plinius Secundus so painstakingly versified were in fact never implemented: he had been caught in the classic trap of assuming practice from legislative theory. Instead, most of the courts he outlined remained a dead letter, and in the same year that he published his pamphlet, even those that had been established were themselves swept away, with a return to a modified version of the old court system – which may explain why *Curiae Canadenses* is not even a footnote in Quebec legal history. Similarly, the impressively large and expensive rural police force and system of stipendiary magistrates established by the Special Council in 1839–40, so different from the void in policing immediately prior to the Rebellions, quickly withered and died in the atmosphere of budgetary constraint that accompanied the transition back to parliamentary rule, with a return to the pre-Rebellions system of justices and bailiffs.[6]

The capacity of the ancien-régime system to affect the lives of the colony's inhabitants was also considerably greater than has been postulated. For all of its internal contradictions, inefficiencies, and irregularities, the system before the Rebellions could and did have a significant impact on those who came in contact with it, for what marked the criminal justice system of the ancien-régime state was in fact a great deal of hidden strength. Consider the high clear rates, or the large proportion of those fined in the court who paid their fines; neither suggests powerlessness. And constables and watchmen went far beyond capturing the odd thief or vagrant, as witnessed by the experience of the tens of thousands of people arrested and imprisoned – for everything from breach of service through assault and battery to murder – by the colony's active, increasingly professional police, let alone the even larger number who were simply arrested and brought before a justice to give bail. The changing impact of the system on the colony's population can be seen from the steady growth in the rate of criminal prosecution in the colony, suggesting the increasing place and power of the criminal justice system across the period. Further, the upsurge in recourse to the criminal justice system in the 1830s, both for cases of interpersonal violence and for those concerning public order, after an only temporary drop in the late 1820s, should be read as the beginning of a fundamental change in the relationship between state and society, not as the last gasp of a resolutely pre-reform system.

While there is little doubt as to the transformation of everyday criminal justice between the Conquest and the Rebellions and the system's increasing place in the lives of the colony's residents in general, and urban dwellers in particular, teasing out the social meaning of the criminal law is more difficult. The classic consensual, conflictual, and marginal views are all grounded in empirical reality, for it is easy to find evidence supporting them in the multitude of stories that make up the criminal justice records. There are thousands of cases in the judicial archives where people willingly used the justices and their courts to resolve their disputes, both cooperatively and vengefully; and there are thousands of examples again of the system used by the state and by privileged groups to dominate others, from militiamen to prostitutes, from servants to petty thieves. Yet these thousands upon thousands of cases pale beside the hundreds of thousands of people who lived in the colony, most of whom never lived the experience of coming before a magistrate as plaintiff or defendant. Even the range of motivations is vast, from domination through greed and revenge to protection, all of which are amply documented in the records of the courts.

In some respects, it is perhaps the problem itself that is ill-posed. Neither consensus, nor conflict, nor marginality can adequately encompass the complex relationship between colonial society and criminal justice between the Conquest and the Rebellions, nor allow for the multiple ways in which the system could serve as a source of social power for the many different and competing groups and institutions in the colony: the administration, propertied white men, local elites, *Canadiens*, women, artisans, *habitants* ... At the level of everyday justice, the meaning of the criminal law was ambiguous, unclear, almost impossible to fit neatly into a concise, theoretically bounded characterization. The large number of cases involving interpersonal violence, the small number involving property, the many where both prosecutors and defendants were similar sorts of people, and the personal nature of many of the issues brought before the justices, often within no more than a day or two, all suggest social consensus and a willingness to use the system to resolve personal disputes. But, though people could use the system, they could also be ill-used by it. The system was not class-neutral, especially in cases in which the interests or values of the elites were threatened, such as breach of service, larceny, or prostitution and vagrancy, where the justices in particular handed down much harsher penalties than the ones they imposed in cases involving interpersonal violence. And, though the effects of class on access to the justice system and on the results are ambiguous, it is certain that elite prosecutors could better afford to pursue their cases through the courts and to hire counsel, and elite defendants more easily pay the fines imposed on them. As well, contact with the system was biased by factors such as geography and sex, though both women and people from outside the cities were not at all absent. At the same time, despite a system riddled with barriers and biases, many people still voluntarily turned to the justices and their police. The structural biases that worked against poorer people and women were evident in their relationship with the justices and their courts, but poor people and women also regularly used the courts. Battered wives are a case in point: they used the system to some extent, having their husbands arrested and put in gaol when the abuse reached a critical level, but did not go much beyond that point. Even some Blacks appear to have believed in the capacity of European law to help them, though again their hopes were not necessarily met. Only Natives seem to have more firmly rejected the legitimacy of the colonial state - the 'Montreal law,' as the Caughnawaga assailants of John Martin put it in 1806.

The relationship between the *Canadien* majority in the colony and the criminal justice system imposed by the British is a perfect illustration of this complexity. *Canadien* elites certainly occupied a smaller place in the colonial administration than their place in the population might warrant. Nevertheless, as a result of the British system of co-opting local communities into local administration, they were in no way excluded, especially at the lower levels of the state, and notably among the magistracy, the police, and judicial officials. This gave the everyday criminal justice system a human face that was far less British than might be expected in a conquered colony; in fact, the system had a strong and, in some periods, dominant francophone, largely *Canadien* presence. At the same time, while *Canadien* magistrates often avowed their belief in the legitimacy of the system, this did not prevent some of them from actively engaging in reform politics, and eventually participating in the Rebellions themselves, and successive governors made fitful attempts to ensure that the magistracy was drawn only from the colony's most loyal of elements. As for the *Canadien* population in general, the ambiguity of their relationship to the justice of the 'anglois' was clear. While they were significantly under-represented among plaintiffs and defendants in comparison to their presence in the population, they did not boycott the criminal courts, at least at the level of the justices. And their under-representation may have been more a reflection of the urban bias of formal criminal justice that was common throughout the Western world and that persisted in Quebec until the mid-twentieth-century at least. The significant presence of *Canadiens* before the justices can be traced in large part to the character of the system itself, not only the nature of the police and the active magistracy but also questions such as language, with the justices' courts largely operating bilingually. Both eased the cultural alienation that would undoubtedly have stemmed from a criminal justice system run by British judges and officials entirely in English, which later historians have often erroneously postulated.

Still, as Douglas Hay has pointed out, the bare fact of popular recourse to a criminal justice system is no proof of its consensual acceptance by a population convinced of its legitimacy, and this applies equally well to the colony's *Canadien* population.[7] The regularity with which people resisted the criminal law in general, and the police in particular, argues strongly against a hegemonic acceptance of the system's legitimacy. Instead, popular recourse to the courts had more to do with another paradox: a criminal justice system based in large part on private prosecutorial initiative, a system where the cases of most defendants never reached a formal conclusion but which was nonetheless not powerless to enforce its orders. The extent to which prosecutors had the discretion to withdraw their actions at almost any stage in the proceedings shows how they could use the system to their own advantage, and this prosecutorial discretion made it appealing to parties whose actions were shaped less by their belief in the legitimacy of the right of the king, and by extension his magistrates, to decide their private disputes, than by the possibility that it might enable them to have their opponent arrested, extract monetary compensation, and so on. These instrumental possibilities also help explain the relatively sparse evidence for a parallel system of infrajudicial resolution of criminal matters by third parties: the justice system of the state was itself flexible enough to fill this role, and, at any rate, the men who were justices of the peace, especially in rural areas, were often members of the very same local elites who otherwise might have been called upon to act as mediators.

It is nevertheless important not to over-emphasize the discretionary nature of the everyday criminal justice system or its instrumentalization by plaintiffs. Even in cases of interpersonal violence, closest to civil matters, discretion was the privilege only of plaintiffs, not defendants, who could end up in court or prison if a plaintiff was willing to persist. And the vagrants and prostitutes increasingly swept up by the urban police forces were dealing not with the discretion of private parties but with that of the state, which operated according to a different logic, conditioned by the desire to impose order on urban space increasingly viewed as dangerous. Here the seeds of the later nineteenth-century system are most clearly evident. The criminal justice system in the later nineteenth century was concentrated heavily on the marginalized and the disorderly, with most prosecutions being for public order and public-morality offences, and the shift towards this emphasis of criminal prosecution had already begun in the 1820s.[8]

In the end, from the point of view of plaintiffs and defendants, it mattered little whether the everyday justice they encountered, embodied in magistrates and police and expressed through structures and practices, conformed to historians' ideal type of the ancien-régime or modern state; nor did they care whether, overall, the system was more consensual, more conflictual, or more marginal. What mattered was what the system could do for them, and what it did to them – how it could serve them, or their opponents, as a source of power. Whatever the true nature of the dispute recounted at the opening of this book, between Michel Asselin and Michel Dubois, which is lost to us, Asselin was nonetheless successful in having Dubois arrested, more than likely by one of the city's professional constables such as Adelphe Delisle or Louis Malo. Dubois had to go to the trouble of assembling Étienne Garceau and Amable Jeaudoin to accompany him to the Police Office to act as his guarantors, probably on short notice. And, though his mark on the bit of paper promising to appear in Quarter Sessions was evidently not worth the paper it was written on, let alone the £10 he had in theory promised to the king, Dubois still had to face the irritation and perhaps ignominy of appearing before Thomas Andrew Turner, in the cramped Police Office in the courthouse decorated with the arms of the king whose grandfather's armies had conquered the land of his forebears.

Notes

Introduction

1 Asselin v. Dubois, QSD 11/8/1830. On the 1763 trial of *La Corriveau*, the literature ranges from scholarly articles to popular films. On McLane's execution in 1797: F. Murray Greenwood, *Legacies of Fear: Law and Politics in Quebec in the Era of the French Revolution* (Toronto: Osgoode Society 1993), 139–70. On the trials of the *Patriotes*: Beverley D. Boissery, *A Deep Sense of Wrong: The Treason, Trials, and Transportation to New South Wales of Lower Canadian Rebels after the 1838 Rebellion* (Toronto: Osgoode Society/Dundurn Press 1995), and F. Murray Greenwood and Barry Wright, eds., *Canadian State Trials. Volume II: Rebellion and Invasion in the Canadas, 1837–1839* (Toronto: Osgoode Society/University of Toronto Press 2002), 207–401.

2 This was the dominant trend in Quebec socio-legal history through to the 1990s, from classics like Hilda M. Neatby, *The Administration of Justice under the Quebec Act* (Minneapolis: University of Minnesota Press 1933), to more recent contributions such as André Morel, 'La réception du droit criminel anglais au Québec (1760–1892),' *Revue juridique Thémis* 13, nos. 2–3 (1978): 449–541; Jean-Marie Fecteau, *Un nouvel ordre des choses: la pauvreté, le crime, l'État au Québec, de la fin du XVIIIe siècle à 1840* (Montreal: VLB 1989); or Evelyn Kolish, *Nationalismes et conflits de droits: le débat du droit privé au Québec, 1760–1840* (LaSalle, Que.: Hurtubise HMH 1994). On Quebec legal history in general, see Donald Fyson, 'Les historiens du Québec face au droit,' *Revue juridique Thémis* 34, no.2 (2000): 295–328.

366 Notes to pages 5–7

3 On England: J.A. Sharpe, *Crime in Early Modern England, 1550–1750* (London: Longman 1999), 5–7, 69–77; Peter King, 'The Summary Courts and Social Relations in England, 1740–1820,' *Past and Present* 183 (2004): 131–4; and Douglas Hay, 'Legislation, Magistrates, and Judges: High Law and Low Law in England and the Empire,' in David Lemmings, ed., *The British and Their Laws in the Eighteenth Century* (London: Boydell and Brewer 2005), 59–79.

4 Concern for everyday justice in pre-Confederation Quebec has become more evident in several theses completed over the last decade; apart from my own, 'Criminal Justice, Civil Society, and the Local State: The Justices of the Peace in the District of Montreal, 1764–1830' (PhD, Université de Montréal 1995), these include Mary Anne Poutanen, '"To Indulge Their Carnal Appetites": Prostitution in Early Nineteenth-Century Montreal, 1810–1842' (PhD, Université de Montréal 1997); Martin Dufresne, 'La justice pénale et la définition du crime à Québec, 1830–1860' (PhD, University of Ottawa 1997); Ian C. Pilarczyk, 'The Law of Servants and the Servants of Law: Judicial Regulation of Labour Relations in Montreal, 1830–1845' (LLM, McGill University 1997) and '"Justice in the Premises": Family Violence and the Law in Montreal, 1825–1850' (PhD, McGill University 2003); and Jean-Philippe Garneau, 'Droit, famille et pratique successorale: les usages du droit d'une communauté rurale au XVIIIe siècle canadien' (PhD, Université du Québec à Montréal 2003).

5 For general reviews of the literature, see Clive Emsley and Louis A. Knafla, eds., *Crime History and Histories of Crime: Studies in the Historiography of Crime and Criminal Justice in Modern History* (Westport, Conn.: Greenwood Press 1996). For a general discussion of power and the state: Michael Mann, *The Sources of Social Power. Volume 1: A History of Power from the Beginning to AD 1760* (Cambridge: Cambridge University Press 1986), 4–10.

6 For the two approaches, see Michael Grossberg, '"Fighting Faiths" and the Challenges of Legal History,' *Journal of Social History* 25, no.1 (1991): 191–201.

7 On the ancien-régime state in general: Mann, *The Sources of Social Power. Volume 1: A History of Power* and *Volume 2: The Rise of Classes and Nation States, 1760–1914* (Cambridge: Cambridge University Press 1993); Pierre Bourdieu, 'Esprits d'État: Genèse et structure du champ bureaucratique,' *Actes de la recherche en science sociale* 96–97 (1993): 49–62, and 'De la maison du roi à la raison d'État: Un modèle de la genèse du champ bureaucratique,' *Actes de la recherche en science sociale* 118 (1997): 55–68; Jean-Philippe Genet, 'La genèse de l'État moderne: les enjeux d'un programme de recherche,' *Actes de la recherche en science sociale* 118 (1997): 3–18; and the

various volumes in Wim Blockmans and Jean-Philippe Genet, eds., *The Origins of the Modern State in Europe* (Oxford: Clarendon Press 1995–). On Quebec: Fecteau, *Nouvel ordre*, 17–26.

8 For simplicity and to avoid anachronism, I generally use the term British to designate the colony's English-speaking population, rather than anglophone.

9 For readability, I use the term Quebec City to distinguish the city from the colony, rather than the more contemporary 'City of Quebec.'

10 The account presented here is necessarily simplified; the best overview is found in John Dickinson and Brian Young, *A Short History of Quebec* (Montreal: McGill-Queen's University Press 2003).

11 Allan Greer and Ian Radforth, eds., *Colonial Leviathan: State Formation in Nineteenth-Century Canada* (Toronto: University of Toronto Press 1992); Allan Greer, *The Patriots and the People: The Rebellion of 1837 in Rural Lower Canada* (Toronto: University of Toronto Press 1993); Fecteau, *Nouvel ordre* and *La liberté du pauvre: sur la régulation du crime et de la pauvreté au XIXe siècle québécois* (Montreal: VLB 2004), 89–139.

12 For example, Fecteau, *Liberté*, or Bruce Curtis, *The Politics of Population: State Formation, Statistics, and the Census of Canada, 1840–1875* (Toronto: University of Toronto Press 2000). On bureaucracy: Gilles Paquet and Jean-Pierre Wallot, *Patronage et pouvoir dans le Bas-Canada (1794–1812)* (Montreal: Presses de l'Université du Québec 1973), and Gérald Bernier and Daniel Salée, *Entre l'ordre et la liberté: Colonialisme, pouvoir et transition vers le capitalisme dans le Québec du XIXe siècle* (Montreal: Boréal 1995). For more nuanced views: Bruce Curtis, 'The Canada "Blue Books" and the Administrative Capacity of the Canadian State, 1822–67,' *Canadian Historical Review* 74, no.4 (1993): 535–65 and 'Comment dénombrer les serviteurs de l'État au Canada-Uni: essai méthodologique,' *Revue d'histoire de l'Amérique française* 46, no.4 (1993): 607–28. On the non-state character of the justices of the peace: Greer, *Patriots*, 96, and Phillip A. Buckner, *The Transition to Responsible Government: British Policy in British North America, 1815–1850* (Westport, Conn.: Greenwood Press 1985), 55–6. For more on *Canadiens* and British institutions, see Donald Fyson, 'The *Canadiens* and British Institutions of Local Governance in Quebec, from the Conquest to the Rebellions,' in Michael Gauvreau and Nancy Christie, eds., *Transatlantic Subjects: Ideas, Institutions, and Identities in Post-Revolutionary British North America* (Montreal: McGill-Queen's University Press, forthcoming).

13 John Brewer, *The Sinews of Power: War, Money and the English State, 1688–1783* (Cambridge, Mass.: Harvard University Press 1990) and 'The Eighteenth-Century British State: Contexts and Issues,' in Lawrence Stone, ed., *An Imperial State at War: Britain from 1689 to 1815* (New York:

Routledge 1994), 52–71; Michael J. Braddick, *State Formation in Early Modern England, c.1550–1700* (Cambridge: Cambridge University Press 2000), 11–27; David Eastwood, *Governing Rural England: Tradition and Transformation in Local Government, 1780–1840* (New York: Oxford University Press 1994), 2; David Philips, 'A"Weak" State? The English State, the Magistracy and the Reform of Policing in the 1830s,' *English Historical Review* 119, no.483 (2004): 873–91.

14 Donald Fyson, 'Les structures étatiques locales à Montréal au début du XIXe siècle,' *Les Cahiers d'histoire* 17, nos.1–2 (1997): 55–75 and 'La paroisse et l'administration étatique sous le Régime britannique (1764–1840),' in Serge Courville and Normand Séguin, eds., *Atlas historique du Québec: La paroisse* (Sainte-Foy, Que.: Presses de l'Université Laval 2001), 25–39.

15 E.P. Thompson, *Whigs and Hunters: The Origin of the Black Act* (Harmondsworth, U.K.: Penguin 1977); Douglas Hay, 'Property, Authority and the Criminal Law,' in Douglas Hay et al., *Albion's Fatal Tree: Crime and Society in Eighteenth-Century England* (Middlesex, U.K.: Penguin 1975), 17–63.

16 The term 'elites' is employed here to refer in a general sense to those groups in society who hold a disproportionate share of political, economic, and social power; the use of the plural reflects the plurality and relative lack of cohesiveness of these groups.

17 The literature is vast, running from classics such as François-Xavier Garneau, *Histoire du Canada depuis sa découverte jusqu'à nos jours* (Quebec: N. Aubin 1845–52), v.3, 295–350, and Lionel Groulx, *Lendemains de conquête* (Montreal: Action française 1920), through Michel Brunet, *Les Canadiens après la Conquête, 1759–1775: de la révolution canadienne à la révolution américaine* (Montreal: Fides 1969), and Gilles Bourque, *Question nationale et classes sociales au Québec, 1760–1840* (Montreal: Parti Pris 1970), to more recent work such as David T. Ruddel, *Québec City 1765–1832: The Evolution of a Colonial Town* (Ottawa: Canadian Museum of Civilization 1987). This view still pervades public discourse in Quebec.

18 Morel, 'Réception,' and Louis A. Knafla and Terry L. Chapman, 'Criminal Justice in Canada: A Comparative Study of the Maritimes and Lower Canada, 1760–1812,' *Osgoode Hall Law Journal* 21, no.2 (1983): 245–74. The Whiggish current is well represented by writers from Edmond Lareau, *Histoire du droit canadien depuis les origines de la colonie jusqu'a nos jours* (Montreal: A. Périard 1888–9), v.1, 307, to Neatby, *Administration*, 298–319.

19 Though there is an extensive literature on phenomenological approaches to the philosophy of history, there is little on applying phenomenological methods to the study of history, as in sociology, for example. Colling-

wood's often-cited notion of historical re-enactment applies more to action than experience (William H. Dray, *History as Re-enactment: R.G. Colling-wood's Idea of History* [New York: Oxford University Press 1995], 57, 109–14); empathetic reconstruction of historical experience is more often explicitly used in the teaching of history (for an overview, see Richard Harris and Lorraine Foreman-Peck, '"Stepping into Other Peoples' Shoes": Teaching and Assessing Empathy in the Secondary History Curriculum,' *International Journal of Historical Learning, Teaching and Research* 4, no.2 [2004]). For a detailed critique of empathy as a form of historical understanding, see Keith Jenkins, *Re-thinking History* (London: Routledge 1991), 47–58.

20 Philip Abrams, 'Notes on the Difficulty of Studying the State (1977),' *Journal of Historical Sociology* 1, no.1 (1988): 58–89.

21 Margaret McCallum, 'Canadian Legal History in the Late 1990s: A Field in Search of Fences?' *Acadiensis* 27, no.2 (1998): 153–4.

22 The main series of judicial records used for the district of Montreal were BAnQ-M TL32 S1 SS11 (Quarter Sessions registers, 1764–; henceforth QSR); TL32 S1 SS1 (Quarter Sessions documents, 1780–; henceforth QSD); TL36 S1 SS11 (Weekly Sessions registers, 1805 and 1829–); TL36 S1 SS1 (Weekly Sessions documents); TL19 S1 SS11 (King's Bench and Oyer and Terminer registers, 1802 and 1812–); and TL19 S1 SS11 (King's Bench and Oyer and Terminer documents, 1812–), to which must be added the Reid notebooks, detailed trial records kept by King's Bench judges between 1807 and 1837 (LAC MG24 B173). For the district of Quebec, the main series were BAnQ-Q TL31 S1 SS1 (Sessions documents, 1802–, as indexed in the *Thémis* 2 database by Archiv-Histo) and TL 18 S1 SS1 and TP 9 S1 SS1 SSS1 (King's Bench and Oyer and Terminer documents, 1765–; these also include Montreal King's Bench records up to 1794). For QSD cases, I used a sample of all cases in the eighteenth century and every five years in the nineteenth, giving approximately 2,900 cases in all; for QSR, all defendants, 1764–1830 and 1835, or about 5,400 in all; for the Weekly Sessions, about 2,600 defendants in all. For the district of Quebec, I used a ten-year sample of Sessions documents from 1805 to 1835, about 3,000 cases in all. For more on sampling and sources, see the methodological appendix in the companion website, currently at http://www.hst.ulaval.ca/profs/dfyson/CrimJust/ and also accessible via the University of Toronto Press website, http://www.utpress.utoronto.ca.

23 The registers are in BAnQ-M E17 S1 SS1 (1826–) and BAnQ-Q E17 (1813–) respectively; the latter have been entered into a database available on the BAnQ website, http://www.banq.qc.ca. The Montreal register can be

370 Notes to page 14

supplemented by the monthly gaol calendars, 1810–28, in LAC RG4 B21,
v.1–4; there are also scattered pre-1810 gaol calendars among the Quarter
Sessions and King's Bench documents. The Montreal Quarter Sessions
documents contain occasional House of Correction calendars; for Quebec
City, House of Correction committals were periodically recorded in the
gaol register (1818–22, 1829–36), and there is also one separate register
covering 1826–7 and 1829–30 (BAnQ-Q E17 1960–01–036/1688, no.318).

24 The Montreal Special Sessions registers (henceforth SSR) and documents
are in Archives de la Ville de Montréal, VM35 (Fonds des juges de paix
de Montréal), along with the documents of Montreal's first City Council
(1833–6), whose registers are in Archives de la Ville de Montréal, VM1
(Fonds du Conseil de ville de Montréal). The road treasurer's accounts are
scattered through several fonds: BAnQ-M P20 (Fonds Ville de Montréal),
P148 (Collection Charles Phillips), TL32 S1 SS11 (Quarter Sessions documents); and Rare Book Room, McGill University, MS469 (Montreal, Road
Committee) and MS719 (Montreal, Municipal Administration, John Reid
fonds).

25 The main series are LAC RG4 A1 (civil secretary's incoming correspondence, henceforth CS); LAC RG7 G15C and RG4 C2 (civil secretary's letter
books, henceforth CSL); LAC RG1 E15A (public accounts, henceforth RG1
E15A); National Archives (UK), CO42 (correspondence and documents
sent to the colonial authorities in England, henceforth CO42), and LAC
RG68 (commissions, henceforth RG68), to which must be added the
equivalent documents in the Haldimand papers, British Library Add.
Mss. 21661–889. I consulted most of these systematically up to 1830, and
selectively thereafter.

26 Notably about 900 justices, 1764–1837; about 600 bailiffs, constables, and
watchmen, 1764–1835; about 1,000 parish bailiffs, 1764–75; and about 1,400
grand jurors, 1764–1833. The prosopographical sources used to construct
these, apart from the sources listed above, include the *Dictionary of Canadian Biography*; the *Dictionnaire des parlementaires du Québec*; the various
databases produced by Robert Sweeney concerning Montreal's residents
in the 1820s; the *Thémis 1* and *Thémis 3* databases, indexing cases heard in
the superior civil terms of the Montreal Common Pleas and King's Bench
through 1827; the Programme de recherche en démographie historique's
Registre de population du Québec ancien (Quebec vital records to 1800); the
Parchemin database of Quebec notarial records up to 1783; the official
documents in the *Early Canadian Online* digital library; and the local histories in the *Our Roots* digital library; along with a wide range of other less
important prosopographical sources.

27 Fyson, 'Criminal Justice.' A brief summary of some of the findings was

published as Donald Fyson. 'The Biases of Ancien Régime Justice: The
People and the Justice of the Peace in the District of Montreal, 1785–1830,'
in Tamara Myers et al., eds., *Power, Place and Identity: Historical Studies of
Social and Legal Regulation in Quebec* (Montreal: Montreal History Group
1998), 11–35; some of the text of this article has been integrated into various parts of this book.

1: English Justice in a Foreign Land

1 Sir Henry Cavendish, *Debates of the House of Commons in the Year 1774, on
the Bill for Making More Effectual Provision for the Government of the Province
of Quebec* ... (London: Ridgway 1839): 126; BAnQ-M TL19 S1 SS11, 9/1826.
Throughout this book, direct quotations preserve the original spelling, but
capitalization has often been modernized.
2 Exceptions include C. Desaulniers, 'La peine de mort dans la législation
criminelle de 1760 à 1892,' *Revue générale de droit* 8, no.1 (1977): 142–6, and
Michel Morin, 'Portalis v. Bentham? The Objectives Ascribed to Codification of the Civil Law and the Criminal Law in France, England and
Canada,' in *Perspectives on Legislation: Essays from the 1999 Legal Dimensions
Initiative* (Ottawa: Law Commission of Canada 2000), 154–7; see also
Fecteau, *Nouvel ordre*, 89–95. For an overview of the legal and constitutional arguments, see J.E. Côté, 'The Reception of English Law,' *Alberta
Law Review* 15, no.1 (1977): especially 37–47, and F. Murray Greenwood
and Barry Wright, 'Introduction: State Trials, the Rule of Law, and Executive Powers in Early Canada,' in F. Murray Greenwood and Barry Wright,
eds., *Canadian State Trials. Volume I: Law, Politics, and Security Measures,
1608–1837* (Toronto: Osgoode Society / University of Toronto Press 1997),
11–23. On Cugnet: Sylvio Normand, 'François-Joseph Cugnet et la reconstitution du droit de la Nouvelle-France,' *Cahiers aixois d'histoire des droits
de l'outre-mer français* 1 (2002): 127–145.
3 Julius Goebel Jr and T. Raymond Naughton, *Law Enforcement in Colonial
New York: A Study in Criminal Procedure (1664–1776)* (Montclair, N.J.:
Patterson Smith 1970 [1944]), 384–413 and passim; Herbert A. Johnson,
'The Advent of Common Law in Colonial New York,'in Herbert A.
Johnson, *Essays on New York Colonial Legal History* (Westport, Conn.:
Greenwood Press 1981), 37–54; Dennis Sullivan, *The Punishment of Crime
in Colonial New York: The Dutch Experience in Albany during the Seventeenth
Century* (New York: Lang 1997), 207–36; Radhika Singha, *A Despotism of
Law: Crime and Justice in Early Colonial India* (Delhi: Oxford University
Press 1998), especially chapters 1–2.
4 Morel, 'Réception'; Douglas Hay, 'The Meanings of the Criminal Law in

Quebec, 1764–1774,' in Louis A. Knafla, ed., *Crime and Criminal Justice in Europe and Canada* (Waterloo, Ont.: Wilfrid Laurier University Press 1981), 77–110.

5 Morel, 'Réception'; Knafla and Chapman, 'Criminal Justice'; more nuanced versions are found in Hay, 'Meanings' and Fecteau, *Nouvel ordre*. See also Jim Phillips, 'Crime and Punishment in the Dominion of the North: Canada from New France to the Present,' in Emsley and Knafla, *Crime History and Histories of Crime*, 164–7.

6 See in particular Fecteau, *Nouvel ordre*, and, for a more nuanced version, *Liberté*, 92–9 and 129–31.

7 Cavendish, *Debates*, 117; *Loix criminelles suivies en Canada* (London: Charles Eyer and Wm. Strahan 1773); Normand, 'François-Joseph Cugnet.'

8 There are exceptions: Hay, for example, points out that the two systems may have been similar in practice, though he emphasizes their differing ideological significance ('Meanings'); and Fecteau notes Alfred Soman's argument for the similarity of English and French criminal justice, though also maintaining that what was imposed was a 'un cadre normatif étranger' (*Nouvel ordre*, 75, 77).

9 These were some of the fundamental texts on the criminal law in use in eighteenth-century England and France: William Blackstone, *Commentaries on the Laws of England* (Oxford: Clarendon Press 1765–9); Matthew Hale, *Historia placitorum coronæ: The History of the Pleas of the Crown* ... (London: F. Gyles 1736); Pierre-François Muyart de Vouglans, *Institutes au droit criminel* (Paris: Le Breton 1757) and *Les lois criminelles de France dans leur ordre naturel* (Paris: Merigot le jeune 1780); Daniel Jousse, *Traité de la justice criminelle de France* (Paris: Debure père 1771).

10 On New France between 1700 and 1759, see André Lachance, *La justice criminelle du roi au Canada au XVIIIe siècle: tribunaux et officiers* (Quebec: Presses de l'Université Laval 1978) and *Crimes et criminels en Nouvelle-France* (Montreal: Boréal Express 1984); Jean-François Leclerc, 'Justice et infra-justice en Nouvelle-France: les voies de fait à Montréal entre 1700 et 1760,' *Criminologie* 18, no.1 (1985): 25–39; Jean-Philippe Garneau, 'Justice et règlement des conflits dans le gouvernement de Montréal à la fin du Régime français' (MA, Université du Québec à Montréal 1995); and John Dickinson, 'Réflexions sur la police en Nouvelle-France,' *McGill Law Journal* 32, no.3 (1987): 497–512. For the British régime, see chapter 5.

11 Lachance, *Crimes et criminels*, 34; *Loix criminelles suivies en Canada*, 162; Joseph-François Perrault, *Questions et réponses sur le droit criminel du Bas-Canada* ... (Quebec: C. Le François 1814), 187–200.

12 For example, the Conquest brought little change in the treatment of

infanticides. See Marie-Aimée Cliche, 'L'infanticide dans la région de Québec (1660–1969),' *Revue d'histoire de l'Amérique française* 44, no.1 (1990): 31–59.

13 Morel, 'Réception,' 472–4; Fecteau, *Nouvel ordre*, 111–12, 233–4, and *Liberté*, 130; Greenwood, *Legacies of Fear*, 20–1; Morin, 'Portalis v. Bentham': 159.

14 See, for example, André-Jean Arnaud et al., *Dictionnaire encyclopédique de théorie et de sociologie du droit* (Paris: Librairie générale de droit et de jurisprudence 1993), 122–6.

15 Greenwood, *Legacies of Fear*, 87–92; Stephen Kenny, 'Cahots and Catcalls: An Episode of Popular Resistance in Lower Canada at the Outset of the Union,' *Canadian Historical Review* 65, no.2 (1984): 184–208.

16 Robert B. Shoemaker, *Prosecution and Punishment: Petty Crime and the Law in London and Rural Middlesex, c. 1660–1725* (Cambridge: Cambridge University Press 1991), 6; Sharpe, *Crime*, 5–7.

17 LAC RG1 E1, v.1, 146–59; Perrault, *Questions et réponses*, 15; Taschereau to Cochran, 8/1/1827, CS, v.247.

18 Seaman Morley Scott, 'Chapters in the History of the Law of Quebec 1764–1775' (PhD, University of Michigan 1933), 84–7; Côté, 'Reception': 77–9; instructions by Suckling, 3/9/1764, CS, v.11: 4360–3; James Marriott, *Plan of a Code of Laws for the Province of Quebec* (1774), in Adam Shortt and Arthur G. Doughty, eds., *Documents Relating to the Constitutional History of Canada, 1759–1791* (Ottawa: Historical Documents Publication Board 1918), 454. On the Poor Laws, see, for example, Eastwood, *Governing Rural England*, 99–165. The only parts of the Poor Laws applied in Quebec and Lower Canada were the bastardy and vagrancy laws, to which we will return.

19 Of about 750 laws passed between 1764 and 1836 (excluding about 150 which simply continued previous laws and another 200-odd which provided only appropriations), over 300 included penal clauses.

20 On forgery and coin-clipping, 4 George III, 'An Ordinance for Regulating and Establishing the Currency of the Province' (1764) and 17 George III c.9 (1777); on petty larceny, 29 George III c.3 (1789).

21 On toll-bridges and the like: 45 George III c.14 (1805) (the first such act); 48 George III c.33 (1808) (Lachine Turnpike); 2 William IV c.58 (1832) (Champlain and St Lawrence Railway); and 6 William IV c.18 (Montreal Gas Light Company). Several people were imprisoned in the Montreal gaol in the early 1830s for setting fire to toll-bridges. On army bills: 52 George III (2) c.1 (1812) and 54 George III c.3 (1814). On aliens: 34 George III c.5 (1794) 43, George III c.2 (1803), and 52 George III c.3 (1812). And on the chartered banks: 1 George IV c.25–27 (1820).

22 Forgery of bank notes, for example, was already arguably covered by

English statutes (Richard Burn, *The Justice of the Peace and Parish Officer* [London: W. Strahan and W. Woodfall 1776], II: 213), though the applicability of these to Lower Canada may have been in question.

23 Burn, *Justice*, III: 263; Blackstone, *Commentaries* IV: 137; Michael D. Gordon, 'The Invention of a Common Law Crime: Perjury and the Elizabethan Courts,' *American Journal of Legal History* 24, no.2 (1980): 145–70; James Oldham, *English Common Law in the Age of Mansfield* (Charlotte: University of North Carolina Press 2004), 268–75.

24 *JHALC* 38 (1828–9), appendix Ee, and 41 (1831–2), appendix A; Bingham to Yorke, 10/8/1830, CS, v.332.

25 Fecteau, *Liberté*, 377n.88; Montreal gaol calendar, c.7/1778, CS, v.23: 7654–7.

26 27 George III c.3 (1787).

27 These laws were passed in 1764 and 1777. In 1791 another law (31 George III c.1) removed most of the restrictions.

28 Compare Luc Lépine, 'La milice du district de Montréal, 1787–1829: essai d'histoire socio-militaire' (PhD, Université du Québec à Montréal 2005), and J.R. Western, *The English Militia in the Eighteenth Century: The Story of a Political Issue* (London: Routledge and Kegan Paul 1965).

29 Pilarczyk, 'The Law of Servants' and '"Too Well Used by His Master": Judicial Enforcement of Servants' Rights in Montreal, 1830–1845,' *McGill Law Journal* 46, no.2 (2000): 491–529; Gillian Hamilton, 'Enforcement in Apprenticeship Contracts: Were Runaways a Serious Problem? Evidence from Montreal,' *Journal of Economic History* 55, no.3 (1995): 551–74; Jean-Pierre Hardy and Thierry Ruddel, *Les apprentis artisans à Québec, 1660–1815* (Montreal: Presses de l'Université du Québec 1977), 169–82; Paul Craven, 'Canada, 1670–1935: Symbolic and Instrumental Enforcement in Loyalist North America,' in Douglas Hay and Paul Craven, eds., *Masters, Servants, and Magistrates in Britain and the Empire, 1562–1955* (Chapel Hill: University of North Carolina Press 2004), 185–92; Carolyn Podruchny, 'Unfair Masters and Rascally Servants? Labour Relations among Bourgeois, Clerks and Voyageurs in the Montreal Fur Trade, 1780–1821,' *Labour / Le travail* 43 (1999): 43–70.

30 Yvon Desloges, 'La corvée militaire à Québec au XVIIIe siècle,' *Histoire sociale / Social History* 15, no.30 (1982): 333–56.

31 François-Joseph Cugnet, *Extraits des edits, declarations, ordonnances et reglemens de Sa Majesté très chrétienne: des reglemens et jugemens des gouverneurs generaux et intendans concernans la justice, et des reglemens et ordonnances de police rendues par les intendans ...* (Quebec: Chez Guillaume Brown 1775), 89–106 and *Traité de la police: qui a toujours été suivie en Canada ...* (Quebec: Guillaume Brown 1775).

32 Thomas Skyrme, *History of the Justices of the Peace* (Chichester: Barry Rose

1991), 2: 59–62; William Edward Nelson, *Americanization of the Common Law: The Impact of Legal Change on Massachusetts Society, 1760–1830* (Cambridge. Mass.: Harvard University Press 1975), 14–15; Ronald Kingman Snell, 'The County Magistracy in Eighteenth Century Massachusetts, 1692–1750' (PhD, Princeton University 1971), 186–7; Goebel and Naughton, *Law Enforcement*, 36–42.

33 *Quebec Gazette*, 16/5/1765; QSR, 13/10/1765 and 10/4/1766; order by Montreal justices, 10/4/1766, CS, v.15: 5762.

34 Dickinson, 'Réflexions sur la police.'

35 17 George III c.15 (1777); Jackson to Lords of Trade, 2/8/1777, CO42, v.8, ff.154–6. Emphasis in original.

36 LAC RG1 E1, v.E, 26/4/1787.

37 31 George III c.3 (1791). The ordinance was unclear on the status of Trois-Rivières, but it was drafted partly in response to a 1790 petition from that town for such powers (CS, v.48: 15952–3 and 16196–207).

38 42 George III c.8 (1802); Fawkener to Sullivan, 17/5/1803, CO42, v.123, ff.113–14; report of Sewell, 22/6/1804, CS, v.84: 26099–101.

39 *JHALC* 19 (1811), 490–2; 51 George III c.13 (1811); 57 George III c.16 (1817); 58 George III c.16 (1818); 4 George IV c.2 (1824); 10 and 11 George IV c.37 (1830).

40 *Parliamentary Register of Lower-Canada*, 6–10.

41 Fletcher to Wilson, 8/6/1816, CS, v.154.

42 42 George III c.11 (1802); 6 William IV c.27 (1836); Pilarczyk, 'The Law of Servants,' 51–9.

43 After the first full sets of regulations in 1766 and 1777, the Montreal justices issued new full sets in 1783, 1786, 1789, 1797, 1800, 1803, 1810, 1817, and 1821. Almost all the regulations are available in QSR.

44 QSR, 20/4/1790 (L'Assomption), 18/11/1791 (William Henry), 19/7/1802 (Berthier), 30/4/1803 (L'Assomption once again), 30/4/1804 (Boucherville), 19/7/1805 (Laprairie), 30/10/1805 (Boucherville once again), 23/10/1806 (Saint-Denis), 19/1/1807 (Berthier), and 29/4/1809 (Terrebonne). Controversy erupted in Terrebonne over the regulations, with petitions for and against (BAnQ-M P1000 D1090; QSR, 1/1809).

45 *Quebec Gazette* 11/5/1780; *Rules and Regulations of Police for the City and Suburbs of Montreal* (Montreal: James Brown 1810); *Rules and Regulations of Police ...* (Quebec: John Neilson 1811); *Rules and Regulations of Police, for the City and Suburbs of Montreal* (Montreal: James Lane 1817); *Rules and Regulations of Police for the City and Suburbs of Montreal* (Montreal: W. Gray 1821). On civil law codification: Brian J. Young, *The Politics of Codification: The Lower Canadian Civil Code of 1866* (Montreal: Osgoode Society / McGill-Queen's University Press 1994).

46 Chisholme to Yorke, 5/6/1830, CS, v.325.
47 On posters: Patricia Lockhart Fleming and Sandra Alston, *Early Canadian Printing: A Supplement to Marie Tremaine's A Bibliography of Canadian Imprints, 1751–1800* (Toronto: University of Toronto Press 1999), appendices A and B. On criers: the various accounts of the Montreal criers scattered through RG1 E15A and the road treasurer's accounts.
48 QSR, 20/7/1779, 17/11/1789; *Quebec Gazette* 11/5/1780, 14/11/1782, 22/5/1783, 28/8/1783, 20/5/1784.
49 QSR, 30/4/1803.
50 QSR, 30/4/1799, 30/4/1803, 19/7/1806, 30/4/1817, 19/1/1821; René Hardy, 'Le charivari dans l'espace québécois,' in Serge Courville and Normand Séguin, eds., *Espace et culture / Space and culture* (Sainte-Foy, Que.: Presses de l'Université Laval 1995), 176–7.
51 Fecteau, *Liberté*, and Dufresne, 'Justice pénale,' both place the change at about the late 1820s or early 1830s.
52 Robert B. Shoemaker, 'Reforming the City: The Reformation of Manners Campaign in London, 1690–1738,' in Lee Davison et al., *Stilling the Grumbling Hive: The Response to Social and Economic Problems in England, 1689–1750* (New York: St Martin's Press 1992), 99–120; David H. Flaherty, 'Law and the Enforcement of Morals in Early America,' *Perspectives in American History* 5 (1971): 203–53; Dickinson, 'Réflexions sur la police': 502.
53 On the English vagrancy laws: Nicholas Rogers, 'Policing the Poor in Eighteenth-Century London: The Vagrancy Laws and their Administration,' *Histoire sociale / Social History* 24, no.47 (1991): 127–47, and Bruce Philip Smith, 'Circumventing the Jury: Petty Crime and Summary Jurisdiction in London and New York City, 1790–1855' (PhD, Yale University 1996), 271–87. On the applicability of the vagrancy laws in Quebec and Lower Canada: Fecteau, *Nouvel ordre*, 250n.214, and Jacques Crémazie, *Les lois criminelles anglaises* ... (Quebec: Fréchette 1842), 61. For the begging regulations: QSR, 10/4/1769; RG1 E15A, v.5, file 'Judicial Establishment 1779,' account of Jacob Kuhn for publishing an order of the justices 'que les pauvres mendiants ne queste plus sans permission'; Fecteau, *Nouvel ordre*, 43. On New France: Dickinson, 'Réflexions sur la police,' 511. For a further discussion of vagrancy in Montreal: Mary Anne Poutanen, 'Regulating Public Space in Early Nineteenth-Century Montreal: Vagrancy Laws and Gender in a Colonial Context,' *Histoire sociale / Social History* 35, no.69 (2002): 35–58.
54 Quebec City justices to Murray, 2/4/1766, CS, v.15: 5748, and to Hamilton, 7/12/1784, CS, v.27: 8912–13; Boncy et al. to Quebec City justices, 18/12/1784, CS, v.27: 8934–5; LAC RG1 E1, 5/4/1766 and 23/12/1784; Hill to

Quebec City justices, 8/7/1783, BAnQ-Q TL18 S1 SS1; Quebec King's
Bench grand jury presentment, 14/5/1789, CS, v.42: 13882–8, and report
of Executive Council thereon, 4/2/1790, CS, v.44: 14660–79; petition of
Quebec City justices, 15/12/1795, *JHALC* 4 (1795–6), 33–41.
55 On houses of correction: 39 Geo III c.6 (1799); 42 George III c.6 (1802);
JHALC 7 (1799), 126, and 13 (1805), 444–60; Fecteau, *Nouvel ordre*, 119–23.
The begging regulations for Montreal are in QSR 19/7/1802, QSD 17/1/
1812, and QSR 30/4/1817. On begging regulations in Quebec City:
Fecteau, *Nouvel ordre*, 43, and Antonio Drolet, *La Ville de Québec: histoire
municipale. Volume II: Régime anglais jusqu'à l'incorporation (1759–1833)*
(Quebec: Société historique de Québec 1965), 42–3. On enforcement:
Joseph Sansom, *Sketches of Lower Canada, Historical and Descriptive* (New
York: Kirk and Mercein 1817), 58, 110–1.
56 QSR, 19/1/1819, 19/1/1821, 30/4/1822; SSR, 25/6/1819, 19/1/1821;
petition of Montreal residents, 19/11/1835, Archives de la Ville de
Montréal, VM35, dossier 64, 1835–1; Poutanen, 'Regulating Public Space':
42–54; Fecteau, *Nouvel ordre*, 189–98. In Quebec City, with no House of
Industry before 1836, licensing provisions continued through the 1820s.
57 There has as yet been no systematic study of the Quebec City regulations.
Complete sets of regulations include *Quebec Gazette*, 11/5/1780, 14/11/
1782, 28/8/1783, 20/5/1784; *Rules and Regulations of Police, with Abstracts of
Divers Ordinances and Statutes Relating Thereto* (Quebec: John Neilson 1811);
Regulations of Police (Quebec, 1815), CS, v.145, file 13–19/6/1815; Thomas
Henri Gleason, *The Quebec Directory for 1822* (Quebec, Neilson and Cowan
1822), 106–22; John Smith, *The Quebec Directory, or, Strangers' Guide in the
City for 1826* (Quebec: T. Cary 1826), 61–94. On the regulation punishing
drunkenness: Dufresne, 'Justice pénale,' 81–2.
58 For example, Hay, 'Meanings,' 81–2, passim; Knafla and Chapman,
'Criminal Justice,' 272; or Fecteau, *Nouvel ordre*, 102–7.
59 For overviews of the system of justices in England: Norma Landau, *The
Justices of the Peace, 1679–1760* (Berkeley: University of California Press
1984); Skyrme, *Justices of the Peace*, especially 2: 1–163; and Eastwood,
Governing Rural England, 43–95. On the justices in colonial settings: A.G.
Roeber, *Faithful Magistrates and Republican Lawyers: Creators of Virginian
Legal Culture, 1680–1810* (Chapel Hill: University of North Carolina Press
1981); Goebel and Naughton, *Law Enforcement*, 42–55, 91–137; and Susan
Dawson Lewthwaite, 'Law and Authority in Upper Canada: The Justices
of the Peace in the Newcastle District, 1803–1840' (PhD, University of
Toronto 2001).
60 Goebel and Naughton, *Law Enforcement*, 46–55; Snell, 'County Magistracy,'

47–8, 60–1; Sandra E. Oxner, 'The Evolution of the Lower Court of Nova Scotia,' in Peter Waite, Sandra Oxner, and Thomas Barnes, eds., *Law in a Colonial Society: The Nova Scotia Experience* (Toronto: Carswell 1984), 61, 63–4. On the civil jurisdiction of the Quebec justices: Donald Fyson with the assistance of Evelyn Kolish and Virginia Schweitzer, *The Court Structure of Quebec and Lower Canada, 1764 to 1860* (Montreal: Montreal History Group 1994/1997; http://www.hst.ulaval.ca/profs/dfyson/courtstr/). On New France: Lachance, *Justice criminelle*, 17–20, and Dickinson, 'Réflexions sur la police.'

61 CS, v.11: 4360–3; Joseph-François Perrault, *Le juge à paix et officier de paroisse, pour la province de Québec* (Montreal: Fleury Mesplet 1789), vi, passim.

62 Greenwood, *Legacies of Fear*, 117, and 34 George III c.5 (1794), 37 George III c.6 (1797), 43 George III (4) c.2 (1803), and 51 George III c.3 (1811). Other examples include 35 George III c.1 (1795) (arrests) and 57 George III c.16 (1817) (summons in master/servant cases).

63 See, for example, *Four Bills, from the Legislative Council, to Consolidate, Amend or Repeal the Laws regarding the Administration of Criminal Justice in Lower Canada* (Quebec, 1829); after failing in the Assembly, these measures were also reintroduced and failed in 1830 and 1831. On the general political climate blocking legislative reform of the criminal justice system, see Fecteau, *Nouvel ordre*, 142–5.

64 The first justices' commissions for the three new districts were 24/7/1788 (Gaspé), 6/7/1790 (Trois-Rivières), and 19/11/1823 (Saint Francis). RG68, Quebec v.3 and Lower Canada v.7.

65 See, for example, 47 George III c.14 (1807) and 57 George III c.14 (1817).

66 *Stanstead British Colonist*, 22/1/1824; 4 George IV c.19 (1824).

67 Landau, *Justices*, 38–43, 240–65; J.H. Aitchison, 'The Development of Local Government in Upper Canada, 1783–1850' (PhD, University of Toronto 1953), 1–14.

68 *JHALC* 28 (1819), 143–5; *JHALC* 33 (1824): appendices Qq and Tt; Montreal King's Bench grand jury presentment, 10/9/1827, CS, v.255; residents of William Henry and Dorchester to Kempt, 26/1/1830, CS, v.309, and 29/1/1830, CS, v.255, file 10–17/9/1827; Dalhousie to Bathurst, 27/5/1827, CO42, v.212, ff.226–9; Kempt to Hay, 30/11/1829, CO42, v.224, ff.316–21; *Bill to Render the Administration of Justice More Easy and Less Expensive to the Inhabitants of the Country Parts ...* (Quebec, 1824); Michel Bibaud, *Histoire du Canada* (Montreal: Lovell et Gibson 1837–78), 281–2; Samuel Hull Wilcocke, *The History of the Session of the Provincial Parliament of Lower Canada for 1828–29* (Montreal, 1829), 110, 137–42; 3 George IV c.17 (1823); 2 William

IV c.66 (1832); William Kennedy and Adam Thom, 'General Report of the Assistant Commissioners of Municipal Inquiry,' in Earl of Durham, *Report on the Affairs of British North America* (London, 1839), appendix C, 13, 17, 18; Fecteau, *Nouvel ordre*, 241.

69 Landau, *Justices*, 209–39.

70 Skyrme, *Justices of the Peace*, 2: 41–5; Eastwood, *Governing Rural England*, 43–95; Roeber, *Faithful Magistrates*.

71 Landau, *Justices*, 23–38, 173–239; Peter King, *Crime, Justice, and Discretion in England 1740–1820* (Oxford: Oxford University Press 2000), 82–128, and 'Summary Courts;' Hay, 'Legislation.'

72 There are occasional traces in RG1 E15A, QSD, QSR, and *JHALC*.

73 RG1 E15A, v.13, file 'Committee on Revenue 1793.'

74 'Rapport de la visite des chemins et ponts de la partie du sud district de Montréal avec les noms des inspecteurs et sousvoyers des differentes paroisses pour l'année 1804–5–6,' QSD 4/1805; Lacroix v. Faribault and Leroux (certiorari), BAnQ-M TL19 S4 SS1 1814 #352; *JHALC* 41 (1831–2), appendix Rr, and 42 (1832–3), appendix Hh.

75 J.M. Beattie, *Crime and the Courts in England, 1660–1800* (Princeton, N.J.: Princeton University Press 1986), 65–7; Ruth Paley, '"An Imperfect, Inadequate and Wretched System"? Policing London Before Peel,' *Criminal Justice History* 10 (1989): 98–102, 105–11; Leon Radzinowicz, *A History of English Criminal Law and Its Administration from 1750* (New York: Macmillan 1948–91), 2: 187–94, and 3: 29–62 and 108–37; Skyrme, *Justices of the Peace*, II:135–48; Richard S. Tompson, 'The Justices of the Peace and the United Kingdom in the Age of Reform,' *Journal of Legal History* 7, no.3 (1986): 276–81; Stanley H. Palmer, *Police and Protest in England and Ireland, 1780–1850* (Cambridge: Cambridge University Press 1988), 99–100; Smith, 'Circumventing the Jury,' 65–72.

76 *Quebec Gazette*, 14/4/1768.

77 CS, v.15: 5712–19; W.P.M. Kennedy and Gustave Lanctot, *Reports on the Laws of Quebec, 1767–1770* (Ottawa: F.A. Acland 1931), 69–70. An exception was the brief appointment of Captain John Schlosser as a salaried justice at Lac-des-Deux-Montagnes in 1767, to prevent the sale of liquor to Kanesatake Natives (LAC RG1 E15A, v.2, file 'Receiver General 1768').

78 Sewell to Jonathan Sewell, 18/9/1794, LAC MG23 GII10, v.3: 875–7; Monk to Dorchester, 18/6/1794, CO42, v.100, ff.52–3; Coffin to Monk, 9/4/1795, CSL; Greenwood, *Legacies of Fear*, 80–3, 106–7.

79 Sewell to Jonathan Sewell, 8/10/1794, LAC MG23 GII10, v.3: 879–82; Coffin to McCord, 20/11/1794, and Coffin to Monk, 9/4/1795, CSL; Coffin to McCord, 20/4/1795; Richardson to Sewell, 3/11/1796, LAC MG23

GII10, v.3: 1010–11; RG1 E15A, v.14, file 'Judicial Establishment 1795' (Police Office accounts). McCord was finally reimbursed the portion of his expenses incurred until November 1794. In Quebec City, Alexis (or P.-L.) Descheneaux received £50 in 1794 and £12/7 in 1795 on account of his salary as 'police magistrate at Quebec,' although his duties and the period covered are unclear (*JHALC* 3 [1795], 83–8, and 4 [1795–6], 147–55). On the constables, see chapter 4. On the 1796 Roads Act riots, see Greenwood, *Legacies of Fear*, 89–92, and Léon Robichaud, 'Le pouvoir, les paysans et la voirie au Bas-Canada à la fin du XVIIIe siècle' (MA, McGill University 1989), 54–67.

80 Quebec King's Bench grand jury presentment, 30/9/1808, CS, v.100: 31640–2; Council minutes, 2/10/1809, CS, v.105: 33366–9; Mondelet to Craig, 12/2/1810, CS, v.107: 33869–72; McGill to Ryland, 19/3/1810, CS, v.107: 34077–8, and 29/3/1810, CS, v.108: 34203–6; Coffin to Brenton, 30/10/1811, CS, v.115: 36682–4; Ryland to Cuthbert, 9/10/1809, Ryland to Lane and Byrne, 3/5/1810, and Brenton to Coffin, 28/10/1811, CSL; Sewell to Prevost, 21/10/1811, and Prevost to Liverpool, 24/10/1811, CO42, v.143, ff.156–9; Ryland to Taylor, 25/1/1813, CS, v.127: 40689. Coffin's salary was initially £200 but was raised to £250 in 1817 (Coffin to Sherbrooke, 14/6/1817, and report of Council, 30/6/1817, CS, v.166).

81 Brenton to Coffin, 28/10/1811, CSL; *JHALC* 30 (1820–1), Appendix R, testimony of W.B. Coltman and A. Caron; Ross to Yorke, 18/6/1829, CS, v.289; Christie to Yorke, 27/6/1829, CS, v.290; Coffin to Yorke, 28/6/1829, CS, v.291. In the text, I use the term 'chairman' throughout.

82 McGill to Ryland, 29/3/1810, CS, v.107: 34203–6; Craig to Liverpool, 17/5/1810, CO42, v.141, ff.89–90; Landau, *Justices*, 100, 279–86; Eastwood, *Governing Rural England*, 55–61; Aitchison, 'Local Government,' 98–102.

83 CS, v.103: 32774–6; Craig to Liverpool, 17/5/1810, CO42, v.141, ff.89–90.

84 CS, v.107: 34203–6, and v.108: 34203–6. On aliens: Greenwood, *Legacies of Fear*; Martin Pâquet, *Tracer les marges de la cité: étranger, immigrant et État au Québec, 1627–1981* (Montreal: Boréal 2005), 78–86.

85 Martin Dufresne, 'La police, le droit pénal et le crime dans la première moitié du XIXe siècle. L'exemple de la ville de Québec,' *Revue juridique Thémis* 34, no.2 (2000): 409–34.

86 McCord and Mondelet to Ryland, 24/5/1810, CS, v.109: 34561–3; Foy to McCord, 28/5/1810, CSL; McCord and Mondelet to Brenton, 25/6/1811 and 9/12/1811, RG1 E15A, v.23, file 'Quarter Sessions of the Peace 1811'; McCord and Mondelet to Prevost, 30/9/1811, CS, v.115: 36556–8; McCord and Mondelet to Cochran, 26/8/1815, CS, v.147; McCord and Mondelet to Dalhousie, 3/7/1820, RG1 E15A, v.37, file 'Quarter Sessions of the Peace

1820'; McCord to Cochran, 18/7/1821, RG1 E15A. v.40, file 'Quarter Sessions of the Peace 1821'; *JHALC* 32 (1823), 193; 34 (1825), 345; and 38 (1828–9), 560. The accounts of the Police Office are scattered through RG1 E15A.

87 On Quebec City: *Rules and Regulations of Police* ... (Quebec: John Neilson 1811), 3–4; *JHALC* 30 (1820–1), appendix R, testimony of Caron, and 39 (1830), appendix, testimony of William Green, 18/3/1830; Christie to Yorke, 27/6/1829, CS, v.290; Christie to Yorke, 23/1/1830, CS, v.309. On Trois-Rivières: Coffin to Brenton, 30/10/1811, CS, v.115: 36682–4; Fraser to Cochran, 1/8/1816, CS, v.155; Trois-Rivières justices to Cochran, 28/10/1822, CS, v.214; Chisholme to Cochran, 18/12/1827, CS, v.258; report of Council, 31/12/1827, CS, v.263, file 'Executive Council 4/1828'; Coffin to Dalhousie, 25/8/1828, with Dalhousie to Murray, 10/11/1828, CO42, v.216; Coffin to Yorke, 28/6/1829, CS, v.291.

88 Fletcher to Dalhousie, 20/4/1823, CS, v.218; Cochran to Fletcher, 2/6/1823, CSL; Mondelet and McCord to Dalhousie, 29/10/1823, CS, v.222; undated note by Dalhousie, at 8/11/1823, CS, v.222; Tremain to Coltman, 3/2/1824, CS, v.224; project of Fletcher, 9/2/1824, CS, v.224; Mondelet and McCord to Cochran, 2/4/1824, CS, v.226.

89 Christie to Cochran, 2/11/1827, CS, v.257; Chisholme to Cochran, 18/12/1827, CS, v.258; Badeaux to Dalhousie, 25/4/1828, CS, v.263; Cochran to D'Estimauville, 5/11/1827, and Yorke to Badeaux, 17/11/1828, CSL.

90 McCord and Mondelet to Prevost, 15/11/1814, CS, v.139: 44451–4; Executive Council report, 30/3/1815, CS, v.143, file 'Executive Council 4/1815'; Drummond to Bathurst, 27/6/1815, CO42, v.162, ff.150–65; Mondelet and McCord to Cochran, 28/12/1816, CS, v.158; *Bill: An Act for the More Effectual Administration of the Office of a Justice of the Peace* ... (Quebec, 1817); *JHALC* 26 (1817): 340–2 and *passim*; McCord to Ready, 4/2/1819, CS, v.184.

91 *Montreal Herald*, 19/11/1814; McCord to Ready, 4/2/1819, CS, v.184.

92 *JHALC* 38 (1828–9), 36, 518–19, and appendices Dd and Ee; *La Minerve*, 25/10/1830; Kempt to Murray, 10/12/1829 and 28/4/1830, CO42, v.225, ff.11–16, and v.229, ff.176–86; Coffin to Yorke, 20/3/1830, CS, v.315; Christie to Yorke, 26/4/1830, CS, v.320; Coffin to Glegg, 19/11/1830, CS, v.343. Mangin and Delaveau were notorious Paris police prefects in the 1820s.

93 Kennedy and Thom, 'General Report,' 17; Walcott to mayors of Montreal and Quebec City, 6/4/1836, CSL. After disappearing in October 1830, professional police magistrates were reappointed for the district of Montreal in November 1837 (Pierre-Édouard Leclère) and for Quebec City in December 1837 (Thomas Ainslie Young). Walcott to Leclère, 11/11/1837, CSL; *Journals of the Special Council of Lower Canada* 2 (1838), appendix

(2); Earl of Durham, *Report on the Affairs of British North America* (London, 1839), 41; RG68, Lower Canada, v.15: 233; Elinor Kyte Senior, *British Regulars in Montreal: An Imperial Garrison, 1832–1854* (Montreal: McGill-Queen's University Press 1981), 26; Allan Greer, 'The Birth of the Police in Canada,' in Greer and Radforth, *Colonial Leviathan*, 17–49.

94 Saint-George Dupré to Kempt, 31/3/1830, CS, v.316; on continuity in other personnel, see chapter 4.
95 *JHALC* 45 (1835–6), 285–6; *La Minerve* 11/9/1834; testimony of Freeman and Delisle with Arnoldi to Gosford, 26/9/1836, CS, v.492. For examples of the continuing use of the term 'Police Office' or 'Bureau de Police,' see the minutes of evidence regarding the Montreal election riots of 1832, *JHALC* 42 (1832–3) and 43 (1834), or, on Quebec City, *JHALC* 45 (1835–6), 286 and appendix EEE, 1/3/1836.
96 See, for example, 'René Gaschet' and 'Pierre Dizy de Montplaisir,' *DCB* 3.
97 Oxner, 'The Evolution,' 70–2; Edith G. Firth, *The Town of York, 1815–1834: A Further Collection of Documents of Early Toronto* (Toronto: Champlain Society 1966), 272–3; T.W. Acheson, *Saint John: The Making of a Colonial Urban Community* (Toronto: University of Toronto Press 1985), 216.

2: Making Justices

1 Murray to Lords of Trade, 3/3/1765, CO42, v.2, f.132; Antrobus to Foy, 26/4/1811, CS, v.113: 35887–9; *JHALC* 38 (1828–9), appendix Dd, 6/2/1829.
2 For example, Garneau, *Histoire du Canada*, 3: 310 and 4: 193, 215; Théophile-Pierre Bédard, *Histoire de cinquante ans (1791–1841): annales parlementaires et politiques du Bas-Canada depuis la Constitution jusqu'à l'Union* (Quebec: Léger Brousseau 1869), 281–83; or Thomas Chapais, *Cours d'histoire du Canada* (Quebec: Librairie Garneau 1919–34), 3: 226–7.
3 Landau, *Justices*, 69–169; Skyrme, *Justices of the Peace*, 2: 12–23, 170–1; Paul Langford, *Public Life and the Propertied Englishman, 1689–1798* (Oxford: Oxford University Press 1991), 390–7; Elizabeth K. Carmichael, 'Jacobitism in the Scottish Commission of the Peace, 1707–1760,' *Scottish Historical Review* 58, no.1 (1979): 58–69; Erwin C. Surrency, 'The Courts in the American Colonies,' *American Journal of Legal History* 11, no.3 (1967): 253–76, and 11, no. (1967): 348.
4 See especially Landau, *Justices*, and Eastwood, *Governing Rural England*.
5 The commissions are scattered through RG68; most were also published in the newspapers, notably the *Quebec Gazette*. On England and Ireland: Landau, *Justices*, 140; Ian Bridgeman, 'The Constabulary and the Criminal

Justice System in Nineteenth-Century Ireland,' *Criminal Justice History* 15 (1994): 99–100.

6 *Montreal Gazette,* 18/10/1830, 25/10/1830; *La Minerve,* 18/10/1830, 21/10/1830, 22/7/1833.

7 The commissions of association are also in RG68; the easiest access is through the general index. On the 1830 law, see below.

8 Ready to Sewell, 10/7/1820, CSL.

9 J.I. Little, *State and Society in Transition: The Politics of Institutional Reform in the Eastern Townships, 1838–1852* (Montreal: McGill-Queen's University Press 1997), 59–60.

10 On England: calculated from Landau, *Justices,* appendix A, using county population figures for England back-derived from the figures for 1801 and 1811 (B.R. Mitchell et al., *British Historical Statistics* [Cambridge: Cambridge University Press 1988], 7–9). On Scotland: Ann E. Whetstone, *Scottish County Government in the Eighteenth and Nineteenth Centuries* (Edinburgh: J. Donald 1981), 39. On Upper Canada: Lewthwaite, 'Law and Authority,' 25. On Ireland: Palmer, *Police and Protest,* 60.

11 See notably Serge Courville, Jean-Claude Robert, and Normand Séguin, *Atlas historique du Québec. Le pays laurentien au XIXe siècle: Les morphologies de base* (Sainte-Foy, Que.: Presses de l'Université Laval 1995), 7–25.

12 Committee minutes, 3/2/1794, CS, v.57: 18660–2; petition to Milnes, 6/3/1805, CS, v.85: 26577–94; Milnes to Camden, 1/8/1805, CO42, v.128; lists of magistrates, 11/9/1820, CS, v.195, c.10/1826, CS, v.244, and c.10/1830, CS, v.340; Jobson to Yorke, 31/8/1829, CS, v.296.

13 Committee report, 11/7/1788, CS, v.39: 12947–51; committee minutes, 18/2/1794, CS, v.57: 18675.

14 Huot to Marshall, 14/3/1820, CS, v.192.

15 On the 1765 commissions: Murray to Lords of Trade, 3/3/1765, CO42, v.2, ff.132–94; Murray to Lords of Trade, 24/6/1765, CO42, v.2, ff.235–8; LAC RG1 E1, 27/6/1765. On the Walker's Ear incident: 'Thomas Walker,' *DCB* 4, and Hilda Neatby, *Quebec: The Revolutionary Age, 1760–1791* (Toronto: McClelland and Stewart 1966), 38–40. On the 1796 commission: Prescott to Portland, 24/10/1796, CO42, v.108, ff.9–11; Sewell to Prescott, 28/10/1796, LAC MG23 GII10, v.10; Greenwood, *Legacies of Fear,* 91. On the 1828 commission: *JHALC* 38 (1828–9), appendices Dd and Ee; *The Seventh Report from the Select Committee of the House of Assembly of Upper Canada on Grievances ...* (Toronto, 1835), 87; *Report from the Select Committee on the Civil Government of Canada* (Quebec, 1829).

16 Shortt and Doughty, *Documents,* 188, 308, 602, 822; Arthur G. Doughty and Duncan A. McArthur, eds., *Documents Relating to the Constitutional History*

384   Notes to pages 61–4

of Canada, 1791–1818 (Ottawa: Public Archives 1914), 20; *Papers relating to Lower Canada viz. 1. Copy of the Instructions Given to the Earl of Gosford ...* (London: HMSO 1838), 7; Murray to Lords of Trade, 3/3/1765, CO42, v.2, f.135, and 24/6/1765, CO42, v.2, ff.235–8; Conway to Murray, 27/3/1766, CO42, v.26, ff.9–12; David Milobar, 'The Origins of British-Quebec Merchant Ideology: New France, the British Atlantic and the Constitutional Periphery, 1720–70,' *Journal of Imperial and Commonwealth History* 24, no.3 (1996): 378–80; *JHALC* 38 (1828–9), appendix Dd, 12/1/1829; Walcott to Morin, 25/6/1836, CSL; *Quebec Gazette* (by authority), 3/8, 10/8, 24/8, 30/8, 21/9, 26/10, and 9/11/1837; LAC RG1 E1, 19–20/10 and 11/11/1837, v.M: 386, 392–3, 403; Gosford to Glenelg, 9/9 and 22/11/1837, in *Copies or Extracts of Correspondence relative to the Affairs of Lower Canada* [23/12/1837] (London: HMSO 1837), 49, 108 (further correspondence on the dismissals is scattered through CSL between June and October); Greer, *Patriots*, 219–20; Jean-Marie Fecteau, 'Mesures d'exception et règle de droit: Les conditions d'application de la loi martiale au Québec lors des rébellions de 1837–1838,' *McGill Law Journal* 32, no.3 (1987): 478n.39.

17 Shortt and Doughty, *Documents*: 188; LAC RG1 E1, 29/8/1764, 28/12/1764.

18 Minutes of Council, 30/6/1788, CS, v.39: 12889, and 22/1/1794, CS, v.57: 18567.

19 Montreal Quarter Sessions grand jury presentment, 1/1765, CS, v.12: 4541–6; Lynd to Finlay, 15/12/1784, CS, v.27: 8928–9; petitions from Trois-Rivières, 8/2/1788, CS, v.36: 11875–6, and 11/3/1789, CS, v.42: 13742–4; Donald Fyson, 'Jurys, participation civique et représentation au Québec et au Bas-Canada: les grands jurys du district de Montréal (1764–1832),' *Revue d'histoire de l'Amérique française* 55, no.1 (2001): 85–120; J.K. Johnson, *Becoming Prominent: Regional Leadership in Upper Canada, 1791–1841* (Montreal: McGill-Queen's University Press 1989), 83–7.

20 Gale to Monk, 4/4/1799, Gale to Monk et al., 4/6/1799, and Ryland to Dechenaux, 16/11/1801, CSL; Sewell to Ryland, 23/8/1797, CS, v.65: 20965–6; report of Council, 2/7/1813, CS, v.129: 41465; Gale to Montizambert, 5/4/1825, CS, v.233.

21 Johnson to Ryland, 9/6/1805, CS, v.87: 26948–9; Ryland to Robertson, 29/12/1800, CSL; Robertson to Ryland, 4/6/1809, CS, v.104: 32920; *JHALC* 38 (1828–9), appendix Dd, testimony of A.W. Cochran, 7/1/1829; Papineau to Montizambert, 27/10/1824, CS, v.230.

22 Johnson, *Becoming Prominent*, 83–97.

23 Poulin to Monk, 24/11/1819, CS, v.189; De Léry to Ready, 10/5/1822, CS, v.209; Cuthbert to Marshall, 9/11/1820, CS, v.196.

24 List of recommendations (dated 18/6/1829 but actually later), CS, v.289.

On Upper Canada: Aitchison, 'Local Government,' 33–53; Lewthwaite, 'Law and Authority,' 15–23; Frances Ann Thompson, 'Local Authority and District Autonomy: The Niagara Magistracy and Constabulatory, 1828–1841' (PhD, University of Ottawa 1996), 61–71. On local civil courts in Quebec and Lower Canada: Fyson, *Court Structure* and 'Paroisse,' 34–5, and Little, *State and Society in Transition*, 52. On the context of petitioning in Lower Canada: Steven Watt, 'Duty Bound and Ever Praying': Collective Petitioning to Governors and Legislatures in Selected Regions of Maine and Lower Canada, 1820–1838' (PhD, Université du Québec à Montréal 2006).

25 Saint-Vallier residents to Quebec judges, 6/9/1813, CS, v.130: 41732–4; Varennes residents to Prevost, 29/2/1812, CS, v.117: 37573–4.
26 Fyson, 'Jurys' and '*Canadiens* and British Institutions'; Watt, 'Duty Bound.'
27 *JHALC* 38 (1828–9), 34–7.
28 Saint-Mathias residents to Monk, 25/10/1819, CS, v.189; Noyan residents to Monk, 15/1/1820, CS, v.191.
29 Residents of Saint-George to Kempt, 15/12/1829 and 26/12/1829, CS, v.304.
30 Saint-Césaire residents to Kempt, 14/10/1828, CS, v.270; Chaffers v. Bouthillier, BAnQ-M TL19 S4 SS1 1828 #1736; pardon petition, 3/9/1829, and judge's report, 12/9/1829, LAC RG4 B20, v.14: 5192–201.
31 Michel Monette, 'Groupes dominants et structure locale du pouvoir à Deschambault et Saint-Casimir, Comté de Portneuf (1829–1870),' *Cahiers de géographie du Québec* 28, nos.73–4 (1984): 73–88; Christian Dessureault and Christine Hudon, 'Conflits sociaux et élites locales au Bas-Canada: le clergé, les notables, la paysannerie et le contrôle de la fabrique,' *Canadian Historical Review* 80, no.3 (1999): 413–39; Jean-René Thuot, 'Élites locales, institutions et fonctions publiques dans la paroisse de Saint-Roch-de-l'Achigan, de 1810 à 1840,' *Revue d'histoire de l'Amérique française* 57, no.2 (2003): 173–208; Christian Dessureault, 'L'élection de 1830 dans le comté de Saint-Hyacinthe: identites elitaires et solidarités paroissiales, sociales ou familiales,' *Histoire sociale / Social History* 36, no.72 (2003): 281–310.
32 Residents of Baie Saint-Antoine and Baie du Fèvre to Sherbrooke, 22/12/1817, CS, v.171; of Williamstown to Kempt, 8/9/1829, CS, v.297; of Longueuil etc. to Dalhousie, 28/6/1828, CS, v.267.
33 Richard Chabot, *Le curé de campagne et la contestation locale au Québec de 1791 aux troubles de 1837–38* (LaSalle, Que.: Hurtubise HMH 1975); Lewthwaite, 'Law and Authority,' 20–3.
34 'Luc Letellier de Saint-Just,' *DCB* 11.
35 Ross to Marshall, 18/1/1820, CS, v.191; Felton to Ready, 26/7/1821, CS, v.202; Eastwood, *Governing Rural England*, 21.

36 *Report from the Select Committee on the Civil Government of Canada*, 139; Aitchison, 'Local Government,' 78–81; Lewthwaite, 'Law and Authority,' 17–18.

37 Coffin to Loring, 15/6/1815, CS, v.145; Loring to Coffin, 19/6/1815, and Ready to Marshall, 20/9/1819, CSL; McCord and Mondelet to Ready, 3/11/1821, CS, v.204.

38 Reid to Ready, 3/9/1821, CS, v.204, file 'Executive Council 10/1821'; Ready to Mondelet, 1/10/1821, Cochran to Gale, 24/10/1825, and Cochran to Christie, 2/6/1827, CSL; *JHALC* 38 (1828–9), appendix Dd, 7/1/1829.

39 Yorke to Saint-Césaire petitioners, 18/10/1828, and Cochran to McCord and Mondelet, 21/9/1822, CSL; Mondelet to Cochran, 3/10/1822, CS, v.213.

40 *Quebec Gazette*, 16/3/1826, 5/1/1829; *JHALC* 38 (1828–9), appendices Dd and Ee; 'Robert Christie,' *DCB* 8; Helen Taft Manning, *The Revolt of French Canada 1800–1835: A Chapter in the History of the British Commonwealth* (Toronto: Macmillan 1962), 146, 294–5, 326–7; Robert Christie, *A History of the Late Province of Lower Canada, Parliamentary and Political …* (Quebec: T. Cary 1848–55), 3: 240–51, 266–7; *La Minerve*, 26/2/1829; Christie to Murray, 10/11/1829, CO42, v.227, ff.113–53; Coffin to Cochran, 24/3/1828, CS, v.261.

41 McKenzie to Yorke, 18/7/1829, CS, v.293; Jobson to Yorke, 31/8/1829, CS, v.296; Morison to Yorke, 17/9/1829, CS, v.298; Allsopp to Yorke, 18/8/1830, CS, v.333; Macrae to Yorke, 21/9/1830, CS, v.336; Kempt to Murray, 10/12/1829, CO42, v.225, ff.11–16, and 12/4/1830, CO42, v.229, ff.155–7; Glegg to Hatt, 4/12/1830, to Corneau and Dumais, 18/3/1831, and to Morin and Quirouet, 11/1/1832, CSL; LAC RG1 E1, report dated 9/10/1830, v.K: 86–7, and report dated 11/11/1837, v.M: 403; Debartzch to Viger, 16/5, 26/5, 16/6 and 23/12/1836, Musée de la civilisation du Québec, Archives du Séminaire de Québec, P32 (Fonds Viger-Verreau), 060/005.3 through 005.6; Walcott to Girouard, 16/2/1836, CSL.

42 Murray to Lords of Trade, 24/6/1765, CO42, v.2, ff.235–8; Gray to Hope, 24/1/1788, LAC MG23 GII3, v.4; Committee minutes, 3/2/1794, CS, v.57: 18660–2; list of justices, 8/2/1810, CS, v.107: 33832–7; report of Council, 29/11/1811, CS, v.115: 36850–7; Landau, *Justices*; Snell, 'County Magistracy,' 84.

43 Circular letters in CSL, 6/11/1815, 14/11/1815, 10/5/1817, 29/5/1826, 27/7/1827, and 31/7/1827, and in CS, 26/7/1830 (v.330) and 2/10/1830 (v.337); Coffin to Loring, 15/6/1815, CS, v.145; Marshall to Ready, 8/7/1820, CS, v.194; Ready to Marshall, 8/1/1820, and Ready to Mondelet, 12/9/1821, CSL; Gamelin to Yorke, 27/11/1830, CS, v.343; Craig to clerks of

the peace, 11/4/1835, CSL; Walcott to clerks of the peace, 4/11/1837, CSL.

44 *JHALC* 38 (1828–9), appendix Dd, 3/1/1829; report of Council, 9/10/1830, CS, v.337.

45 Paquet and Wallot, *Patronage et pouvoir*; Bernier and Salée, *Entre l'ordre et la liberté*, 150–62; Danielle Laudy, 'Les politiques coloniales britanniques et le maintien de l'ancien regime au Bas-Canada (1791–1832),'*Histoire, économie et société* 14, no.1 (1995): 71–88.

46 Murray to Lords of Trade, 3/3/1765, CO42, v.2, ff.133–4. On the rivalries in Montreal, see A.L. Burt, *The Old Province of Quebec* (Toronto: McClelland and Stewart 1968 [1933]), 114–20.

47 The gender of justices was not specified in the governors' instructions before 1791, but that they were to be men was taken for granted, as in the 1764 Quebec Quarter Sessions grand jury presentment (Shortt and Doughty, *Documents*, 188, 212, 602, 822; Doughty and McArthur, *Documents*, 15–16).

48 Neal Garnham, *The Courts, Crime and the Criminal Law in Ireland, 1692–1760* (Dublin: Irish Academic Press 1996), 32–3; Beatriz Betancourt Hardy, 'Papists in a Protestant Age: The Catholic Gentry and Community in Colonial Maryland, 1689–1776' (PhD, University of Maryland College Park 1993), 12–13, 40–1; Geoffrey Plank, *An Unsettled Conquest: The British Campaign against the Peoples of Acadia* (Philadelphia: University of Pennsylvania Press 2001), 96.

49 Report of Council, 9/10/1830, CS, v.337; Aylmer to Murray, 12/11/1830, CO42, v.230, ff.299–339; Aylmer to Stanley, 18/6/1833, CO42, v.244, ff.81–6; Sheldon J. Godfrey and Judith C. Godfrey, *Search out the Land: The Jews and the Growth of Equality in British Colonial America, 1740–1867* (Montreal: McGill-Queen's University Press 1995), 188–9; 'Benjamin Hart' and 'Aaron Ezekiel Hart,' *DCB* 8.

50 Landau, *Justices*, 161–2; Lewthwaite, 'Law and Authority,' 16, 18; Garnham, *Courts*, 33; Whetstone, *Scottish County Government*, 36.

51 *Return to an Address to His Majesty, Dated 6 February 1833 …* (London: HMSO 1834); *Quebec Gazette*, 16/3/1826, 5/1/1829; *JHALC* 38 (1828–9), appendices Dd and Ee, passim; Kempt to Murray, 12/4/1830, CO42, v.229, ff.155–7; 10 and 11 George IV c.2.

52 *Quebec Gazette*, 16/1/1826 and 18/2/1830; for an earlier version of the property debate, see Jean-Pierre Wallot, 'La querelle des prisons dans les Bas-Canada (1805–1807),' in *Un Québec qui bougeait: trame socio-politique au tournant du XIXe siècle* (Montreal: Boréal Express 1973), 47–105, and Fernand Ouellet, *Le Bas-Canada, 1791–1840: changements structuraux et crise* (Ottawa: Éditions de l'Université d'Ottawa 1976), 125–7.

53 *JHALC* 38 (1828–9), 134–7 and appendix Dd; Wilcocke, *History of the Session*, 152–67; Greer, *Patriots*, 219–25; Fyson, 'Jurys'; Ouellet, *Le Bas-Canada*, 329–85; Louis-Georges Harvey, *Le Printemps de l'Amérique française: américanité, anticolonialisme et républicanisme dans le discours politique québécois, 1805–1837* (Montreal: Boréal 2005), 133–93; Eastwood, *Governing Rural England*, 9–16; Aitchison, 'Local Government,' 74–7; Thompson, 'Local Authority,' 69–70.

54 Gale to Hay, 14/4/1828, CO42, v.218, ff.114–22, later printed as *Observations on the Petitions of Grievance, Addressed to the Imperial Parliament, from the Districts of Quebec, Montreal and Three-Rivers* (Quebec: King's Printer 1828); Mackenzie to Yorke, 16/8/1830, CS, v.333; Cartwright, Observations, 25/3/1829, CS, v.282; Bingham to Yorke, 10/8/1830, CS, v.332; *Journals of the Legislative Council of Lower Canada* 15, no.2 (1835–6), 171–2.

55 *Quebec Gazette*, 18/2/1830; Durham, *Report*, 40. Information on Montreal provided by Alan Stewart.

56 Yule to Yorke, 20/8/1830, CS, v.334.

57 Wilcocke, *History of the Session*, 154; *JHALC* 38 (1828–9), appendix Dd.

58 Council minutes, 22/1/1794, CS, v.57: 18567; Kempt to Murray, 17/11/1830, CO42, v.230, f.268.

59 Shortt and Doughty, *Documents*, 840 (a similar clause not referring specifically to justices was in the commissions from Murray forward); Murray to Lords of Trade, 24/6/1765, CO42, v.2, f.238; Mondelet to Cochran, 3/10/1822, CS, v.213; Gale to Hay, 26/3/1828, CO42, v.218, ff.94–108; List of Montreal justices, c.10/1826, CS, v.244; Coffin to Loring, 15/6/1815, CS, v.145.

60 Gale to Montizambert, 28/6/1825, CS, v.234 (Scriver); Burns to Ready, 14/9/1818, CS, v.180 (Odell); R v. Bullock, 3/1819, BAnQ-M TL19 S1 SS1; McGale (qui tam) v. Parker, BAnQ-M TL19 S4 SS1 1822 #624; Marshall to Ready, 8/7/1820, CS, v.194.

61 Mackenzie to Yorke, 16/8/1830, CS, v.333; Carleton to Hillsborough, 25/4/1770, CO42, v.30, ff.43–6; Ross to Yorke, 8/11/1828, CS, v.272; Mercure to Marshall, 2/3/1820, CS, v. 192; Gale to Cochran, 10/1/1827, CS, v.247; report of Mabane and Price, LAC RG1 E1, 27/6/1765; Ross to Marshall, 18/1/1820, CS, v.191; Mondelet to Ready, 6/12/1821, CS, v.203; de LaMothe to Yorke, 28/4/1829, CS, v.285.

62 Lacroix to Marshall, 8/3/1820, CS, v.192; Mondelet and McCord to Cochran, 23/4/1818, CS, v.176; Mondelet to Ryland, 13/6/1808, CS, v.99: 31140–2. On local elites, apart from the Quebec studies already noted, see Landau, *Justices*, 298–318; Philip Jenkins, *The Making of a Ruling Class: The*

Glamorgan Gentry 1640–1790 (Cambridge: Cambridge University Press 1983), 84–7; Ronald K. Snell, '"Ambitious of Honor and Places": The Magistracy of Hampshire County, Massachusetts, 1692–1760,' in Bruce C. Daniels, ed., *Power and Status: Officeholding in Colonial America* (Middletown, Conn.: Wesleyan University Press 1986), 17–35; Thompson, 'Local Authority,' 66–7; Lewthwaite, 'Law and Authority,' 46–7, 56–8.

63 Mondelet to Cochran, 3/10/1822, CS, v.213; Roger Swift, 'The English Urban Magistracy and the Administration of Justice during the Early Nineteenth Century: Wolverhampton 1815–1860,' *Midland History* 17 (1992): 77–83; David Philips, 'The Black Country Magistracy, 1835–60: A Changing Elite and the Exercise of its Power,' *Midland History* 3, no.3 (1976): 165–75.

64 Eastwood, *Governing Rural England*, 79–82; Skyrme, *Justices of the Peace*, 2: 29–36; Langford, *Public Life*, 410–20.

65 Report of Board of Inquiry, 12/7/1787, CS, v.33: 10656–75; A. Couillard Després, *Histoire de Sorel* (Montreal: Imprimerie des Sourds-Muets 1926), 159–61.

66 Garnham, *Courts*, 33; Whetstone, *Scottish County Government*, 39; Lewthwaite, 'Law and Authority,' 43–4.

67 Johnson, *Becoming Prominent*, 95–103.

68 Gaspé to Ryland, 17/10/1812, CS, v.125: 40091–2; Joliette and Loedel to Kempt, 26/12/1828, CS, v.275; Cull to Ryland, 20/5/1807, CS, v.93: 29040–7; Barron to Yorke, 7/12/1829, CS, v.303; David Mills, *The Idea of Loyalty in Upper Canada, 1784–1850* (Montreal: McGill-Queen's University Press 1988); Jane Errington, *The Lion, the Eagle and Upper Canada: A Developing Colonial Ideology* (Montreal: McGill-Queen's University Press 1987).

69 Report of Mabane, 18/3/1766, CS, v.15: 5712–19; Shortt and Doughty, *Documents*: 254; Philip Lawson, *The Imperial Challenge: Quebec and Britain in the Age of the American Revolution* (Montreal: McGill-Queen's University Press 1989), 81–3.

70 Singha, *A Despotism of Law*; Sullivan, *Punishment*, 207–36.

71 Greenwood, *Legacies of Fear*, 177–84.

72 *JHALC* 38 (1828–9), 639, and 43 (1834), 329; Kempt to Murray, 17/11/1830, CO42, v.230, f.268; Aylmer to Goderich, 28/2/1833, CO42, v.241, ff.268–9; Craig to Roy, 31/7/1833, CSL; Debartzch to Viger, 16/5/1836, Musée de la civilisation du Québec, Archives du Séminaire de Québec, P32 (Fonds Viger-Verreau), 060/005.3; 'Archibald Acheson' *DCB* 7; 'Joseph Roy' and 'André Jobin,' *DCB* 8.

73 Cochran to Gale, 24/10/1825, CSL; commission for Montreal, 14/11/1838, RG68, Lower Canada, v.15.

74 Roe to Yorke, 22/9/1830, CS, v.336.
75 Johnson, *Becoming Prominent*, 103–9, 118; Lewthwaite, 'Law and Authority,' 53–4.
76 Walcott to Hotchkiss, 7/8/1837, CSL.
77 McCord to Ready, 18/11/1819, CS, v.189; Marshall to Ready, 8/7/1820, CS, v.194.
78 Burn, *Justice*, III: 19–20; Skyrme, *Justices of the Peace*, 2: 9.
79 Council minutes, 30/6/1788, CS, v.39: 12889; Committee minutes, 12/2/ 1794, CS, v.57: 18659–76.
80 As asserted in Ruddel, *Québec City*, 168–9, 259.
81 Allsopp to Yorke, 31/8/1830, CS, v.334; Sewell to Ryland, 23/8/1797, LAC MG23 GII10, v.10: 4896–7; Perrault, *Le juge à paix*; 'Jonathan Sewell (Sewall),' *DCB* 7; Greenwood, *Legacies of Fear*.
82 Townshend to Christie, 9/6/1824, CS, v.228; *JHALC* 38 (1828–9), appendix Dd, testimony of Leprohon, 9/1/1829.
83 Boucher de Boucherville to Yorke, 16/8/1830, CS, v.333; Quinn to Yorke, 13/9/1830, CS, v.335; Hertel de Rouville to Yorke, 10/8/1830, CS, v.332; 'Jean-Baptiste-René Hertel de Rouville,' *DCB* 8.
84 Norma Landau, 'The Trading Justice's Trade,' in Landau, ed., *Law, Crime and English Society 1660–1830* (Cambridge: Cambridge University Press 2002), 46–70.
85 On urban magistrates and municipal administration: Ruddel, *Québec City*, 161–247. Municipal administration by the Montreal magistracy has yet to be studied in any detail, but see Fyson, 'Les structures étatiques,' and Dany Fougères, *L'approvisionnement en eau à Montréal: du privé au public, 1796–1865* (Quebec: Septentrion 2004), 27–55.
86 Larocque to Yorke, 2/8/1830, CS, v.332; Cuthbert to Brenton, 2/6/1814, CS, v.136: 43530–1; d'Estimauville to Montizambert, 10/12/1824, CS, v.231; Taschereau to Montizambert, 22/6/1825, CS, v.234; Cochran to Marchand, 8/12/1826, CSL; Marchand to Cochran, 16/12/1826, CS, v.246; Reid to Ready, 3/9/1821, CS, v.204, file 'Executive Council 10/1821'; Faribault to Yorke, 18/8/1830, CS, v.333; Jones to Yorke, 19/8/1830, CS, v.334.
87 Cochran to Leprohon, 11/6/1817, CSL; Taschereau to Montizambert, 22/6/1825, CS, v.234; report of Executive Council, 9/10/1830, CS, v.337; 3 George IV c.15 (1823), 4 George IV c.19 (1824), 2 William IV c.26 (1832), 9 George IV c.7 (1829), 6 William IV c.14 (1836); Archambault et al. to Craig, 21/3/1832, CS, v.378.
88 From a sample of parties using the term in Montreal King's Bench (superior civil) cases between 1794 and 1827, as indexed in the *Thémis 1* database.
89 As evoked by Curtis, 'Canada 'Blue Books.'

3: The Character of the Magistracy

1 Chartier de Lotbinière to Reid, 9/4/1806, QSD, 4/1806; Mondelet to Foy, 29/6/1811, CS, v.114: 36210–19; Durham, *Report*, 40–1.

2 Landau, *Justices*.

3 Blackstone, *Commentaries*, IV: 295–6; baptisms of Félicité Decoigne and Louis Decoigne, Les Cèdres, 11/6/1795 (PRDH #712868) and 16/8/1796 (PRDH #712868); BAnQ-M TL19 S1 SS11, 8/1824; Montreal judges to Montizambert, 25/1/1825, CS, v.232; Durham, *Report*, 40–1; Serge Gagnon, *Plaisir d'amour et crainte de Dieu: Sexualité et confession au Bas-Canada* (Quebec: Presses de l'Université Laval 1990), 61 (referring to the seigneur of Vaudreuil in 1789); Sandy Ramos, '"A Most Detestable Crime": Gender Identities and Sexual Violence in the district of Montreal, 1803–1843,' *Journal of the Canadian Historical Association* 12 (2001): 27–48.

4 Mondelet to Dunn 29/6/1811, CS, v.114: 36210–19; Foy to Mondelet, 3/7/1811, CSL; QSR, 4/1811 and 7/1811.

5 The revocation of the justices' civil powers in the 1770s is perhaps the most commonly cited fact about them. On Barker: Cull to Ryland, 20/5/1807, CS, v.93: 29040–7; Conroy et al. to Dunn, 23/6/1807, CS, v.94: 29196–202; report of Council, 29/11/1811, CS, v.115: 36850–7; Cull to Prevost, 29/1/1814, CS, v.134: 42813–14; Barker to Brenton, 2/2/1814, CS, v.134: 42834–5. On Odell: Burns to Ready, 14/9/1818, CS, v.180; Lindsay to Ready, 31/3/1820, CS, v.192. On Scriver: Gale to Montizambert, 28/6/1825, CS, v.234. On tavern-keeper justices: McCord and Mondelet to Ryland, 24/5/1810, CS, v.109: 34561–3. On the fees charged by country justices: QSR, 30/4/1830.

6 Unsigned report on the Trois-Rivières magistracy, c.11/1811, CS, v.115: 36876–82; d'Estimauville to Yorke, 12/11/1828, CS, v.272.

7 See, for example, *La Minerve*, 15/11/1827, 15/1/1829, 1/8/1833, 21/11/1833, 25/11/1833.

8 Sidney Webb and Beatrice Webb, *English Local Government I: The Parish and the County* (Hamden: Archon Books 1963 [1906]), especially 319–86; Skyrme, *Justices of the Peace*, 2: 1–5.

9 See, for example, Scott, 'Chapters,' 294–302; Neatby, *Quebec: The Revolutionary Age*, 50–1, 97–8; Knafla and Chapman, 'Criminal Justice'; Ruddel, *Québec City*, 161–97; Greer, *Patriots*, 92–6; Dufresne, 'Justice pénale,' 30, 69, 115.

10 Scott, 'Chapters' 298; Neatby, *Administration*, 98; Murray to Burton, 9/10/1765, LAC MG23 GII1, series 1, v.2.

11 Dalhousie to Bathurst, 27/5/1827, CO42, v.212, f.226; Greer, *Patriots*, 96; Fecteau, *Nouvel ordre*, 129, 132; Webb and Webb, *English Local Government*, 321; Aitchison, 'Local Government,' 34–5.

12 LAC RG1 E11, v.7.

13 Beattie, *Crime and the Courts*, 59–63; Landau, *Justices*, 137–40 and 392; Garnham, *Courts*, 32–5; Skyrme, *Justices of the Peace*, 2: 26–7; Eastwood, *Governing Rural England*, 76–7; Langford, *Public Life*, 401–7; B.J. Davey, *Rural Crime in the Eighteenth Century: North Lincolnshire, 1740–80* (Hull: University of Hull Press 1995), 58; King, *Crime, Justice*, 110–12; David R. Murray, *Colonial Justice: Justice, Morality and Crime in the Niagara district, 1791–1849* (Toronto: Osgoode Society / University of Toronto Press 2002), 31; John David Phillips, 'Educated to Crime: Community and Criminal Justice in Upper Canada, 1800–1840' (PhD, University of Toronto 2004), 227–8; Lewthwaite, 'Law and Authority,' 62–5.

14 'Daniel Robertson,' *DCB* 5; Dumas et al. to Murray, 15/9/1765, CS, v.14: 5361–2; correspondence regarding billetting, 9–10/1765, CS, v.14: 5421–76, passim; Robertson et al. to Potts, 17/5/1767, CS, v.16: 6018–19; Dumas et al. to Allsopp, 31/7/1769, and Burke to Allsopp, 6/8/1769, CS, v.19: 6541–5; Du Calvet to Hillsborough, 28/10/1770, CO42, v.30, ff.168–99; Ryland to Pownall, 24/9/1799, CSL.

15 'Jean-Marie Mondelet,' *DCB* 7; Carter to Sewell, 4/8/1803, CS, v.81: 25270–2; Mondelet to Craig, 12/2/1810, CS, v.107: 33869–72; Mondelet to Ryland, 9/4/1810, CS, v.108: 34265–7; Mondelet and McCord to Ryland, 11/5/1810 and 21/5/1810, CS, v.108: 34464–70, and v.109: 34551–5; McCord to Foy, 23/7/1810, CS, v.110: 34913–19; Park to Drummond, 3/7/1815, CS, v.146; Mondelet to Loring, 10/7/1815, CS, v.146.

16 'Samuel Gale,' *DCB* 9; Mackenzie to Gale, 8/5/1824, Gale to Stewart, 4/7/1825, and Dalhousie to Gale, 3/3/1827 and 10/7/1829, McCord Museum, Judge Samuel Gale Collection, folders 2 and 5; Gale to Yorke, 8/5/1830, CS, v.322.

17 'Michel-Eustache-Gaspard-Alain Chartier de Lotbinière,' *DCB* 6; 'Michel Chartier de Lotbinière,' *DCB* 4; Sébastien Daviau and Édith Prégent, *Le Musée régional de Vaudreuil-Soulanges: Une histoire passionnante à découvrir* (Vaudreuil-Dorion, Que.: Musée régional de Vaudreuil-Soulanges 2005), 19; Chartier de Lotbinière to Prevost, 21/1/1814, CS, v.134: 42755–63; Chartier de Lotbinière to Reid, 9/4/1806 and 14/10/1809, QSD, 4/1806 and 10/1809.

18 Ivanhoë Caron, *La colonisation de la province de Québec* (Quebec: L'Action Sociale 1923–27), 2: 94, 184, 321; Ferguson et al. to Ryland, 30/1/1802, CS, v.75: 23652–3; Babcock v. Ruiter et al., BAnQ-M TL19 S4 SS1, 1809 #125; Ross to Cochran, 9/10/1823, and Allison to Dalhousie, 8/11/1823, CS, v.222; Cochran to Uniacke, 29/3/1824, and Cochran to May, 30/3/1824, CSL; May to Yorke, 20/9/1830, CS, v.336. For more on the Johnson affair, see chapter 4.

19 'Joseph Bondy, dit Douaire,' in *Dictionnaire des parlementaires du Québec*; *JHALC* 38 (1828–9), appendix Dd; *JHALC* 40 (1831), appendix Aa, Second Report; Montizambert to Bondy, 8/11/1824, CSL.

20 Beattie, *Crime and the Courts*, 61; King, *Crime, Justice*, 111–12.

21 *JHALC* 38 (1828–9), appendix Dd, 9/1/1829.

22 Knafla and Chapman, 'Criminal Justice,' 272; Fecteau, *Nouvel ordre*, 132; Ruddel, *Québec City*, 168–9.

23 BAnQ-Q TL18 S1 SS1.

24 Francis Maseres, *Additional Papers concerning the Province of Quebeck …* (London: W. White 1776), 368.

25 LAC RG1 E11, v.1.

26 Greenwood, *Legacies of Fear*, 21; Knafla and Chapman, 'Criminal Justice': 268.

27 Skyrme, *Justices of the Peace*, 2: 23–37; Landau, *Justices*, 140–4.

28 Johnson, *Becoming Prominent*, 10–11.

29 Landau, *Justices*; Johnson, *Becoming Prominent*, 10–11; Lewthwaite, 'Law and Authority,' 34–5.

30 Lewthwaite, 'Law and Authority,' 29–30.

31 Knafla and Chapman, 'Criminal Justice': 269.

32 Philippe Aubert de Gaspé, *Mémoires* (Ottawa: G.E. Desbarats 1866), 278; Fletcher to Council, 16/12/1830, CS, v.346.

33 Neatby, *Administration*, 93; 'René-Ovide Hertel de Rouville,' *DCB* 4.

34 McCord to Foy, 12/7/1810, CS, v.109: 34871–2; Reid to McCord, 23/12/1815, in McCord Museum, McCord Family Papers, file 208; Mondelet to Burton, 8/12/1824, CS, v.231; certificate of Montreal King's Bench judges, 23/10/1824, CS, v.230; Coffin to Loring, 23/11/1815, CS, v.149.

35 Wilson to Mondelet, 18/3/1817, BAnQ-M TL19 S1 SS1; Walcott to Thurber, 2/6/1837, CSL; Yule to Burton, 15/7/1824, CS, v.228; Grenier v. Levesque dit Basome père, QSD, 28/9/1800; Lecomte v. Heneau dit Deschamps and Chaput, QSD, 22/9/1800.

36 Simon Devereaux, 'The Promulgation of the Statutes in late Hanoverian Britain,' in Lemmings, *The British and Their Laws* 81–5; Scott, 'Chapters,' 296; Sewell McCord, 20/7/1795, and Sewell to Sawers, 23/5/1796, LAC MG23 GII10, v.9; BAnQ-M CN601 S81, 9/8/1831; BAnQ-M CN601 S29, 18/5/1797 #1139; Égide Langlois, 'Livres et lecteurs à Québec: 1760–1799' (MA, Université Laval 1984), 83, 95; Yvan Morin, 'Les niveaux de culture à Québec 1800–1819: étude des bibliothèques privées dans les inventaires après décès' (MA, Université Laval 1979), 98–100; Gilles Labonté, 'Les bibliothèques privées à Québec (*1820–1829*)' (MA, Université Laval 1986), 126–8, 192; Robert Guillemette, 'Les bibliothèques personnelles de Mont-réal entre 1800 et 1820: une contribution à l'histoire sociale du livre' (MA, Université de Montréal 1988), appendix D; Knowlan to Yorke, 30/4/1829, CS, v.285.

37 Perrault, *Le juge à paix*; *Quebec Gazette*, 25/12/1788; *Montreal Gazette*, 23/4/ 1789; Guillemette, 'Bibliothèques personnelles,' appendix H.
38 John A. Conley, 'Doing It by the Book: Justice of the Peace Manuals and English Law in Eighteenth Century America,' *Journal of Legal History* 6, no.3 (1985): 257–98; Perrault, *Questions et réponses*; Sylvio Normand, 'L'imprimé juridique au Québec du XVIIIe siècle à 1840,' http://www. hbic.library.utoronto.ca/vol1normand_en.htm; Lewthwaite, 'Law and Authority,' 92–3.
39 34 George III c.1 (1794), 5 George IV c.5 (1825), 6 George IV c.21 and 22 (1826); Moore to Ryland, 8/11/1807, CS, v.96: 30085–6; Massé to Foy, 3/4/ 1811, CS, v.112: 35805–7; Loring to Wilson, 10/5/1815, CSL; Ross to Yorke, 7/3/1829, CS, v.281; Willard to Yorke, 24/7/1829, CS, v.294; Larue to Yorke, 5/8/1829, CS, v.295; Devereaux, 'The Promulgation of the Statutes,' 89–101.
40 Christine Veilleux, 'Les gens de justice à Québec, 1760–1867' (PhD, Université Laval 1990), 98.
41 RG1 E15A, v.13, file 'Committee on Revenue 1793'; Scott, 'Chapters,' 153– 7, 266–7, 321.
42 RG68, Quebec, v.3, 26/11/1787, and Lower Canada, vol.4, 12/3/1812; 'Sir James Stuart,' *DCB* 8; Reid to Brenton, 9/12/1811, CS, v.116: 36945–9; Brenton to Reid, 5/12/1811, CSL; QSR, 10/1/1812, 22/4/1813, and 19/1/ 1814; Mondelet and McCord to Prevost, 17/8/1814, CS, v.138: 44001–4; Delisle to Prevost, 27/8/1814, CS, v.138: 44067–9.
43 Delisle to Prevost, 27/8/1814, CS, v.138: 44067–9; *La Minerve*, 17/3/1834; *JHALC* 31 (1822), appendix J, 43 and 45 (1835–6), appendix Vv, 4/3/1836. On Alexandre-Maurice: *JHALC* 42 (1832–3), appendix [Montreal election], 26/1/1833, and 'Alexandre-Maurice Delisle,' *DCB* 10. On Jacques-Guillaume: *JHALC* 43 (1834), appendix Q #4. On Adelphe and Benjamin, see chapter 4.
44 'Charles-Elzéar Mondelet,' *DCB* 10; Park to Cochran, 6/8/1815, CS, v.147; McCord and Mondelet to Cochran, 26/8/1815, CS, v.147; RG1 E15A, v.68, file 'Quarter Sessions of the Peace 1829'; McGoogan to Kempt, 14/11/1829, CS, v.301; Mondelet to Yorke, 7/12/1829, CS, v.303; Kentucky Biographies Project, http://www.rootsweb.com/~kygenweb/kybiog/boone/ grant.jf.txt.
45 'James Murray,' *DCB* 4; Scott, 'Chapters,' 153–7, 266; 'James Shepherd,' *DCB* 6; 'David Lynd,' *DCB* 5; 'William Green,' *DCB* 6; 'George Pyke,' *DCB* 8; 'Joseph-Rémi Vallières de Saint-Réal,' *DCB* 7; 'Nicolas-Gaspard Boisseau,' *DCB* 5; 'Joseph-François Perrault,' *DCB* 7; Pierre-Georges Roy,

À travers les Mémoires de Philippe Aubert de Gaspé (Montreal: Ducharme 1943), 173–4; Veilleux, 'Les gens de justice,' 282–4.

46 Gagnon to Sherbrooke, 1/3/1817, CS, v.160; 3 William IV c.10 (1833); 4 George IV c.33 (1824), s.35; Gauvreau to Taylor, 10/12/1815, CS, v.149; Corbeau v. Pinet et al., QSD, 29/1/1830; De Labruère and Vignau to Cochran, 10/9/1827, CS, v.255.

47 Plinius Secundus, *Curiae Canadenses, or, the Canadian Law Courts* (Toronto: H. and W. Rowsell 1843), 35.

48 Memorial from Burke, c.5/1767, CS, v.19: 5466; Fleming and Alston, *Early Canadian Printing*, appendices A and B; Coffin to Cochran, 12/5/1817, CS, v.163.

49 Bowen to Ryland, 19/1/1809, CS, v.102: 32164–7; Walcott to Roe, 26/12/1835, CSL.

50 McCord to Sewell, 5/4/1814, CS, v.135: 43242–4.

51 Fletcher to Ready, 6/5/1819, LAC RG4 B20, v.6: 2156–72.

52 Fyson, 'Jurys': 98, 103; *Le Canadien*, 1/4/1809; *Montreal Herald*, 25/2/1826; Montreal King's Bench grand jury presentment, 10/3/1812, CS, v.118: 37656–7.

53 Edward Abbott of Sorel in the mid-1780s (CS, v.33: 10656–75) and Ignace Bourassa of Laprairie in the late 1790s (Perrier v. Sorelle, QSD, 5/11/1799).

54 Ruddel, *Québec City*, 188–9; Craig to mayor of Quebec City, 27/1/1835, CSL; Fyson, 'Criminal Justice,' 155–7; QSR, 12/11/1791; Lynd to Finlay, 15/12/1784, CS, v.27: 8928–9; Pyke to Ryland, 10/1/1810, CS, v.106: 33704; Fraser to Cochran, 24/4/1815, CS, v.143; Fraser to Coffin, 27/9/1815, CS, v.148; Coffin to Loring, 28/9/1815, CS, v.148; SSR 1831–3, passim.

55 John H. Langbein, 'The Origins of Public Prosecution at Common Law,' *American Journal of Legal History* 17, no.4 (1973): 313–35; Lewthwaite, 'Law and Authority,' 73–124.

56 Uniacke to Loring, 15/3/1816, CS, v.152; Fletcher to Montizambert, 2/7/1825, CS, v.235; Monk to Brenton, 20/1/1813, CS, v.127: 40671–2.

57 Lalanne to McCord and Mondelet, 10/11/1818 and 11/11/1818, and McCord to Lalanne, 17/11/1818, BAnQ-M TL19 S1 SS1; Quebec King's Bench grand jury presentment, 31/3/1823, *Quebec Gazette*, 28/5/1823; Stuart to Cochran, 5/8/1826, CS, v.243, file 'Law Officers 8/1826'; Montreal Oyer and Terminer grand jury presentment, 31/8/1829, CS, v.296; Stuart to Yorke, 19/1/1830, CS, v.308; *Le Canadien*, 1/10/1831.

58 R v. Woods, 3/1828, Hagan to Ogden, 20/2/1827, McGillivray to Delisle, 15/2/1828, Whitney to Gale, 22/8/1825: all in BAnQ-M TL19 S1 SS1. Caldwell to Delisle, 29/8/1822, QSD.

4: The Police before the Police

1 LAC RG1 E1, v.E: 66; CS, v.63: 20420–1; Kennedy and Thom, 'General Report': 33.
2 Greer, 'Birth of the Police'; Fecteau, *Nouvel ordre*, especially 98–101, 162–5, and 228–32; Ruddel, *Québec City*, especially 177–80; Neatby, *Administration*, 299, 306–7; Dufresne, 'La police.'
3 Rivarre v. Prevost, QSD, 2/2/1795; LAC RG4 B45, 419–20. On Kollmyer, see below.
4 Clive Emsley, *The English Police: A Political and Social History* (New York: St Martin's Press 1991), 4–5, and 'Albion's Felonious Attractions: Reflections upon the History of Crime in England,' in Emsley and Knafla, *Crime History and Histories of Crime*, 74–5.
5 Eric H. Monkkonen, 'The Urban Police in the United States,' in Emsley and Knafla, *Crime History and Histories of Crime*, 202–3; Lawrence M. Friedman, *Crime and Punishment in American History* (New York: Basic Books 1993), 67–8. On British North America: Greg Marquis, *Policing Canada's Century: A History of the Canadian Association of Chiefs of Police* (Toronto: University of Toronto Press 1993), 12–39, and Jeffrey Ian Ross, 'The Historical Treatment of Urban Policing in Canada: A Review of the Literature,' *Urban History Review* 24, no.1 (1995): 36–41. More nuanced are John C. Weaver, *Crimes, Constables and Courts: Order and Transgression in a Canadian City, 1816–1970* (Montreal: McGill-Queen's University Press 1995), 28, 50–3, and Acheson, *Saint John*, 214–29.
6 J.M. Beattie, *Policing and Punishment in London, 1660–1750: Urban Crime and the Limits of Terror* (New York: Oxford University Press 2001); Elaine A. Reynolds, *Before the Bobbies the Night Watch and Police Reform in Metropolitan London, 1720–1830* (Stanford, Calif.: Stanford University Press 1998); Andrew T. Harris, *Policing the City: Crime and Legal Authority in London, 1780–1840* (Columbus: Ohio State University Press 2004); Paley, 'Policing London'; David Philips and Robert D. Storch, *Policing Provincial England, 1829–1856: The Politics of Reform* (London: Leicester University Press 1999), 73–92; Garnham, *Courts*, 27–32.
7 Alan D. Watson, 'The Constable in Colonial North Carolina,' *North Carolina Historical Review* 68, no.1 (1991): 1–16; Dennis Charles Rousey, *Policing the Southern City: New Orleans, 1805–1889* (Baton Rouge: Louisiana State University Press 1996), 1–39.
8 Dufresne, 'La police'; Beattie, *Policing and Punishment*, 77–81.
9 Hay and Snyder, 'Using the Criminal Law,' 5–9.
10 RG1 E15A, v.6, file 'Judicial Establishment 1781.'

11 For a more involved discussion, see Fyson, 'Criminal Justice,' 177–85, though the definition adopted here is slightly different. On theories of police, see Carl B. Klockars, 'Police,' in Edgar F. Borgatta, ed., *Encyclopedia of Sociology* (New York: Macmillan 2000), 4: 2107–16, and Peter K. Manning, 'A Dramaturgical Perspective,' in Brian Forst and Peter K. Manning, *The Privatization of Policing: Two Views* (Washington: Georgetown University Press 1999), 55–7.

12 Legal opinions were divided on this: reports of Uniacke (attorney general) and Vanfelson (solicitor general), with Cochran to Burton, 30/1/1823, CS, v.216, file 'Law Officers 1/1823'.

13 4 George III, 'An Ordinance for Regulating and Establishing the Courts of Judicature ...' (1764); LAC RG4 A3, v.1; LAC RG4 B22. For a fuller discussion of the parish bailiffs, see Fyson, '*Canadiens* and British Institutions.'

14 Shortt and Doughty, *Documents*, 208n.1; 4 George III, 'An Ordinance for Regulating and Establishing the Courts of Judicature ...' (1764); 6 George III, 'An Ordinance for Repairing and Amending the High-Ways ...' (1766); 10 George III, 'An Ordinance for the More Effectual Administration of Justice' (1770); circular letters to bailiffs, 26/8/1769 and 27/3/1775, LAC RG4 A3, v.1.

15 References to the parish bailiffs' actions in roads matters are scattered through the papers of the *Grand voyers*, BAnQ-Q E2; see also Robichaud, 'Le pouvoir, les paysans et la voirie,' 41–2, 49–53.

16 17 George III c.5, 8 and 11 (1777); Gerard M.F. Hartley, 'Years of Adjustment: British Policy and the Canadian Militia, 1760–1787' (MA, Queen's University 1993), 99–128; Lépine, 'Milice'; Fyson, '*Canadiens* and British Institutions.'

17 QSR, 22/9/1778; Roy, *Inventaire des procès-verbaux*, 4: 3–4; RG1 E15A, v.9, file 'Judicial Establishment 1786.'

18 RG1 E15A, v.8, file 'Judicial Establishment 1784'; PRDH #s 315994 and 1142756. For more on eighteenth-century civil bailiffs, see Donald Fyson, 'Judicial Auxiliaries across Legal Regimes: From New France to Lower Canada,' in Claire Dolan, ed., *Entre justice et justiciables: les auxiliaires de la justice du Moyen Âge au XXe siècle* (Quebec: Presses de l'Université Laval 2005), 383–403, and '*Canadiens* and British Institutions.'

19 Irene Gladwin, *The Sheriff: The Man and his Office* (London: Gollancz 1974), 348–68 and 383–7; Sharpe, *Crime*, 44–7; Garnham, *Courts*, 94–7; Murray, *Colonial Justice*, 42–51; Scott, 'Chapters,' 149, 267–73; Veilleux, 'Les gens de justice, 99–102; Neatby, *Administration*, passim.

20 LAC MG23 GII3, v.2–3.

21 Burn, *Justice*, I: 98–9, 382.

22 QSR, 10/7/1766. A similar system was apparently implanted in Quebec City at about the same time: *Quebec Gazette*, 17/9/1767.
23 QSR, 10/4/1766, 10/7/1766, 6/7/1767, 23/12/1771, 13/11/1783; Beek to Cramahé, 7/8/1773, CS, v.20: 7020–2; Du Calvet to Governor and Council, 7/8/1769, CS, v.19: 6556–7; account of John Burke, RG1 E15A, v.9, file 'Judicial Establishment 1786'; account of Joseph Gridley, RG1 E15A, v.1, file 'Judicial Establishment 1767'; account of Henry Dunn, v.10, file 'Public Works 1787.'
24 QSR, 9/10/1766, 23/7/1781, 15/4/1784.
25 R v. Bourgoin, 9/1769, BAnQ-Q TL18 S1 SS1.
26 Burn, *Justice*, III: 238–9; Mark Goldie, 'The Unacknowledged Republic: Officeholding in Early Modern England,' in Tim Harris, ed., *The Politics of the Excluded, c. 1500–1800* (New York and Basingstoke: Palgrave 2001), 164.
27 BAnQ-Q TL5 D4289.
28 QSR, 22/7/1769; RG1 E15A, v.8, file 'Judicial Establishment 1785.'
29 BAnQ-Q TL999, 1960–01–343\38, folder 1765–8. It is not clear if this was a civil or criminal arrest.
30 Lawrence Ostola, 'A Very Public Presence: The British Army Garrison in the Town of Quebec 1759–1838' (PhD, Université Laval 2006); Quebec justices to Murray, 24/11/1764, CS, v.11: 4464–5; Jean-Marie Fecteau and Douglas Hay, '"Government by Will and Pleasure Instead of Law": Military Justice and the Legal System in Quebec, 1775–83,' in Greenwood and Wright, *Canadian State Trials. Volume I*, 140–3, 152; Haldimand to Nairne, 1/6/1779, British Library, Add. Mss. 21845, 92–3; Carleton to Mathews, 24/9/1780, and Maclean to Mathews 26/9/1780 and 28/9/1780, British Library, Add. Mss. 21865, 81–7.
31 RG1 E15A, v.3, file 'Judicial Establishment 1772,' v.4, file 'Judicial Establishment 1773,' and v.8, file 'Judicial Establishment 1784.'
32 Lachance, *Justice criminelle*, 29–30, 70; John A. Dickinson, *Law in New France* (Winnipeg: University of Manitoba, Faculty of Law 1992) and 'Réflexions sur la police'; Garneau, 'Justice et règlement des conflits,' 98–101.
33 QSR, 6/5/1765, 9/1/1769; Gray to Gray, 15/11/1784, CS, v.27: 8896–8.
34 LAC RG1 E1, v.E: 125–254; Shortt and Doughty, *Documents*, 907.
35 LAC RG1 E1, v.E: 66–124; 27 George III c.6 (1787).
36 Minutes of the Committee on Public Accounts, 2/2/1788, in RG1 E15A, v.11, file 'Reports on Public Accounts 1788.'
37 Burn, *Justice*, I: 378–84. On Montreal: QSR, 1/8/1787, 10/11/1787. On Quebec City: *Quebec Gazette*, 16/8/1787; Fecteau, *Nouvel ordre*, 100. On Trois-Rivières: 1 George IV c.15 and BAnQ-Q TL 18 S1 SS1, folder 1793.
38 QSR, 8/4/1788, 8/7/1788, 10/1788, passim, 15/11/1788; Burn, *Justice*, I:

380; Radzinowicz, *A History of English Criminal Law*, 2: 184–5, 277–8; Joan
R. Kent, *The English Village Constable, 1580–1642: A Social and Administrative
Study* (Oxford: Clarendon Press 1986), 74; Beattie, *Policing and Punish-
ment*,140–50; Reynolds, *Before the Bobbies*, 9, 46, 54, 67; Robert Storch,
'Policing Rural Southern England before the Police: Opinion and Practice,
1830–1856,' in Hay and Snyder, *Policing and Prosecution*: 223; David
Philips, *Crime and Authority in Victorian England: The Black Country, 1835–
1860* (London: Croom Helm 1977), 54, 60; Garnham, *Courts*, 29–30; Roger
Lane, *Policing the City: Boston, 1822–1885* (Cambridge, Mass.: Harvard
University Press 1967), 9–10; Donna Spindel, *Crime and Society in North
Carolina, 1663–1776* (Baton Rouge: Louisiana State University Press 1989),
36; Watson, 'The Constable,' 6; Douglas Fyfe, 'Transitions in Policing:
Kingston 1816–42,' *Historic Kingston* 34(1986): 72.

39 The Montreal constable lists in QSR are complete for every year but 1794.
On Quebec City: Fecteau, *Nouvel ordre*, 163–4, and Uniacke to Cochran,
12/5/1823, CS, v.219.

40 Occupational information derived from notations in the registers themselves; the 1811, 1813, and c.1817–18 jury lists (LAC RG4 B19); Thomas
Doige's *Alphabetical List of the Merchants, Traders, and Housekeepers Residing
in Montreal* (1819 and 1820); and the *Thémis 1* and *Thémis 3* databases.

41 QSR, 26–28/10/1796; Burn, *Justice*, I: 378.

42 Beattie, *Policing and Punishment*, 140–50.

43 Ruddel, *Québec City*, 178; Fecteau, *Nouvel ordre*, 164n.38. Analysis based on
Denis Racine, 'Les connétables de la ville de Québec (1798–1815),'
L'Ancêtre 6, no.3 (1979): 77–88, and 'Les connétables de la ville de Québec
(1821–1822),' *L'Ancêtre* 6, no.8 (1980): 238–40.

44 QSR, 27/10/1821; McCord and Mondelet to Executive Council, 13/11/
1822, CS, v.216, file 'Executive Council 1/1823.'

45 RG1 E15A, v.50, file 'Quarter Sessions of the Peace 1824.'

46 Uniacke to Cochran, 12/5/1823, CS, v.219; QSR, 10/1819.

47 McCord Museum, Kollmyer Papers; QSR, 17/1/1807; SSR, 1/12/1817.

48 36 George III c.6 (1796); 42 George III c.8 (1802).

49 SSR, 20/3/1819; at least half was paid to police officers of one sort or
another.

50 On England: Radzinowicz, *A History of English Criminal Law*, 2: 182–3. On
Montreal: QSR, 28/10/1795; Sewell to Montreal justices, 31/10/1796, RG1
E15A, v.40, file 'Quarter Sessions of the Peace 1821'; Ryland to Clarke, 22/
11/1802, CSL; Marston to Prevost, 30/8/1812, CS, v.124: 39674–9; comments of inspector general of public accounts and Marston's replies, 19/6/
1817, RG1 E15A, v.40, file 'Quarter Sessions of the Peace 1821.'

51 Road treasurer's accounts; SSR, 29/4/1809 and 22/12/1810; Police Office accounts in RG1 E15A; Jean Turmel, *Premières structures et évolution de la police de Montréal (1796–1909)* (Montreal: Service de la Police de Montréal 1971): 5–6, 20–3.
52 Archives de la Ville de Montréal, VM35, dossier 4, 1809–2, 18/7/1809.
53 Marston to Montreal justices, QSD, 10/7/1817.
54 *Almanach de Québec pour l'année 1789* (Quebec: Guillaume Brown 1788), 54; Cochran to Ryland, 21/11/1815, CSL; D'Estimauville to Drummond, 20/5/1815, CS, v.144; Veilleux, 'Les gens de justice,' 103–4; Fecteau, *Nouvel ordre*, 100; 'John Bentley,' *DCB* 5; 'Robert-Anne d'Estimauville,' *DCB* 6.
55 PRDH #788635; petition of Landry, 9/4/1806, BAnQ-Q TL31 S1 SS1 #2518; Kees v. Johnston, 18/5/1810, BAnQ-Q.TL31 S1 SS1 #4635; Veilleux, 'Les gens de justice,' 109–11, 113, 190.
56 QSR, 7/1815; RG1 E15A, v.41, file 'Road Treasurer 1822'; *JHALC* 27 (1818), 54.
57 Reprinted in *Montreal Gazette*, 9/9/1816.
58 Fletcher to Wilson, 8/6/1816, CS, v.154; on the shift in the meaning of 'police' in Lower Canada, see Dufresne, 'La police,' 420.
59 *JHALC* 25 (1816), 38, 124–6, and 26 (1817): 330–2; Mondelet and McCord to Cochran, 28/12/1816, CS, v.158; QSR, 19/1/1818. A watch was also mentioned in the 1817 petition to incorporate Montreal, CS, v.171.
60 RG1 E15A, v.14, file 'Judicial Establishment 1795'; QSR, 30/7/1779; Mathews to Gray, 5/8/1779, Haldimand Collection, British Library. Add. Mss. 21721, 13. On other temporary watches, apart from the 1783 watch in Montreal mentioned above, see Richardson to Ryland, 1/10/1801, CS, v.74: 23376–9, and McGill University, Rare Book Room, MS 338 (Montreal, 1801); Ruddel, *Québec City*, 177–8.
61 Dufresne, 'Justice pénale,' 69, 253 and passim; Christie to Yorke, 26/3/1829, CS, v.282; Linton et al. to Kempt, 9/2/1830, CS, v.311; Christie to Yorke, 11/2/1830, CS, v.311; *JHALC* 39 (1830), 249–50 and appendix 18/3/1830; constables identified from Dufresne and the *Thémis* 2 database.
62 Hart to Sewell, 23/4/1819, RG1 E15A, v.34, file 'Quarter Sessions of the Peace 1819'; SSR, 4/7/1818, 30/5/1818, 20/3/1819; report of Council, 7/11/1822, CS, v.215, file 'Executive Council 11/1822'; Turmel, *Premières structures*, 20–3.
63 Ready to McCord and Mondelet, 31/8/1818, CS, v.180; QSR, 19/7/1819, 30/10/1819, 30/4/1821, 24/10/1821; Delisle to Ready, 27/10/1821, CS, v.204; Ready to Reid, 2/6/1821, and Ready to Delisle, 1/11/1821, CSL; Hart to Coltman, 24/4/1822, CS, v.208.

64 RG1 E15A, 1819–22; agreement between Marston and Hart, 18/10/1821, CS, v.203; Marston v. Hart, BAnQ-M TL19 S4 SS1 1822 #226.

65 RG1 E15A, v.34, file 'Quarter Sessions of the Peace 1819' and subsequent volumes until 1822; Hart to Ready, 6/4/1822, CS, v.207; Cochran to Police Magistrates, 6/8/1822, CSL; *Canadian Courant*, 12/11/1822, 14/12/1822, 16/1/1823, 22/2/1823, and 15/3/1823; SSR, 29/12/1821; QSR, 19/7/1822; *La Minerve*, 28/3/1833.

66 QSR and SSR, 1823–4, passim; RG1 E15A, v.64, file 'Quarter Sessions of the Peace 1828.'

67 QSR, 28/10/1831; account of clerks of markets, RG1 E15A, v.55, file 'Miscellaneous 1826'; reports of L.-B. Leprohon, 1/11/1833 and 29/6/1835, Archives de la Ville de Montréal, VM35, dossiers 60, 1833–9–2 and 64, 1835–1; *JHALC* 42 (1832–3), appendix M, testimony of Étienne Beneche *dit* Lavictoire, 20/12/1832, and Pierre Auger, 23/1/1833.

68 QSR, 26/10/1833, 28/10/1835; McCarroll v. White, QSD, 3/4/1835; Homonto v. Donnegaro, QSD, 29/8/1835; *La Minerve*, 18/1/1836, 21/7/1836; Turmel, *Premières structures*, 24–34. Biographies of Pierre-Édouard Leclère mistakenly assert that the governor named him superintendent of the Montreal police in 1830 and that he reorganized the police in 1832 (François-Joseph Audet, 'Pierre-Édouard Leclère (1798–1866),' *Cahiers des Dix* 8 (1943): 109–40; 'Pierre-Édouard Leclère (Leclerc),' *DCB* 9.

69 Montreal residents to Dalhousie, 22/9/1823, CS, v.221; Ross to Cochran, 9/10/1823, and Allison to Dalhousie, 8/11/1823, CS, v.222; *Canadian Courant*, 4/10/1823; Cochran to Ogilvie, 20/3/1824, CSL; Murphy v. Delisle and Aumier v. Delisle, QSD, 30/8/1825; *JHALC* 39 (1830), Minutes of Evidence, 18/3/1830; Miville to Kempt, 17/3/1830, CS, v.314; *JHALC* 42 (1832–3), appendix M; *La Minerve*, 17/3/1834; *JHALC* 43 (1834), 201–4; Dufresne, 'Justice pénale,' 70–2; Senior, *British Regulars*, 11–23; Jean-Paul Brodeur, *La délinquance de l'ordre: recherches sur les commissions d'enquête* (LaSalle, Que.: Hurtubise HMH 1984).

70 58 George III c.2 (1818); 3 George IV c.6 (1823); 1 William IV c.54 (1831).

71 On Montreal: SSR, 11/4/1818, 18/4/1818, 24/4/1818; QSR, 24/4/1818; Turmel, *Premières structures*, 8–19, 29–35. On Quebec City: *Rules, Orders and Regulations for the Foreman, Deputy Foreman and Watchmen of the City of Quebec* (Quebec: T. Cary 1827); Frédéric Chevalier, 'Développement et modernisation d'une structure étatique locale, à Québec, au début du XIXe siècle: l'histoire du service du "Guet et des Flambeaux de Nuit," de sa création (1818) jusau'à l'incorporation de la ville (1832)' (unpublished seminar paper, Université Laval 1999).

72 Reynolds, *Before the Bobbies*, and Harris, *Policing*.
73 BAnQ-M TL32 S37 (partly reproduced in E.-Z. Massicotte, 'Le guet à Montréal au XIXe siècle,' *Bulletin des recherches historiques* 36, no.2 [1930]: 68–71, and Fernand Lefebvre, 'L'histoire du guet à Montréal,' *Revue d'histoire de l'Amérique française* 6, no. 2 (1952): 263–73). The function of the grapnels ('creepers' or 'grappins') is unclear.
74 QSR, 30/4/1819, 19/7/1823; SSR, 14/6/1823, 6/12/1823; Quenneville v. Try and Murray, QSD, 18/11/1825; Cusson et al. v. Sweeney et al., QSD, 16/8/1825; *Canadian Courant*, 9/9/1829.
75 Mondelet to Ready, 10/2/1819, CS, v.184; Archives de la Ville de Montréal, VM35, dossier 21, 1818–2, 4/4/1840; QSR, 30/4/1834; *La Minerve*, 5/2/1835.
76 Quebec City justices to Yorke, 25/5/1829, CS, v.287; *Montreal Herald*, 11/9/1824, 12/3/1825; *JHALC* 45 (1835–6), 191; *JHALC* 42 (1832–3), appendix M, testimony of Jacques Viger, 23/2/1833; *JHALC* 31 (1821–2), 142–4, and 45 (1835–6), 191; *La Minerve*, 35/5/1834; Archives de la Ville de Montréal, VM1, série Conseil municipal, procès-verbaux, 30/5/1834, 9/10/1835; Lorne Joseph Ste Croix, 'The First Incorporation of the City of Montreal, 1826–1836' (MA, McGill University 1972), 167; Alan Williams, *The Police of Paris, 1718–1798* (Baton Rouge: Louisiana State University Press 1979), 290.
77 Petition of Macdonell, 18/12/1835, Archives de la Ville de Montréal, VM35, dossier 64, 1835–1; Chevalier, 'Développement et modernisation'; Antonio Drolet, *La Ville de Québec: histoire municipale. Volume III: de l'incorporation à la Confédération (1833–1867)* (Quebec: Société historique de Québec 1967), 3: 40; Pierre-Georges Roy, *Fils de Québec* (Lévis, Que., 1933), 2: 185.
78 'Louis-Nicolas-Emmanuel de Bigault d'Aubreville,' *DCB* 6; petition of MacDonald, 2/10/1835, Archives de la Ville de Montréal, VM35, dossier 64, 1835–1; Rousey, *Policing the Southern City*, 25–9.
79 QSR, 18/1/1823; *La Minerve*, 1/11/1827; *Canadian Courant*, 15/11/1823, 16/3/1825, 29/8/1829; Archives de la Ville de Montréal, VM1, série Conseil municipal, procès-verbaux, 20/2/1835, 20/3/1835, 18/12/1835, 22/1/1836; Ste Croix, *First Incorporation*: 18, 175.
80 D'Aubreville v. Mallard, QSD 27/9/1820; report of watch and light committee, 27/9/1833, Archives de la Ville de Montréal, VM35, dossier 60, 1833–9–2; 'Jean-Philippe Rottot,' *DCB* 13; Ste Croix, 'First Incorporation,' 167–75, 182, 204–9, 233; Turmel, *Premières structures*, 34–5; Dufresne, 'Justice pénale,' 56.
81 *Montreal Herald*, 6/2/1819, 6/2/1821, 10/2/1821; SSR, 6/2/1821; R v. Stephenson et al., 27/10/1821, MG24 B173, v.3; Lauzon et al. v. Sweeney et

al., QSD, 16/8/1825; Dalcour et al. v. Sweeney, QSD, 14/9/1830; Franche
v. McCord, QSD, 20/7/1824; testimony of Pierre Bouthillier, 30/12/1828,
JHALC 38 (1828–9), appendix Ee; *La Minerve*, 5/2/1835, 1/6/1835, 24/3/
1836; 'William King McCord,' *DCB* 8.

82 Calculations for 1827/8 based on the Quebec gaol registers, BAnQ-Q E17;
'Daily report of committals etc.' 1827–8, BAnQ-Q E17; and complaints in
BAnQ-Q TL31 S1 SS1. For 1845 and 1854: 'Statistics of Crime and Offences
in the City of Quebec' (1845) and 'Statistics of Crime, Quebec' (1854), both
in Archives de la Ville de Québec QC1–01B/1370–01. In Montreal, the
arrest rate in the 1840s and 1860s remained at around 100 per 1,000 (*Journal de Québec*, 14/1/1847; *Rapport annuel du Chef de Police* [Montreal: La
Minerve 1864], 24–8).

83 Aubert de Gaspé, *Mémoires*, 475; also 159n.1.

84 Ostola, 'A Very Public Presence'; Senior, *British Regulars*, 11–23; Jean
Pariseau, 'Forces armées et maintien de l'ordre au Canada, 1867–1967: un
siècle d'aide au pouvoir civil' (PhD, Université Paul Valéry III [Mont-
pellier] 1981), 17; BAnQ-M P1000 D1102; account of Ogilvie, 22/3/1824,
BAnQ-M P20 S1 D1; SSR, 30/5/1823 through 13/6/1823.

85 Among others, 34 George III c.1 and c.4 (1794); 47 George III c.14 (1807);
48 George III c.26 (1808); 57 George III c.3 (1817); 1 George IV c.1 (1821);
7 George IV c.3 (1827); 6 William IV c.37 (1836).

86 Hart to Executive Council, 12/4/1822, CS, v.208.

87 Hénault v. Mercier, QSD, 24/8/1814; Craig to Rouville, 19/7 and 28/7/
1834, CSL.

88 Spearman to Dalhousie, 13/9/1823, CS, v.227; *JHALC* 34 (1825), 43;
Spearman to Kempt, 1/2/1830, CS, v.310.; Massé v. Barbier *dit* Pretaboir
fils, QSD, 12/1/1795; QSR, 4/1795; Reid to Monk, 12/6/1794, CO42, v.100,
f.359; QSR, 7/1794; Gale to Saint-Ours, 7/2/1799, CSL; Walcott to
Catenash (Cattenach), 15/3/1836, CSL; Greenwood, *Legacies of Fear*, 80–3.

89 RG1 E15A, v.50, file 'Sheriff 1824'; *JHALC* 43 (1834), 64; Barker to McCord,
18/1/1814, BAnQ-M TL19 S1 SS1; on *Canadien* militia officers, see, for
example, Craig to Panet, 8/11/1835, CSL.

90 Of 192 actions for which Marston and Hart charged in two years from
1817 to 1819, twenty involved travelling into the countryside; of 510 from
1819 to 1820, 82.

91 3 William IV c.10 (1833).

92 Félix Gatien, *Histoire de la paroisse du Cap-Santé* (Quebec: Léger Brous-
seau 1884 [1831]), 171–2; 48 George III c.26 (1808); 1 George IV c.1 (1821);
BAnQ-M TL36 S1 SS1, Séguin v. Choinière dit Sabourin, 2/7/1819; LAC
MG8 F89, v.6: 3683–4, and v.8: 4221–2 (Sorel); QSR, 25/4/1821 (Sainte-

Geneviève); fines by Rémi-Séraphim Bourdages, QSD, 7/1831 (Sainte-Marie-de-Monnoir); BAnQ-Q TL5 D70089: 10 (Saint-Augustin, Ancienne-Lorette, Pointe-Lévy, Saint-Pierre).

93 42 George III c.8 (1802); 47 George III c.14 (1807); QSR, 15/7/1807 (Berthier), 18/7/1807 (L'Assomption), 22/4/1808 (Saint-Denis), 21/10/1809 and 30/10/1810 (Terrebonne), and 22/10/1808 (Caldwell's Manor); 58 George III c.16 (1818); LAC MG8 F89, v.9: 5108–15.

94 BAnQ-Q E17, Événements de 1837–1838, files 59, 61, 68 (Malo) and 118, 587, 602, 844; 'Siméon Marchesseault,' *DCB* 8; 'Pierre-Rémi Narbonne' and 'François-Maurice Lepailleur,' http://cgi2.cvm.qc.ca/glaporte/.

95 At the beginning of November 1837, for example, the administration directed the attorney general to proceed to Montreal to 'inquir[e] into the present state of the Police force in that City with a view to place it on an efficient footing to an extent commensurate with the exigencies of the times, and so as to enable the Civil Authorities to preserve peace & good order and to execute the Laws.' LAC RG1 G15D, 4/11/1837.

96 Greer, *Patriots*, 178–9.

97 In 1865 Montreal had 125 police for a population of about 97, 000, or one per 775 population (Éric Giroux, 'Les policiers à Montréal: travail et portrait socio-culturel, 1865–1924' [MA, Université du Québec à Montréal 1995], 26); this compares to about 37 watchmen and professional constables in the mid-1830s for a population of about 32, 000, or one per 850 population. The police-to-population ratio in Quebec City between 1840 and 1858 varied between 1:715 and 1:1680 (Michael McCulloch, 'Most Assuredly Perpetual Motion: Police and Policing in Quebec City, 1838–58,' *Urban History Review* 19, no. 1 [1990], 105), though this may not count the water police; in the mid-1830s, with a 48-man watch, a high constable, and 3–4 police constables, the ratio was perhaps 1:550.

98 *Canadian Courant*, 17/11/1824.

5: The Relevance of Criminal Justice

1 British Library, Add. Mss., 21734, 593; Pierre Du Calvet, *Appel à la justice de l'État* ... (London, 1784), 166–70; Alexis de Tocqueville, *Regards sur le Bas-Canada* (Montreal: Éditions Typo 2003), 170.

2 Tocqueville, *Regards*, 289–91.

3 John H. Langbein, 'Albion's Fatal Flaws,' *Past and Present* 98 (1983): 96–120; Beattie, *Crime and the Courts*; Shoemaker, *Prosecution and Punishment*; King, *Crime, Justice*.

4 Terry L. Chapman, 'Crime in Eighteenth Century England: E.P. Thomp-

son and the Conflict Theory of Crime,' *Criminal Justice History* 1 (1980): 139–55.

5 Nicole Castan, *Justice et répression en Languedoc à l'époque des lumières* (Paris: Flammarion 1980); Nicole Castan and Yves Castan, 'Une économie de justice à l'age moderne: composition et dissension,' *Histoire économique et sociale* 3 (1982): 361–7; Olwen H. Hufton, 'Le paysan et la loi en France au XVIIIe siècle,' *Annales* 38, no.3 (1983): 679–701.

6 On Quebec in general: Phillips, 'Crime and Punishment'; Vincent Masciotra, 'Quebec Legal Historiography, 1760–1900,' *McGill Law Journal* 32, no.3 (1987): 712–32; and Fyson, 'Historiens.' For the consensual view: Neatby, *Administration*; Scott, 'Chapters.' For a more sophisticated recent version: Pilarczyk, 'The Law of Servants' and 'Justice in the Premises.' On the conflictual view: Morel, 'Réception'; Hay, 'Meanings'; Knafla and Chapman, 'Criminal Justice'; Ruddel, *Québec City*, 176–89; Bernier and Salée, *Entre l'ordre et la liberté*, 158–62; Greenwood, *Legacies of Fear*. On the marginality of criminal justice: Fecteau, *Nouvel ordre* and *Liberté*; Greer, *Patriots*, 91–100.

7 Hay, 'Meanings,' 79.

8 Castan, *Justice et répression*; Allen Steinberg, *The Transformation of Criminal Justice: Philadelphia, 1800–1880* (Chapel Hill: University of North Carolina Press 1989).

9 Sharpe, *Crime*, 59–77.

10 For Montreal, based on King's Bench registers, QSR and QSD, Weekly Sessions registers for 1805, 1829, and 1835, returns of fines imposed in the Weekly and Special Sessions, gaol registers, and gaol and House of Correction calendars. For Quebec, based on Quarter Sessions documents as indexed in the *Thémis* 2 database, clerk of the peace's account, 1766–9 (in RG1 E15A, v.2, file 'Judicial Establishment 1769'), gaol registers, House of Correction calendars, Dufresne, *Justice pénale*, and Fecteau, *Nouvel ordre*.

11 For a more complete methodological discussion, see Donald Fyson, 'The Judicial Prosecution of Crime in the Longue Durée: Quebec, 1712–1965,' in Jean-Marie Fecteau and Janice Harvey, eds., *La régulation sociale entre l'acteur et l'institution: Pour une problématique historique de l'interaction* (Quebec: Presses de l'Université du Québec 2005), 85–119.

12 Sharpe, *Crime*, 69–76. For a contrary view: Douglas Hay, 'Origins: The Courts of Westminster Hall in the Eighteenth Century,' in Philip Girard, Jim Phillips, and Barry Cahill, eds., *The Supreme Court of Nova Scotia, 1754–2004: From Imperial Bastion to Provincial Oracle* (Toronto: Osgoode Society / University of Toronto Press 2004), 20–1.

13 Fecteau, *Nouvel ordre*, 233–52.

14 David Taylor, *Crime, Policing and Punishment in England, 1750–1914* (New York: St Martin's Press 1998), 20–1.

15 *JHALC* 35 (1826), appendix R, and 42 (1832–3), appendix Hh; BAnQ-M TL32 S1 SS1, 'Statement of fines received by John Delisle ...,' 4/1830.

16 *La Minerve*, 25/10/1830.

17 As opposed to what is asserted in Fecteau, *Liberté*, 130. Despite the spike in the number of cases actually tried in Quarter Sessions in 1835, it was not an anomalous year in terms of the total number of complaints brought, judging from the depositions preserved in the case files: about 550 in 1834, 625 in 1835, and 650 in 1836.

18 Douglas Hay, 'War, Dearth and Theft in the Eighteenth Century: The Record of the English Courts,' *Past and Present* 95 (1982): 117–60; Beattie, *Crime and the Courts*, 199–237; Shoemaker, *Prosecution and Punishment*, 64–5; Fernand Ouellet, *Economic and Social History of Quebec, 1760–1850: Structures and Conjunctures* (Ottawa: Carleton Library 1980), 334–7.

19 Peter King, 'Punishing Assault: The Transformation of Attitudes in the English Courts,' *Journal of Interdisciplinary History* 27, no.1 (1996): 53; King, *Crime, Justice*, 132–3; Douglas Hay, 'Dread of the Crown Office: the Magistracy and King's Bench, 1740–1800,' in Landau, *Law, Crime and English Society*, 24; Davey, *Rural Crime*, 9–50; Beattie, *Policing and Punishment*, 17–18; Shoemaker, *Prosecution and Punishment*, 50–1, appendix III.

20 Spindel, *Crime and Society*, 57; Douglas Greenberg, 'Crime, Law Enforcement, and Social Control in Colonial America,' *American Journal of Legal History* 26, no.4 (1982): 310n.39 and 314n.53; Nelson, *Americanization*, 37.

21 Lewthwaite, 'Law and Authority,' 181, and Murray, *Colonial Justice*, 135–49, using the population figures each provides.

22 Steinberg, *Transformation*, 29; Peter Wettmann-Jungblut, 'Penal Law and Criminality in South Western Germany: Forms, Patterns, and Developments 1200–1800,' in Xavier Rousseaux and René Lévy, eds., *Le pénal dans tous ses états: Justice, états et sociétés en Europe (XIIe–XIXe siècles)* (Bruxelles: Publications des Facultés universitaires Saint-Louis 1997), 43–6.

23 CS, v.42: 13853–70; Evelyn Kolish, 'Changements dans le droit privé au Québec Bas-Canada entre 1760 et 1849: attitudes et réactions des contemporains' (PhD, Université de Montréal 1980); *JHALC* 33(1823–4), appendix QQ, and 45 (1835–6), appendix Vv.

24 The calculation of the recidivism rate is based only on defendants' names, so that, if anything, it may be high.

25 BAnQ-Q TL31 S1 SS1, 1802–37 (as indexed in the *Thémis 2* database); Fecteau, *Nouvel ordre*, 133, 237.

26 Nicole Castan, *Les criminels de Languedoc: les exigences d'ordre et les voies du*

ressentiment dans une société pré-révolutionnaire, 1750–1790 (Toulouse: Association des publications de l'Université de Toulouse-Le Mirail 1980), 18–24; Hufton, 'Le paysan et la loi,' 679–701; Thompson, *Whigs and Hunters*; Hay, 'Property, Authority and the Criminal Law'; Shoemaker, *Prosecution and Punishment*, 276; Beattie, *Crime and the Courts*, passim, and *Policing and Punishment*, 17–18; King, *Crime, Justice*, 138–9; Lachance, *Crimes et criminels*, 79. In New France, the same was true for civil cases: Quebec City, with 20 per cent of the population of its district, accounted for three-quarters of the business before the prévôté, the main civil court (John Dickinson, *Justice et justiciables: la procédure civile à la Prévôté de Québec, 1667–1759* [Sainte-Foy, Que.: Presses de l'Université Laval 1982], 142).

27 *La Minerve*, 18/1/1836; Greer, *Patriots*, 91; Clive Emsley, *Crime and Society in England, 1750–1900*, 2nd ed. (London: Longman 1996), 92–120; Shoemaker, *Prosecution and Punishment*, 7; Gregory Thomas Smith, 'The State and the Culture of Violence in London, 1760–1840' (PhD, University of Toronto 1999), 64–5. Information on homicide rates is from an ongoing research project into violence in Quebec and Lower Canada.

28 Hufton, 'Le paysan et la loi'; Greer, *Patriots*, 97–9; Fecteau, *Nouvel ordre*, 77.

29 Sainte-Marguerite-de-Blairfindie residents to Kempt, 5/11/1829, CS, v.301; Massé to Lagueux, 17/1/1825, CS, v.232; de LaMothe to Yorke, 28/4/1829, CS, v.285; Gatien, *Cap-Santé*, 170–1; Allsopp to Yorke, 19/8/1830, CS, v.334.

30 Beaudreau and Dufresne v. Beauchamp, QSD, 29/9/1830; Gatien, *Cap-Santé*, 177–8.

31 LAC MG8 F89: 3657–87.

32 Robert B. Shoemaker, 'Using Quarter Sessions Records as Evidence for the Study of Crime and Criminal Justice,' *Archives* 20, no.90 (1993): 156.

33 Fyson, 'Judicial Prosecution.'

34 Louis A. Knafla, 'Aspects of the Criminal Law, Crime, Criminal Process and Punishment in Europe and Canada, 1500–1935,' in Louis A. Knafla, ed., *Crime and Criminal Justice in Europe and Canada: Essays*, 2nd ed. (Waterloo, Ont.: Wilfrid Laurier University Press 1985), 7.

35 Hay, 'Meanings'; Fecteau, *Nouvel ordre*, 128–9; Greer, *Patriots*, 91–100; Fecteau and Hay, '"Government by Will and Pleasure,"' 132. The same is postulated for the civil law before 1775: André Morel, 'La réaction des Canadiens devant l'administration de la justice de 1764 à 1774: Une forme de résistance passive,' *Revue du Barreau* 20, no.2 (1960): 55–63.

36 Hay, 'Meanings,' 84–5; Fecteau, *Nouvel ordre*, 125–9, 233–9. On plaintiffs and victims: from data kindly supplied me by Jean-Marie Fecteau.

37 *Return to an Address from the Honourable House of Commons, Dated 16 March*

1837, for, Copy of a Report of a Select Committee of the House of Assembly of Lower Canada, respecting Mr. Chisholme, Clerk of the Peace for Three Rivers ... (London: HMSO 1837), 48–58.

38 Fecteau, *Liberté*, 137; Christie, *History*, 2:355–6.

39 Garnham, *Courts*, 63–6.

40 McDonald v. Gagné, 18/4/1810, and Cameron v. Gagné, 19/4/1810, BAnQ-Q TL31 S1 SS1 #s 4349–4650 (Cameron was married to Marie Anne Hill, widow of Henri Kramer and a Catholic); Fecteau and Hay, '"Government by Will and Pleasure"'; Greenwood, *Legacies of Fear*; Jean-Marie Fecteau, F. Murray Greenwood, and Jean-Pierre Wallot, 'Sir James Craig's "Reign of Terror" and Its Impact on Emergency Powers in Lower Canada, 1810–13,' in Greenwood and Wright, *Canadian State Trials. Volume I:* 323–78.

41 Pieter Spierenburg, 'Violence and the Civilizing Process: Does It Work?' *Crime, Histoire & Sociétés* 5, no.2 (2001): 87–105.

42 Poutanen, 'To Indulge Their Carnal Appetites'; Cliche, 'L'infanticide'; Martin Dufresne, 'La reforme de la justice pénale bas-canadienne: le cas des assauts communs à Québec,' *Revue d'histoire de l'Amérique française* 53, no.2 (1999): 247–75; Podruchny, 'Unfair Masters'; Pilarczyk, '"Too Well Used"' and 'The Law of Servants'; Fecteau, *Nouvel ordre*, 129, 238–52.

43 Stephen R. Wilson, 'The Court of Quarter Sessions and Larceny in Sussex, 1775–1820,' *Criminal Justice History* 7 (1986): 75; Davey, *Rural Crime*, 13; Gwenda Morgan and Peter Rushton, *Rogues, Thieves, and the Rule of Law: The Problem of Law Enforcement in North-East England, 1718–1800* (London: University College London Press 1998), 51; King, *Crime, Justice*, 36; George Rudé, *Criminal and Victim: Crime and Society in Early Nineteenth-Century England* (Oxford: Clarendon Press 1985), 10, 17, 26; Philips, *Crime and Authority*, 142; Taylor, *Crime*, 27–43; Emsley, *Crime and Society*, 32–6.

44 Shoemaker, *Prosecution and Punishment*; Jim Phillips and Allyson N. May, 'Female Criminality in 18th-Century Halifax,' *Acadiensis* 31, no.2 (2002): 78; Lewthwaite, 'Law and Authority,' 183; Murray, *Colonial Justice*, 135–7.

45 Mary Anne Poutanen, 'Reflections of Montreal Prostitution in the Records of the Lower Courts, 1810–1842,' in Donald Fyson, Colin Coates, and Kathryn Harvey, eds., *Class, Gender and the Law in Eighteenth and Nineteenth-Century Quebec: Sources and Perspectives* (Montreal: Montreal History Group 1993), 121; RG1 E15A, v.29, file 'House of Correction 1816.'

46 RG1 E15A, v.13, file 'Committee on Revenue 1793.'

47 LAC MG8 F89, v.6: 3657–87.

48 C.W. Brooks, 'Interpersonal Conflict and Social Tension: Civil Litigation in England, 1640–1830,' in A.L. Beier, David Cannadine, and James Rosen-

heim, eds., *The First Modern Society: Essays in English History in Honour of Lawrence Stone* (Cambridge: Cambridge University Press 1989), 391–3; Smith, 'Culture of Violence,' 45; Garneau, 'Justice et règlement des conflits.'

49 Marston v. Berthelet *dit* Savoyard and Mathieu, BAnQ-M TL19 S4 SS1 1796 #123; 'Analytical Index to Cases Determined in the Court of King's Bench for the District of Quebec, from 1808 to 1822,' *Revue de législation et de jurisprudence*, 3, no.2 (1847), 70 citing Peltier v. Miville, 1818 #296.

50 Lajeunesse v. Merckell, 11/1790, BAnQ-M TL16 S2; Judah v. Levy, 3/1781, BAnQ-M TL16 S2.

51 For recent European views, Benoît Garnot, ed., *L'infrajudiciaire du Moyen Age à l'époque contemporaine* (Dijon: Éditions universitaires de Dijon 1996). On Quebec: Scott, 'Chapters,' 293; Hay, 'Meanings,' 88–9; Greer, *Patriots*, 97–100; Fecteau, *Nouvel ordre*, 77; Dufresne, 'Justice pénale.'

52 Minutes of Repentigny and Saint-Sulpice meetings, 24/11/1789 and 6/12/ 1789, CS, v.42: 14374–5 and 14382–3; Bouthillier to Yorke, 13/8/1830, CS, v.333; 'Jean-Antoine Bouthillier,' *DCB*, 6.

53 Benoît Garnot, 'Justice, infrajustice, parajustice et extrajustice dans la France d'ancien régime,' *Crime, Histoire & Sociétés* 4, no.1 (2000): 103–20; Dufresne, 'Justice pénale,' 8, 138. In Canada today, it is estimated that only 37 per cent of non-sexual assaults, and 22 per cent of sexual assaults, are ever reported to police, and only 27 per cent of violent incidents reported lead to a charge being laid. See Karen Mihorean et al., *A Profile of Criminal Victimization: Results of the 1999 General Social Survey* (Ottawa: Statistics Canada 2001), 39–44.

54 Specialists of Lower Canadian notarial records whom I have consulted report seeing few if any cases where potentially criminal disputes were settled.

55 Leclerc, 'Justice et infra-justice.'

56 Tuttle v Bacon, QSD, 13/4/1820.

57 My work in progress on violence suggests that the homicide rate in Lower Canada was about 2 per 100,000 per year.

58 Bouc v. Dupras, QSD, 26/8/1797.

6: Experiencing the Everyday Course of Justice

1 QSR, 22/7/1765; *La Minerve*, 15/11/1827.

2 King, *Crime, Justice*, 1–2, and 'Summary Courts'; Beattie, *Crime and the Courts*, 36–8, 268–71; Shoemaker, *Prosecution and Punishment*, 19–41; Smith, 'Culture of Violence,' 275–335.

3 Lachance, *Justice criminelle*, 115–17; Smith, 'Culture of Violence,' 388–91.

4 For example, Douglas Hay, 'Civilians Tried in Military Courts: Quebec, 1759–64,' in Greenwood and Wright, eds., *Canadian State Trials. Volume I*: 114–28, or Boissery, *A Deep Sense of Wrong*.

5 Tocqueville, *Regards*, 161–5, 181–4, 195–6; for recent examples of the use of this citation, see Danièle Noël, 'Une langue qui ne capitule pas (la justice et les tribunaux),' and John A. Dickinson, 'L'anglicisation,' in Michel Plourde, ed., *Le français au Québec: 400 ans d'histoire et de vie* (Montreal: Fides/Publications du Québec 2000), 76, 83.

6 Goguet v. Bazinet and Brouillet, QSD, 6/9/1800; Martin v. Foucher, 3/5/1800, BAnQ-M TL36 S1 SS1. On Foucher: Pierre-Georges Roy, *Les juges de la province de Québec* (Quebec: R. Paradis 1933), 219.

7 Lauzon v. Duquet, QSD, 20/5/1825; Perrault and Scott to Walcott, 16/9/1836, CS, v.492.

8 QSR, 30/10/1810; Lafleur v. Collin *dit* Laliberté, QSD, 10/5/1815; Frene v. Adam, QSD, 21/7/1815.

9 Shavers to Reid, 11/1/1796, QSD, 4/1799.

10 Archives du séminaire de Saint-Hyacinthe, BSE17 2, 27/7/1819.

11 Garnham, *Courts*, 48–57; King, *Crime, Justice*; Goebel and Naughton, *Law Enforcement*, 339–44, 406–31, 485–553; Lewthwaite, 'Law and Authority,' 73–124; Lachance, *Justice criminelle*, 61–103; Garneau, 'Justice et règlement des conflits'; Dickinson, 'Réflexions sur la police,' 512–15.

12 Shoemaker, *Prosecution and Punishment*, 81–94; King, *Crime, Justice*, 92–3; Smith, 'Culture of Violence,' 37–8, 281–92.

13 RG1 E15A, v.13, file 'Committee on Public Revenue 1793'; Frappier v. Prévost, QSD, 2/2/1795; Grignon v. Sawers, BAnQ-M TL19 S4 SS1 1800 #32; Wright to Yorke, 10/10/1830, CS, v.337; Uniacke to ?, 8/8/1809, CS, v.105: 33177–9.

14 King, *Crime, Justice*, 1, 17–62; Beattie, *Crime and the Courts*, 35–73, and *Policing and Punishment*; Hay and Snyder, 'Using the Criminal Law'; Benoît Garnot, 'Une illusion historiographique: justice et criminalité au XVIIIe siècle,' *Revue historique* 281, no.2 (1990): 369–72.

15 Fecteau, *Nouvel ordre*, 110; Goebel and Naughton, *Law Enforcement*, 319–20 and 620–3; Robert M. Ireland, 'Privately Funded Prosecution of Crime in the Nineteenth-Century United States,' *American Journal of Legal History* 39, no.1 (1995): 43; Jim Phillips, 'The Criminal Trial in Nova Scotia, 1749–1815,' in G. Blaine Baker and Jim Phillips, eds., *Essays in the History of Canadian Law. Volume VIII: In Honour of R.C.B. Risk* (Toronto: Osgoode Society / University of Toronto Press 1999), 478–80; Dufresne, 'La réforme'; Steinberg, *Transformation*.

16 QSR, 10/1785; Kell to Delisle, 11/10/1820, QSD; similarly, see Kell to

Delisle, 4/7/1825, QSD; Smith, 'Culture of Violence,' 64–122; Emsley, *Crime and Society*, 180–4.

17 Bowen to Ryland, 19/2/1809, CS, v.102: 32329–31; Craig to Roe, 8/4/1835, CSL; Dufresne, 'Justice pénale,' 108–9; Norma Landau, 'Indictment for Fun and Profit: A Prosecutor's Reward at Eighteenth-Century Quarter Sessions,' *Law and History Review* 17, no.3 (1999): 510.

18 QSR, 10/11/1787; Fletcher to Ready, 8/11/1819, LAC RG4 B20, v.6: 2250–7.

19 King, 'Summary Courts.'

20 R v. Faribault and Leroux (certiorari), BAnQ-M TL19 S4 SS1 1814 #352; *La Minerve*, 20/9/1827; R v. Cuthbert (certiorari), BAnQ-M TL19 S4 SS1 1816 #949; *La Minerve*, 1/8/1833.

21 For example, R v. McCord and Mondelet (certiorari), BAnQ-M TL19 S4 SS1 1820 #1804.

22 Fyson, 'Jurys'; P.J.R. King, '"Illiterate Plebeians, Easily Misled": Jury Composition, Experience and Behavior in Essex, 1735–1815,' and Douglas Hay, 'The Class Composition of the Palladium of Liberty: Trial Jurors in the Eighteenth Century,' in J.S. Cockburn and Thomas A. Green, eds., *Twelve Good Men and True: The Criminal Trial Jury in England, 1200–1800* (Princeton, N.J.: Princeton University Press 1988), 254–304 and 305–57; François Rivet, 'La vision de l'ordre en milieu urbain chez les élites locales de Québec et Montréal: le discours des grands jurys, *1820–1860*' (MA, Université du Québec à Montréal 2004), 22–5.

23 QSR, 7/1791.

24 For example, *La Minerve*, 1/8/1833.

25 LAC RG1 E1, 18/12/1765; 'Christophe Pélissier,' *DCB* 4.

26 Neatby, *Administration*, 309; John H. Langbein, *The Origins of Adversary Criminal Trial* (Oxford: Oxford University Press 2003), 26–40.

27 McCord and Mondelet to Foy, 8/4/1811, CS, v.113: 35840; Mondelet and McCord to Dalhousie, 29/10/1823, CS, v.222; John Lambert, *Travels through Canada, and the United States of North America, in the Years 1806, 1807, & 1808* (London: C. Cradock and W. Joy 1813), 187–8. While Mondelet and McCord's assertion is perhaps an exaggeration, an 1820 table showing the presence of Montreal attorneys in October Sessions suggests that at least half were present at that session alone, many on several different days (BAnQ-M TL32 S1 SS1 10/1820).

28 *Le Canadien*, 6/5/1809; *La Minerve*, 1/8/1833, 21/11/1833, 25/11/1833; Cornwall to Yorke, 19/11/1829, CS, v.302.

29 Aubert de Gaspé, *Mémoires*, 277–8, 393–9; Morel, 'Réception,' 523–33. In the 1820 list of attorneys in Montreal Quarter Sessions, of the sixteen attorneys listed as appearing, nine were *Canadiens*; overall, about 40 per cent of

attorneys named in the Quarter Sessions registers in the nineteenth century were *Canadiens*.

30 Beattie, *Crime and the Courts*, 352–62; Langbein, *Adversary Criminal Trial*; King, *Crime, Justice*.

31 R v. Duaine, QSR, 1/1780; *La Minerve*, 1/8/1833; Mondelet and McCord to Dalhousie, 29/10/1823, CS, v.222. Examples of legal arguments in Quarter Sessions include R v. Scullion and Hanameny, QSR, 7/1825 (misnomer); R v. Tremblay, QSR, 10/1806 (form of the indictment); Grandmaitre v. Foubert, QSR, 1/1795 (jurisdiction); Mechtler v. Oakes, QSR, 7/1818 (procedure). In Weekly Sessions: *La Minerve*, 21/11/1833.

32 McCord and Mondelet to Cochran, 26/8/1815, CS, v.147.

33 QSR, 19/7/1823.

34 QSR, 24/10/1810, 30/4/1811, 11/1/1831. From 1794, attorneys' fees in the Montreal Quarter Sessions may have been regulated by reference to the fee schedule in 20 George II c.3 (QSR, 27/1/1794), but since that ordinance had expired in 1787, the force of this reference seems doubtful.

35 Smith and Chenette v. Christin *dit* Saint-Amour, QSD, 12/6/1821; QSR, 7/1821.

36 QSR, 11/1/1831.

37 Maurice Lemire et al., *La vie littéraire au Québec. Volume 1: 1764–1805. La voix française des nouveaux sujets britanniques* (Quebec: Presses de l'Université Laval 1991), 108–13; Denis Vaugeois, 'Une langue sans statut,' in Plourde, *Le français au Québec*, 59–71; Michael Dorland and Maurice Charland, *Law, Rhetoric, and Irony in the Formation of Canadian Civic Culture* (Toronto: University of Toronto Press 2002), 89–95; Garneau, *Histoire du Canada* 3: 320; Lareau, *Histoire du droit canadien*, 1: 310–11; Scott, 'Chapters,' 136; Morel, 'Réception,' 534–38; Hay, 'Meanings,' 85–6; Fecteau, *Nouvel ordre*, 109; Noël, 'Une langue,' 78.

38 This is evident from the judges' notebooks in LAC MG24 B173.

39 Babineau v. Chanier, QSD, 24/2/1820; Monk to Ryland, 14/5/1802, CS, v.77: 24035–40.

40 Perrault, *Questions et réponses*, 210–11; Blackstone, *Commentaries*, IV: 318; William Dickinson, *A Practical Guide, to the Quarter, and Other, Sessions of the Peace* (London: Reed and Hunter 1815), 160, 192; Fyson, 'Jurys'; QSR, 10–11/1/1833, 10/7/1834, 21–22/10/1836.

41 Cavendish, *Debates*, 140.

42 *JHALC* 35 (1826), 231–7.

43 *Return to an Address … Respecting Mr. Chisholme …*, 43–5.

44 Johnson to Burton, 26/6/1824, CS, v.228; Yule to Loring, 4/10/1815, CS, v.148; Osborn v. Carden, QSD, 15/3/1825.

45 Brown to Haldimand, 18/9/1783, CS, v.26: 8628.

46 Lampher and Tyler v. Dupré et al., QSD, 13/11/1785.

47 Canadian Centre for Justice Statistics, *Canadian Crime Statistics 2003* (Ottawa: Statistics Canada 2004), 11, 21.

48 *La Minerve*, 21/7/1836; Smith, 'Culture of Violence,' 42–7, 65–6; Landau, 'Indictment'; Beattie, *Crime and the Courts*, 76; King, 'Punishing Assault'; Leclerc, 'Justice et infra-justice'; Garneau, 'Justice et règlement des conflits; Lachance, *Crimes et criminels*, 40; Dickinson, *Justice et justiciables*, 117–18.

49 Landau, 'Indictment,' 514; Fecteau, *Nouvel ordre*, 132–4.

50 Hay, 'Meanings,' 89–90.

51 QSR, 1779–84; TL36 S1 SS11, 1805, 1829, and 1835; CS, v.22: 7564–6, 7568, 7574, 7583–4, and v.25: 8418–35.

52 Pilarczyk, 'The Law of Servants,' 834–5.

53 Bartly to Byrne, 18 and 22/31811, CS, v.112: 35737, 35749–50.

54 Aubert de Gaspé, *Mémoires*, 44–8, 277–8; 'Plan of the Town and Citadel of Quebec with an Actual Survey of the Plains of Abraham ...' (Quebec, 1785), LAC, National Map Collection, (R)H1/340/Quebec/1785; Greenwood, *Legacies of Fear*, 80.

55 Dufresne, 'Justice pénale,' 27–8.

56 QSR, 1/1780, 4/1793, 4/1809, 10/1811.

57 Smith, 'Culture of Violence, 316–17; Landau, 'Indictment,' 515. In eighteenth-century Montreal, about 20 per cent of the fines were one shilling or less.

58 Beaulieu v. Faribault, QSD, 4/4/1820; *Return to an Address ... Respecting Mr. Chisholme ...*, 9; 20 George III c.3 (1780); QSR, 27/1/1794, 19/7/1817, 11/1/1819; report of Council, 2/9/1830, CS, v.334; Dufresne, *Justice pénale*, 97n.220.

59 *Montreal Gazette*, 15/9/1828; Perrault, *Questions et réponses*, 431; Green and Perrault to Sherbrooke, 15/1/1818, CS, v.172; Montreal King's Bench grand jury presentment, 10/9/1824, CS, v.229; anonymous opinion of a crown law officer, 2/12/1824, CS, v.231; *Return to an Address ... Respecting Mr. Chisholme ...*, 8, 47, 62; QSR 30/4/1835; Burn, *Justice*, I: 473–4.

60 Potevin v. Corneau, 20/2/1804, BAnQ-Q TL31 S1 SS1 #s 1456–7, 1471, 1499, and 1648; Dufresne, 'La réforme,' 275, and *Justice pénale*, 117, 129, 138; Landau, 'Indictment,' 517–20.

61 Julien to Sherbrooke, 24/5/1817, LAC RG4 B20, v.6: 1948–50; McClure to Kempt, 18/8/1829, LAC RG4 B20, v.13: 5179–80; Tanguay to Drummond, 22/1/1816, LAC RG4 B20, v.5: 1677–8; Quebec gaol registers, BAnQ-Q E17; BAnQ-Q TL31 S1 SS1 #s 123680, 123680A, 123685.

62 'Analytical Index to Cases Determined in the Court of King's Bench for the District of Quebec, from 1808 to 1822,' *Revue de législation et de jurisprudence*, 3, no.7 (1848), 347 citing Graham v. Whitty, 1818 #1056; petition of

Montreal residents, 18/6/1831, Archives de la Ville de Montréal, VM35, dossier 47, 1831–2.

63 Loizel v. Marchesseau, 10/1800, BAnQ-M TL19 S4 SS1 1800 #59; *La Minerve* 30/10/1828.

64 Dufresne, 'Justice pénale,' 135–6.

65 BAnQ-M TL36 S1 SS1, 6/5/1800; QSR, 10/7/1800.

66 Hay, 'Dread of the Crown Office'; Landau, *Justices*, 344–54; Smith, 'Culture of Violence,' 112–14; Goebel and Naughton, *Law Enforcement*, 154–61, 264–72; King, *Crime, Justice*, 297–333; Jim Phillips, 'The Operation of the Royal Pardon in Nova Scotia, 1749–1815,' *University of Toronto Law Journal* 42, no.4 (1992): 401–49.

67 Reid to Ready, 3/9/1821, CS, v.204; Becquet to Richmond, 9/3/1819 and 15/4/1819, LAC RG4 B20, v.6: 2128–34; Archives de la Ville de Montréal, VM35, dossiers 60–4 (1833–5) and VM1, série Conseil municipal, procès-verbaux, 1833–1836 passim.

68 The petitions themselves and the reports of the chairmen are found mainly in LAC RG4 B20 and CS; other references to these and other petitions are in CSL and in the registers of correspondence received, LAC RG4 A3. Further study of the course of petitions could be accomplished by a detailed study of the latter.

69 Ready to Mondelet, 15/3/1822, Yorke to Ross, 11/12/1828, Walcott to Quebec clerks of the peace, 21/2/1837, and Walcott to Quebec, Montreal and Trois-Rivières clerks of the peace, 4/4/1837, CSL.

70 Ross to Yorke, 8/11/1828, CS, v.268; McCord and Mondelet to Foy, 20/12, CS, v.111: 35486–8. The same discourse of poverty, ignorance, and recognition of guilt underlay the few pardon petitions presented to the Montreal City Council, including one especially amusing petition from a master mason, condemned to a forty-shilling fine for his horse having gone too fast, whose excuse was that it was his teenage son who had taken the horse out without his permission (petition of St-Jean, 30/4/1835, Archives de la Ville de Montréal, VM35, dossier 64, 1835–1).

71 Gale to Yorke, 28/7/1830, CS, v.330.

72 McClure v. Moffet and Dallaire, 17/5/1830, BAnQ-Q TL31 S1 SS1 #s 102793 to 102795.

7: Criminal Justice and Social Power

1 Kennedy and Thom, 'General Report,' 32; Bill v. Lowell, QSD, 29/4/1793; Lowell v. Bill, QSD, 30/4/1793; Bingham v. Burk, QSD, 29/5/1830.

2 *Return to an Address ... Respecting Mr. Chisholme ...*; 'David Chisholme,' DCB 7.

3 On Bingham: 'Michel-Eustache-Gaspard-Alain Chartier de Lotbinière,' *DCB* 6, and *Canadian Courant*, 17/10/1825. For a more extensive discussion of complainants in family-violence cases, and a different take on Burk, see Pilarczyk, 'Justice in the Premises' (178–81 for Burk); arrest information on Burk and Freeman from data kindly provided by Mary Anne Poutanen. Alternately, Freeman may have died in 1831.

4 Fecteau, *Nouvel ordre*; Podruchny, 'Unfair Masters'; Poutanen, 'To Indulge Their Carnal Appetites.'

5 QSR, 30/4/1830.

6 Abbott to Delisle, QSD, 18/6/1825.

7 *Montreal Gazette*, 22/7/1811.

8 Square to Kempt, 27/6/1829, CS, v.290; BAnQ-M TL36 S1 SS11, 23/6/1829; Gale to Yorke, 18/2/1830, CS, v.312; Charmon v. Jenkins, BAnQ-Q TL999 1960-01-343\38, Quebec Weekly and Special Sessions register 1809–1814, 3/3/1813; Dufresne, 'Justice pénale,' 120–9; Douglas Hay, 'Prosecution and Power: Malicious Prosecution in the English Courts, 1750–1850,' in Hay and Snyder, *Policing and Prosecution*, 343–95.

9 Miville to Kempt, 17/3/1830, CS, v.314; Jessica Warner and Frank Ivis, '"Damn You, You Informing Bitch": Vox Populi and the Unmaking of the Gin Act of 1736,' *Journal of Social History* 33, no.2 (1999): 299–330.

10 Robert v. Marois, QSD, 7/6/1815.

11 Anna Clark, 'Humanity or justice? Wifebeating and the Law in the Eighteenth and Nineteenth Centuries,' in Carol Smart, ed., *Regulating Womanhood* (New York: Routledge 1992), 187–206; Margaret Hunt, 'Wife Beating, Domesticity and Women's Independence in Eighteenth-Century London,' *Gender & History* 4, no.1 (1992): 10–33; Jennine Hurl-Eamon, 'Domestic Violence Prosecuted: Women Binding over Their Husbands for Assault at Westminster Quarter Sessions, 1685–1720,' *Journal of Family History* 26, no.4 (2001): 435–54; Roderick Phillips, 'Women, Neighborhood, and Family in the Late Eighteenth Century,' *French Historical Studies* 18, no.1 (1993): 1–12; André Lachance and Sylvie Savoie, 'Violence, Marriage and Family Honour: Aspects of the Legal Regulation of Marriage in New France,' in Jim Phillips, Tina Loo, and Susan Lewthwaite, eds., *Essays in the History of Canadian Law. Volume V: Crime and Criminal Justice* (Toronto: Osgoode Society / University of Toronto Press 1994), 143–73; Pilarczyk, 'Justice in the Premises,' 217–20.

12 Robertson v. Robertson, QSD, 1/3/1830.

13 Pilarczyk, 'Justice in the Premises.'

14 Sery et al. v. Joutras, QSD, 2/1/1800.

15 From Hart's accounts, in RG1 E15A.

16 QSR, 1/1815; Pilarczyk, 'Justice in the Premises,' 240.

17 QSR, 1/1798, 4/1798.
18 Pilarczyk, 'Justice in the Premises,' 241–2; Kathryn Harvey, 'Amazons and Victims: Resisting Wife-Abuse in Working-class Montreal, 1869–1879,' *Journal of the Canadian Historical Association* 2 (1991): 139–42.
19 LAC MG8 F89, v.6: 3657–87; Allard v. Maillou, QSD, 16/9/1820.
20 Pilarczyk, 'Justice in the Premises,' 357.
21 Flynn v. Dogherty, QSD, 5/9/1825.
22 Chartier de Lotbinière to Reid, QSD, 14/10/1809; *La Minerve*, 9/5/1834.
23 Pilarczyk found a slightly higher proportion for the period 1825–50 ('Justice in the Premises,' 261).
24 Gosse v. Skelton, QSD, 2/8/1820;Brais v. Renaud *dit* Desloriers, QSD, 3/12/1830; Saint-Aubin v. Legault dit Delorier, QSD, 2/11/1825; *Montreal Herald*, 5/1/1822; gaol calendars 8/9/1821 and 2/1/1822, LAC RG4 B21; Pilarczyk, 'Justice in the Premises,' 246, 251, 279–84 (on Legault *dit* Delorier), and 362–444 (on spousal murder in general; on the Dewey case, 363–75).
25 QSR, 14/4/1784.
26 Crooks v. Farrell, QSD, 2/11/1835.
27 Burn, *Justice*, I: 173–208; Patricia Bromfield, 'Incidences and Attitudes: A View of Bastardy from Eighteenth-Century Rural North Staffordshire, c.1750–1820,' *Midland History* 27 (2002): 80–98; Cornelia Hughes Dayton, *Women before the Bar: Gender, Law, and Society in Connecticut, 1639–1789* (Chapel Hill: University of North Carolina Press 1995), 157–230.
28 QSR, 8/4/1767; Marie-Aimée Cliche, 'Unwed Mothers, Families, and Society during the French Régime,' in Bettina Bradbury, ed., *Canadian Family History: Selected Readings* (Toronto: Copp Clark Pitman 1992), 33–65; George Okill Stuart, *Reports of Cases Argued and Determined in the Courts of King's Bench and in the Provincial Court of Appeals of Lower Canada...* (Quebec: Neilson and Cowan 1834), 323.
29 QSR, 7/1785, 4/1781, 4/1790.
30 Lisette v. Stodt, QSD, 13/5/1788; Reine v. Petit *fils*, QSD, 21/1/1794; QSR, 10/1792; Constance Backhouse, *Petticoats and Prejudice: Women and Law in Nineteenth-Century Canada* (Toronto: Women's Press 1991), 41–2.
31 QSR, 4/1782, 7/1787, 7/1792.
32 Lavigne v. Monjean, QSD, 30/1/1786; Lacoste v. Daudelin, QSD, 13/1/1794; additional information is from PRDH.
33 QSR, 1/1795, 10/1815; Savary v. Meunier, QSD, 7/8/1815; Craig to Roe, 21/11/1834, CSL.
34 The literature on these biases is immense. For overviews, see, on class inequalities, Dickinson and Young, *A Short History of Quebec*, 65–153; on

gender inequalities, Collectif Clio, *L'histoire des femmes au Québec depuis quatres siècles* (Montreal: Le Jour 1992), 77–148; on racial inequalities, Dorothy W. Williams, *Blacks in Montreal, 1628–1986: An Urban Demography* (Cowansville, Que.: Éditions Yvon Blais 1989), 11–19, and Alain Beaulieu, *Les autochtones du Québec: des premières alliances aux revendications contemporaines* (Saint-Laurent, Que.: Fides 1997), 95–107.

35 Shoemaker, 'Using Quarter Sessions Records,' 151–2.

36 Overall figures for capacity to sign are from Michel Verrette, 'L'alphabé-tisation au Québec 1660–1900' (PhD, Université Laval 1989), appendix 4.1, and Allan Greer, 'The Pattern of Literacy in Quebec, 1745–1899,' *Histoire sociale / Social History* 11, no.22 (1978): 295–335.

37 Fecteau, *Nouvel ordre*, 128. On French translations of Blackstone in the colony: *Quebec Gazette* 7/6/1787.

38 Mary Anne Poutanen, 'The Homeless, the Whore, the Drunkard, and the Disorderly: Contours of Female Vagrancy in the Montreal Courts, 1810–1842,' in Kathryn McPherson, Cecilia Morgan, and Nancy M. Forestell, eds., *Gendered Pasts: Historical Essays in Femininity and Masculinity in Canada* (New York: Oxford University Press 1999), 37.

39 Among many others, see, for example, Malcolm Feeley, 'The Decline of Women in the Criminal Process: A Comparative History,' *Criminal Justice History* 15 (1994): 235–74; André Lachance, 'Women and Crime in Canada in the Early Eighteenth Century, 1712–1759,' in Knafla, *Crime and Criminal Justice in Europe and Canada*, 157–77; Phillips and May, 'Female Criminality.'

40 Fecteau, *Nouvel ordre*, 130, 235, 247.

41 Between 1802 and 1805, almost half of those committed to the House of Correction were women (*JHALC* 13 [1805], 458); between 1811 and 1815, they accounted for 74 of the 141 people committed summarily (RG1 E15A, v.29, file 'House of Correction 1817'); and in four calendars of the House between 1816 and 1826, women accounted for 44 of 52 summary commit-tals (calendars of the House of Correction, 4/1816, 7/1821, 7/1825, 4/1826, in QSD).

42 On the nature of the violence of which men complained, see Donald Fyson, 'Blows and Scratches, Swords and Guns: Violence between Men as Material Reality and Lived Experience in Early Nineteenth-Century Lower Canada,' paper presented to the Annual Meeting of the Canadian Historical Association, Université de Sherbrooke, May 1999, http://www.hst.ulaval.ca/profs/dfyson/Violence.htm.

43 Monjon v. Perrault, QSD, 28/5/1825; Davis v. Oxbey, QSD, 8/8/1835.

44 G.S. Rowe, 'Femmes Covert and Criminal Prosecution in Eighteenth-century Pennsylvania,' *American Journal of Legal History* 32, no.2 (1988): 138–56.

45 Poutanen, 'To Indulge Their Carnal Appetites.'

46 Peter King, 'Gender, Crime and Justice in Late Eighteenth- and Early
    Nineteenth-Century England,' in Margaret L. Arnot and Cornelie
    Usborne, eds., *Gender and Crime in Modern Europe* (London: UCL Press
    1999), 56–7.

47 Lachance, 'Women and Crime in Canada,' 169; Willeen Keough, '"Now
    You Vagabond [W]hore I Have You": Plebeian Women, Assault Cases,
    and Gender and Class Relations on the Southern Avalon, 1750–1860,' in
    Christopher English, ed., *Essays in the History of Canadian Law Volume IX:
    Two Islands, Newfoundland and Prince Edward Island* (Toronto: Osgoode
    Society / University of Toronto Press 2005), 237–71.

48 For example, Singha, *A Despotism of Law*; Derek N. Kerr, *Petty Felony, Slave
    Defiance, and Frontier Villainy: Crime and Criminal Justice in Spanish Louisi-
    ana, 1770–1803* (New York: Garland 1993); Wayne Dooling, *Law and Com-
    munity in a Slave Society: Stellenbosch District, South Africa, c. 1760–1820*
    (Cape Town: Centre for African Studies, University of Cape Town 1992).

49 QSR, 5/1765, 7/1765; Hodossi v. Sacoyatinta and Sacoyatinta, QSD, 18/8/
    1830.

50 The identification of both Blacks and Natives in the criminal court records
    also depends on their being identified as such in the documents, which
    was probably more frequent in the case of defendants (for whom accurate
    identification in a deposition was an essential part of the process leading
    to arrest, and who seem generally to have been identified in prison regis-
    ters) than plaintiffs, though cross-checking names reveals few cases of
    plaintiffs identified as Black or Native in one case and not in another. My
    use of the term 'Black' follows Williams, *Blacks*.

51 Williams, *Blacks*, 11–19.

52 Mercure to Marshall, 12/3/1820, CS, v.192.

53 Sagosennageté v. Ontsientani, QSD, 10/5/1799, Lees to Reid, QSD, 31/7/
    1801.

54 D'Amour v. Lapierre, QSD, 27/11/1795; QSR, 10/1/1796; François v.
    Montgomerie and Johnson, QSD, 29/9/1835.

55 Helen Stone, 'Les indiens et le système judiciare criminel de la Province de
    Québec: les politiques de l'administration sous le régime britannique,'
    Recherches amérindiennes au Québec 30, no.3 (2000): 65–78; Denys Delâge
    and Étienne Gilbert, 'La justice coloniale britannique et les Amérindiens
    au Québec 1760–1820. I – En terres amérindiennes. II – En territoire colo-
    nial,' *Recherches amérindiennes au Québec* 22, no.1 (2002): 63–82, and 22, no.2
    (2002): 107–17.

56 Frank Mackey, *Black Then: Blacks and Montreal, 1780s–1880s* (Montreal:

McGill-Queen's University Press 2004); the Freeman affair is described at 99–103, based on the sources at 216. These can be completed by the depositions and other documents accompanying Arnoldi's petition to Gosford, 26/9/1836, CS, and the judge's notes of the testimony in R v. Grant et al., 6/9/1836, LAC MG24 B173 v.8. Also: Walcott to Arnoldi, 9/9/1836 and 27/10/1836, CSL.

57 'Jacob De Witt,' *DCB* 8.
58 'Louis Perrault,' *DCB* 9; *La Minerve*, 3/11/1836. According to census records available through http://www.ancestry.com, Betsy Ann Freeman, born about 1821, was living in Onslow County, North Carolina, in 1850.
59 'Reflections of Montreal Prostitution,' 106–8.
60 Goder v. Vadeboncoeur and Pilon, QSD, 12/9/1810; QSR, 10/1810.

8: Criminal Justice and State Power

1 Terroux to Montreal judges, 20/4/1815, CS, v.143; Monk to Loring, 3/7/1815, CS, v.146, with estimate and plan of Chevallier, Phillips and Try, 30/6/1815; Charbonneau v. Taylor, QSD, 13/7/1819.
2 Joseph Bouchette, *A Topographical Description of the Province of Lower Canada* (London: W. Faden 1815), 150; 'Estimate of repairs &c.', with Monk to Loring, 3/7/1815, CS, v.146; Foucher to Monk, 1/7/1815. On Marston, see chapter 4.
3 QSR, 19/7/1819, 30/10/1819; Poutanen, 'To Indulge Their Carnal Appetites.'
4 Hay, 'Meanings'; Morel, 'Réception.'
5 For example, Martha J. McNamara, *From Tavern to Courthouse: Architecture and Ritual in American Law, 1658–1860* (Baltimore: Johns Hopkins University Press 2004).
6 Lachance, *Justice criminelle*, 53–4; Luc Noppen, Claude Paulette, and Michel Tremblay, *Québec: trois siècles d'architecture* (Quebec: Libre expression 1979), 292–3; Landau, *Justices*, 231–5; Snell, 'County Magistracy,' 113; McNamara, *From Tavern to Courthouse*, 1–2.
7 Montreal Quarter Sessions grand jury presentment, 1/1765, CS, v.12: 4541–6; notarized protest of English merchants of Montreal, 5/3/1766, CS, v.15: 5682–7; petition of Montgolfier, 16/6/1766, CS, v.16: 5827–9; LAC RG1 E11, 18/6/1766; accounts of James Fraser, RG1 E15A, v.1, file 'Judicial Establishment 1767,' and v.5, file 'Judicial Establishment 1777'; account of John Burke, RG1 E15A, v.5, file 'Judicial Establishment 1778'; *Quebec Gazette*, 28/2/1765, 14/4/1768; accounts of George Young, RG1 E15A, v.10, file 'Judicial Establishment 1787'; Montreal King's Bench grand jury presentment, 3/1797, CO42, v.108, f.260.

8 *Quebec Gazette,* 4/10/1764, 8/11/1764, 24/1/1765, 31/1/1765, 22/12/1766, 6/1/1774; RG1 E15A, v.2, file 'Judicial Establishment 1769,' subfile 'Common Pleas'; Day to Mathews, 29/4/1782, British Library, Add. Mss. 21851, 222; journal of Charles Inglis, 19/6/1789, in *Report of the Public Archives of Canada,* 1913, 237; Martin Lessard, 'La transformation de la place d'Armes de la ville de Québec entre 1799 et 1804' (MA, Université Laval 2002); Alain Parent, 'Entre empire et nation: gravures de la ville de Québec et des environs, 1760–1833' (PhD, Université Laval 2003), 103–41.

9 Accounts of James Fraser, RG1 E15A, v.2, file 'Judicial Establishment 1768,' and v.5, file 'Judicial Establishment 1777.' Of Henry Dunn: v.10, file 'Public works 1787.' Of A.L. Wolff: v.9, file 'Judicial Establishment 1786'; Lessard, 'La transformation de la place d'Armes,' 81; Shortt and Doughty, *Documents*: 604.

10 Parent, 'Entre empire et nation,' 133.

11 Montreal Quarter Sessions grand jury presentment, QSR, 10/11/1791; *JHALC* 2 (1793–4), 136–8, and 4 (1795–6), 203–5; Montreal King's Bench grand jury presentment, 3/1797, CO42, v.108, f.260; Quebec judges to Prescott, c.4/1797, CO42, v.108, f.256.

12 On Quebec City: Noppen et al., *Québec*, 45–54, and Lessard, 'La transformation de la place d'Armes.' On Montreal, Gilles Lauzon and Madeleine Forget, eds., *L'histoire du Vieux-Montréal à travers son patrimoine* (Montreal: Publications du Québec 2004), 114–15. On both: Nathalie Clerk, *Palladian Style in Canadian Architecture* (Ottawa: Parks Canada 1984), 27, 79–80. André Giroux, *Les Palais de justice de la province de Québec de ses origines au début du vingtième siècle* (Ottawa: Parks Canada 1977), is unfortunately unreliable for the period that concerns us. On the North American trend, see McNamara, *From Tavern to Courthouse.*

13 On neo-Palladian style in general and its domination through to the 1780s, see Giles Worsley, *Classical Architecture in Britain: The Heroic Age* (New Haven, Conn.: Yale University Press 1995). On its transplantation to British North America: Clerk, *Palladian Style,* 5–42, though this work underestimates the influence of neo-Palladianism on British official architecture in the second half of the eighteenth century. See also Luc Noppen and Lucie K. Morisset, *La présence anglicane à Québec: Holy Trinity Cathedral, 1796–1996* (Sillery, Que.: Septentrion 1995), 95–102.

14 Bouchette, *Topographical Description,* 434–5.

15 Worsley, *Classical Architecture,* 245, 312; James Stevens Curl, *Georgian Architecture* (Newton Abbot, U.K.: David and Charles 1993), 142–3.

16 Sansom, *Sketches of Lower Canada,* 233; *JHALC* 11 (1803), 132, and 12 (1804), 174.

17 Lessard, *La transformation de la place d'Armes*, 163–8 and figure 50;
Mondelet and McCord to Ryland, 6/2/1813, CS, v.127: 40757–61; QSR, 11/
1/1820; McCord and Mondelet to Brenton, 9/12/1811, RG1 E15A, v.23, file
'Quarter Sessions of the Peace 1811'; *Montreal Herald*, 20/1/1821.

18 *JHALC* 10 (1802), 272–300, 11 (1803), 114–32, and 12 (1804), 172–6.

19 Terroux to Montreal judges, 20/4/1815, CS, v.143, and 20/5/1815, CS,
v.144; Montreal King's Bench grand jury presentment, 10/2/1827, CS,
v.250, file 'Executive Council'; Montreal Quarter Sessions grand jury
presentments, QSR, 19/7/1842 and 19/1/1843; Quebec judges to Prevost,
22/12/1814, CS, v.139: 44577–81; Quebec Quarter Sessions grand jury
presentment, 19/7/1830, in Christie to Yorke, 20/7/1830, CS, v.330.

20 McNamara, *From Tavern to Courthouse*; Worsley, *Classical Architecture*,
278–87.

21 On the gaols in general: Fecteau, *Nouvel ordre*,114–19, 170–2, 239–43; and
Ruddel, *Québec City*, 180–4. The eighteenth-century gaols have yet to be
studied in any depth; the description here is based on, among other
sources, RG1 E15A, v.1, files 'Public Works, Public Buildings 1765,'
'Judicial Establishment 1767,' and 'Judicial Establishment 1768'; Gray to
Carleton, 29/6/1767, CS, v.17: 6121–2; Allsopp to Gray, 21/7/1773, RG1
E14, v.1; *JHALC* 2 (1793–4), 136–8; Montreal King's Bench grand jury
presentment, 10/9/1801, CS, v.74: 23320–1; *JHALC* 12 (1804), 204; Neatby,
Administration, 342–4; and André Charbonneau, Claudette Lacelle, and
Marc Lafrance, *Évolution structurale du Parc de l'Artillerie et du Bastion Saint-
Jean, Québec: 1749–1903* (Ottawa: Parks Canada 1974), 1: 42–3.

22 Wallot, 'La querelle des prisons.'

23 *Montreal Herald*, 30/11/1811; Bouchette, *Topographical Description*, 150.

24 *Montreal Herald*, 1/3/1817.

25 On the nineteenth-century gaols: Bouchette, *Topographical Description*,
150–1, 445; Clerk, *Palladian Style*, 27–8, 81, 83. On Quebec City: Martin
Mimeault, 'Punir, contenir et amender: Les théories carcérales et leurs
applications à la prison des Plaines de Québec, 1863–1877' (MA, Université Laval 1999). On common gaols in Ontario later in the century: Peter
Oliver, *'Terror to Evil-Doers': Prisons and Punishment in Nineteenth-Century
Ontario* (Toronto: Osgoode Society / University of Toronto Press 1998).

26 Account of Joseph Walker, RG1 E15A, v.1, file 'Judicial Establishment
1765'; Proclamation 7/7/1790; *JHALC* 26 (1817), 224–8, 316–18, 422–4, and
30(1820–1), 190–1, appendix Vv; Neatby, *Administration*, 275; Rodolphe
Fournier, *Lieux et monuments historiques des Trois-Rivières et environs* (Trois-
Rivières, Que.: Éditions du Bien public 1978), 102; Clerk, *Palladian Style*, 82.

27 48 George III c.35; 7 George IV c.15; *JHALC* 36 (1827), 179–81; Douglas

Town Quarter Sessions grand jury presentment, 22/9/1824, CS, v.230; Mario Mimeault, 'Le district judiciaire de Gaspé (1788–1988),' *Gaspésie* 26, no.2 (1988): 30.

28 *JHALC* 38 (1828–9), 429–32; judges to Gosford, 30/8/1836, in *Canada: Return to an Address of the Honourable the House of Commons, dated 16 March 1837 ...* (London: HSMO 1837), 133.

29 *JHALC* 45 (1835), appendix M; Kennedy and Thom, 'General Report,' 17; C.-P. Choquette, *Histoire de la ville de Saint-Hyacinthe* (Saint-Hyacinthe, Que.: Richer et fils 1930), 99, 209; Rodolphe Fournier, *Lieux et monuments historiques du sud de Montréal* (Saint-Jean, Que.: Éditions du Richelieu 1970), 100.

30 For example, BAnQ-M TL19 S4 SS1 1814 #352.

31 Beattie, *Crime and the Courts*, 316–18; King, *Crime, Justice*, 334–5; Roeber, *Faithful Magistrates*, 73–111; Jerry Bannister, *The Rule of the Admirals: Law, Custom, and Naval Government in Newfoundland, 1699–1832* (Toronto: Osgoode Society / University of Toronto Press 2003), 90–2, 112.

32 On judges' robes, see, for example, the portraits of Smith, Elmsley, and Sewell in Roy, *Les juges*. On dress rules: Neatby, *Administration*, 308; account of George Young, RG1 E15A, v.10, file 'Judicial Establishment 1787'; *Rules and Orders of Practice, Made for the Court of King's Bench, District of Montreal* (Montreal: Nahum Mower 1811), 8; and *Orders and Rules of Practice in the Court of King's Bench, for the District of Quebec, Lower Canada* (Quebec, 1809), 10–11; Veilleux, 'Les gens de justice,' 116–17. On opening ceremonies: *Quebec Gazette*, 7/7/1766 and 21/7/1766; Morel, 'Les crimes et les peines'; Neatby, *Administration*, 308–9.

33 *Montreal Gazette*, 30/4/1810; QSR, 11/1/1820; *Montreal Herald*, 20/1/1821; *JHALC* 38 (1828–9), appendix Dd, 8/1/1829, testimony of William Henderson.

34 Denaut to Plessis, 18/9/1800 and 25/9/1800, and Somaglia to Plessis, 30/9/1820, summarized in *Rapport de l'archiviste de la province de Québec* 12 (1931–2), 172–3, and 13 (1932–3), 163; Ryland to chief justice, 27/9/1800, CSL; Aubert de Gaspé, *Mémoires*, 446; Lacroix v. Faribault and Leroux (certiorari), BAnQ-M TL19 S4 SS1 1814 #352.

35 Hart to Executive Council, 12/4/1822, CS, v.208; Gatien, *Cap-Santé*, 172; Loizel v. Marchesseau, 10/1800, BAnQ-M TL19 S4 SS1 1800 #59; Grignon v. Sawers, BAnQ-M TL19 S4 SS1 1800 #32; R v. Boright and R v. Charlebois and Charlebois, LAC MG24 B173, v.3, 10/11/1819, and v.5, 8/3/1826; Dubé v. May, QSD, 31/10/1835; R v. Cuvillier, LAC MG24 B173, v.2, 2/9/1817; Parent v. Lake, 31/10/1823, BAnQ-Q TL31 S1 SS1 #8053; Edward Allen Talbot, *Five Year' Residence in the Canadas: Including a Tour through*

Part of the United States of America, in the Year 1823 (London: Longman, Hurst, Rees, Orme, Brown and Green 1824), 302; *JHALC* 42 (1832–3), appendix M, deposition of Théophile Bruneau.

36 Account of François Larivière, RG1 E15A, v.10, file 'Public works 1787'; Quebec judges to Prescott, 4/1797, CO42, v.108, f.256; Quebec King's Bench grand jury presentment 18/5/1785, in BAnQ-Q TL18 S1 SS1; Quebec judges to Prevost, 22/12/1814, CS, v.139: 44577–81; Quebec judges to Cochran, 8/1/1827, CS, v.247; King, *Crime, Justice*, 253; McNamara, *From Tavern to Courthouse*, 6; 'History of the Old Bailey Courthouse,' http://www.oldbaileyonline.org/history/the-old-bailey/.

37 Trois-Rivières justices to Cochran, 28/10/1822, and Chisholme to Yorke, 15/1/1830, CS, vv.214 and 307.

38 Beattie, *Crime and the Courts*, 398–9; King, *Crime, Justice*, 252–7.

39 *JHALC* 42 (1832–3), appendix M, testimony of John Delisle, 11/1/1833; Aubert de Gaspé, *Mémoires*, 397; Hébert v. Floy, QSD, 22/4/1835; Mondelet et al. to Ready, 19/8/1818, CS, v.180; R v. Bower, 1/3/1825, LAC MG24 B173, v.4; Quebec judges to Prevost, 22/12/1814, CS, v.139: 44577–81; Hart to Executive Council, 12/4/1822, CS, v.208; Montreal Quarter Sessions grand jury presentment, QSR, 30/4/1830.

40 Trois-Rivières justices to Cochran, 28/10/1822, CS, v.214.

41 Lewthwaite, 'Law and Authority,' 99–100.

42 Steinberg, *Transformation*, 16–24.

43 Taschereau and Fletcher to Irvine, 30/4/1822, CS, v.209.

44 RG1 E15A, v.13, file 'Committee on Revenue 1793,' and v.39, file 'Clerk of the Peace 1821.'

45 Turmel, *Premières structures*, 24–34.

46 *La Minerve*, 7/1/1830; Fyson, 'Paroisse,' 33–4; Robichaud, 'Le pouvoir, les paysans et la voirie.'

47 Montreal Weekly Sessions register, 1805.

48 The correspondence is scattered through LAC RG4 B28 and CS.

49 Dufresne found the same in Quebec City in the 1830s (*Justice pénale*, 70).

50 BAnQ-M TL36 S1 SS11, 7/4/1829; *La Minerve*, 28/3/1833; Warner and Ivis, '"Damn You, You Informing Bitch."'

51 *La Minerve*, 28/3/1833; Dufresne, 'Justice pénale,' 69–73, 95–6.

52 *JHALC* 39 (1830), appendix, 15/3/1830.

53 Ross to Taylor, 6/4/1813, 5/5/1814, 11/4/1818, and 15/4/1818, CS, vv.128, 136, 176; Rivet, 'La vision de l'ordre,' 85–8.

54 Green and Perrault to Sherbrooke, 18/11/1817, CS, v.170, and 15/1/1818, CS, v.172; RG1 E15A, v.58, file 'Reports on Public Accounts 1827'; *JHALC* 42 (1832–3), appendix M, testimony of John Delisle, 20/3/1833; *JHALC* 45

(1835–6), Appendix Vv, testimony of A.M. Delisle regarding fees paid
Louis Malo; *Return to an Address ... Respecting Mr. Chisholme ...*, 4–6, 11;
Perrault and Scott to Walcott, 16/9/1836, CS, v.492; Dufresne, 'Justice
pénale,' 194.

55 SSR 23/7/1814; Dufresne, 'Justice pénale,' 99.

56 Poutanen, 'To Indulge Their Carnal Appetites,' 166; Fyson, 'Judicial
Prosecution.'

57 Dufresne, 'Justice pénale' and 'La réforme'; Nancy Kay Parker, 'Reaching
a Verdict: The Changing Structure of Decision-Making in the Canadian
Criminal Courts, 1867–1905' (PhD, York University 1999); V.A.C. Gatrell,
'Crime, Authority and the Policeman-State,' in F.M.L. Thompson, ed., *The
Cambridge Social History of Britain, 1750–1950* (Cambridge: Cambridge
University Press 1990), 3: 243–310; Smith, 'Circumventing the Jury';
Shoemaker, *Prosecution and Punishment*; Landau, *Justices*, 173–239; Joanna
Innes, 'Prisons for the Poor: English Bridewells, 1555–1800,' in Francis
Snyder and Douglas Hay, eds., *Labour, Law, and Crime: An Historical
Perspective* (London: Tavistock Publications 1987), 42–122; King, *Crime,
Justice*, 82–103 and 'Summary Courts;' Hay, 'Legislation,' 59–65.

58 Christie to Yorke, 27/6/1829, CS, v.290; R v. Rafferty, QSD, 30/12/1836.

59 *JHALC* 42 (1832–3), appendix Hh; Theodore N. Ferdinand, *Boston's Lower
Criminal Courts, 1814–1850* (Newark, N.J.: University of Delaware Press
1992); Steinberg, *Transformation*; Goebel and Naughton, *Law Enforcement*,
121–37.

60 In Quebec City, in both the year immediately prior to the closing of the
House of Correction in 1827 and the year following its reopening in 1829,
there were about 260 summary committals, almost all to the House of
Correction; during the two years that the institution was closed, there
were about 360 summary committals altogether to the gaol, or about 180
per year. The expiry of the house of correction legislation in May 1835 had
no particular effect on summary commitments in Quebec City, and the
establishment was still functioning in 1837 (Walcott to sheriff of Quebec,
17/4/1837, CSL). The fate of the Montreal House of Correction in the
1830s remains to be explored.

61 Testimony of Louis B. Pinguet, foreman of the Quebec City watch, *JHALC*
31 (1821–2), 142–4; 'Daily report of committals etc.,' 29/5/1827 to 28/5/
1828, and 'Return of Prisoners Committed to the House of Correction,' 3/
1/1826 to 19/4/1827 and 18/5/1829 to 1/4/1830, BAnQ-Q E17 1960–01–
036/1688 #318; Quebec and Montreal gaol registers; petitions of Louis
Marteau and John Godard, 18/4/1834, and deposition of Charles Laberge,
8/4/1835, Archives de la Ville de Montréal, VM35, dossiers 63, 1834–3 and

64, 1835–1; select reports of the Montreal watch, 30/4/1832 to 16/6/1832, *JHALC* 42 (1832–3), appendix M; *La Minerve*, 21/7/1836; Poutanen, 'The Homeless,' 37.

62 BAnQ-M TL32 S1 SS1, House of Correction calendar, 4/1806; BAnQ-Q E17, Quebec gaol register, 18/3/1822.

63 Montreal Oyer and Terminer grand jury presentment, 31/8/1829, CS, v.296; QSR, 19/1/1837.

64 Bowen to Ryland, 19/2/1809, CS, v.102: 32329–31; Caron and Fletcher to Cochran, 27/4/1818, CS, v.176; Fraser to Ready, 17/2/1821, CS, v.197; report of Council, 27/4/1822, CS, v.208, file 'Executive Council 4/1822'; Uniacke to Cochran, 7/3/1823, CS, v.217; Montreal King's Bench grand jury presentment, 10/3/1825, CS, v.233; Stuart to Yorke, 15/1/1830, CS, v.306; Têtu and Archambault to Kempt, 16/1/1830, CS, v.308; Dufresne, 'Justice pénale,' 107–8; Landau, 'Appearance at the Quarter Sessions,' 33–5, 44–6.

65 'Analytical Index to Cases Determined in the Court of King's Bench for the District of Quebec, from 1808 to 1822,' *Revue de législation et de jurisprudence*, 3, no. 7 (1848): 347, citing Graham v. Whitty, 1818 #1056; Burn, *Justice*: 1: 486–7.

66 RG1 E15A, v.13, file 'Committee on Public Accounts 1793.'

67 Abstract of causes against refractory militiamen, c.8/4/1783, CS, v.25: 8418–35.

68 *Montreal Gazette*, 26/11/1810.

69 Montreal justices to Dalhousie, 2/1827, CS, v.248.

70 QSR, 7/1769; Delisle v. Leslie, QSD, 15/9/1830.

71 Jennine Hurl, 'Voices of Litigation; Voices of Resistance: Constructions of Gender in the Records of Assault in London, 1680–1720' (PhD, York University 2001), 290–338.

72 Marstene v. Garoniontée, QSD, 29/4/1806; Meloche v. Cousineau, QSD, 11/1/1820.

73 Daunais et al. v. Dubois, QSD, 18/6/1823; Hurl, 'Voices of Litigation,' 299.

74 R v. Earl et al., 5/1827, MG24 B173; Reid to Dalhousie, 18/9/1828, CS, v.269; Mathons to Kempt, 18/9/1829, CS, v.298.

75 Castonguay v. Sparrow, QSD, 20/12/1799; QSR, 1/1800 and 4/1800.

76 Delisle v. Charbonneau, QSD, 15/10/1835.

77 Inquest on the body of Jane Laughlin, 4/5/1827, BAnQ-Q TL31 S26 SS1. My thanks to Vincent Dusablon for directing me to this. On disorderly women seeking shelter in gaols and houses of correction, see Mary Anne Poutanen, 'Bonds of Friendship, Kinship, and Community: Gender, Homelessness, and Mutual Aid in Early-Nineteenth-Century Montreal,' in

Bettina Bradbury and Tamara Myers, eds., *Negotiating Identities in 19th and 20th Century Montreal* (Vancouver: University of British Columbia Press 2005), 31.

Conclusion

1 Plinius Secundus, *Curiae Canadenses*, 15–16.
2 Storch, 'Policing,' 213. The criticism has been levelled at my own work: Fecteau, *Liberté*, 369n.24.
3 Fyson, 'Judicial Prosecution,' 105–10.
4 This is the case, for example, of both Allan Greer's work on the police and Martin Dufresne's study of criminal justice, and underlies the time-frame chosen for the most important collective work on state formation in British North America, Greer and Radforth, *Colonial Leviathan*, though the premise is criticized in one of that volume's articles (Brian Young, 'Positive Law, Positive State,' 50–1).
5 Derived from an analysis of returns in the annual *Extraits des rapports statistiques judiciaires*.
6 Fyson, *Court Structure*; Greer, 'Birth of the Police,' 39–40. Rural policing and criminal justice in the 1840s remain to be studied.
7 Hay, 'Prosecution and Power,' 389–95.
8 Fyson, 'Judicial Prosecution,' 93–104.

Bibliography

ARCHIVAL SOURCES

Archives du Séminaire de Saint-Hyacinthe
BSE17 2 – Registre de Joseph Porlier, juge de paix, Saint-Hyacinthe, 1819

Archives de la Ville de Montréal
VM1 – Fonds du Conseil de ville de Montréal, série Conseil municipal,
  procès-verbaux
VM35 – Fonds des juges de paix de Montréal

Archives de la Ville de Québec
QC1–01B/1370–01 – Série Sécurité publique, Comité de police, rapports

Bibliothèque et Archives nationales du Québec à Montréal (BAnQ-M)
E17 S1 SS1 – Fonds Ministère de la Justice, Registres de la prison de Montréal
P20 S1 D1 – Fonds Ville de Montréal, Reçus de John Delisle
P148 – Collection Charles Phillips
P1000 D871 – Lois et règlements de la ville de Montréal
P1000 D898 – Municipalité de La Prairie de la Madeleine
P1000 D1090 – Village de Terrebonne
P1000 D1102 – Émeute (charivari) de juin 1823 à Montréal
TL16 – Fonds Cour des plaidoyers communs
TL19 – Fonds Cour du banc du roi/de la reine
TL32 – Fonds Cour des sessions générales de la paix

TL36 – Fonds Cour des sessions spéciales et hebdomadaires de la paix

Bibliothèque et Archives nationales du Québec à Québec (BAnQ-Q)
E2 – Fonds Grands Voyers
E17 – Fonds Ministère de la Justice
TL5 D4289 – Requête de Charles-Philippe Jailliard
TL5 D70089 – Liste des aubergistes ...
TL18 S1 SS1 – Fonds Cour du banc du roi (documents)
TL31 S1 SS1 – Fonds Cour des sessions générales de la paix (documents)
TL999 – Collection Documents de tribunaux du régime anglais

British Library
Add. Mss. 21661–21889 – Haldimand papers

Library and Archives Canada (LAC)
All references in the endnotes are to former reference numbers; new reference numbers are given in parentheses when available. A more complete concordance is available on the companion website: http://www.hst.ulaval.ca/profs/dfyson/crimjust/
MG8 F89 – Fonds de la Seigneurie de Sorel (R11248-0-0)
MG19 A2 Series III – Ermatinger estate fonds, Jacobs-Ermatinger estate (R7712-0-7)
MG23 GII1 – James Murray collection (R6395-0-8)
MG23 GII3 – Edward William Gray fonds (R3233-0-5)
MG23 GII10 – Jonathan Sewell and family fonds (R6199-0-9)
MG23 GII19 – James Monk and family fonds (R5003-0-2)
MG24 B173 – James Reid collection (R2789-0-5)
RG1 E1 – Journals of the Councils of Quebec and Lower Canada (R10808-5-1, R10808-4-X, R10808-6-3, R10870-3-7)
[]RG1 E11 – Oaths of office and allegiance (R10808-0-2, R10870-16-5)
RG1 E14 – Clerk of Council's letterbook (R10808-0-2)
RG1 E15A – Public Accounts (R10808-11-7, R10870-13-X)
RG4 A1 – Civil Secretary, incoming correspondence
RG4 A3 – Civil Secretary, registers and day books
RG4 B19 – Montreal jury lists (R11455-0-5)
RG4 B20 – Applications for pardon or clemency (R11455-0-5)
RG4 B21 – Gaol calendars and prison returns (R11455-0-5)
RG4 B22 – Records relating to the appointment of bailiffs
RG4 B28 – Applications for licences, bonds and certificates
RG4 B45 – Declarations of aliens

RG4 C2 – Provincial Secretary, letterbooks
RG7 G15C – Civil Secretary, letterbooks
RG7 G15D – Civil Secretary, letterbooks (crown law officers)
RG68 – Commissions (R1002–33–9)

McCord Museum
Judge Samuel Gale Collection
Andrew Kollmyer Papers
McCord Family Collection

McGill University, Rare Book Room
MS 338 – Montreal, Night Patrol
MS 469 – Montreal, Road Committee
MS 719 – Montreal, Municipal Administration, James Reid fonds

Musée de la civilisation du Québec
Archives du Séminaire de Québec, P32 – Fonds Viger-Verreau

National Archives (U.K.)
CO 42 – Canada, formerly British North America, Original Correspondence

Université de Montréal, Service des Archives
Collection Baby – Register 74, 'Court of King's Bench. Docket Book of Judgements ...'

NEWSPAPERS

Canadian Courant
Le Canadien
La Minerve
Montreal Gazette
Montreal Herald
Quebec Gazette
Quebec Herald
Stanstead British Colonist

PUBLISHED PRIMARY SOURCES

Only cited published sources are given here; a complete list of published sources consulted is available on the companion website.

Almanach de Québec pour l'année 1789. Quebec: Guillaume Brown 1788.

'Analytical Index to Cases Determined in the Court of King's Bench for the District of Quebec, from 1808 to 1822.' *Revue de législation et de jurisprudence* 1-3 (1845–1848).

Aubert de Gaspé, Philippe. *Mémoires.* Ottawa: G.E. Desbarats 1866.

Blackstone, William. *Commentaries on the Laws of England.* Oxford: Clarendon Press 1765–1769.

Bosworth, Newton. *Hochelaga Depicta: The Early History and Present State of the City and Island of Montreal.* Montreal: W. Greig 1839.

Bouchette, Joseph. *A Topographical Description of the Province of Lower Canada.* London: W. Faden 1815.

Burn, Richard. *The Justice of the Peace and Parish Officer.* 14th ed. London: W. Strahan and W. Woodfall 1776.

Cavendish, Sir Henry. *Debates of the House of Commons in the Year 1774, on the Bill for Making More Effectual Provision for the Government of the Province of Quebec...* London: Ridgway 1839.

Copies or Extracts of Correspondence relative to the Affairs of Lower Canada [23/12/ 1837]. London: HMSO 1837.

Crémazie, Jacques. *Les lois criminelles anglaises* ... Quebec: Fréchette 1842.

Cugnet, François-Joseph. *Extraits des edits, declarations, ordonnances et reglemens de Sa Majesté très chrétienne* ... Quebec: Chez Guillaume Brown 1775.

– *Traité de la police: qui a toujours été suivie en Canada, aujourd'hui province de Québec, depuis son établissement jusqu'à la conquête* ... Quebec: Guillaume Brown 1775.

Dickinson, William. *A Practical Guide, to the Quarter, and Other, Sessions of the Peace.* London: Reed and Hunter 1815.

Doughty, Arthur G., and Duncan A. McArthur. *Documents relating to the Constitutional History of Canada, 1791–1818.* Ottawa: Public Archives 1914.

Doughty, Arthur G., and Norah Story. *Documents relating to the Constitutional History of Canada, 1819–1828.* Ottawa: Public Archives 1935.

Du Calvet, Pierre. *Appel à la justice de l'État* ...Londres: [s.n.] 1784.

Durham, Earl of. *Report on the Affairs of British North America.* London, 1839.

Firth, Edith G. *The Town of York, 1815–1834: A Further Collection of Documents of Early Toronto.* Toronto: Champlain Society 1966.

Four Bills, from the Legislative Council, to Consolidate, Amend or Repeal the Laws regarding the Administration of Criminal Justice in Lower Canada. Quebec, 1829.

Gatien, Félix. *Histoire de la paroisse du Cap-Santé.* Quebec: Léger Brousseau 1884 [1831].

Gleason, Thomas Henri. *The Quebec Directory for 1822.* Quebec, Neilson and Cowan 1822.

Hale, Matthew. *Historia placitorum coronæ. The History of the Pleas of the Crown*
... London: F. Gyles 1736.

Journals of the House of Assembly of Lower Canada, 1793–1836.

Journals of the Legislative Council of Lower Canada, 1792–1836.

Jousse, Daniel. *Traité de la justice criminelle de France* ... Paris: Debure père 1771.

Kennedy, William, and Adam Thom. 'General Report of the Assistant Commissioners of Municipal Inquiry.' In Earl of Durham, *Report on the Affairs of
British North America* (London 1839), appendix C.

Kennedy, W.P.M., and Gustave Lanctot. *Reports on the Laws of Quebec, 1767–
1770.* Ottawa: F.A. Acland 1931.

Lambert, John. *Travels through Canada, and the United States of North America, in
the Years 1806, 1807, & 1808.* 2nd ed. London: C. Cradock and W. Joy 1813.

Loix criminelles suivies en Canada. London: Charles Eyer and Wm. Strahan
1773.

Muyart de Vouglans, Pierre-François. *Institutes au droit criminel, ou Principes
généraux en ces matières* ... *avec un traité particulier des crimes.* Paris: Le Breton
1757.

– *Les loix criminelles de France, dans leur ordre naturel, dédiées au roi.* Paris: La
Société Typographique 1781.

*Orders and Rules of Practice in the Court of King's Bench, for the District of Quebec,
Lower Canada.* Quebec, 1809.

*Papers relating to Lower Canada viz. 1. Copy of the Instructions given to the Earl of
Gosford* ... London: HMSO 1838.

Parliamentary Register of Lower-Canada for the Year 1818. Quebec: John Neilson
1818.

Perrault, Joseph-François. *Le juge à paix et officier de paroisse, pour la province de
Québec.* Montreal: Fleury Mesplet 1789.

– *Questions et réponses sur le droit criminel du Bas-Canada: dédiées aux étudiants
en droit.* Quebec: C. Le François 1814.

Plinius Secundus. *Curiae Canadenses, or, the Canadian Law Courts.* Toronto:
H. and W. Rowsell 1843.

Provincial Statutes of Lower Canada, 1793–1836.

Quebec and Lower Canada proclamations, 1764–1815, *Canadian Archives
Report,* 1917–18, 1919–20.

Quebec ordinances, 1764–92, *Canadian Archives Report,* 1913, 1914–15.

Rapport annuel du Chef de Police. Montreal: La Minerve 1864.

Rapport de l'archiviste de la province de Québec 12 (1931–2) and 13 (1932–3).

Regulations of Police. Quebec, 1815.

Report from the Select Committee on the Civil Government of Canada. Quebec,
1829.

Return to an Address to His Majesty, dated 6 February 1833 ... London: HMSO 1834.

Roy, Pierre-Georges. *Inventaire des procès-verbaux des grands voyers conservés aux archives de la province de Québec.* Beauceville: L'Éclaireur 1923–32.

Rules, Orders and Regulations for the Foreman, Deputy Foreman and Watchmen of the City of Quebec. Quebec: T. Cary 1827.

Rules and Regulations of Police: With Abstracts of Divers Ordinances and Statutes relating Thereto. Quebec: John Neilson 1811.

Rules and Regulations of Police for the City and Suburbs of Montreal. Montreal: James Brown 1810.

Rules and Regulations of Police, for the City and Suburbs of Montreal. Montreal: James Lane 1817.

Rules and Regulations of Police for the City and Suburbs of Montreal. Montreal: W. Gray 1821.

Sansom, Joseph. *Sketches of Lower Canada, Historical and Descriptive.* New York: Kirk and Mercein 1817.

The Seventh Report from the Select Committee of the House of Assembly of Upper Canada on Grievances ... Toronto: M. Reynolds 1835.

Shortt, Adam, and Arthur G. Doughty. *Documents relating to the Constitutional History of Canada, 1759–1791.* Ottawa: Historical Documents Publication Board 1918.

Smith, John. *The Quebec Directory, or, Strangers' Guide in the City for 1826.* Quebec: T. Cary 1826.

Stuart, George Okill. *Reports of Cases Argued and Determined in the Courts of King's Bench and in the Provincial Court of Appeals of Lower Canada* ... Quebec: Neilson and Cowan 1834.

Talbot, Edward Allen. *Five Years' Residence in the Canadas: Including a Tour through Part of the United States of America, in the Year 1823.* London: Longman, Hurst, Rees, Orme, Brown and Green 1824.

Tocqueville, Alexis de. *Regards sur le Bas-Canada.* Montreal: Éditions Typo 2003.

Wilcocke, Samuel Hull. *The History of the Session of the Provincial Parliament of Lower Canada for 1828–29.* Montreal, 1829.

DIGITAL LIBRARIES AND OTHER DIGITAL RESOURCES

Canadiana.org. *Early Canadian Online.* http://www.canadiana.org

Laporte, Gilles, ed. *Les Patriotes de 1837@1838.* http://cgi2.cvm.qc.ca/glaporte/index.shtml

Our Roots. http://www.ourroots.ca

Programme de recherche en démographie historique (PRDH). *Registre de population du Québec ancien.* http://www.genealogie.umontreal.ca
Société Archiv-Histo. *Parchemin* (database)
Société Archiv-Histo. *Thémis 1* (CD-ROM)
Société Archiv-Histo. *Thémis 2* (CD-ROM)
Société Archiv-Histo. *Thémis 3* (CD-ROM)
Sweeney, Robert C.H., ed. *Manuscript Census Returns for Montréal, 1825; Thomas Doige's Directory of 1819; Thomas Doige's Directory of 1820* (databases)

MAJOR PROSOPOGRAPHICAL SOURCES

Audet, F.-J. 'Commissions d'avocats de la province de Québec, 1765 à 1849.' *Bulletin des recherches historiques* 39 (1933): 577–96.
– *Les députés de Montréal (ville et comtés), 1792–1867.* Montreal: Éditions des Dix 1943.
– 'Licenciés des bureaux médicaux du Canada Est de 1788 à 1848.' *Bulletin des recherches historiques* 8 (1902): 175–80, 201–9.
Buchanan, A.W. Patrick. *The Bench and Bar of Lower Canada down to 1850.* Montreal: Burton's 1925.
Bulletin des recherches historiques.
Cahiers des Dix.
Cook, Ramsay and Réal Bélanger, ed. *Dictionary of Canadian Biography* (CD-ROM). Quebec: Université Laval / Toronto: University of Toronto 2000.
Deschênes, Gaston, ed. *Dictionnaire des parlementaires du Québec, 1792–1992.* Sainte-Foy, Que.: Presses de l'Université Laval 1993.
Doige, Thomas. *An Alphabetical List of the Merchants, Traders, and Housekeepers Residing in Montreal* ... 1st and 2nd eds. Montreal: James Lane 1819/1820.
Lafortune, Hélène, Normand Robert, and Serge Goudreau. *Parchemin s'explique.* Montreal: Archives nationales du Québec 1989.
Lefebvre, Jean-Jacques. 'Tableau alphabétique des avocats de la province de Québec 1765–1849.' *Revue du Barreau* 17 (1957): 285–353.
Mémoires de la Société généalogique canadienne-française.
Racine, Denis. 'Les connétables de la ville de Québec (1798–1815) and 'Les connétables de la ville de Québec (1821–1822).' *L'Ancêtre* 6, no.3 (1979): 77–88, and 6, no.8 (1980): 238–40.
Roy, J.-E. *Histoire du notariat au Canada.* Lévis, Que., 1899–1902.
Roy, Pierre-Georges. *Les juges de la province de Québec.* Quebec: R. Paradis 1933.
Turcotte, Gustave. *Le conseil législatif de Québec 1774–1933.* Beauceville: L'Éclaireur 1933.

SECONDARY SOURCES

Abrams, Philip. 'Notes on the Difficulty of Studying the State (1977).' *Journal of Historical Sociology* 1, no.1 (1988): 58–89.

Acheson, T.W. *Saint John: The Making of a Colonial Urban Community*. Toronto: University of Toronto Press 1985.

Aitchison, J.H. 'The Development of Local Government in Upper Canada, 1783–1850.' PhD, University of Toronto 1953.

Arnaud, André-Jean et al. *Dictionnaire encyclopédique de théorie et de sociologie du droit*. 2nd ed. Paris: Librairie générale de droit et de jurisprudence 1993.

Audet, François-Joseph. 'Pierre-Édouard Leclère (1798–1866).' *Cahiers des Dix* 8 (1943): 109–40.

Backhouse, Constance. *Petticoats and Prejudice: Women and Law in Nineteenth-Century Canada*. Toronto: Women's Press 1991.

Bannister, Jerry. *The Rule of the Admirals: Law, Custom, and Naval Government in Newfoundland, 1699–1832*. Toronto: Osgoode Society / University of Toronto Press 2003.

Beattie, J.M. *Crime and the Courts in England, 1660–1800*. Princeton, N.J.: Princeton University Press 1986.

– *Policing and Punishment in London, 1660–1750: Urban Crime and the Limits of Terror*. New York: Oxford University Press 2001.

Beaulieu, Alain. *Les autochtones du Québec: des premières alliances aux revendications contemporaines*. Saint-Laurent, Que.: Fides 1997.

Bédard, Théophile-Pierre. *Histoire de cinquante ans (1791–1841): annales parlementaires et politiques du Bas-Canada depuis la Constitution jusqu'à l'Union*. Quebec: Léger Brousseau 1869.

Bernier, Gérald, and Daniel Salée. *Entre l'ordre et la liberté. Colonialisme, pouvoir et transition vers le capitalisme dans le Québec du XIXe siècle*. Montreal: Boréal 1995.

Bibaud, Michel. *Histoire du Canada*. Montreal: Lovell and Gibson 1837–8.

Blockmans, Wim, and Jean-Philippe Genet, eds. *The Origins of the Modern State in Europe*. Oxford: Clarendon Press 1995–. 7 vols.

Boissery, Beverley D. *A Deep Sense of Wrong: The Treason, Trials, and Transportation to New South Wales of Lower Canadian Rebels after the 1838 Rebellion*. Toronto: Osgoode Society / Dundurn Press 1995.

Bourdieu, Pierre. 'Esprits d'État. Genèse et structure du champ bureaucratique.' *Actes de la recherche en science sociale* 96–7 (1993): 49–62.

– 'De la maison du roi à la raison d'État. Un modèle de la genèse du champ bureaucratique.' *Actes de la recherche en science sociale* 118 (1997): 55–68.

Bourque, Gilles. *Question nationale et classes sociales au Québec, 1760–1840.* Montreal: Parti Pris 1970.

Braddick, Michael J. *State Formation in Early Modern England, c. 1550–1700.* Cambridge: Cambridge University Press 2000.

Brewer, John. 'The Eighteenth-Century British State. Contexts and Issues.' In Lawrence Stone, ed., *An Imperial State at War: Britain from 1689 to 1815* (New York: Routledge 1994), 52–71.

– *The Sinews of Power: War, Money and the English State, 1688–1783.* Cambridge, Mass.: Harvard University Press 1990.

Bridgeman, Ian. 'The Constabulary and the Criminal Justice System in Nineteenth-Century Ireland.' *Criminal Justice History* 15 (1994): 95–126.

Brodeur, Jean-Paul. *La délinquance de l'ordre: recherches sur les commissions d'enquête.* LaSalle, Que.: Hurtubise HMH 1984.

Bromfield, Patricia. 'Incidences and Attitudes: A View of Bastardy from Eighteenth-Century Rural North Staffordshire, c.1750–1820.' *Midland History* 27 (2002): 80–98.

Brooks, C.W. 'Interpersonal Conflict and Social Tension: Civil Litigation in England, 1640–1830.' In A.L. Beier, David Cannadine, and James Rosenheim, eds., *The First Modern Society: Essays in English History in Honour of Lawrence Stone* (Cambridge: Cambridge University Press 1989), 357–99.

Brunet, Michel. *Les Canadiens après la Conquête 1759–1775: de la révolution canadienne à la révolution américaine.* Montreal: Fides 1969.

Buckner, Phillip A. *The Transition to Responsible Government: British Policy in British North America, 1815–1850.* Westport, Conn.: Greenwood Press 1985.

Burt, A.L. *The Old Province of Quebec.* Toronto: McClelland and Stewart 1968 [1933].

Carmichael, Elizabeth K. 'Jacobitism in the Scottish Commission of the Peace, 1707–1760.' *Scottish Historical Review* 58, no.1 (1979): 58–69.

Caron, Ivanhoë. *La colonisation de la province de Québec.* Quebec: L'Action Sociale 1923–7.

Castan, Nicole. *Les criminels de Languedoc: les exigences d'ordre et les voies du ressentiment dans une société pré-révolutionnaire, 1750–1790.* Toulouse: Association des publications de l'Université de Toulouse-Le Mirail 1980.

– *Justice et répression en Languedoc à l'époque des lumières.* Paris: Flammarion 1980.

– and Yves Castan. 'Une économie de justice à l'age moderne: composition et dissension.' *Histoire économique et sociale* 3 (1982): 361–7.

Chabot, Richard. *Le curé de campagne et la contestation locale au Québec de 1791 aux troubles de 1837–38.* LaSalle, Que.: Hurtubise HMH 1975.

Chapais, Thomas. *Cours d'histoire du Canada*. Quebec: Librairie Garneau 1919–34.

Chapman, Terry L. 'Crime in Eighteenth Century England: E.P. Thompson and the Conflict Theory of Crime.' *Criminal Justice History* 1 (1980): 139–55.

Charbonneau, André, Claudette Lacelle, and Marc Lafrance. *Évolution structurale du Parc de l'Artillerie et du Bastion Saint-Jean, Québec: 1749–1903*. Ottawa: Parcs Canada 1974.

Chevalier, Frédéric. 'Développement et modernisation d'une structure étatique locale, à Québec, au début du XIXe siècle: l'histoire du service du "Guet et des Flambeaux de Nuit," de sa création (1818) jusqu'à l'incorporation de la ville (1832).' Unpublished seminar paper, Université Laval 1999.

Choquette, C.-P. *Histoire de la ville de Saint-Hyacinthe*. Saint-Hyacinthe, Que.: Richer et fils 1930.

Christie, Robert. *A History of the Late Province of Lower Canada, Parliamentary and Political* ... Quebec: T. Cary 1848–55.

Clark, Anna. 'Humanity or Justice? Wifebeating and the Law in the Eighteenth and Nineteenth Centuries.' In Carol Smart, ed., *Regulating Womanhood* (New York: Routledge 1992), 187–206.

Clerk, Nathalie. *Palladian Style in Canadian Architecture*. Ottawa: Parks Canada 1984.

Cliche, Marie-Aimée. 'L'infanticide dans la région de Québec (1660–1969).' *Revue d'histoire de l'Amérique française* 44, no.1 (1990): 31–59.

– 'Unwed Mothers, Families, and Society during the French Régime.' In Bettina Bradbury, ed., *Canadian Family History: Selected Readings* (Toronto: Copp Clark Pitman 1992), 33–65.

Collectif Clio. *L'histoire des femmes au Québec depuis quatres siècles*. Montreal: Le Jour 1992.

Conley, John A. 'Doing It by the Book: Justice of the Peace Manuals and English Law in Eighteenth Century America.' *Journal of Legal History* 6, no.3 (1985): 257–98.

Côté, J.E. 'The Reception of English Law.' *Alberta Law Review* 15, no.1 (1977): 29–92.

Couillard Després, A. *Histoire de Sorel*. Montreal: Imprimerie des Sourds-Muets 1926.

Courville, Serge, Jean-Claude Robert, and Normand Séguin. *Atlas historique du Québec. Le pays laurentien au XIXe siècle: Les morphologies de base*. Sainte-Foy, Que.: Presses de l'Université Laval 1995.

Craven, Paul. 'Canada, 1670–1935: Symbolic and Instrumental Enforcement in Loyalist North America.' In Douglas Hay and Paul Craven, eds., *Masters,*

Servants, and Magistrates in Britain and the Empire, 1562–1955 (Chapel Hill: University of North Carolina Press 2004), 175–218.

Curl, James Stevens. *Georgian Architecture*. Newton Abbot, U.K.: David and Charles 1993.

Curtis, Bruce. 'The Canada "Blue Books" and the Administrative Capacity of the Canadian State, 1822–67.' *Canadian Historical Review* 74, no.4 (1993): 535–65.

– 'Comment dénombrer les serviteurs de l'État au Canada-Uni: essai méthodologique.' *Revue d'histoire de l'Amérique française* 46, no.4 (1993): 607–28.

– *The Politics of Population: State Formation, Statistics, and the Census of Canada, 1840–1875*. Toronto: University of Toronto Press 2000.

Davey, B.J. *Rural Crime in the Eighteenth Century: North Lincolnshire, 1740–80*. Hull, U.K.: University of Hull Press 1995.

Daviau, Sébastien and Édith Prégent. *Le Musée régional de Vaudreuil-Soulanges: Une histoire passionnante à découvrir*. Vaudreuil-Dorion, Que.: Musée régional de Vaudreuil-Soulanges 2005.

Dayton, Cornelia Hughes. *Women before the Bar: Gender, Law, and Society in Connecticut, 1639–1789*. Chapel Hill: University of North Carolina Press 1995.

Delâge, Denys, and Étienne Gilbert. 'La justice coloniale britannique et les Amérindiens au Québec 1760–1820. I – En terres amérindiennes.' *Recherches amérindiennes au Québec* 22, no.1 (2002): 63–82. 'II – En territoire colonial.' 22, no.2 (2002): 107–17.

Desaulniers, C. 'La peine de mort dans la législation criminelle de 1760 à 1892.' *Revue générale de droit* 8, no.1 (1977): 141–84.

Desloges, Yvon. 'La corvée militaire à Québec au XVIIIe siècle.' *Histoire sociale / Social History* 30 (1982): 333–56.

Dessureault, Christian. 'L'élection de 1830 dans le comté de Saint-Hyacinthe: identites elitaires et solidarités paroissiales, sociales ou familiales.' *Histoire sociale / Social History* 36, no.72 (2003): 281–310.

– and Christine Hudon. 'Conflits sociaux et élites locales au Bas-Canada: le clergé, les notables, la paysannerie et le contrôle de la fabrique.' *Canadian Historical Review* 80, no.3 (1999): 413–39.

Devereaux, Simon. 'The Promulgation of the Statutes in late Hanoverian Britain.' In David Lemmings, ed., *The British and Their Laws in the Eighteenth Century* (London: Boydell and Brewer 2005), 80–101.

Dickinson, John A. 'L'anglicisation.' In Michel Plourde, ed., *Le français au Québec: 400 ans l'histoire et de vie* (Montreal: Fides/Publications du Québec 2000), 80–91.

- *Justice et justiciables: la procédure civile à la Prévôté de Québec, 1667–1759.*
  Sainte-Foy, Que.: Presses de l'Université Laval 1982.
- *Law in New France.* Winnipeg: University of Manitoba, Faculty of Law 1992.
- 'Réflexions sur la police en Nouvelle-France.' *McGill Law Journal* 32, no.3
  (1987): 497–512.
- and Brian Young. *A Short History of Quebec.* 3rd ed. Montreal: McGill-
  Queen's University Press 2003.
Dooling, Wayne. *Law and Community in a Slave Society: Stellenbosch District,
  South Africa, c. 1760–1820.* Cape Town: Centre for African Studies, Univer-
  sity of Cape Town 1992.
Dorland, Michael, and Maurice Charland. *Law, Rhetoric, and Irony in the
  Formation of Canadian Civic Culture.* Toronto: University of Toronto Press
  2002.
Dray, William H. *History as Re-enactment: R.G. Collingwood's Idea of History.*
  New York: Oxford University Press 1995.
Drolet, Antonio. *La Ville de Québec: histoire municipale. Volume II: Régime anglais
  jusqu'à l'incorporation (1759–1833).* Quebec: Société historique de Québec
  1965.
- *La Ville de Québec: histoire municipale. Volume III: de l'incorporation à la
  Confédération (1833–1867).* Quebec: Société historique de Québec 1967.
Dufresne, Martin. 'La justice pénale et la définition du crime à Québec, 1830–
  1860.' PhD, University of Ottawa 1997.
- 'La police, le droit pénal et le crime dans la première moitié du XIXe siècle.
  L'exemple de la ville de Québec.' *Revue juridique Thémis* 34, no.2 (2000):
  409–34.
- 'La reforme de la justice pénale bas-canadienne: le cas des assauts communs
  à Québec.' *Revue d'histoire de l'Amérique française* 53, no.2 (1999): 247–75.
Eastwood, David. *Governing Rural England: Tradition and Transformation in
  Local Government, 1780–1840.* New York: Oxford University Press 1994.
Emsley, Clive. 'Albion's Felonious Attractions: Reflections upon the History
  of Crime in England.' In Clive Emsley and Louis A. Knafla, eds., *Crime
  History and Histories of Crime: Studies in the Historiography of Crime and
  Criminal Justice in Modern History* (Westport, Conn.: Greenwood Press 1996),
  67–85.
- *Crime and Society in England, 1750–1900.* 2nd ed. London: Longman 1996.
- *The English Police: A Political and Social History.* 2nd ed. London: Longman
  1996.
- and Louis A. Knafla. *Crime History and Histories of Crime: Studies in the
  Historiography of Crime and Criminal Justice in Modern History.* Westport,
  Conn.: Greenwood Press 1996.

Errington, Jane. *The Lion, the Eagle and Upper Canada: A Developing Colonial Ideology*. Montreal: McGill-Queen's University Press 1987.

Fecteau, Jean-Marie. *La liberté du pauvre: sur la régulation du crime et de la pauvreté au XIXe siècle québécois*. Montreal: VLB 2004.

– 'Mesures d'exception et règle de droit: Les conditions d'application de la loi martiale au Québec lors des rébellions de 1837–1838.' *McGill Law Journal* 32, no.3 (1987): 465–95.

– *Un nouvel ordre des choses: la pauvreté, le crime, l'État au Québec, de la fin du XVIIIe siècle à 1840*. Montreal: VLB 1989.

– and Douglas Hay. '"Government by Will and Pleasure Instead of Law": Military Justice and the Legal System in Quebec, 1775–83,' In F. Murray Greenwood and Barry Wright, eds., *Canadian State Trials. Volume I: Law, Politics, and Security Measures, 1608–1837* (Toronto: Osgoode Society / University of Toronto Press 1997), 129–71.

– and F. Murray Greenwood and Jean-Pierre Wallot. 'Sir James Craig's "Reign of Terror" and Its Impact on Emergency Powers in Lower Canada, 1810–13.' In F. Murray Greenwood and Barry Wright, eds., *Canadian State Trials. Volume I: Law, Politics, and Security Measures, 1608–1837* (Toronto: University of Toronto Press 1997), 323–78.

Feeley, Malcolm. 'The Decline of Women in the Criminal Process: A Comparative History.' *Criminal Justice History* 15 (1994): 235–74.

Ferdinand, Theodore N. *Boston's Lower Criminal Courts, 1814–1850*. Newark, N.J.: University of Delaware Press 1992.

Flaherty, David H. 'Law and the Enforcement of Morals in Early America.' *Perspectives in American History* 5 (1971): 203–53.

Fleming, Patricia Lockhart, and Sandra Alston. *Early Canadian Printing: A Supplement to Marie Tremaine's A Bibliography of Canadian Imprints, 1751–1800*. Toronto: University of Toronto Press 1999.

Fougères, Dany. *L'approvisionnement en eau à Montréal: du privé au public, 1796–1865*. Quebec: Septentrion 2004.

Fournier, Rodolphe. *Lieux et monuments historiques du sud de Montréal*. Saint-Jean, Que.: Éditions du Richelieu 1970.

– *Lieux et monuments historiques des Trois-Rivières et environs*. Trois-Rivières, Que.: Éditions du Bien public 1978.

Friedman, Lawrence M. *Crime and Punishment in American History*. New York: Basic Books 1993.

Fyfe, Douglas. 'Transitions in Policing: Kingston 1816–42.' *Historic Kingston* 34 (1986): 68–85.

Fyson, Donald. 'The Biases of Ancien Régime Justice: The People and the Justices of the Peace in the District of Montreal, 1785–1830.' In Tamara

Myers et al., eds., *Power, Place and Identity: Historical Studies of Social and Legal Regulation in Quebec* (Montreal: Montreal History Group 1998), 11–35.

– 'Blows and Scratches, Swords and Guns: Violence between Men as Material Reality and Lived Experience in Early Nineteenth-Century Lower Canada.' Paper presented to the Annual Meeting of the Canadian Historical Association, Université de Sherbrooke, May 1999. http://www.hst.ulaval.ca/profs/dfyson/violence.htm

– 'The *Canadiens* and British Institutions of Local Governance in Quebec, from the Conquest to the Rebellions.' In Michael Gauvreau and Nancy Christie, eds., *Transatlantic Subjects: Ideas, Institutions and Identities in Post-Revolutionary British North America*. Montreal: McGill-Queen's University Press, forthcoming.

– 'Criminal Justice, Civil Society, and the Local State: The Justices of the Peace in the District of Montreal, 1764–1830.' PhD, Université de Montréal 1995.

– 'Les historiens du Québec face au droit.' *Revue juridique Thémis* 34, no.2 (2000): 295–328.

– 'Judicial Auxiliaries across Legal Regimes: From New France to Lower Canada.' In Claire Dolan, ed., *Entre justice et justiciables: les auxiliaires de la justice du Moyen Âge au XXe siècle* (Quebec: Presses de l'Université Laval 2005), 383–403.

– 'The Judicial Prosecution of Crime in the Longue Durée: Quebec, 1712–1965.' In Jean-Marie Fecteau and Janice Harvey, eds., *La régulation sociale entre l'acteur et l'institution: Pour une problématique historique de l'interaction* (Quebec: Presses de l'Université du Québec 2005), 85–119.

– 'Jurys, participation civique et représentation au Québec et au Bas-Canada: les grands jurys du district de Montréal (1764–1832).' *Revue d'histoire de l'Amérique française* 55, no.1 (2001): 85–120.

– 'La paroisse et l'administration étatique sous le Régime britannique (1764–1840).' In Serge Courville and Normand Séguin, eds., *Atlas historique du Québec: La paroisse* (Sainte-Foy, Que.: Presses de l'Université Laval 2001), 25–39.

– 'Les structures étatiques locales à Montréal au début du XIXe siècle.' *Les Cahiers d'histoire* 17, nos.1–2 (1997): 55–75.

– with the assistance of Evelyn Kolish and Virginia Schweitzer. *The Court Structure of Quebec and Lower Canada, 1764 to 1860*. 1st ed. Montreal: Montreal History Group 1994. 2nd ed., revised and corrected. Montreal: Montreal History Group 1997. http://www.hst.ulaval.ca/profs/dfyson/courtstr/

Gagnon, Serge. *Plaisir d'amour et crainte de Dieu: Sexualité et confession au Bas-Canada*. Quebec: Presses de l'Université Laval 1990.

Garneau, François-Xavier. *Histoire du Canada depuis sa découverte jusqu'à nos jours*. Quebec: N. Aubin 1845–52.

Garneau, Jean-Philippe. 'Droit, famille et pratique successorale: les usages du droit d'une communauté rurale au XVIIIe siècle canadien.' PhD, Université du Québec à Montréal 2003.
- 'Justice et règlement des conflits dans le gouvernement de Montréal à la fin du Régime français.' MA, Université du Québec à Montréal 1995.
Garnham, Neal. The Courts, Crime and the Criminal Law in Ireland, 1692–1760. Dublin: Irish Academic Press 1996.
Garnot, Benoît. 'Une illusion historiographique: justice et criminalité au XVIIIe siècle.' Revue historique 281, no.2 (1990): 361–79.
- ed. L'infrajudiciaire du Moyen Age à l'époque contemporaine. Dijon: Éditions universitaires de Dijon 1996.
- 'Justice, infrajustice, parajustice et extrajustice dans la France d'ancien régime.' Crime, Histoire & Sociétés 4, no.1 (2000): 103–20.
Gatrell, V.A.C. 'Crime, Authority and the Policeman-State,' In F.M.L. Thompson, ed., The Cambridge Social History of Britain, 1750–1950 (Cambridge: Cambridge University Press 1990), 2: 243–310.
Genet, Jean-Philippe. 'La genèse de l'État moderne: les enjeux d'un programme de recherché.' Actes de la recherche en science sociale 118 (1997): 3–18. .
Giroux, André. Les Palais de justice de la province de Québec de ses origines au début du vingtième siècle. Ottawa: Parcs Canada 1977.
Giroux, Éric. 'Les policiers à Montréal: travail et portrait socio-culturel, 1865–1924.' MA, Université du Québec à Montréal 1995.
Gladwin, Irene. The Sheriff: The Man and His Office. London: Gollancz 1974.
Godfrey, Sheldon J., and Judith C. Godfrey. Search out the Land: The Jews and the Growth of Equality in British Colonial America, 1740–1867. Montreal: McGill-Queen's University Press 1995.
Goebel, Julius Jr, and T. Raymond Naughton. Law Enforcement in Colonial New York: A Study in Criminal Procedure (1664–1776). Montclair, N.J.: Patterson Smith, 1970 [1944].
Goldie, Mark. 'The Unacknowledged Republic: Officeholding in Early Modern England.' In Tim Harris, ed., The Politics of the Excluded, c. 1500–1800. New York and Basingstoke: Palgrave 2001.153–94.
Gordon, Michael D. 'The Invention of a Common Law Crime: Perjury and the Elizabethan Courts.' American Journal of Legal History 24, no.2 (1980): 145–70.
Greenberg, Douglas. 'Crime, Law Enforcement, and Social Control in Colonial America.' American Journal of Legal History 26, no.4 (1982): 293–325.
Greenwood, F. Murray. Legacies of Fear. Law and Politics in Quebec in the Era of the French Revolution. Toronto: Osgoode Society / University of Toronto Press 1993.
- and Barry Wright. 'Introduction: State Trials, the Rule of Law, and Execu-

tive Powers in Early Canada.' In F. Murray Greenwood and Barry Wright,
eds., *Canadian State Trials. Volume I: Law, Politics, and Security Measures,
1608–1837* (Toronto: Osgoode Society / University of Toronto Press 1997),
3–51.
– and Barry Wright, eds. *Canadian State Trials. Volume I: Law, Politics, and
Security Measures, 1608–1837.* Toronto: Osgoode Society / University of
Toronto Press 1996.
– and Barry Wright, eds. *Canadian State Trials. Volume II: Rebellion and Invasion
in the Canadas, 1837–1839.* Toronto: Osgoode Society / University of Toronto
Press 2002.
Greer, Allan. 'The Birth of the Police in Canada.' In Allan Greer and Ian
Radforth, eds., *Colonial Leviathan: State Formation in Mid-nineteenth-Century
Canada* (Toronto: University of Toronto Press 1992), 17–49.
– *The Patriots and the People: The Rebellion of 1837 in Rural Lower Canada.*
Toronto: University of Toronto Press 1993.
– 'The Pattern of Literacy in Quebec, 1745–1899.' *Histoire sociale / Social History*
11, no.22 (1978): 295–335.
– and Ian Radforth, eds. *Colonial Leviathan: State Formation in Nineteenth-
Century Canada.* Toronto: University of Toronto Press 1992.
Grossberg, Michael. '"Fighting Faiths" and the Challenges of Legal History.'
Journal of Social History 25, no.1 (1991): 191–201.
Groulx, Lionel. *Lendemains de conquête.* Montreal: Action française 1920.
Guillemette, Robert. 'Les bibliothèques personnelles de Montréal entre 1800
et 1820: une contribution à l'histoire sociale du livre.' MA, Université de
Montréal 1988.
Hamilton, Gillian. 'Enforcement in Apprenticeship Contracts: Were Run-
aways a Serious Problem? Evidence from Montreal.' *Journal of Economic
History* 55, no.3 (1995): 551–74.
Hardy, Beatriz Betancourt. 'Papists in a Protestant Age: The Catholic Gentry
and Community in Colonial Maryland, 1689–1776.' PhD, University of
Maryland College Park 1993.
Hardy, Jean-Pierre, and Thierry Ruddel. *Les apprentis artisans à Québec, 1660–
1815.* Montreal: Presses de l'Université du Québec 1977.
Hardy, René. 'Le charivari dans l'espace québécois.' In Serge Courville and
Normand Séguin, eds., *Espace et culture / Space and Culture* (Sainte-Foy,
Que.: Presses de l'Université Laval 1995), 175–86.
Harris, Andrew T. *Policing the City: Crime and Legal Authority in London, 1780–
1840.* Columbus: Ohio State University Press 2004.
Harris, Richard, and Lorraine Foreman-Peck. '"Stepping into Other Peoples'
Shoes": Teaching and Assessing Empathy in the Secondary History Cur-

riculum.' *International Journal of Historical Learning, Teaching and Research* 4, no.2 (2004).

Hartley, Gerard M.F. 'Years of Adjustment: British Policy and the Canadian Militia, 1760–1787.' MA, Queen's University 1993.

Harvey, Kathryn. 'Amazons and Victims: Resisting Wife-Abuse in Working-class Montreal, 1869–1879.' *Journal of the Canadian Historical Association* 2 (1991): 131–48.

Harvey, Louis-Georges. *Le Printemps de l'Amérique française: américanité, anticolonialisme et républicanisme dans le discours politique québécois, 1805–1837.* Montreal: Boréal 2005.

Hay, Douglas. 'Civilians Tried in Military Courts: Quebec, 1759–64.' In F. Murray Greenwood and Barry Wright, eds., *Canadian State Trials. Volume I: Law, Politics, and Security Measures, 1608–1837* (Toronto: University of Toronto Press 1997), 114–28.

– 'The Class Composition of the Palladium of Liberty: Trial Jurors in the Eighteenth Century.' In J.S. Cockburn and Thomas A. Green, eds., *Twelve Good Men and True: The Criminal Trial Jury in England, 1200–1800* (Princeton, N.J.: Princeton University Press 1988), 305–57.

– 'Dread of the Crown Office: The Magistracy and King's Bench, 1740–1800.' In Norma Landau, ed., *Law, Crime and English Society 1660–1830* (Cambridge: Cambridge University Press 2002), 19–45.

– 'Legislation, Magistrates, and Judges: High Law and Low Law in England and the Empire.' In David Lemmings, ed., *The British and Their Laws in the Eighteenth Century* (London: Boydell and Brewer 2005), 59–79.

– 'The Meanings of the Criminal Law in Quebec, 1764–1774.' In Louis A. Knafla, ed., *Crime and Criminal Justice in Europe and Canada* (Waterloo, Ont.: Wilfrid Laurier University Press 1981), 77–110.

– 'Origins: The Courts of Westminster Hall in the Eighteenth Century.' In Philip Girard, Jim Phillips, and Barry Cahill, eds., *The Supreme Court of Nova Scotia, 1754–2004: From Imperial Bastion to Provincial Oracle* (Toronto: Osgoode Society / University of Toronto Press 2004), 13–29.

– 'Property, Authority and the Criminal Law.' In Douglas Hay et al., *Albion's Fatal Tree: Crime and Society in Eighteenth-Century England* (Middlesex, U.K.: Penguin 1975), 17–63.

– 'Prosecution and Power: Malicious Prosecution in the English Courts, 1750–1850.' In Douglas Hay and Francis Snyder, eds., *Policing and Prosecution in Britain 1750–1850* (Oxford: Clarendon Press 1989), 343–95.

– 'War, Dearth and Theft in the Eighteenth Century: The Record of the English Courts.' *Past and Present* 95 (1982): 117–60.

'History of the Old Bailey Courthouse,' http://www.oldbaileyonline.org/
history/the-old-bailey/

Hufton, Olwen H. 'Le paysan et la loi en France au XVIIIe siècle.' *Annales* 38,
no.3 (1983): 679–701.

Hunt, Margaret. 'Wife Beating, Domesticity and Women's Independence in
Eighteenth-Century London.' *Gender & History* 4, no.1 (1992): 10–33.

Hurl, Jennine. 'Domestic Violence Prosecuted: Women Binding over Their
Husbands for Assault at Westminster Quarter Sessions, 1685–1720.' *Journal
of Family History* 26, no.4 (2001): 435–54.

– 'Voices of Litigation; Voices of Resistance: Constructions of Gender in
the Records of Assault in London, 1680–1720.' PhD, York University
2001.

Innes, Joanna. 'Prisons for the Poor: English Bridewells, 1555–1800.' In Francis
Snyder and Douglas Hay, eds., *Labour, Law, and Crime: An Historical Perspective* (London: Tavistock Publications 1987), 42–122.

Ireland, Robert M. 'Privately Funded Prosecution of Crime in the Nineteenth-
Century United States.' *American Journal of Legal History* 39, no.1 (1995): 43–58.

Jenkins, Keith. *Re-thinking History*. London: Routledge 1991.

Jenkins, Philip. *The Making of a Ruling Class: The Glamorgan Gentry 1640–1790*.
Cambridge: Cambridge University Press 1983.

Johnson, Herbert A. 'The Advent of Common Law in Colonial New York.' In
Herbert A. Johnson, *Essays on New York Colonial Legal History* (Westport,
Conn.: Greenwood Press 1981), 37–54.

Johnson, J.K. *Becoming Prominent: Regional Leadership in Upper Canada, 1791–
1841*. Montreal: McGill-Queen's University Press 1989.

Kenny, Stephen. 'Cahots and Catcalls: An Episode of Popular Resistance in
Lower Canada at the Outset of the Union.' *Canadian Historical Review* 65,
no.2 (1984): 184–208.

Kent, Joan R. *The English Village Constable, 1580–1642: A Social and Administrative Study*. Oxford: Clarendon Press 1986.

Keough, Willeen. '"Now You Vagabond [W]hore I Have You": Plebeian
Women, Assault Cases, and Gender and Class Relations on the Southern
Avalon, 1750–1860.' In Christopher English, ed., *Essays in the History of
Canadian Law Volume IX: Two Islands, Newfoundland and Prince Edward Island*
(Toronto: Osgoode Society / University of Toronto Press 2005), 237–71.

Kerr, Derek N. *Petty Felony, Slave Defiance, and Frontier Villainy: Crime and
Criminal Justice in Spanish Louisiana, 1770–1803*. New York: Garland 1993.

King, Peter. *Crime, Justice, and Discretion in England 1740–1820*. Oxford: Oxford
University Press 2000.

– 'Gender, Crime and Justice in Late Eighteenth- and Early Nineteenth-

Century England.' In Margaret L. Arnot and Cornelie Usborne, eds., *Gender and Crime in Modern Europe* (London: UCL Press 1999), 44–74.

– '"Illiterate Plebeians, Easily Misled": Jury Composition, Experience and Behavior in Essex, 1735–1815.' In J.S. Cockburn and Thomas A. Green, eds., *Twelve Good Men and True: The Criminal Trial Jury in England, 1200–1800* (Princeton, N.J.: Princeton University Press 1988), 254–304.

– 'Punishing Assault: The Transformation of Attitudes in the English Courts.' *Journal of Interdisciplinary History* 27, no.1 (1996): 43–74.

– 'The Summary Courts and Social Relations in England 1740–1820.' *Past and Present* 183 (2004): 125–72.

Klockars, Carl B. 'Police.' In Edgar F. Borgatta, ed., *Encyclopedia of Sociology* (New York: MacMillan 2000), 4: 2107–16.

Knafla, Louis A. 'Aspects of the Criminal Law, Crime, Criminal Process and Punishment in Europe and Canada, 1500–1935.' In Knafla, ed., *Crime and Criminal Justice in Europe and Canada: Essays*, 2nd ed. (Waterloo, Ont.: Wilfrid Laurier University Press 1985), 1–15.

– and Terry L. Chapman. 'Criminal Justice in Canada: A Comparative Study of the Maritimes and Lower Canada, 1760–1812.' *Osgoode Hall Law Journal* 21, no.2 (1983): 245–74.

Kolish, Evelyn. 'Changements dans le droit privé au Québec Bas-Canada entre 1760 et 1849: attitudes et réactions des contemporains.' PhD, Université de Montréal 1980.

– *Nationalismes et conflits de droits: le débat du droit privé au Québec, 1760–1840.* LaSalle, Que.: Hurtubise HMH 1994.

Labonté, Gilles. 'Les bibliothèques privées à Québec (1820–1829).' MA, Université Laval 1986.

Lachance, André. *Crimes et criminels en Nouvelle-France.* Montreal: Boréal Express 1984.

– *La justice criminelle du roi au Canada au XVIIIe siècle: tribunaux et officiers.* Quebec: Presses de l'Université Laval 1978.

– 'Women and Crime in Canada in the Early Eighteenth Century, 1712–1759.' In Louis A. Knafla, ed., *Crime and Criminal Justice in Europe and Canada: Essays* (Waterloo, Ont.: Wilfrid Laurier University Press 1985), 157–77.

– and Sylvie Savoie. 'Violence, Marriage and Family Honour: Aspects of the Legal Regulation of Marriage in New France.' In Jim Phillips, Tina Loo, and Susan Lewthwaite, eds., *Essays in the History of Canadian Law. Volume V: Crime and Criminal Justice* (Toronto: Osgoode Society / University of Toronto Press 1994), 143–73.

Landau, Norma. 'Appearance at the Quarter Sessions of Eighteenth-Century Middlesex.' *London Journal* 23, no.2 (1998): 30–52.

- 'Indictment for Fun and Profit: A Prosecutor's Reward at Eighteenth-Century Quarter Sessions.' *Law and History Review* 17, no.3 (1999): 507–36.
- *The Justices of the Peace, 1679–1760.* Berkeley: University of California Press 1984.
- 'The Trading Justice's Trade.' In Landau, ed., *Law, Crime and English Society 1660–1830* (Cambridge: Cambridge University Press 2002), 46–70.

Lane, Roger. *Policing the City: Boston, 1822–1885.* Cambridge, Mass.: Harvard University Press 1967.

Langbein, John H. 'Albion's Fatal Flaws.' *Past and Present* 98 (1983): 96–120.
- *The Origins of Adversary Criminal Trial.* Oxford: Oxford University Press 2003.
- 'The Origins of Public Prosecution at Common Law'. *American Journal of Legal History* 17, no.4 (1973): 313–35.

Langford, Paul. *Public Life and the Propertied Englishman, 1689–1798.* Oxford: Oxford University Press 1991.

Langlois, Égide. 'Livres et lecteurs à Québec: 1760–1799.' MA, Université Laval 1984.

Lareau, Edmond. *Histoire du droit canadien depuis les origines de la colonie jusqu'a nos jours.* Montreal: A. Périard 1888–9.

Laudy, Danielle. 'Les politiques coloniales britanniques et le maintien de l'ancien régime au Bas-Canada (1791–1832).' *Histoire, économie et société* 14, no.1 (1995): 71–88.

Lauzon, Gilles, and Madeleine Forget, eds. *L'histoire du Vieux-Montréal à travers son patrimoine.* Montreal: Publications du Québec 2004.

Lawson, Philip. *The Imperial Challenge: Quebec and Britain in the Age of the American Revolution.* Montreal: McGill-Queen's University Press 1989.

Leclerc, Jean-François. 'Justice et infra-justice en Nouvelle-France: les voies de fait à Montréal entre 1700 et 1760.' *Criminologie* 18, no.1 (1985): 25–39.

Lefebvre, Fernand. 'L'histoire du guet à Montréal.' *Revue d'histoire de l'Amérique française* 6, no.2 (1952): 263–73.

Lemire, Maurice et al. *La vie littéraire au Québec. Volume 1: 1764–1805. La voix française des nouveaux sujets britanniques.* Quebec: Presses de l'Université Laval 1991.

Lépine, Luc. 'La milice du district de Montréal, 1787–1829: essai d'histoire socio-militaire.' PhD, Université du Québec à Montréal 2005.

Lessard, Martin. 'La transformation de la place d'Armes de la ville de Québec entre 1799 et 1804.' MA, Université Laval 2002.

Lewthwaite, Susan Dawson. 'Law and Authority in Upper Canada: The Justices of the Peace in the Newcastle District, 1803–1840.' PhD, University of Toronto 2001.

Little, J.I. *State and Society in Transition: The Politics of Institutional Reform in the Eastern Townships, 1838–1852*. Montreal: McGill-Queen's University Press 1997.

Mackey, Frank. *Black Then: Blacks and Montreal, 1780s–1880s*. Montreal: McGill-Queen's University Press 2004.

Mann, Michael. *The Sources of Social Power. Volume 1: A History of Power from the Beginning to AD 1760* and *Volume 2: The Rise of Classes and Nation States 1760–1914*. Cambridge: Cambridge University Press 1986/1993.

Manning, Helen Taft. *The Revolt of French Canada 1800–1835: A Chapter in the History of the British Commonwealth*. Toronto: Macmillan 1962.

Manning, Peter K. 'A Dramaturgical Perspective.' In Brian Forst and Peter K. Manning, *The Privatization of Policing: Two Views* (Washington: Georgetown University Press 1999), 49–124.

Marquis, Greg. *Policing Canada's Century: A History of the Canadian Association of Chiefs of Police*. Toronto: University of Toronto Press 1993.

Masciotra, Vincent. 'Quebec Legal Historiography, 1760–1900.' *McGill Law Journal* 32, no.3 (1987): 712–32.

Massicotte, E.-Z. 'Le guet à Montréal au XIXe siècle.' *Bulletin des recherches historiques* 36, no.2 (1930): 68–71.

McCallum, Margaret. 'Canadian Legal History in the Late 1990s: A Field in Search of Fences?' *Acadiensis* 27, no.2 (1998): 151–66.

McCulloch, Michael. 'Most Assuredly Perpetual Motion: Police and Policing in Quebec City, 1838–58.' *Urban History Review* 19, no. 1 (1990): 100–12.

McNamara, Martha J. *From Tavern to Courthouse: Architecture and Ritual in American Law, 1658–1860*. Baltimore: Johns Hopkins University Press 2004.

Mihorean, Karen et al. *A Profile of Criminal Victimization: Results of the 1999 General Social Survey*. Ottawa: Statistics Canada 2001.

Mills, David. *The Idea of Loyalty in Upper Canada, 1784–1850*. Montreal: McGill-Queen's University Press 1988.

Milobar, David. 'The Origins of British-Quebec Merchant Ideology: New France, the British Atlantic and the Constitutional Periphery, 1720–70.' *Journal of Imperial and Commonwealth History* 24, no.3 (1996): 364–90.

Mimeault, Mario. 'Le district judiciaire de Gaspé (1788–1988).' *Gaspésie* 26, no.2 (1988): 17–53.

Mimeault, Martin. 'Punir, contenir et amender: Les théories carcérales et leurs applications à la prison des Plaines de Québec, 1863–1877.' MA, Université Laval 1999.

Mitchell, B.R. et al. *British Historical Statistics*. Cambridge: Cambridge University Press 1988.

Monette, Michel. 'Groupes dominants et structure locale du pouvoir à

Deschambault et Saint-Casimir, Comté de Portneuf (1829–1870).'*Cahiers de géographie du Québec* 28, nos.73–4 (1984): 73–88.

Monkkonen, Eric H. 'The Urban Police in the United States.' In Clive Emsley and Louis A. Knafla, eds., *Crime History and Histories of Crime: Studies in the Historiography of Crime and Criminal Justice in Modern History* (Westport, Conn.: Greenwood Press 1996), 201–28.

Morel, André. 'Les crimes et les peines: évolution des mentalités au Québec au XIXe siècle.' *Revue de Droit* 8 (1978): 384–96.

– 'La réaction des Canadiens devant l'administration de la justice de 1764 à 1774: Une forme de résistance passive.' *Revue du Barreau* 20, no.2 (1960): 55–63.

– 'La réception du droit criminel anglais au Québec (1760–1892).' *Revue juridique Thémis* 13, nos.2–3 (1978): 449–541.

Morgan, Gwenda, and Peter Rushton. *Rogues, Thieves, and the Rule of Law: The Problem of Law Enforcement in North-East England, 1718–1800.* London: University College London Press 1998.

Morin, Michel. 'Portalis v. Bentham? The Objectives Ascribed to Codification of the Civil Law and the Criminal Law in France, England and Canada.' In *Perspectives on Legislation: Essays from the 1999 Legal Dimensions Initiative* (Ottawa: Law Commission of Canada 2000), 125–97.

Morin, Yvan. 'Les niveaux de culture à Québec 1800–1819: étude des bibliothèques privées dans les inventaires après décès.' MA, Université Laval 1979.

Murray, David R. *Colonial Justice: Justice, Morality and Crime in the Niagara District, 1791–1849.* Toronto: Osgoode Society / University of Toronto Press 2002.

Neatby, Hilda M. *The Administration of Justice under the Quebec Act.* Minneapolis: Minnesota University Press 1933.

– *Quebec: The Revolutionary Age, 1760–1791.* Toronto: McClelland and Stewart 1966.

Nelson, William Edward. *Americanization of the Common Law: The Impact of Legal Change on Massachusetts Society, 1760–1830.* Cambridge, Mass.: Harvard University Press 1975.

Noël, Danièle. 'Une langue qui ne capitule pas (la justice et les tribunaux).' In Michel Plourde, ed., *Le français au Québec: 400 ans d'histoire et de vie* (Montreal: Fides/Publications du Québec 2000), 72–9.

Noppen, Luc, Claude Paulette, and Michel Tremblay. *Québec, trois siècles d'architecture.* Quebec: Libre expression 1979.

Noppen, Luc, and Lucie K. Morisset. *La présence anglicane à Québec: Holy Trinity Cathedral, 1796–1996.* Sillery, Que.: Septentrion 1995.

Normand, Sylvio. 'François-Joseph Cugnet et la reconstitution du droit de la

Nouvelle-France.' *Cahiers aixois d'histoire des droits de l'outre-mer français* 1 (2002): 127–145
- 'L'imprimé juridique au Québec du XVIIIe siècle à 1840.' http://www. hbic.library.utoronto.ca/vol1normand_en.htm
Oldham, James. *English Common Law in the Age of Mansfield*. Charlotte: University of North Carolina Press 2004.
Oliver, Peter. *'Terror to Evil-Doers': Prisons and Punishment in Nineteenth-Century Ontario*. Toronto: Osgoode Society / University of Toronto Press 1998.
Ostola, Lawrence. 'A Very Public Presence: The British Army Garrison in the Town of Quebec 1759–1838.' PhD, Université Laval 2006.
Ouellet, Fernand. *Le Bas-Canada, 1791–1840: changements structuraux et crise*. Ottawa: Éditions de l'Université d'Ottawa 1976.
- *Economic and Social History of Quebec, 1760–1850: Structures and Conjunctures*. Ottawa: Carleton Library 1980.
Oxner, Sandra E. 'The Evolution of the Lower Court of Nova Scotia.' In Peter Waite, Sandra Oxner, and Thomas Barnes, eds., *Law in a Colonial Society: The Nova Scotia Experience* (Toronto: Carswell 1984), 59–80.
Paley, Ruth. '"An Imperfect, Inadequate and Wretched System"? Policing London Before Peel.' *Criminal Justice History* 10 (1989): 95–130.
Palmer, Stanley H. *Police and Protest in England and Ireland, 1780–1850*. Cambridge: Cambridge University Press 1988.
Paquet, Gilles, and Jean-Pierre Wallot. *Patronage et pouvoir dans le Bas-Canada (1794–1812)*. Montreal: Presses de l'Université du Québec 1973.
Pâquet, Martin. *Tracer les marges de la cité: étranger, immigrant et État au Québec, 1627–1981*. Montreal: Boréal 2005.
Parent, Alain. 'Entre empire et nation: gravures de la ville de Québec et des environs, 1760–1833.' PhD, Université Laval 2003.
Pariseau, Jean. 'Forces armées et maintien de l'ordre au Canada, 1867–1967: un siècle d'aide au pouvoir civil.' PhD, Université Paul Valéry III (Montpellier) 1981.
Parker, Nancy Kay. 'Reaching a Verdict: The Changing Structure of Decision-Making in the Canadian Criminal Courts, 1867–1905.' PhD, York University 1999.
Philips, David. 'The Black Country Magistracy, 1835–60: A Changing Elite and the Exercise of its Power.' *Midland History* 3, no.3 (1976): 161–90.
- *Crime and Authority in Victorian England: The Black Country, 1835–1860*. London: Croom Helm 1977.
- 'A "Weak" State? The English State, the Magistracy and the Reform of Policing in the 1830s.' *English Historical Review* 119, no.483 (2004): 873–91.

– and Robert D. Storch. *Policing Provincial England, 1829–1856: The Politics of Reform*. London: Leicester University Press 1999.

Phillips, Jim. 'Crime and Punishment in the Dominion of the North: Canada from New France to the Present.' In Clive Emsley and Louis A. Knafla, eds., *Crime History and Histories of Crime: Studies in the Historiography of Crime and Criminal Justice in Modern History* (Westport, Conn.: Greenwood Press 1996), 163–99.

– 'The Criminal Trial in Nova Scotia, 1749–1815.' In G. Blaine Baker and Jim Phillips, eds., *Essays in the History of Canadian Law. Volume VIII: In Honour of R.C.B. Risk* (Toronto: Osgoode Society / University of Toronto Press 1999), 469–511.

– 'The Operation of the Royal Pardon in Nova Scotia, 1749–1815.' *University of Toronto Law Journal* 42, no.4 (1992): 401–49.

– 'Women, Crime, and Criminal Justice in Early Halifax, 1750–1800.' In Jim Phillips, Tina Loo, and Susan Lewthwaite, eds., *Essays in the History of Canadian Law. Volume V: Crime and Criminal Justice* (Toronto: Osgoode Society / University of Toronto Press 1994), 174–206.

– and Allyson N. May. 'Female Criminality in 18th-Century Halifax.' *Acadiensis* 31, no.2 (2002): 71–96.

Phillips, John David. 'Educated to Crime: Community and Criminal Justice in Upper Canada, 1800–1840.' PhD, University of Toronto 2004.

Phillips, Roderick. 'Women, Neighborhood, and Family in the Late Eighteenth Century.' *French Historical Studies* 18, no.1 (1993): 1–12.

Pilarczyk, Ian C. 'Justice in the Premises': Family Violence and the Law in Montreal, 1825–1850.' PhD, McGill University 2003.

– 'The Law of Servants and the Servants of Law: Enforcing Masters' Rights in Montreal, 1830–1845.' *McGill Law Journal* 46, no.3 (2000): 791–836.

– 'The Law of Servants and the Servants of Law: Judicial Regulation of Labour Relations in Montreal, 1830–1845.' LLM, McGill University 1997.

– '"Too Well Used by His Master": Judicial Enforcement of Servants' Rights in Montreal, 1830–1845.' *McGill Law Journal* 46, no.2 (2000): 491–529.

Plank, Geoffrey. *An Unsettled Conquest: The British Campaign Against the Peoples of Acadia*. Philadelphia: University of Pennsylvania Press 2001.

Podruchny, Carolyn. 'Unfair Masters and Rascally Servants? Labour Relations among Bourgeois, Clerks and Voyageurs in the Montreal Fur Trade, 1780–1821.' *Labour / Le travail* 43 (1999): 43–70.

Poutanen, Mary Anne. 'Bonds of Friendship, Kinship, and Community: Gender, Homelessness, and Mutual Aid in Early-Nineteenth-Century Montreal.' In Bettina Bradbury and Tamara Myers, eds., *Negotiating Identities in 19th and 20th Century Montreal* (Vancouver: University of British Columbia Press 2005), 25–48.

- 'The Homeless, the Whore, the Drunkard, and the Disorderly: Contours of Female Vagrancy in the Montreal Courts, 1810–1842.' In Kathryn McPherson, Cecilia Morgan, and Nancy M. Forestell, eds., *Gendered Pasts: Historical Essays in Femininity and Masculinity in Canada* (New York: Oxford University Press 1999), 29–47.
- '"To Indulge Their Carnal Appetites": Prostitution in Early Nineteenth-Century Montreal, 1810–1842.' PhD, Université de Montréal 1997.
- 'Reflections of Montreal Prostitution in the Records of the Lower Courts, 1810–1842.' In Donald Fyson, Colin Coates, and Kathryn Harvey, eds., *Class, Gender and the Law in Eighteenth and Nineteenth-Century Quebec: Sources and Perspectives* (Montreal: Montreal History Group 1993), 99–125.
- 'Regulating Public Space in Early Nineteenth-Century Montreal: Vagrancy Laws and Gender in a Colonial Context.' *Histoire sociale / Social History* 35, no.69 (2002): 35–58.
Radzinowicz, Leon. *A History of English Criminal Law and its Administration from 1750.* New York: Macmillan 1948–91.
Ramos, Sandy. '"A Most Detestable Crime": Gender Identities and Sexual Violence in the District of Montreal, 1803–1843.' *Journal of the Canadian Historical Association* 12 (2001): 27–48.
Reynolds, Elaine A. *Before the Bobbies: The Night Watch and Police Reform in Metropolitan London, 1720–1830.* Stanford, Calif.: Stanford University Press 1998.
Rivet, François. 'La vision de l'ordre en milieu urbain chez les élites locales de Québec et Montréal: le discours des grands jurys, 1820–1860.' MA, Université du Québec à Montréal 2004.
Robichaud, Léon. 'Le pouvoir, les paysans et la voirie au Bas-Canada à la fin du XVIIIe siècle.' MA, McGill University 1989.
Roeber, A.G. *Faithful Magistrates and Republican Lawyers: Creators of Virginian Legal Culture, 1680–1810.* Chapel Hill: University of North Carolina Press 1981.
Rogers, Nicholas. 'Policing the Poor in Eighteenth-Century London: The Vagrancy Laws and their Administration.' *Histoire sociale / Social History* 24, no.47 (1991): 127–47.
Ross, Jeffrey Ian. 'The Historical Treatment of Urban Policing in Canada: A Review of the Literature.' *Urban History Review* 24, no.1 (1995): 36–41.
Rousey, Dennis Charles. *Policing the Southern City: New Orleans, 1805–1889.* Baton Rouge: Louisiana State University Press 1996.
Rowe, G.S. 'Femmes Covert and Criminal Prosecution in Eighteenth-Century Pennsylvania.' *American Journal of Legal History* 32, no.2 (1988): 138–56.
Roy, Pierre-Georges. *Fils de Québec.* Lévis, Que.: [s.n.] 1933.
- *À travers les Mémoires de Philippe Aubert de Gaspé.* Montreal: Ducharme 1943.

Ruddel, David T. *Québec City 1765–1832: The Evolution of a Colonial Town.*
Ottawa: Canadian Museum of Civilization 1987.

Rudé, George. *Criminal and Victim: Crime and Society in Early Nineteenth-Century England.* Oxford: Clarendon Press 1985.

Scott, Seaman Morley. 'Chapters in the History of the Law of Quebec 1764–1775.' PhD, University of Michigan 1933.

Senior, Elinor Kyte. *British Regulars in Montreal: An Imperial Garrison, 1832–1854.* Montreal: McGill-Queen's University Press 1981.

Sharpe, J.A. *Crime in Early Modern England, 15501750.* London: Longman 1984. 2nd ed. London: Longman 1999.

Shoemaker, Robert B. *Prosecution and Punishment: Petty Crime and the Law in London and Rural Middlesex, c. 1660–1725.* Cambridge: Cambridge University Press 1991.

– 'Reforming the City: The Reformation of Manners Campaign in London, 1690–1738.' In Lee Davison et al., *Stilling the Grumbling Hive: The Response to Social and Economic Problems in England, 1689–1750* (New York: St Martin's Press 1992), 99–120.

– 'Using Quarter Sessions Records as Evidence for the Study of Crime and Criminal Justice.' *Archives* 20, no.90 (1993): 145–57.

Singha, Radhika. *A Despotism of Law: Crime and Justice in Early Colonial India.* Delhi: Oxford University Press 1998.

Skyrme, Thomas. *History of the Justices of the Peace.* Chichester: Barry Rose 1991. 3 vols.

Smith, Bruce Philip. 'Circumventing the Jury: Petty Crime and Summary Jurisdiction in London and New York City, 1790–1855.' PhD, Yale University 1996.

Smith, Gregory Thomas. 'The State and the Culture of Violence in London, 1760–1840.' PhD, University of Toronto 1999.

Snell, Ronald K. '"Ambitious of Honor and Places": The Magistracy of Hampshire County, Massachusetts, 1692–1760.' In Bruce C. Daniels, ed., *Power and Status: Officeholding in Colonial America* (Middletown, Conn.: Wesleyan University Press 1986), 17–35.

– 'The County Magistracy in Eighteenth Century Massachusetts, 1692–1750.' PhD, Princeton University 1971.

Spierenburg, Pieter. 'Violence and the Civilizing Process: Does It Work?' *Crime, Histoire & Sociétés* 5, no.2 (2001): 87–105.

Spindel, Donna. *Crime and Society in North Carolina, 1663–1776.* Baton Rouge: Louisiana State University Press 1989.

Ste Croix, Lorne Joseph. 'The First Incorporation of the City of Montreal, 1826–1836.' MA, McGill University 1972.

Steinberg, Allen. *The Transformation of Criminal Justice: Philadelphia, 1800–1880.* Chapel Hill: University of North Carolina Press 1989.

Stone, Helen. 'Les indiens et le système judiciare criminel de la Province de Québec: les politiques de l'administration sous le régime britannique.'*Recherches amérindiennes au Québec* 30, no.3 (2000): 65–78.

Storch, Robert. 'Policing Rural Southern England before the Police: Opinion and Practice, 1830–1856.' In Douglas Hay and Francis Snyder, eds., *Policing and Prosecution in Britain 1750–1850* (Oxford: Clarendon Press 1989), 211–66.

Sullivan, Dennis. *The Punishment of Crime in Colonial New York: The Dutch Experience in Albany during the Seventeenth Century.* New York: Lang 1997.

Surrency, Erwin C. 'The Courts in the American Colonies.' *American Journal of Legal History* 11, no.3 (1967): 253–76, and 11, no.4 (1967): 347–76.

Swift, Roger. 'The English Urban Magistracy and the Administration of Justice during the Early Nineteenth Century: Wolverhampton 1815–1860.' *Midland History* 17 (1992): 75–92.

Taylor, David. *Crime, Policing and Punishment in England, 1750–1914.* New York: St Martin's Press 1998.

Thompson, E.P. *Whigs and Hunters: The Origin of the Black Act.* Harmondsworth, U.K.: Penguin 1977.

Thompson, Frances Ann. 'Local Authority and District Autonomy: The Niagara Magistracy and Constabulatory, 1828–1841.' PhD, University of Ottawa 1996.

Thuot, Jean-René. 'Élites locales, institutions et fonctions publiques dans la paroisse de Saint-Roch-de-l'Achigan, de 1810 à 1840.' *Revue d'histoire de l'Amérique française* 57, no.2 (2003): 173–208.

Tompson, Richard S. 'The Justices of the Peace and the United Kingdom in the Age of Reform.' *Journal of Legal History* 7, no.3 (1986): 273–92.

Turmel, Jean. *Premières structures et évolution de la police de Montréal (1796–1909).* Montreal: Service de la Police de Montréal 1971.

Vaugeois, Denis. 'Une langue sans statut.' In Michel Plourde, ed., *Le français au Québec: 400 ans d'histoire et de vie* (Montreal: Fides/Publications du Québec 2000), 59–71.

Veilleux, Christine. 'Les gens de justice à Québec, 1760–1867.' PhD, Université Laval 1990.

Verrette, Michel. 'L'alphabétisation au Québec 1660–1900.' PhD, Université Laval 1989.

Wallot, Jean-Pierre. 'La querelle des prisons dans les Bas-Canada (1805–1807).'In *Un Québec qui bougeait: trame socio-politique au tournant du XIXe siècle* (Montreal: Boréal Express 1973), 47–105.

Warner, Jessica, and Frank Ivis. '"Damn You, You Informing Bitch": Vox

Populi and the Unmaking of the Gin Act of 1736.' *Journal of Social History* 33, no.2 (1999): 299–330.

Watson, Alan D. 'The Constable in Colonial North Carolina.' *North Carolina Historical Review* 68, no.1 (1991): 1–16.

Watt, Steven. '"Duty Bound and Ever Praying": Collective Petitioning to Governors and Legislatures in Selected Regions of Maine and Lower Canada, 1820–1838.' PhD, Université du Québec à Montréal 2006.

Weaver, John C. *Crimes, Constables and Courts: Order and Transgression in a Canadian City, 1816–1970*. Montreal: McGill-Queen's University Press 1995.

Webb, Sidney, and and Beatrice Webb. *English Local Government*. Hamden, U.K.: Archon Books 1963 [1906].

Western, J.R. *The English Militia in the Eighteenth Century: The Story of a Political Issue*. London: Routledge and Kegan Paul 1965.

Wettmann-Jungblut, Peter. 'Penal Law and Criminality in South Western Germany: Forms, Patterns, and Developments 1200–1800.' In Xavier Rousseaux and René Lévy, eds., *Le pénal dans tous ses états: Justice, états et sociétés en Europe (XIIe–XIXe siècles)* (Bruxelles: Publications des Facultés universitaires Saint-Louis 1997), 25–46.

Whetstone, Ann E. *Scottish County Government in the Eighteenth and Nineteenth Centuries*. Edinburgh: J. Donald 1981.

Williams, Alan. *The Police of Paris, 1718–1798*. Baton Rouge: Louisiana State University Press 1979.

Williams, Dorothy W. *Blacks in Montreal, 1628–1986: An Urban Demography*. Cowansville, Que.: Éditions Yvon Blais 1989.

Wilson, Stephen R. 'The Court of Quarter Sessions and Larceny in Sussex, 1775–1820.' *Criminal Justice History* 7 (1986): 73–94.

Worsley, Giles. *Classical Architecture in Britain: The Heroic Age*. New Haven, Conn.: Yale University Press 1995.

Young, Brian. *The Politics of Codification: The Lower Canadian Civil Code of 1866*. Montreal: Osgoode Society / McGill-Queen's University Press 1994.

– 'Positive Law, Positive State.' In Allan Greer and Ian Radforth, eds., *Colonial Leviathan: State Formation in Mid-nineteenth-Century Canada* (Toronto: University of Toronto Press 1992), 50–63.

Illustration Credits

Figure 1.1: Louis Dulongpré, 'Portrait of Thomas McCord' (1816). McCord Museum, Montreal, M8354.

Figure 1.2: Unknown artist, 'Justice Jean-Thomas Taschereau' (c.1815). National Gallery of Canada, 23180.

Figure 3.1: William Berczy, 'Daniel Robertson' (c.1804–1808). National Gallery of Canada, 37004.

Figure 3.2: William Berczy, 'Jean-Marie Mondelet' (c.1807). Collection Musée du Château Ramezay, Montreal, 1998.1142.

Figure 3.3: J.E. Livernois, 'Samuel Gale' (1850s photograph of unknown original). Bibliothèque et Archives nationales du Québec, Centre de Québec, P560 S2 D1 P385.

Figure 3.4 and 3.5: Unknown artist, 'M.E.G.A. Chartier de Lotbinière' (1786, after 1763 miniature). Collection du Musée régional de Vaudreuil-Soulanges, Vaudreuil-Dorion, 2003.73.
William Berczy, 'M.-E.-G.-A. Chartier de Lotbinière' (1809). Collection Centre d'histoire La Presqu'île, Fonds Henry de Lotbinière-Harwood, P6/G2 (original in private hands).

Figure 8.1: Richard Short, 'A View of the Inside of the Jesuits Church' (c.1759, published 1761). Engraved by Anthony Walker. Musée de la civilisation, collection du Séminaire de Québec, fonds Viger-Verreau, 1993.15819.

Figure 8.2: Richard Short, 'A View of the Jesuits College and Church' (c.1759, published 1761). Engraved by Charles Grignion. Musée de la civilisation, collection du Séminaire de Québec, fonds Viger-Verreau, 1993.15818.

Figure 8.3: James D. Duncan, 'Court House' (c.1839). Engraved by P. Christie. In Newton Bosworth, *Hochelaga Depicta: The Early History and Present State of the City and Island of Montreal* (Montreal: W. Greig 1839), 158–9. Courtesy of Musée de la civilisation, bibliothèque du Séminaire de Québec, 25.5.1.

Figure 8.4: James D. Duncan, 'Old Jail' (c.1839). Engraved by P. Christie. In Newton Bosworth, *Hochelaga Depicta: The Early History and Present State of the City and Island of Montreal* (Montreal: W. Greig 1839), 158–9. Courtesy of Musée de la civilisation, bibliothèque du Séminaire de Québec, 25.5.1.

Index

The references in this index are selective. An exhaustive index covering every mention of all institutions, places, individuals, and offences is available on the companion website, currently at http://www.hst.ulaval.ca/profs/dfyson/CrimJust/.

PUBLICATIONS OF THE OSGOODE SOCIETY FOR
CANADIAN LEGAL HISTORY

1981   David H. Flaherty, ed., *Essays in the History of Canadian Law: Volume I*
1982   Marion MacRae and Anthony Adamson, *Cornerstones of Order: Court-houses and Town Halls of Ontario, 1784–1914*
1983   David H. Flaherty, ed., *Essays in the History of Canadian Law: Volume II*
1984   Patrick Brode, *Sir John Beverley Robinson: Bone and Sinew of the Compact*
       David Williams, *Duff: A Life in the Law*
1985   James Snell and Frederick Vaughan, *The Supreme Court of Canada: History of the Institution*
1986   Paul Romney, *Mr Attorney: The Attorney General for Ontario in Court, Cabinet, and Legislature, 1791–1899*
       Martin Friedland, *The Case of Valentine Shortis: A True Story of Crime and Politics in Canada*
1987   C. Ian Kyer and Jerome Bickenbach, *The Fiercest Debate: Cecil A. Wright, the Benchers, and Legal Education in Ontario, 1923–1957*
1988   Robert Sharpe, *The Last Day, the Last Hour: The Currie Libel Trial*
       John D. Arnup, *Middleton: The Beloved Judge*
1989   Desmond Brown, *The Genesis of the Canadian Criminal Code of 1892*
       Patrick Brode, *The Odyssey of John Anderson*
1990   Philip Girard and Jim Phillips, eds., *Essays in the History of Canadian Law: Volume III – Nova Scotia*
       Carol Wilton, ed., *Essays in the History of Canadian Law: Volume IV – Beyond the Law: Lawyers and Business in Canada, 1830–1930*
1991   Constance Backhouse, *Petticoats and Prejudice: Women and Law in Nineteenth- Century Canada*
1992   Brendan O'Brien, *Speedy Justice: The Tragic Last Voyage of His Majesty's Vessel Speedy*
       Robert Fraser, ed., *Provincial Justice: Upper Canadian Legal Portraits from the Dictionary of Canadian Biography*
1993   Greg Marquis, *Policing Canada's Century: A History of the Canadian Association of Chiefs of Police*
       F. Murray Greenwood, *Legacies of Fear: Law and Politics in Quebec in the Era of the French Revolution*
1994   Patrick Boyer, *A Passion for Justice: The Legacy of James Chalmers McRuer*
       Charles Pullen, *The Life and Times of Arthur Maloney: The Last of the Tribunes*
       Jim Phillips, Tina Loo, and Susan Lewthwaite, eds., *Essays in the History of Canadian Law: Volume V – Crime and Criminal Justice*
       Brian Young, *The Politics of Codification: The Lower Canadian Civil Code of 1866*
1995   David Williams, *Just Lawyers: Seven Portraits*

Hamar Foster and John McLaren, eds., *Essays in the History of Canadian Law: Volume VI – British Columbia and the Yukon*

W.H. Morrow, ed., *Northern Justice: The Memoirs of Mr Justice William G. Morrow*

Beverley Boissery, *A Deep Sense of Wrong: The Treason, Trials, and Transportation to New South Wales of Lower Canadian Rebels after the 1838 Rebellion*

1996   Carol Wilton, ed., *Essays in the History of Canadian Law: Volume VII – Inside the Law: Canadian Law Firms in Historical Perspective*

William Kaplan, *Bad Judgment: The Case of Mr Justice Leo A. Landreville*

F. Murray Greenwood and Barry Wright, eds., *Canadian State Trials: Volume I – Law, Politics, and Security Measures, 1608–1837*

1997   James W. St.G. Walker, *'Race,' Rights, and the Law in the Supreme Court of Canada: Historical Case Studies*

Lori Chambers, *Married Women and Property Law in Victorian Ontario*

Patrick Brode, *Casual Slaughters and Accidental Judgments: Canadian War Crimes and Prosecutions, 1944–1948*

Ian Bushnell, *A History of the Federal Court of Canada, 1875–1992*

1998   Sidney Harring, *White Man's Law: Native People in Nineteenth-Century Canadian Jurisprudence*

Peter Oliver, *'Terror to Evil-Doers': Prisons and Punishments in Nineteenth-Century Ontario*

1999   Constance Backhouse, *Colour-Coded: A Legal History of Racism in Canada, 1900–1950*

G. Blaine Baker and Jim Phillips, eds., *Essays in the History of Canadian Law: Volume VIII – In Honour of R.C.B. Risk*

Richard W. Pound, *Chief Justice W.R. Jackett: By the Law of the Land*

David Vanek, *Fulfilment: Memoirs of a Criminal Court Judge*

2000   Barry Cahill, *The Thousandth Man: A Biography of James McGregor Stewart*

A.B. McKillop, *The Spinster and the Prophet: Florence Deeks, H.G. Wells, and the Mystery of the Purloined Past*

Beverley Boissery and F. Murray Greenwood, *Uncertain Justice: Canadian Women and Capital Punishment*

Bruce Ziff, *Unforeseen Legacies: Reuben Wells Leonard and the Leonard Foundation Trust*

2001   Ellen Anderson, *Judging Bertha Wilson: Law as Large as Life*

Judy Fudge and Eric Tucker, *Labour before the Law: The Regulation of Workers' Collective Action in Canada, 1900–1948*

Laurel Sefton MacDowell, *Renegade Lawyer: The Life of J.L. Cohen*

2002   John T. Saywell, *The Lawmakers: Judicial Power and the Shaping of Canadian Federalism*

Patrick Brode, *Courted and Abandoned: Seduction in Canadian Law*

David Murray, *Colonial Justice: Justice, Morality, and Crime in the Niagara District, 1791–1849*

F. Murray Greenwood and Barry Wright, *Canadian State Trials, Volume II: Rebellion and Invasion in the Canadas, 1837–1839*

2003 Robert Sharpe and Kent Roach, *Brian Dickson: A Judge's Journey*
Jerry Bannister, *The Rule of the Admirals: Law, Custom, and Naval Government in Newfoundland, 1699–1832*
George Finlayson, *John J. Robinette, Peerless Mentor: An Appreciation*
Peter Oliver, *The Conventional Man: The Diaries of Ontario Chief Justice Robert A. Harrison, 1856–1878*

2004 Philip Girard, Jim Phillips, and Barry Cahill, *The Supreme Court of Nova Scotia, 1754–2004: From Imperial Bastion to Provincial Oracle*
Frederick Vaughan, *Aggressive in Pursuit: The Life of Justice Emmett Hall*
John D. Honsberger, *Osgoode Hall: An Illustrated History*
Constance Backhouse and Nancy Backhouse, *The Heiress versus the Establishment: Mrs Campbell's Campaign for Legal Justice*

2005 Philip Girard, *Bora Laskin: Bringing Law to Life*
Christopher English, *Essays in the History of Canadian Law: Volume IX – Two Islands: Newfoundland and Prince Edward Island*
Fred Kaufman, *Searching for Justice: An Autobiography*

2006 Donald Fyson, *Magistrates, Police, and People: Everyday Criminal Justice in Quebec and Lower Canada, 1764–1837*
Dale Brawn, *The Court of Queen's Bench of Manitoba, 1870–1950 A Biographical History*
Richard Risk, *A History of Canadian Legal Thought*, ed. G. Blaine Baker and Jim Phillips